Handbook of Multilingualism and Multilingual Communication
HAL 5

Handbooks of Applied Linguistics

Communication Competence
Language and Communication Problems
Practical Solutions

H A L

Editors
Karlfried Knapp and Gerd Antos

Volume 5

Mouton de Gruyter · Berlin · New York

Handbook of Multilingualism and Multilingual Communication

Edited by
Peter Auer and Li Wei

Mouton de Gruyter · Berlin · New York

Mouton de Gruyter (formerly Mouton, The Hague)
is a Division of Walter de Gruyter GmbH & Co. KG, Berlin.

♾ Printed on acid-free paper which falls within the guidelines
of the ANSI to ensure permanence and durability.

Library of Congress Cataloging-in-Publication Data

Handbook of multilingualism and multilingual communication /
edited by Peter Auer, Li Wei.
   p. cm. − (Handbooks of applied linguistics ; 5)
   Includes bibliographical references and index.
   ISBN 978-3-11-018216-3 (hardcover : alk. paper)
   1. Bilingualism.   2. Multilingualism.   I. Auer, Peter, 1954−
II. Wei, Li, 1961−
   P115.H366   2007
   404'.2−dc22
                                2007001159

Bibliographic information published by the Deutsche Nationalbibliothek

The Deutsche Nationalbibliothek lists this publication in the Deutsche Nationalbibliografie;
detailed bibliographic data are available in the Internet at http://dnb.d-nb.de.

ISBN 978-3-11-018216-3

Cover design: Martin Zech, Bremen.
Typesetting: Dörlemann Satz GmbH & Co. KG, Lemförde
Printing and binding: Hubert & Co., Göttingen
Printed in Germany.

Introduction to the handbook series
Linguistics for problem solving

Karlfried Knapp and Gerd Antos

1. Science and application at the turn of the millennium

The distinction between "pure" and "applied" sciences is an old one. According to Meinel (2000), it was introduced by the Swedish chemist Wallerius in 1751, as part of the dispute of that time between the scholastic disciplines and the then emerging epistemic sciences. However, although the concept of "Applied Science" gained currency rapidly since that time, it has remained problematic.

Until recently, the distinction between "pure" and "applied" mirrored the distinction between "theory and "practice". The latter ran all the way through Western history of science since its beginnings in antique times. At first, it was only philosophy that was regarded as a scholarly and, hence, theoretical discipline. Later it was followed by other leading disciplines, as e.g., the sciences. However, as academic disciplines, all of them remained theoretical. In fact, the process of achieving independence of theory was essential for the academic disciplines to become independent from political, religious or other contingencies and to establish themselves at universities and academies. This also implied a process of emancipation from practical concerns – an at times painful development which manifested (and occasionally still manifests) itself in the discrediting of and disdain for practice and practitioners. To some, already the very meaning of the notion "applied" carries a negative connotation, as is suggested by the contrast between the widely used synonym for "theoretical", i.e. "pure" (as used, e.g. in the distinction between "Pure" and "Applied Mathematics") and its natural antonym "impure". On a different level, a lower academic status sometimes is attributed to applied disciplines because of their alleged lack of originality – they are perceived as simply and one-directionally applying insights gained in basic research and watering them down by neglecting the limiting conditions under which these insights were achieved.

Today, however, the academic system is confronted with a new understanding of science. In politics, in society and, above all, in economy a new concept of science has gained acceptance which questions traditional views. In recent philosophy of science, this is labelled as "science under the pressure to succeed" – i.e. as science whose theoretical structure and criteria of evaluation are increasingly conditioned by the pressure of application (Carrier, Stöltzner, and Wette 2004):

Whenever the public is interested in a particular subject, e.g. when a new disease develops that cannot be cured by conventional medication, the public requests science to provide new insights in this area as quickly as possible. In doing so, the public is less interested in whether these new insights fit seamlessly into an existing theoretical framework, but rather whether they make new methods of treatment and curing possible. (Institut für Wirtschafts- und Technikforschung 2004, our translation).

With most of the practical problems like these, sciences cannot rely on knowledge that is already available, simply because such knowledge does not yet exist. Very often, the problems at hand do not fit neatly into the theoretical framework of one particular "pure science", and there is competition among disciplines with respect to which one provides the best theoretical and methodological resources for potential solutions. And more often than not the problems can be tackled only by adopting an interdisciplinary approach.

As a result, the traditional "Cascade Model", where insights were applied top-down from basic research to practice, no longer works in many cases. Instead, a kind of "application oriented basic research" is needed, where disciplines – conditioned by the pressure of application – take up a certain still diffuse practical issue, define it as a problem against the background of their respective theoretical and methodological paradigms, study this problem and finally develop various application oriented suggestions for solutions. In this sense, applied science, on the one hand, has to be conceived of as a scientific strategy for problem solving – a strategy that starts from mundane practical problems and ultimately aims at solving them. On the other hand, despite the dominance of application that applied sciences are subjected to, as sciences they can do nothing but develop such solutions in a theoretically reflected and methodologically well founded manner. The latter, of course, may lead to the well known fact that even applied sciences often tend to concentrate on "application oriented basic research" only and thus appear to lose sight of the original practical problem. But despite such shifts in focus: Both the boundaries between disciplines and between pure and applied research are getting more and more blurred.

Today, after the turn of the millennium, it is obvious that sciences are requested to provide more and something different than just theory, basic research or pure knowledge. Rather, sciences are increasingly being regarded as partners in a more comprehensive social and economic context of problem solving and are evaluated against expectations to be practically relevant. This also implies that sciences are expected to be critical, reflecting their impact on society. This new "applied" type of science is confronted with the question: Which role can the sciences play in solving individual, interpersonal, social, intercultural, political or technical problems? This question is typical of a conception of science that was especially developed and propagated by the influential philosopher Sir Karl Popper – a conception that also this handbook series is based on.

2.   "Applied Linguistics": Concepts and controversies

The concept of "Applied Linguistics" is not as old as the notion of "Applied Science", but it has also been problematical in its relation to theoretical linguistics since its beginning. There seems to be a widespread consensus that the notion "Applied Linguistics" emerged in 1948 with the first issue of the journal *Language Learning* which used this compound in its subtitle *A Quarterly Journal of Applied Linguistics*. This history of its origin certainly explains why even today "Applied Linguistics" still tends to be predominantly associated with foreign language teaching and learning in the Anglophone literature in particular, as can bee seen e.g. from Johnson and Johnson (1998), whose *Encyclopedic Dictionary of Applied Linguistics* is explicitly subtitled *A Handbook for Language Teaching*. However, this theory of origin is historically wrong. As is pointed out by Back (1970), the concept of applying linguistics can be traced back to the early 19th century in Europe, and the very notion "Applied Linguistics" was used in the early 20th already.

2.1.   Theoretically Applied vs. Practically Applied Linguistics

As with the relation between "Pure" and "Applied" sciences pointed out above, also with "Applied Linguistics" the first question to be asked is what makes it different from "Pure" or "Theoretical Linguistics". It is not surprising, then, that the terminologist Back takes this difference as the point of departure for his discussion of what constitutes "Applied Linguistics". In the light of recent controversies about this concept it is no doubt useful to remind us of his terminological distinctions.

Back (1970) distinguishes between "Theoretical Linguistics" – which aims at achieving knowledge for its own sake, without considering any other value –, "Practice" – i.e. any kind of activity that serves to achieve any purpose in life in the widest sense, apart from the striving for knowledge for its own sake – and "Applied Linguistics", as a being based on "Theoretical Linguistics" on the one hand and as aiming at usability in "Practice" on the other. In addition, he makes a difference between "Theoretical Applied Linguistics" and "Practical Applied Linguistics", which is of particular interest here. The former is defined as the use of insights and methods of "Theoretical Linguistics" for gaining knowledge in another, non-linguistic discipline, such as ethnology, sociology, law or literary studies, the latter as the application of insights from linguistics in a practical field related to language, such as language teaching, translation, and the like. For Back, the contribution of applied linguistics is to be seen in the planning of practical action. Language teaching, for example, is practical action done by practitioners, and what applied linguistics can contribute to this is, e.g., to provide contrastive descriptions of the languages involved as a foundation for teaching methods. These contrastive descriptions in turn have to be based on the descriptive methods developed in theoretical linguistics.

However, in the light of the recent epistemological developments outlined above, it may be useful to reinterpret Back's notion of "Theoretically Applied Linguistics". As he himself points out, dealing with practical problems can have repercussions on the development of the theoretical field. Often new approaches, new theoretical concepts and new methods are a prerequisite for dealing with a particular type of practical problems, which may lead to an – at least in the beginning – "application oriented basic research" in applied linguistics itself, which with some justification could also be labeled "theoretically applied", as many such problems require the transgression of disciplinary boundaries. It is not rare that a domain of "Theoretically Applied Linguistics" or "application oriented basic research" takes on a life of its own, and that also something which is labeled as "Applied Linguistics" might in fact be rather remote from the mundane practical problems that originally initiated the respective subject area. But as long as a relation to the original practical problem can be established, it may be justified to count a particular field or discussion as belonging to applied linguistics, even if only "theoretically applied".

2.2.   Applied linguistics as a response to structuralism and generativism

As mentioned before, in the Anglophone world in particular the view still appears to be widespread that the primary concerns of the subject area of applied linguistics should be restricted to second language acquisition and language instruction in the first place (see, e.g., Davies 1999 or Schmitt and Celce-Murcia 2002). However, in other parts of the world, and above all in Europe, there has been a development away from aspects of language learning to a wider focus on more general issues of language and communication.

This broadening of scope was in part a reaction to the narrowing down the focus in linguistics that resulted from self-imposed methodological constraints which, as Ehlich (1999) points out, began with Saussurean structuralism and culminated in generative linguistics. For almost three decades since the late 1950s, these developments made "language" in a comprehensive sense, as related to the everyday experience of its users, vanish in favour of an idealised and basically artificial entity. This lead in "Core" or theoretical linguistics to a neglect of almost all everyday problems with language and communication encountered by individuals and societies and made it necessary for those interested in socially accountable research into language and communication to draw on a wider range of disciplines, thus giving rise to a flourishing of interdisciplinary areas that have come to be referred to as hyphenated variants of linguistics, such as sociolinguistics, ethnolinguistics, psycholinguistics, conversation analysis, pragmatics, and so on (Davies and Elder 2004).

That these hyphenated variants of linguistics can be said to have originated from dealing with problems may lead to the impression that they fall completely into the scope of applied linguistics. This the more so as their original thematic focus is in line with a frequently quoted definition of applied linguistics as "the theoretical and empirical investigation of real world problems in which language is a central issue" (Brumfit 1997: 93). However, in the recent past much of the work done in these fields has itself been rather "theoretically applied" in the sense introduced above and ultimately even become mainstream in linguistics. Also, in view of the current epistemological developments that see all sciences under the pressure of application, one might even wonder if there is anything distinctive about applied linguistics at all.

Indeed it would be difficult if not impossible to delimit applied linguistics with respect to the practical problems studied and the disciplinary approaches used: Real-world problems with language (and to which, for greater clarity, should be added: "with communication") are unlimited in principle. Also, many problems of this kind are unique and require quite different approaches. Some might be tackled successfully by applying already available linguistic theories and methods. Others might require for their solution the development of new methods and even new theories. Following a frequently used distinction first proposed by Widdowson (1980), one might label these approaches as "Linguistics Applied" or "Applied Linguistics". In addition, language is a trans-disciplinary subject par excellence, with the result that problems do not come labelled and may require for their solution the cooperation of various disciplines.

2.3.   Conceptualisations and communities

The questions of what should be its reference discipline and which themes, areas of research and sub-disciplines it should deal with, have been discussed constantly and were also the subject of an intensive debate (e.g. Seidlhofer 2003). In the recent past, a number of edited volumes on applied linguistics have appeared which in their respective introductory chapters attempt at giving a definition of "Applied Linguistics". As can be seen from the existence of the Association Internationale de Linguistique Appliquée (AILA) and its numerous national affiliates, from the number of congresses held or books and journals published with the label "Applied Linguistics", applied linguistics appears to be a well-established and flourishing enterprise. Therefore, the collective need felt by authors and editors to introduce their publication with a definition of the subject area it is supposed to be about is astonishing at first sight. Quite obviously, what Ehlich (2006) has termed "the struggle for the object of inquiry" appears to be characteristic of linguistics – both of linguistics at large and applied linguistics. Its seems then, that the meaning and scope of "Applied Linguistics" cannot be taken for granted, and this is why a wide variety of controversial conceptualisations exist.

For example, in addition to the dichotomy mentioned above with respect to whether approaches to applied linguistics should in their theoretical foundations and methods be autonomous from theoretical linguistics or not, and apart from other controversies, there are diverging views on whether applied linguistics is an independent academic discipline (e.g. Kaplan and Grabe 2000) or not (e.g. Davies and Elder 2004), whether its scope should be mainly restricted to language teaching related topics (e.g. Schmitt and Celce-Murcia 2002) or not (e.g. Knapp 2006), or whether applied linguistics is a field of interdisciplinary synthesis where theories with their own integrity develop in close interaction with language users and professionals (e.g. Rampton 1997/2003) or whether this view should be rejected, as a true interdisciplinary approach is ultimately impossible (e.g. Widdowson 2005).

In contrast to such controversies Candlin and Sarangi (2004) point out that applied linguistics should be defined in the first place by the actions of those who practically *do* applied linguistics:

> [...] we see no especial purpose in reopening what has become a somewhat sterile debate on what applied linguistics is, or whether it is a distinctive and coherent discipline. [...] we see applied linguistics as a many centered and interdisciplinary endeavour whose coherence is achieved in purposeful, mediated action by its practitioners. [...]
> What we want to ask of applied linguistics is less what it is and more what it does, or rather what its practitioners do. (Candlin/Sarangi 2004:1–2)

Against this background, they see applied linguistics as less characterised by its thematic scope – which indeed is hard to delimit – but rather by the two aspects of "relevance" and "reflexivity". Relevance refers to the purpose applied linguistic activities have for the targeted audience and to the degree that these activities in their collaborative practices meet the background and needs of those addressed – which, as matter of comprehensibility, also includes taking their conceptual and language level into account. Reflexivity means the contextualisation of the intellectual principles and practices, which is at the core of what characterises a professional community, and which is achieved by asking leading questions like "What kinds of purposes underlie what is done?", "Who is involved in their determination?" "By whom, and in what ways, is their achievement appraised?", "Who owns the outcomes?"

We agree with these authors that applied linguistics in dealing with real world problems is determined by disciplinary givens – such as e.g. theories, methods or standards of linguistics or any other discipline – but that it is determined at least as much by the social and situational givens of the practices of life. These do not only include the concrete practical problems themselves but also the theoretical and methodological standards of cooperating experts from other disciplines, as well as the conceptual and practical standards of the practitioners who are confronted with the practical problems in the first place. Thus, as Sarangi and van Leeuwen (2003) point out, applied linguists have to become part of the respective "community of practice".

If, however, applied linguists have to regard themselves as part of a community of practice, it is obvious that it is the entire community which determines what the respective subject matter is that the applied linguist deals with and how. In particular, it is the respective community of practice which determines which problems of the practitioners have to be considered. The consequence of this is that applied linguistics can be understood from very comprehensive to very specific, depending on what kind of problems are considered relevant by the respective community. Of course, following this participative understanding of applied linguistics also has consequences for the Handbooks of Applied Linguistics both with respect to the subjects covered and the way they are theoretically and practically treated.

3. Applied linguistics for problem solving

Against this background, it seems reasonable not to define applied linguistics as an autonomous discipline or even only to delimit it by specifying a set of subjects it is supposed to study and typical disciplinary approaches it should use. Rather, in line with the collaborative and participatory perspective of the communities of practice applied linguists are involved in, this handbook series is based on the assumption that applied linguistics is a specific, problem-oriented way of "doing linguistics" related to the real-life world. In other words: applied linguistics is conceived of here as "linguistics for problem solving".

To outline what we think is distinctive about this area of inquiry: Entirely in line with Popper's conception of science, we take it that applied linguistics starts from the assumption of an imperfect world in the areas of language and communication. This means, firstly, that linguistic and communicative competence in individuals, like other forms of human knowledge, is fragmentary and defective – if it exists at all. To express it more pointedly: Human linguistic and communicative behaviour is not "perfect". And on a different level, this imperfection also applies to the use and status of language and communication in and among groups or societies.

Secondly, we take it that applied linguists are convinced that the imperfection both of individual linguistic and communicative behaviour and language based relations between groups and societies can be clarified, understood and to some extent resolved by their intervention, e.g. by means of education, training or consultancy.

Thirdly, we take it that applied linguistics proceeds by a specific mode of enquiry in that it mediates between the way language and communication is expertly studied in the linguistic disciplines and the way it is directly experienced in different domains of use. This implies that applied linguists are able to demonstrate that their findings – be they of a "Linguistics Applied" or "Applied Linguistics"-nature – are not just "application oriented basic research" but can be made relevant to the real-life world.

Fourthly, we take it that applied linguistics is socially accountable. To the extent that the imperfections initiating applied linguistic activity involve both social actors and social structures, we take it that applied linguistics has to be critical and reflexive with respect to the results of its suggestions and solutions.

These assumptions yield the following questions which at the same time define objectives for applied linguistics:

1. Which linguistic problems are typical of what areas of language competence and language use?
2. How can linguistics define and describe these problems?
3. How can linguistics suggest, develop, or achieve solutions of these problems?
4. Which solutions result in what improvements in speakers' linguistic and communicative abilities or in the use and status of languages in and between groups?
5. What are additional effects of the linguistic intervention?

4.   Objectives of this handbook series

These questions also determine the objectives of this book series. However, in view of the present boom in handbooks of linguistics and applied Linguistics, one should ask what is specific about this series of nine thematically different volumes.

To begin with, it is important to emphasise what it is not aiming at:

– The handbook series does not want to take a snapshot view or even a "hit list" of fashionable topics, theories, debates or fields of study.
– Nor does it aim at a comprehensive coverage of linguistics because some selectivity with regard to the subject areas is both inevitable in a book series of this kind and part of its specific profile.

Instead, the book series will try

– to show that applied linguistics can offer a comprehensive, trustworthy and scientifically well-founded understanding of a wide range of problems,
– to show that applied linguistics can provide or develop instruments to for solving new, still unpredictable problems,

– to show that applied linguistics is not confined to a restricted number of topics such as, e.g. foreign language learning, but that it successfully deals with a wide range of both everyday problems and areas of linguistics,
– to provide a state-of-the-art description of applied linguistics against the background of the ability of this area of academic inquiry to provide descriptions, analyses, explanations and, if possible, solutions of everyday problems. On the one hand, this criterion is the link to trans-disciplinary cooperation. On the other, it is crucial in assessing to what extent linguistics can in fact be made relevant.

In short, it is by no means the intention of this series to duplicate the present state of knowledge about linguistics as represented in other publications with the supposed aim of providing a comprehensive survey. Rather, the intention is to present the knowledge available in applied linguistics today firstly from an explicitly problem solving perspective and secondly, in a non-technical, easily comprehensible way. Also it is intended with this publication to build bridges to neighbouring disciplines and to critically discuss which impact the solutions discussed do in fact have on practice. This is particularly necessary in areas like language teaching and learning – where for years there has been a tendency to fashionable solutions without sufficient consideration of their actual impact on the reality in schools.

5.   Criteria for the selection of topics

Based on the arguments outlined above, the handbook series has the following structure: Findings and applications of linguistics will be presented in concentric circles, as it were, starting out from the communication competence of the individual, proceeding via aspects of interpersonal and inter-group communication to technical communication and, ultimately, to the more general level of society. Thus, the topics of the nine volumes are as follows:

1. Handbook of Individual Communication Competence
2. Handbook of Interpersonal Communication
3. Handbook of Communication in Organisations and Professions
4. Handbook of Communication in the Public Sphere
5. Handbook of Multilingualism and Multilingual Communication
6. Handbook of Foreign Language Communication and Learning
7. Handbook of Intercultural Communication
8. Handbook of Technical Communication
9. Handbook of Language and Communication: Diversity and Change.

This thematic structure can be said to follow the sequence of experience with problems related to language and communication a human passes through in the course of his or her personal biographical development. This is why the topic areas of applied linguistics are structured here in ever increasing concentric circles: in line with biographical development, the first circle starts with the communicative competence of the individual and also includes interpersonal communication as belonging to a person's private sphere. The second circle proceeds to the everyday environment and includes the professional and public sphere. The third circle extends to the experience of foreign languages and cultures, which at least in officially monolingual societies, is not made by everybody and if so, only later in life. Technical communication as the fourth circle is even more exclusive and restricted to a more special professional clientele. The final volume extends this process to focus on more general, supra-individual national and international issues.

For almost all of these topics, there already exist introductions, handbooks or other types of survey literature. However, what makes the present volumes unique is their explicit claim to focus on topics in language and communication as areas of everyday problems and their emphasis on pointing out the relevance of applied linguistics in dealing with them.

Bibliography

Back, Otto
   1970   „Was bedeutet und was bezeichnet der Begriff 'angewandte Sprachwissenschaft'?". *Die Sprache* 16: 21–53.
Brumfit, Christopher
   1997   How applied linguistics is the same as any other science. *International Journal of Applied Linguistics*, 7.1: 86–94.
Candlin, Chris N. and Srikant Sarangi
   2004   Making applied linguistics matter. *Journal of Applied Linguistics* 1.1: 1–8.
Carrier, Michael, Martin Stöltzner, and Jeanette Wette
   2004   *Theorienstruktur und Beurteilungsmaßstäbe unter den Bedingungen der Anwendungsdominanz.* Universität Bielefeld: Institut für Wissenschafts- und Technikforschung [http://www.uni-bielefeld.de/iwt/projekte/wissen/anwendungsdominanz.html, last time accessed 05. 01. 2007].
Davies, Alan
   1999   *Introduction to Applied Linguistics. From Practice to Theory.* Edinburgh: Edinburgh University Press.
Davies, Alan and Catherine Elder
   2004   General introduction – Applied linguistics: subject to discipline? In: Alan Davies and Catherine Elder (eds.) *The Handbook of Applied Linguistics*, 1–16. Malden etc.: Blackwell.
Ehlich, Konrad
   1999   Vom Nutzen der „Funktionalen Pragmatik" für die angewandte Linguistik. In: Michael Becker-Mrotzek und Christine Doppler (Hrsg.) *Medium Sprache im Beruf. Eine Aufgabe für* die *Linguistik*, 23–36. Tübingen: Narr.

Ehlich, Konrad
    2006   Mehrsprachigkeit für Europa – öffentliches Schweigen, linguistische Distanzen. In: Sergio Cigada, Jean-Francois de Pietro, Daniel Elmiger und Markus Nussbaumer (Hrsg.) *Öffentliche Sprachdebatten – linguistische Positionen. Bulletin Suisse de Linguistique Appliquée/VALS-ASLA-Bulletin* 83/1: 11–28.
Grabe, William
    2002   Applied linguistics: an emerging discipline for the twenty-first century. In: Robert B. Kaplan (ed.) *The Oxford Handbook of Applied Linguistics*, 3–12. Oxford: OUP.
Johnson, Keith and Helen Johnson (eds.)
    1998   *Encyclopedic Dictionary of Applied Linguistics. A Handbook for Language Teaching.* Oxford: Blackwell.
Kaplan, Robert B. and William Grabe
    2000   Applied linguistics and the Annual Review if Applied Linguistics. In: W. Grabe (ed.) *Applied Linguistics as an Emerging Discipline. Annual Review of Applied Linguistics*, 20: 3–17.
Knapp, Karlfried
    2006   Vorwort. In: Karlfried Knapp, Gerd Antos, Michael Becker-Mrotzek, Arnulf Deppermann, Susanne Göpferich, Joachim Gabowski, Michael Klemm und Claudia Villiger (Hrsg.) *Angewandte Linguistik. Ein Lehrbuch.* 2. Auflage, XIX–XXIII. Tübingen: Francke – UTB.
Meinel, Christoph
    (2000)   Reine und angewandte Wissenschaft. In: *Das Magazin.* Hrsg. vom Wissenschaftszentrum Nordrhein-Westfalen 11/1: 10–11.
Rampton, Ben
    1997/2003   Retuning in applied linguistics. *International Journal of Applied Linguistics*, 7 (1): 3–25, quoted from Seidlhofer (2003), 273–295.
Sarangi, Srikant and Theo van Leeuwen
    2003   Applied linguistics and communities of practice: gaining communality or losing disciplinary autonomy? In: Srikant Sarangi and Theo van Leeuwen (eds.) *Applied Linguistics and Communities of Practice*, 1–8. London: Continuum.
Schmitt, Norbert and Marianne Celce-Murcia
    2002   An overview of applied linguistics. In: N. Schmitt (ed.) *An Introduction to Applied Linguistics.* London: Arnold.
Seidlhofer, Barbara (ed.)
    2003   *Controversies in Applied Linguistics.* Oxford: Oxford University Press.
Widdowson, Henry
    [1980] 1984   Model and fictions. In: Henry Widdowson (1984) *Explorations in Applied Linguistics 2*, 21–27. Oxford: Oxford University Press.
Widdowson, Henry
    2005   Applied linguistics, interdisciplinarity, and disparate realities. In: Paul Bruthiaux, Dwight Atkinson, William G. Egginton, William Grabe, and Vaidehi Ramanathan (eds.) *Directions in Applied Linguistics. Essays in Honor of Robert B. Kaplan*, 12–25. Clevendon etc: Multilingual Matters.

Preface

Peter Auer would like to thank Hanna Beier and Elin Arbin, who did a great job in helping to copy-edit and proof-read the manuscripts. Li Wei is grateful to Zhu Hua who read and commented on some of the chapters and helped with the proofreading. He did his part of the editing work while at Newcastle University. He would like to acknowledge the support his personal assistant Sam Taylor gave him.

Peter Auer, Freiburg
Li Wei, London

Contents

III. Acting multilingual

IV. Living in a multilingual society

Introduction: Multilingualism as a problem? Monolingualism as a problem?

Peter Auer/Li Wei

Applied Linguistics is often conceived as that part of linguistics which deals with practical problems of everyday life concerning language or communication. It deals with issues in language and verbal interaction that arise not out of an academic interest, but out of the needs of language users. Language impairment, reading and writing disabilities, lack of competence in higher stylistic registers which is required in the upper strata of society, inadequate rhetorical skills, misunderstandings in intercultural communication, the struggles of learning a foreign language, communication in high-stress situations or under difficult conditions – there is a long list of potential problems in language and communication. But why should multilingualism be a problem? We estimate that most of the human language users in the world speak more than one language, i.e. they are at least bilingual. In quantitative terms, then, monolingualism may be the exception and multilingualism the norm. Would it not make more sense to look at monolingualism as a problem that is real and consequential, but which can be "cured"? Isn't the very presupposition of a handbook of applied linguistics on multilingualism prejudiced by monolingual thinking in a world which is de facto multilingual? Aren't we turning something into a problem which is the most natural thing in the world? And isn't the only reason for *not* editing a handbook on monolingualism linguists' remarkable lack of interest in the most natural thing in the world?

Indeed, it is a reasonable assumption that the marginal role research on multilingualism has played within linguistics until some decades ago is a result of the monolingual bias of (particularly) European thinking about language which came into being during a phase of European history in which the nation states defined themselves not in the least by the one (standard) language which was chosen to be the symbolic expression of their unity. By and large, the study of linguistics was equal to analysing single languages (even though these were compared, classified, and typified). The fact that languages influence each other through language contact ("borrowing") was acknowledged of course from the very start of linguistics, but this contact was not seen in the context of multilingualism, and it was taken to be a secondary phenomenon which presupposed the existence and stability of the language systems in contact. The European (standard) languages were seen to 'naturally' belong to and justify the existence of the European nations in a one-to-one relationship, such that the establishment of a new nation state almost inevitably entailed the 'invention' of a new standard language. Being part of a nation was equated with being a native speaker of 'its' language. Seen from this perspective, multilingualism deviated from the norm.

Given the intrinsic link between linguistics as a discipline and the nation states, it is, then, not surprising that by and large, there are no multilingual grammars. (There are some exceptions though; for instance, Turkish language books and practical grammars for second language learners written before 1924 sometimes included a grammar of Osmanic and a grammar of Arabic and/or Persian. This reflects the fact that before the Turkish language reform (itself based on the European nation state ideology), educated Turkish was in some ways amalgamated from these three languages, of which the elites had a good knowledge.) The languages described and analysed were regarded as self-contained systems. Multilingualism was considered to be the consequence of some kind of disturbance in the 'language order', such as migration or conquest, which brought language systems into some kind of unexpected and 'unnatural' contact with one another, often leading to structural simplification (which, in the language ideology of the 19th century, usually implied degeneration). Even today, the ease with which the à la mode parlance of hybridity, borrowed from so-called cultural studies, has been taken on in sociolinguistic and multilingualism research, particularly on second and third generation bilinguals and multilinguals with an immigration background, shows that the idea of multilingualism as a derivative fact is still lingering on: what falls between the codified grammars of 'the languages' is fragile, unstable and can only be understood with reference to these languages. Indeed, there is some truth to this conviction in the present language situation in Europe: the large standard languages have been codified over many centuries, their norms are enforced by effective institutions, particularly the school system, and their stability is guaranteed by the fact that they are backed up by a large corpus of written documents which are easily accessible to everybody since the respective societies are literate to a very high degree.

But this does not mean that the European nation states such as the United Kingdom or France were completely monolingual from the very start, or have ever been, for that matter. It took hundreds of years for them to marginalise languages other than 'English' or 'French' in their territories (such as the Celtic languages or Basque), let alone to homogenise their standard varieties at the cost of the structurally related regional languages spoken in the area. However, they succeeded to a remarkable degree, such that only small groups of minority-language speakers remained 50 years ago. Plurilingual states such as the Austrian (Habsburg) Empire did not survive (with the exception of Switzerland with its polyglossic ideology). Immigrant groups (such as the Hugenots in many Protestant countries, or the Poles in industrialising Germany) quickly adapted (or were forced to adapt) to the monolingual majority's language norms. Elite code-switching, which had been widespread until the 18th and in some places until the 19th century, with Latin and French as the two most important languages used in addition to the local vernacular, disappeared in favour of monolingual speech in the (now standardised, and therefore 'tamed') vernacular. At this point, a different view on second language acquisition took over: it was now seen as a means to communicate with foreigners, not with people of one's own (bilingual) community.

Against this background of the rise and dominance of monolingual national standard ideologies, it can be argued that what we perceive as the problems surrounding multilingualism today are to a large degree a consequence of the monolingualism demanded, fostered and cherished by the nation states in Europe and their knock-offs around the world. The idea (which can still be found in the public debates about multilingualism today, and had respectable supporters within linguistics even 50 years ago) that multilingualism is detrimental to a person's cognitive and emotional development can be traced back to this ideology, as can the insistence on 'pure' language and 'pure', 'non-mixed' speech: it goes back to the purism debate which accompanied the emergence of the European standard languages, above all in the 17th, 18th, and 19th centuries, and finds its offspring in present-day debates about the proper use of English in non-English speaking countries. Nobody scolded Martin Luther and his fellow humanist intellectuals for mixing German and Latin in their dinner table conversations, and nobody finds fault with the elite in Kenya who mix Swahili and English in their everyday speech. For both elites, mixing is prestigious and a matter of course, because the idea of a pure language as a value in itself is neither part of 16th century European culture, nor is it part of the language ideology in most of Africa. However, German fashion designers today are criticised by language purists for speaking or writing German interspersed with English words, Danish youngsters are criticised for inserting *shit* into their Danish, and German-Turkish immigrant adolescents are criticised for mixing Turkish and German. In all these cases, language purism is nothing but a symbolic battle field for social conflicts; but the fact that it is a powerful weapon, that it makes sense as an argument at all in public debate, shows that the normative pattern against which language is discussed continues to be that of 'pure', monolingual language.

If, then, this handbook is concerned with problems that arise through and surrounding multilingualism, it should be clear that these problems are not 'natural' problems which are inherent to multilingualism itself: rather, they arise out of a certain context in which this multilingualism is *seen* as a problem or, rather, creates problems. We address these problems in the four sections of this volume which represent four perspectives on multilingualism: multilingual language acquisition (*Becoming Multilingual*), multilingual language maintenance (*Staying Multilingual*), multilingual interaction (*Acting Multilingual*) and, finally, the often problematic relationship between a multi- or monolingual society and a mono- or multilingual individual (*Living in a Multilingual Society*). We will briefly comment on these sections and indicate what kind of issues and problems are discussed in each of them.

Becoming multilingual

Although it is possible at a later stage in life to add another language to one's repertoire, and thus change from a monolingual to a bilingual or from a bi- to a trilingual speaker, for instance as a consequence of migration, many people are bilingual or multilingual already from birth. In genuinely multilingual societies, this is a matter of course, but in a more or less monolingual society (take, as an example, the U.S.A.), the value and importance attached to multilingual upbringing is a debated issue and depends on many factors. It is fair to say that a large part of the attention research on multilingualism has received in public is due to the fact that for more and more people living in monolingual societies, it is a pressing issue whether and how their children should be brought up multilingually. Although many multilingual parents want to maintain their children's knowledge in the 'other' language (i.e. in addition to the dominant, ambient language in the society) for reasons of identity (it may be their own mother tongue) and for practical reasons (ability to talk to the people 'back home') and professional (better job opportunities), they also fear that learning two languages may put extra stress on their child and might delay or even do irrevocable damage to his or her development and scholastic achievement. This is particularly the case when the acquisition of the two languages takes place simultaneously, and not sequentially. Ch. 1 therefore discusses questions of early multilingual language acquisition from a psycholinguistic point of view: does it make a difference whether the child is exposed to two languages at the same time or to one after the other? Under which circumstances will the first (minority) language be lost, or its acquisition process inhibited? Is there, in general, a difference between monolingual and bilingual acquisition of the same language? Ch. 2 takes up the same issue of bringing up a child multilingually from a more interactional perspective: How should the parents behave in order to provide the optimal environment for both languages to be acquired? Should they themselves code-mix when their child does not consistently use one language with them, although they try to follow the "one person – one language" rule? Becoming multilingual involves more than the acquisition of linguistic forms, but also the socialisation to the rules and expectations that accompany the use of those languages. Ch. 3 looks at multilingual acquisition from a language socialisation perspective and addresses questions such as: How do community structures and cultural values impact the process of multilingual acquisition? How are language ideologies developed through linguistic practices in families and communities? And how are identities shaped and reshaped by the language socialisation process? Whereas the first three chapters in this part deal with early multilingual acquisition, Chs. 4 and 5 examine multilingual acquisition in schools and in later life. Instead of focussing on the linguistic processes of second or third language acquisition, Ch. 4 seeks to answer questions such as: How do adult multilinguals feel about their languages? How do adult multilinguals perceive themselves? In what ways do adult multilinguals use emotional speech and react to emotional expressions? Ch. 5 discusses a variety of bilingual education programmes, and asks crucial questions such as: What are the key components of bilingual education? And what are the criteria for the effectiveness of bilingual education?

Staying multilingual

Becoming multilingual in early childhood is one issue – staying multilingual later in life is another. In monolingual social contexts, children who have grown up in a multilingual family often go through a critical phase when they start school. While the second (non-ambient) language is accepted and useful, perhaps even preferred in the family context, the schools are usually dominated by just one language, which is that of the majority – at least in the institutional interactions taking place, for instance in the classroom with the teacher. Certain 'foreign' languages are accepted in the curriculum, and a high amount of time and energy is spent on teaching them to monolingual children (predominantly English), but other languages have no prestige and do not play a role in the sociolinguistic 'market' of the monolingual school. As it happens, the languages of immigrant communities usually belong to the latter group. (And even though some of them may figure among the fairly prestigious languages, such as Italian, the variety of the language spoken in the child's family (the home language) may not be a standard variant, and therefore not valued by the school.) It is, however, not only the school as an institution and its monolingual habitus that puts considerable pressure on the child to shift from early childhood multilingualism (or minority language monolingualism) to majority language monolingualism; the peer group can have the same effect. The more the child is integrated into a peer network in which the majority language is dominant, the more s/he will adapt to this language in everyday language use. On the other hand, multilingual peer groups can play an important role in counteracting the monolingual pressure of the school and in maintaining some version of the minority language, at least in its oral form.

The crucial role of the school in maintaining the weaker language(s) of a multilingual person in a monolingual society is of course generally acknowledged. Together with language maintenance in the family, it is the school which guarantees intergenerational transmission. While the 'old' minorities in Europe today by and large enjoy multilingual (or minority language) schooling and have access to a good educational infrastructure which may be used or not (cf. the situation of Welsh, Irish, Sorbian or Bretonic), the situation of the immigrant languages and their speakers is different. Part II of the handbook deals with school-related problems particularly with regards to these children. The two introductory chapters (6 and 7) look at multilingual children with an immigrant background in monolingual schools from two different angles. Ch. 6 focuses on the situation in Scandinavia but also includes the United States of America; Ch. 7 focuses on the situation in Germany (North Rhine-Westphalia) but includes an outlook to Australia (Victoria State). Both chapters give an overview of existing programmes for immigrant children and how minority languages are treated in monolingual schools. The options range from complete neglect ('sink or swim' submersion) to reception classes which help pupils from a minority language background to acquire sufficient knowledge in the majority language in order to follow a monolingual class in the language, to additional schooling in the minority language, to bilingual programmes for first graders and to monolingual schooling for children from a minority background in the minority language, at least in the first years. The crucial question here is whether schooling in the minority (mother) language only will enable the children to transfer the literacy skills acquired during this period to the majority language in which they are needed to be successful in the monolingual school system in the long run, and whether schooling in the majority language only will lead to 'semilingualism' in the minority language, which in turn will also negatively influence L2 skills (as predicted, among others, by J. Cummins). The counter-position – more popular in some Western discussions about immigrant multilingualism at the moment – claims that minority language teaching leads to the segregation of minority language speakers from the majority school and ultimately to their scholastic failure.

It is often observed that many multilinguals can speak the various languages in their linguistic repertoire but cannot read or write in them. Bi- and multiliteracy has been an issue of concern for many professionals. Ch. 8 deals with this issue. But instead of seeing it as a singular, primarily cognitive knowledge and skill set, the authors demonstrate how literacy practices are enmeshed within and influenced by social, cultural, political, and economic factors, and that literacy learning and use by multilingual speakers varies according to situation and entails complex social interactions. They argue that despite the global flows of people, goods and ideas across national borders in the 21st century, schools around the world still work towards academic monolingualism and national ideologies. Linguistic hierarchies are being created, with some languages having more power and prestige than others. Literacy is symbolic of the new hierarchies, with some languages receiving more institutional and practical support than others as written languages. They point out that educators have the potential to transform values, as well as literacy practices, by giving room to multimodal and plurilingual literacy practices. The authors call for more research into the role of the media and other institutionalised resources in the development of multiliteracies.

Multilingual language acquisition can proceed as fast as monolingual acquisition in the two languages. However, it is also normal for the acquisition of one language to lag somewhat behind the other, and even for the acquisition of both languages to proceed somewhat more slowly than in monolinguals. Since parents and teachers of multilingual children often find it difficult to decide if a child's competence in one of the languages lags behind that of monolingual children in a way which is entirely normal, or whether there are indications of a pathological delay, this part of the handbook also includes chapters on language proficiency testing and language impairment. Ch. 9 looks at the (rare) cases of Special Language Impairment (SLI) in multilingual children and diagnostic options – a delicate issue, since for many of the relevant languages no testing materials are available. Although the chapter argues that SLI in multilingual children may be overlooked more often than in monolingual children, it also shows that SLI is not a *consequence* of multilingualism but entirely independent of it in its pathogenesis.

One of the critical issues in the study of multilingualism is measurement: How do we measure the extent of bilingualism and multilingualism in a country or a community? How do we measure the level of bilingualism and multilingualism in an individual? Ch. 10 deals with the measurement of individual multilingualism, focussing on three key components: linguistic proficiency, linguistic competence and developmental trajectories. As the authors point out, there is no single standard for the measure of individual bilingualism. Instead, a number of different disciplines have developed a whole range of measures that focus on very different aspects of multilingualism. Many of these have never been tested for their compatibility because they are based on rather different concepts. Where the compatibility of different measures has been tested empirically, the results are often difficult to interpret. The authors present a tentative solution to the problem with a cross-linguistic comparative measurement which is based on linguistic profiling, which in turn is based on Processability Theory. However, the authors point out that their proposal is unlikely to answer all the questions at this moment in time. Much more empirical research on a larger scale is needed. They raise a number of questions for a future research agenda.

Acting Multilingual

The third part of the handbook looks at adult multilinguals and how they use their two or more languages in everyday interaction. Chs. 11 and 12 deal with the most obvious manifestation of multilingualism, i.e. the use of more than one language within a conversation, within a speaker's contribution ('turn') or even within a syntactic unit ('sentence'). These forms of switching and mixing may have a bad reputation in some multilingual (and monolingual) communities, and may be looked upon as a 'debased' form of speaking, a sign of laziness, or simply a lack of competence. But it is obvious that this low prestige of mixing and switching is in itself a consequence of a monolingual ideology which pre-scribes 'pure' language use and sanctions 'hybrid' ways of speaking. There are many arguments against such a negative view, one of which is put forward in detail in Ch. 11, where it is shown that code-switching can be highly functional, and does not take place in a random fashion. In an overview of research in this field from the 1960s onwards, the chapter demonstrates how code-switching as a conversational strategy shows a high degree of structuring and can frame (contextualise) utterances in the same way in which monolinguals use prosody or gesture to contextualise what they say. The two or more languages of bi- or multilingual speakers provide an additional resource for meaning-construction in interaction which monolinguals do not have at their disposal. Using the ana-lytic framework provided by Conversation Analysis, the chapter illustrates how code-switching can be used not only to organise face-to-face interaction, but also to construct interpersonal relationships and social identities.

Ch. 12 investigates a more intricate but also more stable way of mixing two languages, i.e. "mixed codes". In this chapter, mixed codes refer to ways of speaking in which substantial amounts of lexical material from at least two lan-guages are combined on the level of the basic syntactic units ('sentences'). The chapter provides a typology of mixed codes which are found in many parts of the world and thereby at the same time sketches a large number of social situ-ations under which such mixing occurs.

While chapters 11 and 12 are more concerned with the structural orderliness of alternating between or combining two languages, Ch. 13 gives another reason why these phenomena occur: their identity-related function. Displaying and ascribing (social) identities (personae) to oneself and others is important for the members of modern and post-modern societies in which social roles are flex-ible and social categorisation is open to negotiation and re-negotiation. This process takes place in interaction, and language is a powerful resource for it. Ch. 13 shows that beyond simple and misleading equations of multilingual talk with ambivalent (hybrid) identities, the situated use of one language or the other can be used in complex and context-dependent ways in order to construe social identities in discourse. These constructions may be subject to negotiation and must therefore be regarded as interactionally based, indexical (context-dependent) and contingent on the unfolding of the interaction.

Ch. 14 takes the issue of identity-construction one step further by looking into one particular case of code-switching which had not been studied extensively until recently: the use of a language by speakers who are not 'entitled' to use this language but who 'transgress' into another social group's linguistic 'territory'. This type of code-switching, often termed "crossing", has recently been noticed and studied, particularly with reference to the use of immigrant languages by adolescent majority speakers, but it can equally be found outside of immigration contexts, e.g. when Afro-American English features are used by white speakers. Closely related but not identical is the use of mock varieties of another language or variety. In both cases, identity is central: speakers play with other identities than their own, with such diverse purposes as accommodation to the group of 'owners' of that variety, or, on the contrary, antagonistic stance-taking towards them.

The last three chapters of this part of the handbook are devoted to more specific domains of multilingual practices. Chs. 15 and 16 look into professional contexts. In Ch. 15, the multilingual speakers belong to the social and economic elites, and their multilingualism is the result of the increasing international mobility of highly skilled labour. Managers, sport professionals, engineers, etc. are drawn to other countries because of their specific skills. They may stay on permanently or travel on to other countries, and they may use second languages (those of the receiving countries or *lingue franche*) in connection with their profession. Ch. 16 gives an insight into the opposite end of work migration: the influx of largely unskilled or semiskilled labour into middle and northern Europe (in this case, England) over the last 50 years, and the concomitant transformation of the workplace from a largely monolingual setting to a multilingual one. Both domains reflect important changes in Europe which have deeply affected and indeed shaken the monolingual identities of the European nation states. Many institutions, from hospitals to supermarkets, from soccer teams to universities, are confronted with new challenges since their employees and their clients increasingly come from different linguistic backgrounds. Their competence in the dominant language of the society may be far from perfect, but they may bring along linguistic resources which the labour market can make use of. Examples range from multilingual personnel in hospitals where the clients are sometimes not able to express themselves in the dominant (majority) language, to management meetings in large international companies in which language proficiency and professional competence become more and more intertwined.

Ch. 17 addresses questions of multilingualism and commerce. In some sense, globalisation offers increased opportunities for language contact and multilingualism. But the reality is very complex. As some of the other chapters in this volume show, many countries in Africa and Asia are in fact losing their multilingualism in favour of global languages such as English. In the meantime, some languages, such as Japanese, Chinese and Spanish, have attracted significantly more learners because of the commercial opportunities they are seen to be able to offer. The chapter discusses the impact of a globalised economy on societal multilingualism. It examines the role of language in a multilingual business environment. The author seeks to address questions such as: How do people from different language backgrounds with varying levels of multilingual proficiencies cope with language-related problems when engaged in commercial activities? What are the costs and benefits of translation in international business transactions? How does the emergence of English as a world lingua franca impact the global market and multilingual individuals in the workplace?

Living in a Multilingual Society

While part three of the handbook is more centred on the individual multilingual speaker and his or her verbal behaviour, the fourth and final part moves on to societal questions and problems. It starts with an overview of the world's most important language constellations on the state, national and societal levels; Ch. 18 discusses diverse issues such as language legislation and language rights, linguistic ecology and language management. The author offers a typological framework of minority language situations based on the distinctions between unique versus non-unique, cohesive versus non-cohesive and adjoining and non-adjoining. The following two chapters (19 and 20) cover the two most important types of multilingual groups in the context of the (European) monolingual nation states, i.e. 'old' (autochthonous) and 'new' (immigrant) minorities. Both were discussed in previous chapters of the handbook as well, but in different contexts. From the societal point of view, matters of linguistic rights, language planning, standardisation and politics enter into the picture.

'Old' or 'autochthonous' regions are those which at one point had their own language(s) and were partly politically independent, but which later joined or were forced to join a nation state which had a different national standard variety. As a consequence, the autochthonous language of the area came under the control of an exoglossic standard which symbolised the power of that nation state. Since the knowledge and use of the majority language was a prerequisite for social and economic success in such an area, the speakers of the minority language had to become proficient in the majority language as well as in their own language; in many cases, strong social pressure against the minority language and its lack of prestige, certainly on the national level, has led to complete language shift, i.e. the disappearance of the minority language. A similar situation emerges when the minority language area is supported by the standard language of another nation state which is structurally related and which can optionally function as an exoglossic 'roof'. (Often, this holds for border areas in which the political border and the language border do not coincide.) An example of the first is Saami in Norway, Sweden and Finland; an example of the second, discussed in detail in this chapter, is Alsatian in France.

The second prototypical constellation – that of 'new' immigrant multilingualism – is discussed from a societal point of view in Ch. 20. The review takes an ecological approach, exploring how the new minorities manage their multilingualism within local, national and global contexts. The author argues that the migratory histories of the minority groups are an important key to their present structures, identities and language ideologies. The author contrasts the government policies towards new linguistic minorities with the community initiatives in language and cultural maintenance. The issue of new multilingual practices is also discussed.

While the preceding chapters have a rather European orientation, the last two chapters broaden this perspective. Ch. 21 looks into the multilingualism of ex-colonial states which is in some way related to their colonial past. However, dealing at length with the examples of Singapore on the one hand, and Mozambique on the other, the chapter shows that the role of the colonial language (English and Portuguese, in this case) in each case is very different, and so is that of the local languages. The commodification of the colonial languages plays an important part in this process, but the role of language is also crucial for the building of new nation states, or its reversal ('retraditionalisation'). The last chapter (22) investigates the ways in which globalised commerce and industry impact multilingualism. While some authors think that globalisation will lead to the worldwide dominance of English, others think that the global mobility of information, ideas, services, goods, tourists and work forces increases the need to communicate, which in turn supports at least certain forms of multilingualism. The chapter argues that globalisation entails a tension between cultural and linguistic diversity on the one hand, and an opposite push towards erasing it on the other.

Tremendous progress has been made in research on multilingualism over the last twenty years, as witnessed in the studies surveyed in this volume. Nevertheless, the monolingual ideology remains dominant in many spheres of society and public life. Many people, including some of those who are themselves bilingual and multilingual, still have misconceived ideas about multilingualism. They fail to see how monolingualism as an ideology is creating restrictions, barriers, and conflicts for us all. Instead, they blame multilingualism for the world's problems. There is clearly a great deal more to be done, not only in researching the fundamentals of multilingualism but also in transferring the knowledge of multilingualism to wider society. This has to be one of the most important challenges for us in the near future. Political authorities in today's world do seem to realise that multilingualism is a sensitive issue. Nevertheless one might wonder how sincere political authorities are when they officially promote bilingualism and multilingualism. Do they really want their citizens to be equally fluent in the national language(s) and minority/immigrant/foreign languages? Or are they using 'double-talk', preferring a minimal bilingualism where knowledge in the minority/immigrant/foreign language is just enough to allow for basic communication but not enough for the speaker to become or to feel bicultural? Since culture and language are so closely intertwined, many politicians may fear that introducing 'foreign' languages/cultures too early might have dire political consequences: i.e. the dilution of the individual's sense of national identity and group membership. They may not want the children to be too attracted to the other language communities, especially in countries where there is tension between communities. It is important that such socio-political issues are addressed head-on.

The increased opportunities for individuals to become bilingual and multilingual are one of the most significant social changes in the last two decades. It has never been easier for people to encounter and learn new languages in schools, through professional contacts, on the internet, through music, arts and other forms of entertainment, and in everyday social interaction. Contacts with people who speak languages other than one's own are increasingly becoming part of the daily routine. Multilingualism in turn brings new opportunities to both the individual and society. Multilingualism offers society a bridge-building potential – bridges between different groups within the nation, bridges with groups beyond the artificial boundaries of a nation, and bridges for cross-fertilization between cultures. Multilingualism also prompts society to rethink the relationship between unity and diversity, to come round for the idea of peaceful co-existence between different linguistic and cultural groups and to observe the rights and obligations of one another. Far from being a problem, multilingualism is part of the solution for our future. Social stability, economic development, tolerance and cooperation between groups is possible only when multilingualism is respected.

I. Becoming bilingual

1. Early bilingual and multilingual acquisition

Johanne Paradis

1. Different kinds of child bilinguals and multilinguals

It has been estimated that the majority of children across the globe grow up speaking more than one language (Tucker 1998), but these bilingual and multilingual children differ from each other in terms of when exposure to each language began, and the sociolinguistic context in which their languages are spoken (Genesee, Paradis and Crago 2004; Goldstein 2004a). These differences have consequences for acquisition patterns and rates of the languages, as well as for ultimate proficiency in each language. Furthermore, the research issues and questions surrounding dual and multiple language acquisition are often different depending on the kind of child bilingual/multilingual. Genesee et al. (2004) present a categorization of dual language children based on two intersecting variables: simultaneous or sequential exposure to two languages, and the minority or majority status of those two languages. Simultaneous bilingual children are those whose dual language learning experiences began at birth or at least before the age of 3;0 (de Houwer 1995; McLaughlin 1978). The majority of simultaneous bilinguals studied in the research are children acquiring their two languages at home where each parent speaks their native language to the child; however, some simultaneous bilinguals acquire both languages from both parents who freely alternate between them, or acquire one language mainly at daycare and the other at home. The process of simultaneous bilingualism is commonly referred to as bilingual first language acquisition (BFLA). Sequential bilingualism is distinct from simultaneous bilingualism in that one language is introduced after the other language has become somewhat established, e.g., after the age of 3;0. Sequential bilingual children typically speak their first language (L1) language at home with both parents, and their second language (L2) at school.

For some simultaneous and sequential bilingual children, one of their two languages is a minority language, meaning it is not widely spoken outside the home, and has little or no cultural, political or educational status in the broader society. For simultaneous bilinguals this means that the parent who speaks that language is the primary and sometimes solitary source of that language, a situation referred to as 'family bilingualism' (Lanza 1997). Sequential bilinguals with a minority L1 are often children from immigrant families where both parents speak the L1 at home, and the child learns the majority societal language in the community and in school. In contrast, for some bilinguals, both their languages have majority status. French-English bilinguals in Montréal, Canada can be considered majority language bilinguals because both their languages are widely spoken in the community and enjoy similar social status. Sequential bilingual children who speak the societal language at home and in the community, like English in Canada or the United States, but attend immersion school in another language such as French or Spanish by choice, can be considered L1 majority – L2 minority children. It is important to note that the minority-majority distinction is really a gradient rather than categorical concept (Suyal 2002). For example, both French and English have majority status in the Canadian provinces of Québec and New Brunswick, Spanish has varying levels of status depending on the region in the United States (see Oller and Eilers 2002), and a language like Nepali is a highly minority language in most centres in North America.

In the context of early multilingual development, the categorization of Genesee et al. (2004) expands to include more possibilities. For example, children in the Basque region of Spain may have learned the majority languages of their community, Basque and Spanish, either simultaneously or sequentially, and also be acquiring a minority third language (L3), English, in school (Cenoz 2001). Alternatively, children may acquire two minority L1s at home from immigrant parents, and will also acquire the majority language of the host country simultaneously or sequentially through daycare or schooling (Hoffmann 1985; Maneva 2004).

In this review, simultaneous and early sequential bilingual acquisition is presented in separate sections, but commonalities between these two groups are discussed in the final section. Section 2 is focused primarily on research pertaining to simultaneous bilinguals' development in the preschool years, with some mention of outcomes in the early school years, and section 3 on sequential bilinguals mainly reports research conducted with L1 minority L2 learners. For more information on school age children who experienced BFLA, or who are majority L1 children learning an L2 at school, see additional readings in section 5, and Baker (this volume). Research on early multilingualism is very limited, but findings from available studies are included in both sections on simultaneous and sequential bilingualism. In addition, how issues raised in research on bilinguals might impact on multilingual development is discussed even in the absence of available research. In most cases throughout this chapter, the issues raised and findings reported for bilingual children would also apply to multilingual children, and thus, use of the term 'bilingual' is meant to include multilinguals as well.

2.   Simultaneous bilingual children

2.1.   Patterns and rates of acquisition in simultaneous bilinguals

Unlike sequential bilinguals, simultaneous bilinguals are exposed to two languages as infants and toddlers, thus, they receive this dual input before they are old enough to explicitly or consciously understand that their input comes from two linguistic sources. For this reason, researchers have asked whether these children forge an initial unitary linguistic system that later must be differentiated into two systems (Genesee 1989; Leopold 1949; Volterra and Taeschner 1978). Currently, researchers have shifted from the 'one system or two?' question to more nuanced questions about degrees of contact and separation between the two developing languages of these children (e.g., see contributions in Döpke 2000). Another central issue in BFLA research has been how bilinguals compare to their monolingual age-peers in their learning patterns and linguistic achievements in each language. Bilingual children have to acquire two linguistic systems in the same amount of time that monolinguals acquire one. Moreover, they seldom receive equal amounts of input in both languages, and often one language is more proficient or 'dominant' than the other. Therefore, it is possible that bilinguals acquire their languages at different rates than monolinguals. With respect to trilingualism in the preschool years, the issues of amount of input and linguistic achievement in each language are heightened in importance. Case studies of early trilingualism have found that the least dominant language, e.g., the language for which the child receives the smallest amount of input, may display incomplete acquisition of some grammatical aspects, or become more a passive than an active language in the child's repertoire (Hoffman 1985; Maneva 2004). In this section, we examine how phonological, lexical and morphosyntactic acquisition unfold in children learning two or more languages at one time in order to address the following questions: (1) Do bilingual children have a unitary or dual/multiple linguistic system at the early stages? (2) What is the nature of crosslinguistic influence between the developing languages of a bilingual child? (3) How do bilinguals compare with monolingual age-mates? Do they display unique developmental patterns? Do they lag behind monolinguals in their acquisition rates in one or both their languages?

2.1.1.   *Phonological acquisition in simultaneous bilinguals*

Speech perception abilities in infants with monolingual exposure show the following patterns. Initially, infants can discriminate most phonetic contrasts that are used phonemically in the world's languages, like [pa] vs. [ba], [da] vs. [ɖa], or [e] vs. [ɛ]. These language-general perception abilities shift to language-specific abilities between 6 to 12 months of age such that the infant can only discriminate contrasts present in the ambient language, with the shift occurring for vowels before consonants (see Werker and Curtin 2005 for review). With respect to infants exposed to dual language input, researchers have found that the shift to language specific abilities follows the same vowels-before-consonants pattern as monolinguals, but that it occurs a few months later (Bosch and Sebastián-Gallés, 2003; Burns, Werker and McVie 2003). For a minority of contrasts, such as [d] vs. [ð] in English, discrimination requires language experience, and Sundara, Polka and Genesee (in press) found that French-English bilingual four-year-olds lagged slightly behind monolingual English children in their ability to discriminate this contrast. Taken together, these findings for bilinguals highlight the role of amount of language exposure in the development of speech perception.

Regarding production of sounds, determining whether bilingual toddlers have two distinct phonological systems is complicated by several factors: immense variation in young children's phonetic productions of individual segments, crosslinguistic universality of substitution processes, language-specific segments often being the marked or late-acquired ones, and the possibility that early linguistic organization consists of an inventory of individual word forms, without an abstract phonemic system (Deuchar and Quay 2000; Johnson and Lancaster 1998; Paradis 2001; Vihman 2002). For example, if a bilingual child substitutes stops for fricative consonants in words from both languages, this may not constitute pertinent evidence addressing the "one system or two?" question because two monolinguals acquiring both languages might display the same pattern. Given these complications for the toddler years, consistent evidence of separate phonological systems in production emerges from research with bilingual children older than 2;0 (Johnson and Wilson 2002; Kehoe, Lleó and Rakow 2004; Paradis 2001; except see Keshavarz and Ingram 2002). Turning to patterns and rates of development, studies looking at a range of phonological properties, from acoustic cues to the prosodic structure of words, have found some bilingual children to lag behind monolinguals in their acquisition rates (Kehoe, 2002; Kehoe, Lleó and Rakow 2004; Lleó 2002), and to display crossover effects from one phonological system to the other (Ball, Müller and Munro 2001; Kehoe et al. 2004; Keshavarz and Ingram 2002; Paradis, 2001). The presence of bilingual/monolingual differences and crossover effects may be predicted by whether the target structure is marked or late-acquired, as well as by bilingual children's dominance (Ball et al. 2001; Kehoe 2002; Lleó 2002; Paradis 2001).

2.1.2.   Lexical acquisition in simultaneous bilinguals

Volterra and Taeschner (1978) claimed that bilingual toddlers do not have translation equivalents, e.g. *horse* and *cheval* for a French-English child, in their early productive vocabularies, and that this constituted evidence for a unitary lexicon. Subsequent research with larger numbers of children contradicts Volterra and Taeschner's empirical claim since bilingual toddlers' early lexicons consist of 3.9% to 67% translation equivalents, depending on children's ages and methods used to determine vocabulary composition (Deuchar and Quay 2000; Johnson and Lancaster 1998; Nicoladis and Secco 2000; Pearson, Fernández and Oller 1995; Quay 1995;Vihman 1985). However, there is no consensus about whether the presence of translation equivalents alone constitutes evidence for differentiation at the lexical level (see Deuchar and Quay 2000; Johnson and Lancaster 1998; Pearson et al. 1995).

Bilingual children employ the same word learning mechanisms as monolinguals to build their lexicons; however, their developmental timetable may be somewhat altered by the dual language experience (Fennell, Polka and Werker 2002; Hoff and Mackay 2005). For example, Fennell et al. (2002) found that bilingual and monolingual toddlers both showed the ability to learn new words for novel objects when the words differed only slightly phonetically (minimal pairs), but this ability emerged approximately three months later in the bilinguals than in the monolinguals. For older bilingual children, the dual language experience may confer some advantages over monolinguals in cognitive abilities underlying literacy-based lexical skills (see Bialystok 2004 for review). Regarding word formation rules like compounding, bilinguals can create novel compounds at the same ages as monolinguals; however, the actual compounds they produce and the stages they pass through show evidence of crosslinguistic interference (Nicoladis 2002; 2003). For instance, deverbal compounds in English follow an object-verb-*er* pattern, e.g., *pencil sharpener*; whereas in French, they follow a reversed verb-object pattern, *taille-crayon* 'sharpen-pencil'. French-English bilingual children produced more verb-object novel compounds in English than English monolinguals, which Nicoladis (2003) attributed to the influence of French. Importantly, Nicoladis (2003) observed no parallel crosslinguistic effects on a compound comprehension task, suggesting crosslinguistic transfer to be a production phenomenon only.

Another facet of crosslinguistic interaction is crosslanguage interdependence to facilitate the process of lexical development (cf. Cummins 2000). For example, learning a translation equivalent for an already lexicalized concept might be faster than learning a new label for a new concept. Research conducted to date does not show strong support for this hypothesis. Using data from standardized measures of vocabulary and early grammatical development, Marchman, Martínez-Sussmann and Dale (2004) found that relationships between lexical and grammatical measures are stronger within each language of a bilingual toddler than between them. Pearson et al. (1995) argued that their data showed little evidence for a preference to learn translation equivalents among Spanish-English bilingual toddlers and two-year-olds. In school-age bilingual children, Cobo-Lewis, Eilers, Pearson and Umbel (2002) and Pearson (2002) found crosslanguage inter-relationships for literacy-based lexical skills and narrative skills in Spanish and English, but found no compelling crosslanguage inter-relationships for receptive and expressive vocabulary size and diversity.

Possibly the most significant and long-standing finding emerging from research on lexical development in simultaneous bilinguals is that on standardized measures of expressive and receptive vocabulary development, simultaneous bilinguals, as a group, score lower than monolingual age-mates in each language. This effect has been shown in toddlers, preschool and school age children, acquiring English together with Spanish or French (Cobo-Lewis, Pearson, Eilers and Umbel 2002; Doyle, Champagne and Segalowitz 1978; Marchman et al. 2004; Nicoladis and Genesee 1996a; Pearson, Fernandez and Oller 1993; Umbel, Pearson, Fernandez and Oller 1992). Vocabulary size reflects quantity of input in each language, and therefore, bilingual preschoolers can score closer to monolinguals in the language in which they receive more input (Marchman et al. 2004; Patterson and Pearson 2004; Pearson et al. 1993; Pearson, Fernández, Lewedeg and Oller 1997). For school age bilinguals, input quantity variables, such as language(s) spoken at home and language(s) of instructional program, were associated with lexical achievements and how closely these children's performance resembled that of monolinguals (Cobo-Lewis, Pearson et al. 2002). Regarding vocabulary size as a clinical measure of developmental progress, Pearson et al. (1993) and Pearson (1998) show that bilingual children are not delayed in their ability to accumulate lexicalized concepts; when bilingual children's total conceptual vocabulary is taken into account across both languages, they perform on par with monolinguals age-mates. It is probable that multilingual development in the preschool years would render children's vocabularies even more susceptible to this 'distributed' effect (Oller and Eilers 2002), where lexicalized concepts are spread across three or more languages, and thus, vocabulary size in each language would be smaller than for monolinguals. However, to date, research on early multilingual children has not included comparisons with monolinguals based on standardized measures.

2.1.3. *Morphosyntactic acquisition in simultaneous bilinguals*

There is some debate concerning whether bilingual toddlers have differentiated morphosyntactic systems since it is possible that even monolingual children do not have a grammar per se organizing their earliest word combinations (Meisel 1994a; Deuchar and Quay 2000). When bilingual children are reliably using word combinations and some grammatical morphology in their speech, researchers have found evidence for two separate morphosyntactic systems (Meisel 1989; Meisel 1994a; Paradis and Genesee 1996; 1997). Meisel (1989) demonstrated that two French-German bilingual children's verb placement followed appropriate language-specific patterns beginning as early as 2;0. Paradis and

Genesee (1996) examined the distribution of pronouns and finite/nonfinite verbs in the spontaneous speech of three French-English bilingual two-year-olds and found that they displayed the same distinct and language-specific patterns of development as monolingual children. In a case study of a multilingual child, Maneva (2004) reported that her first word combinations in the flexible word order languages of Bulgarian and Arabic were mainly verb + subject in construction; whereas, her first word combinations in French, which has fixed word order, were subject + verb in construction. Thus, the child's first word combinations reflected typical patterns of her three input languages.

Crosslinguistic influence between the two developing grammatical systems of bilingual children has recently been the focus of many studies. Researchers have found examples of crosslinguistic structures in children acquiring French or Italian along with German and Dutch, and German, Italian, Spanish, French or Cantonese along with English (Döpke 1998, 2000; Hulk 2000; Müller 1998; Müller and Hulk 2001; Paradis and Navarro 2003; Serratrice, Sorace and Paoli 2004; Yip and Matthews 2000). Researchers who examined these effects over time have found that they are temporary, and concentrated between the ages of 2;0 to 3;6. To give an example, German is a verb-second language that has variable but rule-governed word order, and both verb-object and object-verb word orders are possible; whereas, English has rigid verb-object word order. Döpke (1998) studied children acquiring English and German simultaneously in Australia and found that they went through a stage where they overused the verb-object word order in German. Since this kind of word order error is very rare in monolingual German children, Döpke (1998) argued that the quantitative effect of verb-object structures in the English input constituted competing cues to those from the German input, and caused the children to take longer to converge on the appropriate German word order rules. Müller and Hulk (2001) put forward a similar argument in their claim that crosslinguistic effects are likely to happen where there is structural ambiguity between bilingual children's two languages such that language A allows for more than one option for a structure, but language B only allows for only one. In this case, the more rigid system (language B) may influence the system with options, but not the other way around. Paradis and Navarro (2003) found evidence consistent with Müller and Hulk's proposal by examining the use of overt and null subjects by a Spanish-English bilingual. This child produced more redundant overt subjects in her Spanish than monolingual children, possibly due to the non-null subject nature of English. In contrast, Yip and Matthews (2000) found evidence for crosslinguistic transfer in a Cantonese-English child that was not traceable to structural ambiguity, and was more likely explained by dominance in Cantonese. For example, this child sometimes produced head-final relative clauses in English, e.g. *where's the [Santa Claus give me] the gun*? 'where's the gun [that Santa Claus give(gave) me]?' (Yip and Matthews 2000: 204). It is important to point out that not all researchers have found crosslinguistic influence to be apparent in bilingual children's morphosyntactic development (Hulk and Müller 2000; Paradis and Genesee 1996). Whether crosslinguistic influence is an individual or a group trait, and whether it is the result of structural ambiguity or dominance, is currently being debated and researched.

As with both phonological and lexical developmental, researchers have compared morphosyntactic outcomes of bilingual and monolingual age mates in order to determine if bilinguals lag behind monolinguals due to their reduced exposure time to each language. Results of such comparisons have been mixed, with some studies showing no evidence for delayed development in bilinguals (Paradis and Genesee 1996; Paradis, Crago, Genesee and Rice 2003; Paradis, Crago and Genesee 2005/2006), while others have found bilinguals to be less advanced in their development than monolingual age-mates for particular aspects of morphosyntax (Gathercole 2002; Gathercole and Thomas 2005; Marchman et al. 2004; Nicoladis, Palmer and Marentette in press). Such mixed findings suggest that morphosyntactic development may be less vulnerable to the effects of reduced input than vocabulary accumulation.

2.2.   Language choice and codeswitching in simultaneous bilinguals

A salient and unique characteristic of bilingual as opposed to monolingual development is that these children must learn to choose which language to speak, and whether or not to mix the two languages, according to the discourse situation. Bilingual children's sensitivity to their interlocutors' linguistic preferences and needs is displayed by their language choice overall; within the broad concept of language choice, there are different types of language mixing. Mixing can take the form of inter- or intra-utterance codeswitching. Inter-utterance codeswitching consists of shifting from one language to another between utterances. Intra-utterance codeswitching consists of producing elements from both languages in one utterance, e.g., *where's the* mitaine *go?* 'mitten', and *we bring* saucisses à la garderie *yesterday*, 'sausages to the daycare' (Paradis and Nicoladis, in press: 17).

Early models claimed that indiscriminate language choice characterized bilingual development before 3;0, and this constituted evidence for a unitary linguistic system (Leopold 1949; Volterra and Taeschner 1978). In contrast, more recent research has shown that bilingual children can differentiate their two languages according to their interlocutor, at least from the age of 2;0 and possibly earlier for some (Deuchar and Quay 2000; Genesee, Nicoladis and Paradis 1995; Lanza, 1997; Nicoladis and Genesee 1996b). Further demonstration of pragmatic differentiation is shown by bilingual and multilingual children's ability to accommodate the language preference of familiar versus unfamiliar interlocutors (Genesee, Boivin, Nicoladis 1996; Maneva 2004; Suyal 2002), and to accommodate shifts in the amount of language mixing initiated by the interlocutor across different play sessions (Comeau, Genesee and Paquette 2003). However, pragmatic differentiation is subject to development because four-year-olds show superior interlocutor sensitivity to two-year-olds (Suyal 2002; Paradis and Nicoladis in press). Finally, anecdotal evidence for children's early awareness of their dual or multiple linguistic systems can be found in overt metalinguistic statements, for example, *az govar'a na* balgarski *frenski I arabski* 'I speak Bulgarian, French and Arabic' at age 2;7 (Maneva, 2004: 116), or behaviour such as translating for parents at age 2;3 (Hoffmann 1985).

Both child-internal and child-external factors have been proposed to explain variations in bilingual children's ability to pragmatically differentiate their languages. First, children's interlocutor sensitivity is constrained by their degree of proficiency in each language. Genesee et al. (1995) found that English dominant two-year-olds used more French with their French-speaking parent than with their English-speaking parent, but used a lot of English with both. Examinations of children's language choice as a function of their lexical knowledge in each language have shown that children are more likely to codeswitch when they do not know the word for the referent in that language, in other words, when they have a lexical gap (Deuchar and Quay 2000; Nicoladis and Secco 2000; Nicoladis and Genesee 1996b). With respect to intra-utterance codeswitching in particular, some researchers have suggested that bilingual children use mixing to increase their morphosyntactic expression in their weaker language, which can be construed as a grammatical gap-filling strategy (Bernardini and Schlyter 2004; Gawlitzek-Maiwald and Tracy 1996; Lanvers 2001; Lanza 1997; Petersen 1988). With respect to external factors, Lanza (1997; this volume) argued that through their reactions to children's mixing, parents may be consciously or unconsciously negotiating a bilingual versus monolingual discourse context, and in turn, influencing their children's language choices (see also Lanvers 2001; Maneva 2004). Other environmental factors, such as, the usual language of a physical location, or which family members are participating in the discourse, can influence bilingual children's language choice (Deuchar and Quay 2000; Vihman 1998). Finally, Paradis and Nicoladis (in press) and Suyal (2002) argued that for older preschool bilingual children, understanding of the language patterns in the community and the sociolinguistic status of the languages might influence their language choice (see also Hoffmann 1985; Maneva 2004; Pan 1995).

Since language choice patterns change over time in bilingual children as they develop more proficiency in each language, researchers have also asked whether the structure of their intra-utterance codeswitches changes over time also as a function of language development. Adult models of bilingual codeswitching emphasize that combining elements from both languages in one sentence is a systematic or rule-governed process, although the particular rules proposed differ between models (e.g. Myers-Scotton 1993; Poplack 1980; see Muysken this volume). If adult codeswitching is the end point for child bilingual code-switching, then it is relevant to examine the structural aspects of bilingual children's codeswitching to ascertain when in development they demonstrate adult-like rules. Most investigations addressing this question have examined the syntactic categories of single-items in mixed utterances because in adult codes-witching open class words like nouns and verbs are freer to mix into a host language sentence than closed class elements (Vihman 1985; Lanza 1997; Meisel 1994b; Köppe 1996; Deuchar and Quay 2000; Nicoladis and Genesee 1998). All studies except Nicoladis and Genesee (1998) found that young bilingual children initially showed the reverse pattern to the adults; however, bilingual children's patterns may appear distinct from adults' not because their codes-witching is constrained by different underlying principles, but because their lexicons have not developed sufficiently to show the same proportions of open class and closed class words as adults (see Paradis, Nicoladis and Genesee 2000 for further discussion). Meisel (1994b) also discusses the possibility that early in development, bilingual children may appear to violate adult rules of code-switching indirectly because they have not yet acquired the morphosyntactic structures and lexical items to obey them. Paradis et al. (2000) tested this hypothesis by examining codeswitched utterances in a semi-longitudinal corpus of 15 French-English bilingual children aged 2;0 to 3;6. They found that from 2;0, the children's mixed utterances were consistent with the constraints proposed in the Matrix-Language Frame Model (Myers-Scotton 1993) nearly 90% of the time, and violations could be explained by the absence of sufficient morphosyntactic development. Other studies of older preschool bilingual children have found that the patterns in their codeswitched utterances mirrored those of the adult models to which they were compared (Paradis and Nicoladis in press; Vihman 1998). In sum, while there is some dispute about the nature of codeswitching patterns in very young bilinguals, most research shows that by 3;0, bilingual children display rule-governed and adult-like patterns.

3.   Sequential bilingual children

3.1.   Patterns and rates of acquisition in sequential bilinguals

Unlike simultaneous bilinguals, early sequential bilinguals and multilinguals have one or two languages established before they learn their second or third one. This raises the question of how children's L1 influences their L2, or in turn, their L3 development. Also unlike simultaneous bilinguals, sequential bilinguals and multilinguals are learning one of their languages when they are more cognitively mature, although much younger than adult language learners. This could potentially speed up the process of acquisition for the target language and permit them to quickly 'catch up' with their monolingual native speaker peers. It could also mean that age effects on ultimate attainment may be less apparent than with adult language learners. In this section, phonological, lexical and morphosyntactic acquisition in early sequential bilinguals and multilinguals is discussed with a view to addressing the following questions: (1) What is the role of the L1 in child L2 and L3 acquisition? (2) How does child L2 acquisition compare to the monolingual acquisition of the same target language? (3) When, if ever, do child L2 learners catch up to their native-speaker age peers?

3.1.1.   Phonological acquisition in sequential bilinguals

Flege (1999) argues that the starting point for L2 speech development is the L1 phonetic categories. This perspective is supported by research showing that Spanish L1-English L2 children aged 4–7 years are more accurate in their production of phonemes that are shared between the two languages than for phonemes that are only in English (Goldstein 2004b). Furthermore, the effects of the L1 phonology may extend across a sequential bilingual's lifespan. Flege (2004) reports research examining foreign accent ratings of Korean and Japanese L1 children acquiring English, and found that after five years experience with English, these children still did not rate identically to native English-speaker peers. Retrospective developmental studies show that adults who began to acquire their L2 as early as 6–8 years of age can have a perceptible foreign accent (Flege 1999). Furthermore, phonological distance between the L1 and the L2 can make a difference in ultimate attainment. Flege and Fletcher (1992) found that Chinese L1 adults had more perceptible foreign accents than Spanish L1 adults, even though both groups had been immersed in a majority English environment from 5–8 years of age. With respect to acoustic properties like voice onset time, Watson (1991) reported that language-specific production systems can develop for L1 and L2 (see also Flege 1991), but that the perceptual systems might be permanently unified between the two languages of early sequential bilinguals. Essentially, in the phonological domain, L1 and L2 may always be interconnected, and so child L2 learners may never completely 'catch up' to their monolingual peers in the sense that they may always have a distinct and composite sound system. However, early sequential bilinguals tend to pronounce the L2 more like monolinguals than L2 adults (Winitz et al. 1995; Flege 2004).

3.1.2.   Lexical acquisition in sequential bilinguals

Child L2 learners, with both majority and minority L1s, need to stretch meager lexical resources in the target language to meet the needs of complex and demanding environments like a classroom. Thus, L2 children are often in a situation where the communicative task outstrips the L2 vocabulary they have learned. Harley (1992) documented phenomena associated with this situation in English L1 children in French immersion schools, as compared to French monolingual children. In describing a cartoon strip, the L2 children more often used non-specific nominals e.g. *une chose* 'a thing', or non-specific verbs, e.g., *il va dans l'eau* 'he goes into the water' instead of *il plonge dans l'eau* 'he dives into the water' than the native-speakers. The L2 children were also more likely to use sound symbolism or codeswitching to get the meaning across for a word they did not know in French. Golberg, Paradis and Crago (under review) looked at minority L1 children's non-specific versus appropriate uses of the verb *do* over time in their English L2. For example, *he do a baseball* instead of *he throws a baseball* is a non-specific usage. Frequencies of non-specific uses decreased steadily from the interval when the children had 9 months exposure to English until they had 34 months exposure.

The lexical compensatory strategies used by children acquiring their L3 raise the question of which of their other two languages would act as the source language for interference in the L3: the children's L1, their more proficient language whether L1 or L2, or the language that is typologically closer to the L3? Cenoz (2001) examined story-telling data in the English L3 of Basque-Spanish bilingual school-age children. She found that Spanish, which is typologically closer to English, was the predominant source language for lexical interference in English, regardless of whether Spanish was the children's L1 or L2.

Because vocabulary size is important for success in literacy, researchers have been highly concerned with understanding when L2 children catch up to their monolingual peers in this domain. Regarding rate of development, it is possible that L2 learners accumulate vocabulary more rapidly the second time round because they are more cognitively mature when the process starts, and also have an existing lexicon in their L1 to draw upon for insight into conceptual-lexical mappings. Winitz et al. (1995) found that a Polish L1 child advanced four developmental years in vocabulary knowledge within one chronological year of exposure to English, as shown by age-equivalency scores on the Peabody Picture Vocabulary Test (PPVT). Following the same logic, Golberg et al. (under review) compared age equivalency scores from the PPVT with months of exposure to English for 19 L2 children. The children gained 3.24 mental age equivalency years in less than three years of exposure to English, suggesting somewhat more rapid development in L2 than might be expected in L1; however, age-equivalency scores only outpaced months of exposure during the last 12 month interval.

Turning to comparisons with monolingual age-mates, Umbel et al. (1992) studied the receptive vocabulary knowledge of 1st grade Spanish L1 children in Miami who had been introduced to English in kindergarten. These English L2 learners scored lower than the monolingual norming sample mean on the PPVT;

however, they scored at the mean for the equivalent test in Spanish. This study indicates that vocabulary accumulation in the majority language is very gradual for sequential bilinguals, and subsequent research with Spanish-L1-English-L2 children in Miami showed that these children scored below monolingual English children on standardized tests for productive and receptive vocabulary until 5th grade, at which point the gap narrowed (Cobo-Lewis et al. 2002). Golberg et al. (under review) also compared English L2 children's performance to the monolingual norming sample for the PPVT, and found that the children had nearly caught up to their monolingual peers after just 3 years of full-time schooling in English, as their mean standard score was 97 at that time. A possible reason for the more rapid lexical acquisition displayed by the children in Golberg et al.'s study than for the children in Miami could be opportunities to use the native language. Spanish-speakers form a large community in Miami and consequently, Spanish is widely-spoken in social, educational and economic spheres in the city. In contrast, the English L2 children in Golberg et al.'s study were residing in an English majority community where they may have only rarely spoken their L1 outside the home, and thus, had more opportunities to use and hear English (see section 3.2). Cobo-Lewis et al. (2002) also found that L2 children were more likely to lag behind monolinguals on tests of productive than receptive vocabulary, and this is consistent with research on lexical processing in sequential bilinguals. Windsor and Kohnert (2004) examined word recognition and picture naming in Spanish L1-English-L2 learners and English native speakers aged 8–13. The L2 learners performed similarly to the native speakers in both accuracy and response time for word recognition; however, the English native speakers outperformed the English L2 group for picture naming accuracy and response time.

What is the role of the L1 in L2 lexical acquisition? Unlike phonology, researchers have paid less attention to L1 influence in lexical acquisition. This is due in part to the uncertainty about how transfer from one language to the other would take place in this domain. Patterson and Pearson (2004) suggested that older sequential bilingual children may take advantage of cognates to enhance L2 vocabulary acquisition, for literacy in particular.

3.1.3. *Morphosyntactic acquisition in sequential bilinguals*

The majority of research on L2 children's acquisition of morphosyntax has been concentrated on grammatical morphology in general, finite verb morphology in particular. The findings show that children tend to acquire L2 grammatical morphology more quickly in the nominal than the verbal domain, regardless of target language, and that this sequence parallels L1 acquisition of morphosyntax (Dulay and Burt 1973, 1974; Grondin and White 1996; Haznedar 2001; Ionin and Wexler 2002; Paradis 2005; Paradis and Crago 2000, 2004; Paradis, Le

Corre and Genesee 1998; Prévost and White 2000). For example in L2 English, children generally are more accurate in producing plural [-s] on nouns than they are in producing third person singular [-s] on verbs. Also like L1, omission errors are more common than commission or substitution errors with grammatical morphology in L2 English and French (Ionin and Wexler 2002; Jia 2003; Paradis 2004, 2005; Paradis and Crago 2000). English L2 children are more likely to make errors like *he want some ice cream* (want → wants) than errors like *I didn't sawed* (sawed → see) (Genesee et al. 2004: 124–125).

Research on the role of the L1 in L2 morphosyntax has shown mixed results. On the one hand, Dulay and Burt (1973) found that 85 % of the errors made by Spanish L1-English L2 children were developmental in origin, in other words, not the result of transfer from Spanish. On the other hand, Paradis (2004) found that error patterns with object pronouns in child L2 French reflected transfer from English. Harley (1989) reported transfer in the use of prepositions in the French L2 of English L1 children in immersion schools. Regarding the source language for transfer in L3 acquisition, Hoffmann (1985) found that a Spanish-German bilingual girl transferred German grammatical elements into her English L3 even though she was dominant in Spanish, presumably because German and English are more closely related languages (cf. Cenoz, 2001). With respect to rate of development, Dulay and Burt (1974) found that Chinese L1 children displayed lower levels of accuracy with grammatical morphemes than Spanish L1 children; however, Paradis (2005) found that accuracy with a variety of tense-marking morphemes in L2 English, such as auxiliary verbs and inflections, was not related to whether the children's L1 was richly inflected or not. Retrospective developmental studies have also shown conflicting findings as to whether typological distance between the L1 and the L2 influences ultimate attainment in early sequential bilinguals. Bialystok and Miller (1999) found that when exposure to English began before 8 years of age, adult Chinese L1 and Spanish L1 speakers of English performed virtually the same on a grammaticality judgment task as English native speakers. In contrast, McDonald (2000) found that Vietnamese L1 adults had less accurate grammaticality judgments in English than Spanish L1 adults; both groups had been living in an English majority setting from the age of 5 years.

Akin to lexical acquisition, researchers have examined how L2 children compare to monolinguals in their rates and achievements in morphosyntactic development. Jia (2003) compared the average length of exposure time to English needed to master the use of plural [-s] in L1 and L2 learners. She found that individual variation was possibly larger for the L2 children, but that the average rate was nearly the same. Thus, it is unsurprising that it takes years for L2 children to display morphosyntactic abilities comparable to their native-speaker age-peers. Gathercole (2002) compared grammaticality judgments for English morphosyntax given by Spanish-English sequential bilinguals and English native-speakers. She found that the L2 children were less accurate than native speakers in their judgments in 2nd grade, but had nearly caught up by 5th grade. Gathercole and Thomas (2005) examined performance on a variety of grammatical tasks in Welsh from a cross-sectional sample of children aged 3–9 years. Some children only spoke Welsh at home and some only spoke English at home; both groups were in Welsh schools. Gathercole and Thomas (2005) found that for some structures, only the Welsh L2 children in the nine-year-old group displayed similar abilities to the Welsh L1 children; however, relatively less opaque/complex structures were acquired earlier by the Welsh L2 learners. Paradis (2005) and Paradis and Crago (2005) measured minority L1 English L2 learners' performance on a test of grammatical morpheme development normed on monolinguals. Even after 34 months exposure to English, only half of these children achieved a score in the range of typically-developing monolingual age-mates. These are the same children that Golberg et al.(under review) studied, so it seems that catching up to monolingual peers may be slower for grammatical morphology than it is for the lexicon.

It is pertinent to ask whether sequential bilinguals ever develop completely parallel morphosyntactic knowledge to monolingual speakers of the target language. As with phonological acquisition, there appears to be age effects in morphosyntactic ultimate attainment for sequential bilinguals when exposure to the L2 begins in middle childhood rather than before (Bialystok and Miller 1999; Jia 2003; McDonald 2000; Weber-Fox and Neville 1999; 2001). Weber-Fox and Neville (1999, 2001) found monolingual-bilingual differences in both ERP measurements of closed class word processing and in grammaticality judgments of syntactic violations for Chinese-English bilinguals whose onset of L2 acquisition occurred between ages 7–10 years old. Interestingly, they did not find such differences for open class word processing or in grammaticality judgments of semantic (lexical choice) violations.

3.2.   Individual differences in sequential bilinguals

Sources of individual differences in acquisition are possibly more pronounced in L2 and L3 acquisition than in L1, since additional sources of variation are found in the L2/L3 situation, such as, divided input time, presence of other languages, and variable age of onset for learning. The impact of age of onset and L1 typology on L2 and L3 development has already been discussed in section 3.1. In this section, we examine some other factors, both internal and external to the child, that have been found to underlie individual differences in L2 acquisition.

Language aptitude and personality characteristics are two learner-internal factors thought to underlie variation in outcomes between learners. Language aptitude is a composite of analytic and working memory skills relevant to acquiring compositional structures (e.g. morphosyntax) and words, and is somewhat related to verbal and non-verbal intelligence (Dörnyei and Skehan 2003; Sawyer and Ranta 2001). Language aptitude is widely considered to be one of the most reliable factors explaining individual differences in language development (Dörnyei and Skehan 2003; Skehan 1991). Ranta (2002) examined language analytic aptitude and English L2 attainment in 6th grade French-speaking children enrolled in a five-month English immersion program. She found that high and low language aptitude was associated with high and low L2 attainment. Genesee and Hamayan (1980) also found that a more general analytical skill, nonverbal reasoning, predicted success in French by English L1 children in 1st grade immersion. In contrast, research investigating the relationship between personality variables and L2 outcomes have shown mixed results (Dornyei and Skehan 2003; Sawyer and Ranta, 2001), but Strong (1983) claims that significant relationships between personality variables and L2 outcomes have been found more often when natural communicative language was measured. Strong (1983) examined such a relationship in L1 minority children in an English kindergarten. He found that personality variables associated with amount of social contact with native speakers, namely talkativeness, responsiveness and gregariousness, were significantly correlated with better English grammar, vocabulary and pronunciation as measured through spontaneous language production in child-to-child interactions.

Two learner-external, or environmental, factors found to influence differential achievement in child L2 learners are socio-economic status (SES) of the family, and quantity and quality of L2 input. SES is typically measured through parental levels of education or income, and is a key predictor of outcomes in L1 acquisition (see Oller and Eilers, 2002). Cobo-Lewis, Pearson et al. (2002) and Gathercole (2002) found that high SES Spanish L1-English-L2 children performed better on vocabulary and morphosyntactic measures than their low SES counterparts. Golberg et al. (under review) found mother's level of education to be the most significant predictor of L2 vocabulary growth in L1 minority children. Finally, Hakuta, Goto Butler and Witt (2000) examined global oral English proficiency in L1 minority children in schools with varying percentages of children qualifying for free lunch programs, which are based on family income. The development of English proficiency lagged behind in schools where 70% of the children were enrolled in free lunch programs.

Child L2 learners receive different amounts of L2 input in their instructional programs and outside the classroom; they also receive differential quality of input depending on their input sources. The studies with Spanish-L1-English-L2 children in Miami showed that children in Spanish-English bilingual programs lagged behind children in English only programs in their vocabulary and morphosyntactic acquisition in English (but certainly not in Spanish) (Cobo-Lewis, Pearson et al. 2002; Gathercole 2002). These researchers, Gathercole in particular, argue that the results point to input frequency as a highly important predictor of L2 acquisition rates. Gathercole and Thomas (2005) discuss similar effects for children in Welsh-only and Welsh-English bilingual programs. Both the Miami and Wales research also found an enhancing effect on acquisition when the target language was spoken at home and at school, although it is difficult to know from their descriptions whether the children whose families spoke both English and Spanish or English and Welsh in the home were simultaneous or early sequential bilinguals. Jia (2003) and Jia and Aaronson (2003) examined input factors using a fine-grained measure, richness of the English L2 environment outside the classroom. Using a composite score based on information about hours of English TV watched weekly, number of English books read, number of English native-speaker friends, and the percentage of time children spoke English at home, Jia (2003) found that faster acquisition of the plural [-s] in English by Chinese L1 children was associated with increasing richness of the L2 environment over time. Finally, it is important to take into account quality as well as quantity. Golberg et al (under review) examined the relationship between use of English in the home by all family members, and children's vocabulary growth in their L2. Use of English in home was not correlated with receptive and productive vocabulary growth, which appears on the surface to contradict the above-mentioned findings. However, what needs to be taken into consideration is that language use in the home includes the parents' use of English, and none of the parents this study were fluent English speakers, according to self-report and authors' observation. Therefore, the English input the children were receiving in the home most likely differed qualitatively from what the children in the Miami studies were hearing from their parents, many of whom spoke English fluently (Oller and Eilers 2002).

3.3.   First/minority language attrition in sequential bilinguals

Under certain circumstances, L1 minority children acquiring a majority L2 may stagnate in their L1 development, or begin to lose L1 proficiency, and inevitably become more proficient in the majority L2. Losing an L1 has been thought to be detrimental for various social-psychological reasons, as well as impacting negatively on children's L2 outcomes in school (Cummins 2000; Wong Fillmore 1991). In this section, the shift in dominance from L1 to L2, the markers of attrition in L1, as well as the circumstances under which L1 attrition occurs, are discussed.

Kohnert and colleagues looked at Spanish-L1-English-L2 children's lexical processing skills at various ages and years of exposure to English. Their results showed that speed and accuracy were superior in the Spanish L1 until children had had approximately 7 to 10 years experience with English, indicating that dominant language shift can be very gradual in this domain (Kohnert and Bates

2002; Kohnert, Bates and Hernandez 1999). The younger children are when L2 exposure begins, the faster the turnover in dominance to the L2. For example, Mägiste (1992) found that German L1 learners of Swedish shifted dominance on a lexical processing task to the Swedish L2 after 4 years' residence if they were young children, but after 6 years if they were adolescents (see also Jia and Aaronson 2003).

Sequential bilinguals whose dominant language is the majority L2 often display distinct characteristics of attrition in their minority L1. Anderson (2004) summarizes such characteristics across several studies of Spanish L1 children acquiring English in the United States. The lexical characteristics are mainly compensatory strategies used when the child does not know the precise word in Spanish, for example, non-specific demonstrative pronouns like *esto* 'this one', or lexical borrowing and code-switching, which parallel the lexical processes in early stages of L2 acquisition discussed in section 3.1. Grammatical changes include those due to direct influence from English, such as rigid Subject-Verb-Object word order, as well as other changes like simplification of inflectional paradigms, where the third person singular/verb stem is substituted for other persons, as a possible default verb form. It is not always possible to tease apart the effects of incomplete acquisition of the L1 and attrition of the L1 (Anderson 2004; Montrul 2002)

Researchers have investigated many factors predictive of L1 attrition (see Anderson 2004 for review). Wong Fillmore (1991) argued on the basis of a large-scale survey in the United States that onset of English acquisition by minority L1 children in the preschool years was predictive of more rapid L1 attrition. In contrast, Winsler, Diaz, Espinosa and Rodriguez (1999) compared Spanish language proficiency in two groups of kindergarten children, one that attended English preschool and one that did not, and found no deleterious effects on L1 maintenance due to early onset of English acquisition. Jia and Aaronson (2003) claim that L1 maintenance can be best explained by a dynamic model of factors, including age of L2 onset. In the Chinese L1 children they studied, they noted that there was an interrelationship between age of L2 onset, positive attitudes toward the L2 and host culture, the social network in the L2, and L1 proficiency over time. The earlier the age of onset, the more likely a child is to have positive attitudes toward the host culture and language, which in turn increases the likelihood of a larger social network of L2 speakers. This increases experiences with the L2, and results in a shift in preference and superior proficiency from L1 to L2. Dominant language shift then becomes another factor causing increased experience with the L2 and host culture. An additional important factor has to do with language spoken in the home and attitudes toward language maintenance by the parents themselves, which is related to the immigration depth of the family, e.g., how many generations were born in the host culture (Hakuta and D'Andrea 1992; Hakuta and Pease-Alvarez 1994).

Although more studied in the context of sequential bilingualism, simultaneous bilinguals and multilinguals may also experience loss of a minority language. Maneva (2004) reports that her trilingual daughter increasingly spoke the majority language, French, more often in the home after the age of three years, possibly because she became aware of the status of French *vis à vis* her other two languages, Arabic and Bulgarian. As a result, her input and proficiency in Arabic diminished considerably after that time (see also Hoffmann 1985).

4.   Commonalities between simultaneous and sequential bilingual acquisition

The research reviewed in sections 2 and 3 above suggest that there are important differences between simultaneous and sequential bilinguals, most notably in differential proficiency levels between the languages. L2 learners at the early stages have a proficiency gap between their two languages that is larger than the gap between a simultaneous bilingual's dominant and non-dominant language. In addition, sequential bilinguals who begin learning in middle childhood may not achieve the same levels of native-speaker attainment as children whose exposure to both languages began at birth. These differences are important to take into account in educational and clinical settings, as well as for participant selection in research. On the other hand, it is noteworthy that differences in abilities in both languages between simultaneous and sequential bilinguals may diminish by the end of elementary school if both languages are highly supported in the community and educational systems, and sequential bilinguals began learning the L2 at least in kindergarten (Oller and Eilers 2002; Gathercole and Thomas 2005). In other words, initial ability differences between simultaneous and sequential bilinguals emerging from variation in onsets of acquisition and amounts of exposure time may only be manifest until a certain threshold of language experience has been reached (Oller and Eilers, 2002).

The distinction between simultaneous and sequential bilingualism at the early stages has lead to different issues becoming prominent in the research on these populations. For example, the 'one system or two?' question is applied mainly to BFLA, and examination of sources for individual differences has been researched more thoroughly in child SLA. However, some issues of concern to researchers overlap between these two groups of children. First, crosslinguistic influence in simultaneous bilinguals and transfer from L1 to L2/L3 in sequential bilinguals share many of the same properties. Second, both simultaneous and sequential bilinguals are frequently compared to their monolingual peers. The questions asked are often framed differently, for example, 'does simultaneous bilingualism cause delay?' or 'when do child L2 learners catch up to native-speakers?', but they display a common underlying concern about measuring developmental progress, and how bilinguals may come up short when compared with monolinguals. Both these issues of crosslinguistic influence/transfer and delay/catch up are indicative of how patterns and rates in bilingual acquisition can be different from those of monolingual acquisition. This difference may persist in some domains throughout the lifespan, as Grosjean suggests: "Bilinguals are not the sum of two complete or incomplete monolinguals, but have a unique and specific linguistic configuration" (1995: 259). It is hoped that future research will more often recognize that bilingual and multilingual development have characteristics that make them simply different, rather than deviant, from monolingual development.

References

Anderson, Raquel
  2004   First language loss in Spanish-speaking children: Patterns of loss and implications for clinical practice. In: Brian Goldstein (ed.), *Bilingual Language Development and Disorders in Spanish-English Speakers*, 187–212. Baltimore: Brookes.
Ball, Martin, Nicole Müller and Siân Munro
  2001   The acquisition of the rhotic consonants by Welsh-English bilingual children. *International Journal of Bilingualism* 5: 71–86.
Bernardini, Petra and Suzanne Schlyter
  2004   Growing syntactic structure and code-mixing in the weaker language: The Ivy Hypothesis. *Bilingualism: Language and Cognition* 7: 49–70.
Bialystok, Ellen
  2004   The impact of bilingualism on language and literacy Development. In: Tey Bhatia and William Ritchie (eds.), *The Handbook of Bilingualism*, 577–601. Oxford: Blackwell.
Bialystok, Ellen and Barry Miller
  1999   The problem of age in second language acquisition: Influences from language, structure and task. *Bilingualism: Language and Cognition* 2: 127–145.
Bosch, Laura and Nuria Sebastián-Gallés
  2003   Simultaneous bilingualism and the perception o a language-specific vowel contrast in the first year of life. *Language and Speech* 46: 217–243.
Burns, Tracey, Janet Werker and Karen McVie
  2003   Development of phonetic categories in infants raised in bilingual and monolingual environments. In: Barbara Beachley, Amanda Brown, and Frances Conlin (eds.) *BUCLD 27 Proceedings*, 173–184. Somerville, MA: Cascadilla Press.
Cenoz, Jasone
  2001   The effect of linguistic distance, L2 status and age on cross-linguistic influence in third language acquisition. In: Jasone Cenoz, Britta Hufeisen and Ulrike Jessner (eds.), *Cross-linguistic Influence in Third Language Acquisition: Psycholinguistic Perspectives*, 9–20. Clevendon: Multilingual Matters.

Cobo-Lewis, Alan, Rebecca Eilers, Barbara Pearson, and Vivian Umbel
  2002   Interdependence of Spanish and English knowledge in language and literacy among bilingual children. In: D. Kimbrough Oller and Rebecca Eilers (eds.), *Language and Literacy in Bilingual Children*, 118–134. Clevendon: Multilingual Matters.
Cobo-Lewis, Alan, Barbara Pearson, Rebecca Eilers, and Vivian Umbel
  2002   Effects of bilingualism and bilingual education on oral and written English skills: A multifactor study of standardized test outcomes. In D. Kimborough Oller and Rebecca Eilers (eds.), *Language and Literacy in Bilingual Children*, 64–97. Clevendon: Multilingual Matters.
Comeau, Liane, Fred Genesee and Lindsay Lapaquette
  2003   The modeling hypothesis and child bilingual code-mixing. *International Journal of Bilingualism* 7: 113–126.
Cummins, Jim
  2000   *Language, Power and Pedagogy: Bilingual Children in the Crossfire.* Clevendon: Multilingual Matters.
De Houwer, Annick
  1995   Bilingual language acquisition. In: Paul Fletcher and Brian MacWhinney (eds.), *The Handbook of Child Language*, 219–250. Oxford: Blackwell.
Deuchar, Margaret and Suzanne Quay
  2000   *Bilingual Acquisition: Theoretical Implications of a Case Study.* Oxford: Oxford University Press.
Döpke, Susanne
  2000   Generation of and retraction from cross-linguistically motivated structures in bilingual first language acquisition. *Bilingualism: Language and Cognition* 3: 209–226.
Döpke, Susanne (ed.)
  2000   *Cross-linguistic Structures in Simultaneous Bilingualism.* Amsterdam: Benjamins.
Döpke, Susanne
  1998   Competing language structures: The acquisition of verb placement by bilingual German-English children. *Journal of Child Language* 25: 555–584.
Dörnyei, Zoltán and Peter Skehan
  2003   Individual differences in second language learning. In: Catherine Doughty and Michael Long (eds.), *The Handbook of Second Language Acquisition*, 589–630. Oxford: Blackwell.
Doyle, Anna-Beth, Mireille Champagne, and Norman Segalowitz
  1978   Some issues in the assessment of linguistic consequences of early bilingualism. In: Michel Paradis (ed.), *Aspects of Bilingualism*, 13–21. Columbia, SC: Hornbeam Press.
Dulay, Heidi and Marina Burt
  1974   Natural sequences in child second language acquisition. *Language Learning* 24: 37–53.
Dulay, Heidi and Marina Burt
  1973   Should we teach children syntax? *Language Learning* 24: 245–258.
Flege, James
  2004   Second language speech learning. Paper presented at *Laboratory Approaches to Spanish Phonology and Phonetics.* Indiana University.

Flege, James
  1999   Age of learning and second language speech. In: David Birdsong (ed.), *Second Language Acquisition and the Critical Period Hypothesis,* 101–132. Mahwah, NJ: Lawrence Erlbaum.
Flege, James
  1991   Age of learning affects the authenticity of voice-onset time (VOT) in stop consonants produced in a second language. *Journal of the Acoustical Society of America* 89: 395–411.
Flege, James and Kathryn Fletcher
  1992   Talker and listener effects on degree of perceived foreign accent. *Journal of the Acoustical Society of America* 91: 370–389.
Chris T. Fennell, Linda Polka and Janet Werker
  2002   Bilingual early word learner's ability to access phonetic detail in word forms. Paper presented at the Fourth *International Symposium on Bilingualism,* Tempe, AZ.
Gathercole, Virginia
  2002   Monolingual and bilingual acquisition: Learning different treatments of that-trace phenomena in English and Spanish. In: D. Kimbrough Oller and Rebecca Eilers (eds.), *Language and Literacy in Bilingual Children,* 220–254. Clevendon: Multilingual Matters.
Gathercole, Virginia and Enlli M. Thomas
  2005   Minority language survival: Input factors influencing the acquisition of Welsh. In: James Cohen, Kara T. McAlister, Kellie Rolstad and Jeff Mac-Swan (eds.) *ISB4: Proceedings of the 4ᵗʰ International Symposium on Bilingualism,* 852–874. Somerville, MA: Cascadilla Press.
Gawlitzek-Maiwald, Ira and Rosemarie Tracy
  1996   Bilingual bootstrapping. *Linguistics* 34: 901–926.
Genesee, Fred
  1989   Early bilingual development: One language or two? *Journal of Child Language* 16: 161–180.
Genesee, Fred and Elizabeth Hamayan
  1980   Individual differences in second language learning. *Applied Psycholinguistics* 1: 95–110.
Genesee, Fred, Johanne Paradis and Martha Crago
  2004   *Dual Language Development and Disorders: A Handbook on Bilingualism and Second Language Learning.* Baltimore: Brookes.
Genesee, Fred, Isabelle Boivin and Elena Nicoladis
  1996   Bilingual children talking with monolingual adults: A study of bilingual communicative competence. *Applied Psycholinguistics 17*: 427–442.
Genesee, Fred, Elena Nicoladis and Johanne Paradis
  1995   Language differentiation in early bilingual development. *Journal of Child Language* 22: 611–631.
Golberg, Heather, Johanne Paradis and Martha Crago
  under review   Lexical acquisition over time in L1 minority children learning English as second language.
Goldstein, Brian (ed.)
  2004a   *Bilingual Language Development and Disorders in Spanish-English Speakers.* Baltimore: Brookes.

Goldstein, Brian
  2004b   Phonological development and disorders. In: Brian Goldstein (ed.), *Bilingual Language Development and Disorders in Spanish-English Speakers*, 259–286. Baltimore: Brookes.
Grondin, Nathalie and Lydia White
  1996   Functional categories in child L2 acquisition of French. *Language Acquisition* 5: 1–34.
Grosjean, François
  1995   A psycholinguistic approach to code-switching: The recognition of guest words by bilinguals. In: Leslie Milroy and Pieter Muysken (eds.), *One Speaker, Two Languages: Cross-disciplinary Perspectives on Code-Switching*, 259–275. Cambridge: Cambridge University Press.
Hakuta, Kenji and Daniel D'Andrea
  1992   Some properties of bilingual maintenance and loss in Mexican background high-school students. *Applied Linguistics* 13: 72–99.
Hakuta, Kenji and Lucinda Pease-Alvarez
  1994   Proficiency, choice and attitudes in bilingual Mexican-American children. In: Guus Extra and Ludo Verhoeven (eds.), *The Cross-Linguistic Study of Bilingual Development*, 145–164. Amsterdam: Royal Netherlands Academy of Arts and Sciences.
Hakuta, Kenji, Y. Goto Butler and D. Witt
  2000   *How Long Does it Take English Learners to Attain Proficiency?* Policy Report, the University of California Linguistic Minority Research Institute. Retrieved March 31, 2004, from http://www.stanford.edu/~hakuta/.
Harley, Birgit
  1992   Patterns of second language development in French immersion. *French Language Studies* 2: 159–183.
Harley, Birgit
  1989   Transfer in the written compositions of French immersion students. In H. Dechert and M. Raupach (eds.), *Transfer in Language Production*, 3–19. Norwood NJ: Ablex Publishing Corporation.
Haznedar, Belma
  2001   The acquisition of the IP system in child L2 English. *Studies in Second Language Acquisition* 23: 1–39.
Hoff, Erika and Jodi McKay
  2005   Phonological memory skill in monolingual and bilingual 23-month-olds. In: James Cohen, Kara T. McAlister, Kellie Rolstad, and Jeff Macswan (eds.), *ISB4: Proceedings of the 4th International Symposium on Bilingualism*, 1041–1044. Somerville, MA: Cascadilla Press.
Hoffmann, Charlotte
  1985   Language acquisition in two trilingual children. *Journal of Multilingual and Multicultural Development* 6: 479–495.
Hulk, Aafke and Natascha Müller
  2000   Bilingual first language acquisition at the interface between syntax and pragmatics. *Bilingualism: Language and Cognition* 3: 227–244.
Hulk, Aafke
  2000   Non-selective access and activation in child bilingualism: the syntax. In:

38   Johanne Paradis

        Susanne Döpke (ed.), *Cross-Linguistic Structures in Simultaneous Bilingualism*, 57–78. Amsterdam: Benjamins.

Ionin, Tania and Kenneth Wexler
2002   Why is 'Is' easier that '-s'? – Acquisition of tense/agreement morphology by child L2-English learners. *Second Language Research* 18: 95–136.

Jia, Gisela
2003   The acquisition of the English plural morpheme by native Mandarin Chinese-speaking children. *Journal of Speech, Language and Hearing Research* 46: 1297–1311.

Jia, Gisela and Doris Aaronson
2003   A longitudinal study of Chinese children and adolescents learning English in the United States. *Applied Psycholinguistics* 24: 131–161.

Johnson, Caroline and Paige Lancaster
1998   The development of more than one phonology: A case study of a Norwegian-English bilingual child. *International Journal of Bilingualism* 2: 265–300.

Johnson, Caroline and Ian Wilson
2002   Phonetic evidence for early language differentiation: Research issues and preliminary data. *International Journal of Bilingualism* 6: 271–290.

Kehoe, Margaret
2002   Developing vowel systems as a window to bilingual phonology. *International Journal of Bilingualism* 6: 315–334.

Kehoe, Margaret, Conxita Lleó and Martin Rakow
2004   Voice onset time in bilingual German-Spanish children. *Bilingualism: Language and Cognition* 7: 71–88.

Keshavarz, Mohammed and David Ingram
2002   The early phonological development of a Farsi-English bilingual child. *International Journal of Bilingualism* 6: 255–270.

Kohnert, Kathryn and Elizabeth Bates
2002   Balancing bilinguals II: Lexical comprehension and cognitive processing in children learning Spanish and English. *Journal of Speech, Language and Hearing Research* 45: 347–359.

Kohnert, Kathryn, Elizabeth Bates and Arturo Hernandez
1999   Balancing bilinguals: Lexical-semantic production and cognitive processing in children learning Spanish and English. *Journal of Speech, Language and Hearing Research* 42: 1400–1413.

Köppe, Regine
1996   Language differentiation in bilingual children: the development of grammatical and pragmatic competence. *Linguistics* 34: 927–954.

Lanvers, Ursula.
2001   Language alternation in infant bilinguals: a developmental approach to code-switching. *International Journal of Bilingualism* 5: 437–464.

Lanza, Elizabeth
1997   *Language Mixing in Infant Bilingualism*. Oxford: Oxford University Press.

Leopold, Werner
1949   *Speech Development of a Bilingual Child: A Linguist's Record*. (Vols. 1–4). New York: AMS press.

Lleó, Conxita
    2002   The role of markedness in the acquisition of complex prosodic structures by
            German-Spanish bilinguals. *International Journal of Bilingualism* 6: 291–314.
Mägiste, Edith.
    1992   Second language learning in elementary and high school students. *Euro-
            pean Journal of Cognitive Psychology* 4: 355–365.
Maneva, Blagovesta
    2004   'Maman, je suis polyglotte' [Mommy, I'm a polyglot]: a case study of
            multilingual language acquisition from 0 to 5 years. *The International Jour-
            nal of Multilingualism* 1: 109–122.
Marchman, Virginia, Carmen Martínez-Sussmann, and Philip Dale
    2004   The language-specific nature of grammatical development: evidence from
            bilingual language learners. *Developmental Science* 7: 212–224.
McDonald, Janet L.
    2000   Grammaticality judgments in a second language: influences of age of ac-
            quisition and native language. *Applied Psycholinguistics* 21: 395–423.
Meisel, Jürgen
    1994a   Getting FAT: Finiteness, agreement and tense in early grammars. In Jürgen
            Meisel (ed.), *Bilingual First Language Acquisition: French and German
            Grammatical Development*, 89–130. Amsterdam: Benjamins.
Meisel, Jürgen
    1994b   Code-switching in young bilingual children: the acquisition of grammatical
            constraints. *Studies in Second Language Acquisition, 16*, 413–441.
Meisel, Jürgen
    1989   Early differentiation of languages in bilingual children. In Kenneth Hylten-
            stam and Lorraine Obler (eds.), *Bilingualism Across the Lifespan: Aspects
            of Acquisition, Maturity, and Loss,* 13–40. Cambridge: Cambridge Univer-
            sity Press.
McLaughlin, Barry
    1978   *Second Language Acquisition in Childhood.* Hillsdale, NJ: Lawrence Erl-
            baum.
Montrul, Silvina
    2002   Incomplete acquisition and attrition of Spanish tense/aspect distinctions in
            adult bilinguals. *Bilingualism: Language and Cognition* 5: 39–68.
Müller, Natascha
    1998   Transfer in bilingual first language acquisition. *Bilingualism: Language
            and Cognition* 1: 151–171.
Müller, Natascha and Aafke Hulk
    2001   Crosslinguistic influence in bilingual acquisition: Italian and French as re-
            cipient languages. *Bilingualism: Language and Cognition* 4: 1–21.
Myers-Scotton, Carole
    1993   *Duelling Languages: Grammatical Structure in Codeswitching.* Oxford,
            UK: Clarendon.
Nicoladis, Elena
    2003   Cross-linguistic transfer in deverbal compounds of preschool bilingual
            children. *Bilingualism: Language and Cognition* 6: 17–31.
Nicoladis, Elena
    2002   What's the difference between 'toilet paper' and 'paper toilet'? French-

English bilingual children's crosslinguistic transfer in compound nouns. *Journal of Child Language,* 29: 843–863.

Nicoladis, Elena and Fred Genesee
1998   Parental discourse and codemixing in bilingual children. *International Journal of Bilingualism 2:* 85–99.

Nicoladis, Elena and Fred Genesee
1996a   Word awareness in second language learners and bilingual children. *Language Awareness 5:* 80–90.

Nicoladis, Elena and Fred Genesee
1996b   A longitudinal study of pragmatic differentiation in young bilingual children. *Language Learning 46:* 439–464.

Nicoladis, Elena, A. Palmer and Paula Marentette
in press   The importance of a critical mass of past tense verbs in using past tense morphemes correctly. *Developmental Science.*

Nicoladis, Elena and Giovanni Secco,
2000   The role of a child's productive vocabulary in the language choice of a bilingual family. *First Language 58:* 3–28.

Oller, Kimbrough D. and Rebecca Eilers (eds.)
2002   *Language and Literacy in Bilingual Children.* Clevendon: Multilingual Matters.

Pan, Barbara A.
1995   Code negotiation in bilingual families: 'My body starts speaking English'. *Journal of Multilingual and Multicultural Development 16:* 315–327.

Paradis, Johanne
2005   Grammatical morphology in children learning English as a second language: implications of similarities with specific language impairment. *Language, Speech, and Hearing Services in Schools* 36: 172–187.

Paradis, Johanne
2004   On the relevance of specific language impairment to understanding the role of transfer in second language acquisition. *Applied Psycholinguistics* 25: 67–82.

Paradis, Johanne
2001   Do bilingual two-year-olds have separate phonological systems? *International Journal of Bilingualism* 5: 19–38.

Paradis, Johanne and Martha Crago
2005   Grammatical morphology in English second language learners over time. Paper presented at the 10th Congress of the *International Association for the Study of Child Language*, Berlin, Germany.

Paradis, Johanne and Martha Crago
2004   Comparing L2 and SLI grammars in French: Focus on DP. In: Philippe Prévost and Johanne Paradis (eds.) *The Acquisition of French in Different Contexts: Focus on Functional Categories*, 89–108. Amstcrdam: Benjamins.

Paradis, Johanne and Martha Crago
2000   Tense and temporality: similarities and differences between language-impaired and second-language children. *Journal of Speech, Language and Hearing Research* 43: 834–848.

Paradis, Johanne, Martha Crago and Fred Genesee
2005/2006   Domain-specific versus domain-general theories of the deficit in SLI:
             object pronoun acquisition by French-English bilingual children. *Language
             Acquisition*, 13, 33–62.
Paradis, Johanne, Martha Crago, Fred Genesee and Mabel Rice
2003   Bilingual children with specific language impairment: how do they com-
        pare with their monolingual peers? *Journal of Speech, Language and Hear-
        ing Research* 46: 1–15.
Paradis, Johanne and Fred Genesee
1997   On continuity and the emergence of functional categories in bilingual first
        language acquisition. *Language Acquisition 6*: 91–124.
Paradis, Johanne and Fred Genesee
1996   Syntactic acquisition in bilingual children: Autonomous or interdependent?
        Studies in Second Language Acquisition 18: 1–15.
Paradis, Johanne, Mathieu Le Corre and Fred Genesee
1998   The emergence of tense and agreement in child L2 French. *Second Lan-
        guage Research* 14: 227–257.
Paradis, Johanne and Samuel Navarro
2003   Subject realization and crosslinguistic interference in the bilingual acquisi-
        tion of Spanish and English. *Journal of Child Language* 30: 371–393.
Paradis, Johanne and Elena Nicoladis
in press   The role of dominance and sociolinguistic context on the language choice
            of bilingual preschoolers. *International Journal of Bilingualism and Bilin-
            gual Education.*
Paradis, Johanne, Elena Nicoladis and Fred Genesee
2000   Early emergence of structural constraints on code-mixing: evidence from
        French-English bilingual children. *Bilingualism: Language and Cognition*
        3: 245–261.
Patterson, Janet and Barbara Pearson
2004   Bilingual lexical development: influences, contexts, and processes. In:
        Brian Goldstein (ed.), *Bilingual Language Development and Disorders in
        Spanish-English Speakers*, 77–104. Baltimore: Brookes.
Pearson, Barbara
2002   Narrative competence among monolingual bilingual school children in
        Miami. In: D. Kimbrough Oller and Rebecca Eilers (eds.), *Language and
        Literacy in Bilingual Children*, 135–174. Clevendon: Multilingual Matters.
Pearson, Barbara
1998   Assessing lexical development in bilingual babies and toddlers. *Inter-
        national Journal of Bilingualism* 2: 347–372.
Pearson, Barbara, Sylvia Fernández and D. Kimbrough Oller
1995   Cross-language synonyms in the lexicons of bilingual infants: one language
        or two? *Journal of Child Language 22*: 345–368.
Pearson, Barbara, Sylvia Fernández and D. Kimbrough Oller
1993   Lexical development in bilingual infants and toddlers: Comparison to
        monolingual norms. *Language Learning 43*: 93–120.
Pearson, Barbara, Sylvia Fernández, Vanessa Lewedag and D. Kimbrough Oller
1997   The relation of input factors to lexical learning by bilingual infants (ages 10
        to 30 months). *Applied Psycholinguistics 18*: 41–58.

42   Johanne Paradis

Petersen, Jennifer
    1988   Word-internal code-switching constraints in a bilingual child's grammar. *Linguistics 26*: 479–493.
Poplack, Shana
    1980   'Sometimes I start a sentence in English y termino en Espanol': Toward a typology of code-switching. *Linguistics 18*: 581–618.
Prévost, Philippe and Lydia White
    2000   Accounting for morphological variation in second language acquisition: truncation or missing inflection? In: Marc-Ariel Friedemann and Luigi Rizzi (eds.), *The Acquisition of Syntax*, 202–235. Harlow: Longman.
Quay, Suzanne
    1995   The bilingual lexicon: implications for studies of language choice. *Journal of Child Language 22*: 369–387.
Ranta, Leila
    2002   The role of learners' language analytic ability in the communicative classroom. In: Peter Robinson (ed.), *Individual Differences and Instructed Language Learning,* 159–181. Amsterdam: Benjamins.
Sawyer, Mark and Leila Ranta
    2002   Aptitude, individual differences, and instructional design. In: Peter Robinson (ed.), *Cognition and Second Language Instruction,* 319–353. Cambridge: Cambridge University Press.
Serratrice, Ludovica, Antonella Sorace and S. Paoli
    2004   Crosslinguistic influence at the syntax-pragmatics interface: subjects and objects in English-Italian bilingual and monolingual acquisition. *Bilingualism: Language and Cognition 7*: 183–206.
Skehan, Peter
    1991   Individual differences in second language learning. *Studies in Second Language Acquisition 13*: 275–298.
Strong, Michael
    1983   Social styles and the second language acquisition of Spanish-speaking kindergartners. *TESOL Quarterly 17*: 241–258.
Sundara, Megha, Linda Polka, and Fred Genesee
    in press   Language-experience facilitates discrimination of /d – ð/ in monolingual and bilingual acquisition of English. *Cognition.*
Suyal, Cinnamon
    2002   *Bilingual First Language Acquisition: Code-Mixing in Children Who Speak a Minority Language.* Unpublished Master's thesis, Department of Linguistics, University of Alberta, Edmonton, Canada.
Tucker, Richard
    1998   A global perspective on multilingualism and multilingual education. In: Jasone Cenoz and Fred Genesee (eds.), *Beyond Bilingualism: Multilingualism and Multilingual Education,* 3–15. Clevedon: Multilingual Matters.
Umbel, Vivian, Barbara Pearson, Maria Fernández and D. Kimborough Oller
    1992   Measuring bilingual children's receptive vocabularies. *Child Development 63*: 1012–1020.
Vihman, Marilyn
    2002   Getting started without a system: from phonetics to phonology in bilingual development. *International Journal of Bilingualism*, 6, 239–254.

Vihman, Marilyn
 1998   A developmental perspective on codeswitching: conversations between
           a pair of bilingual siblings. *International Journal of Bilingualism 2*: 45–
           84.
Vihman, Marilyn
 1985   Language differentiation by the bilingual infant. *Journal of Child Lan-
           guage 12*: 297–324.
Volterra, Virginia and Taute Taeschner
 1978   The acquisition and development of language by bilingual children. *Jour-
           nal of Child Language 5*: 311–326.
Watson, Ian
 1991   Phonological processing in two languages. In: Ellen Bialystok (ed.),
           Language Processing in Bilingual Children, 25–48. Cambridge: Cam-
           bridge University Press.
Weber-Fox, Christine and Helen Neville
 2001   Sensitive periods differentiate processing of open- and closed-class words:
           an ERP study of bilinguals. *Journal of Speech, Language and Hearing Re-
           search* 44: 1338–1353.
Weber-Fox, Christine. and Helen Neville
 1999   Functional neural subsystems are differentially affected by delays in second
           language immersion: ERP and behavioral evidence in bilinguals. In: David
           Birdsong (ed.), *Second Language Acquisition and the Critical Period Hy-
           pothesis*, 23–38. Mahwah, NJ: Lawrence Erlbaum.
Werker, Janet and Suzanne Curtin
 2005   PRIMIR: A developmental framework of infant speech processing. *Lan-
           guage Learning and Development* 1: 197–234.
Windsor, Jennifer and Kathryn Kohnert
 2004   The search for common ground: part I. Lexical performance by linguisti-
           cally diverse learners, *Journal of Speech, Language and Hearing Research*
           47: 877–890.
Winitz, Harris, Brenda Gillespie and Jennifer Starcev
 1995   The development of English speech patterns of a 7-year-old Polish-speak-
           ing child. *Journal of Psycholinguistic Research* 24: 117–143.
Winsler, Adam, Rafael Díaz, Linda Espinosa and James Rodríguez
 1999   When learning a second language does not mean losing the first: bilingual
           language development in low-income, Spanish-speaking children attending
           bilingual preschool. *Child Development* 70: 349–362.
Wong Fillmore, Lily
 1991   When learning a second language means losing the first. *Early Childhood
           Research Quarterly* 6: 323–346.
Yip, Virginia and Stephen Matthews
 2000   Syntactic transfer in a Cantonese-English bilingual child. *Bilingualism:
           Language and Cognition* 3: 193–208.

Recommended readings

Baker, Colin
  2000   *A Parents' and Teachers' Guide to Bilingualism* (2nd Edition). Clevedon:
            Multilingual Matters.
Genesee, Fred
  2004   What do we know about bilingual education for majority language stu-
            dents? In: Tey Bhatia and William Ritchie (eds.), *The Handbook of Bilin-
            gualism*, 547–576. Oxford: Blackwell.
Genesee, Fred and Elena Nicoladis
  in press Bilingual first language acquisition. In: Erika Hoff and Marilyn Shatz
            (eds.), *Handbook of Language Acquisition.* Oxford: Blackwell.
Meisel, Jürgen
  2004   The bilingual child. In: Tey Bhatia and William Ritchie (eds.), *The Hand-
            book of Bilingualism*, 91–113. Oxford: Blackwell.
Paradis, Johanne
  in press Child second language acquisition. In Erika Hoff and Marilyn Shatz (eds.),
            Handbook of Language Acquisition. Oxford: Blackwell.

2.   Multilingualism and the family

Elizabeth Lanza

1.   Introduction

Multilingualism has been the norm throughout the ages in most of the world. Nonetheless the phenomenon is perhaps relatively speaking more recent in Western society. With the greater mobility of people and consequent cross-linguistic and cross-cultural relationships, an increasing number of children are growing up with early exposure to two languages in the family. Indeed *more* than two languages may be in the linguistic repertoire of the family, rendering a case of family multilingualism (cf. Quay 2001). Multilingualism has increasingly come in focus with, for example, studies emphasizing trilingualism and how it may differ from bilingualism (cf. Hoffmann and Ytsma 2004). Nonetheless, in the following I will use the term *bilingualism* to refer to the acquisition and use of two, or more, languages, similar to the general use in the literature. I will, however, employ the term *multilingualism* when referring to specific cases involving more than two languages.

   In this chapter, I will address the issue of bilingualism and the family with a focus on the influence of the family environment on early bilingual language acquisition, in the framework of individual bilingualism – that is, in an environment in which the minority language does *not* have community support. While Ch. 1 of this handbook addressed psycholinguistic aspects of early multilingual language acquisition, this chapter will specifically address what is often referred to as the *input* for acquisition, although arguably it is difficult to assess the child's processing and production of language without considering the input. If the parents choose to raise their children bilingually, this implies a positive attitude towards bilingualism. However, attitudes towards bilingualism in general and bilingualism in early childhood in particular may vary considerably and have an impact on parents' conception of their linguistic practices. In the following, I will first present the family as an important sociolinguistic environment, specifically as a community of practice, and discuss the issue of language socialization in light of language choice patterns in the family. Thereafter, I will present and discuss various applied linguistic approaches to studying the bilingual family in a society in which the minority language does not have community support. These approaches are illustrated through studies that have employed survey data and in-depth interviews of bilingual families, those examining language ideology as a significant factor in bilingual acquisition, and finally interactional studies investigating parent-child conversations. Recom-

mended readings are provided at the end of chapter. These include relevant literature and journals that publish work related to the topic of this chapter. Furthermore, publications are presented that have as a goal to enlighten parents on the
issue of bilingualism and to present ways to stimulate bilingualism in the family.

2.   The family as an important sociolinguistic environment

The family is a vital social unit for acquiring language. Corsaro (1997: 88)
points out "the utility of conceptualizing families as local cultures in which
young children actively participate, contribute to their own social development,
and affect the participation of all other family members". Although the family
is an integral part of society and as such should not be separated from it, the
focus in this chapter will be on the family with the term *family bilingualism*
used for analytical purposes to refer to individual bilingualism within the family
(Lanza 1997: 10). In such a case, the one language is the majority language
of the outside community while the other language is not spoken in the community.

A focus on the family will allow us to explore issues that foster bilingualism
in cases in which there is no community support for the minority language(s) in
contrast to cases of societal bilingualism, which comprises not only bilingual
communities such as in Quebec but also immigrant contexts, typically characterized by closed networks. Examples of the type of families that will be the
focus of this article include a family living in France in which the mother is Japanese and the father French, or a family living in Germany in which the father is
bilingual in Catalan and Spanish while the mother speaks German. In each case,
the parent may address the child in his/her respective language(s) and potentially contribute to establishing the child's individual bilingualism in his or her
formative years. Although many of the relevant issues are important for both
family and societal bilingualism, the focus in this chapter will nonetheless be on
individual bilingualism/multilingualism in the family.

The distinction drawn above between societal bilingualism and family bilingualism has often been referred to as a distinction between *folk bilingualism* and
elitist bilingualism. Although the distinction is a real one, the notion of an elitist
bilingualism truly undermines the fact that many parents face problems as they
attempt to raise their children bilingually. Many receive unfounded advice and
lack the general support from any bilingual community, and hence abandon any
attempts to establish individual bilingualism in the home. As Harding and Riley
(1986) point out, some of the important social repercussions of this failure include the inability of the child to communicate with grandparents and other
family in the immigrant parent's homeland. Moreover, they state, "someone will
lose their linguistic identity – and it is usually the mother" (25).

We may consider the family as a *community of practice,* a social unit that has its own norms for language use. According to Eckert and McConnell-Ginet (1999: 186), a community of practice is "an aggregate of people who, united by common enterprises, develop and share ways of doing things, ways of talking, beliefs, and values – in short, practices". This notion bears resemblance to other sociolinguistic concepts such as the speech community and social network and includes issues of language attitudes. However, it captures the reality that even smaller groups can have their own ways of speaking, acting and believing. Moreover, it provides a focus on praxis that is a cornerstone for language socialization theory.

The community of practice approach is part of a social theory of learning (Lave and Wenger 1991; Wenger 1998) that addresses how individuals gradually become members of the community. By considering the family as a community of practice, we may examine the ways in which gaining membership "interacts with the process of gaining control of the discourse appropriate to it" (Holmes and Meyerhoff 1999: 175). The family as a community of practice provides us a focus on a particular setting for language socialization although language socialization occurs in a broader social context.

2.1.   Language socialization

Various theories of socialization have perceived the child as either an active or passive participant in the process. Traditional theories of socialization emphasize the process by which children adapt to, and internalize, society. The child is, from this perspective, perceived as something that needs to be molded and guided by society in order to become a fully-fledged member. As Corsaro (1997) notes, the term *socialization* has an individualistic and forward-looking connotation that is inescapable, the notion of training and preparing the individual child for the future. However, children are active, creative social agents who produce their own unique children's cultures, all the while contributing to the production of adult society. Constructivist and interpretive theoretical perspectives in sociology have given rise to new ways of conceptualizing children (James and Prout 1990; Corsaro 1997; James, Prout, and Jenks 2002). Corsaro proposes the term *interpretive reproduction* as a replacement for *socialization.* His term incorporates the idea that children actively contribute to societal preservation (or reproduction) as well as to societal change through interpretation. Despite the use of the term *socialization,* language socialization studies have held similar conceptions of the child as an active social agent (cf. Schieffelin and Ochs 1986a, 1986b; Ochs and Schieffelin 1995). Schieffelin (1990: 17) has pointed out that "socialization is a product of interaction". In this approach there is an emphasis on the dialogic nature of socialization that is in line with the new sociology of childhood. Moreover, this tunes in well with the community of practice approach to investigating family bilingualism (cf. Garrett and Baquedano-López 2002). In 3.3, studies concentrating on the interactional basis for studying family bilingualism will be examined. However, before addressing various approaches to studying the bilingual family, we will first consider how language choice figures generally in cases of childhood bilingualism.

2.2.   Language choice patterns in the home

In an attempt to explain variation in language acquisition among young bilingual children, scholars have given special attention to language use patterns in the home. The language choice pattern that has received the most attention in family bilingualism is that of *One Person – One Language* (cf. Döpke 1992; Barron-Hauwaert 2004), which typically results in family bilingualism. First discussed in the work of the linguist Ronjat (1913), it is also referred to as the Grammont Formula after the linguist of the same name. Grammont advised Ronjat, who was French, and his wife, a German, to address their child Louis each in their native languages. It was held that separating the languages from infancy would help the child learn both languages without any effort or confusion. This strategy figures in the typology of language choice patterns in the home set up by Romaine (1995: 183–185). Reviewing the field of early childhood bilingualism and basing her typology on Harding and Riley (1986), Romaine proposed six basic types of language choice patterns in the family that vary according to the native languages of the parents, the language(s) of the community, and the strategy the parents employ with the child. The six types are the following:
1.   One Person – One Language
2.   Non-dominant Home Language/ One Language – One Environment
3.   Non-dominant Home Language without Community Support
4.   Double Non-dominant Home Language without Community Support
5.   Non-native Parents
6.   Mixed Languages
Certain types more easily render simultaneous bilingualism (for example, the One Person – One Language strategy) while other types in which the non-dominant language is spoken at home and the dominant language outside the home may render sequential bilingualism. And yet another type in which the child is exposed to two languages in the home and another later outside the home may render both simultaneous and sequential bilingualism (e.g. Quay 2001). There are, however, other aspects of family bilingualism not covered in Romaine's typology such as the parents' and the community's ideology of language, the language the parents use to communicate with each other, as well as peer or sibling language use. Moreover, the sixth type, concerning mixing languages, can

actually overlap with the other types, for example when parents claim to adhere to the One Person/ Parent – One Language principle yet code-switch (see Ch. 11 of this handbook). We will return to this issue in 3.3. below.

3.   Approaches to studying the bilingual family

Various approaches to studying the child's development of individual bilingualism in the family have prevailed in the field. Although case studies of early bilingualism, or the simultaneous acquisition of two languages, have dominated, some studies have taken a more comprehensive approach to mapping out important factors for fostering bilingualism through the use of surveys and interviews. An important factor that has an impact on the parents' language choice and indeed on the child's bilingual acquisition concerns language ideology. The attitudes of the environment and the parents will play a role in language choice patterns. Finally, a closer look at parent-child interaction can provide us with a deeper understanding of the role of the family in the child's acquisition of two or more languages.

3.1.   Surveys of bilingual and multilingual families:
Mapping out important factors

A revealing example of the value of written survey data is found in De Houwer (2004) in her study of input and children's language use in trilingual families in Flanders, which is officially monolingual Dutch-speaking. Although the children who were targeted were somewhat older (6–9 years of age) than those usually studied regarding early bilingualism, the results provide insight into family bilingualism. The data come from over 18,000 surveys that were returned. Some of the families were bilingual with Dutch outside the home, while many families were trilingual. The data revealed 14 individual input patterns, an input pattern being "a configuration of reported spoken home language use by mother and father combined (the parent pair), or by either mother or father in single parent families" (123). The children, on the other hand, "exhibit five different home language use patterns: (1) Dutch and two other languages X and Y, (2) two languages X and Y but no Dutch, (3) Dutch and one other language X, (4) one language X only and (5) only Dutch" (123). An investigation was made into the possible relationship between parental input patterns and children's language use. As the study was mainly concerned about issues of trilingualism, the children were classified as "actively trilingual" or "not actively trilingual". The active trilinguals (42 % of the sample) were those who spoke both languages X and Y in addition to Dutch, while the others only spoke Dutch, and possibly also one other language X. A statistically highly significant result indicated that the presence of Dutch in the input was strongly associated with the lack of active trilingualism. Another significant variable was whether or not both parents used languages X and Y. Active trilingualism was associated with the use of both languages in the family by the parents. These two factors could account for 84% of the variation in whether the children were actively trilingual or not in the 244 trilingual families in the sample, with the remaining percentage unaccountable through the survey data. Hence survey data can isolate important main variables contributing to active multilingualism. De Houwer (132), furthermore, notes that other potentially important factors are the relative frequencies with which the home languages are spoken as well as the interactional strategies parents use in communication with their children.

Another example of written survey data that also included follow-up interviews is Yamamoto's (2001) study of what she refers to as "interlingual families" in Japan. The research questions concerned the child's language choice, particularly concerning under which circumstances a child is likely to speak the minority language to the native-speaking parent. Over 1,000 written questionnaires were sent out to international families while the final sample to be analyzed totaled 118. Over one-half of the sample did not respond and of those who did, many were disqualified because they did not meet the criteria which included each parent's having a native language as either Japanese or English, that the family reside in Japan, and that the youngest child be three years of age or older. Follow-up interviews were held with six of the families. The two major promoting factors for the child's use of the minority language were attendance at an English-medium school and not having siblings. More generally, the results indicated that the more the parents use the minority language and the less the minority-language speaking parent uses the majority language to the child, the greater the likelihood the child will use the minority language to the parent who is the native speaker of that language. Yamamoto (127–128) claims that this finding undermines the One Parent – One Language principle as this language use pattern does not provide "the most optimal linguistic environment for promoting children's active use of the non-mainstream language in cross-native/ community language families". Moreover, this language use pattern was not the most commonly adopted pattern and even when adopted did not guarantee the child's use of the minority language to the parent speaking it. In conclusion, Yamamoto (129) points out that the prestige of the languages involved can play a role: English enjoys high status in Japan. An interesting complement to this work is the survey study of Okita (2002), which provides a broad overview of Japanese-British families' language choice decisions and childrearing practices in England and how conflicting pressures can render language maintenance difficult.

Survey data as discussed in the above-mentioned studies can contribute to mapping out important factors involved in fostering bilingualism in the family.

These factors may be investigated in more depth through follow-up studies. As noted, the relative status of the languages involved can affect the degree to which the minority-language speaking parent speaks his/her language to the child. This was also the case in a study of mixed couples in France and Germany (Varro 1997). Indeed societal ideology can play a role in bilingual acquisition, as well as the local ideologies of a community of practice such as a family. The next section will examine the notion of language ideology.

3.2.   Language ideology: Attitudes and beliefs of the parents and the environment

Language ideology may be defined quite generally as "shared beliefs of commonsense notions about the nature of language in the world" (Rumsey 1990: 346). And as Woolard (1998: 3) states succinctly, "there is as much cultural variation in ideas about language and about how communication works as a social process as there is in the very form of language". The issue of language ideology has gained prominence in recent years with the field of linguistic anthropology. However, its core matter has been of interest for quite some time through the study of language attitudes, world views in language, and language planning, among others.

Ideologies about language are of course not about language alone, rather they reflect issues of social and personal identity. Language ideologies are manifested in linguistic practice itself, that is, in how people talk, their language choice. Moreover, these ideologies are expressed in explicit talk about language, that is, in metalinguistic or metapragmatic discourse, as well as in what Woolard (1998: 9) refers to as "implicit metapragmatics": "linguistic signaling that is part of the stream of language use in process and that simultaneously indicates how to interpret that language-in-use". This idea is similar to Gumperz's (1982) notion of contextualization cues – the message is not only in what is said, but also in how it is said. Thus a person's language ideology may be recoverable in what he or she says about language, both explicitly and implicitly, and in the language choices he or she makes. There is a multiplicity of language ideologies in various social orders, and indeed as Gal (1998) points out, ideas about language can also be contradictory.

Various families may have different language ideologies. Parental beliefs and attitudes about language and language learning play an important role in early bilingual development and are intrinsically tied with language use, as discussed in De Houwer (1999). She builds on the assumption that these beliefs and attitudes fit within the larger framework of general belief systems concerning children's overall development, and that there is considerable variation. Okita (2001: 232) also notes that language use in bilingual families is "deeply intertwined with the experience of childrearing".

Parents may have positive or negative attitudes towards bilingualism, towards specific bilingual praxis such as code-switching, towards particular languages, or even towards particular types of interactional strategies. De Houwer (1999: 83) refers to an "impact belief", which she defines as "the parental belief that parents can exercise some sort of control over their children's linguistic functioning". Such impact beliefs may be strong as when parents, for example, provide negative sanctioning to certain linguistic practices, and thus employ control over the child's language use, or they may be fairly weak in that there is an attitude of 'anything goes'. Hence, as De Houwer points out, parental beliefs and attitudes will influence parents' own linguistic practice and interaction strategies with their child, and this in turn will have an impact on the child's language development. De Houwer concludes (92) that the best chances for active bilingualism will come about in family situations in which the parents "have an impact belief concerning their own possible role in the language acquisition process, and where there is a general positive attitude towards the languages involved and to being bilingual". Such beliefs and attitudes shared by parents we may generally refer to as a local language ideology within the community of practice of the family. It is, however, important to point out that parents may share the same language ideology overtly, yet covertly make different linguistic choices (Lanza 1997/2004). Moreover, they may in fact hold different ideological stances, which could potentially lead to conflict in language planning in the family, as discussed in Piller (2002).

We may ask how such an ideology concerning bilingualism is formed. King and Fogle (forthc.) investigated the relationship between parents' beliefs about how to successfully raise children bilingually, the various types of advice given in the media, and current findings in empirical research in the field. They focused on four recurrent themes in the media and popular literature, and indeed concerns of parents: language delay, language confusion, language learning materials, and the connection between bilingualism and intelligence. 24 families were interviewed and recurrent themes were documented in the discourse. Furthermore, a systematic review of popular literature published in the last five years was carried out. What they discovered was that parental ideologies tended to coincide with the information and advice given in the media and popular literature, including newspaper articles, parenting magazines, websites pertaining to bilingual parenting as well as popular parenting books. Moreover, there were significant mismatches between parental beliefs and the popular literature on the one hand, and the findings in empirical research on the other. As King and Fogle (26) note: "Thus, although parents and many popular writers espouse the idea that bilingualism is a good thing for children's cognitive development, they – and we – are still left with the hangover of earlier, now out of date, research – especially in terms of the language delay and confusion issue". King and Fogle also noted that parent language ideologies were closely connected

with other cultural-specific notions of good parenting and childrearing practices, also the case noted in Okita's (2001) study of Japanese-English families in
England, cited above.

Parental language ideologies are vital in that they are linked to language
use patterns in the home. The language ideologies of parents may be overtly
expressed through metalinguistic comments; however, they may find covert expression through language choice. Moreover, there may be a mismatch. Goodz
(1994) showed clearly the mismatch between parents' purported language use
patterns in the home and their actual language use in interaction with their
children. Although claiming to use the One Person – One Language strategy, the
parents in fact used both languages. Mapping out general parental ideology towards language acquisition and bilingualism is an important contribution of survey questionnaires and interviews. However, the examination of how parents
actually do talk to their children can only be accomplished through an interactional analysis of parent-child conversations. Hence we move from more
macro-oriented approaches to studying bilingual families to micro-approaches
in the examination of factors involved in fostering early bilingualism.

3.3.   Interactional analysis: Parent-child conversations

In his work on language maintenance and language shift in immigrant communities, Fishman (1991) stresses the decisive role of the micro-level of face-to-
face interaction and social life within the intimate family and local community.
A look at the micro-level of the community of practice in cases of family bilingualism can help us understand why some children establish bilingualism at a
very early age while others do not. This involves looking at what Okita (2001)
has referred to as the "invisible work" in bilingual childrearing.

Insightful examples and references to interactional strategies in the bilingual
home can be found in the earlier literature on the simultaneous acquisition of
two languages, for example, in Leopold's (1939–1949) four volume diary on his
daughters' bilingual development. However, systematic analyses of bilingual
conversations between caregiver and child have only emerged in recent years
in the field. Lanvers (2001: 444) notes that "whilst micro-focused analyses of bilingual conversations have been adopted to switching data in children, especially
in formal schooling environments (…), the approach remains little used with data
from younger children". Indeed there is a paucity of studies in the field of bilingual first language acquisition that focus on conversational interaction in the
family, compared to studies examining other aspects of bilingual development. In
the following, the point of departure will be on two in-depth studies that do focus
on conversational interaction (Döpke 1992; Lanza 1997/2004). Many studies do
not necessarily focus on this type of interaction, yet examples and relevant findings are often brought up in the discussion, and will be mentioned below.

In her study of the discourse structures of parents in bilingual families, Döpke (1992) illustrates quite effectively the complexity of the One Person – One Language strategy of interaction. This research was based on data from bilingual German-English families in Australia, including recordings of four children, aged 2;4 or 2;8 at the onset of the study, in naturally occurring interactions with their parents. The goal of the study was to investigate the type of input that could result in the child's use of the minority language. What Döpke's analyses revealed is that the greater the degree of child-centeredness the parent's interactional strategies were, the greater the chance that the child would become an active bilingual, using the minority language. A child-centered mode of interaction was defined as the use of various discourse structures that encouraged the child's contributions in conversation. The overall idea is that *quality* is more important than *quantity* in parent-child interaction. These findings have been an important contribution to the study of language socialization in the bilingual family. Nonetheless a closer examination of methodological issues can highlight the implications of such findings.

The parents in Döpke's study were advised to pursue their regular interactional routines and hence the recorded mother-child conversations and father-child conversations involved different routines and activities. Indeed such an approach renders the study a naturalistic and thus more suitable one for investigating the child's language socialization. However, since free play lends itself to more child-centered speech, as Döpke herself states, one could equally interpret the findings as support for the hypothesis that the more the parent speaking the minority language engages in play with the child, the greater the chance the child will become an active bilingual. Hence it appears that the social construct of the mother and father in various cultures would have an impact on the results. In other words, one may ask whether the decisive factor is that the minority-language speaking parent has a more child-centered mode of interaction or that s/he is more often engaged in child-centered activities. Döpke suggests that the adult's choice to engage in playful activities and talk-oriented interactions is also related to individual personality and not just a result of the traditional roles in the family. However, it is clear that societal constructions of gender roles, and hence the role of the father and the mother, will also affect individual performance.

A particular aspect of the parents' interaction in the minority language was the use of what Döpke called "insisting strategies" to use the one language or the other with the parent. Only those children in the study who acquired active command of German were in fact met with high-constraint insisting strategies such as unspecified clarification requests and requests for translation. Kasuya (1998) also noted in her study of Japanese-English bilingual families that the parents' use of a discourse strategy that made their preference for the use of Japanese explicit had the highest success rate in securing the child's subsequent choice of Japanese. A closer examination of how parents who profess to use the One Person – One Language strategy of interaction actually react to the child's introduction of the other language into the conversation can provide us with insight into the child's language socialization into bilingualism – whether the child is socialized into language separation according to interlocutor, or code-switching.

Döpke's study reported on parental discourse structures used in conversations with the bilingual child. These structures were not explicitly linked with the child's contributions in the conversation. Rather they were reported on globally and linked to the assessment of whether or not the child was an active bilingual. In contrast with Döpke's study, Lanza (1992, 1997/2004, 2001) presents a *sequential* analysis of the child's language mixing in interaction with each parent and how the parent reacts to that mixing. Mixing was defined as the use of mixed utterances as well as utterances in the other language than that used by the parent who claims using the One Person – One Language strategy of interaction. An interpretive framework is presented for analyzing the discourse context of the young bilingual language mixing; the parental interactional strategies were assessed as to what extent they contributed to a context that was more or less monolingual or bilingual.

The data upon which this study builds are conversational exchanges between a two-year-old girl named Siri and her parents, a bilingual family in Norway in which the parents claimed to use the One Person – One Language strategy. Siri's mother was American and spoke English with her daughter while her father was Norwegian. Recordings were made from just prior to Siri's second birthday until she was 2;7. Siri mixed languages throughout the entire period of the study. A distinction, however, was made between grammatical mixing and lexical mixing. Elsewhere I have argued that Siri's grammatical mixing may be attributed to her language dominance in Norwegian (cf. Lanza 1993, 1997, 2000).[1] Despite this dominance she mixed lexically more often with her Norwegian-speaking father than with her English-speaking mother. A micro-analysis of her parents' discourse strategies in response to Siri's mixing provided some interesting results. Siri's mother used strategies that opened negotiations for a context that was more or less monolingual whereas her father employed strategies that contributed to negotiating a context that was more or less bilingual. Table 1 lists the discourse strategies that can serve to propose a context which is more or less monolingual or bilingual. These interactional strategies cover the parental reactions found in the data.

Table 1. Parental discourse strategies towards child language mixing (Lanza 1997: 262)

1. **Minimal Grasp Strategy** (Ochs 1988):   Adult indicates no comprehension of the child's language choice.   2. **Expressed Guess Strategy** (Ochs 1988):   Adult asks a yes-no question using the other language.   3. Adult **Repetition** of the content of the child's utterance, using the other language.   4. A **Move On Strategy**: the conversation merely continues.   5. Adult **Code-Switches**.

In discussions of discourse strategies, one is often led to think that there is conscious calculation on the part of the interactant. Studies of conversational code-switching, a particular type of discourse strategy, however, have shown that even adult bilinguals may be unaware of what language they are actually using as they are so immersed in the interaction. Discourse strategies may thus at times operate below the level of consciousness and playback techniques may even surprise the individual of his or her own language use. Therefore, although there may be degrees of consciousness with which the parents employ various discourse strategies, what is of particular interest is the children's response to these strategies, and the discourse the parent and child co-construct, and over time the interactional style they create. The child's response to these strategies may indicate the child's perception of the context but this needs to be grounded in the discourse. The child's degree of mixing can thus be evaluated in relation to the extent to which the parent creates a monolingual or bilingual context with the child. In so doing, the parent highlights his or her role of a monolingual or a bilingual. And thus we may see to what extent the parent socializes the child into language separation or code-switching.

The strategies listed in Table 1 can be placed on a continuum, as done in Figure 1, indicating their potential for making a bid for a monolingual or bilingual context once the child has opened negotiations for a bilingual context through mixing. Note that I employ the word 'open', as negotiations are indeed an interactional process and must be sequentially analyzed.

MONOLINGUAL				**BILINGUAL**
CONTEXT				**CONTEXT**
Minimal Grasp	Expressed Guess	Adult Rep.	Move On Strategy	Code- Switching

Figure 1. Parental strategies toward child language mixes (Lanza 1997: 268)

Let us now turn to some examples of these parental strategies in other bilingual parent-child interactions. In (1) below we find an example of the minimal grasp where the parent provides minimal support for the child's utterance through a request for clarification, leaving her to reformulate the utterance. Recall that Döpke (1992) noted in her study that only those bilingual children who were met with so-called high-constraint insisting strategies (such as the minimal grasp) actively used the minority language. In this example we note the effect of the repeated sequencing of the mother's minimal grasp that eventually results in the child's switching to German, the language choice of the mother.

(1) **Minimal Grasp Strategy**
   Giulia (2;4): Mother speaks German, Father speaks Italian. They live in Rome. In the following, Giulia addresses her German-speaking mother continually in Italian until the last reply (Taeschner 1983: 201).
   G: Mami *aple*.   ('Mommy open'.)
→ M: Wie bitte?   ('What, please?')
   G: Mami *aple*.
→ M: Wie bitte?
   G: Mami *aple*.
→ M: Wie?
   A: *APLEEEEEEE*!!!!
→ M: (covers her ears) Wie bitte?
   G: Aufmachen?   ('Open?')

In (2) the reply of Jacob's mother is an instance of an expressed guess. With an expressed guess the child can either confirm or disconfirm the guess. Note that with the expressed guess the parent subtly reveals his or her role as a bilingual through the translation of the child's mix. Hence this shifts the child even further along the language mode continuum towards the bilingual end of it.

(2) **Expressed Guess Strategy**
   Jacob (2;8) is bilingual in German and English and lives in Australia. He is talking with his German-speaking mother (Döpke 1992: 95).
   C: *do it again*
→ M: noch mal?
      ('again?')
   C: yeah.

With a repetition, the parent repeats the child's meaning, using the other language in a non-question form, which implicitly does not require an answer of the child. Hence the repetition strategy, as in (3), places less of an interactional demand on the child than the expressed guess and the minimal grasp.

(3) **Adult Repetition**

Andreu (2;2.22) is bilingual in English and Catalan; he lives in Spain. He and his Catalan-speaking mother are looking at a picture book (Juan-Garau and Pérez-Vidal 2001: 74).

A: *a bucket.*

→   M: un cubell. ('a bucket.')

A: *a boat!*

→   M: una barca, i una cadira. ('a boat, and a chair.')

With the move on strategy the caregiver merely continues the conversation thereby implicitly indicating comprehension and acceptance of the child's mixing. The conversational excerpt in (4) illustrates this strategy.

(4) **Move On**

OLI is bilingual in French and English and lives in Montréal. She is speaking with his anglophone mother (Nicoladis and Genesee 1998: 92).

Child: *il est où ma pomme?*
         ('where is my apple?')

→   Mother: Mommy put it away in the kitchen.

Finally, with code-switching the parent either switches over completely to the other language or employs intra-sentential code-switching. This strategy is illustrated in the following example:

(5) **Code-switching**

Freddy (1;8.22) is trilingual in English, German, and Japanese. He lives in Japan. He and his English-speaking mother are looking at a book (from Quay 2001: 184).

MOT: what's that?

FRE: *nya.* (Japanese baby word for 'cat')

→   MOT: *nya nya.*

MOT: that's right.

These short excerpts of discourse need to be anchored within the ongoing conversation in order to be fully analyzed. In many studies of language choice in bilingual families, the language used by the individual parent is considered the 'context' for the child's language choice and hence used to evaluate to what extent the child uses the languages appropriately. However, we cannot determine whether a parent is behaving 'monolingually' just because he or she is only speaking one language. In Lanza (1997/2004), a more dynamic notion of context was invoked by examining the evolving discourse achieved between parent and child, resulting in contexts that were more or less monolingual or bilingual.

Each strategy noted above functions as a contextualization cue (Gumperz 1982) and how the cue is interpreted requires its anchoring in the discourse. Siri's language mixing was evaluated developmentally and interactionally. Every instance of lexical mixing was examined sequentially in context. Moreover, the parents' variation in strategy use in relation to Siri's linguistic development was also followed. By doing this, one can determine the degree to which Siri was socialized into maintaining a monolingual context with her mother, and into a bilingual context with her father. Hence Siri's parents had different approaches to their daughter's language socialization.

Siri's mother was her sole source of input for English and hence her negotiation of a monolingual strategy with her daughter created a natural context for the use of the language. This stimulated Siri's active use of English, which in turn contributed to her acquisition of the language in spite of the dominance of Norwegian in her environment. Moreover, the father's negotiation of a bilingual context, opening up for the use of English and in fact encouraging Siri's use of English, further contributed to Siri's acquisition of the minority language. At times he even provided a correct adult model for Siri's attempted pronunciation of English lexical items (cf. Lanza 2004: 283).

The approach to analyzing parent-child conversations and hence language socialization that I have advocated is a qualitative sociolinguistic one. Psycholinguistic approaches, however, have basically dominated the field of bilingual first language acquisition and focused on quantitative measures of investigating 'parental input'. Accordingly, Nicoladis and Genesee (1998) attempted to quantify the use of the discourse strategies outlined above in order to determine a causal relationship between discourse strategy and degree of mixing by the child. The results were negative; in other words, statistical analyses did not reveal any support of a relationship between parental strategy and level of mixing. In Nicoladis and Genesee's study, elements of discourse were pooled across various developmental periods and conversations involving different interlocutors in the quantifications. In other words, neither a developmental nor an interactional analysis was performed. Deuchar and Muntz (2003) also attempted quantification of their data on a Spanish-English bilingual child. Such quantification, however, is at odds with a sequential approach to analyzing conversation, which is an important analytical perspective in language socialization theory since "socialization is a product of interaction", as noted in 2.1 above.

In Lanza (2001, 2005) I discussed problems in quantifying interactional phenomena. In some quantifications, in order to determine a causal relationship between strategy use and the child's subsequent language choice, the next or following conversational turn was employed. Example 1 illustrated quite clearly the need to examine larger units of relevant discourse. A mere turn-by-turn quantification of the child's mixing in the conversation and the parent's response would miss the cumulative effect of the parent's strategy, which is important from a language socialization perspective. Moreover, consider the following example:

(6) Jens (2;9) is bilingual in French and German. Here he is trying to attract his German-speaking father's attention (Kielhöfer 1987: 147).

1	Jens:	Guck' mal, eine *mouche*!
		('Look, a *fly*!')
2	Father:	Eine ... was?
		('A ... what?')
3	Jens:	Eine *mouche*! Da, guck!
		('A *fly*! There, look!')
4	Father:	Ach so, eine Fliege!
		('Oh, a fly!')
5	Jens:	Ja, eine Fliege!
		('Yes, a fly!')

In his excitement Jens initially responds to his father's minimal grasp in line 2 with a continued mixed utterance repeating the mix from line 1. His father then replies with a repetition in line 4 and Jens confirms in line 5, repeating the German equivalent himself. In this excerpt we once again see the importance of a sequential account in evaluating the parent and child's contributions to the discourse. An analysis that restricts itself to the immediate turn following the parental strategy would not capture the effect of the parental strategy in light of the rest of the conversation. Juan-Garau and Pérez-Vidal (2001) employed the strategies discussed above in their study of a young child's acquisition of English and Catalan in Spain. The father changed his strategy towards his child's mixing at a certain point in the child's development and the authors showed how this had an impact on the child's subsequent language choice. They note that had the data on the young child Andreu's dramatic shift in mixing rates and his father's change in parental strategy in mixing been confounded with data from other children, the patterns found in their case study would not have been recoverable.

Deuchar and Quay (2000) have convincingly argued for the case study approach, which allows us to explore certain phenomena in depth while assessing the validity of existing models of analysis. Only by carefully analyzing interaction developmentally in many cases of the language socialization of bilingual children can we truly assess the role of interaction in establishing and fostering bilingualism or multilingualism in the family. Moreover, this includes looking at multiparty family interactions and not merely dyadic interactions, which has indeed been the focus in the research in bilingual first language acquisition. As noted in Lanza (2001: 222–224), a close look at triadic interactions might in fact reveal multilingual practices that are absent in dyadic interaction. In two-year-old Siri's family, interactions including the mother and father in conversation with their daughter showed that Siri's mother would actually encourage Siri's use of Norwegian, while in dyadic conversations she would give negative sanction in the form of clarification requests to Siri's use of Norwegian. In the family dinnertime conversations, Norwegian was often prompted by Siri's mother as Siri recounted her day's activities. Hence Siri's mother would display her bilingual identity in triadic interactions by usually moving on in the conversation and allowing Siri's father to pick up on the Norwegian bids for conversation. Methodologically speaking, this contrast in Siri's mother's interactional style implies that triadic interactions cannot be used to build dyadic models of communication. Indeed triadic interactions are not merely a series of dyadic exchanges.

In order to investigate the interaction between language socialization processes and language acquisition in the family as a community of practice, more work remains to be done on a larger variety of family interactions, including with siblings. The work in bilingual first language acquisition, including my own, has strongly focused on the first-born child, often in families without siblings for the child. The child's parents are not necessarily the only individuals involved in language socialization. Furthermore, there is a need to further embed interactional analyses within a larger socio-cultural framework as exemplified in Li Wei's (1994) study of three generations and two languages in one family among the Chinese community in Britain. Li Wei's study is not one of individual bilingual/multilingualism in the family, as defined in this chapter, but rather of societal bilingualism. Nonetheless it provides insights into how language choice in the family at the conversational level can be related to social networks at a socio-cultural level, and in turn cast light on the issue of language maintenance and shift. Thus a focus on the family can reveal factors that impact on children's multilingual development and multilingual practices.

4.   Conclusion

In this chapter I have examined various applied linguistic approaches to studying family bilingualism in order to gain insight into the factors that contribute to fostering bilingualism and multilingualism in the young child in the formative years. Illustrative examples were given of studies using surveys and questionnaires to map important environmental factors in this regard. The significance of language ideology was highlighted. Parents express their ideology covertly in their language choice in interaction and hence socialize their children into this ideology – for example, the extent to which code-switching is acceptable in interaction. An appeal was made to the theoretical framework of language socialization, which emphasizes the dialogic nature of socialization in the process of interaction. It is through micro-analyses of parent-child conversations that we can gain insight into what can contribute to active bilingualism in the child. Controversies in the field of bilingual language acquisition were referred to in regards to how to treat conversational data. These controversies involve theoretical implications and have methodological consequences. There is a need for more case studies examining the micro-level of face-to-face interaction in the bilingual family. As the conversation analyst Schegloff (1993: 102) reminds us, *one* is also a number, and "in examining large amounts of data, we are studying *multiples or aggregates of single instances*". Hence quantitative analysis is not an alternative to a single case analysis, but rather should be built upon it. Only by carefully analyzing interaction developmentally in many cases of family bilingualism can we truly test the relationship between parental discourse strategies and their impact on the child's language socialization. And this includes the study of a variety of interaction types, both dyadic and triadic.

In addition, there is a need to enlarge the scope of inquiry in the study of multilingualism in the family to include case studies of larger families, not just those with only first-born children and not just those in which the parents are the sole caregivers. Conversational analyses of multiparty interactions in bilingual/multilingual first language acquisition are a neglected source of data in the study of language socialization. These aspects can provide further insight into issues concerning language maintenance and language shift. Indeed the applied linguist has many challenges to meet in the study of multilingualism and the family.

Notes

1. This dominance was manifested not only in her directionality of mixing but also in her greater linguistic development in Norwegian, her language preference, her lexical accessing problems in English, and finally her parents' own evaluation of Norwegian being her 'stronger' language. Within Levelt's (1989) model, we may say that grammatical mixing is not at the level of conceptualization, but rather occurs at the lower or automatized levels of production. Moreover, lexical mixing is more characteristic of bilingual adult speech (Myers-Scotton 1997; Poplack and Meechan 1998).

References

Barron-Hauwaert, Suzanne
    2004   *Language Strategies for Bilingual Families. The One-Parent-One-Language Approach.* Clevedon: Multilingual Matters Ltd.
Corsaro, William
    1997   *The Sociology of Childhood.* Thousand Oaks: Sage/Pine Forge Press.

De Houwer, Annick
  1999   Environmental factors in early bilingual development: The role of parental
          beliefs and attitudes. In: Guus Extra and Ludo Verhoeven (eds.), *Bilin-
          gualism and Migration,* 75–95. Berlin: Mouton de Gruyter.
De Houwer, Annick
  2004   Trilingual input and children's language use in trilingual families in Flanders.
          In: Charlotte Hoffmann and Jehannes Ytsma (eds.), 118–35.
Deuchar, Margart and Suzanne Quay.
  2000   *Bilingual Acquisition. Theoretical Implications of a Case Study.* Oxford:
          Oxford University Press.
Deuchar, Margaret and Rachel Muntz
  2003   Factors accounting for code-mixing in an early developing bilingual. In:
          Natascha Müller (ed.), *(In)vulnerable Domains in Multilingualism,* 161–190.
          Amsterdam/Philadelphia: John Benjamins.
Döpke, Susanne
  1992   *One Parent One Language: An Interactional Approach.* Amsterdam/Phil-
          adelphia: John Benjamins.
Eckert, Penelope and Sally McConnell-Ginet
  1999   New generalizations and explanations in language and gender research.
          Language in Society 28 (2): 173–183.
Fishman, Joshua
  1991   *Reversing Language Shift.* Clevedon: Multilingual Matters Ltd.
Gal, Susan
  1998   Multiplicity and contention among language ideologies: A commentary. In:
          Bambi Schieffelin, Kathryn Woolard, and Paul Kroskrity (eds.), *Language
          Ideologies. Practice and Theory,* 317–331. Oxford: Oxford University Press.
Garrett, Paul B. and Patricia Baquedano-López
  2002   Language socialization: Reproduction and continuity, transformation and
          change. *Annual Review of Anthropology* 31: 339–361.
Goodz, Naomi
  1994   Interactions between parents and children in bilingual families. In: Fred
          Genesee (ed.), *Educating Second Language Children. The Whole Child, the
          Whole Curriculum, the Whole Community,* 61–81. Cambridge: Cambridge
          University Press.
Gumperz, John J.
  1982   *Discourse Strategies.* Cambridge: Cambridge University Press.
Harding, Edith and Phillip Riley
  1986/2003   *The Bilingual Family: A Handbook for Parents.* Cambridge: Cambridge
          University Press.
Hoffmann, Charlotte and Jehannes Ytsma (eds.)
  2004   *Trilingualism in Family, School and Community.* Clevedon: Multilingual
          Matters Ltd.
Holmes, Janet and Miriam Meyerhoff
  1999   The community of practice: Theories and methodologies in language and
          gender research. *Language in Society* 28 (2): 173–183.
James, Allison and Alan Prout
  1990   *Constructing and Reconstructing Childhood: Contemporary Issues in the
          Sociological Study of Childhood.* London: Falmer Press.

James, Allison, Alan Prout, and Chis Jenks
    2002   *Theorizing Childhood.* Oxford: Polity Press.
Juan-Garau, M. and Carmen Pérez-Vidal
    2001   Mixing and pragmatic parental strategies in early bilingual acquisition. *Journal of Child Language* 28: 59–87.
Kasuya, Hiroko
    1998   Determinants of language choice in bilingual children. *International Journal of Bilingualism* 2 (3): 327–346.
Kielhöfer, Bernd
    1987   Le 'bon' changement de langue et le 'mauvais' mélange de langues. In: Georges Lüdi (ed.), *Devenir bilingue – parler bilingue*, 135–155. Tübingen: Max Niemeyer Verlag.
King, Kendall and Lyn Fogle
    forth-   Raising bilingual children: Parent ideologies and strategies. Paper pre-
    coming   sented at the International Symposium on Bilingualism 5, Barcelona. Ms. submitted for publication. [To appear as: Bilingual parenting as good parenting, in: International Journal of Bilingualism.]
Lanza, Elizabeth
    1993   Language mixing and language dominance in bilingual first language acquisition. In: Eve V. Clark (ed.), *The Proceedings of the Twenty-fourth Annual Child Language Research Forum. Center for the Study of Language and Information Conference Series,* 197–208. Stanford University.
Lanza, Elizabeth
    1997/2004 *Language Mixing in Infant Bilingualism: A Sociolinguistic Perspective.* Oxford: Oxford University Press.
Lanza, Elizabeth
    2000   Concluding remarks: Language contact – a dilemma for the bilingual child or for the linguist? In: Susanne Döpke (ed.), *Crosslinguistic Structures in Simultaneous Bilingualism,* 227–245. Amsterdam/Philadelphia: John Benjamins.
Lanza, Elizabeth
    2001   Bilingual first language acquisition. A discourse perspective on language contact in parent-child interaction. In: Jasone Cenoz and Fred Genesee (eds.), *Trends in Bilingual Acquisition,* 201–229. Amsterdam/Philadelphia: John Benjamins.
Lanza, Elizabeth
    2005   Language socialization of infant bilingual children in the family: Quo vadis? In: Xoan Paulo Rodriguez-Yanez, Anxo M. Lorenzo Suarez, and Fernando Ramallo (eds.), 21–39.
Lanvers, Ursula
    2001   Language alternation in infant bilinguals: A developmental approach to codeswitching. *International Journal of Bilingualism* 5 (4): 437–464.
Lave, Jean and Etienne Wenger
    1991   *Situated Learning: Legitimate Peripheral Participation.* Cambridge: Cambridge University Press.
Leopold, Werner
    1939–1949 *Speech Development of a Bilingual Child: A Linguist's Record,* Volumes I–IV. Evanston, Ill.: Northwestern University Press.

Levelt, Wilhelm
  1989   *Speaking. From Intention to Articulation.* Cambridge, Mass.: MIT Press.
Li Wei
  1994   *Three Generations, Two Languages, One Family: Language Choice and Language Shift in a Chinese Community in Britain.* Clevedon: Multilingual Matters Ltd.
Myers-Scotton, Carol
  1997   Code-switching. In: F. Coulmas (ed.), *Handbook of Sociolinguistics,* 217–237. Oxford: Blackwell.
Nicoladis, Elena and Fred Genesee
  1998   Parental discourse and codemixing in bilingual children. *International Journal of Bilingualism* 2 (1): 85–99.
Ochs, Elinor
  1988   *Culture and Language Development: Language Acquisition and Language Socialization in a Samoan Village.* Cambridge: Cambridge University Press.
Ochs, Elinor and Bambi Schieffelin
  1995   The impact of language socialization on grammatical development. In: Paul Fletcher and Brian MacWhinney (eds.), *The Handbook of Child Language,* 73–94. Oxford: Blackwell.
Okita, Toshie
  2001   *Invisible Work. Bilingualism, Language Choice and Childrearing in Inter-married Families.* Amsterdam/Philadelphia: John Benjamins.
Piller, Ingrid
  2002   *Bilingual Couples Talk. The Discursive Construction of Hybridity.* Amsterdam/Philadelphia: John Benjamins.
Poplack, Shana and M. Meechan
  1998   How languages fit together in codemixing. *International Journal of Bilingualism.* Special issue: Instant loans, easy conditions: The productivity of bilingual borrowing 2: 127–138.
Quay, Suzanne
  2001   Managing linguistic boundaries in early trilingual development. In: Jasone Cenoz and Fred Genesee (eds.), *Trends in Bilingual Acquisition,* 149–199. Amsterdam/Philadelphia: John Benjamins.
Rodríguez-Yañez, Xoán Paulo, Anxo M.Lorenzo Suarez, and Fernando Ramallo (eds.)
  2005   *Bilingualism and Education: From the Family to the School.* Munich: Lincom Europa.
Romaine, Suzanne
  1995   *Bilingualism.* Oxford: Blackwell.
Ronjat, Jean
  1913   *Le Développement du Langage Observé chez un Enfant Bilingue.* Paris: Champion.
Rumsey, A.
  1990   Wording, meaning and linguistic ideology. *American Anthropologist* 92: 346–361.
Schegloff, Emmanuel
  1993   Reflections on quantification in the study of conversation. *Research on Language and Social Interaction* 26 (1): 99–128.

Schieffelin, Bambi
   1990   *The Give and Take of Everyday Life. Language Socialization of Kaluli Children.* Cambridge: Cambridge University Press.
Schieffelin, Bambi and Elinor Ochs
   1986a   *Language Socialization Across Cultures.* Cambridge: Cambridge University Press.
Schieffelin, Bambi and Elinor Ochs
   1986b   Language socialization. *Annual Review of Anthropology* 15: 163–191.
Taeschner, Traute
   1983   *The Sun is Feminine. A Study on Language Acquisition in Bilingual Children.* Berlin: Springer-Verlag.
Varro, Gabrielle
   1997   *Les Couples Mixtes et Leurs Enfants en France et en Allemagne.* Paris: Armand Colin.
Wenger, Etienne
   1998   *Communities of Practice.* Cambridge: Cambridge University Press.
Woolard, Kathryn
   1998   Language ideology as a field of inquiry. In: Bambi Schieffelin, Kathryn Woolard, and Paul Kroskrity (eds.), *Language Ideologies. Practice and Theory,* 3–47. Oxford: Oxford University Press.
Yamamoto, Masayo
   2001   *Language Use in Interlingual Families: A Japanese – English Sociolinguistic Study.* Clevedon: Multilingual Matters Ltd.

Recommended readings

In addition to the works cited in this chapter, there are volumes that address bilingualism in the family. Xoán Paulo Rodríguez-Yañez, Anxo M. Lorenzo Suarez and Fernando Ramallo's edited volume, *Bilingualism and Education: From the Family to the School* (München: Lincom Europa, 2005), contains noteworthy contributions. Of particular interest is Part Two on bilingual socialization in the family, edited by Gabrielle Varro. As noted in this chapter, there are relatively speaking few studies dedicated to investigating parent-child interaction in the bilingual family; however, valuable insights are often presented in articles investigating the young bilingual child's simultaneous acquisition of two languages. The *International Journal of Bilingualism* published by Kingston Press publishes such articles. Comeau, Genesee and Lapaquette's (2003) article published in the journal, "The modeling hypothesis and child bilingual codemixing", is relevant to the discussion in this chapter. Also of interest is Mishina (1999), "The role of parental input and discourse strategies in the early language mixing of a bilingual child", *Multilingua,* 18 (4): 317–342.

There are currently many books on the market targeting parents of bilingual children as well as those interested in the field. A highly readable contribution to this collection which focuses on interactional issues is the recent book by Barron-Hauwaert (2004), *Language Strategies for Bilingual Families. The One-Parent-One-Language Approach.* Multilingual Matters, which publishes this book, also publishes the *Bilingual Family Newsletter* in which parent-child interaction and language choice is a recurrent theme of concern. Hardy and Riley's (1986) classic, *The Bilingual Family: A Handbook for Parents* (Cambridge University Press) has been updated and appeared in 2003. All of these works provide insight into fostering bilingualism in the family. Another classic Saunder's (1988) *Bilingual Children: From Birth to Teens* (Multilingual Matters Ltd.) presents an interesting case study of a bilingual family in Australia in which both parents are native speakers of English. They adopted the One Person – One Language strategy; however, the father is a non-native speaker of German. For readers of French, Christine Deprez's (1995) *Les Enfants Bilingues: Langues et Familles* (Paris: Didier) presents interesting cases of families involving both individual and societal bilingualism studied within the context of a large metropolis.

3. Growing up in a multilingual community: Insights from language socialization

Patricia Baquedano-López and Shlomy Kattan

1. Introduction

Becoming multilingual involves not only the acquisition of linguistic forms in two or more languages, but also the socialization to the rules and expectations that accompany the usage of those languages. Learning these forms does not occur independently of their meaning in their social contexts. At the same time, the very use of those forms creates a context in which those very forms acquire their meaning, both the immediate and broader contexts, the spatial and the temporal (Goodwin and Duranti 1992; Hanks 1996; Haviland 1996; Ochs 1996; Whorf [1941] 1995). Children and other language learners develop competencies across linguistic, social, cultural, and historical domains. These competencies are rooted in the practices of the community of which individuals become members and reproduce or transform those same standards of competence. The field of Language Socialization[1], along with Sociolinguistics and Linguistic Anthropology, has sought to understand the complexities of the relationships between languages, individuals, contexts, communities, and cultures and thus shed light on the affordances and limitations of the traditional methods of linguistics and applied linguistics in understanding the processes of becoming multilingual.

Language Socialization, as a field of study, offers a unique perspective for understanding the development of these competencies in bilingual and multilingual contexts, especially since language contact is the predominant condition in most societies. In this chapter, as is common in Language Socialization studies, we do not draw a clear demarcation between bilingualism and multilingualism. While it is true that by definition the former is restricted to two languages and the latter implies the possibility of speaking two or more codes, this distinction is not of great theoretical importance for the arguments offered here and in the works reviewed. We therefore use the terms bilingual, multilingual, and their derivatives interchangeably. Language Socialization along with the related fields of Linguistic Anthropology and Sociolinguistics has consistently called into question long-standing assumptions prevalent in mainstream child language acquisition studies. While Language Socialization studies do not set out to disprove theories and hypotheses from linguistics and psycholinguistics, which have traditionally studied child language acquisition, the methods of study afford opportunities to observe differences between what is proposed in the literature and actual language development and use *in situ*. This approach to the study of multilingualism has profited from understanding multilingualism not as an individual trait, but rather as an interdependent relationship between the individual and the community. Language Socialization and related disciplines thus understand language acquisition as a social phenomenon affected by and affecting situations and processes such as language contact and shift, language ideologies, and identity formation.

In this chapter we examine the social, cultural, and linguistic aspects of growing up in a multilingual community from the perspectives afforded primarily from a Language Socialization perspective, with concepts that have been informed as well by Linguistic Anthropological and Sociolinguistic studies. We begin with a brief introduction covering concepts central to understanding how Language Socialization views the process of 'becoming multilingual'. To gain a better understanding of the ways in which the notions of bilingualism and multilingualism have evolved within Language Socialization and in other fields, we discuss how language and community as subjects of study have been conceived across related disciplines (Section 2). We then provide a historical review of the field of Language Socialization, its theoretical and methodological underpinnings, as well as its interdisciplinary trajectory (Section 3). In the following section (Section 4) we examine the distinction between 'communities of practice' (Lave and Wenger 1991) and 'practices of communities' (Schieffelin and Ochs 1986), terms that have come to be used increasingly in Language Socialization research. More centrally, our chapter critically reviews recent child language socialization studies in multilingual communities. Given that much recent work in the field of Language Socialization has been carried out in postcolonial, transnational, and globalized settings, we also discuss the three interrelated concepts of language contact and shift, language ideology (the social and symbolic processes entailed in choosing between languages or in privileging one language over another), and identity formation which have been instrumental in shaping how Language Socialization studies contribute a more comprehensive view of growing up in a multilingual community (Section 5). Finally, we provide a summary of the ways in which Language Socialization research contributes to the study of multilingualism and outline future research trajectories (Section 6). Throughout the chapter we aim to illustrate how Language Socialization studies have reconsidered long-standing concerns to the study of language acquisition, especially in multilingual settings. Language Socialization, of course, is not the only area of research concerned with these questions, and in fact, these areas of investigation have been long-enduring ones in Linguistic Anthropology and Sociolinguistics, as well as other disciplines concerned with language in its social use. However, the field of Language Socialization has been crucially informed by, and has itself made significant contributions to these areas of study.

2.   Speech community

The analysis of the individual in the community is a long-standing concern of Sociolinguistic, Linguistic Anthropology, and Language Socialization research for its relevance to understanding how social norms are passed on from one generation to the next as individual persons also change those norms or create new ones. Folk notions of community understand the term as referring to any group which shares certain characteristics, resources, or spaces. Usually, these notions rest on the assumption that community is synonymous with homogeneity and that it exists in fixed points in time. For example, the term 'ethnic community' is often used to refer to groups that share the same cultural heritage where it is assumed that few differences exist among community members. Neighborhoods are also often thought of as communities in that residents share a geographical space despite the fact that they may not participate in the same speech or cultural practices. While these notions of community are commonly used, they do not capture the heterogeneous and fractal characteristics of community adopted in Sociolinguistic and Language Socialization studies. In speaking of growing up in multilingual communities, then, it is particularly important to discuss how different understandings of speech community may shape the way we understand the competencies involved in becoming multilingual and how multilingualism is a socially constituted phenomenon. In this section we trace the genealogy of the term 'speech community' and how it is intricately related to notions of competence and performance, as well as notions of social reproduction.

The term speech community was first proposed by Leonard Bloomfield ([1933] 1984: 42), who defined it as "a group of people who interact by means of speech." According to Bloomfield ([1933] 1984: 42), "all the so-called higher activities of man – our specifically human activities – spring from the close adjustment among individuals which we call society, and this adjustment, in turn, is based upon language; the speech-community, therefore, is the most important kind of social group." This understanding of speech community, however, posits language as an unbreakable bond between people. That is, it does not allow for a full understanding of communities that differ from one another despite similarities in linguistic code and language usage, nor does such a definition allow for simultaneous membership in multiple communities (Morgan 2004). Such a gap is especially noticeable when we consider how Bloomfield's definition of speech community would apply to bilingual individuals. Under Bloomfield's model, such persons pose a problem in that they do not fit into only one social aggregate. They thus put into question this model which assumes monolingualism. Bloomfield's model also reflects a bias towards opposing typical and atypical situations in which monolingualism, homogeneity, and uniformity are the presumed norm.

Discussions of linguistic or speech communities waned during the height of Chomskian linguistics, which had called into question the behaviorist foundations of the Bloomfieldian paradigm (Morgan 2004). However, the notion of speech community was again taken up in early sociolinguistic work done by John Gumperz and Dell Hymes. In his landmark publication, "The Speech Community," Gumperz (1968) wrote of the importance of studying languages in their communal use. Gumperz, challenging the notion that language should be studied as a closed system, wrote: "In analyzing linguistic phenomena within a socially defined universe, however, the study is of language usage as it reflects more general behavior norms: This universe is the speech community: any human aggregate characterized by regular and frequent interaction by means of a shared body of verbal signs and set off from similar aggregates by significant differences in language usage" (Gumperz 1968: 381). In his definition of the speech community, Gumperz resolves the first limitation of Bloomfield's definition of the speech community, allowing for the fact that speakers of the same language are not necessarily members of the same community. Still, Gumperz's definition, as Bloomfield's before him, suggests that individuals belong to only one community at a time.

It is important to note as well the critique of Chomskian linguistics that forms the crux of the Sociolinguistic argument while also acknowledging Gumperz's deviation from a strict behaviorist approach. The former concern was the driving force of Sociolinguistics, as expressed in the writings of Dell Hymes. Departing from Chomskian notions which contended that "linguistic theory is concerned primarily with an ideal speaker-listener, in a completely homogenous speech community who knows his language perfectly and is unaffected by such grammatical irrelevant conditions as memory limitations, distractions, shifts of attention and interest, and errors (random or characteristic) in applying his knowledge of the language in actual performance" (Chomsky 1965: 2), Hymes and Gumperz argued that all language, as a socially defined means of communication, must be studied as it is used by social beings in socially appropriate situations. Chomsky (1965: 3) writes that competence is the innate ideal knowledge that every person has of a particular language. Complementarily, performance is the actual use of the language, and, unless it can be used under ideal conditions, will not approximate competence. This competence-performance model and the theory of syntax developed within it became the guiding principles for the development of theories of language acquisition and learning. Within the Chomskian paradigm, children are born with the ability to acquire any language, an ability derived from each individual's innate linguistic capabilities which Chomsky termed 'universal grammar' (more specifically, linguistic principles and rules that enable children to acquire any language).

Hymes (1972) argued against the notion that *language use* is purely performance. Under Chomskian linguistics the notions of 'competence' and 'performance' do not clearly explain the variability that is found among speakers of the same speech community. Due to this perceived lack of explanatory power of the Chomskian perspective in 'actual' settings, Hymes called for a new theory of competence that included a theory of language *use*, that is, knowing what is appropriate to say and when it is appropriate to say it, in addition to a theory of grammar (Hymes 1972: 281). According to Hymes, "competence is dependent upon both (tacit) *knowledge* and (ability for) *use*" (1972: 282, emphasis in original). By redefining competence and performance, Hymes illustrates the central role played by sociality in determining what it means to speak a language. It is important to note, however, that Gumperz's "universe," this speech community, is not only defined by its use of language but by a system that reflects and constructs and therefore "constitutes meaningful participation in a society and culture" (Morgan 2004: 3). Gumperz and Morgan are not only alluding to the primacy of interaction or the social nature of language, but also to the myriad competencies that are involved in community membership. This departure from Chomskian linguistics, therefore, is multiple in that it both reconsiders what a language is and what it means to know a language, two changes that have had significant consequences for our understanding of what it is to grow up multilingual.

More recent models of community prominent in Language Socialization and Sociolinguistics research have advocated for views which front the inherent diversity of any collectivity. This includes the possibility of participation in multiple, sometimes overlapping, sometimes conflicting communities. In this sense individuals belong to and constitute both proximal and distal, co-present and imagined communities. Membership in community thus crosses over traditional analytic categories such as nationality, ethnicity, and race in favor of a more fluid, multiple, and shifting notion of community. The notion of communities as "imagined" has been specially influential in expanding the boundaries of what a speech community is. For Anderson, the nation is imagined "because the members of even the smallest nation will never know most of their fellow-members, meet them, or even hear of them, yet in the minds of each lives the image of their communion" (Anderson 1991: 6). Spitulnik's (1996, 1998) study of Zambian radio programming's reflection of state ideologies and influence upon popular culture illustrates how mass-mediated symbols and culturally shared meanings expand our understanding of community to include translocality, non-copresence, intertextuality, and transposability of contexts as part and parcel of our understanding of community membership. In so doing, Spitulnik departs from the earlier sociolinguistic notions of speech community while also problematizing the homogeneous and egalitarian undertones of Anderson's work in postcolonial settings (Spitulnik 1996). This more fluid and expanded notion of community allows us to understand bilinguality in ways not afforded by previous models. That is, in every day practices members of various communities may invoke the practices and beliefs of their numerous affiliations.

3.   Language Socialization

Language Socialization as a field of study grew out of these efforts to understand language as socially situated activity whereby cultural and community norms are both passed on and reworked from one generation to the next. Conscious that there are numerous scholars who adopt the concept of language socialization, we clarify that the view of Language Socialization taken here, then, is of the paradigm that follows Ochs and Schieffelin's (1984; Ochs 1986; Schieffelin and Ochs 1986) first conceptualization of this theory and method. Therefore, when we discuss Language Socialization as a discipline, we intend that it follows certain theoretical and methodological tenets. Studies not modeled after these tenets, then, may be studies of socialization practices in which language may figure prominently, but they are not, in our understanding of the field, Language Socialization studies (Garrett in press; Garrett and Baquedano-López 2002; Kulick and Schieffelin 2004).

Rooted in sociological, psychological, and anthropological approaches to the study of human development, Language Socialization takes as its goal the explication of the ways younger or newer members of communities are socialized to the beliefs and sociocultural and linguistic practices of their communities, both explicitly and implicitly, *through* the use of language, while also being socialized *to* community-specific ways of using language (Ochs 1986, 1988; Ochs and Schieffelin 1984; Schieffelin 1990; Schieffelin and Ochs 1986). In this sense, language is both the means by which to reach the end of socialization and an end of socialization in itself (Ochs and Schieffelin 1995). The idea that individuals are socialized both *to the use of language* and *through the use of language*, however, cannot be seen as two separable ways of socialization. To do so would fail to capture one of the central tenets of Language Socialization: the ways in which language is the main socializing tool of the culturally organized means-ends language socialization paradigm.[2]

Unlike traditional theories of language development, Language Socialization sees the processes of acquisition and socialization as integrated and bidirectional (Schieffelin and Ochs 1986). This perspective elaborates on the notion of communicative competence proposed by Hymes (1972) and discussed above in that it inquires into how the integrated domains of linguistic and sociocultural knowledge are learned by individuals in communities. A distinguishing feature of the Language Socialization paradigm is its concern with theories of social reproduction and social structures, drawing especially on the work of Bourdieu (1977, 1990, 1991), Bernstein (1972), and Giddens (1979, 1984). Departing from theories of enculturation (Mead 1956) which view the individual as a passive recipient of social norms, Language Socialization sees socialization as a bidirectional process where both adults and children are agents of socialization. That is, there are no preconceived socialization roles which individuals fill.

Rather, the identities of individuals are constructed over time in the moment-to-moment interactions of social actors. Additionally, Language Socialization views socialization as a life-long process that begins as soon as babies participate (or are present in) social interactions. For example, parents who decorate their children's rooms prior to the child's birth, already socialize themselves and the child to family life and, in many cases, gendered expectations are also conveyed and displayed. In this way, Language Socialization views the relationship between individuals and social structures in ways akin to Bourdieu's (1977) notion of *habitus* and Giddens' (1979, 1984) concept of *structuration* (cf. Ochs 1986). Significantly, Language Socialization methods provide a means by which to observe and analyze the enduring and emergent patterns of social reproduction and change (Garrett and Baquedano-López 2002).

It is important to distinguish between Language Socialization as a field of study and studies which look at language socialization practices. Socialization, as both a conscious and unconscious practice, is a ubiquitous phenomenon. Language Socialization studies are characterized by four main methodological tenets. First, they are longitudinal. That is, Language Socialization studies look at development of individuals across time in order both to see the development that is taking place and to see how developmental change occurs. Without this temporal perspective, studies could only speak to isolated events as they are related to other events occurring at the same time. They would not be able to make claims to broader perspectives of whether or not practices change over time. Secondly, Language Socialization studies are ethnographic. This means that these studies are concerned with the long-term description of everyday practices of communities arrived at through sustained observation by the researcher. Studies which are not ethnographic, could only speak again to the description of isolated events. Additionally, Language Socialization studies are cross-cultural in that they are concerned with how culturally distinct practices are acquired. Finally, Language Socialization studies are descriptive and analytic. They do not prescribe methods for how to socialize or teach children, but rather illustrate the range of practices by which language and culture are acquired (for a review see Garrett and Baquedano-López 2002).[3]

Language Socialization studies take as their primary concern the routine and everyday life of social actors (Ochs 1986; Peters and Boggs 1986; Schieffelin and Ochs 1986; Watson-Gegeo and Gegeo 1986). Routine activities provide opportunities to observe recurrent linguistic patterns which give clues as to how cultural perspectives are organized for young children in particular. This focus on the routine was instrumental in one of the earlier contributions of Language Socialization studies to the field of child development. The first was the recognition that 'baby talk', the phonologically, syntactically, and semantically simplified talk used when addressing young children, and which was first observed in White middle class American households, is not a universal phenomenon, but rather one which reflects a social group's expectations of the role of children in conversation (Ochs and Schieffelin 1984). The second major contribution, and related to the first, was that there appeared to be two main ways that cultural groups organized the participation of young children and adults in what were termed 'child-centered' or 'situation-centered' social environment. In a child-centered environment, young children are the focus of attention and accommodations towards them are frequent. These accommodations included simplified talk directed to the child, elaborations on the intentions and meanings of children's (unintelligible) utterances, and spatial and material arrangements considered suitable for the child (e.g. baby furniture, toys). In contrast, a situation-centered approach to child-adult interactions does not consider children as suitable partners of conversation so that simplified register is not frequent and children's utterances which do not approximate accepted words are not interpreted for them. In this perspective, children are expected to accommodate to the talk and the activities around them. It is important to note that these two perspectives are by no means ends of a pole, or that they stand in opposition. Social groups that could be said to employ one of these perspectives more strongly, depending on the occasion, will employ elements of the other (Ochs and Schieffelin 1984). Some interpretations of this typology (cf. Zentella 1997) have critiqued the model for creating an either-or dichotomy. However, this was never the intention. Rather, the model was always seen as allowing for shift, so the question was never one of *which* orientation a cultural group employed, but rather the degree of "*intensity* of the orientation" (Ochs and Schieffelin 1984: 304 emphasis in original). In this regard, the typology is meant to provide a general means by which to organize child-caregiver observations, rather than to predict steadfast rules for different communities.

In recent years, numerous publications have emerged addressing similar concerns to those raised by Language Socialization, in particular, an attention to socializing interactions, but which depart from the methodological and theoretical orientation of the paradigm (Kulick and Schieffelin 2004). Studies such as those reported in Bayley and Schecter (2004; also Schecter and Bayley 2002), and Watson-Gegeo (2004) contribute to our understanding of language in its social context in that they examine how language is used in interaction. Yet, as Kulick and Schieffelin (2004) point out, there is a difference between these studies and Language Socialization research in that while both are concerned with socializing interactions, they are nonetheless fundamentally different in how they situate their language acquisition findings in relation to the broader sociocultural context observed in longitudinal, ethnographic studies.

There are presently several interpretations of where Language Socialization is headed as theoretically and methodologically across a span of disciplines concerned with language acquisition and use (cf. Bayley and Schecter 2003; Watson-Gegeo 2004; Wortham 2005). While this propensity to adopt the term *lan-*

guage socialization is indicative of the spread of the paradigm, it also represents a potential departure from the tenets of Language Socialization research. This puts the field in a quandary, for while we may expect the application of all theories or paradigms to take place in ways which alter the original, in itself a sign of the productivity of the field, many of the current reconsiderations of Language Socialization deviate so considerably from the original paradigm as to warrant a closer examination of their claims to be Language Socialization studies. This is not to say that studies of language socialization practices must follow the tenets of Language Socialization, only that their theoretical and methodological contributions might lie more centrally in other fields.

4.   Communities of practice and practices of communities

Our discussion of community must take into account an important distinction between the concept of 'communities of practice' (Lave and Wenger 1991) and that of 'practices of communities' (Schieffelin and Ochs 1986). These two concepts, while overlapping and interrelated, are not synonymous. The concept of communities of practice derives from the study of apprenticeship among tailors in Liberia. For Lave and Wenger (1991: 98) "a community of practice is a set of relations among persons, activity, and world, over time and in relation with other tangential and overlapping communities of practice." It is important to recognize that *communities of practice* is a specific concept that is not meant to be generalized to broader notions of community in the anthropological, linguistic, or even colloquial sense. That is, communities of practice are situated within specific goal-oriented economic activity. In this sense, communities of practice, and the attendant notions of Legitimate Peripheral Participation and situated learning are not meant to be understood as recipes for pedagogical implementation (Lave and Wenger 1991: 40). Legitimate peripheral participation, as used by Lave and Wenger, indicates that newcomers to professional or trade communities become full participants by learning the knowledgeable skills and sociocultural practices of the community through their interaction with old-timers and other newcomers (1991: 29).

The concepts of legitimate peripheral participation and communities of practice differ from the notion of practices of communities. While both consider the processes by which members of communities become more knowledgeable of the competencies expected of them as their participation increases and is closer to target norms, the former defines communities through their economic activities and practices. The latter, on the other hand, understands communities as social aggregates which can be studied by an analysis of their everyday and varied cultural practices and activities which may be, but are not necessarily defined by those shared practices (e.g. tailoring as a profession).

Activity is a central unit of analysis in Language Socialization research as it is one of the principal loci where children and their caregivers, novices and experts participate in culturally organized ways in their communities. The notion of activity draws on the Lave and Wenger studies, but it also more directly builds on the principles of Activity Theory (Chaiklin 1996; Engeström 1999; Leont'ev 1978; Luria 1976). Activity is not understood simply as participation in local exchanges, but rather as a system which "integrates the subject, the object, and the instruments (material tools as well as signs and systems) into a unified whole" (Engström 1996: 67). While a study of language socialization would focus on activity and the engagement of tasks, it is also inclusive of the larger historical and social frameworks in which the activity being observed is situated. Many such studies have provided invaluable insights into how *habitus* is both historically and locally organized (Schieffelin 2000, 2002). In so doing, Language Socialization studies also attend to participation frameworks (Goffman 1974; M. Goodwin 1990; Philips 1972), or the organization of talk and task in collaborative activity.[4]

Over the last decade, Language Socialization research and research in related disciplines, has become increasingly concerned with socializing practices in multilingual settings. These studies have provided a unique perspective on the notions of community, socialization, practice, and activity discussed above. We now turn to discussing recent analytical trends that have come to the fore in these studies.

5.   Recent trends in Language Socialization research

The focus of this section is to provide an up-to-date description of Language Socialization studies carried out in recent years in multilingual settings. We also discuss some studies from the related fields of Linguistic Anthropology and Sociolinguistics inasmuch as they inform the same research questions. However, we do not include studies of language socialization practices which are not longitudinal, ethnographic, descriptive, and analytic. This is not to say that such studies cannot show socializing practices, but that they do not address the theoretical and methodological questions of concern to us here.

In this review we present three broad themes that represent recent efforts to provide an integrative perspective of the individual in society and the processes of becoming multilingual. We discuss how these themes contribute to seeing language socialization as a lifelong process that involves both reproduction and change. In what follows we examine these concepts in turn and look at how they have constructed a notion of multilingualism particular to the field of Language Socialization. However, it is important to keep in mind that the analytic categories of language contact and shift, ideology, and identity do not stand alone, but rather overlap in complex ways. Thus, the separation of these categories in this chapter is meant to provide a quick guide for identifying and explaining these themes at a foundational level. Since socialization to language and socialization through language is a lifelong process, and since community, as discussed above, is to be understood as a fluid set of relationships, growing up in a bilingual community cannot be understood separately from schooling, family life, work, and other institutional settings (see other contributors, this volume). Nonetheless, we focus on studies which have looked at socialization earlier in life and in particular settings.

5.1.   Language contact and shift

To speak of language contact generally entails speaking as well of cultural contact. Language contact has long been understood as a situation that is characterized by the distribution of two or more languages or codes for discursive space (Weinreich 1964; Garrett 2004). Language contact may oftentimes come about in contexts of migration or colonization where groups of different cultural and linguistic backgrounds are brought into contact because of geographic movement, military conquest, or dissemination of mass media. These situations usually lead to more marked power asymmetries that often translate into differential valuations of the languages of the different groups. Thinking of settings exhibiting language contact causes us to understand multilingualism as a social and cultural, rather than individual and mentalistic phenomenon. That is to say, while innatist approaches may view bilingualism as something which develops within the child, Linguistic Anthropological, Sociolinguistic, and Language Socialization studies conceive of this process as a social one.

   In such situations of linguistic and cultural contact it is common to witness language shift, or the gradual or rapid transition by speakers of one language (usually the language with less symbolic value or capital) to another (usually the language of greater symbolic value or capital). Beginning with Don Kulick's (1992) study of language contact and shift in Gapun, Papua New Guinea, a number of Language Socialization studies have been centrally concerned with how shift occurs as children are socialized to the use of languages in their communities (Crago, Annahatak and Ningiuruvik 1993; Field 1998; Garrett 1999, 2000, 2003, 2005; Howard 2003; Paugh 2001, 2005; Pease-Alvarez and Vasquez 1994; Romero 2003; Vasquez, Pease-Alvarez, Shannon and Moll 1994; Zentella 1997). Language shift is not necessarily the linear transition from one language to another, but can involve the creation of new varieties or the shift to either bilingualism or monolingualism. The notion of shift broadly encompasses these ideas as well as the ideas of language loss, attrition, maintenance, dormancy, and extinction. Yet, as with the notion of contact, language shift is best viewed as a social process rather than one of the individual alone. As we discuss in the following sections, these questions of contact and shift are intertwined with notions of ideology and identity. We will first focus on how shift has figured in Language Socialization, Linguistic Anthropological, and Sociolinguistic studies.

The Language Socialization paradigm views language shift as both a product of and an influence upon practices of socialization. Language shift coincides with sociocultural change in multifaceted and dynamic ways. The dynamism of language shift is illustrated in the reconsideration of long-standing notions of domain-specificity of languages. Garrett's (2005) reevaluation of the notion of diglossia (Fishman 1965, 1972) (i.e. the strict compartmentalization of codes according to domain) is particularly useful for understanding the ways in which Language Socialization can reframe the study of multilingualism in ways that provide a more socioculturally situated view of this process. In his long-term ethnographic study of St. Lucian children growing up in the multidialectal community of Morne Carré, where three codes, English, Vernacular English of St. Lucia [VESL], and Kwéyòl, are in contact, Garrett (1999, 2000, 2003, 2005) documents the processes of language shift as dominant forms and local varieties acquire varying degrees of prestige and power. Garrett asks how it is that in a setting in which English has acquired more symbolic power (Bourdieu 1991), less valued dialects or languages, such as Kwéyòl, are maintained, retained and reproduced. Garrett argues that speech genres (Bakhtin 1986) which are code-specific but not necessarily domain-specific serve in passing on the less valued codes. This explains the use of less expected codes in domains that have traditionally been seen as sites for use only of dominant codes. Garrett's research thus illustrates that the persistence of less-valued codes and varieties is a result of the relevance of those codes to particular cultural practices. Taking an example of the routine cultural practice of cursing, a practice that is prevalent across a wide variety of cultures and classes (Paugh 2002, MacDonald 1973), Garrett examines how children learn to curse in Kwéyòl, the devalued language, while they are generally expected to communicate predominantly in English, the language of prestige. Thus, while the local expectation for St. Lucian children is to learn English, they often participate in Kwéyòl exchanges around culturally and linguistically defined social practices. Children's participation in these exchanges illustrates more pointedly the persistence of code-specific genres that have implications for understanding language acquisition as a deeply contextualized and cultural activity which changes over time. In the following excerpt from Garrett (2005), Tonia, a three year-old child, is prompted by her aunt to curse. Tonia's mother and aunt (Noelicia) are conversing in Kwéyòl while Paul Garrett videotapes their interaction. During this exchange Noelicia prompts Tonia to 'fling a curse' at Paul Garrett.

1 Noelicia: Di Paul "Bat tjou'w," ah
   [to Tonia] 'Tell Paul "Beat your ass," eh'

2 Tonia: Bat tjou mama'w
   [to Paul] 'Beat your mother's ass'

3 Mother: Bondou
   [variant of *Bondyé* 'God'; an exclamation of surprise/shock]

4 Paul: Sa i di mwen?!
   'What did she say to me?!'

5 Mother: "Bat tjou mama'w"!

This example illustrates how young children display not only knowledge of the language, but also of competency in when to use the language in question. Tonia displays appropriate knowledge of the code (note her use of the appropriate grammatical construction when she adds *mama* in line 2) as well as appropriate knowledge of the genre and the social situation being negotiated (as is evidenced by her appropriately inappropriate participation). This example also illustrates a fluid and multiple notion of community membership in a language contact setting. As their talk continues, Mother (Paya) now admonishes Tonia in VESL (underlined utterances in the transcript below) not to curse.

12 Mother: <u>Paul naat koming in yoh bofdee patii</u>
    'Paul is not going to come to your birthday party'

13 Noelicia: Di'y las bat djòl li ah,
    'Tell her quit running her mouth'

    di'y sa, di Paya "Las bat djòl ou," ah
    'tell her that, tell Paya "Quit running your mouth," eh'

14 Tonia: Paya, bat tjou mama'w
    'Paya, beat your mother's ass'

15 Mother: <u>Wai yuu seeying dat, Tonia?!</u>
    'Why are you saying that, Tonia?!'

16 Noelicia: "Las bat djòl ou," mwen di'w di'
    '"Quit running your mouth," I told you to say'

The switch to VESL illustrates the code-specificity of genres. That is to say, the cursing routine is carried out in Kwéyòl while admonishing and other disciplinary measures are done in VESL. This phenomenon of generic code-specificity is also supported by the findings of Paugh's (2005) study of the use of Patwa and English in Dominica and in Kulick's (1998) study of Taiap and English in Papua New Guinea, both of whom found that both maintenance and shift of the local vernacular were tied to the use of the language in particular speech genres and routines.

Other studies have also shown that language shift does not follow a linear trajectory from monolingualism in one language to bilingualism and then to monolingualism in another language, a model of shift which had been assumed as the norm for some time. Drawing on an earlier longitudinal study of the socialization and interactional practices of Mexican-descent families in Northern California, Pease-Alvarez (2002) reports on interviews conducted with informants from that study to illustrate parents' perceptions of the changing linguistic abilities of their children (in English and Spanish). From these reports she concludes that there are competing values accorded to language use and the potential for language shift across generations (see also González 2001).

Language shift brings about other cultural changes such as alterations in child rearing practices. For example, a study of language shift conducted in Inuit communities in Northern Quebec also illustrated dramatic concomitant shifts in culturally specific child-rearing practices (Crago et al. 1993). Based on ethnographic interviews with mothers of different age groups, Crago and her colleagues illustrated that participants' reports of language use reflected differences in language socialization patterns. Generational differences among the mothers reflected different competencies in English and Inuktitut, the older generation of mothers being monolingual in the Inuit language, the younger mothers speaking either French or English in addition to Inuktitut. Crago et al.'s informants, as well as the researchers' ethnographic observations of the community, revealed that local socializing routines that included genres of affectionate and child-directed speech waned as the dominance of English, coupled with changes in economic and social patterns of the communities, became more salient.

The focus on language shift has also generated findings that resonate with the long-standing Language Socialization tenet that children are agents of socialization and change. A particularly notable example is the research by students of Language Socialization and Sociolinguistics on language and cultural brokering, in which children act as mediators between home, community, and other social institutions (cf. González 2001; Orellana, Reynolds, Dorner and Meza 2003; Pease-Alvarez and Vasquez 1994; Valdes 2003; Vasquez et al. 1994). Such findings illustrate the complexities of immigration, language and cultural contact, and the acquisition of competencies. In these settings, a Sociolinguistic, Anthropological, Language Socialization perspective allows us to document and analyze the emergence of new needs and competencies as existing norms change under novel circumstances.

Across geographic and political boundaries, language shift is also often promoted by legislation and educational policy. In the United States, the privileging of one language is reflected in educational policy such as the passage of English-only laws and in the goals of transitional bilingual programs for mainstreaming students rather than promoting sustainable bilingualism. These policies are often tied up with general anti-immigrant sentiments and have consequences for language use both in institutional settings and the home (Baquedano-López 1998, 2004). Pease-Alvarez and Vasquez's (1994; see also Vasquez et al. 1994) longitudinal study of Mexican-descent families in the Northern California city of Eastside takes a nuanced look at the contexts of language use and learning across home and school. The authors describe in detail the socialization experiences of Eastside community members and, finding schools to be a main agent of shift, argue for a non-deficit approach to the education of immigrant children. The passage of legislation and policies that limit bilingualism is of course a reflection of deep-rooted ideologies about languages and their speakers. In the next section we turn to discussing the problem of looking at the effects of the dispositions of individuals towards languages and the groups that use them.

5.2.   Language ideologies

The study of language contact and language shift in Language Socialization, Linguistic Anthropological, and Sociolinguistic research has fruitfully benefited from the concept of 'language ideologies' in examining notions of how and why speakers choose one language over another in multilingual situations. Over the last quarter century there has been little agreement over what exactly the concept of language ideologies should mean as a theoretically organizing unit of investigation, and in fact, different terms, such as 'language ideology', 'linguistic ideologies', or 'ideologies of language' have been used to describe the same concept over the years (see Kroskrity 2004 and Woolard 1998 for discussions). Silverstein's (1979: 193) classic definition understands language ideology as "sets of beliefs about language articulated by users as a rationalization or justification of perceived language structure and use." Yet, as he and others point out, language ideologies not only express views of speakers about the structure of their language, but can actually change that linguistic structure (Silverstein 1979; Woolard 1998). In multilingual settings, this can be seen in how code switching or borrowing affect the routine use of two or more languages (Rindstedt and Aronsson 2002; Zentella 1997).

Kroskrity (2004), in a review of the anthropological literature on language ideologies, examines five levels of organization or "converging dimensions" (2004: 501) which exemplify language ideologies. Kroskrity first states that "language ideologies represent the perception of language and discourse that is constructed in the interest of a specific social or cultural group"(2004: 501). That is, speakers' perceptions of language are rooted in their social and cultural experiences and often both reflect and reproduce particular economic interests. Second, language ideologies are multiple (2004: 503). Also, members of communities or social groups "may display varying degrees of awareness of local language ideologies" (2004: 505). Fourth, according to Kroskrity (2004: 507), and in consonance with Silverstein's (1979) and Woolard's (1998) observations, "language ideologies mediate between social structures and forms of talk." Finally, as will be discussed in the next section of this chapter, language ideologies are intricately involved in the construction of identity. Language ideologies are thus central in understanding the processes of growing up in multilingual communities from a Language Socialization and Sociolinguistic perspective since they enable researchers to see how the views and beliefs group members have of the languages they use and of how they use them affect their usage of those languages.

As Ochs and Schieffelin (1995) note, language ideologies come to the fore in Language Socialization studies of bilingual and multidialectal communities because of the discipline's attention to the cultural organization of speech and development:

> A language socialization perspective yields a more sophisticated model of grammatical development, that is, one tuned into certain cultural realities that influence when, how, and why young children use and understand grammatical forms. Such a model of grammatical development takes an informed look at ideology and social order as forces that organize children's use and comprehension of grammatical forms (Ochs and Schieffelin 1995: 73).

Within such an understanding of the acquisition of grammatical forms as an ideologically situated process, one can see how and why young speakers may attain varying degrees of grammatical competence in the multiple languages spoken in their community. The appropriateness of children's speaking one language or dialect and not the other, usually a reflection of the language ideologies of the group, may be equally as important a factor as the children's exposure to the different languages. In this sense, if young children in a bilingual community speak only one of the languages of their group, this can be understood as reflective of local beliefs about children's linguistic needs rather than as a result of deficiencies in the linguistic environment of the children. Such divisions can be based on ideologies not only of age, but also of gender and ethnicity, and may be related to notions of 'correct' or 'pure' forms of the language.

In line with Ochs and Schieffelin's comments, recent Language Socialization and Sociolinguistic studies have gained both theoretically and methodologically from looking at the language ideologies of the communities they are investigating (cf. Fader 2000, 2001; Field 2001; Garrett 2005; Jaffe 2001; Kulick 1992, 1998; Paugh 2005; Rindstedt and Aronsson 2002; Schieffelin 2000; Schieffelin and Doucet 1994; Zentella 1997). The analysis of language ideologies has also been instrumental in studies of literacy and socialization (Fader 2000, 2001; Schieffelin 2000; Schieffelin and Doucet 1994). In a study of the interface between language orthography and language ideology in Haiti, Schieffelin and Doucet (1994: 176) found "that arguments about orthography reflect competing concerns about representations of Haitianess at the national and international level." Fader (2000, 2001), for example, in her Language Socialization study of Hasidic Jews in New York City, has noted that language ideologies and beliefs about gender roles, assimilation, and religious integrity were central in the community's decisions on literacy instruction and availability of reading materials for girls and boys, as well as the differential use of Yiddish and English among the two gender groups. She has examined in great detail how local ideologies influenced community decisions to let girls learn to read in English while boys only learned to read and write in Yiddish and Hebrew.

Rindstedt and Aronsson (2002) also found local ideologies of language, gender, and ethnicity to be a determining factor in the shift from Quichua-Spanish bilingualism to Spanish monolingualism in an Andean community in Ecuador. In line with Kulick's findings in Gapun (1998; discussed below), Rindstedt and Aronsson (2002: 737) observed that the perception of Quichua as associated with "Indianness, rural life, poverty, and femininity" and of Spanish as associated with urban maleness contributed to the shift towards monolingualism. More significantly, the shift toward monolingualism was generational and often reflected and resulted from intergenerational linguistic practices. Thus, as the authors report, "bilingual practices are clearly linked not only to gender hierarchies but, above all, to position in the age hierarchy" (Rindstedt and Aronsson 2002: 738), a finding also reported in Kulick (1992). In Rindstedt and Aronsson's ethnographic study, adults routinely spoke to each other in both Quichua and Spanish while speaking directly to their children only in Spanish because of their perceptions of their children's needs beyond the community and of their children's competence in Quichua.

Language Socialization studies have long been interested in activities and routines as sites of socializing practices (Garrett and Baquedano-López 2002; Ochs 1986; Peters and Boggs 1986; Watson-Gegeo and Gegeo 1986). Routines and activities are to be understood as ideologically informed cultural practices. Field (2001), drawing on her ethnographic fieldwork in an Athabaskan community, has examined why certain ideologies about language use, as reflected in interactional routines, may be more resistant to change than is language code. Field found that despite a shift from Navajo to English, the use of triadic directives, in which adults may direct one child to tell another child to do something, has persisted. Field understands this persistence to indicate that while "a speech community's linguistic and ideological systems interpenetrate one another [...]

the two systems are also separate" (2001: 252), so that the persistence of this routine is an ideological one. Kulick (1998) examines a case in which the distribution of discourse genres among community members serves not only to expound the ideologies and customs concerning anger management and gender identity, but also to promote certain types of language shift. Looking at two of the ways in which villagers from the village of Gapun in Papua New Guinea deal with or rather express anger (*kroses* and oratories), Kulick contends that "at certain periods in the history of a language and its speakers, the links that exist among discourses on affect, gender, and language may come to salience and work to compel speakers to engage in linguistic practices that may result in changes in the language itself" (Kulick 1998: 87–88). For Kulick, these configurations of discourses or linguistic practices and the languages associated with them, in this case Taiap with *kros* and Tok Pisin with oratory, as well as the connections of those languages to other phenomena, such as tradition and Christianity, the land and money, women and men, leads village members to select the use of one over the other and thus "[move] the village vernacular (Taiap) towards extinction" (Kulick 1998: 100). In this regard, it is again fruitful to review Garrett's illustrative example of a girl learning to curse. The persistence of Kwéyòl through this speech genre results both from ideologies which limit the use of Kwéyòl (e.g. adults' beliefs that their children would benefit more from learning English and their perceptions of Kwéyòl as a dispreferred language) and from ideologies which perpetuate the use of the local vernacular in ideologically marked routines.

Local language ideologies are instrumental in understanding language use and socialization in multilingual communities as they relate to community members' views on code switching, borrowing, and 'correct' or 'pure' languages. Zentella (1997), for example, found that adults lamented the community's children's use of 'incorrect' Spanish. In her study of a Puerto Rican neighborhood in New York, she noted that these views reflected more generally perceived ideologies of code switching or code mixing as evidence of lack of competence. Rather than view 'Spanglish'[5] as a 'degenerate' language, Zentella demonstrated the myriad and complex competencies involved in knowing how, when, and with whom to code switch. Views of language purism such as those expressed by some of the adults in Zentella's study, however, are usually closely related to language shift in that community members in bilingual settings may refrain from using one of the codes with speakers who are perceived to speak it incorrectly (see also Bhimji 2001; Kroskrity 1998, 2000; Rindstedt and Aronsson 2002). Kroskrity, looking at the ritual Kiva speech of the Arizona Tewa, examines how ideologies of language maintain the 'linguistic purity' of Tewa in ways that cannot be accounted for by theoretical positions that claim it as a form of "linguistic conservatism" (Kroskrity 1998: 104). For Kroskrity, the preservation of Tewa in Kiva talk is regulated by "convention, indigenous purism, strict compartmental-ization, and linguistic indexing of identity" (Kroskrity 1998: 105).

The concept of language ideologies has been most central in understanding language choice and language shift as linked to notions of ethnicity and, as will be discussed in greater detail in the next section, to notions of identity (Echeverria 2003; Heller 2001; Jaffe 2001; Kulick 1992, 1998; Paugh 2005; Rindstedt and Aronsson 2002; Zentella 1997). The question of ethnic authenticity has been especially important in this regard and a number of studies in this topic are advancing newer understandings from a more ethnographically based perspective. Jaffe (2001) notes that the Corsican ethno-regionalist movement used language revitalization and a discourse of linguistic identity as means by which to authenticate Corsican identity. Echeverria (2003) found in her study of the Basque Autonomous Community that use of Euskera, the Basque language, was differentially seen by teenagers of the area as either necessary or not for developing a Basque identity and ethnicity.

To summarize, the concept of language ideologies is important in understanding growing up in multilingual communities, both of the local community and of the broader society, because they influence the ways in which languages are used by the group. They are instrumental in determining the amount and areas of exposure to languages that younger community members have to the codes spoken in the community and thus in determining the ways in which children growing up in these communities become bilingual or not. In thus influencing the linguistic landscape, language ideologies are also central in the construction of identity among community members. We now turn to discussing this area of concern in language socialization and sociolinguistic research.

5.3.   Language and identity

Scholarly attention to the study of identity across related disciplinary fields supports the premise that identity is fluid, dynamic and discursively created according to the cultural systems in which people are located both spatially and temporally. Moreover, the construction of identity is embedded in a matrix of relations of power that organize participation in discourses and activities (Bucholtz and Hall 2004; Butler 1997; Kroskrity 1993, 1998; Ochs 1993; Ochs and Capps 1996). Speakers, as social actors, construct identities and at the same time find themselves performing identities that have been constructed by others, often in the context of historical forces that shape both the actions and the conditions for articulating such identities. As a result, much of identity politics rests not just in highlighting similarities but also in recognizing what makes individuals different (Bucholtz and Hall 2004). From this perspective, the construction of identity through discourse and practice is not a neutral, value-free activity. Language Socialization research has addressed the ways in which the study of language in situated practice informs our understanding of the construction of locally situated identities, but, more importantly, of how speakers' actions have consequences for the larger, global politics of identity and language learning and use.

The process of identity formation involves a complex social structure that is sustained through collaborative efforts of self and others. Individuals construct social identities at any one point in social interaction and social life. Children or novices' claims to social identities are negotiable not only across situations but also across the life span. In this respect, identities are more like candidate personae that are only ratified by other participants during interaction. Claims and requests for the development or display of particular identities are carried out through the socialization of linguistic forms, as well as through relevant cultural orderings of stances, acts, activities, and genres (Ochs 1993). As Ochs and Schieffelin (1995: 74) note, "A language socialization approach relates children's use and understanding of grammatical forms to complex yet orderly and recurrent dispositions, preferences, beliefs, and bodies of knowledge that organize how information is linguistically packaged and how speech acts are performed within and across socially recognized situations." Participants in language socialization encounters have at their disposal grammatical, lexical, and phonological resources to construct and socialize identities. As a socialization act par excellence, narrative provides a particularly rich site for understanding the socialization of identity.

A number of cornerstone Language Socialization studies have already illustrated the role of narrative in the reproduction of expected identities, including gendered roles (Andersen 1986; Peters and Boggs 1986). In their analysis of lullabies in Kwara'ae, Peters and Boggs describe in compelling detail the mixed genre of children's bedtime stories and lullabies which narrate the imagined adult activities of two young girls in this way projecting the expectancy of roles in their community. In another study of narrative socialization in working-class communities in the U.S. (Heath, 1983), children acquire skills that make them competent participants of their home community but which may not necessarily ensure a continuity of these practices across other language socialization domains, particularly in the public school. While this situation has the potential for creating conflict and tension in the construction of a coherent self across contexts, and most importantly, in the display of appropriate linguistic and cultural competencies across dissimilar contexts, it is not the only outcome. Studies in other multilingual settings illustrate the construction of linguistic identities through narrative practices (Baquedano-López 1997, 2000; Moore 2004). Baquedano-López has described how immigrant Mexican children enrolled in Spanish-language *doctrina* classes in Los Angeles, California, are socialized to a Mexican collective identity through religious narratives about Our Lady of Guadalupe (a primarily Mexican Catholic symbol). Through a comparison of these narrative practices and those in an English-language catechism class in the same parish, she demonstrates how, through these story-telling activities, teachers socialize children to particular social identities in a transnational context (Mexican, Indian, (Mexican) Catholic, American). The narratives in the *doctrina* classes, for example, draw both historical and social connections between the students in the classroom and their cultural and religious heritage and experiences outside the classroom and beyond 20th-century Los Angeles. In her Language Socialization study of Fulfulde folktale practices in Cameroon, a genre and practice that was predicted to disappear due to increased cultural and linguistic contact (French public education, Kuranic instruction in Arabic, Fulfulde home practices), Moore (2004) documented that while the genre of folktale persists in Fulfulde children's multilingual environment, the means to socialize it does in fact reflect influences from other codes and genres, namely Kuranic instruction practices. Moore's Language Socialization study is a particularly illustrative example of the process of growing up in a multilingual society and of the identities that children learn to invoke and successfully display across situations and linguistic codes. Thus, an important outcome of the language socialization process is to create a coherent 'self' out of a multiplicity of identities that are socially and culturally relevant to particular social events.

A number of Linguistic Anthropological and Sociolinguistic studies illustrate the construction of youth identities vis-à-vis ethnic groups in multilingual settings and institutions (Lo 1999; Rymes 1996; Rampton 2001). Lo (1999), for example, illustrates the heteroglossic, although sometimes conflicting, environment of Asian immigrant youth in Los Angeles. Through interviews and discourse analyses of exchanges between three male college students, a second generation Chinese American, Chazz, a 1.5 generation[6] Korean-American, Ken, and an African-American Rob, Lo demonstrates the ways in which the Asian males display linguistic and cultural affiliation and disavowal. As her data illustrate, while learning multiple codes is possible, and highly desirable for young Asian-Americans in Los Angeles, linguistic competence alone does not guarantee cultural competence or ethnic group affiliation. Rather, affiliation must be ratified by other community members in order to make it legitimate. Thus, identity formation in language contact situations is an ideologically informed process that changes over time while also reproducing social norms and expectations. Language Socialization studies have, therefore, for the last decade, revealed a productive line of investigation into the processes of language acquisition and multilingualism.

6.   Future trajectories

This chapter has offered a perspective of 'growing up' as socialization to and through language over the entire lifespan of the individual. Likewise, community has been framed here not as a geographically or ethnically bound group of people, but rather as sets of relationships between individuals who share symbolic and material resources. Finally, multilingualism was presented as a social phenomenon of contact between persons, their languages, and ideologies, all of which have repercussions for individual and collective senses of self. As individuals interact with each other, they reproduce and change local and extra-local communal goals, norms, beliefs, and expectations. The lens of Language Socialization views growing up in a multilingual community to be a comprehensive, interrelated, historical, enduring, as well as novel and emergent set of cultural and linguistic accomplishments. For students of language, such a perspective affords opportunities for understanding language use in its multiple and nested contexts. For students of human development, it provides ways in which to demonstrate processes of growth across several dimensions.

While the Language Socialization paradigm and the fields of Linguistic Anthropology and Sociolinguistics provide a comprehensive means to study multilingualism specifically and language acquisition more generally, the field has yet to fully develop a principled way to document and analyze the complexities of historical process that impinge on current practices. For example, discussions of language contact often gloss over the violent practices and residues of colonization. Likewise, studies of immigrant experiences in industrialized states such as the U.S., while acknowledging the inherently oppressive attitudes towards newcomers' use of their home languages, have generally neglected to analytically engage discussions of race and language use.[7] The fields of language study reviewed here have proven to be productive in complicating the process of growing up multilingual and they have reached an important conceptual and methodological juncture to engage even more deeply the social and historical complexities of the acquisition process. The reproductive and potentially transformative process of growing up multilingual can no longer be studied from the perspective of a linear language development; as the Language Socialization studies reviewed here illustrate, the process is complex and illustrates dynamic developmental and socio-historical trajectories.

Notes

1. In this chapter, when we refer to Language Socialization as a discipline or a field of study, we capitalize the terms. When we refer to language socialization as a process carried out by individuals and social groups, we do not capitalize the terms. We elab-

orate on this distinction in Section 3 below. Additionally, readers familiar with Language Socialization research may have more often read of it being referred to as a paradigm rather than as a field or discipline. To call Language Socialization a discipline is not to claim that it is necessarily on par with the more established fields of Linguistic Anthropology or Sociolinguistics. Rather, it is to recognize that fields and disciplines are formed over time. LS, as a historically interdisciplinary field, has, especially in recent years, spawned its own approaches and theories that, while drawing on other disciplines, have begun to make a contribution in their own right.

2. Luykx (2005), for example, writes that "the field of language socialization comprises two broad areas of interest: socialization *to use* language, and socialization *through the use of* language (Schieffelin & Ochs, 1986). Within both areas, most research has focused on children; analyses of the language socialization of adults are relatively rare, though they have increased in recent years. Within the first area, studies of adults have focused mainly on second language acquisition – occasionally with some attention to social factors, but only inasmuch as these affect speakers' developing competency in the L2 [...] The second area – socialization through the use of language – has produced more culturally situated examinations of how adults' differing social roles are manifested in their linguistic practice" (Luykx 2005: 1407). This interpretation of the paradigm does not understand the connection between language and socialization as a recursive means-ends hypothesis, but rather as two disconnected areas of inquiry, a view which, as we have discussed, diverges drastically from the view of Language Socialization adopted here.

3. These four characteristics, however, are not set in stone. Kulick and Schieffelin (2004), for example, set out *three* criteria for Language Socialization studies: that they be longitudinal, ethnographic, and that they demonstrate acquisition of sociocultural knowledge across time and contexts. In this sense, the third and fourth categories enumerated by Garrett and Baquedano-López (2002) are folded into one criterion that focuses on the outcomes of analysis.

4. The notion of 'participation frameworks' (Goffman 1974), and the related concepts of 'participant frameworks' (M. Goodwin 1990) and 'participant structures' (Philips 1970), while differing slightly, do share in common a concern with joint attention, sequentiality of action, and goal-oriented activity.

5. A largely derogatory term used to indicate codeswitching in Spanish and English.

6. Generation 1.5 refers to immigrant youth who moved to the United States with their families in late childhood or early adolescence (cf. Park 1999; Portes and Rumbaut 2001).

7. A possible exception would be Urciuoli's (1996) treatment of Puerto Rican experiences in New York City. However, from our perspective, this study does not situate its findings within a larger scholarly debate on racialization and race theory.

References

Andersen, Elaine S.
    1986   The acquisition of register variation by Anglo-American children. In *Language Socialization Across Cultures*, Bambi B. Schieffelin and Elinor Ochs (eds.), 153–161, Cambridge: Cambridge University Press.

Anderson, Benedict
1991   *Imagined Communities*. London: Verso.
Bakhtin, Mikhael M.
1986   The problem of speech genres. In *Speech Genres and Other Late Essays*, Carol Emerson and Michael Holquist (eds.), 60–102, Austin: University of Texas Press.
Baquedano-López, Patricia
1997   Creating social identities through *doctrina* narratives. *Issues in Applied Linguistics* 8 (1): 27–45.
1998   Language socialization of Mexican children in a Los Angeles Catholic parish, PhD. diss., University of California Los Angeles.
2000   Narrating community in *Doctrina* classes. *Narrative Inquiry* 10 (2): 429–452.
2004   Traversing the center. *Anthropology and Education Quarterly* 35 (2): 212–232.
Bayley, Robert and Sandra R. Schecter (eds.)
2003   *Language Socialization in Bilingual and Multilingual Societies*. Clevedon, UK: Multilingual Matters.
Bernstein, Basil
1972   Social class, language and socialization. In *Language and Social Context: Selected Readings*, Pier Paolo Giglioli (ed.), 157–178, Harmondsworth: Penguin.
Bhimji, Fazila
2001   'Dile Family': Socializing language skills with directives in three Mexican families in South Central Los Angeles. PhD. diss., University of California Los Angeles.
Bloomfield, Leonard
1984   *Language*. Chicago: University of Chicago Press. Original edition 1933.
Bourdieu, Pierre
1977   *Outline of a Theory of Practice*. Cambridge: Cambridge University Press.
1990   *The Logic of Practice*. Cambridge: Polity Press.
1991   *Language and Symbolic Power*. Cambridge, MA: Harvard University Press.
Bucholtz, Mary and Kira Hall
2004   Language and identity. In *A Companion to Linguistic Anthropology*, Alessandro Duranti (ed.), 369–394, Oxford: Blackwell Publishers.
Butler, Judith P.
1997   *Excitable Speech: A Politics of the Performative*. New York: Routledge.
Chaiklin, Seth
1996   Understanding the social scientific practice of *Understanding Practice*. In *Understanding Practice: Perspectives on Activity and Context*, Seth Chaiklin and Jean Lave (eds.), 377–402, Cambridge: Cambridge University Press.
Chomsky, Noam
1965   *Aspects of the Theory of Syntax*. Cambridge, MA: M.I.T. Press.
Crago, Martha, Betsy Annahatak and Lizzie Ningiuruvik
1993   Changing patterns of language socialization in Inuit homes. *Anthropology and Education Quarterly* 24 (3): 205–223.
Echeverria, Begoña
2003   Schooling, language, and ethnic identity in the Basque Autonomous Community. *Anthropology and Education Quarterly* 34 (4): 351–372.

Engeström, Yrjö
1996   Developmental studies of work as a testbench of activity theory: The case
          of primary care medical practice. In *Understanding Practice: Perspectives
          on Activity and Context*, Seth Chaiklin and Jean Lave (eds.), 64–103, Cam-
          bridge: Cambridge University Press.
1999   Activity theory and individual and social transformation. In *Perspectives
          on Activity Theory*, Yrjö Engeström, Reijo Miettinen and Raija-Leena Pu-
          nämaki (eds.), 19–38, Cambridge: Cambridge University Press.
Fader, Ayala
2000   *Morality, Gender, and Language: Socialization Practices in a Hasidic com-
          munity.* PhD diss., New York University.
2001   Literacy, bilingualism, and gender in a Hasidic community. *Linguistics and
          Education* 12 (3): 261–283.
Field, Margaret
1998   Maintenance of indigenous ways of speaking despite language shift: lan-
          guage socialization in a Navajo preschool, PhD. diss., University of Cali-
          fornia Santa Barbara.
2001   Triadic directives in Navajo language socialization. *Language in Society* 30
          (2): 249–263.
Fishman, Joshua A.
1965   Who speaks what language to whom and when? *La Linguistique* 2: 67–88.
1972   Domains and the relationship between micro- and macrosociolinguistics.
          In *Directions in Sociolinguistics*, John Gumperz and Dell Hymes (eds.),
          435–453, New York: Holt, Rinehart and Winston.
Garrett Paul B.
1999   Language socialization, convergence, and shift in St. Lucia, West Indies.
          PhD diss. New York University.
2000   'High' Kwéyòl: The emergence of a formal creole register in St. Lucia. In
          John H. McWhorter (Ed.) *Language Change and Language Contact in
          Pidgins and Creoles.* 63–101, Amsterdam: John Benjamins.
2003   An 'English creole' that isn't: On the sociohistorical origins and linguistic
          classification of the vernacular English of St. Lucia. In Michael Aceto
          and Jeffrey Williams (Eds.) *Contact Englishes of the Eastern Caribbean.*
          155–210, Amsterdam: John Benjamins.
2004   Language contact and contact languages. In Alessandro Duranti (Ed.) *A
          Companion to Linguistic Anthropology.* 46–72, Oxford: Blackwell Pub-
          lishers.
2005   What a language is good for, *Language in Society* 34 (3): 327–361.
in press Language socialization. In *Elsevier Encyclopedia of Language and Lin-
          guistics* (2nd, completely revised edition), Volume 6, 604–613
Garrett, Paul B. and Patricia Baquedano-López
2002   Language socialization: reproduction and continuity, transformation and
          change. *Annual Review of Anthropology* 31: 339–361.
Giddens, Anthony
1979   *Central Problems in Social Theory: Action, Structure, and Contradiction in
          Social Analysis.* Berkeley: University of California Press.
1984   *The Constitution of Society: Outline of the Theory of Structuration*, Berke-
          ley: University of California Press.

Goffman, Erving
  1974   *Frame Analysis: An Essay on the Organization of Experience.* Cambridge, Mass.: Harvard University Press.
González, Norma
  2001   *I Am My Language.* Tucson, AZ: Arizona University Press.
Goodwin, Charles and Alessandro Duranti
  1992   Rethinking context: An introduction. In *Rethinking Context: Language as an Interactive Phenomenon,* Alessandro Duranti and Charles Goodwin (eds.), 1–42, Cambridge: Cambridge University Press.
Goodwin, Marjorie H.
  1990   *He-said-she-said: Talk as social organization among Black children.* Bloomington: Indiana University Press.
Gumperz, John J.
  1968   The speech community. *International Encyclopedia of the Social Sciences,* 381–386, New York: Macmillan.
Hanks, William F.
  1996   *Language and Communicative Practices.* Boulder, CO: Westview Publishers.
Haviland, John B.
  1996   Projections, transpositions, and relativity. In *Rethinking Linguistic Relativity,* John J. Gumperz and Steven C. Levinson (eds.), 271–323 Cambridge: Cambridge University Press.
Heath, Shirley B.
  1983   *Ways with Words: Language, Life, and Work in Communities and Classrooms,* Cambridge: Cambridge University Press.
Heller, Monica
  2001   Legitimate language in a multilingual school. In *Voices of Authority: Education and Linguistic Difference,* Monica Heller and Marilyn Martin-Jones (eds.), 381–402, Westport, Connecticut: Ablex Publishing.
Howard, Kathryn M.
  2003   Language socialization in a Northern Thai bilingual community, PhD. diss., University of California Los Angeles.
Hymes, Dell
  1972   On communicative competence. In J.B. Pride and Janet Holmes (eds.), 269–293, *Sociolinguistics: Selected Readings.* Harmondsworth, Middlesex: Penguin.
Jaffe, Alexandra
  2001   Authority and authenticity: Corsican discourse on bilingual education. In *Voices of Authority: Education and Linguistic Difference,* Monica Heller and Marilyn Martin-Jones (eds.), 269–296 Westport, Connecticut: Ablex Publishing.
Kroskrity, Paul V.
  1993   *Language, History, and Identity: Ethnolinguistic Studies of the Arizona Tewa.* Tucson, AZ: University of Arizona Press.
  1998   Arizona Tewa Kiva speech as a manifestation of a dominant language ideology. In *Language Ideologies: Practice and Theory,* Bambi B. Schieffelin, Katherine A. Woolard and Paul V. Kroskrity (eds.), 103–122, New York: Oxford University Press.

2000   Language ideologies in the expression and representation of Arizona Tewa ethnic identity. In *Regimes of Language: Ideologies, Polities, and Identities*, Paul V. Kroskrity (ed.), 329–360, Santa Fe, NM: School of American Research Press.

2004   Language ideologies. In *A Companion to Linguistic Anthropology*, Alessandro Duranti (ed.), 496–517, Oxford: Blackwell Publishing.

Kulick, Don

1992   *Language Shift and Cultural Reproduction.* Cambridge: Cambridge University Press.

1998   Anger, gender, language shift, and the politics of revelation in a Papau New Guinean village. In *Language Ideologies: Practice and Theory*, Bambi B. Schieffelin, Katherine A. Woolard and Paul V. Kroskrity, (eds.), 87–102, New York: Oxford University Press.

Kulick, Don and Bambi B. Schieffelin

2004   Language socialization. In *A Companion to Linguistic Anthropology*, Alessandro Duranti (ed.), 349–368, Oxford: Blackwell Publishing.

Lave, Jean and Etienne Wenger

1991   *Situated Learning: Legitimate Peripheral Participation.* Cambridge: Cambridge University Press.

Leont'ev, Aleksei N.

1978   *Activity, Consciousness and Personality.* Engelwood Cliffs: Prentice Hall.

Lo, Adrienne

1999   Codeswitching, speech community membership, and the construction of ethnic identity. *Journal of Sociolinguistics* 3(4): 461–479.

Luria, Aleksandr R.

1976   *Cognitive Development: Its Cultural and Social Foundations.* Cambridge: Harvard University Press.

Luykx, Aurolyn

2005   Children as socializing agents: family language policy in situations of language Shift. In *ISB4: Proceedings of the 4th International Symposium on Bilingualism*, James Cohen, Kara T. McAlister, Kellie Rolstad, and Jeff MacSwan, (eds.), 1407–1414, Somerville, MA: Cascadilla Press.

Macdonald, Judy Smith

1973   Cursing and context in a Grenadian fishing community. *Anthropologica* 15: 89–128.

Mead, George H.

1956   *On Social Psychology.* Chicago: University of Chicago Press.

Moore, Leslie C.

2004   Learning languages by heart: second language socialization in a Fulbe community (Maroua, Cameroon), PhD. Dissertation, University of California Los Angeles.

Morgan, Marcyliena M.

2004   speech Community. In *A Companion to Linguistic Anthropology*, Alessandro Duranti (ed.), 3–22, Oxford: Blackwell Publishers.

Ochs, Elinor

1986   Introduction. In *Language Socialization Across Cultures*, Bambi B. Schieffelin and Elinor Ochs (eds.), 3–17, Cambridge: Cambridge University Press.

1988   *Culture and Language Development: Language Acquisition and Sociali-zation in a Samoan Village.* New York: Cambridge University Press.

1993   Constructing social identity: a language socialization perspective, *Research on Language and Social Interaction* 26 (3): 287–306.

1996   Linguistic resources for socializing humanity. In *Rethinking Linguistic Relativity*, John J. Gumperz and Steven C. Levinson (eds.), 407–437, Cambridge: Cambridge University Press.

Ochs, Elinor and Lisa Capps

1996   Narrating the self. *Annual Review of Anthropology* 25: 19–43.

Ochs, Elinor and Bambi B. Schieffelin

1984   Language acquisition and socialization: three developmental stories. In *Culture Theory: Essays on Mind, Self, and Emotion*, Richard A Schweder and Robert A. LeVine (eds.), 276–320, Cambridge: Cambridge University Press.

1995   The impact of language socialization on grammatical development. In *The Handbook of Child Language*, Paul Fletcher and Brian MacWhinney (eds.), 73–94, Oxford: Blackwell Publishing.

Orellana, Marjorie F., Jennifer Reynolds, Lisa Dorner, and María Meza

2003   In other words: translating or "Para-Phrasing" as a family literacy practice in immigrant households. *The Reading Research Quarterly* 38 (1): 12–35.

Park, Kyeyoung

1999   'I really do feel I'm 1.5': The construction of self and community by young Korean-Americans. *Amerasia Journal*, 25(1): 139–163.

Paugh, Amy

2001   'Creole day is every day': language socialization, shift, and ideologies in Dominica, West Indies, PhD diss., New York University.

2002   Child language socialization in working families, UCLA Center for the Everyday Lives of Families Working Papers.

2005   Multilingual play: children's code-switching, role play, and agency in Dominica. *Language in Society* 34 (1): 63–86.

Pease-Alvarez, Lucinda

2002   Moving beyond linear trajectories of language shift and bilingual language socialization, *Hispanic Journal of Behavioral Sciences* 24 (2): 114–137.

Pease-Alvarez, Lucinda and Olga Vásquez

1994   Language socialization in ethnic minority communities. In *Educating Second Language Children: The Whole Child, the Whole Curriculum, the Whole Community*, Fred Genessee (ed.), 82–102, Cambridge: Cambridge University Press.

Peters, Ann M. and Steven T. Boggs

1986   Interactional Routines as cultural influences upon language acquisition. In *Language Socialization Across Cultures*, Bambi B. Schieffelin and Elinor Ochs (eds.), 80–96, Cambridge: Cambridge University Press.

Philips, Susan U.

1972   Participant structures and communicative competence: Warm Springs children in community and classroom. In *Functions of Langauge in the Classroom*, C.B. Cazden, V.P. John and D. Hymes (eds.), 370–394, New York: Teacher's Collage.

Portes, Alejandro and Rubén G. Rumbaut
　　2001　　*Legacies: The Story of the Immigrant Second Generation*. Berkeley: University of California Press.

Rampton, Ben
　　2001　　Youth, race and resistance in multilingual Britain: a sociolinguistic perspective. In *Voices of Authority: Education and Linguistic Difference*, Monica Heller and Marilyn Martin-Jones (eds.), 403–418, Westport, Connecticut: Ablex Publishing.

Rindstedt, Camilla and Karin Aronsson
　　2002　　Growing up monolingual in a bilingual community: The Quichua revitalization paradox, *Language in Society* 31 (5): 721–742.

Romero, Mary E.
　　2003　　Perpetuating the Cochiti Way of Life: A Study of Child Socialization and Language Shift in a Pueblo Community, PhD. diss., University of California Berkeley.

Rymes, Betsy
　　1996　　Naming as social practice: the case of Little Creeper from Diamond Street. *Language in Society* 25: 237–260.

Schecter, Sandra R. and Robert Bayley
　　2002　　*Language as Cultural Practice: Mexicanos en el Norte*. Mahwah, NJ: Lawrence Erlbaum.

Schieffelin, Bambi B.
　　1990　　*The Give and Take of Everyday Life: Language Socialization of Kaluli Children*. New York: Cambridge University Press.
　　2000　　Introducing Kaluli literacy: a chronology of influences. In *Regimes of Language: Ideologies, Polities, and Identities*, Paul V. Kroskrity (ed.), 293–328, Santa Fe, NM: School of American Research Press.
　　2002　　Marking time: the dichotomizing discourse of multiple temporalities. *Current Anthropology* 43: S5–S17.

Schieffelin, Bambi B. and Rachelle Charlier Doucet
　　1994　　The 'real' Haitian Creole: ideology, metalinguistics, and orthographic choice. *American Ethnologist* 21(1): 176–200.

Schieffelin, Bambi B. and Elinor Ochs
　　1986　　Language socialization. *Annual Review of Anthropology* 15: 163–191.

Silverstein, Michael
　　1979　　Language structure and linguistic ideology. In *The Elements: A Parasession on Linguistic Units and Levels*, Paul R. Clyne, William F. Hanks, and Carol L. Hofbauer (eds.), 193–247, Chicago: Chicago Linguistic Society.

Spitulnik, Deborah
　　1998　　Mediating unity and diversity: the production of language ideologies in Zambian broadcasting. In *Language Ideologies: Practice and Theory*, Bambi B. Schieffelin, Katherine A. Woolard and Paul V. Kroskrity (eds.), 163–188, New York: Oxford University Press.
　　1996　　The social circulation of media discourse and the mediation of communities. *Journal of Linguistic Anthropology*, 6(2): 161–187.

Urciuoli, Bonnie
　　1996　　*Exposing Prejudice: Puerto Rican Experiences of Language, Race, and Class*. Boulder, CO: Westview.

Valdés, Guadalupe
    2003   *Expanding Definitions of Giftedness: The Case of Young Interpreters from Immigrant Communities.* Mahwah, NJ: Lawrence Erlbaum Associates.
Vásquez, Olga, Lucinda Pease-Alvarez, Sheila M. Shannon, and Luis C. Moll
    1994   *Pushing Boundaries: Language and Culture in a Mexicano Community,* Cambridge: Cambridge University Press.
Watson-Gegeo, Karen-Ann
    2004   Mind, language, and epistemology: toward a language socialization paradigm for SLA. *The Modern Language Journal* 88: 331–350.
Watson-Gegeo, Karen-Ann and David W. Gegeo
    1986   Calling-out and repeating routines in Kwara'ae children's language socialization. In *Language Socialization Across Cultures,* Bambi B. Schieffelin and Elinor Ochs (eds.), 17–50, Cambridge: Cambridge University Press.
Weinreich, Uriel
    1956   *Languages in Contact: Findings and Problems.* The Hague: Mouton.
Whorf, Benjamin Lee
    1995   The relation of habitual thought and behavior to language. In *Language, Culture, and Society: A book of readings,* Ben G. Blount (ed.), 64–84, Prospect Heights, IL: Waveland Press. Originally published in 1941.
Woolard, Katherine A.
    1998   Introduction: language ideology as a field of inquiry. In *Language Ideologies: Practice and Theory,* Bambi B. Schieffelin, Katherine A. Woolard and Paul V. Kroskrity (eds.), 3–47, New York: Oxford University Press.
Wortham, Stanton E.F.
    2005   Socialization beyond the speech event. *Journal of Linguistic Anthropology* 15 (1): 95–112.
Zentella, Ana Celia
    1997   *Growing Up Bilingual.* Malden, MA: Blackwell Publishing.

Recommended readings

de León, Lourdes
    1998   The emergent participant: interactive patterns in the socialization of Tzotzil (Mayan) Infants, *Journal of Linguistic Anthroplogy* 8(2): 131–161.
Duranti, Alessandro, Elinor Ochs, and Elia K. Ta'ase
    1995   Change and tradition in literacy instruction in a Samoan American Community. *Educational Foundations* 9 (1): 57–74.
Gal, Susan
    1998   Multiplicity and contention among language ideologies: a commentary. In *Language Ideologies: Practice and Theory,* Bambi B. Schieffelin, Katherine A. Woolard and Paul V. Kroskrity (eds.), 317–332, New York: Oxford University Press.
Hill, Jane H.
    1998   Language, race, and white public space. *American Anthropologist* 100 (3): 680–689.

Hymes, Dell
    1974   *Foundations in Sociolinguistics.* Philadelphia: University of Pennsylvania
            Press.
Irvine, Judith T. and Susan Gal
    2000   Language ideology and linguistic differentiation. In *Regimes of Language:
            Ideologies, Polities, and Identities,* Paul V. Kroskrity (ed.), 35–84, Santa
            Fe, NM: School of American Research Press.
Jacoby, Sally and Patrick Gonzales
    1991   The constitution of expert-novice in scientific discourse. *Issues in Applied
            Linguistics* 2 (2): 149–181.
Kramsch, Claire
    2002   Introduction: "How can we tell the dancer from the dance?" In *Language
            Acquisition and Language Socialization: Ecological Perspectives.* Claire
            Kramsch (ed.), 1–30, London: Continuum Press.
Rogoff, Barbara
    1990   *Apprenticeship in Thinking: Cognitive Development in Social Context.*
            New York: Oxford University Press.
Zentella, Ana Celia
    1990   El impacto de la realidad socio-económica en las comunidades hispanopar-
            lantes de los Estados Unidos: Reto a la teoria y metodologia linguistica. In
            Spanish in the United States: Sociolinguistic Issues, J.J. Bergen (ed.),
            152–166, Washington, D.C.: Georgetown University Press.

4.   Becoming bi- or multi-lingual later in life

Jean-Marc Dewaele

1.   Introduction

The present chapter proposes an exploration of the literature on individual differences in bi- and multilingual experience in adulthood. One might be tempted
to think that bilingualism research focuses more on early bi- and multilingualism (cf. Genesee 2003; Paradis, this volume) than on adult bi- and multilingualism. We would like to argue that this is probably a false perception based on the
fact that 'child bilingualism' exists as a recognized subfield with bi- and multilingualism research; has journals that focus specifically on child bilinguals; has
its own association (IACL) that organises international conferences regularly
and had a very active Scientific Commission within AILA convened by the
leading researchers in the field. No such specific groupings exist for adult bi-
and multilingualism and no conferences have been organised – as far as we
know – that focused exclusively on this specific and large age group.

   As a result, findings of research involving adult multilinguals are scattered
over a much wider area, the core of it being the bilingualism and multilingualism
paradigms, with a vast 'periphery' including cognitive psychology, social and
cultural psychology, anthropology, cognitive linguistics, neurolinguistics, neuroimaging, psycholinguistics, sociolinguistics, pragmatics, intercultural pragmatics, education, and second language acquisition. As researchers in these
fields usually publish in their own journals[1] and present papers at their own
specialist conferences, their work is less accessible to the rest of the bilingualism
community.

   It is thus fair to say that researchers active in adult bi- and multilingualism
may be numerous but are part of a much looser network with no clear common
identity. Moreover, researchers in these different paradigms use very different
research methodologies and perspectives which may seem hermetic to outsiders.
There have been initiatives to establish informal networks between researchers
from various background focusing on adult bi- and multilinguals. The five international symposia in bilingualism (ISB) organized so far have allowed a certain amount of contact between researchers interested in adult bi- and multilingualism. Smaller scale conferences and colloquia have been organised on more
specific issues of adult bi- and multilingualism which have resulted in special issues in journals and edited volumes. To name but a few of the topics: L1 attrition
(Schmid et al. 2004), third language acquisition (Jessner, Hufeisen and Cenoz
2001), gender issues in bilingualism (Pavlenko et al. 2003), negotiation of bilin-

gual identities (Pavlenko and Blackledge 2004), bilingual memory (Pavlenko, Schrauf and Dewaele 2003), bilingualism and emotions (Pavlenko and Dewaele 2004a, b, Pavlenko 2005). Although there is no specific field labeled 'adult' bi- and multilingualism, there is a kernel of researchers that focus specifically on aging and bilingualism (typically dealing with participants over the age of 65, cf. Schrauf 2000).

The present chapter will cover a relatively wide area of research that considered adult bi- and multilinguals who became multilingual later in life. The focus will be specifically on the communication of emotion in adult bi- and multilingualism. Affect and emotion are inextricably linked to issues of presentation of self and identity. Misunderstandings between individuals on factual information in non-emotional communication does not necessarily lead to loss of face. However, pragmatic failures in phatic communication where personal opinions and beliefs are expressed are much more likely to embarrass the interlocutors. SLA learners in formal instruction engage much more in the first type of exchange than adult L2 users for whom phatic communication is linked to the socialisation process in the L2. Our argument is that the stakes are much higher in L2 phatic communication and that it relates directly to "the psychological heart of bilingualism" (Edwards 2003: 40). We will thus consider social and psychological aspects of bi- and multilinguals' feelings and their verbalisation in different languages.

We will highlight three overlapping questions about adult bi- and multilingualism and see how they have been addressed by various researchers, and what tentative answers have been formulated:
1. What do adult bi- and multilinguals feel about their languages?
2. How do adult bi- and multilinguals perceive themselves?
3. How do adult bi- and multilinguals use emotional speech and react to emotional expressions?
4. What do we know about the representation of emotion words in the bi- and multilingual mental lexicon?

Rather than addressing each research question separately, we will organise the overview of studies on adult bi- and multilingualism according to their position on the qualitative-quantitative continuum of research methodologies. After defining the concepts on which this chapter is based, we will discuss the phenomenon of transformation in individual bi- and multilingualism, arguing in favor of triangulation to capture the dynamic nature of the phenomenon. We will then present an overview of the findings of qualitative research based on autobiographical literature from adult bi- and multilinguals. Next, we will review the findings of so-called mixed design studies (combining both qualitative and quantitative research methods). Finally, we will look at studies that rely more on quantitative analyses in quasi-experimental or experimental designs before concluding.

2.   Some definitions

The title of the present chapter, 'becoming a bi- or multilingual', requires a short analysis of these three key terms.

2.1.   Becoming and un-becoming

The verbal form *becoming*, is an accomplishment verb in terms of inherent lexical aspect (Vendler 1967) and a progressive in terms of grammatical aspect. Accomplishment verbs are [– punctual], implying that the verb's meaning is not inherently instantaneous, because it refers to a durative process. Accomplishment verbs are [+telic], implying a transition from one state to another, whereby the temporal endpoint of the action brings about the transition. Finally, accomplishment verbs are [+dynamic], because of the energy needed to carry out their action. The progressive form of the verb stresses the on-going nature of the event at the time of speaking (Bayley 1994). In other words, the form *becoming* means an on-going process that started from a point in time that could be described as i+1 (1 referring to the hours of input in another language) with no clear end-point. Paradoxically, 'becoming' could also imply 'un-becoming'. One could wonder whether a bi- and multilingual in the process of losing a language retains the right to the term bi- and multilingual? Does that person become an ex-bi- and multilingual, or a monolingual? This leads us to the second key-term, bilingual, which is equally fuzzy.

2.2.   Bilingualism

The term 'bilingual' is ubiquitous yet abstruse, muddied by varying uses in the general media, education, and politics (Sia and Dewaele 2006). It is often assumed to be understood by the reader, and remains therefore undefined. Researchers in second language acquisition, language teaching pedagogy, sociolinguistics, or psycholinguistics, may all be applying different definitions to the concept, and readers may be applying yet other ones. We noted that a further problem with such a widely-used but difficult to define concept is that laypeople's perception of who is and who is not a bilingual may quite different from the linguists' perception. We were personally struck by the different existing interpretations of the concept of bilingualism when promoting the 'bilingualism and emotion' online web questionnaire (Dewaele and Pavlenko 2001). Many non-linguist bi- and multilingual friends and colleagues whom we asked to fill out the questionnaire declined, saying they did not consider themselves to be bilinguals. It may have been a convenient excuse to escape a time-consuming exercise in metalinguistic awareness and soul-searching, but it may also reflect a gap between linguists' current understanding of the concept of bilingualism and the laypeople' view. The latter's view is probably influenced by early restrictive definitions of bilingualism such as the ones by Bloomfield, i.e. "native-like control of two languages" (1935: 56) and Ducrot and Todorov (1972), who stipulate that to qualify as bilingual an individual needs to master two languages, both acquired as mother tongues, and needs to speak them "perfectly well" (Ducrot and Todorov 1972: 83).

It is also possible that the term 'bilingualism' retains negative connotations outside the circle of language professionals. As Baetens Beardsmore (2003) stated:

> there is a deep-seated and widespread fear of bilingualism. Moreover, there is an all-pervading tendency to couple the notion of 'problems' to that of bilingualism, a connotation that never comes to mind in discussions on unilingualism. (Baetens Beardsmore 2003: 10)

Thankfully, the situation is evolving. Edwards (2003) observed that misconceptions about bilingualism have gradually disappeared in academic writing:

> Older ideas that bilingualism meant a splitting of finite cognitive potential or, worse, a diminution of intellectual capacities, have long since been retired by research, to be replaced by the view that bilingualism does not mean loss; indeed, some have argued that increases in linguistic repertoire correlate with heightened sensitivity, enhanced cultural awareness, perhaps even greater cognitive flexibility and all-round *nous*. (Edwards 2003: 28)

The new perspective of bi- and multilingualism has been promoted in journals for the general public like the *Bilingual Family Newsletter,* in numerous books on family bilingualism destined for a wide audience (Baker 2000; Barron-Hauwaert 2003) and in 'Readers' containing the seminal papers on bilingualism aimed at undergraduates (Wei 2000). Bilingual writers do underline the positive aspects of their bi- and multilingualism and their observations seem to be backed up by hard psycholinguistic evidence. For instance, Nancy Huston states that bilingualism is "une stimulation intellectuelle de tous les instants" [a constant intellectual stimulation] (Nancy Huston *Nord Perdu* 1999: 46).

The problem that remains is that of the criteria an individual has to fulfill in order to define him or herself as bilingual. Baetens Beardsmore (1982) noted that is difficult to "[posit] a generally accepted definition of the phenomenon that will not meet some sort of criticism" (1982: 1). We have argued in favor of a broad definition of bilingualism that includes:

> not only the 'perfect' bilingual (who probably does not exist) or the 'balanced' ambilingual (who is probably rare) but also various 'imperfect' and 'unstable' forms of bilingualism, in which one language takes over from the other(s) on at least some occasions and for some instances of language use. (Dewaele, Wei and Housen 2003: 1)

The decision not to set a higher level of proficiency in the L2 as a prerequisite for being categorized as a bilingual is based on Cook's (2002) observation that researchers need to abandon the Platonic ideal of the perfect bilingual. He therefore advocates the term 'L2 user' namely "a person who knows and uses a second language at any level" (Cook 2002: 4). This L2 user is in no ways exceptional; it is "the average person who uses a second language for the needs of his or her everyday life" (Cook 2003: 5). This average L2 user is situated somewhere in the middle of the proficiency continuum, with users of the Basic Variety on one end (Klein and Perdue 1997), and L2 users which are undistinguishable from native speakers of the target language on the other end. L2 users are typically adult bi- and multilinguals, who are generally no longer actively learning the second language in a formal setting.

But do all L2 users consider themselves to be bilingual? We addressed this question in Sia and Dewaele (2006) where we looked specifically whether adults' self-categorization as a bilingual was linked to certain sociobiographical and self-reported linguistic factors. The sample consisted of 45 adult participants, all of whom had at least a working knowledge of a second language, yet less than half categorized themselves as bilinguals. Self-reports on 10-point proficiency scales (for speaking, listening, reading, writing and pragmatic competence) revealed that although the self-categorised bilinguals scored significantly higher on these scales, the self-categorised not-bilinguals used nearly the full range of scores. We found that younger participants were more likely to label themselves 'bilingual', possibly because they were less influenced by the older, more restrictive definitions of bilingualism. The length of time spent in the L2 environment in the present or in the past was not linked to self-categorization as a bilingual. However, recency of stay in the L2 environment did affect the decision (the more recent, the more likely to define oneself as bilingual) and negatively linked to current study of the second language (those engaged in study of the second language were less likely to self-categorization as a bilingual). We concluded that any definition of individual bilingualism based on strict linguistic criteria would be doomed to failure as some people see themselves as bilingual and others do not, even if their abilities, experiences and exposures to their L2s appear to be similar.

Should the term 'bilingual' therefore be discarded in favour of the term 'L2 user'? The decision depends on the perspective adopted by the researcher. The problem with the term of 'L2 user' is that it refers primarily to the second language(s) of the individual. Of course, any L2 user is by definition also an L1 user; but the term L2 user still suggests it is the L2 that matters. Cook (2003) showed that the L1 of the bi- and multilingual presents an equally rich area of investigation. The L1 can be affected by the L2 and the L1 can occupy any place on the continuum of activation (cf. Green 1986): at one end it could be the clearly dominant and most highly activated language of the individual, and the opposite end it could be dormant, partly or even completely attrited (Cook 2003; Kecskes and Papp 2000; Schmid et al. 2004). It thus seems preferable to use the word 'bilingual', considering the individual's conceptual and linguistic systems as a unique fusion of different languages, rather than trying to dissect it in its various components. By 'older' bi- and multilinguals we mean people aged 20 or older.

2.3.   Multilingualism

One of the key questions in bi- and multilingualism research relates to the categorization of individuals according to the number of language they know. We have just seen that the L2 proficiency criterion is rather fuzzy in the deciding who is a bi- and multilingual. There is equal uncertainty about the number of languages a bi- and multilingual actually knows. Etymologically bilingual means a person knowing two languages. It has been used indiscriminately however to refer to any individual knowing more than one language. The argument is that any language acquired after the first one can be labeled L2, and that one can possess several L2s (Cook 2002, 2003). The implication of such a decision is that these 'foreign' languages may have been acquired at different times in the individual's life, up to varying degrees of proficiency, but that the numbering of these languages is not really important. Such a perspective is typical for researchers who worked on bilinguals (L1+L2), or on monolinguals in the process of acquiring a second language. There was no need for these researchers to use a more fine-grained distinction between the first L2 and any language acquired subsequently. Their research designs typically had two categories: a monolingual control group and the experimental group with bilinguals or second language learners (cf. Bialystok 2002). Whether these bilinguals were in fact trilinguals, quadrilinguals or pentalinguals did not matter to them. These researchers constitute the majority in the field of applied linguistics. A need for finer distinctions and categorizations emerged with the onset of trilingualism research (Cenoz and Jessner 2000; Cenoz et al. 2001; De Angelis 2005a, b). Trilingualism researchers set out to investigate whether trilinguals differed from bilinguals. The research thus far does seem to confirm the seminal work of Voorwinde who concluded that "phenomena related to trilingualism (are) more complex than, rather than basically different from, those related to bilingualism" (Voorwinde 1981: 25). Differences between bilingualism and trilingualism are mainly of a quantitative nature as the same processing mechanisms operate (Hoffmann 2001). Strong debates erupted with the trilingualism community on the need to focus on trilingual individuals only, or whether trilingual meant any person knowing more than two languages. Jasone Cenoz and Ulrike Jessner who started the journal attached to the association (*International Journal of Multilingualism*) opted for the latter option. They state in the description of the journal that it "seeks to go beyond bilingualism and second language acquisition by developing the understanding of the specific characteristics of acquiring, processing and using more than two languages" (www.multilingual-matters.com/multi/journals/journals_ijm.asp).

Multilinguals have been found to differ from bilinguals (L1+L2) in that they suffer less from communicative anxiety (Dewaele 2002; Dewaele, Petrides and Furnham 2006) and develop higher levels of metapragmatic awareness, i.e. the ability to see language as an object which can be analysed, and to switch between focusing on meaning and focusing on form (Kemp 2001). They also benefit from higher levels of pragmatic awareness (Safont-Jordà 2005).

3.   Uncovering the causes of change in individual bi- and multilingualism: the need for triangulation

We have argued in Dewaele (2005b) that researchers in Second Language Acquisition ideally need triangulation, i.e. a combination different research methodologies, in order to answer common research questions. Such an approach is also crucial in the search for the factors that determine the development or deterioration of the languages of the bi- and multilingual. Just as in SLA, the interaction of various independent variables affecting the state of a language in the bi- and multilingual's mind is so complex that only a combination of approaches can start to shed some light on the process. There are strong arguments for including an emic perspective in our research on bi- and multilingualism as it can provide an excellent complement to quantitative empirical analysis. Researchers adopting, or adding, this perspective view participants not merely as passive objects, a 'bunch of variables', but also as active subjects, capable of meta-linguistic insights on their bi- and multilingualism. This emic perspective allows bi- and multilinguals' voices and opinions to be "heard on a par with those of the researchers" (Pavlenko 2002a: 297), at least in domains where they can help complement a global picture. There is less need for an emic perspective in certain types of research like brain imaging studies or reaction time experiments, for example, where activation levels may vary independently of conscious control and where the participants' comments might be less relevant in the interpretation of the data.

Adult bi- and multilinguals' feelings about their language can determine the answer to the many questions concerning language behaviour and language affect. In bi- and multilingualism, just as in second language acquisition, attitudes towards a target language, its speakers and the motivation to study or use that language is a crucial variable in the development or maintenance of the linguistic system (Dörnyei 2001; Gardner 1985). Affective variables determine how much energy a bi- and multilingual individual is prepared to spend on his/her languages. Hyltenstam and Viberg (1993) pointed out that the languages of a bilingual are inherently dynamic, in a constant state of flux and change, linked to the social context in which they are used. Bilinguals adapt their languages according to their communicative needs. In other words, bi- and multilinguals probably assess their linguistic skills at regular intervals and readjust the level of effort according to their specific needs. This may involve a reactivation of a lesser used language through reading or viewing of films in that language prior to a journey to the country where that language is spoken, or prior to an interview in that language. Bilinguals may judge their skills in the second language sufficient at different levels of proficiency. They may be aware that their proficiency is still some way of from native speaker norms, but they may also decide that they can simply not afford the extra tuition because of financial or time pressure. Bilinguals may also judge that an extra effort is simply not warranted because they feel proficient enough to function socially. For example, the North-African immigrants described in the ESF project who used a Basic Variety of French were fully functional in their socioprofessional environment in the south of France (Giacomi, Stoffel and Véronique 2000). There was no pressing need for them to invest extra energy in developing their second language. One of the participants, Abdelmalek, had a rudimentary knowledge of French was but it was good enough for him to work as a waiter in Marseille. His second language developed slowly through daily contact with his customers (Giacomi, Stoffel and Véronique 2000).

The situation of these North African immigrants in Marseille is quite different from the Russian immigrants in Israel described in Aronin (2004). These Russian Jews were often highly educated individuals who realized that in order to attain a socioprofessional status comparable to the one they had enjoyed at home, they needed to become highly fluent in Hebrew; hence their high levels of motivation and the increased effort into the development of this language, as well as English, the international language.

We would argue that underlying the social context and changing communicative needs of the bi- and multilingual are a basic desire to engage in interactions with people in specific contexts and a conscious decision to improve proficiency if it is felt that the communicative needs justify an extra effort. Of course, the bi- and multilingual can decide to give up at any point, if he/she judges that progress is too slow or unwarranted after all. The law of the least effort and maximal efficiency rules over linguistic systems just as it does over any system. As communicators we expect the highest possible return for the energy invested in the system. If insufficient effort is made to develop a system, it will remain rudimentary. If no more effort is made to maintain an existing system, it will gradually fade and dissolve. In the case of a bi- and multilinguals' language that is no longer used and not felt worth maintaining, it may become dormant (Green 1986) and it may gradually attrite (Schmid 2002). Language attrition among adult bi- and multilinguals may not strike with the same speed and thoroughness as in child bi- and multilinguals where the L1 can be dramatically eroded

(Köpke and Schmid 2004: 9) but complete language loss (or at least inaccessibility of that language) is perfectly possible among adults. One major study to have highlighted the effect of personal attitudes on L1 attrition among adult bi- and multilinguals is that of Schmid (2004). She interviewed 35 German Jews who emigrated from Germany under the Nazi regime. She discovered that the forced emigration and brutal persecution "led to identity conflicts which, for some of the informants, resulted in a wish to distance themselves from Germany, the Germans and consequently also the German language" (2004: 41). The degree of L1 attrition was linked to the period during which the emigration had happened. The group who had left before 1935 (when the Nuremberg laws were introduced) still used German and displayed positive attitudes towards that language. Their lexicon was slightly smaller than monolingual speakers but sounded perfectly native-like. However, those who left 1935 were more reluctant to use German and their language system had attrited to some degree. The group who experienced the 1938 pogrom had developed such a distaste for German that their L1 had attrited to the point of marking them as 'non-native speakers' (Schmid 2004: 54). These findings reinforce earlier observations by bi- and multilinguals who lost their L1, such as Gerda Lerner – a German refugee, who later became an American scholar, and writer:

> The truth was, I no longer wanted to speak German; I was repelled by the sound of it; for me as for other Americans it had become the language of the enemy. [...] I ceased speaking German altogether. (cited in Pavlenko 2002b: 49).

The case of language maintenance and/or development in bi- and multilinguals is not fundamentally different from that of monolinguals. Some monolinguals may develop a wider range of registers than others, or lose certain registers after prolonged periods of non-use. Research on the French *verlan*[2], very popular among the young in France, shows that fluent speakers of *verlan* are highly admired among their young peers (Doran 2004). However, as they grow older and move into different social circles where fluency in *verlan* is no longer considered prestigious, they no longer use *verlan* which attrites accordingly. Similarly, one could expect a monolingual language professional to invest more energy in widening and deepening his/her knowledge of the language compared to the monolingual for whom an average linguistic proficiency and vocabulary is felt to be sufficient. The monolingual's vocabulary size may depend on factors such as reading newspapers, novels, technical reports, but also on factors such a playing scrabble or filling out crosswords regularly. My argument is that linguistic systems are permanently in a state of flux, in monolinguals as well as in bi- and multilinguals, and that this variation is linked to environmental factors (immigration, holiday) as well as affective and emotional factors. We will further consider these factors in more detail in the next section.

4.   Evidence from qualitative research

Linguistic autobiographies and narratives by adult bi- and multilinguals offer a valuable source of information on the perceptions of laypeople (i.e. non-linguists) on their bi- and multilingualism. (Besemeres 2004; Pavlenko 1998, 2001, 2002b). The increased meta-linguistic awareness of bi- and multilinguals means that those who tap into this reservoir of bi- and multilingual experience over a life-time may provide valuable insights on the affective and psychological dimensions of their language use. A recurrent theme in these autobiographies is that of personality and identity shifts linked to language shifts.

> A change of language brings with it a change of role. When I speak French, I can't stop making gestures with my hands. I learnt Danish at Oxford, because my wife-to-be, who is Danish, didn't like my Anglophone personality: when I was speaking English, I was becoming too intellectual. Fortunately, she liked my Danish personality. (Harbsmeier, quoted in Wierzbicka 2004: 94)

The second language of the adult bi- and multilingual is often described as being more intellectual, more precise, more detached. This is illustrated by the Mexican-American author Ilan Stavans who immigrated to New York as a young adult. He describes his perception of his second language, English and compares it to his first, Spanish:

> English is almost mathematical. Its rules manifest themselves in an iron fashion. This is in sharp contrast to Spanish of course, whose Romance roots make it a free-flowing, imprecise language, with long and uncooperative words. As a language, it is somewhat undeserving of the literature it has created [...] For me, mastering English was, as I convinced myself, a ticket to salvation. (Stavans 2001: 223)

Whether his statement is true in a scientific sense is beyond the point. Saying that one language is more precise than another would probably make any linguist cringe. What is revealing in the paragraph is that for the author the second language somehow appears to be more rule-driven, more disciplined, and that at some point during his youth in Mexico, he convinced himself that the knowledge of English could help him attain the goals he had set to himself.

Samuel Beckett presents a mirror image of Stavans. He started as an author of texts in English that overflowed with pathos and emotion, and then switched to write exclusively in French after World War II, the language he learned as a schoolboy and studied at Trinity College in Dublin. This decision to write in French has been interpreted by literary critics as an attempt to gain a greater simplicity and objectivity and to "restrain his native verbal profligacy" (Kellman 2000: 28). Knowlson (1996) adds that for Beckett: "Writing poetry in French allowed him to get away [...] from the dense allusiveness, wide erudition and 'intimate at arms length' quality of his English poems" (Knowlson

1996: 293–294). Using French enabled him "to cut away the excess, to strip away the color" (Knowlson 1996: 357).

Nancy Huston is an Anglo-Canadian author who emigrated from Calgary to Paris as a student. French became the preferred language for writing novels and producing academic discourse. In her analysis of Huston's work, Kinginger (2004) observed that for Huston, the French language offers an alternative frame associated with "adult affect, self-control, and subtle artistry, but also with history, refinement, and civilization". French offered a life-line to Huston, an "escape from the "unavoidable" emotional residue of a childhood of "violent surprises" (Kinginger 2004: 173).

> Oui, je crois que c'était là l'essentiel: la langue française (et pas seulement ses mots tabous) était, par rapport à ma langue maternelle, moins chargée d'affect et donc moins dangereuse. Elle était froide, et je l'abordais froidement. Elle m'était égale. C'était une substance lisse et homogène, autant dire neutre. Au début, je m'en rends compte maintenant, cela me conférait une immense liberté dans l'écriture – car je ne savais pas par rapport à quoi, sur fond de quoi, j'écrivais. (Huston 1999: 63)
> [Yes, I think that was the essential thing: compared to my mother tongue, the French language was less burdened with emotion and therefore less dangerous. She was cold and I approached her coldly. She was uniform. It was a smooth and homogeneous substance, one might say neutral. In the beginning, I realize now, this conveyed an enormous liberty to me in writing – because I didn't know with respect to what, or against what background I was writing.] (Huston 1999: 63, translated by Kinginger 2004: 171).

The cases of Harbsmeier, Stavans, Beckett and Huston suggest that the perceived 'objective' quality of the second language is not so much an intrinsic quality of the language but rather a common view that adult bi- and multilinguals have of their second language. In her overview of studies of linguistic autobiographies by bi- and multilinguals, Aneta Pavlenko found that this is exactly the pattern that emerges, namely that second languages that are learned after onset of puberty do not have the same emotional impact, they feel more distant, more detached, and seem to have less emotional hold on the individual (Pavlenko 2002b).

Does it matter at what age the immigration takes place? The tentative answer is yes. Nancy Huston moved to France as a young adult, Eva Hoffman, emigrated at 13 from Poland to Canada, and both report the less visible but strong emotional bond with their first language: Hoffman's inner speech seems to be mostly in English, but Polish phrases emerge in a emotional context: "Occasionally, Polish words emerge unbidden […]. They are usually words from the primary palette of feeling: 'I'm so happy,' a voice says with bell-like clarity […]" (Hoffman 1989: 272). Yet, Eva Hoffman seems to have acculturated much faster than her parents, displaying behaviour more typical of Canadian than Polish teenagers: "My mother says I'm becoming "English". This hurts me, because I know she means I'm becoming cold ..." (Hoffman 1989: 146). Hoffman's "Polish" self is romantic while her 'English' self is pragmatic and rational, the answer to the big questions vary according to the language in which they are formulated:

> – Should you marry him? the question comes in English. – Yes. – Should you marry him? the question echoes in Polish. – No. […] […] – Should you become a pianist? the question comes in English. – No, you mustn't. You can't. – Should you become a pianist? the question echoes in Polish. – Yes, you must. At all costs. (Hoffman 1989: 199)

Jerzy Kosinski, who emigrated from Poland to the United States as an adult, is convinced that there is an age effect in bi- and multilinguals' perception of their languages:

> I think had I come to the United States at the age of nine I would have become af- fected by this traumatizing power of language. […] When I came to the United States I was twenty-four. Hence, I am not traumatized by my English – no part of my Eng- lish affects me more or less than any other one. (Kosinski and Teicholz 1993: 46–47)

Besemeres (2004) also looked what adult bi- and multilinguals think about their languages, their bi- and multilingualism and their sense of self. She considered the question of cultural differences in the experience and expression of emotion by bi- and multilinguals. Using the texts of Eva Hoffman, Tim Parks, Lilian Ng, Nino Ricci, and Stanislaw Baranczak and Zhengdao Ye, she focused on "their treatment of the role played in their own or their protagonists' lives by forms of emotional expression that do not readily translate between their two languages" (Besemeres 2004: 140) and on the extent to which nonverbal communication of emotion translate, or fail to. She concludes that "different languages make pos- sible distinct emotional styles, which engage different parts of a bilingual's self" (Besemeres 2004: 140). Bilinguals who migrate to a culture where emotional behaviour is quite different from their original culture often realize that "feel- ings that were previously felt to be purely personal are at least partly dependent on cultural forms" (Besemeres 2004: 157). As a consequence, bi- and multilin- guals may struggle to choose between different ways of feeling and differing cultural norms of expression, and hence transcending a particular emotional world. She concludes that for bi- and multilinguals "different languages may indeed mean different emotions" (Besemeres 2004: 157). Besemeres (2006), in a follow-up study on the narratives of the same authors – including also Peter Skrzynecki –, wonders whether the bi- and multilingual's feelings or the emo- tional resonance of a word comes first. She concludes that it is a "chicken and egg proposition, practically irresolvable" (Besemeres 2006: 55). Indeed, emo- tional vocabulary shapes a speaker's feeling: "In particular, the emotion con- cepts that are available to us contribute to how we interpret what we feel, how we experience it, even how we act on it" (Besemeres 2006: 55).

Wierzbicka (2004) refers to her own personal bilingual experience to illustrate to what extent the L1 and the L2 can differ in their emotionality, and how using the L2 to communicate with a baby is somehow incompatible with her emotional world. She has a granddaughter who lives far away, but she visits her often. When she comes backs, she is asked by her Anglophone friends, how her grandchild is, and this is where she is often stuck for words:

> I just can't find English words suitable for talking about my tiny granddaughter. It is not that I am not familiar with the register of English used for talking about babies but I feel that this register does not fit the emotional world to which this baby belongs for me. No doubt one reason is emotional force that English doesn't have for me. But this is not the only reason. Another reason is that Polish words that I could use to talk about my baby granddaughter do not have exact semantic equivalents in English and therefore feel irreplaceable. (Wierzbicka 2004: 100)

5.   Evidence from combined qualitative and quantitative studies

Evidence for the emotionality of the mother tongue comes also from studies on the psychological counseling of bilinguals. One of the seminal works is the study by Gonzales-Reigosa (1976) who found that Spanish-English bilingual patients employed English when discussing anxiety-arousing topics, and used English for portraying a persona of self-confidence, calm, and emotional reserve.

Panayiotou (2004) addressed similar issues using a different methodology. She focused more specifically on the verbal construction of emotions with 10 adult bilingual/bicultural American English and Cypriot Greek professionals. Panayiotou examined whether her participants expressed different emotions in their respective languages. Two culturally similar scenarios were presented to them first in English and a month later in Greek and their verbal reactions were recorded. The story is centered on American work ethic, with the male protagonist spending little time with family and friends because of work pressure. Participants were asked if the protagonist was a person close to them. Reactions to the same story differed depending on the language it was read in, with participants offering culturally appropriate emotional responses in both languages. The verbal responses were not direct translations of each other (Panayiotou 2004: 134). She argues that participants changed their social code, i.e. sociocultural expectations, with the change in linguistic code. She concludes that "the bilingual self may be contextual, one which is found and founded in two languages. The self can be multi-layered, both English and Greek, both satisfied and confused, both at home and at a loss" (Panayiotou 2004: 134). Panayiotou (2006) explored the verbal construction of English 'guilt' (translated in Greek as *enohi*) and the Greek *ntropi* (linguistically translated as 'shame') in a follow-up study with the same participants. While these terms have linguistic equivalents in both languages, they have different meanings in both cultures. Her participants reported that they borrow emotion terms from two emotional universes but "that these universes are interconnected and guided by one unified 'experiencer' of the terms" (Panayiotou 2006: 204). One participant noted that bilingualism gives him the chance to 'fine-tune (his) emotions':

> When you are a bilingual/bicultural person, I think that you can move the needle of your emotions a little bit to the left or a little bit to the right until you land on the most precise description of what you are trying to say [...] maybe monolingual people have the same needle but it's the ability to move this needle yourself that makes one a bilingual person. (Panayiotou 2006: 204)

Koven (1998) studied how 23 French-Portuguese bilinguals, children of Portuguese immigrants in France display affect in their two languages. She used three complementary approaches. First she interviewed the bilinguals about their intuitions of how they feel speaking each language. Secondly, she compared Portuguese and French versions of the same event (a personal experience) told each time to a different bilingual of the same age, and background. Thirdly, she collected a corpus of five demographically similar bilinguals' reactions to audiorecordings of the original corpus of the same stories told twice. This corpus allowed her to investigate how others perceived the speakers and inferred emotional states from their speech. The results showed important differences in the use of lexical and morphosyntactic resources and linguistic repertoires in the two languages. The bilinguals perceived themselves differently when using French or Portuguese and were judged to be different people (in terms of social background) by the listeners. Their Portuguese self was more likely to be judged as rural, while their French self – influenced by peer socialization – was seen as more sophisticated. Koven (2006) presents a detailed quantitative and qualitative case study of Linda, a French–Portuguese bilingual daughter of Portuguese migrants in France, focusing on her different kinds of affective displays in her two languages in two sociolinguistic contexts. She is perceived as a more angry and intense person in French, using profanity, while she comes across as a calmer and more reserved person in Portuguese. Linda says that she restrains herself more in Portuguese. Koven speculates that being away from the Portuguese context, Linda may recognize she is no longer one of them, and therefore not "free to perform an aggressive persona in Portuguese" (Koven 2006: 108).

Pavlenko (2004) combined quantitative and qualitative methods using the large database set up through an on-line questionnaire (Dewaele and Pavlenko 2001) to investigate the effects of perceived language emotionality and affective repertoires offered by particular languages in language choice and use in parent-child communication, in particular in emotional expression. A quantitative analysis of the responses from 389 participants showed language dominance as the principal variable affecting language choices, overall and in emotional expression. Parents dominant in the L1 were more likely to use the L1 with the children, but those dominant in another language or in two or more languages, were less likely to use the L1. A more detailed analysis of narratives of 141 bilingual parents revealed that perceived language emotionality and affective repertoires do play in important role in the choice of the L2 for praising or disciplining children: parents who perceived their L2 to be highly emotional were more likely to use that language for emotional speech with their children. A qualitative analysis of narratives showed that L1 is not always the preferred language of emotions for bilingual parents. Pavlenko argues that "Adult second language socialisation in the private space of the family may make other languages seem equally / if not more / emotional than the first" (Pavlenko 2004: 200). Many bi- and multilingual parents reported code-switching for emotion speech with their children, which is evidence that language choice is fluid and that many parents draw on multiple linguistic repertoires.

This finding suggests that the higher emotional resonance of the L1 is not a law of nature but rather a reflection of averages. The bi- and multilingual's dominant language is usually the language of emotion, and in our database about 90 % of the participants declared themselves to be dominant in their L1 (Dewaele and Pavlenko 2001).

In her overview of studies of dual selves in psychology, Pavlenko (2006) points out that when tested in their respective languages, bicultural bi- and multilinguals may perform differently on a variety of verbal tasks, including self-ratings. A common observation is that bicultural bilinguals are often perceived and rated differently by other individuals when they use their different languages in the same context. This finding is linked to differences in language socialization experiences that instill distinct cultural values and frames of expectation in each language (Pavlenko 2006). Pavlenko's own investigation into the self-perceptions of 1039 bi- and multilinguals about their linguistic selves revealed that two thirds do perceive a personality change when switching languages, at least in some contexts. An even larger proportion of respondents reported having experienced this at some point in the past. A typical illustration would be the following testimony by a participant, GCM, a 43 year-old female (English L1, French L2, German L3):

> I remember in the first years I was working and using L2 that I did feel as though I were playing a part but now I would feel as though part of my life were missing if I were to return to a monolingual environment. I think in some ways I have become a different person through using other languages – but this is difficult to differentiate from the experience of living in a different culture.

Pavlenko's (2006) Bakhtinian analysis of (double-)voicing[3] in participants' responses suggests that interlocutors seem to notice the changes in their verbal and non-verbal performances, while the respondents themselves remain unaware of the shifts. Further analysis of participants' responses showed that these personality changes were interpreted in terms of the linguistic and cultural contexts in which the languages had been learned and were being used. Other aspects were mentioned such as levels of emotionality attached to these languages, self-perceived proficiency, verbal and non-verbal repertoires offered to them by the respective languages. Pavlenko concludes firstly that "the perception of different selves is not restricted to late or immigrant bilinguals, but is a more general part of bi- and multilingual experience" (Pavlenko 2006: 27) and, secondly that "similar experiences (e.g. change in verbal and non-verbal behaviours accompanying the change in language) may be interpreted differently by people who draw on different discourses of bi/multilingualism and self" (Pavlenko 2006: 27).

6.   Evidence from the quantitative paradigm

6.1.   The personality psychological paradigm

Ervin (1964) is one the first studies to have investigated personality differences in bilinguals. A group of French–English bilinguals did the Thematic Apperception Test in English and French. It appeared that females focused more on achievement themes in English than in French. Overall Ervin found more verbal aggression towards in peers in the French stories than in the English stories, which the author attributes to differences between both cultures.

Further evidence of a link between language and personality was provided by Hull (1996). His Spanish-English bilinguals filled out the California Personality Inventory in Spanish and English. Scores on the *Good impression* factor were higher in Spanish than in English, which the author attributes to the emphasis put on interpersonal harmony in collectivist cultures as opposed to more individualistic cultures. Scores on the *Intellectual efficiency* dimension were higher for English than for Spanish which would reflect the achievement aspirations of the Anglo-American culture.

Bicultural bilinguals have also been found to obtain different scores on basic personality dimensions. Ramirez-Esparza et al. (2006) showed that adult Spanish–English bilinguals, located in the US and Mexico obtain higher scores for Extraversion, Agreeableness, and Conscientiousness in the English version of the test. The scores of the bilinguals approached those of the Anglo-American monolingual control group in the English version of the test and those of the Mexican monolingual control group for the Spanish version. The authors conclude that:

> bicultural individuals (i.e., people who have internalized two cultures, such as bilinguals) (…) change their interpretations of the world, depending upon their internalized cultures, in response to cues in their environment (e.g., language, cultural icons). (Ramírez-Esparza et al. 2006: 118)

An investigation using the same database as Pavlenko (2006) but with the full 1500 participants rather than the first 1039 is being carried out by Wilson (in progress). Using the answer to the question "do you feel different when you use different language?" as a dependent variable, she carried out a quantitative analysis of the data and found that significantly more females reported feeling different when speaking different languages, and significantly more highly educated participants perceived themselves to shift in their different language. The predominant emotions expressed were of feeling more confident and less constrained by convention when operating in a foreign language. Wondering whether the answer to the question of 'feeling different' might be linked to personality variables, Wilson designed a questionnaire with 29 questions on the perception of personality change in different languages which was submitted to 34 language learners, the majority of whom rated their proficiency in one or more foreign languages as intermediate level. The participants also completed a standard personality questionnaire (OCEAN). Statistical analysis showed that introversion and neuroticism were significant predictors of the 'feeling different' score. Highly introvert and more nervous bi- and multilinguals were more likely to feel a personality shift when switching languages.

In a larger survey of over 100 participants, a similar relationship with introversion was shown although it was not statistically significant. In contrast, a survey of another 120 language learners who rated their foreign language proficiency at a very low level showed no such relationship.

6.2.   The word-priming paradigm

Altarriba and Santiago-Rivera (1994) used the word-priming paradigm to investigate the representation that bilingual individuals have of emotion words in their two languages linking it to cross-linguistic differences and language histories.

Altarriba (2003) investigated this topic further and used rating scales to uncover critical word characteristics for concrete, emotion, and abstract words in the Spanish of 21 adult Spanish-English bilinguals. Emotion words were rated as less concrete but more easily pictured than abstract words, bilinguals provided equal ratings for both word types in terms of context-availability. This suggests that when individuals learn emotion words in a L1 those words are stored at a deeper level of representation than their L2 counterparts. Altarriba attributes this difference to the fact that emotion words in the L1 have been experienced in many more contexts and have been applied in varying ways specifically in the case of late bilinguals. As a consequence, multiple traces are created in memory for these words, which strengthens their semantic representation. On the other hand, emotion words learned in a L2 may not be as deeply encoded, if they are practiced much less and applied in fewer contexts. As a consequence, an emotion word in the L2 is less likely to activate as many different associations as is the same word in the more dominant language: "Emotion words in the first language may carry a broader range of expression and may be more highly associated to specific contexts than their presumed counterparts in a second language" (Altarriba 2003: 318). Altarriba and Canary (2004) analysed the effect of emotional arousal on affective priming on English monolinguals and Spanish-English bilinguals. They discovered positive priming effects for both groups in high and medium arousal conditions. The arousal condition did produce longer latencies for bilinguals than for monolinguals. The study showed that "arousal components are activated in a subordinate though native language when processing emotion-related words in the dominant language" (Altarriba 2006: 252).

Eilola, Havelka and Sharma (2006) used an emotional Stroop task (using emotionally charged words instead of colour words) to investigate the automatic emotional response to word stimuli with 41 proficient Finnish-English bilinguals. The stimuli were neutral, positive, negative and taboo words in both Finnish and English. The findings suggest that, at least for highly proficient bilinguals, the negative and taboo words produce the same pattern and magnitude of interference in both languages. These threatening word stimuli are equally capable of activating the emotional response and thus interfering with the cognitive processes involved in responding to colour.

6.3.   Bilingual autobiographical memories

Immigrants' childhood memories are generally more emotionally charged and more vivid when described in their native language (Schrauf 2000). However, recent research shows that the memories recalled in the first language are not necessarily always the most emotional ones. Marian and Kaushanskaya (2004) analysed autobiographical memories in Russian and English of 47 bicultural adult Russian-English bilinguals who had immigrated to the US as teenagers. The bilinguals' language choice was found to affect their self-construal. The recall of memories in English, a language associated with a more individualistic culture, resulted in more individualistic narratives, whereas memories in Russian, a language associated with a more collectivist culture, produced more collectivist narratives, regardless of language of encoding or main agent in the narrative. The researchers also found that bilinguals expressed more intense affect when speaking the same language at the time of retrieval that they spoke at the time when the event took place. Age also affected the valency of the memories, with memories encoded later in life being rated as more positive than memories encoded earlier in life.

Schrauf and Rubin (2004) uncovered similar patterns in their study of 30 older Spanish-English speaking Puerto Ricans (average age: 69) who had emigrated to the US in early adulthood. Their participants rated the emotional intensity of memories at recall as more emotional in the second language than those in the first language. The authors suggest that is could be linked to the phenomenon of ethnopsychological acculturation to the emotional register of the second language and culture-of-adoption which renders second-language memories more salient at retrieval (Schrauf and Rubin 2004: 28). In their recent review of methodologies and theories on bilingual autobiographical memory and emotion, Schrauf and Durazo-Arvizu (2006) conclude that both emotion and language are present in memories. A bilingual recalling a particular memory engages in the mental reconstruction of some event that was originally encoded into memory in a particular sociocultural and linguistic environment. Memories are tagged by language and the emotional tone of the experience is encoded as well:

> In the moment of recalling the memory, these various bits of information are reintegrated into the whole narratively structured memory again, and some of them are vividly re-experienced, while others are almost or merely conceptual in status (much of this depends on the sociocultural and linguistic context of retrieval). (Schrauf and Durazo-Arvizu 2006: 307)

Schrauf and Durazo-Arvizu (2006) also plead for the use of more sensitive statistical techniques such as multilevel modeling rather than traditional regression and analysis of variance because of the complex nature of autobiographical memories, nested within individual minds (Schrauf and Durazo-Arvizu 2006: 307).

6.4.   Self-reports from bi- and multilinguals

The studies by Pavlenko (cf. supra) showed that bi- and multilinguals usually feel that their L1 is most emotional, although some report that languages learnt later in life can acquire equally strong emotional resonance. Dewaele (2004a) focused on language choice for swearing among 1039 bi- and multilinguals in up to five languages. The expected pattern emerged, namely that participants generally preferred the dominant language (often the L1) for swearing. Multilinguals who had started to learn the language as children and who used the language frequently usually preferred that language for swearing. Dewaele (2004b) focused on variation in perceived emotional force of swear words and taboo words in 1039 bi- and multilinguals' different languages. A statistical analysis showed that the perceived emotional force is highest in the L1 and gradually lower in languages learned later. Highly proficient and frequent users of languages reported significantly higher levels of emotional force of swear words and taboo words. Participants who had started learning an L2 at a younger age tended to rate the emotional force of swear words and taboo words more highly in that L2. Strong positive correlations appeared between scores on perception of emotional force of swear words and values for frequency of use of swear words in the different languages. Narratives by participants revealed that despite a general preference for swearing in the L1 and the stronger emotional resonance of swear words in that language did not prevent participants from occasionally using their other languages, depending on the intended perlocutionary effects and the identity of the interlocutor.

In Dewaele (2005a), we focused on the effect of context of acquisition on language choice for swearing and perception of emotional force of swear words and taboo words in a bi- and multilingual's multiple languages. The results showed that instructed language learners used the target language less frequently for swearing and gave lower ratings on emotional force of swear words and taboo words in that language compared to mixed learners (i.e. a combination of classroom instruction and naturalistic contact) and naturalistic learners (i.e. who had not benefited from any classroom instruction). Dewaele (2006) uncovered similar patterns for the language choice for the expression of anger among 1454 bi- and multilinguals. The L1 was generally the preferred language for expression of anger. However, another language could become the preferred language to express anger after a period of intense socialization. Mixed learners and participants who had started learning a language early used that language more frequently to express anger than those who started later. A clear positive link emerged also between self-perceived proficiency in a language and frequency of use of that language to express anger.

The last study included in this section is the one by Dewaele (2004c) that dealt with L1 attrition among adult bi- and multilinguals. The same corpus with 1039 participants revealed that perceived L1 attrition significantly affected self-related proficiency in the L1, frequency of use of the L1 for the expression of feelings, anger and swearing to different interlocutors and in different modalities, in silent and articulated speech. L1 attrition was also found to alter the perceptions of certain characteristics of the L1, but not the perception of its emotional and poetic character, and the perception of emotional force of swear words. Even bi- and multilinguals who reported strong attrition in their L1 showed that the L1 did retain powerful emotional connotations, which could be either positive or negative.

6.5.   The psychophysiological paradigm

Harris and her associates considered the emotionality of the bilinguals' languages using a brain-based perspective. Their aim was to establish whether psychophysiological measures and the subjective reports of bilinguals are congruent.

Harris, Ayçiçegi and Gleason (2003) analysed the emotional impact of words in the L1 and L2 through their effect on autonomic reactivity, as manifested in skin conductance. The researchers used electrodermal monitoring (i.e. fingertip electrodes) to compare reactivity for reprimands, taboo words, aver-sive, positive and neutral words presented visually and auditorily in the L1 and the L2 of 32 Turkish L1-English L2 bilinguals. Physiological reactions to taboo words presented auditorily in the L1 were found to be much stronger than their translation equivalent in the L2. That said, responsiveness to English (L2) taboo words was also high, showing that taboo words in either language activate emotionally-arousing conceptual structures. Childhood reprimands in the L1 were found to be the most physiologically arousing while similar expressions in their L2 had very little effect. A final exploratory analysis was carried out to verify whether sociobiographical variables predicted skin conductance responses. Neither age, gender, age of exposure to English, age of arrival in the US, length of stay in the US, self-rated proficiency, nor English verbal proficiency significantly predicted skin conductance responses. Harris et al. (2003) observe that the anxiety aroused by taboo words has frequently been attributed to punishment from parents for saying these words during childhood. In contrast, taboo words learned in a L2, after childhood or outside of interaction with parents, have fewer associations with punishment. The authors finally emphasise that the broader concept of societal disapproval may be more important than punishment by parents.

Harris (2004) used the same methodology in follow-up study with a larger number of emotional expressions, intermixed with 36 less emotional items, half in English, half in Spanish, with half of the items in each language being presented visually, and the other half auditorily. The participants were 15 Spanish-English bilinguals who had grown up in the US (early learners). The early L2 learners of English showed stronger reactions to both Spanish and English taboo words. The author explains that this is consistent with the proposal that when two languages are learned early, emotion-laden terms activate the autonomic nervous system equally (2004: 241). No such difference was obtained for the 21 bilinguals who were first exposed to English during middle childhood (late learners), indicating that age of acquisition of the second language and proficiency modulate speakers' physiological reaction to emotional language. These results show that the L1 is not always more emotional. Harris concludes that because the early learners reported greater proficiency in their L2, "the data are consistent with the proposal that the L1 is more emotional when it is the more proficient language" (2004: 241).

In a further follow-up study, Harris et al. (2006), using the same dependent variable, concentrated on 31 early and 21 late learners of English, with Spanish as L1. Again, late learners of a L2 had greater skin conductance amplitudes to emotional phrases (including taboo words and reprimands) in their L1, while those who acquired both languages in childhood displayed similar skin conductance responses in both languages. It thus seems that the L2 is not invariably experienced as less emotional than the L1. The authors stress that if the L2 is acquired in childhood, and to greater proficiency than L1, it will be experienced as more, or equally emotional to L1. The authors argue that to explain why a first language was not more emotional than a second language which was acquired in childhood, we proposed a mechanism independent of age: the emotional contexts of learning hypothesis; where language is experienced as emotional when it is acquired and used in an emotional context. (Harris et al. 2006: 277)

7.   Conclusion

We set out to answer a number of questions addressed by researchers in different fields using different approaches concerning various aspects of phatic communication, perception and reaction to emotional stimuli in different languages, images of self, attitudes towards one's languages and speculation about the representation of emotion words and expressions in the bilingual mind. The overview has revealed some common trends such as the strong emotional power and the emotional connotations of the first language(s) of the bi- and multilingual. It has also shown that while on average the first language(s) may seem more involved to the bi- and multilingual, languages learnt later in life may acquire equally strong emotional resonance for some bi- and multilinguals. This may be the opportunity to reconsider the words in the title 'becoming a bi- and multilingual later in life'. It is probably unfair to use the word 'become', at it implies that the achievement of bi- and multilingual status is some kind of crowning after a very long process of acquisition and socialisation into the L2. One 'becomes' bi- and multilingual from the moment that the first words are used in a meaningful interaction. At that point it would be appropriate to talk about "being" bi- and multilingual, with a emphasis on the progressive form which signals a never-ending process (which could be either a development or a deterioration of the L2). The crucial point is that the languages of the bi- and multilinguals, as well as the individual selves are in slow but constant motion. The perception of the world and the presentation of the self can switch together with the bi- or multilingual's language switch. The dynamic character of individual adult bi- and multilingualism is particularly clear in phatic communication. Attitudes towards languages evolve just as the person develops, yet some visceral link with the L1 can remain even though the L1 may have attrited to a large degree. Different emotions may be experienced and expressed in different languages in reaction to a similar stimulus. Not surprisingly, this dissociation may lead to different perceptions of the bi- and multilingual by their interlocutor(s). The preference for particular languages to express emotions is linked to a myriad of independent variables. Among the most important factors are the frequency of use of a language, and – linked to that – the proficiency in that language. High frequency and high proficiency in a language are in themselves indicative of intense socialisation in that language. However, low frequency and loss of proficiency among L1 attriters seems to affect their choice of language for emotional communication but not the perception of some emotional characteristics of the L1. Other factors, buried in the bi- and multilinguals' past, such as age of acquisition and context of acquisition seem to continue to exert an influence on the linguistic behaviour and physiological reactions of bi- and multilinguals many years on.

Despite the abundance of research into adult bi- and multilinguals, one cannot escape the impression that researchers have merely scratched the surface. A number of apparently crucial pieces of the puzzle may have been unearthed, but it is clear that many remain to be discovered. Only a concerted interdisciplinary effort will allow a more global and profound understanding of the feelings and behaviour of adult bilinguals.

Notes

1. It must be said that the new journals such as *Bilingualism: Language and Cognition*, the *International Journal of Bilingualism*, the *International Journal of Bilingualism and Bilingual Education* have provided an excellent platform for researchers from different disciplines and theoretical backgrounds to present their studies on various issues involving bilingualism.
2. Originally a French language game involving syllabic inversion, now used as "an umbrella term for a more elaborated code which has become a recognizable sociolect over the past two decades" (Doran 2004: 97).
3. Voicing is an intertextual strategy where the speech of others is rendered directly or indirectly. Double voicing allows respondents to bring in the voices of others but also to impose their own meaning on them by appealing to irony or sarcasm or by challenging their opinions directly (Pavlenko 2006).
4. The present research was supported by a grant (SG-40768) from the British Academy.

References

Altarriba, Jeanette
    2003   Does cariño equal 'liking'? A theoretical approach to conceptual nonequivalence between languages. *International Journal of Bilingualism* 7 (3): 305–322.
Altarriba, Jeanette
    2006   Cognitive approaches to the study of emotion-laden and emotion words in monolingual and bilingual memory. In: Aneta Pavlenko (ed.), *Bilingual Minds: Emotional Experience, Expression, and Representation*, 232–256. Clevedon: Multilingual Matters.
Altarriba, Jeanette and Tina M. Canary
    2004   Affective priming: The automatic activation of arousal. *Journal of Multilingual and Multicultural Development* 25 (2/3): 248–65.

Altarriba, Jeanette and Azara L. Santiago-Rivera
    1994   Current perspectives on using linguistic and cultural factors in counseling the Hispanic client. *Professional Psychology: Research and Practice* 25: 388–397.
Aronin, Larisa
    2004   Multilinguality and emotions: Emotional experiences and language attitudes of trilingual immigrant students in Israel. *Estudios de Sociolingüística* 5 (1): 59–82
Baetens Beardsmore, Hugo
    1982   *Bilingualism: Basic Principles*. Clevedon: Multilingual Matters.
Baetens Beardsmore, Hugo
    2003   Who is afraid of bilingualism? In: Jean-Marc Dewaele, Li Wei, and Alex Housen (eds.), *Bilingualism: Beyond Basic Principles*, 10–27. Clevedon: Multilingual Matters.
Baker, Colin
    2000   *A Parents' and Teachers' Guide to Bilingualism* (2nd edition) Clevedon: Multilingual Matters.
Baker, Colin and Sylvia Prys Jones
    1998   *Encyclopedia of Bilingualism and Bilingual Education*. Clevedon: Multilingual Matters.
Bayley, Robert
    1994   Interlanguage variation and the quantitative paradigm: Past-time marking in Chinese-English. In Elaine Tarone, Susan Gass and Andrew Cohen (eds.), *Research Methodology in Second Language Acquisition*, 157–181. Hillsdale, NJ: Erlbaum.
Barron-Hauwaert, Suzanne
    2003   *Language Strategies for Bilingual Families: The One-Parent-One-Language Approach*. Clevedon: Multilingual Matters.
Besemeres, Mary
    2004   Different languages, different emotions? Perspectives from autobiographical literature. *Journal of Multilingual and Multicultural Development* 25 (2/3): 140–158.
Besemeres, Mary
    2006   Language and emotional experience: The voice of translingual memoir. In: Aneta Pavlenko (ed.), *Bilingual Minds: Emotional Experience, Expression, and Representation*, 34–58. Clevedon: Multilingual Matters.
Bialystok, Ellen
    2002   Cognitive processes of L2 users. In: Vivian Cook (ed.) *Portraits of the L2 User*, 145–165. Clevedon: Multilingual Matters.
Bloomfield, Leonard
    1935   *Language*. London: George Allen and Unwin LTD.
Cenoz, Jasone and Ulrike Jessner
    2000   *English in Europe: the Acquisition of a Third Language*. Clevedon: Multilingual Matters.
Cook, Vivian
    2002   Background to the L2 user. In: Vivian Cook (ed.), *Portraits of the L2 User*, 1–28. Clevedon: Multilingual Matters.

Cook, Vivian
  2003   Introduction: The changing L1 in the L2 user's mind. In: Vivian Cook (ed.),
            Effects of Second Language on the First, 1–18. Clevedon: Multilingual
            Matters.
Crystal, David
  2003   *A Dictionary of Linguistics and Phonetics.* Oxford: Blackwell Publish-
            ing.
De Angelis, Gessica
  2005a   Multilingualism and non-native lexical transfer: an identification problem.
            International Journal of Multilingualism 2 (1): 1–25.
De Angelis, Gessica
  2005b   Interlanguage influence of function words. *Language Learning* 55 (3):
            379–414.
Dewaele, Jean-Marc
  2002   The effect of multilingualism and socio-situational factors on communi-
            cative anxiety of mature language learners. In Jehannes Ytsma and Marc
            Hooghiemstra (eds.), *Proceedings of the Second International Conference
            on Trilingualism.* Leeuwaarden: Fryske Akademie (CD Rom).
Dewaele, Jean-Marc
  2004a   Blistering barnacles! What language do multilinguals swear in?!" *Estudios
            de Sociolingüística* 5 (1): 83–106.
Dewaele, Jean-Marc
  2004b   The emotional force of swearwords and taboo words in the speech of multi-
            linguals. *Journal of Multilingual and Multicultural Development* 25 (2/3):
            204–222.
Dewaele, Jean-Marc
  2004c   Perceived language dominance and language preference for emotional
            speech: The implications for attrition research. In: Monika S. Schmid, Bar-
            bara Köpke, Merel Kejser and Lina Weilemar (eds.), *First Language Attri-
            tion: Interdisciplinary Perspectives on Methodological Issues*, 81–104.
            Amsterdam/Philadelphia: John Benjamins.
Dewaele, Jean-Marc
  2005a   The effect of type of acquisition context on perception and self-reported
            use of swearwords in the L2, L3, L4 and L5. In: Alex Housen and Michel
            Pierrard (eds.), *Investigations in Instructed Second Language Acquisition*,
            531–559. Berlin: Mouton De Gruyter.
Dewaele, Jean-Marc
  2005b   Investigating the psychological and the emotional dimensions in instructed
            language learning: Obstacles and possibilities. *The Modern Language Jour-
            nal* 89 (3): 367–380.
Dewaele, Jean-Marc
  2006   Expressing anger in multiple languages. In: Aneta Pavlenko (ed.), *Bilingual
            Minds: Emotional Experience, Expression, and Representation*, 118–151.
            Clevedon: Multilingual Matters.
Dewaele, Jean-Marc, Alex Housen and Li Wei
  2003   *Bilingualism: Beyond Basic Principles.* Clevedon: Multilingual Matters.
Dewaele, Jean-Marc and Aneta Pavlenko
  2001   Web questionnaire *Bilingualism and Emotions.* University of London.

Dewaele, Jean-Marc, Dino Petrides and Adrian Furnham
    2005   An investigation of the relationship between communicative anxiety and
            trait emotional intelligence on a sample of adult polyglots. University of
            London, unpublished manuscript.
Doran, Meredith
    2004   Negotiating between bourge and racaille: Verlan as youth identity practice
            in suburban Paris. In: Aneta Pavlenko and Adrian Blackledge (eds.), *Ne-
            gotiation of Identities in Multilingual Contexts*, 93–124. Clevedon: Multi-
            lingual Matters.
Dörnyei, Zoltan
    2001   *Motivational Strategies: Creating and Maintaining Student Motivation in
            the Foreign Language Classroom.* New York: Cambridge University Press.
Ducrot, Oswald and Todorov, Tzvetan
    1972   *Dictionnaire encyclopédique des sciences du langage.* Paris: Seuil.
Edwards, John
    2003   The importance of being bilingual. In: Jean-Marc Dewaele, Li Wei, and
            Alex Housen (eds.), *Bilingualism: Beyond Basic Principles*, 28–42. Cleve-
            don: Multilingual Matters.
Eilola, Tiina M., Jelena Havelka and Dinkar Sharma
    2006   Emotional activation in the first and second language. Manuscript sub-
            mitted for publication.
Ervin, Susan M.
    1964   Language and TAT content in bilinguals. *Journal of Abnormal and Social
            Psychology* 68: 500–507.
Gardner, Robert C.
    1985   *Social Psychology and Second Language Learning: The Roles of Attitudes
            and Motivation.* London: Edward Arnold.
Genesee, Fred
    2003   Rethinking bilingual acquisition. In: Jean-Marc Dewaele, Li Wei, and Alex
            Housen (eds.), *Bilingualism: Beyond Basic Principles*, 204–228. Clevedon:
            Multilingual Matters.
Giacomi, Alain, Henriette Stoffel and Daniel Véronique (eds.)
    2000   *Appropriation du français par des Marocains arabophones à Marseille.*
            Aix en Provence: Publications de l'Université de Provence.
Gonzales-Reigosa, Fernando
    1976   The anxiety-arousing effect of taboo words in bilinguals. In Charles D.
            Spielberger and Rogelio Diaz-Guerrero (eds.), *Cross-Cultural Anxiety*,
            89–105. Washington, DC: Hemisphere.
Green, David W.
    1986   Control, activation and resource: A framework and a model for the control
            of speech in bilinguals, *Brain and Language* 27: 210–223.
Harris, Catherine L.
    2004   Bilingual speakers in the lab: Psychophysiological measures of emotional
            reactivity. *Journal of Multilingual and Multicultural Development* 25 (2/3):
            223–247.
Harris, Catherine L., Ayse Ayçiçegi, and Jean B. Gleason
    2003   Taboo words and reprimands elicit greater autonomic reactivity in a first
            than in a second language. *Applied Psycholinguistics* 24: 561–579.

Harris, Catherine L., Jean B. Gleason, and Ayse Ayçiçegi
    2006   Why is a first language more emotional? Psychophysiological evidence from bilingual speakers. In: Aneta Pavlenko (ed.), *Bilingual Minds: Emotional Experience, Expression, and Representation*, 257–283. Clevedon: Multilingual Matters.
Hoffman, Eva
    1989   *Lost in translation. A life in a New Language*. New York: Dutton.
Hoffmann, Charlotte
    2001   Towards a description of trilingual competence. *International Journal of Bilingualism* 5 (1): 1–17.
Hull, Philip V.
    1996   Bilingualism: Some personality and cultural issues. In Dan I. Slobin, Julie Gerhardt, Amy Kyratzis, Jiansheng Guo and Susan M. Tripp (eds.), *Social Interaction, Social Context, and Language: Essays in Honor of Susan Ervin-Tripp*, 419–434. New Jersey: Lawrence Erlbaum Associates.
Hyltenstam, Kenneth and Åke Viberg (eds.)
    1993   *Progression and regression in language*. Cambridge: Cambridge University Press.
Jessner, Ulrike, Britta Hufeisen, and Jasone Cenoz (eds.)
    2001   *Cross-Linguistic Influence in Third Language Acquisition: Psycholinguistic Perspectives*. Clevedon: Multilingual Matters.
Kecskes, Istvan and Tünde Papp
    2000   *Foreign Language and Mother Tongue*. Hillsdale, NJ/ London: Lawrence Erlbaum.
Kellman, Steven G.
    2000   *The Translingual Imagination*. Lincoln: University of Nebraska Press.
Kemp, Charlotte
    2001   Metalinguistic awareness in multilinguals: Implicit and explicit grammatical awareness and its relationship with language experience and language attainment. Unpublished PhD thesis, University of Edinburgh.
Kinginger, Celeste
    2004   Bilingualism and emotion in the autobiographical works of Nancy Huston. *Journal of Multilingual and Multicultural Development* 25 (2/3): 159–178.
Klein, Wolfgang and Clive Perdue
    1997   The Basic Variety. *Second Language Research* 13 (4): 301–347.
Knowlson, James
    1996   *Damned to Fame. The Life of Samuel Beckett*. London: Bloomsbury.
Köpke, Barbara and Monika Schmid
    2004   Language attrition: The next phase. In: Monika S. Schmid, Barbara Köpke, Merel Kejser and Lina Weilemar (eds.), *First Language Attrition: Interdisciplinary Perspectives on Methodological Issues*, 6–30. Amsterdam/Philadelphia: John Benjamins.
Kosinski, Jerzy N. and Tom Teicholz
    1993   *Conversations with Jerzy Kosinski*. Jackson: University Press of Mississippi.
Koven, Michèle E. J.
    1998   Two languages in the self/the self in two languages: French-Portuguese bilinguals' verbal enactments and experiences of self in narrative discourse. *Ethos* 26 (4): 410–455.

Koven, Michèle E. J.
   2006   Feeling in two languages: A comparative analysis of a bilingual's affective
           displays in French and Portuguese. In: Aneta Pavlenko (ed.), *Bilingual
           Minds: Emotional Experience, Expression, and Representation*, 84–117.
           Clevedon: Multilingual Matters.
Mackey, William
   2002   Changing paradigms in the study of bilingualism. In: Li Wei, Jean-Marc
           Dewaele and Alex Housen (eds.), *Opportunities and Challenges in Bilin-
           gualism*, 328–344. Berlin: Mouton de Gruyter.
Marian, Viorica and Margarita Kaushanskaya
   2004   Self-construal and emotion in bicultural bilinguals. *Journal of Memory and
           Language* 51: 190–201.
Panayiotou, Alexia
   2004   Switching codes, switching code: Bilinguals' emotional responses in Eng-
           lish and Greek. *Journal of Multilingual and Multicultural Development* 25
           (2/3): 124–139.
Panayiotou, Alexia
   2006   Translating guilt: An endeavour of shame in the Mediterranean? In: Aneta
           Pavlenko (ed.), *Bilingual Minds: Emotional Experience, Expression, and
           Representation*, 183–208. Clevedon: Multilingual Matters.
Pavlenko, Aneta
   1998   Second language learning by adults: testimonies of bilingual writers. *Issues
           in Applied Linguistics* 9 (1): 3–19.
Pavlenko, Aneta
   2001   Language learning memoirs as a gendered genre. *Applied Linguistics* 22
           (2): 213–240.
Pavlenko, Aneta
   2002a   Poststructuralist approaches to the study of social factors in L2. In: Vivian
           Cook (ed.), *Portraits of the L2 User*, 277–302. Clevedon: Multilingual
           Matters.
Pavlenko, Aneta
   2002b   Bilingualism and emotions. *Multilingua* 21 (1): 45–78.
Pavlenko, Aneta
   2004   'Stop doing that, la Komu Skazala!': Language choice and emotion in par-
           ent-child communication. *Journal of Multilingual and Multicultural Devel-
           opment* 25 (2/3): 179–203.
Pavlenko, Aneta
   2005   *Emotions and Multilingualism.* New York: Cambridge University Press.
Pavlenko, Aneta
   2006   Bilingual selves. In: Aneta Pavlenko (ed.), *Bilingual minds: Emotional ex-
           perience, expression, and representation*, 1–33. Clevedon: Multilingual
           Matters.
Pavlenko, Aneta and Adrian Blackledge (eds.)
   2004   *Negotiation of Identities in Multilingual Contexts.* Clevedon: Multingual
           Matters.
Pavlenko, Aneta, Adrian Blackledge, Ingrid Piller and Maria Teutsch-Dwyer (eds.)
   2003   *Multilingualism, Second Language Learning, and Gender.* Berlin: Mouton
           De Gruyter.

Pavlenko, Aneta and Jean-Marc Dewaele (eds.)
2004a   *Bilingualism and Emotion.* Special issue of *Estudios de Sociolingüística* 5 (1).
Pavlenko, Aneta and Jean-Marc Dewaele (eds.)
2004b   *Languages and Emotions: A Crosslinguistic Perspective.* Special double issue of *Journal of Multilingual and Multicultural Development* 25 (2/3).
Pavlenko, Aneta, Robert W. Schrauf and Jean-Marc Dewaele (eds.)
2003   *New Directions in the Study of Bilingual Memory.* Special issue of *International Journal of Bilingualism* 7 (3).
Ramírez-Esparza, Nairán, Samuel D. Gosling, Verónica Benet-Martínez, Jeffrey P. Potter and James W. Pennebaker
2006   Do bilinguals have two personalities? A special case of cultural frame switching. *Journal of Research in Personality* 40 (2): 99–120.
Safont-Jordà, Maria Pilar
2005   *Third Language Learners. Pragmatic Production and Awareness.* Clevedon: Multilingual Matters.
Schmid, Monika S.
2002   *First Language Attrition, Use and Maintenance: The case of German Jews in Anglophone Countries.* Amsterdam and Philadelphia: John Benjamins.
Schmid, Monika S.
2004   Identity and first language attrition: A historical approach. Bilingualism and Emotion. *Estudios de Sociolingüística* 5 (1): 41–58
Schrauf, Robert W.
2000   Bilingual autobiographical memory: Experimental studies and clinical cases. *Culture and Psychology* 6: 387–417.
Schrauf, Robert W. and David C. Rubin
2004   The 'language' and 'feel' of bilingual memory: Mnemonic traces. *Estudios de Sociolingüística* 5 (1): 41–58.
Schrauf, Robert W. and Ramon Durazo-Arvizu
2006   Bilingual autobiographical memory and emotion: theory and methods. In: Aneta Pavlenko (ed.), *Bilingual Minds: Emotional Experience, Expression, and Representation,* 284–311. Clevedon: Multilingual Matters.
Stavans, Ilan
2001   *On Borrowed Words. A Memoir of Language.* New York: Viking Penguin.
Sia, Jennifer and Jean-Marc Dewaele
2006   Are you bilingual? *Birkbeck Studies in Applied Linguistics*/www.bbk.ac.uk/llc
Vendler, Zeno
1967   Verbs and times. In: Zeno Vendler (ed.), *Linguistics in Philosophy.* Ithaca, NY: Cornell University Press, 97–121.
Voorwinde, Stephen
1981   A lexical and grammatical study in Dutch-English-German trilingualism. *ITL Review of Applied Linguistics* 52: 3–30.
Wei, Li
2000   *The Bilingualism Reader.* London: Routledge.
Wierzbicka, Anna
2004   Bilingual lives, bilingual experience. *Journal of Multilingual and Multicultural Development* 25 (2/3): 94–104.

Wilson, Rosemary
    in progress   'Another language is another soul': the presentation of self through a
        foreign language. PhD thesis. University of London.

Recommended readings

Bamberg, Michael
    1997   Language, concepts and emotions: The role of language in the construction
        of emotions. *Language Sciences* 19 (4): 309–340.
Fussell, Susan (ed.)
    2002   *The Verbal Communication of Emotions: Interdisciplinary Perspectives.*
        Mahwah, NJ: Lawrence Erlbaum Associates.
Mori, Kyoko
    1997   *Polite Lies: On Being a Woman Caught Between Two Cultures.* New York:
        Henry Holt and Company.
Piller, Ingrid
    2002   *Bilingual Couples Talk: The Discursive Construction of Hybridity.* Amster-
        dam: Benjamins.
Schumann, John
    1997   *The Neurobiology of Affect in Language.* Boston: Blackwell.
Ye, Veronica Zhengdao
    2003   La Double Vie de Veronica: Reflections on my life as a Chinese migrant
        in Australia. *Mots Pluriels* 23. On WWW at http://www.arts.uwa.edu.au/
        motspluriels/MP2303vzy.html.

5.   Becoming bilingual through bilingual education

Colin Baker

1.   Introduction

Given that many children spend around 15,000 hours in school, there is potentially ample opportunity for bilingualism and biliteracy to develop. In many countries (e.g. Canada, Scandinavia, South Africa), bilingual and multilingual education delivers such bilingualism. The aim of this chapter is to explore how children become bilingual at school through bilingual education. It starts by examining the meaning of 'bilingual education' and how there are different kinds of dual language education.

'Bilingual education' is an ambiguous, generic term. It is attributed to many different schools that teach bilingually, or merely teach bilingual students. The phrase 'bilingual education' is used to cover schools where children move quickly from minority language dominance to majority language dominance as well as for schools that help children become bilingual and biliterate.

To reduce ambiguity, 'bilingual education' is ideally reserved for those schools and classrooms that teach some, most or all subject content through two languages. This is termed a 'strong' version of bilingual education (Baker 2006). In contrast, there are 'weak' forms that allow children to use their home language for a short, temporary, transitional period. The language of instruction quickly moves from a minority language to being in the majority language only. There is also the case of an absence of any bilingual instruction, yet because there are bilingual children present, the word 'bilingual education' is wrongly applied.

The term 'bilingual education' does not refer to school contexts where an individual is taught a second language, but where that language is used for content teaching. Thus, second language lessons (e.g. French in the US and UK) and the teaching of English as a foreign language (TESOL / TEFL) would not count as bilingual education. However, although some children become bilingual through second language lessons, this chapter contends that children best become bilingual at school via 'strong' forms of bilingual education. But what comprises 'strong' forms of bilingual education?

2.   'Strong' types of bilingual education

There are different types of 'strong' bilingual education. For example, one of the most well researched models derives from Canada. Termed *immersion education* or *immersion bilingual education*, children from English medium homes in Canada learn through the medium of French (Johnstone 2002). They are immersed in a second language, and become fluent in that language through content learning. Such immersion schools enrol majority language children, and teach through two majority languages. In the United States, an increasingly researched form of bilingual education is *Dual Language Schools* (Lindholm-Leary 2001). Such schools teach, for example, the subject curriculum through one language on one day, and through a different language the next day, in strict alternation. In many, but not all cases, the two languages are English and Spanish. The children in such schools approximate an equal number of language majority (e.g. English L1) and language minority (e.g. U.S. Spanish L1) speakers.

A third type of bilingual education mostly contains indigenous language minority children and is currently commonly entitled *heritage language education* (Wiley 2001). Such children are typically taught in their home (heritage) language for at least 50% of curriculum time, often more to begin with. Other types of 'strong' bilingual education include mainstream schools that teach through two or more majority languages, as in the European Schools movement (Mejia 2002). Such children may derive from a variety of language backgrounds, and many will become multilingual and multicultural.

Baker (2006) provides a ten-fold typology of bilingual education: structured immersion, mainstreaming with withdrawal classes, segregationist, transitional, mainstream with foreign language teaching, separatist, immersion, heritage language, dual language and mainstream bilingual education. While this portrays the major types of bilingual education in the world, there are limitations to such typologies. For example, the schools themselves rarely use these terms; some schools are a mixture of, for example, immersion and heritage language education, typologies do not reveal variety within a model, and there are individual bilingual schools that do not fit neatly into such a typology. This chapter continues by outlining the main forms of bilingual education in this typology, and then portrays the key dimensions of such schooling that lie beneath this typology.

3.   Major types of bilingual education

This section outlines the three major 'strong' versions of bilingual education that each have a strong tradition of research and are internationally eminent. A detailed examination of different types of bilingual education that includes a consideration of mainstream bilingual education (e.g. the European Schools movement, International Schools) is found in Baker (2006) and Baker and Jones (1998). However, before discussing 'strong' versions of bilingual education, it is important to contrast 'weak' and 'strong' forms of bilingual education.

3.1.   'Weak' forms of bilingual education

'Weak' forms of bilingual education refer to the mainstreaming of children from minority language communities who are not allowed to use their home language in the school after a short adaptation period. For example, in immigrant communities where mainstream education is through a majority language, then 'weak' forms of bilingual education include the use of language assistants (language support staff) who help children move from their home language to the majority language of the classroom. In United States, transitional bilingual education allows a child to use their home language in the classroom for between one and six years, with the underlying aim of moving that child away from their home language to sole use of the majority language in the classroom. Thus, the term 'weak' is used as the aim is only the temporary use of the home language, with outcomes being relative monolingualism and enculturation in the majority language.

Such 'weak' forms of bilingual education have tended to be criticised by academics, yet supported by many politicians, policymakers and the public (Crawford 2003, 2004). For academics, such weak forms of bilingual education tend to result in lower achievement, poorer self-esteem, increased school absences and dropping out, the loss of the home language, and a slow acquisition of the majority language (Ovando, Collier and Combs 2003). One root cause of such negative outcomes is that the child's cognitive and scholastic ability that has been gained through the home language tends to be denied when they are made to operate through the majority language in the classroom. The child is expected to learn through a language that may be insufficiently developed to understand an increasingly complex and abstract curriculum. The child not only has to learn a new language, but learn through that new language, and may therefore find that understanding the subject curriculum is not easy.

For example, the language of the teacher and the curriculum is not the same as conversational 'street' language. Cummins (2000) defines this as the differences between (1) context reduced and context embedded communication, and (2) cognitively demanding and cognitively undemanding communication. Classroom language tends to be more context reduced and cognitively demanding. Conversational language, in contrast, is relatively more cognitively embedded and cognitively undemanding. The teacher may assume that conversational competence implies classroom language competence. Such an assumption may place a linguistic barrier to classroom learning and achievement.

Other social and emotional factors also appear to operate in 'weak' forms of bilingual education where there is a denial of the child's home language, heritage culture and cognitive abilities. When the child's home language is disallowed in the curriculum, there is an increased possibility of a child's self-esteem, self-confidence and self-concept suffering. The symbolism is that previous learning, early literacy skills, coming from a different culture and diverse life experiences are not valued by the school or its teachers. The child, its parents and extended family, community and religion may each be seen as rejected through the home language being denied. The educational environment becomes subtractive, even stressful. The chances of underachievement, even failure, are made more probable (Tse 2001).

In contrast, the viewpoint of politicians, policymakers and elements of the public is that such 'weak' forms of bilingual education are essential for many language minority children. Despite the evidence that minority language children tend to show an achievement gap with such forms of education, the political logic is as follows. Such children need to function economically, socially and culturally in majority language society (e.g. English in the United States). Therefore, they must learn the majority language at the earliest opportunity, and learn it well so as to maximize equality of educational and employment opportunity. This translates as maximal majority language experience as soon as the child enters kindergarten.

The political argument is ostensibly that only by education through the majority language will a child be given the greatest economic, social and cultural opportunities. However, underlying such a political belief is often the need to make a language minority group well assimilated, subordinate and governable. A key latent political aim is frequently to ensure that there is social control of the language minority, such that it stays subservient, docile and manageable. This applies typically to immigrant groups who in terms of culture, religion and potential power may be seen as potentially subversive. It can also apply to indigenous groups, whose potential rise to power is seen as producing potential contest, conflict and challenge.

Thus, the conclusion is that children do not typically become bilingual through 'weak' forms of bilingual education, As neither their home language, culture nor their motivation to become bilingual is supported. In contrast, three forms of 'strong' bilingual education are now portrayed. Each produces bilingual, bicultural and biliterate children.

3.2.   Immersion bilingual education

In Canadian immersion schooling, children from English-language homes take much of their elementary schooling through French. While there are different models of immersion education, from early total immersion to late immersion (see Baker 2006), the desired outcome is the same: children become fully bilingual and biliterate in French and English, operate in the subject curriculum in either language, and appreciate the two language solitudes of Canada. While early total immersion tends to be the form that maximally delivers these expected outcomes, success can still occur with older children (middle and late immersion) and less of the curriculum taught through French (partial immersion). Not only does immersion schooling occur in Canada as a success story, but (with variations to suit local and historical contexts) language immersion education has shown effectiveness in Finland, Colombia, Scotland, Switzerland, Wales and Ireland (Johnstone 2002; Baker 2006).

Immersion bilingual education in Canada is an additive experience. That is, the child's first language English does not suffer as the result of a learning French or through the medium French. Immersion teachers also are usually fully bilingual, providing a powerful role model of successful bilingualism. Canadian immersion bilingual education has robust research support not only in terms of overall achievement of its graduates, but also in strategies for language teaching, curriculum delivery and language allocation (Johnstone 2002).

3.3.   Dual Language Schools

There is research backing and an increasing volume of supportive literature for Dual Language education in the United States (Thomas and Collier 2002; Lindholm-Leary 2001). Sometimes called Two Way bilingual education, a typical dual language program has approximately equal numbers of language minority and language majority students in the same classroom. The policy is usually for both languages to be used to teach the curriculum, but in ways that keep clear boundaries between those languages. For example, in some Dual Language schools, the curriculum is taught through one language on one day, a different language on the next day, in strict rotation. Instead of whole days, the alternating period can be half days or even whole weeks. For both minority and majority language children, the second language is learnt almost entirely through content rather than by direct language instruction. However, specific attention to syntax and vocabulary, for example, may be effective and efficient.

Such Dual Language schools tend to produce children with proficiency in both languages, with higher academic achievement than comparable minority language children who are mainstreamed, and children who have positive intercultural attitudes (Thomas and Collier 2002; Lindholm-Leary 2001). Such children may also have value-added language and cultural attributes for the employment market, such that Dual Language schools can produce economic gains for their children (Genesee *et al.* 2005).

While Dual Language schools mostly exist in the United States, similar approaches have been documented outside of the United States. In Israel and

Macedonia there are examples of dual language peace schools (Bekerman 2005; Tankersley 2001). For example, the research of Bekerman (2005) in Israeli Dual Language (Arabic and Hebrew) schools depicts such bilingual education as an attempt to enable Jewish and Palestinian children and their families to live together peacefully, cooperatively and harmoniously. Such schools represent bottom-up attempts to deliver peace at community level. As will be discussed later, language education is closely linked with political ideology and objectives.

3.4.   Heritage language bilingual education

Heritage language bilingual education attempts to maintain, even revitalise language minority and minority languages. Essentially, such bilingual education enrols children from language minority homes and teaches, at least in the early years, most of the curriculum through the medium of a heritage language. For example, in the United States, some Navajo children attend heritage language schools whose aims include reversing language shift, maintaining one of the many indigenous languages of United States, as well as delivering quality education (McCarty 2003, 2004; McCarty and Bia 2002). Such heritage language schools may also have a small proportion of language majority children (Hickey 2001). Thus under one roof there may be the immersion of majority language speakers in a minority language, and heritage language learning.

In such heritage language schools, more rather than less of the curriculum may be taught through the minority language, sometimes reducing through the grades. For example, 90 % or more of the curriculum content may be through the home language when a child commences school, reducing to around 50 % with a child leaves for secondary schooling.

In such schools, curriculum content may also reflect the desire to preserve heritage culture, inculcate values and understandings from heritage cultural traditions, preserve indigenous and occasionally immigrant literacies and lifestyles. A heritage language school will also ensure that the child develops bilingually, with full competence in the majority language. Biliteracy or multiple literacies are typically encouraged (Blackledge 2000). In many countries, children in heritage language bilingual education at the elementary level move to relatively monolingual secondary education through the medium of the majority language. However, there are examples in the Basque region, Catalonia and Wales where children can take all their education, from preschool through to university, through the minority language. Such a decision may affect a chance language balance. When a child continues in a 'strong' former bilingual education through to secondary schooling, then bilingual language development, biliteracy, biculturalism, the status of the minority language, and dark earnings potential of being bilingual are all increased.

A bilingual education typology is a valuable starting point for a specification of key components around which school systems differ, and which locate varying aims, strategies and politics. However, these schools also have many elements in common. The following selection of major components of bilingual education helps portray the variety in the nature, aims, outcomes and ethos of a bilingual school. Baker and Jones (1998) and Baker (2006) provide a more exhaustive portrayal. Such components will affect a child becoming more or less bilingual in 'strong' forms of bilingual education.

4.   The components of bilingual education

4.1.   The type of child

A first component around which bilingual schools differ is the type of child attending that school. When a majority language child learns a new language, the home language is unlikely to be replaced by a new school language. In such an additive language context, the child becomes bilingual or multilingual at no expense to their first language. In contrast, there are children who come from a minority language background, and for whom the school language experience is likely to be mostly or totally monolingual in a majority language. This particularly occurs with immigrant children and those from non-indigenous language communities, but also from 'native' language groups (e.g. Native American Indians in the United States). For such children, bilingual education is a misnomer. It is the children attending the school that are bilingual, not the mission, learning approach or outcome of the school. In contrast, minority language children may alternatively experience a 'strong' form of bilingual education that encourages the fruition of their minority language as well as the development of one or more majority languages.

A consideration of the type of children attending bilingual education indicates the complexity of a school profile. A bilingual school may have a mixture of majority and minority language children, such that the language experience within the school may be different for children of different home backgrounds. In Celtic bilingual schools, one classroom may contain a combination of English first language children and children from homes where Irish, Gaelic, Manx Gaelic or Welsh is the first language. Immersion and heritage language models are combined within one classroom and one school.

4.2.   The language balance of children

This first component leads on to the language balance of the children within a classroom. For example, are all or most of the children from a language majority background (as in immersion bilingual education)? Is there an attempt, as in dual language schools, for a balance between majority and minority language children? Are most or all of the children from language minority homes? Are such children from indigenous, or long-standing or recent immigrant language homes and communities?

This is particularly important, not only in teaching strategies, but also in the status of languages within schools (Lindholm-Leary 2000, 2005; Hickey 2001). Where majority language children predominate, then the higher status of that language tends to be reinforced. Even when the teacher attempts to ensure that learning is through a minority language, once children talk informally in the classroom, then the majority language may be higher status and most used. This majority language dominance is often apparent in the playground. When one child does not prefer to speak in the minority language, children may switch to using the majority language, as that language becomes the common denominator.

Researching in Ireland, Hickey (2001) found that in mixed language classrooms, children from minority language homes tended to switch to English. Such children had less language effect on majority language speakers than those English-only speakers had on Irish speakers. Majority language students immerse native speakers in the majority language. Teachers tended to tailor their language to accommodate second language (Irish) learners. This dual effect tends to support the development of bilingualism in majority language speakers rather than minority language speakers.

This suggests that the numerical balance of minority language native speakers and learners of a minority language is important, possibly being tilted to a predominance of minority language speakers. Also, it is important to support and enrich the first language competences of native speakers of a minority language in such schools. This implies the possible separation of children of different language abilities for 'language instruction' sessions while avoiding language group separation and discrimination.

United States dual language classrooms have a mixture of majority language speakers who are learning through the minority language and native speakers of that minority language. This can mean two different language agenda: minority language speakers acquiring the high status majority language; majority language acquiring the minority language. The language balance of the classroom is important in achieving such dual aims.

4.3.   The balance of languages in the classroom

The third component in bilingual education is the balance in the use of two or more languages in the school and classroom. There are a number of subcomponents, for example the relative amount of use of two or more languages on walls, announcements, in non-curriculum activities such as school assemblies, the language of the playground, as well as the language of the classroom. In the classroom, what is the balance between the use of two languages? Is the majority language used almost entirely, or is the minority language also used systematically and comprehensively, or for temporary scaffolding? One variety of immersion education (early total immersion) teaches almost entirely through the second language in the first grade, moving gradually to around 50:50 usage in the final grades of elementary schooling. Many Dual language schools in the U.S. attempt to use each language on a 50:50 rotational basis. Heritage language schools may initially teach almost 100% through the minority language, slowly introducing the majority language as children proceed through elementary schooling.

Typically, in bilingual education, as children move through the grades, less use is made of the minority language and more use is made of the majority language. However, some heritage language schools maintain a strong balance towards the minority language throughout the elementary, even secondary (high school) curriculum. This is to attempt to counter-balance the higher status and use of the majority language outside the school. However, literacy in the majority language is typically regarded as essential, with induction around the ages of seven to eight common, with full biliteracy desired by the ages of nine and ten.

4.4.   The allocation of languages in the curriculum

A key and sometimes controversial issue is: what curriculum areas, subjects and topics are taught through the majority and minority language? For example are mathematics and science only taught through the majority language? What role is given to the minority language in 'modern' pursuits such as computing and in less literacy based areas (e.g. sports, craft and design technology)? The attraction is sometimes to teach mathematics and science in the majority language (e.g. English). This may be defended as scientific publications and higher education science courses tend to be in a majority and not minority language. However, such a decision serves to reduce the status of the minority language. It may send signals to the children that the majority language has more functional and prestigious value. The minority language may be perceived to have a restricted usage that connects more with the past than the present, heritage and history rather than modernity and progression.

Dual Language schools strategically use both languages to teach the curriculum. By alternation, status issues are mostly avoided, with the added advantage of children becoming comfortable in both languages in the curriculum. There are dual language school exceptions, for example where different languages are allocated for different content areas (Gómez, Freeman and Freeman 2005).

4.5.   School personnel

The fifth component concerns the language profile (and hence role models)
of teachers, teacher support staff, administrative staff and Headteachers / Principals. Key issues include: to what extent such staff are bilingual or multilingual? Do such staff use both of their languages and encourage children to do the
same? Or does the school hire minority language personnel who only use the
majority language in school and become 'internal colonisers'? If staff use both
languages with children, are they good role models for both of those languages,
or are they fluent in one language, not so fluent in the other? Are the senior staff
in school monolingual, providing a strong signal that only the majority language
is important in employment, promotion and affluence?

Thus a foundational ingredient into a bilingual school is the characteristics
and language proficiency of the teachers and other support staff, their own biculturalism or multiculturalism, attitudes to minority languages and minority
students, and their professional and personal identity (Morgan 2004; Varghese
2004; Varghese, Morgan, Johnston and Johnson 2005; Howard *et al.* 2005).
Such teachers need to be positive towards students' language and cultural backgrounds, sensitive to their home and community contexts, responding to
children's language and cultural needs, celebrating diversity and recognizing
the linguistic and cultural gifts of such children (Benson 2004).

As Benson (2004) reminds us in the context of developing countries, bilingual teaching is often more challenging than monolingual teaching, frequently
occurring in relatively economically deprived locations with power and status
divisions between language / ethnic groups. Teachers are expected to address
such inequalities, provide cultural and linguistic capital, meet high stakes test
standards for oracy, literacy and numeracy, bridge the home and school gap,
become respected members of the community, and campaign for educational
reform and innovation. The roles include "pedagogue, linguist, innovator, intercultural communicator, community member, and even advocate of bilingual
programmes" (Benson 2004: 207–8).

This school personnel component also engages a question about the training
of teachers for bilingual education. Educating teachers to work in the bilingual
environment, and particularly to use both languages in a well-designed manner
in the classroom, is internationally quite rare. For example, training teachers to
allocate two or more languages within the same time period (e.g. in Williams'
(2000) 'translanguaging' notion of input (e.g. reading) in one language with
output (e.g. writing) in a different language) is quite rare in teacher training.
Emphasis is often placed on teachers establishing working relationships with
minority language homes and communities, yet teacher induction into styles
and approaches in successfully doing this is not always apparent in teacher
professional development. There are exceptions, with the training of immersion

teachers in Canada and Finland, and the detailed advice that is available to teachers in Dual Language schools in the United States, providing models for progression (Baker 2006).

4.6.   The nature of curriculum resources

The next component concerns the nature of curriculum resources. Are most curriculum materials experienced by children only in the majority language (e.g. science and mathematics textbooks)? How plentiful, professionally produced, high-quality are the resources produced for minority language content areas? Are the minority language materials mostly home produced, local and dated? How is the minority language represented when instruction is aided by modern technology, for example use of the World Wide Web and e-learning? In multilingual situations, does the curriculum celebrate the diversity of multiple languages (e.g. South Africa; community language contexts in the United Kingdom and Germany; immigrant language situations in the United States)? Are some languages promoted more than others (e.g. indigenous rather than immigrant languages)?

Immersion schools access curriculum resources in both majority languages (e.g. French and English in Canada). This tends to provide relatively greater choice, and up to date good-quality material. It is heritage language schools, in contrast, that tend to find it more difficult to access modern, glossy and comprehensive curriculum materials. In some heritage languages, there may be a stronger oral than literacy tradition, relatively sparse materials in that language, requiring hard-pressed teachers to create their own local offerings. When a region has a variety of heritage languages (e.g. over 300 languages in London), then such challenges can be compounded.

4.7.   The aims of bilingual education

On the surface, 'strong' forms of bilingual education aim to create bilingualism, biliteracy and sometimes multiculturalism in their children. Effective bilingual schools, particularly when compared with mainstream monolingual schools, are typically expected to show that their children have (i) comparable majority language achievement to those in mainstream monolingual schools (ii) literacy in the majority language, and (iii) performance throughout the curriculum that is at least equal to that of peers in mainstream schools. Value-addedness in bilingual education is achieved by children becoming competent in minority language oracy and literacy, with personality (e.g. self-esteem) and social adjustment (e.g. tolerance of diversity) also being desirable.

Thus bilingual children are typically expected to show the same levels and types of success as their peers in monolingual (mainstream) schools, but in addition, to achieve bilingualism and biliteracy at no cost to general academic achievement. 'Strong' forms of bilingual education have been remarkable in delivering this expectation, and this will be considered later.

Below the surface, bilingual education is expected to deliver much more this. There are underlying aims and ambitions, latent missions and political pressures.

For example, heritage language schools are a major component in language planning. The survival, maintenance and revitalization of the large number of dying languages in the world requires bilingual education to play its part in producing new speakers (Baker 2000). That is, part of the *raison d'être* of heritage language schools is reversing language shift (Fishman 1991). Families tend to produce a shortfall in reproducing a heritage language in their children. Some minority language parents raise their children in the majority language only. Bilingual education then has the function of addressing this shortfall by producing sufficient language speakers in school to replenish the heritage language stock. Language lessons may produce a few new language speakers, but a more secure and effective language production line is 'strong' bilingual education.

That heritage language education is part of the politics of language planning exemplifies a crucial point: there is no understanding of bilingual education without understanding local and national politics. The aims, mission, targets and objectives of a bilingual school typically relate to the expectations and pressures of politicians, central and local policymakers, and sometimes parents as stakeholders and customers.

The aims of a school reflect deeper underlying politics and pressures. A school or education system may announce that it aims for full bilingualism and biliteracy, or for limited bilingualism, for monolingualism in a majority language or for multilingualism. Behind this declaration will be the demands of those in power, and the pressure of national and local politics. Bilingual education directly relates to political ideologies, for example, the assimilation of immigrants, the integration of disparate cultural and ethnic groups, indigenous language maintenance, or cultural pluralism.

'Weak' forms of bilingual education, and particularly movements that attempt to eradicate bilingual education (e.g. Proposition 227 in California), are based less on education than on politics. In immigrant communities and community language contexts, there is often pressure on schools to move children not only from the home language into the majority language, but also particularly to move each child from their heritage and home culture into enculturation in the majority language society. The political pressure will often be for assimilation of recent and long-standing immigrant populations into mainstream society, attempting to replace their heritage identity with a new identity that is loyal to the dominant language, culture and politics. Social cohesion, a common identity, minimising potentially subversive minority groups is a latent political ideology that is translated into school systems, the subject curriculum and school ethos. Children become more than bilingual through bilingual education.

Alternatively, a bilingual school may work for an additive experience, linguistically, culturally and socially. In such schools there is maintenance of a home language and a cultural enrichment, with an emphasis on maintenance of minority languages and cultures, and additive rather than subtractive approaches to language and culture. But politics lurks behind immersion education. Such immersion programs are regarded as giving the majority group in society (e.g. English speaking Canadian children) the bilingual proficiency to maintain their socioeconomic dominance in Canada. Quebec politicians sometimes argue that French first language speakers' historic dominance in obtaining French speaking jobs is threatened by such immersion students. Immersion education can be perceived as giving English-speaking first language children an economic and vocational advantage, making the motivation less about education and language, and more about having value-addedness in the jobs and promotion market, and providing an opportunity for monetary advancement.

4.8.   The economic value of bilingual education

A little-discussed component of bilingual education is its economic attributes, including for children. Dutcher's (2004) analysis of heritage language education shows the importance of this dimension. From international evidence from Haiti, Nigeria, the Philippines, Guatemala, Canada, New Zealand, United States (Navajo), Fiji, the Solomon Islands, Vanuatu and Western Samoa, she concludes that there are similar costs for bilingual education as for mainstream (monolingual) programs. Bilingual education is not a more costly option, and has comparable expenditure costs to mainstream programs. However, 'strong' forms of bilingual education have cost benefits (e.g. reducing dropout rates, and the number of children repeating grades). 'Strong' forms of bilingual education provide higher levels of achievement in less years of study. Student progress is faster and their higher achievement benefits society by less unemployment and a more skilled work force.

A World Bank cost-effectiveness study on bilingual education in Guatemala estimated that cost benefits due to bilingual education were in the order of 33.8 million US dollars per year (World Bank 1997; Dutcher 2004). Also, individual earnings rose by approximately 50 % when individuals received a 'strong' form of bilingual education.

5.   The effectiveness of bilingual education

Generally, strong forms of bilingual education have been shown by research to produce success stories at the individual, institutional and systems levels (Baker 2006). The evidence from both Canadian immersion and United States Dual Language schools is relatively strong in supporting the effectiveness of such models of bilingual education. As an overview, the findings tend to be that children learn another language and literacy at no cost to their overall academic achievement nor to their first language skills. Indeed, there is evidence to suggest that Canadian immersion students tend to outperform their peers in mainstream monolingual programs (Swain 1997).

Similarly, United States research evaluations tend to suggests that dual language students show superior performance to minority language children who are mainstreamed not only in content areas but also in English-language competency (Thomas and Collier 2002; Lindholm-Leary 2001). Such a finding regarding English-language development appears illogical to many parents and politicians. Their expectation is that children educated solely through the medium of English would develop the strongest English-language competence. Research tends to suggests this is not the case. Dual language schools build on the language competence of children rather than rejecting it (as does mainstreaming and transitional bilingual education for example). Given that such Dual Language schools produce an additive linguistic and cultural environment, and given the acceptance of the child's home language rather than disparagement as in 'weak' forms of bilingual education, then linguistically and psychologically the child appears to gain from such strong forms of bilingual education, including in English-language development in the United States.

While scholars are mostly agreed that effectiveness research generally supports 'strong' forms of bilingual education, nevertheless there is criticism that such research tends to be too small-scale, unsophisticated in statistical analysis, narrow in measures of school and individual success, and insufficiently objective (Baker 2006).

One research limitation that is difficult to resolve is that the children who attend strong forms of bilingual education tend to be self-selecting, or at least their parents are self selecting. That is, the children who attend bilingual education are not a random sample of the population, but rather a group that may be more enthusiastic about becoming bilingual, biliterate and multicultural. The random assignment of children to experimental groups that is required in a pure experiment is ethically suspect. Therefore, there is a chance of an immediate sampling bias towards finding success in bilingual education.

Another criticism of such bilingual education effectiveness research is that researchers may commence with inherent beliefs that strong forms of bilingual education will be superior. Scholars who are committed to linguistic diversity, cultural pluralism, language minority politics and empowerment may commence with a hidden agenda. Do personal ideologies among researchers lead to biases in the research design and analysis, such that researchers tend to deliver findings that fit their own beliefs and preferences (Hakuta 2002)?

6.   Effective bilingual classrooms

As discussed above, research has examined the effectiveness of different models of bilingual education. Such research tends to be aimed at those who decide policy and provision. These macro evaluations do not tend to address the practical bilingual classroom issues that teachers daily encounter (e.g. teaching and learning classroom strategies using two languages). Examples of major and current strategies for effective bilingual schools and classrooms follow. Each of these is important in producing bilingual children through bilingual education.

6.1.   Shared vision, mission and goals among staff

A consensus, clarity, consistency in application and collaboration in realizing the language aims and targets of the bilingual school is needed among school staff. What language learning outcomes are desired and achieved? Do the process strategies (e.g. allocation of two languages across the content curriculum) optimize achievement across different subjects?

6.2.   Leadership

The leadership of the school is a crucial factor, and ideally the appointee is expert in bilingualism, bilingual education, language learning plus has a fine understanding of the local community's language networks. Having a clarity of purpose while empowering all staff in decision-making processes tends to be a fine balance with rich rewards. Effective leaders may extend their leadership into the community, liaising with families and community leaders.

6.3.   Staff professional development and training

Staff professional development can be designed to help all staff effectively serve language minority and language majority students. For example, staff development programs can sensitize teachers to students' language and cultural backgrounds, increase their knowledge of second language development and help develop effective curriculum approaches in teaching language minority students (Howard *et al.* 2005). Wong Fillmore and Snow (2000) define specific teacher competencies that bilingual teachers need based on their multiple roles as classroom communicators, educators, evaluators and community workers.

6.4.   Literacy, biliteracy and multiliteracies

An effective curriculum tends to include bilingual and biliteracy development across the curriculum (including in sciences and information technology), with smooth transitions across ages and stages. Biliteracy or multiliteracies can be developed throughout the subject curriculum.

An effective bilingual school typically emphasizes biliteracy because there are multiple advantages at the individual and societal levels. For individuals, biliteracy reinforces and develops both oral languages in terms of, for example, vocabulary and fluency. At both the individual and the group level, minority language literacy gives that language increased functions, usage and status. It also helps standardize the corpus of a minority language. Literacy in the minority language enables knowledge, ideas, wisdom and understandings to be accessed and reproduced. Reading literature in two or more languages may be for education and recreation, instruction and gratification. Whether minority language literature is regarded as aiding moral or religious teaching, of value as an artistic form, or as a means of vicarious experience, literacy becomes both an emancipator and an educator.

6.5.   Assessment

An equitable testing and assessment policy that is based on desired learning outcomes is a key part of the curriculum. Such assessment may be driven by national accountability, standards-driven requirements (e.g. high stakes testing in the U.S.). A political focus is sometimes on whether bilingual 'immigrant' children are 'failing' (e.g. the emphasis on English language proficient in the U.S.), and on the 'achievement gap' among 'immigrant' bilingual children that has nothing to do with their bilingualism. Assessment also concerns screening, diagnosis, record keeping, feedback to parents, children and teachers, selection and certification and not just the current emphasis on monitoring standards and accountability. Such uses emphasize the more individual and humanistic treatment of bilingual children in school.

6.6.   Supportive ethos and environment

The language minority child may experience prejudice and discrimination resulting from the subordinate status of their language minority group. Such negative experiences (inside and outside school) may lower their self-esteem and create low expectations. This makes the monitoring of group integration and academic achievement in school important. A supportive language and cultural environment is needed where students feel they are cared for as well as educated, an environment that values cultural, ethnic and racial diversity (Montecel and Cortez 2002).

6.7.   High expectations

High expectations for language minority children are important among teachers, parents and the children themselves. When bilingual students come from materially impoverished homes, with relatively low aspirations present in the family and community, then low expectations may too easily and implicitly be embedded in a schools' ethos. Instead, high expectations need to be communicated to such students, with a celebration of their linguistic and cultural diversity.

6.8.   Parents

Plentiful parental involvement, with home–school collaboration is typically a major dimension of bilingual school effectiveness. Regular two-way communication can ensure a synthesis and harmonization in bilingual and biliteracy development (e.g. parents helping their child to read and write in both the majority and minority language). Parents can also become partners with the teachers. Moll (1992) encouraged parents to bring their 'funds of knowledge' into the classroom, to extend the curriculum. For example, parents are repositories of family and community history and heritage, wisdom and cultural understandings, and can share these in the classroom.

6.9.   Code-switching in the classroom

Codeswitching is frequent if not normal in most bilingual classrooms. Ferguson (2003) suggests that codeswitching "is not only very prevalent across a wide range of educational settings but also seems to arise naturally, perhaps inevitably, as a pragmatic response to the difficulties of teaching content in a language medium over which pupils have imperfect control" (2003: 46). Yet Lin (1996) has shown that codeswitching in Hong Kong classrooms is predictable and patterned, and has important pedagogic and social functions (e.g. signaling the start of a lesson or a transition in the lesson, specify an interaction with a particular student, or when move disciplining).

7.   Conclusions

There are many potential societal, ethnic group and community benefits of 'strong' forms of bilingual education such as: continuity of heritage, language maintenance and revitalization, cultural transmission and cultural vitality, empowered and informed citizenship, raising school and national achievement levels, social and economic inclusion, socialization, social relationships and networking, ethnic identity, and ethnic group self-determination and distinctiveness. However, perhaps the strongest support for bilingual education tends to derive from eight interacting potential advantages of bilingual education that are claimed for children (Baker 2006).

First, bilingual education frequently enables a student's two languages to attain higher levels of language competency enabling children to engage in wider communication across generations, regions and cultural groups. Second, bilingual education can develop a broader enculturation, a more sensitive view of different ethnicities, religions and cultures. Third, 'strong' forms of bilingual education frequently lead to a child engaging in literacy practices in two or more languages. This adds more uses to an individual's language (e.g. employment), widening the choice of literature for enjoyment, giving more opportunities for understanding different perspectives and viewpoints, and leading to a deeper understanding of history and heritage, traditions and territory.

Fourth, research on Dual Language schools, Canadian immersion education and heritage language education all indicate that classroom achievement is increased through dual language curriculum strategies (Cummins 2000). Fifth, research suggests that children with two well-developed languages share cognitive benefits (e.g. metalinguistic abilities, divergent and creative thinking). Sixth, children's self-esteem may be raised in bilingual education for minority language students (Cummins 2000). The opposite occurs when a child's home language is replaced by the majority language.

Seventh, bilingual education can aid the establishment of a more secure identity at a local, regional and national level. Achieving Welsh or Native American identities may be enhanced by the heritage language and culture being celebrated and respected in the classroom. Eighth, in some regions (e.g. Catalonia, Scandinavia) there are economic advantages for having experienced bilingual (or trilingual) education. Being bilingual can be important to secure employment, particularly when there is a customer interface that requires more than one language. Thus, bilingual education is increasingly seen as delivering relatively more marketable employees than monolingual education.

These eight advantages make 'strong' forms of bilingual education child-centered, value-added over mainstream education, and worthy of expansion. It also leave the uncomfortable question of whether any child who is denied the chance to become bilingual through the family or the school is being linguistically, culturally, cognitively deprived.

References

Baker, Colin
   2000   Three perspectives on bilingual education policy in Wales: Bilingual education as language planning, bilingual education as pedagogy and bilingual education as politics. In: R. Daugherty, R. Phillips and G. Rees (eds.), *Education Policy in Wales: Explorations in Devolved Governance.* 102–126. Cardiff: University of Wales Press.
Baker, Colin
   2006   *Foundations of Bilingual Education and Bilingualism* (4th edition). Clevedon: Multilingual Matters.
Baker, Colin and Sylvia Prys Jones
   1998   *Encyclopedia of Bilingualism and Bilingual Education.* Clevedon: Multilingual Matters.
Bekerman, Z.
   2005   Complex contexts and ideologies: bilingual education in conflict-ridden areas. *Journal of Language, Identity, and Education* 4,1: 1–20.
Benson, Carol
   2004   Do we expect too much of bilingual teachers? Bilingual teaching in developing countries. *International Journal of Bilingual Education and Bilingualism* 7, 2 and 3: 204–221.
Blackledge, Adrian
   2000   *Literacy, Power and Social Justice.* Stoke on Trent: Trentham.
Crawford, James
   2003   *Hard Sell: Why is Bilingual Education so Unpopular with the American Public?* (EPSL-0302–102-LPRU). Tempe: Arizona State University, Language Policy Research Unit. http://www.asu.edu/educ/epsl/LPRU/features/brief8.htm
Crawford, James
   2004   *Educating English Learners: Language Diversity in the Classroom.* Los Angeles: Bilingual Education Services.
Cummins, Jim
   2000   *Language, Power and Pedagogy: Bilingual Children in the Crossfire.* Clevedon: Multilingual Matters.
Dutcher, Nadaline
   2004   *Expanding Educational Opportunity in Linguistically Diverse Societies* (2nd edition). Washington, DC: Center for Applied Linguistics.
Ferguson, G.
   2003   Classroom code-switching in post-colonial contexts. In S. Makoni and U.H. Meinhof (eds), *Africa and Applied Linguistics.* AILA Review 16, 38–51. Amsterdam: John Benjamins.
Fishman, Joshua.A.
   1991   *Reversing Language Shift.* Clevedon: Multilingual Matters.

Genesee, Fred, Kathryn J. Lindholm-Leary, W. Saunders and Donna Christian
    2005   *Educating English Language Learners: A Synthesis of Empirical Evidence.*
            New York: Cambridge University Press.
Gómez, L., D. Freeman, and Y. Freeman
    2005   Dual language education: a promising 50–50 model. *Bilingual Research Journal* 29, 1, 145–164.
Hakuta, Kenji
    2002   Comment. International Journal of the Sociology of Language 155/156, 131–136.
Hickey, Tina
    2001   Mixing beginners and native speakers in minority language immersion: who is immersing whom? *Canadian Modern Language Review* 57, 3, 443–474.
Howard, E.R., J. Sugarman, Donna Christian, Kathryn Lindholm-Leary, D. Rogers
    2005   *Guiding Principles for Dual Language Education.* Washington, DC: Center for Applied Linguistics. http://www.cal.org/twi/guidingprinciples.htm
Johnstone, Richard
    2002   *Immersion in a Second or Additional Language at School: A Review of the International Research.* Stirling (Scotland): Scottish Centre for Information on Language Teaching. http://www.scilt.stir.ac.uk/pubs.htm
Lin, A.M.
    1996   Bilingualism or linguistic segregation? Symbolic domination, resistance and code switching in Hong Kong schools. *Linguistics and Education* 8,1, 49–84.
Lindholm-Leary, Katherine.J.
    2000   *Biliteracy for Global Society: An Idea Book on Dual Language Education.* Washington, DC: NCBE.
Lindholm-Leary, Katherine.J.
    2001   *Dual Language Education.* Clevedon: Multilingual Matters.
Lindholm-Leary, Katherine.J.
    2005   Review of Research and Best Practices on Effective Features of Dual Language Education Programs. http://www.lindholm-leary.com/resources/review_research.pdf
McCarty, Theresa L.
    2003   Revitalising indigenous languages in homogenizing times. *Comparative Education* 39, 2, 147–163.
McCarty, Theresa L.
    2004   Dangerous difference: a critical-historical analysis of language education policies in the United States. In J.W. Tollefson and A.B.M. Tsui (eds) *Medium of Instruction Policies: Which Agenda? Whose Agenda?* 71–96. Mahwah, NJ: Erlbaum.
McCarty, Theresa L. and F. Bia
    2002   *A Place To Be Navajo: Rough Rock and the Struggle for Self-Determination in Indigenous Schooling.* Mahwah, NJ: Lawrence Erlbaum.
Mejia, Anne-Marie de
    2002   *Power, Prestige and Bilingualism: International Perspectives on Elite Bilingual Education.* Clevedon: Multilingual Matters.
Moll, L.C.
    1992   Bilingual classroom studies and community analysis. *Educational Researcher* 21 (2), 20–24.

Montecel, M.R. and J.D. Cortez
2002   Successful bilingual education programs: development and the dissemination of criteria to identify promising and exemplary practices in bilingual
education at the national level. *Bilingual Research Journal* 26, 1, 1–10.
http://brj.asu.edu/content/vol26_no1/html/art2.htm

Morgan, B.
2004   Teacher Identity as Pedagogy: Towards a Field-Internal Conceptualisation
in Bilingual and Second Language Education. *International Journal of Bilingual Education and Bilingualism* 7, 2 and 3, 172188.

Ovando, Carlos J., Virginia P. Collier and M.C. Combs
2003   *Bilingual and ESL Classrooms: Teaching in Multicultural Contexts* (3rd
edition). New York: McGraw Hill.

Swain, Merrill
1997   French immersion programs in Canada. In J. Cummins and D. Corson (eds),
Bilingual Education. Volume 5 of the *Encyclopedia of Language and Education*. Dordrecht: Kluwer.

Tankersley, Dawn
2001   Bombs or bilingual programmes? Dual language immersion, transformative education and community building in Macedonia. *International
Journal of Bilingual Education and Bilingualism* 4, 2, 107–124

Thomas, Wayne P. and Virginia P. Collier
2002   *A National Study of School Effectiveness for Language Minority Students'
Long-Term Academic Achievement. Final report.* Washington, DC: Center
for Research on Education, Diversity and Excellence.

Tse, Lucy
2001   *"Why Don't they Learn English?" Separating Fact from Fallacy in the U.S.
Language Debate.* New York: Teachers College Press.

Varghese, M.
2004   Professional development for bilingual teachers in the United States: A site
for articulating and contesting professional roles. *International Journal of
Bilingual Education and Bilingualism* 7, 2 and 3, 222–237.

Varghese, M., B. Morgan, B. Johnston, and K.A. Johnson
2005   Theorizing language teacher identity: Three perspectives and beyond. *Journal of Language, Identity, and Education* 4, 1, 21–44.

Wiley, Terrence G.
2001   On Defining Heritage Language Education and Their Speakers. In J.K. Pey-
ton, D.A. Ranard and S. McGinnis (eds.), *Heritage Languages in America:
Preserving a National Resource*. 29–36. McHenry, IL: Delta Systems.

Williams, Cen
2000   Welsh-medium and bilingual teaching in the further education sector. *International Journal of Bilingual Education and Bilingualism* 3, 2, 129–148.

Wong Fillmore, L. and C. Snow
2000   *What Elementary Teachers Need to Know About Language.* Washington: Center for Applied Linguistics. http://www.cal.org/resources/digest/
0006fillmore.html

World Bank
1997   *Project Appraisal Document, Guatemala, Basic Education Reform Project.*
Washington, DC: World Bank.

Recommend readings

Baker, Colin
  2006   *Foundations of Bilingual Education and Bilingualism* (4th edition). Cleve-
          don: Multilingual Matters.
Cummins, Jim
  2000   *Language, Power and Pedagogy: Bilingual Children in the Crossfire.*
          Clevedon: Multilingual Matters.
Genesee, Fred, Kathryn J. Lindholm-Leary, W. Saunders and Donna Christian
  2005   *Educating English Language Learners: A Synthesis of Empirical Evidence.*
          New York: Cambridge University Press.
Mejia, Anne-Marie de
  2002   *Power, Prestige and Bilingualism: International Perspectives on Elite Bi-
          lingual Education.* Clevedon: Multilingual Matters.

II. Staying bilingual

6.   Bilingual children in monolingual schools

J. Normann Jørgensen and Pia Quist

1.   Introduction

In this paper we present research into and discussions about the language development of bilingual children in monolingual schools, particularly linguistic minority children attending majority schools. The bulk of research in this theme has been done in the industrialized societies which have received a growing number of immigrants (and refugees) over the past four decades. We claim that only one comprehensive theory has been developed which involves both linguistic, socio-political, and general educational aspects. This is the so-called threshold hypothesis (or rather a set of similar and specific hypotheses of which the threshold hypothesis is the most profiled version). We further claim that although the threshold hypothesis has been refuted, it has played a constructive role in our understanding of the issues involved. Its place has been taken by studies which are less oriented towards a comprehensive theory, but which are either focussed on language development and language use, or on educational issues and school achievement. The whole theme of minority children in majority schools has had quite extensive public attention in Europe and North America, sometimes in very negative ways. We present the different arguments, and the different approaches to them, before we conclude that being a minority student in a majority school is becoming increasingly hard.

2.   The Threshold Hypothesis

Around 1980 the only overarching theory about monolingual children in bilingual schools was developed. It contained an important perspective on the language development of school children, particularly children whose mother tongue was not usually the medium of instruction in their school. In some forms it was called the "threshold hypothesis" (for instance, Skutnabb-Kangas 1981), in other forms the "BICS-CALP distinction" (by Cummins 1979) which was later developed into a two-dimensional framework (Cummins 1981). In its original form the threshold hypothesis was suggested by Cummins (1976) and contained three levels of language development with two clear-cut thresholds in between. The crucial element of the theory was that there is a level of bilingual development, the lower threshold, under which the speaker is "semi-lingual" (a term later explicitly abandoned by Cummins, see Cummins 2000) with negative cognitive effects. Furthermore, there is a level, the upper threshold, above which the speaker enjoys "additive bilingualism" with positive cognitive effects. Between the two levels the speaker is a "dominant bilingual" with a strong L1 and a weak L2; according to the hypothesis, dominance-bilingualism has no specific cognitive effects. The implication for schooling lies in the idea that the level of L1 development of a minority student predicts the chances of an L2-medium teaching to succeed in helping the student become an "additive" bilingual. If the child in question has not developed her or his mother tongue to the lower threshold, teaching in L2 will have negative effects on the child's bilingualism and cognitive development. According to this line of thinking linguistic minority children should be taught through their mother tongue, at least until they have reached the lower threshold.

A long range of empirical studies which found that linguistic minority students generally did worse than majority students in the school systems was cited as evidence in favor of the threshold hypothesis. Skutnabb-Kangas (1981) (English version 1984) is a good example, listing a number of studies as support for the hypothesis. Skutnabb-Kangas also distinguishes between "elite" bilingualism in which children of high-SES parents pass the thresholds of language development with ease, and "popular" bilingualism in which children of low-SES parents struggle to reach just the lower threshold. The results of the studies quoted were also to a certain extent related to socio-economic differences, not least because linguistic minority students in the westernized industrial world more often than not belong to low-prestige, low-income families.

Cummins' distinction defines two basically different types of linguistic competence or proficiency. The one comprises the so-called "basic interpersonal communicative skills", and the other type covers "cognitive-academic language proficiency". The distinction has become known as the BICS-CALP distinction, and it differentiates between, on the one hand, the linguistic competence it takes to engage in everyday conversational language use and, on the other hand, the linguistic competence it takes to successfully participate in and benefit from the more abstract practices of the school, particularly through literacy.

These hypotheses, whether we consider them a related theoretical set or independent hypotheses, aim to describe the bilingual (and cognitive!) development of school children and to explain it in terms of a hierarchy of development which depends on, inter alia, socio-economic factors. They attempt to present an integrated view of socio-economic factors, language, cognitive development, and school achievement with respect to bilingual children in general, and linguistic minority children in majority societies in particular (this is in fact the only theoretical work to do so). The resulting conclusion for good educational planning is that schools should emphasize the teaching both in and of linguistic minority children's L1 until it has reached the lower threshold, and from then on the L2 can be gradually introduced, but not before. This has had concrete influence in several educational systems, or at least in the thinking of educators and education planners (such as North America, see Cline and Frederickson 1996, and Scandinavia, see Pedersen and Skutnabb-Kangas 1983). However, practical implications in overall systematic reorganization of school systems did not materialize in very many places (one such example being the Finnish-speaking minority in Sweden, see Paulston 1982).

The group of hypotheses had another effect, however. They inspired a wide range of criticism and thus challenged a good many scholars to look into the field. They were also integrated into the sometimes harsh political debates around bilingualism and linguistic minority students in schools in North America and Europe.

The hypotheses were criticized for being primitive because they tended to describe linguistic development as one-dimensional ("a half-baked theory of communicative competence", see Martin-Jones and Romaine 1986), and CALP has been attacked for probably being little more than another word for test wiseness (see Edelsky 1990). The group of hypotheses has also been criticized for being deficit hypotheses (Edelsky 1983), and for being very primitive in their view of education, seeing children as containers who could be more or less filled (Martin-Jones and Romaine 1986), and in the same vein for being too abstract and too sketchy for any practical purposes (Wiley 1996). The empirical evidence for the threshold hypothesis and the BICS-CALP distinction was weak in the first place. All the studies cited by Skutnabb-Kangas (1981) are certainly not inconsistent with her hypothesis, but they lend no specific, at best indirect, support to it. Toukomaa's and her studies (Toukomaa and Skutnabb-Kangas 1977; Skutnabb-Kangas and Toukomaa 1976) have been quoted both by Skutnabb-Kangas (1981) and by Cummins (2000) as empirical evidence for the threshold hypothesis, but with these studies as the only ones lending specific support to the relationship between language development and thresholds, the threshold hypothesis has little empirical support.

As theory of language and language skills, this group of hypotheses has been robustly refuted (although Cummins has taken up some elements of the discussion (2000, chapter 4) and defended some of his stances) and empirically there is little to say for it. Nevertheless it deserves credit for being the only general attempt at theorizing these issues in relation to each other, and it deserves credit for inspiring opposition. It should also be remembered that elements of the hypotheses are still quoted in educational debates.

3.   Multilingual practices in monolingual schools

Sociolinguistic discussions about the big issues have faded out somewhat. These include the relationship between social structures in society, as educational systems, and individual language development, including its relations to eventual school success. Controversial issues such as the general suppression of minorities and inequality in education have yielded to a greater emphasis on individuals and smaller groups and their individual relations. We have therefore not seen the construction of overarching theories involving the sociolinguistic aspects of language variation and the school success or failure of linguistic minority students. Likewise, discussions about linguistic development have more or less been detached from the discussions about school success. There are thus a couple of strands of work that can claim their legacy from the threshold hypothesis years.

First of all we have seen empirical studies of real-life minority children and their language development in majority schools (and in their homes), for instance Extra and Yağmur (2004). We have seen a number of studies dealing with the language practices of speakers who grow up with a minority mother tongue and attend school in a majority language, sometimes even with one or several foreign languages on the curriculum. Often these studies concentrate on the linguistic behavior of grade school students outside official classroom activity. Examples are Kotsinas (1998), Rampton (1995, 1999) and Cromdal (2000). Few studies have concentrated on the actual long-term language development of linguistic minority children in majority schools. In the following we shall go into detail with the largest of these, the so-called Køge Project.

The Køge Project is a longitudinal study of the linguistic development of Turkish-Danish grade school children from the beginning to the end of their school careers. During these years the project students, the majority of whom spoke little Danish at school start, were subjected to a typical Danish curriculum including mother tongue classes 3–4 hours a week (these classes were abolished nationwide in 2001), with one exception: the Turkish classes were integrated with the rest of the curriculum, while minority language classes in Denmark generally were not. The data from the Køge project include group conversations among the minority students, group conversations with majority peers, face-to-face conversations with Turkish-speaking adults and with Danish-speaking adults, and much more. One result is the gradually growing, but complex, importance of Danish vis-a-vis Turkish, see figure 1.

Figure 1 shows the percentage of Danish-based utterances (i.e. utterances which are entirely in Danish, or which involve non-Danish loanwords, but only Danish grammar) in group conversations among Turkish-Danish grade school students for each grade level, 1 through 9. By grade 9 Danish plays a much more important role than in grade 1. Interestingly, the graph does not show a steady

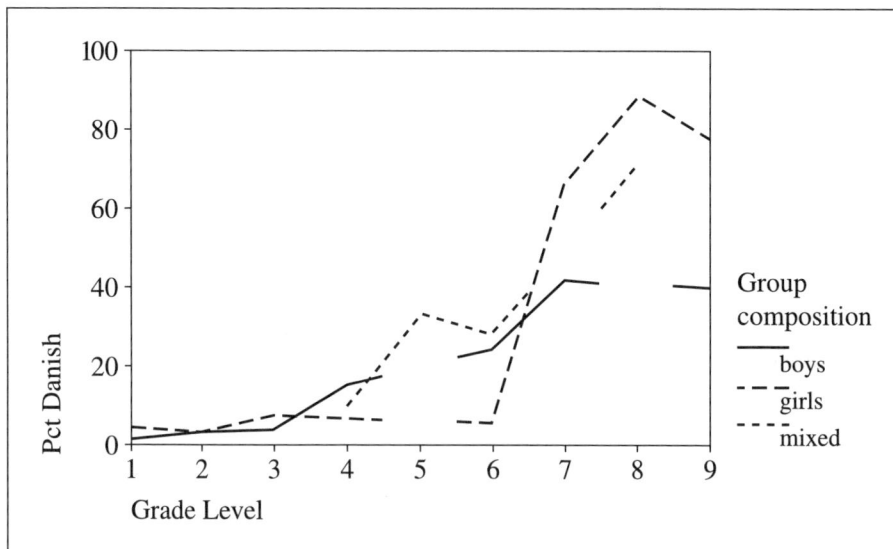

Figure 1. The percentage of Danish-based utterances in the group conversations among Turkish-Danish grade school students, grade 1–9. The solid line represents the boys' groups, the dashed line girls' groups, and the dotted line gender-mixed groups.

and continuous growth of the use of Danish. There is a peak in grade 5, and there is a fall in the use of Danish in grade 6. The gender composition of the groups is a likely explanation. The boys-only groups begin to use Danish in grade 4, and they continue to use some Danish, but by grade 9 they still use at least as much Turkish as Danish. The girls-only groups use almost no Danish at all until grade 7, but from then on they use almost only Danish. As it happens, in grade 5 we only have gender-mixed groups, and here all of the bilingual students use a certain amount of Danish – not very different from the amount of Danish used by the boys in grade 4 and 6. In other words, when girls are among girls, they speak Turkish – until grade 7 when they shift into Danish. But when girls are among boys, they do as the boys do. Boys, on the other hand, do not seem to change their way of speaking nearly as much as the girls do. The opposite seems to be the case in grade 8. We have compared the amount of Danish used by the boys in grades 7–9. In grade 8 when the boys are all in company with girls, they speak more Danish than in grade 7 and grade 9 when they are among boys (for instance, the boy Bekir uses 49 % Danish-based utterances in grade 7, 85 % in grade 8, and 56 % in grade 9; the boy Murat uses 47 % Danish-based utterances in grade 7, 77 % in grade 8, and 41 % in grade 9).

The explanation presented by the Køge Project is that there is identity work involved. A sociogram of the adolescent group that these speakers belong to was drawn when they were in the grade 8. Quist (1998: 113) finds that the most important boundary within the group is not ethnic, but gender-based. There are many friendship connections between monolinguals and bilinguals, i.e. across the ethnic boundary. However, there is only one single connection involving a boy and a girl, i.e. across the gender boundary. This may be part of the explanation why the use of Danish increases among girls in grade 5 and among boys in grade 8. The presence of classmates who are to a certain extent out-group members – or perhaps members of a different in-group – coincides with an increase in the use of the L2. In other words, an individual Turkish-Danish boy may have one in-group of Turkish-Danish boys, and another in-group of Turkish-Danish classmates, male or female, and the different in-groups are characterized by different linguistic behavior. Consequently, in these cases it is debatable whether Danish represents a "they-code" in Gumperz' (1982) terms. It would probably be more precise to describe different "we-codes" reserved for the different groups which the speakers belong to. But there is little doubt that their behavior with respect to code-choice is linked to their social relations.

There are several peaks in the bilingual students' language development in grade 5. The use of third languages, particularly English, increases in grade 5 and recedes afterwards. The Køge Project explains this by the fact that English was introduced to these students in grade 4, so by the beginning of grade 5 they were in the process of adding another code to those they already had. This involved a lot of language play (Crystal 1998) with this new linguistic toy (see Jørgensen 2003a). In grade 5 the amount of intersentential code-switching also peaks with about 40 per cent of the utterances being based in another language than the immediately preceding utterance (Jørgensen 2003a: 130).

This leads us to the development of code-switching patterns which has been studied extensively in the Køge project (for instance, Hansen 2003; Jørgensen 2003b). Hansen analyzes the code-switching practices of the bilingual students using Auer's (1995) categories. Hansen finds that the students seem to follow the same developmental path and that there is an implicational relationship between the categories suggested by Auer. The earliest code-switching is Auer's type I in which the interlocutors speak one language until a certain point at which time one of the speakers starts speaking another language, thereby contextualizing a point of reference or a point of view. The conversation may continue (for a while) in this language. All of the Turkish-Danish students use this practice very early in their school career, i.e. almost immediately after beginning systematic instruction in and through Danish. Auer's type IV, i.e. the insertion of lexemes and phrases from one language into a stretch of speech in another language, is almost simultaneous with type I. Type III appears somewhat later, for some as late as grade 6. In type III switching the speakers use both languages in their contributions, i.e. they code-switch intrasententially. Auer's type II – so-called language negotiation sequences in which the interlocutors for a while use different languages – is the latest one to appear, and not all students reach this point of the implicational scale. Hansen compares this development with the students' development of their Danish L2 as determined by Quist (1998, see below) and finds a surprising similarity in developmental patterns and eventual achievement. He argues that code-switching skills should be a central part of all assessments of individual bilingual proficiency.

Quist (1998) studies the acquisition of Danish structures by the Turkish-Danish students from grade 1 through 8. She uses Holmen's (1990; see also Holmen 1993) developmental line for the acquisition of Danish by linguistic minority students. Based on the first appearance of certain features in their "interactional focus", Quist ranks the minority students on a 5-point scale, grade by grade. Eventually all students reach the highest point, but they do so by different ages (the earliest in grade 1, the latest not before grade 10). In a separate sub-study, a quasi-matched guise test, Quist collects evaluations of 12 students, 10 of whom are Turkish-Danish. The evaluations were given by adult native speakers of Danish. The ranking of the speakers is quite close to the eventual ranking according to L2 development (see also Jørgensen and Quist 2001). Quist compares these differences in L2 development with the students' individual ranking in the social hierarchy of the group studied. She concludes that there is a strong relationship between language achievement and status in the social hierarchy. She refrains from deciding which is cause and which is effect, but the relationship is clear.

Jørgensen (2003b) finds that in general the girls lead the boys in the development of code choice patterns and that this holds true throughout their school years. The girls also use a wider range of different patterns in their code-switching practices than the boys do. The differences in bilingual behavior are related to differences in social status. The strongest individuals are girls who show great flexibility and creativity in their code-switching. The girls are (somewhat against received wisdom) more linguistically aggressive toward each other than toward boys, and more aggressive than boys are toward each other (see Jørgensen 2001 and Madsen 2003). This means that the strongest girls are very strong indeed and have a varied range of linguistic means at their disposal, while the lowest ranking individuals in the hierarchy are those girls whose code-switching skills are least developed.

The main conclusions to the Køge Project are that Danish gradually takes an increasingly prominent place in the language use of the linguistic minority students. But this does not happen along a nice straight line, or even in one dimension. Secondly, social relations among the students constitute a clearly visible non-linguistic factor relating to their language use, their L2 development, and their eventual school success. Thirdly, achievement in one (language) dimension is a good indicator of achievement on other and traditional measures (quasi-matched-guise test, school leaving grades in written Danish and oral Danish, teacher evaluations, etc.). Fourthly, the circumstances under which these students go to school seem to divide them into two groups. One is the group of high achievers who score very well on almost all measures, often at the very top. The other is a less homogenous group, where all members score below or well below average on all traditional measures of achievement. They do not rank very highly in the social hierarchy among their peers.

4.   Scholarly discussions about minority children in majority schools

A second thread of work relates to debates about and experiments with the organization of the education of linguistic minority children. Debates about these issues seldom reach a scholarly level. Most professional arguments about the schooling of linguistic minority students have cited linguistic, psychological, and educational aspects. On the more popular side there has been reference to ideological, political, and moral aspects. There are, however, also more scientifically sound discussions. We will go into one particular example of a scholarly debate, namely in Norway, which has seen a qualified and civilized discussion that has nevertheless included the political issues involved, and we shall take a brief look at Denmark and Sweden.

4.1.   The Norwegian debate

In 1983 the city government of Oslo decided to introduce a new concept into the school system. This was the so-called bicultural class which included an integrated bilingual education of linguistic minority children (at that time about 20 per cent of the school beginners), primarily in the beginning of their school careers. The council's decision was politically controversial and a bold move. It was not always successfully implemented, but by and large Oslo became a mirror against which other Scandinavian and international efforts in the same field were measured. Ten years later, the bicultural classes were abolished in a complex process of budget politics in the city government. This led to intense discussions, some of which were quite qualified. We have a good example in Brox (1995) and Hvenekilde (1994). Both publications originated in a scientific seminar which split apart in disagreement. The most important difference is characteristic of discussions which have been going on in the field in most European societies with post-World War II immigration and has to do with attitudes to the ultimate goal of schooling. On one side (in this case, Brox) the center of interest is the acquisition of the majority language as L2 by minority students. The argument for the concentration on Norwegian is given by Brox: "A shared language is a prerequisite for a functioning democracy. If we can not *discuss* with each other, it does not help with formally democratic institutions" (1995: 10, our translation). The focus on Norwegian does not exclude mention of the minority languages, although they are mostly not treated as an asset in themselves. It is argued that not only is a minimum of linguistic competence necessary for participation in social practice, but some degree of participation in social practice is also necessary for developing linguistic competence. The opposite side (Hvenekilde) argues that the political discourse about the education of linguistic minority students in Norway is biased, nationalist and sometimes even xenophobic. This side attempts, with references to ideological frameworks, to describe the strong desire among politicians to get rid of the minorities' languages and cultures. The minorities disturb the nation's unity and harmony, and the majority elite considers their cultures inefficient and useless in a modern industrialized society. The distinction between 'their' children and 'our' children – common among majority parents, teachers, and politicians – has been linked (Loona and Myklebust 1994) to the discourse in the late 1800s about working class children in the cities whose parents had migrated from the countryside. The authorities found that these parents did not value education and that 'bad homes' were taken to be the cause of many a child's school failure. The actions of the Oslo school authorities in the 1990s are "two steps backwards" to the 1850s and the prevailing educational ideology of that time: mainstreaming, normalizing, patronizing.

The bicultural classes were systematically supported starting in 1978, and their number gradually grew during the following years. The demolition began with a decision to decentralize the decision making process and to assign all students to the nearest district school. Hvenekilde (1994) notes that this looks nice as a pedagogical principle, but it effectively destroys the possibility of organizing minority groups, who are scarcely represented in the city. Later it was made voluntary for the schools to offer minority education, and in 1994–1995 the schools in Oslo were instructed not to give it at all.

The disagreement between Brox and Hvenekilde led to a so-called consensus conference in Norway in 1996 which further led to the publication of Hyltenstam et al. (1996) suggesting a clear and distinct role for the minority languages in the school, while at the same time emphasizing the great importance of Norwegian L2. This academically-oriented attempt to reach agreement never resulted in any political changes, and this experience is shared by scholars elsewhere, at least in Scandinavia (see Jørgensen 2005). In this process of discussion in Norway a vast array of issues, studies, and viewpoints were presented. Political standpoints were also analyzed and put into context. The debate is, if not unique, then rare with respect to its level of quality. However, minority mother tongue teaching has never re-appeared. In this respect Norway is probably typical of industrialized societies in which scholarship recommends multilingualism, and decision makers strive to maintain monolingualism.

4.2.   European Debates

Hegelund (2002) compares the official educational policies in Sweden and Denmark. She concludes that both countries have decided on policies strongly influenced by "a Herderian equation of nation, state and language" (Hegelund 2002: 170). Therefore, neither state "can currently be seen to plan for lasting minority multilingualism for the allochthonous minorities" (Hegelund 2002: 170–171). Sweden does indeed offer more generous minority language mother tongue teaching than Denmark (and indeed, since Hegelund finished her manuscript, Denmark has abolished the provision altogether), but the education foreseen in the basic Home Language Reform Act of 1977 has been systematically reduced ever since. It is thus characteristic of all the three Scandinavian states that an original attempt at securing the minority mother tongues a place in the educational system has utterly and totally failed with respect to what are considered non-indigenous minority languages. In Sweden's case this attempt apparently has had whole-hearted political support, although perhaps not always popular support. In Denmark and Norway the attempt had only half-hearted political and popular support.

It is a shared experience of many educational systems in the industrialized part of the world that children of linguistic minorities reach below average achievement in majority schools. At least since the 1960s this fact has been the cause of concern, and a range of policies have emerged, including educational experiments, largely in vain. The Council of Europe issued a number of resolutions which led to, among other things, the organization of special reception classes for immigrated linguistic minority children (Wittek 1992: 2). In 1977 the European Community Commission issued directive 77/486 which is a crucial document in official European policy. Article 2 of the directive states that the official languages must be taught, and teacher training should be provided for this special task. Article 3 requires support for the teaching of minority languages and cultures. In principle, these articles refer to the children of migrants who have migrated internally in the European Community, but in a separate document the ministers of education acknowledge that the articles should also be extended to cover children of other migrant minorities.

In the 1980s a range of educational experiments in member countries were carried out, and in the overall evaluation the conclusions strongly recommended continuation of teaching experiments involving minority languages (Reid and Reich 1992: 249–250). The European Parliament later adopted resolutions to the same effect, emphasizing the need to integrate the languages involved into the school curriculum. Local governments, typically at a sub-national level, sometimes also set in initiatives to solve the complicated set of problems surrounding the education of minority students. An excellent example is Reich et al. (2002) which was commissioned by the Landesregierung in Hamburg, a local German state. This publication cites a number of international studies and presents a series of "commonly accepted insights" (our translation).

First of all, individual and societal bilingualism is normal – not an aberration. Secondly, individual bilingualism has no negative cognitive effects. Thirdly, the first language and the second language of bilingual students can perfectly well work efficiently in co-operation in the individual's development. Fourthly, personal problems with the bilingualism of an individual do not stem from bilingualism, but from the (narrow or wide) social circumstances. Reich et al. (2002: 41) adds, importantly, that "the scientific systematization of the connection is however not yet so far progressed that general statements can be made" (our translation). Fifthly, the success or failure of bilingual students is related to the "interactional histories" between school and minority student. It is important to realize that changing school systems from concentrating on majority students to also cater to bilingual students, is a long and difficult process which must nevertheless be pursued. Sixthly, the report concludes that the best indicators of school success seem to be the students' socioeconomic status and command of the school language. Seventhly, and equally important, the Reich report finds that on the schools' side there are a range of factors which influence the chances of minority school success. The general atmosphere at the school, the curriculum and its meaningfulness to minorities, and teacher education are all relevant factors. Under all circumstances, the involvement of minority students' mother tongue seems to be a crucial and often forgotten element.

It is characteristic of the European scene that there is a difference between the supra-national and the national levels. At the supra-national level there is a well-documented and clear understanding of the issues involved, and there is a certain amount of political support for additive bilingualism and for the maintenance of minority languages in majority schools. However, at the national level national romanticist ideologies have proven harder to beat (cf. Hegelund's remark about Hegel's ongoing influence in Sweden and Denmark), and it is just as characteristic of this level that directive 77/486 has only been implemented in a few places. One of them was Denmark, which had officially introduced the directive, but for decades the Danish Ministry of Education systematically sabotaged mother tongue teaching of minority languages (Kristjánsdóttir 2003), and in 2001 the government abolished minority mother tongue teaching altogether. By and large, the strong national romanticist ideology of one nation – one language has undermined directive 77/486. School systems everywhere have nevertheless experimented with different ways of organizing the education of linguistic minority students, with developing special teaching materials, with teacher education, etc. Characteristically, the evaluation reports – when such reports exist – tend to support the involvement of minority languages. Hyltenstam et al. (1996) is a good example, concluding a long Norwegian debate by recommending integration of minority mother tongues into the school as school subjects. Hetmar (1991) is another good example – an evaluation study of a range of grade school development projects dealing with linguistic minority children in Denmark. Hetmar (1991: 179) specifically states that there are too few projects involving minority languages "and in the relationship between mother tongue teaching and the remaining school subjects. This should be taken up in the future" (our translation). Yet, whereas nation states at least in Europe often do not hesitate to provide teaching of – and through – foreign languages, particularly English, for their majority students, there is little and diminishing support for supporting the mother tongues of minority students. At a sub-national level (Hamburg, Oslo), we can sometimes also observe a certain understanding of the issues – but generally the impact does not last for very long. Particularly in Germany with its Länder-based education, sub-national authorities with very little understanding of issues of bilingualism can be found.

4.3.   North American Debates

In the United States the National Clearinghouse for Bilingual Education has supported the use of minority languages and assisted in the development of bilingual education. The political support on the national level has changed with the political color of the administration, but the educational establishment has been positive. The Collier and Thomas (1997, 2001) reports form a good example. These reports study and compare a number of educational programs designed for linguistic minority students in the USA. In a longitudinal study they compared several types of school organization. Enrichment bilingual programs were those which aimed at additive bilingualism for the students. So-called remedial bilingual programs also involved the minority language, but the eventual goal was focussed on English, i.e. transitional bilingualism. Different types of English-only programs were also involved. Collier and Thomas compare test results in standardized tests for a large cohort of students in these different programs. Their results unequivocally favor the programs which involve the minority mother tongue the most and disfavor the English-only programs.

As in Europe, however, there is a strong politically motivated resistance against accepting the educational implications of such studies. Motivated and financed by a private millionaire crusader with a right-wing political agenda, a political move to abolish bilingual education was adopted by a popular vote in California in 1998. Later, a couple of other states followed, and the resistance grew elsewhere in the early 2000s. Both in the United States and in Europe these developments cannot be fully understood if we do not consider the general political trends in society, i.e. a clear move in a direction which supports nationalism even at the cost of rejecting scholarly evidence.

5.   Public debates about linguistic minority children in majority schools

The discrepancy between scholarly insight and political and educational reality is sometimes much more obvious elsewhere than what we have observed in Oslo. This leads us to a third phenomenon with affinity to the threshold hypothesis, i.e. the peculiarly aggressive debate between scholars and linguists on the one hand, and lobbyists, politicians, and decision makers on the other hand. This debate has sometimes turned ugly and seems to be shared by several, if not all, societies in the western world. It has been utterly harsh in the USA, but we have also witnessed a shrill tone and a sharp front between scholars and politicians elsewhere.

Two major issues are involved in these discussions. The first one is the relationship between the majority language and the minority language (or minority languages) in the educational system, and in society at large. Both the English-only movement in the United States and similar movements elsewhere express themselves vehemently against any official public use of other languages than the majority language (Crawford 2000). The strong trend in the media (cf. Galindo 2003) is also against the protection of minority languages and against bilingual education. Arguments can be both nationalist (Herder inspired) and liberalist.

The second issue is the distinction between learning a language and learning through a language. This has a peculiar place in the debate in general. Even advanced L2 users of languages will sometimes learn through their L1, and as the Norwegian consensus report states, this affects the relevance of the organization of schools. Schools may be organized without any regard to the mother tongue of the students in so-called submersion curricula. But schools could also be organized to provide the students with some access to teachers and other adults who share their mother tongue, and schools could be organized to provide classes in the mother tongue of minority students, i.e. as a subject. This distinction between language as a topic and language as a means of instruction is quite clearly understood and lies behind the opening of a small but growing number of experimental schools in significant places in the European Union. These schools are so-called immersion schools, and they teach majority children through an L2, e.g. Finnish in Sweden or English in Germany (Laurén 1999).

The consequence of these discussions and decisions about school organization is a rather clear hierarchy of languages (cf. Jørgensen 2000) which does not go unnoticed by minorities. Thus, liberalist and conservative governments have profoundly changed the educational landscape and in the process also the educational atmosphere. This is to a certain extent a reaction to so-called globalization, but in local communities and at the national level it means that there is very little support for minority languages, minority cultures, or minority viewpoints. It is becoming more difficult to be a child with a minority mother tongue attending school in the majority tongue. At the supra-national level we do see some understanding, and based on that fact one may take a more optimistic view (cf. Extra, this volume). However, supra-national entities tend to become lofty and abstract – in practical educational terms, the past 20 years have not been good for minority languages in many parts of Europe or, as we have seen, North America.

This does indeed affect the individual marginalization of linguistic minority students in the majority schools, especially if their acquisition of L2 is below average. Rahbek (1987) is an ethnographic classroom study of social and educational integration in a majority school. She reports how minority students are physically marginalized – they occupy the seats in the periphery of the classroom, and they only participate in common activities on a low scale and in low-prestige functions. Almost 10 years later Quist (1998) reports how Eda, the lowest-achieving student in the Køge Project, is also thoroughly marginalized and ranks lowest of all in the hierarchy. The social psychological effect of collective marginalization obviously has a profound negative effect on the individual in these cases. As Quist (1998) speculates, individual self-esteem and feelings of individual identity are affected in a very counterproductive manner for Eda and minority students in similar circumstances.

6.   Conclusions

There are two different lines of thought which have an impact on educational decision making, especially when liberalist and conservative (and to a certain extent also 'third way') politicians are involved. One is the threshold hypothesis (and similar hypotheses), and the other one is national romanticism. These two lines of thinking do sometimes meet in educational decision making processes. Educators sometimes entertain the intuitively satisfying, simple view of language development of the threshold hypothesis (little, more, or much) and its clear linkage to cognitive development and school success (little, more, or much). This has been used as an argument to provide mother tongue classes for minority students. However, according to this understanding of the hypotheses children will only need to reach the lower threshold in their mother tongue development. Then they have 'learned enough' and they do not need to learn any more of their mother tongue – now they can continue with learning in the majority language, their L2. Their mother tongue development is considered complete and in need of no more support. Therefore the hypotheses have been used as an argument to close minority mother tongue classes after grade 4.

Our conclusion is that the only coherent theory which covers both socioeconomic aspects, educational aspects, and linguistic aspects is the group of hypotheses around the threshold hypothesis. They involve an understanding of individual language development, of individual cognitive development, and of socioeconomic differences. However, the view of language which characterizes these hypotheses is a gross oversimplification. That in itself is enough to refute them, even if there were no other reasons. This does not alter the fact that the threshold hypothesis, for good and for bad, has inspired both linguists and educators to work with various aspects of the issue.

However, over the past decades we have seen a division of the studies of these issues. The study of individual bilingual language development has taken a much more social-psychologically oriented perspective than that very closely connected to individual cognitive development which the threshold hypothesis offered. On the other hand, the study of schooling has been less interested in specifically latching on to language. With respect to education we see two ongoing debates. One is more or less professional and discusses pedagogical issues, including intercultural education, but with little emphasis on language. The other one is political, and although it has profound implications for minority language users, it has little to show in understanding of either linguistic or cognitive development.

The linguistically oriented studies show us that social relations are surprisingly clearly reflected in not only the language use and language attitudes of the individual, but also in language acquisition, general cognitive development, and eventual school success. We cannot know whether this is a causal relation, but there is a connection.

References

Auer, Peter
   1995   The pragmatics of codeswitching: A sequential approach. In: Ann Lesley Milroy and Pieter Muysken (eds.), *One speaker, Two languages,* 115–135. Cambridge: Cambridge University Press.
Brox, Ottar (ed.)
   1995   *Integrasjon av minoriteter. Kan Carmen og Khalid bli gode i norsk?* Oslo: Tano Aschehoug.
Cline, Tony and Norah Frederickson (eds.)
   1996   *Curriculum Related Assessment, Cummins and Bilingual Children.* Clevedon, Avon: Multilingual Matters.
Collier, Virginia P. and Wayne P. Thomas
   1997   *School Effectiveness for Language Minority Students.* Washington, DC: National Clearinghouse for Bilingual Education, George Washington University.
   2001   *A National Study of School Effectiveness for Language Minority Students: Long-Term Academic Achievement.* www.crede.ucsc.edu or www.crede.org

Crawford, James
2000   *At War With Diversity: U.S. Language Policy in an Age of Anxiety*. Cleve-
        don, Avon: Multilingual Matters.
Cromdal, Jakob
2000   *Code-switching for all Practical Purposes*. Linköpings Universitet.
Crystal, David
1998   *Language Play*. London: Penguin.
Cummins, Jim
1976   The influence of bilingualism on cognitive growth: A synthesis of research
        findings and explanatory hypotheses. *Working Papers on Bilingualism* 9:
        1–43.
1979   Cognitive/academic language proficiency, linguistic interdependence, the
        optimum age question and some other matters. *Working Papers on Bilin-
        gualism* 19: 121–129.
1981   The role of primary language development in promoting educational suc-
        cess for language minority students. In: California State Department of
        Education (ed.), *Schooling and Language Minority Students: A Theoretical
        Framework*, 3–48. Los Angeles: California State University.
2000   *Language, Power and Pedagogy. Bilingual Children in the Crossfire*.
        Clevedon, Avon: Multilingual Matters.
Edelsky, Carol
1986   Educational Linguistics. Review of Charlene Rivera (1984): Lan-
        guage proficiency and academic achievement. *Language in Society* 15:
        123–128.
1990   *With Literacy and Justice for All: Rethinking the Social in Language and
        Education*. London: Falmer Press.
Extra, Guus and Kutlay Yağmur (eds.)
2004   *Urban Multilingualism in Europe. Immigrant Minority Languages at Home
        and School*. Clevedon, Avon: Multilingual Matters.
Galindo, Rene
2003   Newspaper Editorial Response to California's Post-Proposition 227 Test
        Scores. Unpublished paper, University of Colorado at Denver.
Gumperz, John J.
1982   *Discourse Strategies*. Cambridge University Press.
Hansen, Jesper
2003   The development of bilingual proficiency – A sequential analysis. *Inter-
        national Journal of Bilingualism* 7: 379–406.
Hegelund, Lone
2002   *A Comparative Policy Analysis of Minority Mother Tongue Education in
        Denmark and Sweden*. (Copenhagen Studies in Bilingualism, vol. 33). Co-
        penhagen: Danish University of Education.
Hetmar, Tytte
1991   *Tosprogede elever – en undervisning i udvikling*. (Københavnerstudier i
        tosprogethed, vol. 15). København: Danmarks Lærerhøjskole.
Holmen, Anne
1990   *Udviklingslinjer i tilegnelsen af dansk som andetsprog – en kvalitativ,
        kvantitativ analyse*. (Københavnerstudier i tosprogethed, vol. 12). Køben-
        havn: Danmarks Lærerhøjskole.

1993   Syntactic development in Danish L2. In: Kenneth Hyltenstam and Åke Viberg (eds.), *Progression and Regression in Language*, 267–288. Cambridge: Cambridge University Press.

Hvenekilde, Anne (ed.)
1994   *Veier til kunnskap og deltakelse.* Oslo: Novus.

Hyltenstam, Kenneth, Ottar Brox, Thor Ola Engen and Anne Hvenekilde
1996   *Tilpasset språkopplæring for minoritetselever. Rapport fra en konsensus-
konferanse.* Oslo: Norge Forskningsråd.

Jørgensen, J. Normann
2000   Language hierarchies, bilingualism and minority education in the Nordic
countries. In: Elite Olshtain and Gabriel Horenczuk (eds.), *Language, Identity and Migration*, 219–238. Jerusalem: Magnes Press.

2003a   Languaging among fifth graders: Code-switching in Conversation 501 of
the Køge Project. In: J. Normann Jørgensen (ed.), *Bilingualism and Social
Relations*, 126–148. Clevedon, Avon: Multilingual Matters.

2003b   Gender differences in the development of language choice patterns in the
Køge Project. *International Journal of Bilingualism* 7: 353–378.

2005   Sociolingvistikken og *native* speaker i Skandinavien. In: Petter Dyndahl and
Lars Anders Kulbrandstad (eds.), *High fidelity eller rein jalla? Purisme som
problem I kultur, språk og estetikk*, 33–52. Vallset: Oplandske Bokforlag.

Jørgensen, J. Normann (ed.)
2001   *En køn strid. Sprog, magt og køn hos tosprogede børn og unge.* Frederiks-
berg: Roskilde Universitetsforlag.

Jørgensen, J. Normann and Pia Quist
2001   Native speakers' judgements of second language Danish. *Language Awareness* 10: 41–56.

Kotsinas, Ulla-Britt
1988   Immigrant children's Swedish – a new variety? *Journal of Multicultural
and Multilingual Development* 9: 129–140.

Kristjánsdóttir, Bergþóra
2003   Viljen til undervisning i tosprogede elevers modersmål. In: Christian Horst
(ed.), *Interkulturel pædagogik*, 85–110. Vejle: Kroghs Forlag.

Laurén, Christer
1999   *Språkbad. Forskning og praktik.* Vaasa: Vasa Universitet.

Loona, Sunil and Randi Myklebust
1994   Historien om mine barn og andres unger – nok en gang. In: Anne Hvenekilde (ed.), Veier til kunnskap og deltakels, 25–52.

Madsen, Lian Malai
2003   Power relationships, interactional dominance and manipulation strategies
in group conversations of Turkish-Danish children. In: J. Normann Jørgensen (ed.), *Bilingualism and Social Relations*, 90–101. Clevedon, Avon:
Multilingual Matters.

Martin-Jones, Marilyn and Suzanne Romaine
1986   Semilingualism: A half-baked theory of communicative competence. *Applied Linguistics* 7: 26–38.

Paulston, Christina Bratt
1982   *Swedish Research and Debate about Bilingualism.* Stockholm: Swedish
National Board of Education.

Pedersen, Birgitte Rahbek and Tove Skutnabb-Kangas
   1983   *God, bedre, dansk? – om indvandrerbørns integration i Danmark.* København: Forlaget Børn and Unge.
Quist, Pia
   1998   *Ind i gruppen – ind i sproget. En undersøgelse af sammenhænge mellem andetsprogstilegnelse og identitet.* (Københavnerstudier i tosprogethed Køgeserien, vol. K5). København: Danmarks Lærerhøjskole.
Rahbek, Birgitte
   1987   *Børn mellem to kulturer.* København: Hans Reitzel.
Rampton, Ben
   1995   *Crossing: Language and Ethnicity Among Adolescents.* London: Longman.
   1999   *Deutsch* in Inner London and the animation of an instructed foreign language. *Journal of Sociolinguistics* 3: 480–504.
Reich, Hans H. and Hans-Joachim Roth in cooperation with Ø. Dirim, J. N. Jørgensen, Gundula List, Günther List, U. Neumann, G. Siebert-Ott, U. Steinmüller, F. Teunissen, T. Vallen, V. Wunig
   2002   *Spracherwerb zweisprachig aufwachsender Kinder und Jugendlicher.* Hamburg: Behörde für Bildung und Sport.
Reid, Euan and Hans H. Reich (eds.)
   1992   *Breaking the Boundaries. Migrant Workers' Children in the EC.* Clevedon, Avon: Multilingual Matters.
Skutnabb-Kangas, Tove
   1981   *Tvåspråkighet.* Lund: Liber.
   1984   *Bilingualism or Not?* Clevedon, Avon: Multilingual Matters.
Skutnabb-Kangas, Tove and Pertti Toukomaa
   1976   *Teaching Migrant Children's Mother Tongue and Learning the Language of the Host Country in the Context of the Socio-cultural Situation of the Migrant Family.* University of Tampere: Dept. of Sociology and Social Psychology Research reports, vol. 15.
Toukomaa, Pertti and Tove Skutnabb-Kangas
   1977   *The Intensive Teaching of the Mother Tongue to Migrant Children at Pre-school Age.* University of Tampere: Dept. of Sociology and Social Psychology Research reports, vol. 26.
Wiley, Terrence G.
   1996   *Literacy and Language Diversity in the United States.* Washington, DC: Center for Applied Linguistics.
Wittek, Fritz
   1992   The historical and international context for current action on intercultural education. In: Euan Reid and Hans H. Reich (eds.), *Breaking the Boundaries. Migrant Workers' Children in the EC,* 1–14.

Additional sources

Baetens Beardsmore, Hugo
   1994   *European Models of Bilingual Education.* Clevedon, Avon: Multilingual
            Matters.
Baker, Colin
   2006   *Foundations of Bilingual Education and Bilingualism.* Fourth edition.
            Clevedon, Avon: Multilingual Matters.
Feinberg, Rosa Castro
   2002   *Bilingual Education. A Reference Handbook.* Santa Barbara, California:
            ABC-CLIO.
Paulston, Christina Bratt
   1988   *International Handbook of Bilingual Education.* Greenwood Press.
Journal of Multicultural and Multilingual Development. Clevedon, Avon: Multilingual
   Matters.
Bilingual Research Journal. Washington, DC: National Association for Bilingual Edu-
   cation. Online version: http://brj.asu.edu
International Journal of Bilingual Education and Bilingualism. Clevedon, Avon: Multi-
   lingual Metters.
Language, Culture and Curriculum. Clevedon, Avon: Multilingual Matters.
A wide range of publications by the National Association for Bilingual Education, 1030
   15th St NW, Suite 470, Washington, DC 20005, USA. Website: http://www.nabe.org/

7. From minority programmes to multilingual education

Guus Extra

1. Introduction

Language transmission usually occurs both in the domestic and in the public domain. Prototypical of these two domains are the home and the school, respectively. Viewed from the perspectives of majority *versus* minority language speakers, language transmission becomes a very different issue. In the case of majority language speakers, language transmission at home and at school are commonly taken for granted: at home, parents speak this language usually with their children, and at school, this language is usually the only or major subject and medium of instruction. In the case of minority language speakers, however, there is usually a mismatch between the language of the home and the language of the school. Whether parents in such a context continue to transmit their language to their children is strongly dependent on the degree to which these parents, or the minority group to which they belong, conceive of this language as a core value of their cultural identity.

The focus of this Chapter is on minority groups in education, in particular – but not exclusively – on immigrant minority (henceforward IM) groups in a European context of immigration and intergenerational minorization. Section 2 goes into the semantics or nomenclature of our field of concern. In Sections 3 and 4, case studies of educational policies and practices will be presented with respect to IM languages in two widely different and distant contexts, i.e. North Rhine-Westphalia in Germany and Victoria State in Australia. In each of these federal states, interesting affirmative action programmes have been set up in this domain, although the nomenclature and educational policies are very different. The focus in North Rhine-Westphalia is on *Muttersprachlicher Unterricht* for IM children, whereas the focus in Victoria State is on the learning and teaching of *Languages Other Than English* (LOTE) for all children. Section 5 goes into the crossnational educational outcomes of the *Multilingual Cities Project*, carried out in six European cities/countries, as described in Extra and Yağmur (2004). Section 6 is aimed at an outline and reconciliation of the top-down European elite discourse on trilingualism for all European citizens and the bottom-up plea of minority groups for a similar approach.

2.   The semantics of our field of concern

Europe has a rich diversity of languages (Haarmann 1975). This fact is usually illustrated by reference to the national languages of Europe. However, many more languages are spoken by the inhabitants of Europe. Examples of such languages are Welsh and Basque, or Arabic and Turkish. These languages are usually referred to as minority languages, even when in Europe as a whole there is no one-majority language because all languages are spoken by a numerical minority. The languages referred to are representatives of regional minority (RM) and immigrant minority (IM) languages, respectively.

RM and IM languages have much in common, much more than is usually thought. On their sociolinguistic, educational, and political agendas, we find issues such as their actual spread; their domestic and public vitality; the processes and determinants of language maintenance versus language shift towards majority languages; the relationship between language, ethnicity, and identity; and the status of minority languages in schools, in particular in the compulsory stages of primary and secondary education. The origin of most RM languages as minority languages lies in the nineteenth century, when, during the processes of state formation in Europe, they found themselves excluded from the state level, in particular from general education. Only in the last few decades have some of these RM languages become relatively well protected in legal terms, as well as by affirmative educational policies and programmes, both at the level of various nation-states and at the level of the European Union (henceforward EU).

There have always been speakers of IM languages in Europe, but these languages have emerged only recently as community languages spoken on a wide scale in north-western Europe, due to intensified processes of migration and intergenerational minorization. Turkish and Arabic are good examples of so-called 'non-European' languages that are spoken and learned by millions of inhabitants of the EU member-states. Although IM languages are often conceived of and transmitted as core values by IM language groups, they are much less protected than RM languages by affirmative action and legal measures in, for example, education. In fact, the learning and certainly the teaching of IM languages are often seen by speakers of mainstream languages and by policy makers as obstacles to integration. At the European level, guidelines and directives regarding IM languages are scant and outdated.

Despite the possibilities and challenges of comparing the status of RM and IM languages, amazingly few connections have been made in the sociolinguistic, educational, and political domains. In the *Linguistic Minorities Project* of the early 1980s, which was restricted to England, an observation was made which still applies to the situation today: "The project has been struck by how little contact there still is between researchers and practitioners working in bilingual areas and school systems, even between England and Wales. Many of the newer minorities in England could benefit from the Welsh experience and expertise" (Linguistic Minorities Project 1985: 12). In our opinion, little has improved over the past decades, and contacts between researchers and policy makers working with different types of minority groups are still scarce. Examples of publications which focus on both types of minority language are the dual volumes on RM and IM languages by Alladina and Edwards (1991), and more recently the integrated volumes by Ammerlaan et al. (2001) and Extra and Gorter (2001).

As yet, we lack a common referential framework for the languages under discussion. As all of these RM and IM languages are spoken by different language communities and not at a statewide level, it may seem logical to refer to them as community languages, thus contrasting them with the official languages of European nation-states. However, the designation 'community languages' is already in use to refer to the official languages of the EU, and in that sense occupied territory. From an inventory of the different terms in use, we learn that there are no standardized designations for these languages across nation-states. Table 1 gives a nonexhaustive overview of the nomenclature of our field of concern in terms of reference to the people, their languages, and the teaching of these languages. The concept of 'lesser-used languages' has been adopted at the EU level; the *European Bureau for Lesser Used Languages* (EBLUL), established in Brussels and Dublin, speaks and acts on behalf of "the autochthonous regional and minority languages of the EU." Table 1 shows that the utilized terminology varies not only across different nation-states, but also across different types of education.

There is much published evidence on the status and use of RM languages, both in Europe and abroad (e.g. Gorter et al. 1990). Baetens Beardsmore (1993) focused on RM languages in western Europe, whereas the focus of Synak and Wicherkiewicz (1997), Bratt-Paulston and Peckham (1998), and Hogan-Brun and Wolff (2003) was on RM languages in central and eastern Europe. Given the overwhelming focus on mainstream language acquisition by IM groups, there is much less evidence on the status and use of IM languages across Europe as a result of processes of immigration and intergenerational minorization. In contrast to RM languages, IM languages have no established status in terms of period and area of residence. Obviously, typological differences between IM languages across EU member-states do exist, e.g. in terms of the status of IM languages as EU languages or non-EU languages, or as languages of formerly colonialized source countries. Taken from the latter perspective, Indian languages are prominent in Great Britain, Maghreb languages in France, Congolese languages in Belgium, and Surinamese languages in the Netherlands.

Tosi (1984) offered an early case study on Italian as an IM language in Great Britain. Most studies of IM languages in Europe have focused on a spectrum of IM languages at the level of one particular multilingual city (Kroon 1990; Baker

Table 1. Nomenclature of the field

Reference to the people
■ national/historical/regional/indigenous minorities *versus* non-national/non-historical/non-territorial/non-indigenous minorities
■ non-national residents
■ foreigners, *étrangers, Ausländer*
■ (im)migrants
■ new-comers, new Xmen (e.g. new Dutchmen)
■ co-citizens (instead of citizens)
■ ethnic/cultural/ethnocultural minorities
■ linguistic minorities
■ allochthones (e.g. in the Netherlands), allophones (e.g. in Canada)
■ non-English-speaking (NES) residents (in particular in the USA)
■ *anderstaligen* (Dutch: those who speak other languages)
■ coloured/black people, visible minorities (the latter in particular in Canada)

Reference to their languages
■ community languages (in Europe *versus* Australia)
■ ancestral/heritage languages (common concept in Canada)
■ national/historical/regional/indigenous minority languages *versus* non-territorial/non-regional/non-indigenous/non-European minority languages
■ autochthonous *versus* allochthonous minority languages
■ lesser used/less widely used/less widely taught languages (in EBLUL context)
■ stateless/diaspora languages (in particular used for Romani)
■ languages other than English (LOTE: common concept in Australia)

Reference to the teaching of these languages
■ instruction in own language (and culture)
■ mother tongue teaching (MTT)
■ home language instruction (HLI)
■ community language teaching (CLT)
■ regional minority language instruction *versus* immigrant minority language instruction
■ enseignement des langues et cultures d'origine (ELCO: in French/Spanish primary schools)
■ enseignement des langues vivantes (ELV: in French/Spanish secondary schools)
■ Muttersprachlicher Unterricht (MSU: in German primary schools)
■ Muttersprachlicher Ergänzungsunterricht (in German primary/secondary schools)
■ Herkunftssprachlicher Unterricht (in German primary/secondary schools)

and Eversley 2000), one particular nation-state (Linguistic Minorities Project 1985; Alladina and Edwards 1991; Extra and Verhoeven 1993a; Caubet, Chaker and Sibille 2002; Extra et al. 2002), or one particular IM language at the European level (Tilmatine 1997 and Obdeijn and De Ruiter 1998 on Arabic in Europe, or Jørgensen 2003 on Turkish in Europe). A number of studies have taken both a crossnational and a crosslinguistic perspective on the status and use of IM languages in Europe (e.g. Husén and Opper 1983; Jaspaert and Kroon 1991; Extra and Verhoeven 1993b, 1998; Extra and Gorter 2001). Churchill (1986) offered an early crossnational perspective on the education of IM children in the OECD countries, whereas Reid and Reich (1992) carried out a crossnational evaluative study of 15 pilot projects on the education of IM children supported by the European Commission.

In the European public discourse on IM groups, two major characteristics emerge (Extra and Verhoeven 1998): IM groups are often referred to as *foreigners* and as being in need of *integration*. First of all, it is common practice to refer to IM groups in terms of *non-national* residents and to their languages in terms of *non-territorial*, *non-regional*, *non-indigenous* or *non-European* languages. The call for integration is in sharp contrast with the language of exclusion. This conceptual exclusion rather than inclusion in the European public discourse derives from a restrictive interpretation of the notions of citizenship and nationality. From a historical point of view, such notions are commonly shaped by a constitutional *ius sanguinis* (law of the blood) in terms of which nationality derives from parental origins, in contrast to *ius solis* (law of the soil) in terms of which nationality derives from the country of birth. When European emigrants left their continent in the past and colonized countries abroad, they legitimised their claim to citizenship by spelling out *ius solis* in the constitutions of these countries of settlement. Good examples of this strategy can be found in English-dominant immigration countries like the USA, Canada, Australia and South Africa. In establishing the constitutions of these (sub)continents, no consultation took place with native inhabitants, such as Indians, Inuit, Aboriginals and Zulus respectively. At home, however, Europeans predominantly upheld *ius sanguinis* in their constitutions and/or perceptions of nationality and citizenship, in spite of the growing numbers of newcomers who strive for an equal status as citizens.

A second major characteristic of the European public discourse on IM groups is the focus on *integration*. This notion is both popular and vague, and it may actually refer to a whole spectrum of underlying concepts that vary over space and time. Miles and Thränhardt (1995), Bauböck, Heller and Zolberg (1996), and Kruyt and Niessen (1997) are good examples of comparative case studies on the notion of integration in a variety of EU countries that have been faced with increasing immigration since the early 1970s. The extremes of the spectrum range from assimilation to multiculturalism. The concept of assimilation is based on the premise that cultural differences between IM groups and established majority groups should and will disappear over time in a society which is proclaimed to be culturally homogeneous. On the other side of the spectrum, the concept of multiculturalism is based on the premise that such differences are an asset to a pluralist society, which actually promotes cultural diversity in terms of new resources and opportunities. While the concept of assimilation focuses on unilateral tasks for *newcomers*, the concept of multiculturalism focuses on multilateral tasks for *all* inhabitants in changing societies (Taylor 1993; Cohn-Bendit and Schmid 1992). In practice, established majority groups often make strong demands on IM groups for integration in terms of assimilation and are commonly very reluctant to promote or even accept the notion of cultural diversity as a determining characteristic of an increasingly multicultural environment.

It is interesting to compare the underlying assumptions of 'integration' in the European public discourse on IM groups at the national level with assumptions at the level of cross-national cooperation and legislation. In the latter context, European politicians are eager to stress the importance of a proper balance between the loss and maintenance of 'national' norms and values. A prime concern in the public debate on such norms and values is cultural and linguistic diversity, mainly in terms of the national languages of the EU. National languages are often referred to as core values of cultural identity. It is a paradoxical phenomenon that in the same public discourse IM languages and cultures are commonly conceived as sources of problems and deficits and as obstacles to integration, while national languages and cultures in an expanding EU are regarded as sources of enrichment and as prerequisites for integration.

The public discourse on integration of IM groups in terms of assimilation vs. multiculturalism can also be noticed in the domain of education. Due to a growing influx of IM pupils, schools are faced with the challenge of adapting their curricula to this trend. The pattern of modification may be inspired by a strong and unilateral emphasis on learning (in) the language of the majority of society, given its significance for success in school and on the labour market, or by the awareness that the response to emerging multicultural school populations can not be reduced to monolingual education programming (Gogolin 1994). In the former case, the focus will be on learning (in) the national language as a second language only, in the latter case on offering more than one language in the school curriculum.

3.   Case study 1: Mother Tongue Education in North Rhine-Westphalia, Germany

There are large differences between different states in the Federal Republic of Germany concerning the educational policy and practice of teaching IM languages (Gogolin and Reich 2001; Hunger 2001), referred to as *Muttersprachlicher Unterricht* (henceforward MSU). As an example of affirmative practice, in this section, the situation in North Rhine-Westphalia (henceforward NRW) is described. It should, however, be stressed that language policy in this domain is vulnerable to political changes in government. This holds for NRW and for other states, both in Germany and elsewhere. For a description and analysis of the demographic development concerning migration and minorization of IM groups in NRW, the report of the *Interministerielle Arbeitsgruppe Zuwanderung* (2000) is most relevant. This publication contains detailed information on the intake figures of IM children in education.

Against the background of internationalisation and globalisation of society, the development and promotion of multilingualism (*Förderung der Mehrsprachigkeit*) are taken as a point of departure in the state policy of NRW. Illner and Pfaff (2001) give a comprehensive overview of educational policies on this matter. The development of multilingualism at the primary school level is increasingly considered within a spectrum of the following four learning tasks:

- proficiency in German as L1 or L2 should give access to school success and social participation at large;
- MSU should value and promote the available diversity of languages in NRW;
- English should give access to international communication;
- *Begegnung mit Sprachen* ('Meeting with languages') should function as a window to other languages with which children come into contact.

Common principles for language teaching should be taken into account, such as building upon previous skills and knowledge, offering meaningful contexts for communication, and stimulating metalinguistic awareness across the boundaries of any particular language. All of these measures are meant to put language teaching in the overarching perspective of a multicultural and multilingual Germany and Europe.

According to recent NRW school statistics, more than 30% of children in this state grow up speaking two or more languages. They speak the languages of their parents in varying degrees and these languages are used in various media, such as newspapers, TV, radio, and so on. German is the mainstream language used with German-speaking people and in most of the media. The language competencies of IM children vary, but the early experience with multilingual communication is a basic experience for most of them. Against this background, on August 1, 2000, a new MSU policy and curriculum for all state schools of NRW were decreed. According to this policy, in order to meet the needs of multilingual children, schools must offer MSU as an elective course for grades 1 to 10. The new curriculum was developed by the *Landesinstitut für Schule und Weiterbildung* (LSW, Soest). The LSW has a statewide task in promoting multilingualism in the NRW school system, derived from experiences abroad (Landesinstitut für Schule und Weiterbildung 2001). This educational policy is based on the following arguments (Ministerium für Schule und Weiterbildung 2000):

- MSU contributes to the maintenance and development of contacts and bonds with the country of origin;
- MSU is an expression of the public value attached to the linguistic and cultural heritage of IM children and their parents;
- children who have spoken and written competencies in their mother tongues will be ready and capable of learning better German;
- the promotion of multilingualism is important both from a cultural and an economic perspective.

On the basis of the above arguments, at the end of grade 6, children are expected to achieve the following educational objectives: a spoken and written language proficiency that is adequate for various contexts of language use, and a sensitivity to multilingualism and knowledge of other languages with an ambition to learn German and other languages that are important to the future of a multilingual and multicultural Europe. Children must learn to

- value cultural diversity;
- look at their cultural background from their own and from other people's perspectives;
- understand the behaviour of others to solve problems arising from cultural misunderstandings;
- develop strategies and techniques to handle concrete conflicts arising from different expectations, interests, and values;
- act on the basis of human rights against discrimination directed at minorities;
- in the case of Muslim children, learn about Islamic tradition and history, be able to function effectively in a dominantly Christian society, and acquire knowledge about a secular society with freedom of religion.

This ambitious curriculum is set for grades 1–6 and it is also valid for MSU in grades 7–10 of secondary schooling. The target groups for MSU are pupils who have learned languages other than German as a first, second, or foreign language: as a first language before German, as a second language next to or after German, or as a foreign language learned abroad. The languages to be offered in MSU are identified by the Ministry of Education and valid for the whole state of NRW.

In 2003, 19 different languages were offered. Schools can offer a maximum of 5 hours of MSU per week, provided that there are at least 15 primary school children or 18 secondary school children for a certain language group from one or more schools, that parents demand instruction for their children, and that there is a qualified teacher available. Admission to MSU classes is independent of the pupils' or parents' nationality. Even though participation in MSU classes is on a voluntary basis, participation is obligatory after approved parental application.

MSU is offered on a statewide basis and MSU classes are part of the school inspection system. Irrespective of their nationality, the teachers are in the service of the state, and they receive a salary that is earmarked statewide for MSU. Most of the teachers serve at more than one school, and one school usually acts as a base school for the teachers. In-service training of teachers and the development of learning materials are also covered by the state. These are the responsibility of the *Landesinstitut für Schule und Weiterbildung* (LSW) in Soest. The quality control of the learning materials and the approval for their use in schools are also part of the duties of the LSW. Turkish teachers are trained by and receive their qualifications from the Turkish Department at Essen University. The organisation of MSU in primary schools is the responsibility of *Schulämter*. In practice, in terms of cultural background, language proficiency, age, and grade, very heterogeneous groups make use of these MSU classes. These circumstances put high demands on the teachers, who must reconcile the didactic principles of first, second, and foreign language teaching. Intercultural experiences and management skills are used as a common basis for didactic principles. MSU teachers must be well informed of the characteristics of their pupils and, in cooperation with the class teachers, they should shape the curriculum of the whole school. Recently, efforts have been made to coordinate bilingual education (i.e. German plus MSU) during primary schooling on the basis of experiences in Berlin with the KOALA project (*Koordinierte Alphabetisierung im Anfangsunterricht*). These experiences have been adapted to NRW conditions. In 2003, about 40 primary schools in NRW participated in the KOALA project with coordinated efforts in teaching German/Turkish, German/Italian, and German/Arabic (see also *www.raa.de*).

On a yearly basis, the Ministry of Education publishes statistics on IM pupils and MSU teachers on the basis of nationality criteria. Table 2 presents an overview of relevant figures for the 2001/2002 school year. It clearly shows the leading position of Turkish compared to all the other languages. For this reason, Turkish acts as a role model for the implementation of other languages in the context of MSU in NRW.

Table 2. MSU figures in North Rhine-Westphalia in the 2001/2002 school year (source:
Ministerium für Schule und Weiterbildung, Amtliche Schuldaten 2001/2002,
Statistische Übersicht nr. 330, Düsseldorf 29-1-2002)

Language	Total number of classes	Total number of pupils	Total number of class hours	Total number of teachers
Albanian	137	1,689	501	15
Arabic	374	4,799	1,271	70
Bosnian	65	758	235	35
Greek	385	4,671	1,606	86
Italian	548	6,661	1,998	122
Croatian	140	1,588	612	54
Macedonian	17	239	58	14
Polish	59	884	207	14
Portuguese	193	2,574	811	38
Russian	189	2,785	606	27
Serbian	78	786	309	31
Slovenian	6	70	23	3
Spanish	218	3,154	850	55
Turkish	5,747	80,375	15,576	790
Other languages	147	2,119	580	47
Total	8,298	113,152	25,243	1,401

During the primary 2002/2003 school year, 1,377 MSU teachers were employed
at the NRW state level. Due to general budget cuts, however, a reduction occurred to less than 900 MSU teacher positions. This reduction is meant to be
temporary; MSU continues to be positively valued for its contribution to the
maintenance and development of multilingualism.

Educational attainments obtained in MSU classes are periodically and systematically evaluated. Given the heterogeneous nature of the classes, pupils'
achievements are not reported in the form of subject grades but verbalised in the
form of expected future achievement. The following are the concrete guidelines
for such reports:

– at the end of the first and second grades, the attainments are described in the
  form of a short text;
– in the third grade, pupils are given subject grades for each semester, provided
  that the pupils receive grades for other subjects as well;
– in grades four to six, pupils receive subject grades for each semester.

At the end of the sixth grade, the level of achievement attained in MSU is taken
into consideration for the final level assessment of primary school pupils at large.

In 2003, language proficiency testing was introduced in NRW for all primary school entrants in grade 1. From the 2003/2004 school year onwards, a digital bilingual proficiency test was introduced for all entrants on the basis of pilot experiences in primary schools in the municipality of Duisburg. This digital bilingual proficiency test consists of four parts with increasing levels of difficulty, and deals with such domains as receptive vocabulary, phonological awareness, and text comprehension. The test is the result of cooperation between the Dutch Central Institute for Test Development (CITO) and the NRW *Landesinstitut für Schule und Weiterbildung*. The handling of the digital test is made easy for children. It takes about one hour for each language, and the outcomes are available immediately. On the basis of the outcomes, a bilingual profile is constructed for each child, and recommendations are made for both MSU and the teaching of German. Initially, pilot experiences have been limited to measuring German/Turkish proficiency.

In secondary schools, MSU is offered as an elective course, which can replace a second or third foreign language. Pupils who attend MSU classes on a regular basis can complete a language test. The results obtained from such tests are reported in school reports, and in some cases these grades are taken as substitutes for traditional foreign language results. For Turkish and Greek, the Ministry of Education organises end-of-school exams. In the 1998/1999 school year, more than 9,000 pupils attended MSU classes instead of foreign language classes. Around 7,000 pupils completed final school examinations in 33 different languages. For a discussion of spoken and written language proficiency requirements for end-of-school exams in secondary schools, we refer to Bebermeier et al. (1997).

The example of NRW is remarkable in many respects:

- MSU is part of a state-supported educational philosophy in favour of multilingualism and multiculturalism in both a nationwide and European context;
- MSU is offered in a broad spectrum of languages and for a broad spectrum of target groups, independent of the pupils' or parents' nationalities;
- languages are offered on demand, given a sufficient enrolment of pupils and the availability of qualified teachers;
- evaluation of achievement through MSU is carried out by measuring the bilingual proficiencies of children rather than proficiency in German only;
- parental interest and involvement in providing MSU for their children is stimulated;
- MSU is offered under the supervision and control of the regular school inspection system;
- MSU is provided by teachers who are appointed and paid by the state, not by source country agencies;

– teacher training and in-service training for MSU are taken seriously, and
  MSU teachers must fulfil the same requirements as any other teacher;
– learning materials are subject to quality control, and developed and/or published with state support.

All of these measures are meant to encourage a positive attitude towards language diversity, both in schools and in NRW at large. The involvement of parents in the schooling of their children is encouraged. Also, knowing that IM languages and cultures are respected by the school system and by mainstream
society, educational authorities hope that pupils will develop a higher self-esteem and respect for themselves and for others. In this way, intercultural communication and tolerance is promoted as well. Finally, the NRW example shows
that, instead of taking a 'deficit' perspective, policy makers opted for multicultural and multilingual education. Rather than taking language diversity and heterogeneity as phenomena of crisis and burden, they are taken as normal and
challenging. The latter perspective was taken even earlier and in a more out-
spoken way in the next case study.

4.   Case study 2: Languages Other Than English in Victoria State, Australia

MSU in North Rhine-Westphalia is an example of positive action in the European context. In order to present another example, a more distant context is
chosen. Before focusing on Victorian State at the federal level, some background
information is presented on the development of multiculturalism and multilingual policies in the Australian national context so that readers can gain a deeper
insight into the arguments of social cohesion *versus* cultural and linguistic pluralism. For an overview of Australia's policy on languages from the end of
World War II until recent times, we refer to Clyne (1991) and Ozolins (1993).
Acceptance of the concepts and practices of multiculturalism and multilingualism is rather recent in Australian history. The 1950s and 1960s, especially, were
years of fierce assimilationist policies. The Australian governments of that time
wanted to create a country that would be culturally and linguistically homogenous, based on British heritage and traditions, and with English as the *only* subject
and medium of instruction at school. The education sector played an important
role in promoting the values and customs of the mainstream Anglo-Australian
culture.

In the early 1970s, there were many inquiries and reports into assimilationist
policies. The Karmel Report on Schooling in Australia (1973) indicated that assimilationist policies not only disadvantaged IM groups from different language
backgrounds but also that such policies were basically wasteful of the potential,

talents, and resources IM groups could contribute to society. As a result of these reports, the policy of assimilation was gradually replaced by a policy of integration. The latter intended to enable people of all cultural backgrounds to participate equally in mainstream social, political, and economic institutions. *English as a Second Language* (ESL) programmes and special teacher-training programmes were set up to reach that goal.

It was only after the influential Galbally Report (1978) that the Australian government opted for fully-fledged multicultural policies in all walks of life. The Galbally Report saw schools as critical actors in the creation of a climate in which the concepts of multiculturalism and multilingualism could be understood and promoted. As a result, special programmes in *Languages Other Than English* (henceforward LOTE) for mother-tongue maintenance and development, for second language development, and for bilingual education were developed. Special plans for the recognition of multicultural perspectives across the school curriculum and the development of projects to encourage the participation of parents from non-English-speaking backgrounds in school life were developed. There were also special programmes to fight against prejudice, stereotyping, and racism.

Australia has now had a *National Policy on Languages* (NPL) since 1987. The NPL's main focus has been on realizing four principles which reflect those of all the major policy documents of the 1980s:

– English for all;
– a language other than English for all;
– support for Aboriginal and Torres Strait Island languages;
– equitable and widespread language services.

The NPL has had to survive in an often unsupportive or suspicious environment (Ozolins 1993: 250). This holds in particular for the last mentioned principle in such domains as language translation services and broadcasting services. At the federal level, the various NPL programmes had differing results in different states in Australia. Especially the multicultural State of Victoria implemented such programmes. In the view of the State of Victoria, an effective multicultural policy is a policy that promotes respect by all cultures for all cultures, one that allows Australians the freedom to maintain and celebrate their languages and cultures within a socially cohesive framework of shared values, including respect for democratic processes and institutions, the rule of law, and acknowledgment that English is the nation's common language.

In multicultural Victoria, schools play an important role in the development of attitudes, values, and critical thinking with respect to these principles. The role of education in the implementation of a multicultural policy is to ensure that racism and prejudice do not develop to hinder individuals' participation, and that all pupils are assisted in developing the understandings and skills that will enable them to achieve their full potential, and to participate effectively and successfully in a multicultural society. These understandings and skills derive from education programmes and processes that accurately and positively reflect cultural pluralism, promote cultural inclusiveness, and help all pupils to develop

- proficiency in English;
- competence in a language other than English;
- in-depth knowledge and awareness of their own and other cultures;
- an understanding of the multicultural nature of Australia's past and present history, and of the interdependence of cultures in the development of the nation;
- an awareness of the reality of the global village and national interdependence in the areas of trade, finance, labour, politics, and communications, and an awareness that the development of international understanding and cooperation is essential.

With this change of ideology and policy, educational institutions in Victoria State created a totally new system. Previously, only French, German, Italian, and, sometimes, Latin were offered as modern foreign languages in secondary schools. In primary schools, English was the only language used as the subject and medium of instruction. Facilities for LOTE were considered to be superfluous and threatening to social cohesion. However, in line with the developments described above, special programmes for LOTE and ESL were developed. In 1993, the Department of Education in Victoria established a Ministerial Advisory Council on LOTE (MACLOTE). In the same year, a LOTE Strategy Plan was published (MACLOTE 1993). According to this long-term plan, in the year 2000, all primary school pupils and at least 25 % of all secondary school pupils should take part in LOTE classes. In 1994, the School Council made a number of suggestions concerning the implementation and organisation of LOTE (MACLOTE 1994). These suggestions resulted in the development of a *Curriculum and Standard Framework* (CSF). The CSF acted as a base document for the development of attainment targets for spoken and written proficiency in different languages, and made a considerable contribution to curriculum development and the placement of pupils in LOTE programmes.

The multicultural education policy of Victoria not only targets IM pupils, but strives to reach out to all pupils with the following learning objectives:

- knowledge and consciousness of the multicultural character of the society, and knowledge and competence in intercultural communication;
- proficiency in English as a first or second language;
- proficiency in one or more languages other than English.

Concerning LOTE, a differentiation is no longer made between the status of languages as home language, heritage language, or foreign language. Moreover, *priority languages* are specified that can be taught as LOTE for which statewide budgets are earmarked in order to develop curricula, learning materials, and teacher training programmes. In LOTE programmes, schools need to ensure that multicultural perspectives are included in the content of the provision, and the culture of the target language should be explored in depth both in the LOTE class and across other curriculum areas. LOTE programmes should deal with other cultures – in addition to the LOTE being studied – in a culturally sensitive, non-stereotypical way. This is particularly important in bilingual programmes where other curriculum areas are taught in and through the LOTE.

The ultimate goal of achieving multiculturalism is realised in Victoria mostly because learning more than one language is not only the task of IM children but of all pupils in the state. Apart from English as a first or second language, all children learn at least one LOTE at school. Depending on demand, LOTE programmes are offered at government mainstream schools, at the *Victorian School of Languages* (VSL), or at after-hours ethnic schools. The VSL is a central government school in Melbourne with a record in LOTE teaching for over sixty years (see its website for recent information). The school is committed to the provision of language programmes for pupils in grades 1–12 who do not have access to the study of those languages in their mainstream schools in all sectors. The school also caters to international students. Language programmes are delivered through face-to-face classes (in metropolitan and regional centres across the state) and through distance education.

In order to achieve the above objectives, the state does not limit multicultural school policy to language education only. The understanding and promotion of multiculturalism is taught in all subjects across the curriculum. These objectives are gradually implemented across all domains of primary education. Accordingly, teacher-training institutions are restructured along the given principles. The VSL offers high-quality in-service training for its teachers and publishes series of training documents, some of which are available on the Internet. The Department of Education regularly provides detailed information on the number of pupils attending language classes both in mainstream schools and in the VSL. Table 3 presents figures for pupils attending LOTE classes in the year 2000.

Table 3. Pupils attending LOTE classes in the year 2000 (Department of Education 2001: 77)

Languages	Primary education			Secondary education			
	Main-stream schools	VSL	Subtotal	Main-stream schools	VSL	Subtotal	Total
Indonesian	85,394	4	85,398	27,959	287	28,246	113,644
Italian	77,914	22	77,936	22,223	257	22,480	100,416
Japanese	56,732	36	56,768	21,824	420	22,244	79,012
German	24,230	28	24,258	17,182	312	17,494	41,752
French	15,761	29	15,790	23,584	339	23,923	39,713
Chinese	7,669	836	8,505	3,615	1,072	4,687	13,192
Greek	2,696	422	3,118	1,042	272	1,314	4,432
Vietnamese	1,745	367	2,112	1,137	645	1,782	3,894
Spanish	1,779	100	1,879	800	333	1,133	3,012
Sign Language	2,444	–	2,444	192	–	192	2,636
Turkish	442	682	1,124	357	790	1,147	2,271
Arabic	397	141	538	698	220	918	1,456
Macedonian	209	170	379	541	265	806	1,185
Korean	298	23	321	421	19	440	761
Koorie lang.	447	–	447	9	–	9	456
Croatian	95	15	110	–	289	289	399
Serbian	–	75	75	–	283	283	358
Polish	–	126	126	–	192	192	318
Latin	–	–	–	222	37	259	259
Khmer	17	23	40	92	115	207	247
Singhalese	–	99	99	–	17	17	116
Farsi	–	39	39	–	76	76	115
Portuguese	–	31	31	–	61	61	92
Russian	–	3	3	–	88	88	91
Hindi	–	33	33	–	56	56	89
Norwegian	75	–	75	–	–	–	75
Albanian	–	21	21	–	11	11	32
Hungarian	–	14	14	–	6	6	20
Bengali	–	6	6	–	13	13	19
Bosnian	–	7	7	–	9	9	16
Dari	–	8	8	–	8	8	16
Hebrew	–	–	–	–	16	16	16
Slovenian	–	1	1	–	10	10	11
Dutch	–	–	–	–	10	10	10
Other languages	–	9	9	–	33	33	42
Total	278,344	3,370	281,714	121,898	6,561	128,459	410,173

In the year 2000, classes were offered in 41 languages in primary and/or secondary schools. The six most-chosen languages were Indonesian, Italian, Japanese, German, French, and Chinese. At 96 % of all primary schools, LOTE facilities were offered (68 % in 1994) and 87 % of all primary school pupils took part in LOTE classes. All secondary schools (apart from 6) offered LOTE facilities in 2000. Table 4 presents the supply of language classes in various school types in the year 2000.

Table 4. Language programmes in various educational institutions in 2000
(* not in Table 3)

Educational institutions		N languages
Government primary schools	Mainstream schools	18
	Victorian School of Languages	30
	Distance education only	6
Government secondary schools	Mainstream schools	17
	Victorian School of Languages	37
	Distance education only	1
After-hours ethnic schools *		52

The major conclusion that can be drawn from the two case studies presented in Sections 3 and 4 is that NRW offers good practice for mother-tongue teaching in Germany but, compared to Victorian State in Australia, still has a great distance to cover. In NRW, enrolment in classes is on a voluntary basis but, in Victoria State, learning a LOTE is compulsory for all children. Victoria State in Australia has taken firm steps towards achieving a multilingual environment where all children, including Anglo-Australian children, learn another language.

5.   Crossnational perspectives on community language teaching in Europe

Across Europe, large contrasts occur in the status of IM languages at school, depending on particular nation-states, or even particular federal states within nation-states (as in Germany), and depending on particular IM languages being national languages in other European (Union) countries or not. Most commonly, IM languages are not part of mainstream education. In Great Britain, for example, IM languages are not part of the so-called national curriculum, and they are dealt with in various types of so-called "complementary" education in out-of-school hours (see e.g. Martin et al. 2004).

```
┌─────────────────────────────────────────────────────────────────────────┐
│   Dominant Germanic        Mixed form   Dominant Romance                  │
│          /│\                    │            /\                           │
│         / │ \                   │           /  \                          │
│  Swedish  German   Dutch              French      Spanish                 │
│     │       │        \         /        \           │                     │
│     │       │         \       /          \          │                     │
│  Göteborg Hamburg  The Hague  Brussels   Lyon      Madrid                 │
└─────────────────────────────────────────────────────────────────────────┘
```

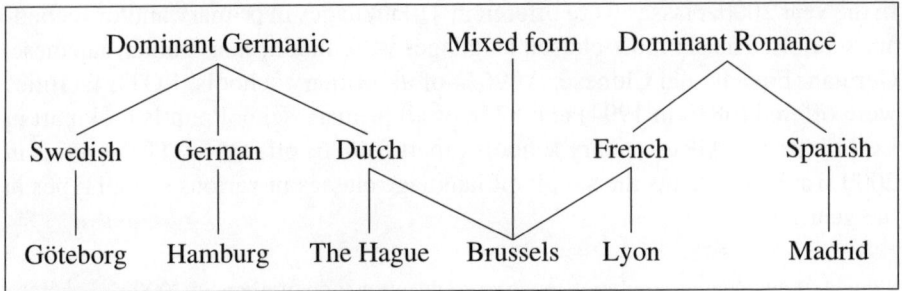

Figure 1. Outline of the Multilingual Cities Project (MCP)

Here we present the most salient educational outcomes of the *Multilingual Cities Project* (MCP), a multiple case study in six major multicultural cities in different EU member-states (Extra and Yağmur 2004). The aims of the MCP were to gather, analyze, and compare multiple data on the status of IM languages at home and at school. In the participating cities, ranging from northern to southern Europe, Germanic and/or Romance languages have a dominant status in public life. Figure 1 gives an outline of the project.

Being aware of crossnational differences in denotation (see Table 1), we use the concept of *community language teaching* (CLT) when referring to this type of education. Our rationale for using the concept of CLT rather than the concepts of mother tongue teaching or home language instruction is the inclusion of a broad spectrum of potential target groups. First of all, the status of an IM language as a 'native' or 'home' language can change through intergenerational processes of language shift. Moreover, in secondary education, both minority and majority pupils are often *de jure* (although seldom *de facto*) admitted to CLT.

In all countries involved in the MCP, there has been an increase in the number of IM pupils who speak a language at home other than or in addition to the mainstream language in primary and secondary education. Schools have largely responded to this home–school language mismatch by paying more attention to the learning and teaching of the mainstream language as a second language. A great deal of energy and money is being spent on developing curricula, teaching materials, and teacher training for second-language education. CLT stands in stark contrast to this, as it is much more susceptible to an ideological debate about its legitimacy. While there is consensus about the necessity of investing in second-language education for IM pupils, there is a lack of support for CLT. IM languages are commonly considered sources of problems and deficiencies, and they are rarely seen as sources of knowledge and enrichment. Policy makers, local educational authorities, school principals, and teachers of 'regular' subjects often have reservations or negative attitudes towards CLT. On the other hand, parents of IM pupils, CLT teachers, and IM organizations often make a case for including IM languages in the school curriculum. These differences in top-down and bottom-up attitudes were found in all the cities and countries investigated.

From a historical point of view, most of the countries show a similar chronological development in their argumentation in favour of CLT. CLT was generally introduced into primary education with a view to family remigration. This objective was also clearly expressed in *Directive 77/486* of the European Community, on July 25, 1977. The directive focused on the education of the children of "migrant workers" with the aim "principally to facilitate their possible reintegration into the Member State of origin." As is clear from this formulation, the directive excluded all IM children originating from non-EU countries, although these children formed a large part of IM children in European primary schools. At that time, Sweden was not a member of the European Community, and CLT policies for IM children in Sweden were not directed towards remigration but modelled according to bilingual education policies for the large minority of Finnish-speaking children in Sweden.

During the 1970s, the above argumentation for CLT was increasingly abandoned. Demographic developments showed no substantial signs of remigrating families. Instead, a process of family reunion and intergenerational minorization came about in the host countries. This development resulted in a conceptual shift, and CLT became primarily aimed at combating disadvantages. CLT had to bridge the gap between the home and the school environment, and to support school achievement in 'regular' subjects. Because such an approach tended to underestimate the intrinsic value of CLT, a number of countries began to emphasize the importance of CLT from a cultural, legal, or economic perspective:

– from a cultural perspective, CLT contributes to maintaining and advancing a pluriform society;
– from a legal perspective, CLT meets the internationally recognized right to language transmission and language maintenance, and acknowledges the fact that many IM groups consider their own language as a core value of cultural identity in a context of migration and minorization;
– from an economic perspective, CLT leads to an important pool of profitable knowledge in societies, which are increasingly internationally oriented.

The historical development of arguments for CLT in terms of remigration, combating deficiencies, and multicultural policy is evident in some German states, in particular North Rhine-Westphalia and Hamburg (see also Section 3 of this Chapter). In most other countries in our study, cultural policy is tied in with the mainstream language to such an extent that CLT is tolerated only in the margins. Cultural motives have played a rather important role in Sweden. It should, however, be noted that multicultural arguments for CLT have not led to an educational policy in which the status of IM languages has been substantially advanced in any of the countries involved in our study.

Derived from Extra and Yağmur (2004), we give a crossnational overview of nine parameters of CLT in primary and secondary education that were taken into account in each of the six countries involved. CLT for primary school children came to an abrupt nationwide end in the Netherlands in 2004 for being "in contradiction with integration", and the information presented is therefore completely in retrospect.

Target groups

The target groups for CLT in primary schools are commonly IM children, defined as such in a narrow or broad sense. Narrow definitions commonly relate to the range of languages taught and/or to children's proficiency in these languages. The most restrictive set of languages is taught in Spain, i.e. Arabic and Portuguese only, for Moroccan and Portuguese(-speaking) children respectively. A wide range of languages is taught in Sweden and Germany. The Netherlands, Belgium, and France take/took an intermediate position. Sweden and France demand from the target groups an active use of the languages at home and a basic proficiency in these languages. Special target groups in Sweden are adopted children; in Germany, ethnic German children from abroad; and in France, speakers of recognized RM languages. Sweden has had the most explicit policy for access to CLT in terms of 'home language' (nowadays, back to 'mother tongue') instead of socio-economic status. The target groups for CLT in secondary schools are commonly those who participated in CLT in primary schools. *De jure*, all pupils were elligible for CLT in the Netherlands, independent of ethnolinguistic background; *de facto*, most commonly, a subset of IM pupils took part. CLT for secondary school pupils is almost nonexistent in Belgium, and limited to Arabic and Portuguese in a few secondary schools in Spain.

Arguments

The arguments for CLT are formulated in terms of a struggle against deficits and/or in terms of multicultural policy. Whereas the former type of argument predominates in primary education, the latter type predominates in secondary education. The vague concept of 'integration' utilized in all countries under discussion may relate to any of these arguments. Deficit arguments may be phrased in terms of bridging the home–school gap, promoting mainstream language learning, promoting school success in other ('regular') subjects, preventing educational failure, or overcoming marginalization. Multicultural arguments may be phrased in terms of promoting cultural identity and self-esteem, promoting cultural pluralism, promoting multilingualism in a multicultural and globalizing society, and avoiding ethnic prejudice. Whereas in the Netherlands and Belgium deficit arguments dominate(d), multicultural arguments tend to play a greater role in the other countries. Deficit arguments for CLT are almost absent in secondary schools, and multicultural arguments are commonly favoured in all countries in this type of education.

Objectives

The objectives of CLT in primary schools are rarely specified in terms of language skills to be acquired. The vague concept of 'active bilingualism' has been a common objective in Sweden, whereas in Germany and Spain, reference is made to the development of oral and written language skills, language awareness, and (inter)cultural skills. In none of these cases have more particular specifications been introduced. In contrast, the objectives of CLT in secondary schools are commonly specified in terms of particular oral and written skills to be reached at intermediate stages and/or at the end of secondary schooling.

Evaluation

The evaluation of achievement through CLT may take place informally and/or formally. Informal evaluation takes place by means of subjective oral and/or written teachers' impressions or comments, meant for parents at regular intervals, e.g. once per semester or year. Formal evaluation takes place using more or less objective language proficiency measurement and language proficiency report figures, e.g. once per semester or year. Informal evaluation may occur in lower grades of primary schooling, formal evaluation in higher grades (e.g. in Sweden). In most countries, however, no report figures for CLT are provided throughout the primary school curriculum, and report figures for 'language' commonly refer implicitly to proficiency in the mainstream language. If CLT report figures are given (e.g. in France), such figures commonly do not have the same status as report figures for other subjects. The evaluation of achievement through CLT in secondary schools takes place formally through assessment instruments and examinations. Here, report figures may have a regular or a peripheral status. The former holds in particular for Sweden, Germany, and the Netherlands.

Minimal enrolment

Minimal enrolment requirements for CLT may be specified at the level of the class, the school, or even the municipality at large. The latter is common practice only in Sweden, and the minimal enrolment requirement for children from different classes/schools in Sweden was five in 2003/2004. Secondary schools in Sweden may also opt for CLT if at least five pupils enrol; four pupils are required in the Netherlands. All other countries are more reluctant, with minimal requirements for primary school pupils ranging between 10 and 20 (Germany, Belgium, France), or without any specification (the Netherlands and Spain). In the latter case, enrolment restrictions are commonly based on budget constraints.

Curricular status

In all countries, CLT at primary schools takes place on a voluntary and optional basis, provided at the request of parents. Instruction may take place within or outside regular school hours. The latter is most common in Sweden, Belgium, and France. Germany, the Netherlands (until 2004), and Spain allow(ed) for two models of instruction, either within or outside regular school hours, depending on the type of language (in Germany), the type of goal (auxiliary or intrinsic in the Netherlands), and the type of organization (in integrated or parallel classes in Spain). The number of CLT hours varies from 1–5 hours per week. If CLT takes place at secondary schools, it is considered a regular and optional subject within school hours in all countries under consideration.

Funding

The funding of CLT may depend on national, regional, or local educational authorities in the country/municipality of residence and/or on the consulates/embassies of the countries of origin. In the latter case, consulates or embassies commonly recruit and provide the teachers, and they are also responsible for teacher (in-service) training. Funding through the country and/or municipality of residence takes/took place in Sweden and the Netherlands. Funding through the consulates/embassies of the countries of origin takes place in Belgium and Spain. A mixed type of funding occurs in Germany and in France. In Germany, the source of funding is dependent on particular languages or organizational models for CLT. In France, source countries fund CLT in primary schools, whereas the French ministry of education funds CLT in secondary schools.

Teaching materials

Teaching materials for CLT may originate from the countries of origin or of residence of the pupils. Funding from ministries, municipalities, and/or publishing houses occurs in Sweden, Germany, and the Netherlands, although limited resources are available. Source country funding for CLT occurs in Belgium and Spain. In France, source countries fund teaching materials in primary schools, whereas the French ministry of education funds teaching materials in secondary schools.

Teacher qualifications

Teacher qualifications for CLT may depend on educational authorities in the countries of residence or origin. National or statewide (in-service) teacher training programmes for CLT at primary and/or secondary schools exist in Sweden, Germany, and the Netherlands, although the appeal of these programmes is limited, given the many uncertainties about CLT job perspectives. In Belgium and Spain, teacher qualifications depend on educational authorities in the countries of origin. France has a mixed system of responsibilities: source countries are responsible for teacher qualifications in primary schools, whereas the French ministry of education is responsible for teacher qualifications in secondary schools.

The presented overview of given parameters shows that there are remarkable crossnational differences in the status of CLT. There are also considerable differences between primary and secondary education in the status of CLT. A comparison of all nine parameters makes clear that CLT has gained a higher status in secondary schools than in primary schools. In primary education, CLT is generally not part of the 'regular' or 'national' curriculum, and, therefore, becomes a negotiable entity in a complex and often opaque interplay between a variety of actors. Another remarkable difference is that, in some countries, CLT is funded by the consulates or embassies of the countries of origin. In these cases, the national government does not interfere in the organization of CLT, or in the requirements for and the selection and employment of teachers. A paradoxical consequence of this phenomenon is that the earmarking of CLT budgets is often safeguarded by the above-mentioned consulates or embassies. National, regional, or local governments often fail to earmark budgets, so that funds meant for CLT may be appropriated for other educational purposes.

The higher status of CLT in secondary education is largely due to the fact that instruction in one or more languages other than the national standard language is a traditional and regular component of the (optional) school curriculum, whereas primary education is mainly determined by a monolingual *habitus* (Gogolin 1994). Within secondary education, however, CLT must compete with 'foreign' languages that have a higher status or a longer tradition. It should further be noted that some countries provide instruction and/or exams in nonstandard language varieties. In France, for instance, pupils can take part in examinations in several varieties of Arabic and several Berber languages (Tilmatine 1997); Sweden offers Kurdish as an alternative to Turkish.

From mid-2004 on, the EU has been expanded with the inclusion of the national languages of 10 new EU countries. This leads to the paradoxical situation that the national languages of, for example, the three Baltic states are supported by more positive action ('celebrating linguistic diversity') in multilingual Europe than IM languages such as Turkish, spoken by many more people across Europe. CLT may be part of a largely centralized or decentralized educational policy. In the Netherlands, national responsibilities and educational funds are gradually being transferred to the municipal level, and even to individual schools. In France, government policy is strongly centrally controlled. Germany has devolved most governmental responsibilities to the federal states, with all their differences. Sweden grants far-reaching autonomy to municipal councils in dealing with educational tasks and funding. In general, comparative crossnational references to experiences with CLT in the various EU member-states are rare, or they focus on particular language groups. With a view to the demographic development of European nation-states into multicultural societies, and the similarities in CLT issues, more comparative crossnational research would be highly desirable.

6.   Beyond bilingualism: Dealing with multilingualism at school

In Europe, language policy has largely been considered a domain which should be developed within the national boundaries of the different EU nation-states. Proposals for an overarching EU language policy were laboriously achieved and are noncommittal in character (Coulmas 1991). The most important declarations, recommendations, or directives on language policy, each of which carries a different charge in the EU jargon, concern the recognition of the status of (in the order mentioned):

– national EU languages;
– 'indigenous' or RM languages;
– 'non-territorial' or IM languages.

On numerous occasions, the EU ministers of education declared that EU citizens' knowledge of languages should be promoted (Baetens Beardsmore 1993). Each EU member-state should promote pupils' proficiency in at least two 'foreign' languages, and at least one of these languages should be the official language of an EU state. Promoting knowledge of RM and/or IM languages was left out of consideration in these ministerial statements. The European Parliament, however, accepted various resolutions which recommended the protection and promotion of RM languages and which led to the foundation of the *European Bureau for Lesser Used Languages* (EBLUL) in 1982. Another result of the European Parliament resolutions was the foundation of the *European Mercator Network*, aimed at promoting research into the status and use of RM languages. In March 1998, the *European Charter for Regional or Minority Languages* came into operation. The charter is aimed at the protection and promotion of RM languages, and it functions as an international instrument for the comparison of legal measures and other facilities of the EU member-states in this policy domain (Craith 2003).

Bilingual education in national majority languages and RM languages has been an area of interest and research for a long time (Baker 2001). More recently, local and global perspectives are taken into consideration that go beyond bilingualism and focus on multilingualism and multilingual education. Apart from national majority and RM languages, the focus is commonly on the learning and teaching of English as a third language, and in this way on promoting trilingualism from an early age (Cenoz and Genesee 1998; Cenoz and Jessner 2000; Beetsma 2002; Ytsma and Hoffmann 2003). As yet, no affirmative initiatives have been taken in the European policy domain of IM languages. It is remarkable that the teaching of RM languages is generally advocated for reasons of cultural diversity as a matter of course, whereas this is rarely a major argument in favour of teaching IM languages. The 1977 guideline of the Council of European Communities on education for IM children (*Directive 77/486*, July 25, 1977) is now completely outdated. It needs to be put in a new and increasingly multicultural context; it needs to be extended to pupils originating from non-EU countries; and it needs to be given greater binding force in the EU member-states.

There is a great need for educational policies in Europe that take new realities of multilingualism into account. Processes of internationalization and globalization have brought European nation-states to the world, but they have also brought the world to European nation-states. This bipolar pattern of change has led to both convergence and divergence of multilingualism across Europe. On the one hand, English is on the rise as the *lingua franca* for international communication across the borders of European nation-states at the cost of all other national languages of Europe, including French. In spite of many objections against the hegemony of English (Phillipson 2003), this process of convergence will be enhanced by the extension of the EU in an eastward direction. Within the borders of European nation-states, however, there is an increasing divergence of home languages due to large-scale processes of migration and intergenerational minorization.

The call for differentiation of the monolingual *habitus* of primary schools across Europe originates not only bottom-up from IM parents or organizations, but also top-down from supranational institutions which emphasize the increasing need for European citizens with a transnational and multicultural affinity and identity. Multilingual competencies are considered prerequisites for such an affinity and identity. Both the European Commission and the Council of Europe have published many policy documents in which language diversity is cherished as a key element of the multicultural identity of Europe – now and in the future. This language diversity is considered to be a prerequisite rather than an obstacle for a united European space in which all citizens are equal (not the same) and enjoy equal rights (Council of Europe 2000). The maintenance of language diversity and the promotion of language learning and multilingualism are seen as essential elements for the improvement of communication and for the reduction of intercultural misunderstanding.

The European Commission (1995) opted in a so-called *White Book* for trilingualism as a policy goal for all European citizens. Apart from the 'mother tongue,' each citizen should learn at least two 'community languages.' In fact, the concept of 'mother tongue' referred to the national languages of European nation-states and ignored the fact that mother tongue and national language do not coincide for many inhabitants of Europe. At the same time, the concept of 'community languages' referred to the national languages of two other EU member-states. In later European Commission documents, reference was made to one foreign language with high international prestige (English was deliberately not referred to) and one so-called *neighbouring* language. The latter concept related commonly to neighbouring countries, never to next-door neighbours.

In a follow-up to the first *European Year of Languages*, proclaimed in 2001, the heads of state and government of all EU member-states gathered in 2002 in Barcelona and called upon the European Commission to take further action to promote multilingualism across Europe, in particular by the learning and teaching of at least two foreign languages from a very young age (Nikolov and Curtain 2000). The final Action Plan 2004–2006, published by the European Commission (2003), may ultimately lead to an inclusive approach in which IM languages are no longer denied access to Europe's celebration of language diversity. In particular, the plea for the learning of three languages by all EU citizens, the plea for an early start to such learning experiences, and the plea for offering a wide range of languages to choose from open the door to such an inclusive approach. Although this may sound paradoxical, such an approach can also be advanced by accepting the role of English as a *lingua franca* for intercultural communication across Europe.

Against this background, the following principles are suggested for the enhancement of multilingual education at the primary school level:

1. In the primary school curriculum, three languages are introduced for all children:
   - the standard language of the particular nation-state as a major school subject and the major language of communication for the teaching of other school subjects;
   - English as a lingua franca for international communication;
   - an additional third language chosen from a variable and varied set of priority languages at the national, regional, and/or local level of the multicultural society.

2. The teaching of these languages is part of the regular school curriculum and subject to educational inspection.
3. Regular primary school reports provide, formally or informally, information on the children's proficiency in each of these languages.
4. National working programmes are established for the priority languages referred to under (1) in order to develop curricula, teaching methods, and teacher training programmes.
5. Part of these priority languages may be taught at specialized language schools.

This set of principles is aimed at reconciling bottom-up and top-down pleas in Europe for multilingual education, and is inspired by large-scale and enduring experiences with the learning and teaching of English (as L1 or L2) and one language other than English (LOTE) for all children in the State of Victoria, Australia (see Section 4 of this Chapter). When each of the above-mentioned languages should be introduced in the curriculum, and whether or when they should be subject or medium of instruction, should be spelled out depending on particular national, regional, or local contexts. Derived from an overarching conceptual and longitudinal framework, priority languages could be specified in terms of both RM and IM languages for the development of curricula, teaching methods, and teacher-training programmes. Moreover, the increasing internationalization of pupil populations in European schools requires that a language policy be introduced for all school children in which the traditional dichotomy between foreign language instruction for indigenous majority pupils and home language instruction for IM pupils is put aside. Given the experiences abroad (e.g. the Victorian School of Languages in Melbourne, Australia), language schools could become centers of expertise where a variety of languages are taught, in particular if the number of children requesting instruction in these languages is low and/or spread over many schools. In line with the proposed principles for primary schooling, similar ideas could be worked out for secondary schools where learning more than one language is already an established practice. The above-mentioned principles would recognize multilingualism in an increasingly multicultural environment as an asset for all children and for society at large. The EU, the Council of Europe, and UNESCO could function as leading transnational agencies in promoting such concepts. The UNESCO *Universal Declaration of Cultural Diversity* (2002) is in line with the inclusive views expressed here, in particular in its plea to encourage language diversity, to respect the mother tongue at all levels of education, and to foster the learning of several languages from the youngest age.

References

Alladina, S. and V. Edwards (eds.)
  1991   *Multilingualism in the British Isles.* (Vol. 1: The older mother tongues and Europe; Vol. 2: Africa, the Middle East and Asia.) London/New York: Longman.
Ammerlaan, T., M. Hulsen, H. Strating and K. Yağmur (eds.)
  2001   *Sociolinguistic and Psycho-linguistic Perspectives on Maintenance and Loss of Minority Languages.* Münster/New York: Waxmann.
Baetens Beardsmore, H.
  1993   *European Models of Bilingual Education.* Clevedon: Multilingual Matters.
Baker, C.
  ³2001   *Foundations of Bilingual Education and Bilingualism.* Clevedon: Multilingual Matters.
Baker, Ph. and J. Eversley (eds.)
  2000   *Multilingual Capital. The Languages of London's School Children and Their Relevance to Economic, Social and Educational Policies.* London: Battlebridge Publications.
Bauböck, R., A. Heller and A. Zolberg (eds.)
  1996   *The Challenge of Diversity. Integration and Pluralism in Societies of Immigration.* European Centre Vienna: Avebury.
Bebermeier, H., E. Thürmann, J. Illner and U. Pfaff
  1997   *Sprachprüfung (Feststellungsprüfung) anstelle von Pflichtfremdsprachen oder Wahlpflichtfremdsprachen.* Soest: LSW.
Beetsma, D. (ed.)
  2002   *Trilingual Primary Education in Europe.* Leeuwarden: Fryske Akademie.
Bratt-Paulston, C. and D. Peckham (eds.)
  1998   *Linguistic Minorities in Central and Eastern Europe.* Clevedon: Multilingual Matters.
Caubet, D., S. Chaker and J. Sibille (eds.)
  2002   *Codification des langues de France.* Paris: l'Harmattan.
Cenoz, J. and F. Genesee (eds.)
  1998   *Beyond Bilingualism. Multilingualism and Multilingual Education.* Clevedon: Multilingual Matters.
Cenoz, J. and U. Jessner (eds.)
  2000   *English in Europe. The Acquisition of a Third Language.* Clevedon: Multilingual Matters.
Churchill, S.
  1986   *The Education of Linguistic and Cultural Minorities in the OECD Countries.* Clevedon: Multilingual Matters.
Clyne, M.
  1991   *Community Languages: The Australian Experience.* Cambridge: Cambridge University Press.
Cohn-Bendit, D. and Th. Schmid
  1992   *Heimat Babylon. Das Wagnis der multikulturellen Demokratie.* Hamburg: Hoffmann and Campe.

Coulmas, F.
1991   *A Language Policy for the European Community. Prospects and Quan-daries*. Berlin/New York: Mouton de Gruyter.
Council of Europe
2000   *Linguistic Diversity for Democratic Citizenship in Europe. Towards a Framework for Language Education Policies. Proceedings Innsbruck (Austria) May 1999*. Strasbourg: Council of Europe.
Craith, M.
2003   Facilitating or generating linguistic diversity. The European charter for regional or minority languages. In: G. Hogan-Brun and S. Wolff (eds.), *Minority Languages in Europe. Frameworks, Status, Prospects*, 56–72. Hampshire: Palgrave Macmillan.
Department of Education
2001   *Languages Other than English in Government Schools, 2000*. State Government Victoria.
Directive 77/486
1977   *Directive 77/486 of the Council of the European Communities on the Schooling of Children of Migrant Workers*. Brussels: CEC.
European Commission
1995   *Whitebook. Teaching and learning: Towards a Cognitive Society*. Brussels: COM.
European Commission
2003   *Promoting Language Learning and Linguistic Diversity. An Action Plan 2004–2006*. Brussels: COM. Retrieved from www.europa.eu.int/comm/education/policies/lang/languages/actionplan_en.html.
Extra, G., R. Aarts, T. van der Avoird, P. Broeder and K. Yağmur
2002   *De andere talen van Nederland: Thuis en op school*. Bussum: Coutinho.
Extra, G. and D. Gorter (eds.)
2001   *The Other Languages of Europe. Demographic, Sociolinguistic, and Educational Perspectives*. Clevedon: Multilingual Matters.
Extra, G. and L. Verhoeven (eds.)
1993a   *Community Languages in the Netherlands*. Amsterdam: Swets and Zeitlinger.
1993b   *Immigrant Languages in Europe*. Clevedon: Multilingual Matters.
1998   *Bilingualism and Migration*. Berlin: Mouton De Gruyter.
Extra G. and K. Yağmur (eds.)
2004   *Urban Multilingualism in Europe. Immigrant Minority Languages at Home and School*. Clevedon: Multilingual Matters.
Galbally Report
1978   *Migrant Services and Programmes*. Canberra: Australian Government.
Gogolin, I.
1994   *Der monolinguale Habitus der multilingualen Schule*. Münster/New York: Waxmann.
Gogolin, I. and H. Reich
2001   Immigrant languages in Federal Germany. In: G. Extra and D. Gorter (eds.), *The Other Languages of Europe. Demographic, Sociolinguistic and Educational Perspectives*, 193–214. Clevedon: Multilingual Matters.

Gorter, D., J. Hoekstra, L. Jansma and J. Ytsma (eds.)
1990   *Fourth International Conference on Minority Languages* (Vol. 1: General papers; Vol. 2: Western and Eastern European papers.) Clevedon: Multilingual Matters.
Haarmann, H.
1975   *Soziologie und Politik der Sprachen Europas.* München: Deutscher Taschenbuch Verlag.
Hogan-Brun, G. and S. Wolff (eds.)
2003   *Minority Languages in Europe. Frameworks, Status, Prospects.* Hampshire: Palgrave Macmillan.
Hunger, U.
2001   Schulerfolg und bildungspolitische Integrationsmodelle im Vergleich der Zuwanderungsnationalitäten und Bundesländer. In: J. Illner and E. Thürmann (eds.), *Zweisprachigkeit und Schulerfolg. Beiträge zur Diskussion,* 123–152. Soest: LSW.
Husén, T. and S. Opper (eds.)
1983   *Multicultural and Multilingual Education in Immigrant Countries.* Oxford: Pergamon Press.
Illner, J. and U. Pfaff
2001   Migrantinnen und Migranten an den Schulen in NRW. In: J. Illner and E. Thürmann (eds.), *Zweisprachigkeit und Schulerfolg. Beiträge zur Diskussion,* 153–168. Soest: LSW.
Interministerielle Arbeitsgruppe 'Zuwanderung' der Landesregierung
2000   *Zuwanderung und Integration in Nordrhein-Westfalen.* Düsseldorf: Ministerium für Arbeit und Soziales, Qualifikation und Technologie.
Jaspaert, K. and S. Kroon (eds.)
1991   *Ethnic Minority Languages and Education.* Amsterdam/Lisse: Swets and Zeitlinger.
Jørgensen, J. (ed.)
2003   *Turkish Speakers in North Western Europe.* Clevedon: Multilingual Matters.
Karmel, P. (chair)
1973   *Karmel Report on Schooling in Australia.* Canberra: Australian Government Printing Service.
Kroon, S.
1990   *Opportunities and Constraints of Community Language Teaching.* Münster/New York: Waxmann.
Kruyt, A. and J. Niessen
1997   Integration. In: H. Vermeulen (ed.), *Immigrant Policy for a Multicultural Society. A Comparative Study of Integration, Language and Religious Policy in Five Western European Countries.* Brussels: Migration Policy Group.
Landesinstitut für Schule und Weiterbildung (eds.)
2001   *Zweisprachigkeit und Schulerfolg. Die Wirksamkeit von Schulischen Modellen zur Förderung von Kindern aus zugewanderten Sprachminderheiten. Ergebnisse der (Schul)forschung.* Soest: LSW.
Linguistic Minorities Project
1985   *The Other Languages of England.* London: Routledge and Kegan.
MACLOTE
1993   *LOTE Strateg Plan.* Melbourne: Directorate of School Education.

MACLOTE
  1994   *Report to the Minister for Education.* Melbourne: Directorate of School
          Education.
Martin, P., A. Creese, A. Bhaff and N. Bhojani
  2004   *Complementary Schools and their Communities in Leicester. Final Report.*
          School of Education, University of Leicester.
Miles, R. and D. Thränhardt (eds.)
  1995   *Migration and European Integration. The Dynamics of Inclusion and Ex-
          clusion.* London: Pinter Publ.
Ministerium für Schule und Weiterbildung
  2000   *Lehrplan für den muttersprachlichen Unterricht.* Soest: LSW.
Nikolov, M. and H. Curtain (eds.)
  2000   *An Early Start. Young Learners and Modern Languages in Europe and
          Beyond.* Strasbourg: Council of Europe.
Obdeijn, H. and J.J. de Ruiter (eds.)
  1998   *Le Maroc au coeur de l'Europe. L'enseignement de la langue et culture
          d'origine (ELCO) aux élèves marocains dans cinq pays européens.* Tilburg:
          Tilburg University Press, Syntax Datura.
Ozolins, U.
  1993   *The Politics of Language in Australia.* Cambridge: Cambridge University
          Press.
Phillipson, R.
  2003   *English-Only Europe? Challenging Language Policy.* London/New York:
          Routledge.
Reid, E. and H. Reich
  1992   *Breaking the Boundaries. Migrant Workers' Children in the EC.* Clevedon:
          Multilingual Matters.
Synak, B. and T. Wicherkiewicz (eds.)
  1997   *Language Minorities and Minority Languages in the Changing Europe.*
          University of Gdansk.
Taylor, Ch.
  1993   *Multikulturalismus und die Politik der Anerkennung.* Frankfurt: Fischer.
Tilmatine, M. (ed.)
  1997   *Enseignment des langues d'origine et immigration nord-africaine en Eu-
          rope: langue maternelle ou langue d'état?* Paris: INALCO/CEDREA-CRB.
Tosi, A.
  1984   *Immigration and Bilingual Education. A Case Study of Movement of Popu-
          lation, Language Change and Education Within the EEC.* Oxford: Perga-
          mon Press.
UNESCO
  2002   *Universal Declaration of Cultural Diversity.* Paris. Retrieved from
          www.unesco.org/culture/pluralism/diversity.
Ytsma, J. and C. Hoffmann (eds.)
  2003   *Sociolinguistic Perspectives in Third Language Acquisition.* Clevedon:
          Multilingual Matters.

Recommended readings

Baetens Beardsmore, H.
  1993   *European Models of Bilingual Education.* Clevedon: Multilingual Matters.
Baker, C.
  ³2001   *Foundations of Bilingual Education and Bilingualism.* Clevedon: Multilingual Matters.
Cenoz, J. and F. Genesee (eds.)
  1998   *Beyond Bilingualism. Multilingualism and multilingual education.* Clevedon: Multilingual Matters.
Coulmas, F.
  1991   *A Language Policy for the European Community. Prospects and quandaries.* Berlin/New York: Mouton de Gruyter.
Extra, G. and D. Gorter (eds.)
  2001   *The Other Languages of Europe. Demographic, Sociolinguistic, and Educational Perspectives.* Clevedon: Multilingual Matters.
Extra G. and K. Yağmur (eds.)
  2004   *Urban Multilingualism in Europe. Immigrant Minority Languages at Home and School.* Clevedon: Multilingual Matters.
Hogan-Brun, G. and S. Wolff (eds.)
  2003   *Minority Languages in Europe. Frameworks, Status, Prospects.* Hampshire: Palgrave Macmillan.
Phillipson, R.
  2003   *English-only Europe? Challenging Language Policy.* London/New York: Routledge.

8.   From biliteracy to pluriliteracies

Ofelia García, Lesley Bartlett and JoAnne Kleifgen

1.   Introduction

Literacy is, as Gee (1996: 22) has aptly described, "a socially contested term." Sociocultural studies of literacy have problematized the tendency to define literacy as a singular knowledge or developmentally ordered skill set; as unvarying across contexts and situations; and as primarily cognitive. Instead, they have demonstrated that literacy entails much more than the ability to read and write, that literacy practices are enmeshed within and influenced by social, cultural, political, and economic factors, and that literacy learning and use varies by situation and entails complex social interactions. If literacy is a socially contested term, the situation that has, in the literature to date, been dubbed 'biliteracy' is surely doubly contested, since the inclusion of more than one language system clearly points to power differentials and tensions about linguistic rights.

Yet, at this historical moment, people around the world engage daily in the complicated social, political, cultural, and psychological work of learning and using literacies in multiple languages and scripts that are enmeshed within other channels or modes of communication and diverse semiotic systems. In many parts of African, Asian, and Latin American post-colonial societies, multilingualism has long been the norm. However, in the 21st century, global flows of people, goods, and ideas across national borders have created complex forms of multilingualism in developed countries as well. Naturally, in each situation there are carefully negotiated linguistic hierarchies, with some languages (often colonial ones) having more power than others, and with schools often working towards academic monolingualism.

Ironically, the spread of English throughout the world and the important role it has assumed in globalized encounters (Brutt-Griffler 2004; Crystal 2003; Phillipson 2003) have been important mechanisms for the complex ways in which multilingualism is used today. Given the prestige granted English by its use in international business, tourism, and global communications, people around the world are increasingly obliged to incorporate English in their communicative and literacy practices. English has become both boon and threat to multilingualism, for English also threatens to overwhelm national and regional languages, especially in situations where language education policies privilege English over local or national languages (as, for example, the case of Tanzania). And yet, the prominence of English and the increased familiarity with multilingualism has bent the rigid power of some national languages, allowing other languages voice and power within society. This is best seen in the context of Latin America where countries, such as Guatemala and Bolivia, have official-ized indigenous languages (López 2006). It is seen worldwide, too, as immi-grants use their many languages not only in ethnolinguistic communities, but also in more public spaces such as the web, and to communicate not only with their own local community, but also with others who speak their languages worldwide, and who do so, because of contact with other languages, in very dif-ferent ways. The increased presence in public domains, including the web, of languages that had been previously relegated to private domains accentuates the variability, hybridity, and sense-making processes of literacy practices today.

In this context, it has become clear that, instead of bilingualism and biliter-acy, the terms *plurilingualism* and *pluriliteracies* more accurately describe the complex language practices and values of speakers in multilingual communities of the 21st century (Beacco and Byram 2003; Conseil d'Europe, 2000; Clyne 2003; Coste 2001; Hélot 2004).[1] In terms of language use, plurilingualism entails "proficiency, of varying degrees, in several languages and experience of several cultures" (*Common European Framework of Reference for Languages*, p. 168). For Coste (2001: 15), plurilingualism involves practices and values that are not equivalent or even homologous in different languages, but that are *inte-grated, variable, flexible, and changing*. Further, scholars aver that plurilingual-ism should entail the awareness that all language varieties have equal value, although different functions (Beacco and Byram 2003). Plurilingualism, then, requires the *integration* of *unevenly developed* competences in a variety of lan-guages, dialects, and registers, as well as the *valuing of linguistic tolerance*.

In this chapter, we review the existing literature on what has been called 'bi-literacy' and the central concepts and theoretical approaches that have been used for its study. We include a section on the pedagogy of literacy and bilin-gualism, a topic that has received much attention because of the important role that school has played in the development of literacy. We pay special attention to Hornberger's landmark framework, which discusses the continua of biliter-acy, and we consider new work on multilingual literacies. Then, reviewing scholarship in New Literacy Studies, multiliteracies, and multimodal literacies, and adding a plurilingual perspective, we reframe and extend the biliteracy scholarship to recognize more dynamic and hybrid uses of literacies in and out of schools, influenced by the new ways of using languages and literacies that are the result of new technologies and increased movements of people, services and goods in a globalized world. By integrating the different theoretical perspec-tives that surround biliteracy and sociocultural studies of literacy, we develop a *pluriliteracies approach* that, we argue, promises to address more accurately contemporary sociolinguistic practices.

2.   Biliteracy

Biliteracy in schools is often focused only on a skills-based view of an individual's literacy in one or the other language. But biliteracy is much more than what is learned in schools. Biliteracy, even more than monolingual literacy, also develops in families, homes, and communities (see Farr 1994a, 1994b; Gregory and Williams 2000 for biliteracy; and Hull and Schultz 2002 for monolingual literacy). Children and adults surrounded by different scripts in out-of-school settings often acquire the ability to read and write in two languages in functionally appropriate ways. They also acquire different attitudes and values about different literacy practices, including how these are associated with particular situated identities and social positions.

2.1.   Biliteracy definitions

Early scholars of biliteracy, such as Goodman, Goodman and Flores (1979), as well as Fishman (1980), defined biliteracy as *mastery* of reading and writing in two languages. Some scholars, retaining the notion of literacy as singular, did not refer to the term biliteracy and spoke instead of *literacy and bilingualism* (Williams and Snipper 1990) or of *literacy across languages and cultures* (Ferdman, Weber and Ramirez 1994). Most of these studies, as we will see below, focused on the acquisition of literacy in a powerful second language. Dworin (2003: 171) defined biliteracy as "children's literate competencies in two languages, to whatever degree, developed either simultaneously or successively." Reyes (2001: 98) also defined biliteracy as mastery, but she extended the concept to mean:

> mastery of the fundamentals of speaking, reading, and writing (knowing sound/ symbol connections, conventions of print, accessing and conveying meaning through oral or print mode, etc.) in two linguistic systems. It also includes constructing meaning by making relevant cultural and linguistic connections with print and the learners' own lived experiences […] as well as the interaction of the two linguistic systems to make meaning.

Broader definitions of biliteracy have been proposed by Pérez and Torres-Guzmán (1996) and Lüdi (1997). Pérez and Torres-Guzmán (1996: 54) defined biliteracy as "the acquisition and learning of the decoding and encoding of and around print using two linguistic and cultural systems in order to convey messages in a variety of contexts."

Basing his understandings on Street's work (discussed below), Lüdi (1997: 207) proposed a broad definition of biliteracy as

> *the possession of, or access to, the competences and information required to accomplish literacy practices which an individual wishes to – or is compelled to – engage*

in in everyday situations in two languages, with their corresponding functions and in the corresponding cultural contexts, independently of the degree of mastery and the mode of acquisition (italics in the original).

Biliteracy, as defined by Hornberger, its most perceptive scholar, describes "the use of two or more languages in and around writing" (Hornberger 2003: xii) or "any and all instances in which communication occurs in two or more languages in or around writing" (Hornberger 1990: 213). Hornberger adapts the definition of "literacy event" given by Heath (1982: 83) as "any occasion in which a piece of writing is integral to the nature of participants'interactions and their interpretative processes" in a bilingual context. But precisely because bilingualism and biliteracy are so complex, Hornberger speaks of biliteracy "instances," encompassing not only events, but also "biliterate actors, interactions, practices, activities, programs, situations, societies, sites, worlds" (Hornberger 2003: xiii; Hornberger and Skilton-Sylvester 2000: 98; Hornberger 2000: 362). And Hornberger proposes a multifaceted model of a "continua of biliteracy," which we describe below.

2.1.   Sequential biliteracy

Just as the definitions of biliteracy have shifted over time, theories regarding the acquisition of biliteracy and approaches to biliteracy pedagogy have also changed substantially. The most popular position at the end of the 20th century was that literacy in the first language (L1) had to be developed prior to literacy in the second (L2). UNESCO suggested in 1953 that there were advantages in using the child's mother tongue to teach initial literacy. This was the position of the early proponents of bilingual education, especially for children of linguistic minorities (Modiano 1968). The idea was not to develop biliteracy per se, but rather to advance literacy in the dominant societal language by teaching children to read in a language they understood. Most bilingual education programs of the transitional kind teach children to read and write in their mother tongue initially, with full transition to reading and writing in the child's second language only after the child has oral proficiency in the language to be read, as shown in Figure 1.

literacy in L1 and oral proficiency in L2 →	literacy in L2 and oral proficiency in L2

Figure 1. Literacy education in transitional bilingual education programs

Cummins (1981 and 1991), writing about second language acquisition, and Bernhardt and Kamil (1995), writing about second language reading research, have proposed that there is an interdependence across languages. Cummins refers to this as the *Common Underlying Proficiency* and the *Developmental Interdependence Hypothesis*. Bernhardt and Kamil speak of the *Linguistic Interdependence Hypothesis*. Both hypotheses posit that successful readers in L1 must reach a *threshold* of second language competence for transferability of literacy skills to occur (Bossers 1991; Brisbois 1992). They argue that there should be fluency and literacy in L1 before embarking on such instruction in L2; that is, that *sequential biliteracy* is necessary (Collier and Thomas 1989; Hakuta 1986; Wong Fillmore and Valadez 1986). Many correlational studies have indeed shown that at least reading proficiency transfers between languages (Carson et al. 1990; Elley 1984; Goldman, Reyes and Varnhagen 1984; Groebel 1980; Reyes 1987; Tregar and Wong 1984). Heath (1986) has referred to this same concept as *transferable generic literacies*.

This *sequential view of biliteracy* posits that literacy in the second language should not be introduced until a child has competence in speaking, reading, and writing the first language (Wong, Fillmore and Valadez 1986). This is consistent with research findings on the academic failure of indigenous peoples and immigrants who most often are given their initial reading instruction in a second language (Skutnabb-Kangas 1981, 2000; Francis and Reyhner 2002).

2.2. Simultaneous biliteracy

The success of immersion bilingual education programs in Canada where anglophone children learned to read in French, a second language, without any adverse effects challenged the position that literacy in L1 was essential to acquire literacy in L2 (Cummins 1979; Lambert and Tucker 1972; Genesee 1980). Furthermore, in their studies of ethnic mother tongue schools, Fishman and colleagues (Fishman 1980; Fishman et al. 1985) and García (1988) found that children were able to *simultaneously* acquire literacy in two languages, even when languages differed significantly in script and discourse mode. Similar findings have resulted from studies of community language classes and complementary schools in Great Britain (Kenner 2000; Creese et al. forthcoming), as well as heritage language programs in Canada (Beynon and Toohey 1991).

Proponents of simultaneous biliteracy argue that children can learn to read in two languages at once, even as they are still developing cognitive-oral skills in L2 (Anderson and Roit 1996; Barrera 1983; Gersten 1996; Hudelson 1984; Reyes 2001; Weber 1991). This position has been supported by Edelsky's (1986) excellent study of children's writing in Spanish and English, as well as research by Hudelson (1984) and Dworin (2003). Dworin (2003: 179) posits the *bidirectionality* of biliteracy development, pointing to the "dynamic, flexible process in which children's transactions with two written languages mediate their language learning for both languages."

Notably, in all of these studies, children acquired literacy in the two languages simultaneously, but in different educational spaces, that is, in different classrooms, with different teachers, or with the same teacher but at different times. This instructional situation is very different from the more integrated approach of plurilingual literacy practices that we describe in section 3.

2.3.   The pedagogy of biliteracy

The view of sequential or simultaneous biliteracy holds that each language develops separately, even if simultaneously, and thus each literacy should be taught as monolingual literacy. Most handbooks to teach biliteracy propose reading and writing approaches that are similar to those that are used to teach literacy in one or the other language. This is so, especially, for the English-speaking world, and particularly in the United States for the teaching of literacy in Spanish and English (see, for example, Ada 2003; Brisk and Harrington 2000; Carrasquillo and Segan 1998; Freeman and Freeman 1996; Pérez and Torres-Guzmán 1996.)

Other texts focus on teaching literacy in a dominant language, most often English, to second language learners, especially immigrants (Gibbons 2002; Gregory 1996; Hawkins 2004; Peregoy and Owen 1996). Pérez (1998: 36) suggests that studies of reading in bilingual contexts have found that second language learners require:

- careful pre-reading preparation to activate and expand background knowledge for comprehension,
- use of good meaning-making strategies, such as ability to relate the text to prior experience or learning, and familiarity with genre and kinds of questions that students are asked (Langer et al. 1990),
- use of metacognitive strategies, such as self-questioning (Muñiz-Swicegood 1994),
- activation of three types of schemata – linguistic schemata, based on prior language development; content schemata, based on prior knowledge of content; and text schemata, based on knowledge of rhetorical structure of the text (Carrell 1987),
- explicit instruction in previewing, skimming, adjusting reading rate, recognizing the author's purpose, making inferences, and separating fact from opinion (Jensen 1986),
- reading extensively to become productive readers.

The use of process approaches to teach writing are favored with language minority children because of their focus on developing voice and fluency, although these approaches have been challenged (Delpit 1991). Derewianka (1990) has identified four stages of explicit literacy teaching that are important for second language learners:

- building up the field
- modeling the text type
- joint construction
- independent writing

Pedagogical approaches to literacy in a second language rely heavily on the concept of *scaffolding* social interaction so as to create contexts for linguistic and academic learning in the *Zone of Proximal Development*, that is, "the distance between the actual developmental level as determined by independent problem solving and the level of potential development as determined through problem solving under adult guidance or in collaboration with more capable peers" (Vygotsky 1978: 86). According to Van Lier (2005) and Walqui (2002: 6), scaffolding in educational settings has six features:

- the tasks are repeated, with variations, and connected to one another,
- exploration is encouraged in a safe, supportive environment with contextual support,
- there is encouragement and participation in a shared community of practice,
- tasks are adjusted depending on actions of learners,
- there is an increasing role for the learner as skills and confidence increase,
- participants are focused on the task.

Walqui (2002) identifies six main types of instructional scaffolding to use with second language learners:

- modeling
- bridging
- contextualization
- schema building
- text re-presentation
- metacognitive development

2.4.   Beyond sequential and simultaneous biliteracy to the continua of biliteracy

As Hornberger and Skilton-Sylvester (2000) have pointed out, studies of biliteracy most often focus on the development of literacy in a second language in school, and are accompanied by a skills-based view of literacy. Biliteracy pedagogies often continue to demand two separate, evenly developed competencies corresponding to equal contexts and separate identities, with literacy in one language often being more valued (and more assessed) than literacy in the other.

Hornberger's (1989) *continua of biliteracy* has created an integrated way of analyzing complex phenomena, including the contexts, development, media, and more recently (Hornberger and Skilton-Sylvester 2000) the content of biliteracy. According to these authors, the continua of biliteracy include the following, with the left representing the less powerful end of the continuum and the right representing the more powerful end of the continuum:

Contexts of biliteracy
- The micro - macro continuum
- The oral -literate continuum
- The bilingual - monolingual continuum

Biliterate development in the individual
- The reception - production continuum
- The oral language - written language continuum
- The L1 - L2 transfer continuum

Media of biliteracy
- The simultaneous - - - - - - - - - - - - - - - - - -successive exposure continuum
- The dissimilar - - - - - - - - - - - - - - similar language structures continuum
- The divergent - convergent scripts continuum

Content of biliteracy
- Minority -majority continuum
- Vernacular - literacy continuum
- Contextualized - - - - - - - - - - - -decontextualized language texts continuum

This most recent version of the model (Hornberger and Skilton-Sylvester 2000) emphasizes that not only are all points in a particular continuum interrelated, but that all points across the continua are also interrelated. This revision integrates a critical perspective, positing that there tends to be a privileging of one end of the continua over the other because of differences in power relations, and that biliteracy is better obtained when learners can draw on all points of the continua (Hornberger 1989: 289). The interrelated nature of Hornberger's continua supports the potential for positive transfer across literacies, but its nested nature also shows how transfer can be promoted or hindered by different contextual factors (Hornberger 2003: 25).

Hornberger's continua of biliteracy identifies the major social, linguistic, political, and psychological issues that surround the development of biliteracy, as they relate to each other. The framework has been most influential in studies of biliteracy and multilingual literacies throughout the world (see Hornberger 2003). What makes Hornberger's continua of biliteracy powerful and different from all other studies we have referenced is that it captures the complexity of biliteracy. It builds on the *differences* that are the result of the degree to which groups or societies have power; live in monolingual or bilingual societies; speak languages that have literacies, or that have similar/dissimilar language structures or scripts; have schools in which their languages are used or taught; have opportunities to receive or produce texts with different varieties of diverse languages. And yet, schools have ignored the complexity of Hornberger's continua, and pedagogical frameworks informed by the model have yet to be developed.

In an effort to emphasize the coexistence of not just two but multiple languages and literacies, Martin-Jones and Jones (2000) have proposed the term *multilingual literacies*. For these authors, the term highlights the "multiplicity and complexity of individual and group repertoires" (p. 5) and the "multiple ways in which people draw on and combine the codes in their communicative repertoire when they speak and write" (p. 7). With this term, Martin-Jones and Jones wish to signal: that people use more than two "spoken or written languages and language varieties in their communicative repertoire"; that the communicative purposes associated with different spoken and written languages are multiple and complex; that there are "multiple paths to the acquisition of the spoken and written languages within the group repertoire, and people have varying degrees of expertise in these languages and literacies"; and that "people draw on and combine the codes in their communicative repertoire when they speak and write" in multiple ways (2000: 5–7).[2]

Yet, as we noted in the introduction, the contemporary proliferation of not only languages, scripts, dialects, and registers but also modes, channels of communication and semiotic systems requires an integration of the sociolinguistically grounded work being done in biliteracy and multilingual literacies, the sociocultural scholarship of new literacy studies and multimodal literacies, and the burgeoning field of plurilingualism. We turn now to that task.

3.   A pluriliteracies approach

In this section, we argue that the work being developed in the field of biliteracy can be enriched by integrating and adapting ideas from New Literacy Studies, multimodal literacies, and plurilingualism. Our *pluriliteracies* approach builds on and extends the continua of biliteracy and the concept of multilingual literacies by integrating key insights from other literatures. For us, a *pluriliteracies approach* captures not only literacy continua with different interrelated axes, but also an emphasis on *literacy practices in sociocultural contexts,* the *hybridity* of literacy practices afforded by new technologies, and the increasing *interrelationship of semiotic systems.*

The use of two or more languages in reading and writing makes evident the importance of the social contexts of literacy learning – that is, it reveals that literacy is not an *autonomous* set of skills stripped of its cultural contexts and social purposes (Street 1984, 1993). Situations of multilingual literacies need to be researched and understood within a sociocultural framework, which emphasizes that making meaning from and with print varies according to different sociocultural contexts (Hornberger 1989; Pérez 1998) and media. As such, biliteracy is most appropriately studied within an *ideological* framework (Street 1984: 3). One of the important ideas we adopt from New Literacy Studies is the focus on *literacy practices* which are "the socially regulated, recurrent, and patterned things that people do with literacy as well as the cultural significance they ascribe to those things" (Brandt and Clinton 2002: 342; see also Baynham

1995: 1). The notion of *plurilingual literacy practices* emphasizes that social and cultural contexts are integral to doing literacy, even as it acknowledges the transfer between contexts of ways of knowing and doing.

Recent scholarship (New London Group 1996; Cope and Kalantzis 2000; Jewett and Kress 2003; Kleifgen 2001, forthcoming; Kress 2003) has proposed that multiple literacies are not only associated with different cultural contexts and social structures, but also with different channels or modes of communication. These studies recognize that literacy practices are increasingly *multimodal* – that is, that written-linguistic modes of meaning are intricately bound up with other visual, audio, and spatial semiotic systems. On this basis, the New London Group (1996) has proposed a *multiliteracies pedagogy* consisting of *situated practice, overt instruction, critical framing, and transformed practice*. This insight highlights the fact that, in the 21st century where new media are occasioning increased variation in multimodal discourses, biliteracy and multilingual literacies are practiced, as Coste (2001) averred, in an *integrated* fashion. Our pluriliteracies approach moves away from the dichotomy of the traditional L1/L2 pairing, emphasizing instead that languages and literacies are interrelated and flexible, and positing that all literacy practices have equal value.

The concept of *hybridity* is important in our understanding of plurilingual literacy practices. Extending the work of Bakhtin (1981) on the hybridity of the dialogue of languages, of Anzaldúa (1987) on the hybridity of being in the "borderlands," and of Bhabha (1994) on the hybridity of postcoloniality, we follow Shohat and Sham's (1994: 42) definition of hybridity as "an unending, unfinalizable process [...] [that] is dynamic, mobile, less an achieved synthesis, or prescribed formula than an unstable constellation of discourses." We agree with Gutiérrez and her colleagues (Gutiérrez, Baquedano-López and Alvarez, 2001: 128) that "hybrid language use is more than simple code-switching as the alternation between two codes. It is more a systematic, strategic, affiliative, and sense-making process [...]" A pluriliteracies approach acknowledges the agency involved in doing literacy and the dynamic transfer between different contexts in ways of being, knowing and doing (Bartlett, forthcoming). And although grounded in the social, political, and economic processes of globalization, a pluriliteracies approach has the potential for transformation and change, precisely because of the dynamism and flexibility of integrated hybrid practices.

Gutiérrez and her colleagues (Gutiérrez et al., 1999a, Gutiérrez, Baquedano-López and Tejada, 1999b, Gutiérrez et al. 2001), as well as Reyes (2001) have demonstrated the diversity of, and interplay between linguistic codes and literacy practices in multilingual classrooms. The hybridity of plurilingual literacy practices is also abundantly evident in studies of biliteracy in the home and community, and especially among adult immigrants. For example, Kalmar (2000) demonstrated how Latino adult migrants' developed their own hybrid writing system that used the Spanish alphabet to capture English speech sounds.

Guerra (1998) and Farr and Guerra (1995) examined the interplay between English and Spanish literacy strategies among transnational populations as they moved between Mexico and Chicago.

A pluriliteracies approach better captures the sociolinguistic realities of the current epoch. Sridhar (1996) posits that, in 21st century plurilingual societies, languages are not compartmentalized in a diglossic situation, but rather they overlap, intersect, and interconnect. A fusion of languages, dialects, scripts, registers, and semiotic systems characterize how people communicate today. As political and economic alliances are shaped and technology advances, literacy practices and literacy identities are variable and integrated.

Practices of plurilingual literacies are not simply markers of national or ethnic identity, but have become a form of economic and social capital in integrated markets and a globalized world (Bourdieu 1991; Heller 1999). It is pluriliteracy that is being marketed as a unifying capacity for European citizens in the 21st century. For example, the European Union is actively seeking to develop its citizen's plurilingual literacy practices and values. To do so, it emphasizes the role of school not simply in teaching languages to a certain level of proficiency, but also in recognizing and valuing the plurilingual language and literacy practices of students in their full range. The development of the European Language Portfolio (ELP) is one attempt to record and recognize these practices, regardless of whether they are learned or valued in school (Common European Framework of Reference for Languages 2002).

Our pluriliteracies approach, then:

- emphasizes the integrated, hybrid nature of plurilingual literacy practices;
- values all plurilingual literacy practices equally;
- highlights the continuous interplay of multiple languages, scripts, discourses, dialects, and registers;
- calls attention to the ways in which multilingual literacies are enmeshed and rely upon multiple modes, channels of communication, and semiotic systems;
- adopts from new literacy studies a constant awareness of the ways in which cultural contexts and social relations influence literacy practices;
- and attends to the development of literacy practices beyond the school, even as work within this vein endeavors to bring theoretical insight to bear on pedagogical developments.

3.1.   Pedagogies for plurilingual literacy practices

A pluriliteracies approach, or integrated plurilingual literacy practices, is one way for educators to resist the hegemony of dominant national languages. Whereas in traditional language enrichment, language maintenance, or transitional bilingual education programs, practices of literacies in the two languages were always kept separate, the heterogeneity of linguistic profiles in contemporary classrooms allows plurilingual literacy practices to naturally emerge. The linguistically integrated space of the classroom, coupled with the possibilities afforded to all languages by new technologies, fosters the development of pedagogies for plurilingual literacy practices that will increase the potential for communication, knowledge and understandings among all participants.

Even in the United States and other dominant English-speaking societies, where homogenizing literacy practices into 'standard English' is increasingly being imposed in schools (see García and Menken 2006; Hornberger 2006), emerging pedagogies are moving away from strict language compartmentalization. For example, in an interesting study of teaching ESL in Chinatown, Fu (2003) describes how she encouraged teachers to let students write in Chinese mixed with English as they were developing English writing. Manyak (2001, 2002), working in a primary grade English immersion class in California post-proposition 227, examined the blending of not only Spanish and English but also home and school registers in an elementary classroom, although he warned that hybrid literacy pedagogy did not benefit all students equally. Gutiérrez et al. (1999a, 1999b, 2001) suggested that the "commingling of and contradictions among different linguistic codes and registers" offered significant resources for learning (1999b: 289).

In the United States, the growth and development of dual language bilingual education programs also nurture and develop plurilingual literacy practices, despite the fact that teachers try to keep the two languages separate (see, for example, García 2006). Because in these classrooms children of different linguistic profiles are together, plurilingual literacy practices evolve informally, as children communicate around writing in two languages trying to make sense of who they all are, what they understand and know, and what they're doing.

Working on the design of learning environments for a new economy (Early, Cummins and Willinsky 2002), Cummins describes the use of "identity texts" as a way of highlighting the important role of negotiation of identities in students' learning (Cummins 2001, 2006). He builds on the four components of the multiliteracies pedagogy proposed by The New London Group (1996) – situated practices, overt instruction, critical framing, and transformed practices – but proposes an "academic expertise framework," which argues that *maximum identity investment* on the part of students is key to optimal academic development. In a school setting described by Cummins (2006), young students of diverse linguistic background create stories in English that are then translated with the help of older students, parents and teachers into their home languages. These multilingual stories are then published on the web, accompanied by images; spoken, musical, and dramatic renderings; or combinations of these in multimodal form.

Pedagogical work that incorporates pluriliteracies is especially evident in multilingual European contexts. In Wales *translanguaging and transliteracy* techniques are increasingly used to develop both English and Welsh, with students hearing or reading a lesson in one language, and developing their work in the other. Cen Williams, who coined the Welsh term *trawysieithu* [translanguaging] to refer to this pedagogy, sees four advantages to translanguaging and transliteracy: deeper understanding of the subject matter, development of competence in the weaker language, home-school cooperation, and integration of fluent speakers with early-level learners (as discussed by Baker, 2001: 280–284). Baker (2003) clarifies that translanguaging is not about code-switching, but rather about an arrangement that normalizes bilingualism without diglossic functional separation.

A pluriliteracies approach better describes the ways in which the practices of literacies are being supported pedagogically in the European Union. We have already referred to the European Language Portfolio (ELP) as an attempt to record and recognize plurilingual literacy practices, beyond those learned in schools. *CLIL/EMILE (Content and Language Integrated Learning)* is different from Traditional bilingual education or immersion pedagogy in that it allows for uneven but integrated competencies in different languages[3]. In addition, *language awareness* pedagogy, which is used in many European school contexts today to familiarize students with many different languages and to teach students to value them (see Hélot and Young 2006), does not in itself promote plurilingualism or plurilingual literacy practices, but it does build a social context in which such practices would be valued and recognized.

4.   Conclusion

Despite the potential to build on the integrated plurilingual literacy practices that are prevalent among peoples in the 21st century and facilitated through new media, schools reflect a national ideology that is at best multilingual in the sense of separate languages, but that is rarely multimodal or truly plurilingual. There are issues of resources for schools, but the core of the resistance lies in the lack of will to change the status quo of situations in which dominant languages and literacies hold power and privilege. The pedagogies that we have described in this chapter are most often accepted as "bridges" and "stepping stones" to monolingual literacy, or at best multilingual literacy. But we are still far removed from a stable use of pedagogies in schools, which would build on the plurilingual literacy practices that are prevalent among plurilingual individuals in informal settings, and which are today widespread in their personal use of technology. And yet, educators have the potential to transform values, as well as literacy practices, by giving room to these plurilingual literacy practices in a context other than the informal ones.

An important question is whether schools, regarded as the most influential educational domain, will continue to protect literacy in standard national languages and in traditional media, or will begin to build on the flexible and multimodal plurilingual literacy practices that characterize the world today.

Notes

1. Although this trend characterizes most of the world, it is absent in the United States where even bilingualism has been silenced in the 21st century (see García 2006; Hornberger, 2006.)
2. In the afterword to the Martin-Jones and Jones volume, Hornberger (2000) clarifies that her concept of biliteracy encompasses multilingual literacies, as well as the practices of multiple literacies, vernacular literacies, indigenous literacies, everyday literacies, and multiliteracies.
3. For more on CLIL/EMILE visit www.clilcompendium.com

References

Ada, Alma Flor
    2003   *A Magical Encounter: Latino Children's Literature in the Classroom.* 2d ed. Boston: Pearson Education.
Anderson, Valerie and Marsha Roit
    1996   Linking reading comprehension instruction to language development for language minority students. *Elementary School Journal* 96: 295–310.
Anzaldúa, Gloria
    1997   *Borderlands/La Frontera: The New Mestiza.* San Francisco: Aunt Lute Books.
Baker, Colin
    2001   *Foundations of Bilingual Education and Bilingualism.* Avon, UK: Multilingual Matters.
    2003   Biliteracy and transliteracy in Wales: Language planning and the Welsh National Curriculum. In *Continua of Biliteracy,* Nancy Hornberger (ed.), 71–90. Clevedon, Avon: Multilingual Matters.
Bakhtin, Mikhail M.
    1981   *The Dialogic Imagination.* Austin: University of Texas Press.
Barrera, Rosalind
    1983   Bilingual reading in the primary grades: Some questions about questionable views and practices. In *Early Childhood Bilingual Education: A Hispanic Perspective,* Teresa H. Escobedo (ed.), 164–183. New York: Teachers College Press.
Bartlett, Lesley
    forth-   To seem and to feel: Situated identities and literacy practices. *Teachers Col-*
    coming   *lege Record.*
Baynham, Mike
    1995   *Literacy Practices.* New York: Longman.

Beacco, Jean-Claude and Myram Byram
    2003   Guide for the development of language education policies in Europe. From linguistic diversity to plurilingual education. Strasbourg: Council of Europe (April, 2003). www.coe.int/lang.

Bernhardt, Elizabeth and Michael Kamil
    1995   Interpreting relationships between L1 and L2 reading: Consolidating the linguistic threshold and the linguistic interdependence hypotheses. *Applied Linguistics* 16: 15–34.

Beynon, June and Katherine Toohey
    1991   Heritage language education in British Columbia: Policy and programmes. *Canadian Modern Language Review* 47 (4): 606–616.

Bhabha, Homi K.
    1994   *The Location of Culture*. London: Routledge.

Bossers, B.
    1991   On thresholds, ceilings and short-circuits: The relation between L1 reading, L2 reading and L2 knowledge. *AILA Review* 8: 45–60.

Bourdieu, Pierre
    1991   *Language and Symbolic Power*. Cambridge: Harvard University Press.

Brandt, Deborah and Clinton, Katie
    2002   Limits of the local: Expanding perspectives on literacy as social practice. *Journal of Literacy Research* 34 (3): 337–356.

Brisbois, Judith E.
    1995   Connections between first- and second-language reading. *Journal of Reading Behavior* 27: 565–584.

Brisk, María Estela and Margaret M. Harrington
    2000   *Literacy and Bilingualism. A Handbook for All*. Mahwah, New Jersey: Lawrence Erlbaum.

Brutt-Griffler, Janina
    2004   *World English. A Study of Its Development*. Clevedon, Avon: Multilingual Matters.

Carson, Joan Eisterhold, Patricia L. Carrell, Sandra Silberstein, Barbara Kroll, and Phyllis A. Kuehn
    1990   Reading–writing relationships in first and second language. *TESOL Quarterly* 24 (2): 245–266.

Carrasquillo, Angela and Philip Segan (eds.)
    1996   *The Teaching of Reading in Spanish to the Bilingual Student*. 2d ed. Mahwah, New Jersey: Lawrence Erlbaum.

Carrell, Patricia L.
    1987   Content and formal schemata in ESL reading. *TESOL Quarterly* 21: 461–481.

Clyne, Michael
    2003   *Dynamics of Language Contact*. Cambridge: Cambridge University Press.

Collier, Virginia P. and William P. Thomas
    1989   How quickly can immigrants become proficient in school English? *Journal of Educational Issues of Language Minority Students* 5: 26–38.

Common European Framework of Reference for Languages
    2002   [http://www.coe.int/T/E/Cultural_Cooperation/education/Languages/ Language_Policy/Common_Framework_of_Reference/1cadre.asp# TopOfPage]

Conseil de l'Europe
   2000   *Cadre européen commun de référence pour les langues. Apprendre, enseigner, evaluer.* [Common European frame of reference on languages: Learn, teach, evaluate.] Division des Langues Vivantes Strasbourg: Didier.

Coste, David
   2001   La notion de compétence plurilingue. Actes du séminaire: L'enseignement des langues vivantes, perspectives. [The notion of plurilingual competence. Seminar proceedings: The teaching of living languages, perspectives.] Paris: Ministère de la Jeunesse de l'Education et de la Recherche, DES. [http://www.eduscol.education.fr/DOO33/langviv-act10.htm]

Cope, Bill and Mary Kalantzis
   2000   *Multiliteracies. Literacy Learning and Design of Social Futures.* London: Routledge.

Creese, Angela, Arvind Bhatt, Nirmala Bhojani and Peter Martin
   forth-   Multicultural, heritage and learner identities in complementary schools.
   coming

Crystal, David
   2003   *English as a Global Language.* 2d ed. Cambridge: Cambridge University Press.

Cummins, Jim
   1979   Linguistic interdependence and the educational development of bilingual children. *Review of Educational Research* 49: 222–251.
   1981   Four misconceptions about language proficiency in bilingual education. *NABE Journal* 5: 31–45.
   1991   Conversational and academic language proficiency in bilingual contexts. *AILA Review* 8: 75–89.
   2001   *Negotiating Identities: Education for Empowerment in a Diverse Society.* 2d ed. Los Angeles: California Association for Bilingual Education.
   2006   Identity texts: The imaginative construction of self through multiliteracies pedagogy. In *Imagining Multilingual Schools: Languages in Education and Globalization,* Ofelia García, Tove Skutnabb-Kangas and María Torres-Guzmán (eds.), 51–68. Clevedon, Avon: Multilingual Matters.

Delpit, Lisa
   1991   The silenced dialogue: Power and pedagogy in educating other people's children. In *Language Issues in Literacy and Bilingual/Multicultural Education,* Masahiko Minami and Bruce P. Kennedy (eds.), 483–502. Cambridge, MA: Harvard Educational Review.

Derewianka, B.
   1990   *Exploring How Texts Work.* Portsmouth, NH: Heinemann.

Dworin, Joel
   2003   Insights into biliteracy development: Toward a bidirectional theory of bilingual pedagogy. *Journal of Hispanic Higher Education* 2: 171–186.

Early, Margaret, Jim Cummins and John Willinsky
   2002   From literacy to multiliteracies: Designing learning environments for knowledge generation within the new economy. Proposal funded by the Social Sciences and Humanities Research Council of Canada.

Edelsky, Carole
  1986   Writing in a bilingual program: Había una vez. Norwood, NJ: Ablex Pub-
            lishing.
Elley, Warwick B.
  1984   Exploring the reading difficulties of second language learners and second
            languages in Fiji. In *Reading in a Foreign Language,* Charles J. Alderson
            and Alexander H. Urquhart (eds.), 281–297. London: Longman.
Farr, Marcia
  1994a   Biliteracy in the home: Practices among mexicano families in Chicago. In
            Adult Biliteracy in the United States, David Spener (ed.), 89–110 Washing-
            ton, D.C.: Center for Applied Linguistics.
  1994b   En los dos idiomas: Literacy practices among mexicano families in Chi-
            cago. [In both languages]. In *Literacy Across Communities,* Beverly Moss
            (ed.), 9–48. Cresskill, NJ: Hampton Press.
Farr, Marcia and Juan Guerra
  1995   Literacy in the Community: A Study of 'Mexicano' Families in Chicago.
            Discourse Processes 19 (1): 7–19.
Ferdman, Bernardo M., Rose-Marie Weber and Arnulfo G. Ramirez (eds.)
  1994   *Literacy across Languages and Cultures.* Albany: SUNY Press
Fishman, Joshua A.
  1980   Ethnocultural dimensions in the acquisition and retention of biliteracy.
            Journal of Basic Writing 3: 48–61.
Fishman, Joshua A., Michael Gertner, Esther Lowy and William Milán
  1985   *The Rise and Fall of the Ethnic Revival: Perspectives on Language and
            Ethnicity.* Berlin: Mouton.
Francis, Norbert and Jon Reyhner
  2002   *Language and Literacy Teaching for Indigenous Education: A Bilingual
            Approach.* Clevedon, Avon: Multilingual Matters.
Freeman, Yvonne and David Freeman
  1996   *Teaching Reading and Writing in Spanish in the Bilingual Classroom.*
            Portsmouth, NH: Heinemann.
Fu, Danling
  2003   *An Island of English: Teaching ESL in Chinatown.* Portsmouth, NH: Heine-
            mann.
García, Ofelia
  1988   The education of biliterate and bicultural children in ethnic schools in the
            United States. *Essays by the Spencer Fellows of the National Academy of
            Education* 4, 19–78.
  2006   Lost in transculturation: The case of bilingual education in New York City.
            In *'Along the Routes to Powe': Explorations of the Empowerment through
            Language,* Pütz, Martin, Joshua A. Fishman and JoAnne Neff-van Aertse-
            laer (eds.), 157–178. Berlin/New York: Mouton de Gruyter.
García, Ofelia and Kate Menken
  2006   The English of Latinos from a plurilingual transcultural angle: Impli-
            cations for assessment and schools. In *Dialects, Other Englishes, and
            Education,* Shondel Nero (ed.), 167–184. Mahwah, New Jersey: Law-
            rence Erlbaum.

Gee, James Paul
    1996   *Social Linguistics and Literacies. Ideology in Discourses*. London and
            Bristol, Pa.: Taylor and Francis.
Gersten, Russell
    1996   Literacy instruction for language minority students. The transition years.
            The Elementary School Journal 96: 228–244.
Gibbons, Pauline
    2002   *Scaffolding Language. Scaffolding Learning: Teaching Second Language
            Learners in the Mainstream Classroom*. Portsmouth, NH: Heinemann.
Goldman, Susan R., M. Reyes and Connie K. Varnhagen
    1984   Understanding fables in first and second languages. *NABE Journal* 8: 35–66.
Goodman, Kenneth, Yetta Goodman and Barbara Flores
    1979   *Reading in the Bilingual Classroom: Literacy and Biliteracy*. Rosslyn, VA:
            National Clearinghouse for Bilingual Education.
Gregory, Eve
    1996   *Making Sense of a New World: Learning to Read in a Second Language*.
            London: Paul Chapman.
Gregory, Eve and Ann Williams
    2000   *City Literacies: Learning to Read across Generations and Cultures*. New
            York: Routledge.
Groebel, Lillian
    1980   A comparison of students' reading comprehension in the native language
            with their reading comprehension in the target language. *English Language
            Teaching Journal* 35: 54–59.
Guerra, Juan
    1998   *Close to Home: Oral and Literate Practices in a Transnational Mexicano
            Community*. New York: Teachers College Press.
Gutiérrez, Kris D., Patricia Baquedano-López and Héctor H. Alvarez
    2001   Literacy as hybridity: Moving beyond bilingualism in urban classrooms.
            In *The Best for our Children: Critical Perspectives on Literacy for Latino
            Students,* María de la Luz Reyes and John J. Halcón (eds.), 122–141. New
            York and London: Teachers College Press.
Gutiérrez, Kris, Patricia Baquedano-López, Héctor Alvarez, and Ming Ming Chiu
    1999   Building a Culture of Collaboration through Hybrid Language Practices.
            Theory into Practice 38 (2): 87–93.
Gutiérrez, Kris, Patricia Baquedano-López and Carlos Tejada
    1999   Rethinking diversity: Hybridity and hybrid language practices in the third
            space. *Mind, Culture and Activity* 6 (4): 286–303.
Hakuta, Kenji
    1986   *Mirror of Language: The Debate on Bilingualism*. New York: Basic Books.
Hawkins, Margaret
    2004   Researching English language and literacy development in schools. *Edu-
            cational Researcher* 33 (3): 14–25.
Heath, Shirley Brice
    1986   Sociocultural contexts of language development. *Beyond Language: Social
            and Cultural Factors in Schooling Language Minority Students*, 145–186.
            Los Angeles: California State University, Evaluation, Dissemination and
            Assessment Center.

Heller, Monica
1999   *Linguistic Minorities and Modernity: A Sociolinguistic Ethnography.* London and New York: Longman.
Hélot, Christine
2004   Bilinguisme des migrants, bilinguisme des élites, analyse d'un écart en milieu scolaire. [Bilingualism of migrants, bilingualism of elites, analysis of a gap in the school environment] In *Les Cahiers de la Recherche,* A. Akkari (ed.), 8–27. Neuchâtel, Suisse: HEP Bejune.
Hélot, Christine and Andrea Young
2006   Imagining multilingual education in France: A language and cultural awareness project at primary level. In *Imagining Multilingual Schools: Languages in Education and Globalization,* Ofelia García, Tove Skutnabb-Kangas, and María Torres-Guzmán (eds.), 69–90. Clevedon, U.K.: Multilingual Matters.
Hornberger, Nancy H.
1989   Continua of biliteracy. *Review of Educational Research* 59: 271–296.
1990   Creating successful learning contexts for bilingual literacy. *Teachers College Record* 92 (2): 212–229.
2000   Multilingual literacies, literacy practices, and the continua of biliteracy. In *Multilingual Literacies,* Marilyn Martin-Jones and Kathryn Jones (eds.), 353–368. Amsterdam: John Benjamins.
2003   *Continua of Biliteracy: An Ecological Framework for Educational Policy, Research and Practice in Multilingual Settings.* Clevedon, U.K.: Multilingual Matters.
2006   Nichols to NCLB: Local and global perspectives on U.S. language education policy. In *Imagining Multilingual Schools: Languages in education and globalization,* Ofelia García, Tove Skutnabb-Kangas, and María Torres-Guzmán (eds.), 223–237. Clevedon, U.K.: Multilingual Matters.
Hornberger, Nancy H. and Ellen Skilton-Sylvester
2000   Revisiting the continua of biliteracy: International and critical perspectives. *Language and Education: An International Journal* 14 (2): 96–122.
Hudelson, Sarah
1984   Kan yu ret and rayt en Ingles: Children become literate in English as a second language. *TESOL Quarterly* 18: 221–238.
Hull, Glynda and Katherine Schultz (eds.)
2002   *School's out! Bridging Out-of-School Literacies with Classroom Practice.* New York: Teachers College Press.
Jensen, Linda
1986   Advanced reading skills in a comprehensive course. In *Teaching Second Language Reading for Academic Purposes,* Fraida Dubin, David E. Eskey and William Grabe (eds.), 103–124. Reading, Ma. Addison-Wesley.
Jewett, Carey and Gunther Kress
2003   *Multimodal Literacy.* New York: Peter Lang.
Kalmar, Tomás
2000   *Illegal Alphabets and Adult Biliteracy: Latino Migrants Crossing the Linguistic Divide.* Mahwah, NJ: Erlbaum Associates.

Kenner, Charmian
  2000   Biliteracy in a monolingual school system? English and Gujarati in South
            London. *Language, Culture and Curriculum* 13: 13–30.
Kleifgen, JoAnne
  2001   Assembling talk: Social alignments in the workplace. *Research on Language and Social Interaction* 34 (3): 279–308.
  forth-   Affordances and constraints of technology: Variation in multimodal dis-
  coming   course. In *Multimodal discourse in practice*, Sigrid Norris and Laurent Filliettaz (eds.), 238–261. London: Routledge.
Kress, Gunther
  2003   *Literacy in the New Media Age.* New York: Routledge.
Langer, Judith, Lillia Bartolomé, Olga A. Vásquez and Tamara Lucas
  1990   Meaning construction in school literacy tasks: A study of bilingual students. *American Educational Research Journal* 27: 427–471.
López, Luis Enrique
  2006   Cultural diversity, multilingualism and indigenous education in Latin America. In *Imagining Multilingual Schools: Languages in education and globalization,* Ofelia García, Tove Skutnabb-Kangas, and María Torres-Guzmán (eds.), 238–261. Clevedon, U.K.: Multilingual Matters.
Lüdi, Georges
  1997   Towards a better understanding of biliteracy. In *Writing Development: An Interdisciplinary View,* Clotilde Pontecorvo (ed.), 205–219. Amsterdam: John Benjamins.
Manyak, Patrick
  2001   Participation, Hybridity, and Carnival: A Situated Analysis of a Dynamic Literacy Practice in a Primary-Grade English Immersion Class. *Journal of Literacy Research* 33 (3): 423–65.
  2002   'Welcome to Salon 110': The consequences of hybrid literacy practices in a primary-grade English classroom. *Bilingual Research Journal* 26 (2): 421–442.
Martin-Jones, Marilyn and Katherine Jones (eds.)
  2000   *Multilingual Literacies: Comparative Perspectives on Research and Practice.* Amsterdam: John Benjamins.
Modiano, Nancy
  1968   National or mother language in beginning reading: A comparative study. *Research in the Teaching of English* 2 (1): 39.
Muñiz-Swicegood, M.
  1994   The effects of metacognitive reading strategy training on the reading performance and student reading analysis strategies of third grade bilingual students. *Bilingual Research Journal* 18: 83–98.
New London Group
  1996   A pedagogy of multiliteracies: Designing social futures. *Harvard Educational Review* 66 (1), 60–92.
Peregoy, Suzanne F. and Owen. F. Boyle
  1996   *Reading, Writing and Learning in ESL: A Resource Book for K-12 Teachers.* New York: Longman.

Pérez, Bertha (ed.)
1998   *Sociocultural Contexts of Language and Literacy.* Mahwah, NJ: Lawrence Erlbaum Associates.
Pérez, Bertha and María Torres-Guzmán
1996   *Learning in Two Worlds: An Integrated Spanish/English Biliteracy Approach.* 2d ed. New York: Longman.
Phillipson, Robert
2003   *English-Only Europe? Challenging language policy.* London: Routledge.
Reyes, María de la Luz
1987   Comprehension of content area passages: A study of Spanish/English readers in third and fourth grade. In *Becoming Literate in English as a Second Language,* S. Goldman and H. Trueba (eds.), 107–126. Norwood, New Jersey: Ablex.
1992   Challenging venerable assumptions: Literacy instruction for linguistically different students. *Harvard Educational Review* 62: 427–446.
2001   Unleashing possibilities: Biliteracy in the primary grades. In *The Best for our Children: Critical Perspectives on Literacy for Latino Students,* María de la Luz Reyes and John J. Halcón (eds.), 96–121. New York and London: Teachers College Press.
Reyes, María de la Luz and L. Constanzo, L.
2002   On the threshold of biliteracy: A first grader's personal journey. In *Making a Difference in the Lives of Bilingual-Bicultural Children,* Lourdes Díaz Soto, 145–156. New York: Peter Lang.
Shohat, Ella and Robert Stam
1994   *Unthinking Eurocentrism: Multiculturalism and the Media.* New York and London: Routledge.
Skutnabb-Kangas, Tove
1981   *Bilingualism or Not: The Education of Minorities.* Clevedon, Avon: Multilingual Matters.
2000   *Linguistic Genocide in Education – or Worldwide Diversity and Human Rights?* Mahwah, NJ: Lawrence Erlbaum.
Sridhar, Kamil K.
1996   Societal multilingualism. In *Sociolinguistics and Language Teaching,* Sandra. L. McKay and Nancy H Hornberger (eds.), 47–70. Cambridge: Cambridge University Press.
Street, Brian
1984   *Literacy in Theory and Practice.* New York: Cambridge University Press.
Street, Brian (ed.)
1993   *Cross-cultural Approaches to Literacy.* Cambridge: Cambridge University Press.
Tregar, B. and Wong, B.F.
1984   The relationship between native and second language reading comprehension and second language oral ability. In *Placement Procedures in Bilingual Education; Education and Policy Issues,* Charlene Rivera (ed.), 152–164. Clevedon, England: Multilingual Matters.
UNESCO
1953   *The Use of Vernacular Languages in Education.* Paris: UNESCO.

Van Lier, Leo
    2005   *The Ecology and Semiotics of Language Learning.* Dordrecht, NL: Kluwer
            Academic.
Vygotsky, Lev S.
    1978   *Mind in Society.* Cambridge, MA: Harvard University Press.
Walqui, Aída
    2002   Conceptual Framework. Scaffolding instruction for English learners. San
            Francisco: WestEd (unpublished).
Weber, Rose
    1991   Linguistic diversity and reading in American society. In *Handbook of Read-
            ing Research.* Vol. 2., R. Barr, M. L. Kamil, P. Mosenthal and P. David Pear-
            son (eds.), 97–119. New York: Longman.
Williams, James and Grace Capizzi Snipper
    1990   *Literacy and Bilingualism.* New York: Longman.
Wong Fillmore, Lily and Concepción Valadez
    1986   Teaching bilingual learners. In *Handbook of Research on Teaching,* M.C.
            Wittrock (ed.), 648–685. New York: Macmillan.

Recommended readings

Cope, Bill and Kalantzis, Mary
    2000   *Multiliteracies: Literacy Learning and Design of Social Futures.* London:
            Routledge.
Hornberger, Nancy H.
    2003   *Continua of Biliteracy: An Ecological Framework for Educational Policy,
            Research and Practice in Multilingual Settings.* Clevedon, U.K.: Multilin-
            gual Matters.
Kenner, Charmian
    2004   *Becoming Biliterate: Young Children Learning Different Writing Systems.*
            Stoke on Trent, UK: Trentham Books.
Martin-Jones, Marilyn and Katherine Jones (eds.)
    2000   *Multilingual Literacies: Comparative Perspectives on Research and Prac-
            tice.* Amsterdam: John Benjamins.
Reyes, María de la Luz and John J. Halcón (eds.)
    2001   *The Best for Our Children: Critical Perspectives on Literacy for Latino Stu-
            dents.* New York: Teachers College Press.
Street, Brian (ed.)
    2000   *Literacy and Development: Ethnographic Perspectives.* London: Routledge.

9. Multilingualism and Specific Language Impairment (SLI)

Monika Rothweiler

1. Introduction

In monolingual language acquisition, the distinction between normal and deviant language development is easy to make – at least from a theoretical point of view. If the acquisition of a given language is studied in many children, we know the normal developmental sequence and the normal range of variation. If a child does not fall within this range, his or her language acquisition is delayed (too slow) and/or impaired (deviant). There are several possible causes for delayed or impaired language acquisition, for example hearing loss, mental retardation, traumatic brain injury or social deprivation. For a special group of children with language deficits, none of these causes apply, however. In these children the language deficits appear to result from a central developmental problem. Such Specific Language Impairment – SLI – is assumed to be genetically based (Choudhury and Benasich 2003). The identification of SLI in children is based on (1) the exclusion of other causal factors for language disorders (see above), and (2) on an assessment made against the background of normal acquisitional sequences.

Compared to monolingual acquisition, language disorders in multilingual children are a far more complex issue. Obviously, factors like hearing loss, mental retardation, traumatic brain injury or social deprivation will affect simultaneous and successive multilingual development as well. Whether multilingual language acquisition aggravates the problems caused by such factors is not clear. The same holds for SLI. Although practitioners often claim that multilingualism is an additional impediment to acquisition under conditions of impairment, the first detailed studies focussing on linguistic characteristics of SLI in bilingual children have not confirmed this claim (see sections 5 and 7 below). Furthermore, it is evident that SLI cannot be caused by a multilingual context since SLI has congenital causes, and is not an acquired disorder. SLI can on the other hand be expected to influence the acquisition of both languages of a bilingual person. As children with SLI form a fairly large group (3 % to 10 % of all children according to Leonard 1998, see section 2 below), the same prevalence should hold for multilingual children (cf. Goldstein 2004 for Spanish-English children in the United States).

As multilingual development takes place under a variety of social and individual conditions with a vast amount of factors influencing grammatical structures, sequences and speed of acquisition, the outcome may differ from mono-lingual acquisition and only a non-native proficiency may be achieved. Multilingual children may need educational language support; this, of course, does not mean they suffer from specific language impairment (cf. Restrepo and Guitiérrez-Clellen 2004). Nevertheless, there seems to be an overlap between the structures affected in multilingual language development and the structures typically affected in monolinguals with SLI (see section 5 below). This may lead to an over- or underrepresentation of multilingual children in speech and language pathology institutions. Multilingual children without SLI may be falsely diagnosed as suffering from SLI, while multilingual children with SLI may be overlooked. As will be pointed out below, the misdiagnosis of SLI in multilingual contexts is related to inappropriate clinical practices, particularly the use of developmental norms based on monolinguals (cf. Restrepo and Gui-tiérrez-Clellen 2004).

Dealing with SLI and multilingual acquisition involves a variety of topics. The first topic relates to the definition and description of Specific Language Im-pairment (SLI) (see section 2), especially with respect to different languages (see section 3). Language deficits caused by SLI manifest themselves in lan-guage-specific ways cross-linguistically. Therefore, multilingual individuals suffering from SLI should show different language problems in the respective languages. This raises practical as well as theoretical questions which are the topic of section 4. The comparison of SLI and second language acquisition pro-vides the necessary criteria needed for evaluating deviations in bilingual children and for a diagnosis of SLI in bilinguals (sections 5 and 7). The central section on SLI in bilingual individuals (section 6) is followed by a discussion of the relevant issues in diagnosis and intervention (section 7).

2.   Specific Language Impairment (SLI) in monolingual children

Specific Language Impairment (SLI) has been studied for more than 40 years. The diagnostic term SLI refers to a type of language development which signifi-cantly lags behind the general intellectual, auditory, neuromotoric and socio-emotional development of non-affected children. The diagnosis of SLI is based on exclusionary criteria, i.e. the child shows normal performance in non-verbal IQ assessment as well as normal hearing, and no deviant social behaviour. At the same time, SLI children show limitations in a wide range of language abil-ities (Rice 2000). This implies that SLI might be biologically or even genetic-ally based, a view which is strengthened by family and twin studies as well as by the fact that two to three times as many boys than girls are affected (Bishop 1997; Choudhury and Benasich 2003; Leonard 1998: 149ff). The biological basis of SLI may be best explained in terms of an early disorder in neurological development. Nevertheless, the causes of SLI and the way in which brain functions are affected are still unknown.

Children with SLI have considerable difficulties in acquiring the language they are exposed to. Both expressive language (production) and receptive language (comprehension) are affected, yet problems in production seem to be more dominant. Typically, SLI children are late talkers, i.e. they show a delay of several months in the onset of word production, and vocabulary growth is slow. Although the acquisitional problems are heterogeneous and many SLI children have phonological disorders, the most obvious and serious problems concern the acquisition of grammar. Children with a phonological disorder only are excluded from the category of SLI (Leonard 1998: 13f).

SLI is far more than a delay. Language acquisition is not only slow but also deviant from normal acquisition. This does not mean that SLI children produce forms which never occur in normal language development, but rather refers to an unbalanced development resulting in an acquisition profile different from that of non-impaired children. Grammatical structures which are acquired more or less simultaneously by unimpaired children may be acquired only partly or not simultaneously by SLI children. Although language proficiency increases over time, especially by means of therapeutic intervention, the language problems of many SLI children are persistent. About 50% of SLI children have problems in the acquisition of literacy. Even in some adults, language deficits are still visible.

Early identification and intervention are considered the best practices in order to minimise possible risks. Early indicators of SLI are (a) late talking, i.e. a vocabulary of less than 50 words at the age of 2, (b) no vocabulary spurt, and (c) phonological disorders. Although a lot of late talkers develop into late bloomers, i.e. their language development starts late but catches up at the age of 3, the late talker criterion is a quite robust early indicator of SLI. The diagnosis of SLI may be supported if language or literacy problems also occur in other family members. Diagnosis of SLI entails the assessment of language skills as well as a non-verbal IQ assessment. By definition, SLI is diagnosed if verbal IQ scores are at least one standard deviation below the mean, whereas non-verbal IQ is within age-appropriate limits. The availability of diagnostic means, especially of standardised language tests, varies with respect to different languages. For many languages, no studies of SLI are available. This is one major problem in the assessment of SLI in multilingual children. In the following paragraph, some grammatical features of SLI in various languages are discussed.

3.   SLI across languages

SLI is language specific. This means that the structure of the target language determines the kind of grammatical problems which an SLI child faces in acquiring the respective language. Cross-linguistic studies on SLI reveal that the most dominant grammatical problems relate to morpho-syntax and the use of function words (see Leonard 1998: 89–117, 2000 for a comprehensive overview). The language specifity of SLI has been shown by a number of studies of SLI in various languages (see for German: Clahsen 1991; Clahsen and Rothweiler 1993; Rice, Ruff Noll and Grimm 1997; for English see the general overview by Leonard 1998; for French: Jakubowicz, Nash and van der Velde 1999; Paradis and Crago 2000; for Hebrew: Dromi, Leonard and Shteiman 1993; Leonard et al. 2000; for Italian: Bottari et al. 1998; Leonard, Caselli and Devescovi 2002; and for Swedish: Håkansson 2001; this is just a selection, for a more detailed overview see Leonard 1998, 2000). In Greek, the clinical marker for SLI is a deficit in the use of special clitics (Tsimpli and Mastropavlou 2004, to appear). In Spanish, article and clitic pronoun use is affected, i.e. SLI children exhibit article omissions and difficulties with gender and number agreement in articles (Restrepo and Guitiérrez-Clellen 2004). While English SLI-children have special problems with regular past tense-marking (Rice and Wexler 1996), the clinical markers for SLI in German are deficits in the morphological marking of subject-verb agreement and finite verb morphology, and in verb placement (Clahsen, Bartke and Göllner 1997; Hamann, Penner and Lindner 1998).

The following example of a monolingual German boy (age 7;5) with diagnosed SLI illustrates a typical grammatical phenotype of SLI in German. The short passage is part of a dialogue about last year's Christmas Eve.

Child

Interviewer
Was macht ihr denn Weihnachten so?
'What are you doing on Christmas Eve?'

1   *nur nich in die stube dürfen*$_{inf/1stpl}$
     'just not in the living room
     allowed to'
     correct:
     Wir dürfen nur nicht in die Stube.
     'We are not allowed to enter the
     living room.'

2   *un dann warten müssen*
     'and then wait have to'
     correct:
     Und dann müssen wir warten. /
     Und müssen dann warten.

'And then we have to wait.' /
'And have to wait then.'

> *Habt ihr 'nen Tannenbaum zu Hause?*
> 'Do you have a christmas tree at home?'

3   *ja*
   'yes'

> *Wie sah der denn letztes Jahr aus?*
> 'How did it look last year?'

4   *groß*
   'big/tall'
5   *pieksig*
   'prickly'
6   *Kati ne?*
   'Kati (name of the female
   family cat) TAG'
7   *die immer den so rumgeht*$_{3rdsg}$
   'she always him so around goes'
   correct:
   Die ist immer so um den herum-
   gegangen.
   'She was always walking around it.'

> *Spielt die mit dem Tannenbaum?*
> 'Did she play with the christmas tree?'

8   *ja*
   'yes'

> *Mit den Kugeln?*
> 'With the (Christmas tree) balls?'

9   *ja*
   'yes'
10   *eine ne von letzten jahr kaputt*
   'one TAG of last year broken'
   correct:
   Eine vom letzten Jahr ist kaputt.
   'One of last year's is broken.'
11   *die katze kaputt machen*$_{inf}$
   'the cat broken make'
   correct:
   Die Katze hat sie kaputt gemacht.
   'The cat broke it.'

This example illustrates several characteristics of SLI in German:
- preference for verb last structures (1, 2, 7, 11) (German is a verb second language),
- subject-verb agreement is not consistent (correct in (7), incorrect in (11), unclear in (1) and (2)),
- subject omission (1, perhaps 2),
- omissions of function words like prepositions (7) or copula (10).

Unimpaired German children acquire subject-verb agreement (i.e. finiteness) and the verb-second rule between age 2 and 3. Even children who start to acquire German around the age of 3, acquire these central structural properties after 6 to 18 months of exposure to German (Rothweiler 2006). Children with SLI, on the contrary, have considerable problems in the acquisition of this part of German grammar.

SLI children clearly have problems in using inflected forms, but in most cases this does not mean that inflections do not occur at all. In English and French, for example, SLI children have substantial difficulties in applying tense-bearing morphemes (Paradis, Crago, Genesee and Rice 2003; Leonard 1998). Leonard et al. (1997) found that English SLI children tend to produce over-regularised past tense forms like *catched* (for *caught*). This shows that these children are able to extract and apply the regular rule for creating past tense forms. Nevertheless, they use the past tense -ed in only 32 % of the obligatory contexts (compared to 62 % in MLU controls).

The language specifity of SLI becomes even more evident when inflection errors are compared across languages. SLI children produce relatively less inflectional errors when acquiring a language with a rich inflectional morphology. Comparing the percentages of third person singular inflection in English, German and Italian, Leonard (2000: 121) showed that in English they were lower than in German (21 % and 53 %) in SLI children, and in both languages, SLI percentages were lower than in MLU-controls. Moreover, Italian SLI children produced 94 % third person singular inflections and did not differ from their MLU-controls. These results are preliminary however due to the fact that no objective criterion exists which is capable of measuring inflection in a language with little morphology and comparing this to a language with rich morphology. The status and syntactical functions of inflectional morphology in these languages differ substantially.

4.   Multilingual acquisition and Specific Language Impairment

The interest in analysing the relation and possible interaction of SLI and multilingualism is at least two-fold. Following the assumption that about 3 % to 10 %

of all children are affected by SLI, this should also hold for multilingual children. The definition of SLI predicts that typical language deficits show up in both languages, and that the structures affected by the language impairment are determined by the respective languages. Early identification of SLI is based on accurate assessment. In a bilingual setting, this means assessment in both languages. In this context, it is important to know whether and how the presence of another language affects the acquisitional problems of SLI children. Special diagnostic criteria of SLI in multilingual children are needed. However, there has been little research focusing on SLI in multilingual contexts so far (cf. Goldstein 2004).

The second point of interest is psycho-linguistic. The study of language acquisition, specifically in SLI or in bilingual contexts, is a source of insight into developmental patterns and interdependencies hidden in unimpaired monolingual first language acquisition. Both impaired language acquisition and second language acquisition differ from monolingual unimpaired acquisition in crucial aspects, and the difference relates to theoretical questions. These are – among others – questions concerning inborn capacities and the critical period for language aquisition, questions of acquisitional strategies in different populations and/or age groups, and the question of proficiency in second language acquisition as well as in SLI.

The following section will give an overview of studies in which SLI and multilingual acquisition are compared.

5.   SLI and second language acquisition in childhood

When traditional language assessment measures are used, a considerable overlap appears between monolingual SLI children and adult second language learners (Kohnert 2006). A number of linguistic studies comparing language acquisition in SLI children and L2 acquisition in childhood also found striking similarities. The same structural domains or structures seem to be affected in both groups, and error types and/or frequencies seem to be the similar (Crago and Paradis 2003; Grüter 2004; Håkansson 2001; Håkansson and Nettelbladt 1993, 1996; Paradis and Crago 2000, 2004; Schöler, Ljubešić and Kovačević 1998; Kohnert 2006).

For instance, Håkansson and Nettelbladt (1993, 1996) report that the same developmental errors occur in Swedish children with SLI and in unimpaired children acquiring Swedish as a second language. The Swedish grammar develops in the same sequence in both groups, following a language specific developmental profile. Håkansson (2001) investigated the development of tense morphology and verb-second placement in three preschool groups of learners of Swedish (unimpaired L1 children, age 3;1–3;7; language-matched impaired L1 children, age 4;0–6;3; L2 children, age-matched to the SLI group, age 3;6–6;0). She found no significant differences in tense marking. The main difference between the groups concerned verb-second placement and subject-verb inversion. The unimpaired group of first language learners had already acquired verb-second placement in topicalised declaratives, whereas both L2 children and children with SLI produced verb-third structures (XSV). Six months later, both L2 children and SLI children had improved in such a manner that there were no longer any statistically significant differences between the groups.

Paradis and Crago (2000) compared the acquisition of tense and subject verb agreement in monolingual French SLI children and in unimpaired children acquiring French as a second language in kindergarten and school. Children of both groups were about seven years old, and the control group of monolingual French-speaking children was age-matched. Both experimental groups scored significantly lower in the use of finite, i.e. tensed, verbs in obligatory contexts. The past tense and future tense forms were more often replaced by nonfinite or – sometimes – by present tense forms, when compared to the monolingual controls. But Paradis and Crago also found differences between L2 learners and SLI children: while L2 children preferred to use present tense forms, SLI children chose more nonfinite forms.

Paradis (2005) investigated unimpaired minority children who had been learning English as a second language for an average of 9.5 months. In spontaneous and elicited data, she counted accuracy and error types in the production of grammatical morphemes such as third person singular -*s*, past tense -*ed*, irregular past tense, *be* as a copula and auxiliary verb, *do* as an auxiliary, progressive -*ing*, prepositions *in* and *on*, plural -*s*, and determiners. She compared the results to those of age-matched monolingual English SLI children and found strong similarities.

Paradis and Crago (2004) compared the acquisition of noun morphology in French SLI children to that of English children acquiring French as a second language. Both groups had no difficulties with determiners and adjective placement. Only with respect to gender marking did the two groups differ significantly from the respective monolingual unimpaired French controls. Paradis and Crago relate this finding to the lexical nature of gender as an inherent property of nouns. After having reached MLU values of about 3.6 to 4.0, noun morphosyntax was almost completely mastered by all three groups.

Using grammatical judgement tests and error correction tasks (inflections) in school children (grade 1 to 4), Schöler, Ljubešić and Kovačević (1998) found that the answer patterns of Croatian children acquiring German as an early second language were more similar to the patterns of monolingual SLI children of both languages than to those of unimpaired monolinguals. Although bilingual and SLI children detected many inflectional errors, children of both groups scored significantly lower than monolingual controls in error correction.

Rothweiler and Kroffke (in prep.) compared the early successive L2 acquisition of German by four Turkish-speaking children with data of three older monolingual SLI children. The bilingual children had acquired German successively from the age of three onwards, and were recorded for at least 18 months. The study focused on the acquisition of verb placement (in main clause and subordinate clause) and of subject verb agreement and finiteness, since these structures are known to be vulnerable in German SLI. In fact, the SLI children produced sentences with correct verb placement and correct verb forms, but they also placed non-finite verb forms in the finite V2 position, in main as well as in subordinate clauses. This kind of verb placement error almost never occurs in unimpaired L1 acquisition (Clahsen, Bartke and Göllner 1997). In contrast, Rothweiler and Kroffke found that the bilingual children acquired finiteness and verb placement similar to monolingual unimpaired children. The authors interpret this finding as evidence for early successive bilingual acquisition being a mere variant of simultaneous bilingual acquisition.

Grüter (2004) studied comprehension and elicited production of French object clitics. She compared three groups of children (age 6 to 8): monolingual French-speaking children, French L2 learners with English as a first language (time of exposure about 18 months), and monolingual French SLI children. SLI and L2 learners scored significantly lower in the production task than the control group, whereas comprehension of object clitics was intact in all three groups, with slightly better results in the monolingual controls. In examining the individual results in both tests in more detail, Grüter found one individual pattern in a subgroup of the SLI group which did not appear in L2 or L1 learners. This pattern – no clitic production, but good performance in comprehension of clitics – seems to be unique to the SLI group.

The studies reported here differ in methodological designs and experimental groups; additionally, the grammatical structures investigated differ in crucial details. One main difference between the studies is the age of onset of L2 acquisition in the bilingual groups, and the time and amount of exposure to the second language. The main overlap of certain deviant structures is found between SLI and L2 development, while early L2 acquisition equals simultaneous acquisition of the two languages (cf. Rothweiler and Kroffke, in prep.). Paradis (2005) concludes that as a consequence, normally-developing second language learners could be wrongly diagnosed as being language impaired.

It would be unjustified to conclude from these results that language acquisition by SLI children and that of L2 learners are subject to the same restrictions in access to acquisition devices or strategies. As has been pointed out before, the overlap might be due to the fact that some grammatical structures of a language are more vulnerable to problems in acquisition in general than others (cf. Platzack 2001: *vulnerable domains*). Exactly these structural domains are affected under exceptional conditions, such as second language acquisition, SLI (or, for that matter, aphasia). This neither means that the errors are identical nor that the cause for the respective acquisitional pattern is the same. The studies by Grüter (2004) and Paradis and Crago (2000) show that although the same grammatical domains are affected, a more fine-grained comparison of L2 and SLI acquisition may reveal more qualitative differences. SLI children are considered to have less efficient language-learning systems than unimpaired monolinguals. In contrast, second language learning may be complicated by external factors, such as reduced input (cf. Kohnert 2006). Another possibility is that the inborn language acquisition faculty changes over time. The critical period is defined as a limited life span in which certain language specific learning devices are available. The accessibility of these learning mechanisms fades out when the critical periods ends (cf. Hyltenstam and Abrahamsson 2003; Meisel 2004; Rothweiler 2006). This predicts that second language learning differs from monolingual acquisition, leading to L2 typical acquisitional stages and structures. Despite these different explanations, the assumption of language specific vulnerable domains suggests that the same structures are affected in SLI children and in L2 acquisition.

6.   SLI in bilingual children

One of the first authors pointing out the problems in distinguishing between language disorders and specific structures arising in bilingual development was Miller (1984). However, it was not until the late 1990s that well-designed studies on SLI in bilinguals were done.

There are at least two relevant groups of bilingual children to be considered. The first group consists of children who acquire two languages simultaneously. In many cases, unimpaired simultaneous acquisition mirrors L1 acquisition in both languages (Meisel 2004; see ch. 1, this volume). The second group are children who learn a second language after they have acquired a first (family) language. Child L2 learners are a very heterogeneous group since a number of variables may influence L2 acquisition, i.e. age of onset, amount and quality of input, social situation of the family and/or the ethnic group or language community the children belong to, to name just a few. In many western societies, a relevant group of child L2 learners are children with an immigrant background (for more details see ch. 20, this volume). As Paradis et al. (2003) and Restrepo and Guitiérrez-Clellen (2004) point out, it is important to consider the role of language dominance in multilingual contexts. The acquisition of morpho-syntax in the nondominant language can be slow and therefore resemble monolingual SLI. On the other hand, a bilingual SLI child may display morphosyntactic errors parallel to monolingual SLI children only in the dominant language (cf. Paradis, Crago, Genesee and Rice 2003).

One general methodological problem for the study of SLI in bilingual children is testing. In simultaneous acquisition, SLI children may be identified by the same assessment methods used for monolinguals in both languages (cf. Paradis, Crago, Genesee and Rice 2003). But a problem arises with L2 learners. If we want to examine how SLI and L2 acquisition interact, the usual assessment procedures are not applicable. Tests which have been standardised for monolinguals cannot be used to assess successive bilinguals.

We may be dealing with a bilingual SLI child if several of the following criteria apply: (a) language development in both languages is delayed and deviant, as diagnosed by informal assessment by an expert, or by standardised tests in the first language if available, (b) non-verbal intelligence is within normal range, (c) the child suffers from a phonological disorder, and (d) speech and language disorders in the family are reported by the parents (Rothweiler, Kroffke and Bernreuter 2004).

6.1.   SLI in simultaneous acquisition

SLI in children acquiring two languages simultaneously has been studied by Paradis et al. (2003) and by Paradis, Crago and Genesee (2004). The aim of their studies was to find out whether bilingual SLI children show the same language impairment in each language as their monolingual peers. The study concentrated on French-English bilingual children and analysed spontaneous speech data. Paradis et al. (2003) compared eight bilingual SLI children with two control groups of age-matched monolingual SLI children in each language. The authors examined tense-bearing and non-tense-bearing verbal morphology. The main result was that bilingual and monolingual SLI children exhibit the same developmental patterns. In all groups, tense morphology raises greater problems than non-tense morphemes, and the error scores were similar in monolingual and bilingual children. The authors conclude that, with respect to the grammatical morphology examined, bilingual SLI children are similar to their monolingual SLI peers. This result also holds for object clitics. Paradis, Crago, and Genesee (2004) compared the use of object pronouns in French and English. They found that bilingual children, both with and without SLI, used more pronouns in English than in French, and accuracy was higher in English than in French in both groups. Problems with pronouns are typical for French SLI children, and for this language, SLI bilinguals are equal to monolingual children with SLI. The authors conclude that problems with object clitics are specific for French, and are caused by their morpho-syntactic complexity. The results of both studies strongly suggest that the simultaneous acquisition of two languages does not cause a special problem for SLI children, since their learning deficits do not increase. The authors underline that this conclusion is restricted to grammatical morphology.

6.2.   SLI in child L2 learners

The population of bilingual children acquiring a second language successively is larger and more heterogeneous than the group of simultaneous learners. Therefore, as has been pointed out in section 5, the study of SLI in these children is much more difficult than the study of SLI in simultaneous bilinguals. Successive acquisition need not mirror monolingual acquisition. In SLI children who acquire a second language, two kinds of deviations from unimpaired monolingual acquisition are therefore in danger of being confounded, namely differences between L1 and L2 acquisition and differences between unimpaired and impaired acquisition. Child L2 learning involves complex interactions between the first language, the second language, the developing child, and his or her experiences. Language assessments in either the first or the second language may underestimate the skills of immigrant children when comparing performance to monolingual normative data (cf. Kohnert 2006).

Crutchley, Conti-Ramsden and Botting (1997) compared the linguistic performance of monolingual and bilingual SLI children acquiring English as an (early) second language. Using a standardised language assessment battery for English, the authors found that the bilinguals scored lower than the monolinguals. It remains unclear whether these lower scores are due to the fact that the L2 proficiency was not as far advanced as the L1 competence of the peers, or whether L2 acquisition increases the language problems of SLI children.

Håkansson, Salameh and Nettelbladt (2003) studied two groups of Arabic-Swedish preschool children, one normally developing and the other SLI children, matched for age (4 to 7 years) and exposure to Swedish in preschool. The bilingual SLI children were diagnosed as severely language impaired. They had great difficulties with grammar and were below expectations in both languages. The authors conducted specific tasks in both languages. They evaluated the results against a developmental sequence of structures for measuring grammatical development. The main result of the study was that bilingual SLI children showed low levels of grammatical development in both languages, whereas the unimpaired controls reached a level comparable to monolingual peers in at least one of the two languages.

Restrepo and Guitiérrez-Clellen (2004) report preliminary results of studies of Spanish-English SLI children in the United States. They differentiate between SLI in contexts of subtractive bilingualism (i.e. Spanish is suppressed or at least not supported in the same way as English) and SLI in additive bilingualism (i.e. educational support and teaching of literacy skills are given in both languages). First findings indicate that grammatical performance in additive bilinguals with SLI did not differ from monolingual SLI. This result supports the findings on simultaneous bilinguals reported in 6.1. The results of two children in a subtractive bilingual context provide evidence that SLI children might run a higher risk of language loss than SLI children in additive contexts. Furthermore, these children produced typical L2 errors like subject ellipsis in English.

The results of these few studies on SLI in child L2 learners provide evidence that bilingual development per se does not cause language impairment. This will turn out to be relevant for diagnosis and therapy (see section 7).

The fact that many children acquiring a second language – especially in migration contexts – are not very successful in their L2, or even in both languages, is not bound to the fact that they are exposed to more than one language. Such problems are linked to socio-cultural and socio-economic factors which may lead to situations with a qualitatively and quantitatively insufficient amount of language input during critical phases of language development. Also, motivational factors and questions of socio-cultural identity of the parents and the children are involved.

7.   Consequences for diagnosis and therapy

For practitioners, the most important question is whether bilingualism is an impediment to SLI children. If a bilingual child is suspected to be language impaired, it should be self-evident that both languages are tested. Children with reduced proficiency in only one of the languages spoken in their environment do not have SLI. The main problem in identifying SLI in bilingual children is that no multilingual assessment tools are available. Furthermore, for most of the first languages of L2 learners, suitable test material is not available. Håkansson et al. (2003) report that there are approximately 140 different mother tongues in Swedish schools. This holds for most western societies. Even if standardised tests were available for these first languages, trained professionals who could administer the tests or interpret the results are lacking.

One consequence of these missing assessment tools is that children learning two languages sequentially may be overrepresented or underrepresented in language remediation and special education programs (Kohnert 2006; Winter 1999). Paradis (2005) has coined the expression *mistaken identity* which refers to the fact that interlanguage phenomena of L2 learners might be misinterpreted as language deficits. *Missed identity* occurs when an L2 learner has a language impairment which is not identified as such, but falsely reduced to L2 development. Crutchley et al. (1997) and Salameh et al. (2004) show that bilingual children run a higher risk of later assessment and SLI diagnosis, and they have a higher risk of being diagnosed as severely language impaired. An obvious reason for these misinterpretations is a lack of information about bilingual children in speech and language therapy services and schools. This has clear implications for the training of the staff of educational and therapeutic institutions. Genesee et al. (2004: 194) point out that teachers with vast experience are able to identify SLI in multilingual children because they can compare the development of these children to that of non-impaired children with the same language background. Nevertheless, more research is necessary in order to shed light onto the interaction of SLI and bilingual development. Especially SLI in child L2 learners is in need of thorough investigation.

With regard to simultaneous acquisition, the results of Paradis et al. (2003) suggest that assessment and intervention materials used for monolinguals are adequate for this group of bilingual children as well. They may even be helpful if assessment tools are available in one language only (Rothweiler 2004). With regard to second language learners, the assessment conditions are quite different. The use of standardised tests designed for monolinguals in non-native speaker populations is not a good practice.

Advisors and counsellors in health care institutions and schools should no longer advise parents to restrict themselves to one language. The acquisition of more than one language is not an a priori risk factor for language development, not even for SLI children. But the restriction to one language may have negative consequences for educational and career opportunities and for the social and ethnic identity of a child. Therefore, bilingual intervention is needed so that bilingual children can achieve long term social, emotional, and cognitive well-being as well as academic and vocational success (cf. Kohnert 2006).

References

Bishop, Dorothy
    1997   *Uncommon Understanding: Development and Disorders of Language Comprehension in Children*. Hove: Psychology Press.
Bottari, Piero, Paola Cipriani, Anna Maria Chilosi and Lucia Pfanner
    1998   The determiner system in a group of Italian children with SLI. *Language Acquisition* 7: 285–315.
Choudhury, Naseem and April A. Benasich
    2003   A family aggregation study: The influence of family history and other risk factors on language development. *Journal of Speech, Language, and Hearing Research* 46: 261–272.
Clahsen, Harald
    1991   *Child Language and Developmental Dysphasia: Linguistic Studies of the Acquisition of German*. Amsterdam: John Benjamins.
Clahsen, Harald, Susanne Bartke and Sandra Göllner
    1997   Formal features in impaired grammars: a comparison of English and German SLI children. *Journal of Neurolinguistics* 10: 151–171.
Clahsen, Harald and Monika Rothweiler
    1993   Inflectional rules in children's grammars: Evidence from German participles. In: Geert Booij and Jaap van Marle (eds.), *Yearbook of Morphology 1992*, 1–34. Dordrecht: Kluwer.

Crago, Martha and Johanne Paradis
   2003   Two of a kind? Commonalities and variation in languages and language
           learners. In: Yonata Levy and Jeannette Schaeffer (eds.), *Language Com-
           petence Across Populations: Towards a Definition of Specific Language Im-
           pairment*, 97–110. Mahwah, NJ: Lawrence Erlbaum.
Crutchley, Alison, Gina Conti-Ramsden and Nicola Botting
   1997   Bilingual children with specific language impairment and standardized as-
           sessments: Preliminary findings from a study of children in language units.
           International Journal of Bilingualism 1, 2: 117–134.
Dromi, Esther, Laurence B. Leonard and Michal Shteiman
   1993   The grammatical morphology of Hebrew-speaking children with specific
           language impairment: Some competing hypotheses. *Journal of Speech and
           Hearing Research* 36: 760–771.
Genesee, Fred, Johanne Paradis and Martha Crago
   2004   *Dual Language Development and Disorders: A Handbook on Bilingualism
           and Second Language Learning*. Baltimore: Brookes.
Goldstein, Brian A.
   2004   Bilingual language development and disorders. Introduction and overview.
           In: Brian A. Goldstein (ed.), *Bilingual Language Development and Dis-
           orders in Spanish-English Speakers*, 3–19. Baltimore: Brookes.
Grüter, Theres
   2004   Teasing apart L2 and SLI: Will comprehension make the difference? In:
           Alejna Burgos, Linnea Micciulla and Christine E. Smith (eds.), *BUCLD 28
           Proceedings*, 220–231. Somerville, MA.: Cascadilla Press.
Håkansson, Gisela
   2001   Tense morphology and verb-second in Swedish L1 children, L2 children
           and children with SLI. *Bilingualism: Language and Cognition* 4: 85–99.
Håkansson, Gisela and Ulrika Nettelbladt
   1993   Developmental sequences in L1 (normal and impaired) and L2 acquisition in
           Swedish syntax. *International Journal of Applied Linguistics* 3: 131–157.
Håkansson, Gisela and Ulrika Nettelbladt
   1996   Similarities between SLI and L2 children: Evidence from the acquisition of
           Swedish word order. In: Carolyn E. Johnson and John H. V. Gilbert (eds.),
           Children's Language. Volume 9, 135–151. Mahwah, N.J.: Erlbaum.
Håkansson, Gisela, Eva-Kristina Salameh and Ulrika Nettelbladt
   2003   Measuring language development in bilingual children: Swedish-Arabic
           children with and without language impairment. *Linguistics* 41: 255–288.
Hamann, Cornelia, Zvi Penner and Katrin Lindner
   1998   German impaired grammar: The clause structure revisited. *Language Ac-
           quisition* 7: 193–245.
Hyltenstam, Kenneth and Niclas Abrahamsson
   2003   Maturational constraints in SLA. In: Catherine J. Doughty and Michael H.
           Long (eds.), *The Handbook of Second Language Acquisition,* 539–588.
           Malden/Oxford: Blackwell.
Jakubowicz, Celia, Lea Nash and Marlies van der Velde
   1999   Inflection and past tense morphology in French SLI. In: Annabell Green-
           hill, Heather Littlefield and Cherly Tano (eds.), *BUCLD 23 Proceedings*,
           289–300. Somerville, MA.: Cascadilla Press.

Kohnert, Kathryn
  2006   Primary language impairments in bilingual children and adults. In: Jeanette
 (in press)   Altarriba and Roberto R. Heredia (eds.), *Introduction to Bilingualism:*
              Principles and Processes. Mahwah, NJ: Erlbaum.
Leonard, Laurence B.
  1998   *Children With Specific Language Impairment*. Cambridge, Mass.: MIT
              Press.
Leonard, Laurence B.
  2000   Specific language impairment across languages. In: Dorothy Bishop and
              Laurence B. Leonard (eds.), *Speech and Language Impairments in Children.*
              Causes, Characteristics, Intervention and Outcome, 115–129. Hove: Psy-
              chological Press.
Leonard, Laurence B., Maria Christina Caselli and Antonella Devescovi
  2002   Italian children's use of verb and noun morphology during the preschool
              years. *First Language* 22: 287–304.
Leonard, Laurence B., Esther Dromi, Galit Adam and Sara Zadunaisky-Ehrlich
  2000   Tense and finiteness in the speech of children with specific language im-
              pairment acquiring Hebrew. *International Journal of Language and Com-*
              munication Disorders, 35: 319–335.
Leonard, Laurence B., Julia A. Eyer, Lisa M. Bedore and Bernard G. Grela
  1997   Three accounts of the grammatical morpheme difficulties of English-speak-
              ing children with specific language impairment. *Journal of Speech, Lan-*
              guage and Hearing Research 40: 741–753.
Meisel, Jürgen
  2004   The bilingual child. In: Tej K. Bhatia and William C. Ritchie (eds.), *The*
              Handbook of Bilingualism, 91–113. Malden/ Oxford: Blackwell.
Miller, Niklas
  1984   Language problems and bilingual children. In: Niklas Miller (ed.), *Bilin-*
              gualism and Language Disability. Assessment and Remediation, 81–103.
              London/Sydney: Croom Helm.
Paradis, Johanne
  2005   Grammatical morphology in children learning English as a second lan-
              guage: Implications of similarities with specific language impairment. *Lan-*
              guage, Speech and Hearing Services in the Schools 36: 172–187.
Paradis, Johanne and Martha Crago
  2000   Tense and temporality: A comparison between children learning a second
              language and children with SLI. *Journal of Speech, Language, and Hearing*
              Research 43: 834–847.
Paradis, Johanne and Martha Crago
  2004   Comparing L2 and SLI grammars in French: Focus on DP. In: Philippe Pré-
              vost and Johanne Paradis (eds.), *The Acquisition of French in Different*
              Contexts: Focus on Functional Categories, 89–108. Amsterdam: John Ben-
              jamins.
Paradis, Johanne, Martha Crago, Fred Genesee and Mabel Rice
  2003   French-English bilingual children with SLI: How do they compare with
              their monolingual peers? *Journal of Speech, Language, and Hearing Re-*
              search 46: 113–127.

Paradis, Johanne, Martha Crago and Fred Genesee
   2003   Object clitics as a clinical marker of SLI in French: Evidence from French-English bilingual children. In: Barbara Beachley, Amande Brown and Frances Conlin (eds.), *BUCLD 27 Proceedings [Proceedings of the 27th Boston University Conference on Language Development]*, 638–649. Somerville, MA: Cascadilla Press.

Pienemann, Manfred
   1998   Developmental dynamics in L1 and L2 acquisition: Processibility theory and generative entrenchment. *Bilingualism: Language and Cognition* 1: 1–20.

Platzack, Christer
   2001   The vulnerable C-domain. *Brain and Language* 77: 364–377.

Restrepo, Maria Adelaida and Vera F. Guitiérrez-Clellen
   2004   Grammatical impairments in Spanish-English bilingual children. In: Brian A. Goldstein (ed.), *Bilingual Language Development and Disorders in Spanish-English Speakers*, 213–234. Baltimore: Brookes.

Rice, Mabel
   2000   Grammatical symptoms of specific language impairment. In: Dorothy Bishop and Laurence B. Leonard (eds.), *Speech and Language Impairments in Children. Causes, Characteristics, Intervention and Outcome*, 17–34. Hove: Psychology Press.

Rice, Mabel, Karen Ruff Noll and Hannelore Grimm
   1997   An extended optional infinitive stage in German speaking children with specific language impairment. *Language Acquisition* 6: 255–295.

Rice, Mabel and Kenneth Wexler
   1996   Toward tense as a clinical marker of specific language impairment in English-speaking children. *Journal of Speech and Hearing Research* 39: 1239–1257.

Rothweiler, Monika
   2004   Spezifische Sprachentwicklungsstörung und früher Zweitspracherwerb. Begründende Überlegungen zu einem Forschungsprojekt. *VHN – Vierteljahresschrift für Heilpädagogik und ihre Nachbargebiete* 73: 167–178.

Rothweiler, Monika
   2006   The acquisition of V2 and subordinate clauses in early successive acquisition of German. In: Conxita Lleó (ed.), *Interfaces in Multilingualism: Acquisition, Representation and Processing*, 93–115. Amsterdam: John Benjamins.

Rothweiler, Monika and Solveig Kroffke
   (in prep.) Same or different? Differentiating specific language impairment and early second language acquisition in German.

Rothweiler, Monika, Solveig Kroffke and Michael Bernreuter
   2004   Grammatikerwerb bei mehrsprachigen Kindern mit einer Spezifischen Sprachentwicklungsstörung. Voraussetzungen und Fragen. *Die Sprachheilarbeit* 49: 25–31.

Salameh, Eva-Kristina, Gisela Håkansson and Ulrika Nettelbladt
   2004   Developmental perspectives on bilingual Swedish-Arabic children with and without language impairment: a longitudinal study. *International Journal of Language and Communication Disorders* 39: 65–91.

Schöler, Hermann, Martha Ljubešić and Martha Kovačević
  1998   Eine Störung, zwei Sprachen, verschiedene Fehler? Die Spezifische Sprach-
          entwicklungsstörung im Sprachvergleich. In: Hermann Schöler, Waldemar
          Fromm and Werner Kany (eds.), *Spezifische Sprachentwicklungsstörung
          und Sprachlernen. Erscheinungsformen, Verlauf, Folgerungen für Dia-
          gnostik und Therapie*, 251–274. Heidelberg: C. Winter.
Tsimpli, I.-M. & Mastropavlou, M.
  (in press) Clitics and Determiners in child L1, child L2 and SLI: evidence from
          Greek. In: H. Goodluck, J. Liceras and H. Zobl (eds.), *Features and Mini-
          malism in Language Acquisition*, Amsterdam: John Benjamins.
Winter, Kirsten
  1999   Speech and language therapy provision for bilingual children: aspects of
          the current service. *International Journal of Language and Communication
          Disorders* 34: 85–98.

Recommended readings:

Genesee, Fred, Johanne Paradis and Martha Crago
  2004   *Dual Language Development and Disorders: A Handbook on Bilingualism
          and Second Language Learning.* Baltimore: Brookes.
Kohnert, Kathryn
  2006   Primary language impairments in bilingual children and adults. In: Jeanette
  (in press) Altarriba and Roberto R. Heredia (eds.), *Introduction to Bilingualism:
          Principles and Processes.* Mahwah, NJ: Erlbaum.
Leonard, Laurence B.
  2000   Specific language impairment across languages. In: Dorothy Bishop and
          Laurence B. Leonard (eds.), *Speech and Language Impairments in Children.
          Causes, Characteristics, Intervention and Outcome*, 115–129. Hove: Psy-
          chological Press.

10. Measuring bilingualism

Manfred Pienemann and Jörg-U. Keßler

1. Introduction

The measurement of bilingualism is a vexed issue because the object of measurement is not well-defined and because the potential purposes of the measurement can be manifold. First of all, there is an abundance of terms that reflect the attempt to characterise different types of bilingualism, such as ideal vs. partial bilingualism and coordinate vs. compound bilingualism (Weinreich 1953), incipient bilingualism (Diebold 1964), receptive bilingualism and semi-bilingualism (Hockett 1958). Some of these terms refer to conditions of bilingualism that are external to the bilingual individual or the bilingual speech community, while other terms are based on the assumption that there are differences in the representation of the two languages in the speaker's mind. Overall, there is no consensus on what constitutes bilingualism and how bilingual competence is represented. Many researchers have implicitly or explicitly assumed Haugen's (1953) 'minimalist' position which defines bilingualism to start with the early stages of second language acquisition.

Even this minimal position implies a whole host of issues for the measurement of bilingualism, many of which have not been resolved. Haugen's minimalist position avoids a comparison of the bilingual individual with the monolingual norms of the language, but it introduces the process of becoming bilingual (i.e. acquiring the two languages as L1 or L2) into the formula. In other words, the measurement of bilingualism requires valid constructs for the notions 'language' and 'language acquisition'. However, there is no universally agreed and operationalisable set of concepts that can represent these two key notions.

For the purpose of measurement the notion 'language' would need to be operationalised at the phonological, lexical, semantic, morphological, syntactic, discourse and interactional level in a manner that is typologically plausible. At present, there is no generally accepted theory of language that integrates all of these aspects and that can readily be operationalised for a given set of two languages. The field of language testing has been keenly aware of this deficit and has developed indirect and yet global approaches to the measurement of linguistic abilities such as proficiency rating scales (e.g. Bachman 1990, Brindley 1998). Apart from the issue of construct validity and reliability of rating scales, any reliance on rating scales in the measurement of bilingualism raises the question whether language proficiency measured in this way does represent the speaker's linguistic competence. In other words, one of the key issues in the measurement of language is whether proficiency relates to linguistic competence in a systematic way. On the other hand, accuracy-based measures of proficiency (cf. Valette 1967) provide only a partial and eclectic snapshot of the speaker's linguistic ability.

The second key concept implied in the measurement formula is equally dicey. The acquisition processes present in emerging bilingualism are far from straightforward. Depending on the age of contact with the L1 and the L2, native or second language acquisition processes may be invoked. In other words, a number of language acquisition researchers have provided empirical evidence and put forward theoretical reasons supporting a fundamental difference between first and second language acquisition (e.g. Bley-Vroman 1990; Clahsen 1990; Meisel 1991), and these fundamentally different acquisition processes may result in different developmental trajectories (cf. Pienemann 1998b). Therefore language samples would need to be screened against the background of either the L1 or the L2 developmental schedule in order to achieve a reliable linguistic profile of the languages of a bilingual speaker.

As this brief discussion has shown, there are at least three different 'yardsticks' that are implicit in the measurement of language in bilingualism:

- linguistic proficiency,
- linguistic competence and
- developmental trajectories.

And it is not clear how these can be related to each other at a conceptual level.

Given this heterogeneous state of affairs in the measurement of bilingualism, we will not be able to resolve these conceptual mismatches, contradictions and gaps in this chapter. Instead, we will sketch different approaches to the measurement of bilingualism from the perspective of the disciplines that have shown most interest in bilingualism, i.e. sociolinguistics, education, linguistics, psychology and cognitive neuroscience. Each of these fields reflects a specific kind of interest in the phenomenon of bilingualism, which ranges from more utilitarian to theoretical. For instance, language policy makers have an interest in the distribution of languages in bilingual communities and in related factors. Educationists have an interest in the effect of different educational approaches on bilingualism and in the assessment of bilingual school populations for the purpose of streaming students into different classes. The primary interest of linguists in bilingualism is to understand how two languages are represented in one mind, whereas psychologists and psycholinguists study how two languages are processed in one mind, and cognitive neuroscientists study the neural correlates of bilingual representation or processing. Naturally, there is a certain amount of overlap between these fields, but due to the specific questions that are studied in each of them and due to their own history, each of these fields has made its own specific contribution to the measurement of bilingualism that can best be understood from within its own tradition.

2.   Previous approaches to the measurement of bilingualism

In the proceedings of a 1967 conference on the "Description and Measurement of Bilingualism" Kelly (1969: 6) made the following observation:

> Bilingualism has been measured according to the function, stability, and distribution of the languages involved, in relation to their location, origin and dominance. These dimensions can apply both to the individual and the group.
>
> Most measures presuppose the creation of units. In the measurement of bilingualism, this is rendered difficult by the fact that these units are not self-evident. They are, therefore, often simply measures of indices which are assumed to reflect certain variables of bilingualism-dominance, skill, regression, etc. Are these true indications of such variables? What does the presence of a certain feature really indicate?
>
> Before being used as the basis for units of measurement, such indices require validation.

As we noted in the introduction to this chapter, the need for the validation of measures is still a key issue in the measurement of bilingualism. Many of the key concepts used in research on bilingualism are mere taxonomies of factors external to bilingualism. Naturally, such taxonomies give little leverage for the study of the nature of bilingualism. Many of these taxonomies of bilingualism are easy enough to measure. The following are just two examples:

Factor: age (Hamers and Blanc 2000: 25)
a) Childhood bilinguality (1. simultaneous; 2. consecutive)
b) Adolescent bilinguality
c) Adult bilinguality.

Factor: environment (Hamers and Blanc 2000: 26; also Paradis 1987: 7)
a) Endogenous bilinguality (i.e. presence of L2 community)
b) Exogenous bilinguality (i.e. absence of L2 community).

It is straightforward to ascertain whether a second or third language was added in childhood, adolescence or adulthood. But this tells us little about differences in the representation or processing of the bilingual individuals or about principled differences in the social dynamics leading to different types of bilingualism. One can connect these taxonomies to measures of proficiency or some other linguistic measure. However, even potential performance differences in these groups reveal little about the internal mechanics of the two languages in the bilingual's mind or their social environment. Further taxonomies are based on the following external factors (cf. for instance Hamers and Blanc 2000; Paradis 1987; Romaine 1989; Baetens Beardsmore 1982):

- age of acquisition
- context of acquisition
- relative status of the two languages
- group membership and cultural identity
- motivation
- context of use

The measurement of bilingual ability has in the past ranged from tests that are aimed at maximum scope, such as rating scales, to discrete point tests aiming at maximum precision. Examples of the latter category include the Peabody Picture Vocabulary Test (Dunn 1959) which focuses on receptive vocabulary, Reynell's syntactic complexity test (Reynell 1969) or varieties of the c-test (Oller 1979). Although these tests were originally designed to measure monolingual competence, some researchers nevertheless advocate utilizing those tests for the assessment of bilingual competence (cf. Hamers and Blanc 2000).

One of the key issues in the measurement of bilingual ability is the comparison of the level of ability in each of the languages involved. Global measures such as rating scales are not specific to individual languages. However, before proficiency measures are compared across different languages one needs to be sure that levels on a proficiency rating scale describe the same degree of ability across different languages. In the case of discrete item tests, the comparability of measures is difficult to achieve because the lexicon and grammar are specific to the individual. In other words, one of the key issues for both types of measures is their cross-linguistic validity (cf. Daller, van Hout and Treffers-Daller 2003).

In an attempt to overcome these limitations, behavioural measures of bilingual competence have been developed that are based on the assumption that for specific behavioural parameters the performance of a bilingual subject in language A can be compared to the subject's performance for the same parameter in language B. The following are examples of bilingual tests based on behavioural parameters some of which are still in use today:

- verbal association tests (Lambert 1955),
- interlingual verbal flexibility (Lambert, Havelka and Gardner 1959),
- use of interlingual ambiguity (Lambert, Havelka and Gardner 1959),
- reaction-time measures (e.g. Macnamara 1969),
- completion and word-detection tests (Baetens Beardsmore 1982).

All these tests permit a direct comparison of the subjects' performance in the two languages for which they are designed. However, it is not clear how the overall bilingual ability of the informants can be measured using these very narrow parameters. To put it more generally, it is not clear exactly which aspect of bilingualism they measure – apart from the trivial observation that a verbal association test measures verbal association. In addition, most of these tests are designed for specific language pairs, and they are difficult to relate to factors that are valid cross-linguistically.

3.   The state of the art

3.1.   Sociolinguistics/ language policy

One of the key questions in sociolinguistics has been "who speaks what language to whom and when?" (Fishman 1965). In the bilingual context this question includes the study of fundamental notions such as 'code-switching' and 'domain' as well as attitudinal and political factors in the choice of language. In other words, this line of research focuses on bilingual language use and its relationship to factors in society. One of the key measurement instruments in the study of this question has been the use of questionnaires for the collection of *census data* (cf. Baetens Beardsmore 1982; Romaine 1989). Typically such questionnaires contain questions such as "what is your native language?" or "which language do you speak in the home?", and mostly they are distributed to communities of bilingual speakers or they may be included in a general census administered by government agencies for the residents and citizens of a country or region.

Census data form the empirical basis of many sociolinguistic studies of bilingualism in Australia (e.g. Clyne 1982), the United States (Fishman 1971; Haugen 1956), Canada and many other countries. Governments often rely on census data in their planning of community services and in educational and language policies. One example is the National Policy on Languages of the Australian government (cf. Lo Bianco 1987). Governments and education authorities often assume that census data provide a reliable basis for policies and planning decisions. However, several authors have pointed out the shortcomings of census data (e.g. Kelly 1969; Baetens Beardsmore 1982). The basic two problems with census data are (1) the assumption that the questions will be unambiguous and (2) that the respondents give truthful answers.

Both these assumptions are not necessarily warranted. For instance, a second-generation Dutch immigrant in Australia who arrived in the country at the age of six, who has a good command of Dutch and who is perceived as a native-speaker of English may not be sure how to respond to the question "what is your native language?" Also, which inference will the bureaucrat make from answers to this question? Is the alleged native language the 'strongest' language of the respondent, is it the 'most natural' or the 'preferred' language? Notions such as 'native language' are notoriously difficult to define even for the specialist (cf. Romaine 1989). Therefore their inclusion in questionnaires is bound to introduce ambiguity and thus errors of measurement.

Census data are often collected in situations that are associated with the respondents' social identity. When an official government-released questionnaire includes the question "which language do you speak in the home?" the immigrant respondent may be inclined to give a response that reflects more his or her desired status in society that is related to language choice rather than a factually correct answer. Or even worse, the respondent may not even be aware of his or her actual choice of language. In all of these cases census data are unreliable. Baetens Beardsmore (1971, 1982) discusses the case of censuses in Belgium. He shows that due to the regional status of the languages Dutch, French and German in Belgium and the associated social identity of the respective residents, census questionnaires have in the past been perceived by respondents as a referendum on language use and related political issues. As a result, responses are biased by this perception. In other words, attitudinal variables may enter into the data collected on the basis of questionnaires, and informants have been shown not to reveal their true attitudes in questionnaires (cf. Dawes 1972).

Linguistic census data often include data on the level of language skill, and these data are based on self-evaluation using intuitive rating scales (e.g. on scales of 0–4). Census data and self-rating were already used by Fishman (1968; 1971) for the validation of such key notions as domain (of language use), which was crucial for an understanding of language choice in bilingual communities. Given that this type of data is based on large populations, they lend themselves to statistical methods developed in psychometrics. For instance, Fishman (1971: 26) subjected his census data on language preference to a factor analysis that revealed a particular loading of factors that can be taken to support his notion of domain in the given study.

The so-called 'portfolio' is a current form of self-evaluation that is promoted particularly by EU agencies. The language policy of the EU is aimed at competence in three languages by the citizens of its member states. Various measures have been taken by the member states to achieve this goal. The European "Common Framework of Reference" established the portfolio as an assessment tool that is promoted for the purpose of implementing the EU language policy. The following quotation from the "Common Framework of Reference" describes the objectives of the European Language Portfolio as follows:

> The development of a *European Language Portfolio (ELP)* enabling an individual to record and present different aspects of his or her language biography [...] is designed to include not only any officially awarded recognition obtained in the course of learning a particular language but also a record of more informal experiences involving contacts with languages and other cultures. (Common Framework of Reference[1], p. 175)

Romaine (1989) showed that the self-evaluation of a bilingual's 'level' of language is biased by attitudinal factors relating particularly to the prestige of the language to be evaluated. In other words, the level of competence in a desirable language is evaluated higher and that of a less desirable language is evaluated lower. In the same vein, Daller et al. (2003: 199) found self-assessment to be "notoriously unreliable".

In his research Li Wei (1996; in press) utilised the concept of social networks to define ethnic identity and to predict language choice in bilingual communities. In this approach social networks are measurable entities. The strength of a network can be measured on the basis of the intensity of contact, and the overall structure of the network with its participants serves to define ethnic identity. Li Wei demonstrated that language choice can be predicted on the basis of ethnic identity defined in this way. In this approach the definition of the social dimension is fully operationalised and thus readily measurable.

3.2.   Education

Educational research on bilingualism focuses on the cognitive, social and academic effect of bilingual programs and bilingualism in society. Therefore it entails the measurement of school performance (partly in relation to measures of bilingualism), cognitive development and linguistic development.

To make a case for bilingual programs it was essential to test the school performance of students enrolled in bilingual programs. Many of the influential educational studies carried out in the context of the Canadian bilingual programs at the Ontario Institute of Studies in Education (OISE) (for a summary see Swain and Lapkin 1982) focused on demonstrating that bilingual education is not detrimental to academic achievement, to cognitive development (cf. Cummins 1976) and to bilingual language acquisition. The measures used in these studies include tests of academic achievement in different school subjects and a range of L1 and L2 proficiency measures. For instance, to measure the effects of immersion programmes on the development of English language skills, Swain and Lapkin (1982) used standardized tests, including the Canadian Test of Basic Skills and the Peabody Picture Vocabulary Test. The tests included items relating to word knowledge, word discrimination, reading, spelling and punctuation. Other tests also included listening and speaking skills (cf. Genesee 1978d). Swain and Lapkin (1982) also summarise analyses of errors made in cloze tests. Written data were based on students' short stories, and oral data were collected using storytelling tasks. These data were subjected to a range of quantitative linguistic analyses, mostly measures of accuracy.

Oller (1991) studied the role of language in intelligence testing for bilinguals and monolinguals. One proficiency measure used in this study is based on a multiple choice instrument. Other linguistic measures include the Revised Illinois Test of Psycholinguistic Abilities (designed by Charles Osgood), the Peabody Picture Vocabulary Test and the Bellugi Syntax Measure. Oller (1991) compared data from IQ tests and linguistic measures and concluded that language skills play a central role in the non-linguistic measures.

Rating scales are one of the key instruments of measuring language in educational programs. Rating scales seek to describe language ability in global terms and tend to be based on 'real communication'. Trained raters evaluate samples of oral or written language on the basis of their training and a set of descriptors for the different levels of the rating scale. Most rating scales are designed to provide a global assessment of the speaker's level of linguistic ability in the four basic skills. However, the precise empirical and theoretical basis of published rating scales is often unclear (cf. Brindley 1998) although serious attempts were made by theorists to develop a valid theoretical framework for the definition of descriptors of linguistic ability (for instance, Bachman 1990). In other words, the relationship between descriptor, actual measurement and theoretical concept is not always clear.

Brindley (1998) points out that some designers of rating scales claim that their scales describe the course of L2 development. However, the exact relationship between proficiency rating and L2 development is at present unclear. This is not surprising because the two concepts are based on fundamentally different research traditions, and rating scales are aimed at maximum scope, whereas the profiling of language development is aimed at maximum precision. At present this constitutes a dilemma in language testing, because with rating scales scope is achieved at the expense of precision whereas in profiling precision is achieved at the expense of scope. A way out of this dilemma can be found only if the relationship between the two underlying concepts, proficiency and language development, can be clarified.

Lexical richness is another key concept in the measurement of bilingualism that is relevant in the educational context. Tidball and Treffers-Daller (2005: 1) argue as follows: "Because of the importance of vocabulary for the everyday lives of speakers in general, and because vocabulary knowledge is one of the major predictors of school success (Verhallen and Schoonen 1998), researchers are interested in developing reliable and valid vocabulary measures."

A widely used measure of lexical richness is the *type-token ratio* (TTR), which measures the ratio of the total number of words in a text and the number of different words. It can easily be applied to corpora of spontaneous or written learner data. However, empirical studies (e.g. Richards 1987) have shown that the TTR declines with the length of the text. Various methods have been proposed to counter-act the length effect. Daller et al. (2003) utilise the Index of Guiraud, which uses the square root of the tokens in the denominator.

It may at first glance appear simple enough to compare lexical richness across languages. However, languages vary considerably in morphology and in the use of certain word classes. For instance, many function words (e.g. *in, the* or *a*) used in isolating languages such as English correspond to affixes in agglutinative languages such as Finnish[2] or Turkish (cf. Daller et al. 2003). Therefore cross-linguistic comparisons have to incorporate such typological differences. In other words, these adjustments need to be made separately for every given language pair. The enormous effort entailed in this exercise is reflected in the title of a paper by Tidball and Treffers-Daller (2005): "Exploring measures of vocabulary richness [...]: a quest for the Holy Grail?" Below we will return to the issue of a universal cross-linguistic matrix for the comparative measurement of bilingualism.

3.3.   Linguistics

In linguistics many types of measures of bilingual (or monolingual) development are based on corpora of naturalistic speech. This tradition goes back to pioneers of language acquisition research such as Leopold (1939; 1947), who kept a diary of the speech of his German-English bilingual child. The main purpose of the corpus approach is to ensure that the regularities inherent in the child's language are described in their own terms rather than in terms of the adult language or merely in terms of the distance to the adult language.

This basic philosophy was supported by the development of recording technology and was refined in research on child language (cf. Bowerman 1973; Brown 1973) and in typological field work (cf. Samarin 1967). In a number of approaches these trends converged with sociolinguists' interest in accounting for the dynamics of linguistic systems in social and historical variation (e.g. Labov 1969; DeCamp 1973; Bickerton 1971). These scholars found that the linguistic system used by a speech community is neither static nor homogenous, and they attempted to account for linguistic variation present in the corpora they collected. Language acquisition follows similar dynamics. Therefore the most general objective of language acquisition research is to describe and explain how a learner moves from not knowing a language to near target-like use of the language, and most language acquisition research is based on some notion of a transitional paradigm.

To account for linguistic variability Labov (1969) developed a quantitative approach to 'variable rules', and DeCamp (1973) accounted for linguistic dynamics using *implicational scaling* (cf. Guttman 1944) which is described for students of language acquisition by Hatch and Lazaraton (1994: 204ff. cf. also Rickford 2002). The implicational scaling technique was advocated for the description of linguistic dynamics in corpora of language learners by Meisel, Clahsen and Pienemann (1981) and was used extensively by these authors, their collaborators and other language acquisition researchers (cf. for instance, Clahsen, Meisel and Pienemann 1983; Meisel 1990; Pienemann 1998; 2005).

The basic point of implicational scaling is this: cumulative learning processes can be represented by successive additions of linguistic rules to the interlanguage system: rule 1 + rule 2 + rule 3, etc. In this way changes in the interlanguage system can be accounted for by the addition of rules. When analysing interlanguage corpora one can apply the following logic of implicational scales to individual interlanguage samples. For any set of rules that is learned in a cumulative fashion the following is true: if sample A contains rule 3, then it will also contain rule 2 and rule 1. This fact is usually expressed in the format of table 1.

Table 1. Implicational scale

	time 1	time 2	time 3	time 4
rule 3	–	–	–	+
rule 2	–	–	+	+
rule 1	–	+	+	+

In other words, rules that are learned later imply the presence of rules that are learned earlier. This has a number of advantages for the description of linguistic dynamics. Implicational scales make it possible to describe complex acquisition processes on a continuum, as in Table 1. The rules of the interlanguage system are listed on one axis, while the samples (here identical with points in time) are listed on the other axis. This presentation amounts to a systematic account of a linguistic system (grammar axis) in relation to developmental time. In other words, this system is a non-static grammar which describes dynamic aspects of the learning process.

When it comes to accounting for cross-sectional data, implicational scaling has a further advantage. As long as one limits oneself to cumulative learning processes, interlanguage samples from different speakers can be represented on what is the time axis in Table 1. If such an exercise produces a valid implicational relationship of individual interlanguage rules (cf. Hatch and Lazaraton 1994 for a calculation of 'scalability'), then the chronological development of these rules can be hypothesised to follow the implicational pattern.

This dynamic description of interlanguage development goes far beyond a mere description of orders of accuracy, as for instance in the 'morpheme order studies' (e.g. Dulay and Burt 1973; 1974; Rosansky 1976) where linguistic development is expressed in one numeric value that is based on the suppliance of morphemes in obligatory contexts. This value is based on group mean scores of accuracy, which are calculated for different grammatical morphemes and arranged into rank orders of accuracy which are then interpreted as the order of acquisition.

The main problem with this procedure is that it is based on the assumption that accuracy rates uniformly describe progress in acquisition. However, there is no guarantee that the accuracy of morpheme insertion will increase steadily in relation to any two morphemes or in relation to any two learners. On the contrary, it is quite likely and well attested in empirical studies (Meisel et al. 1981; Pienemann 1998) that accuracy rates develop with highly variable gradients in relation to grammatical items and individual learners. These observations are represented in Figure 1, which illustrates the point that for any given learner and for any given structure, suppliance in obligatory contexts may develop in quite different patterns. A, B and C represent three different structures. The rate of suppliance increases in different ways for A, B and C. Structure B increases in a linear way; C increases exponentially with a steep gradient; A has a flat gradient. The interesting point is that cross-sections at different rates of suppliance would result in different accuracy orders as shown in Figure 1.

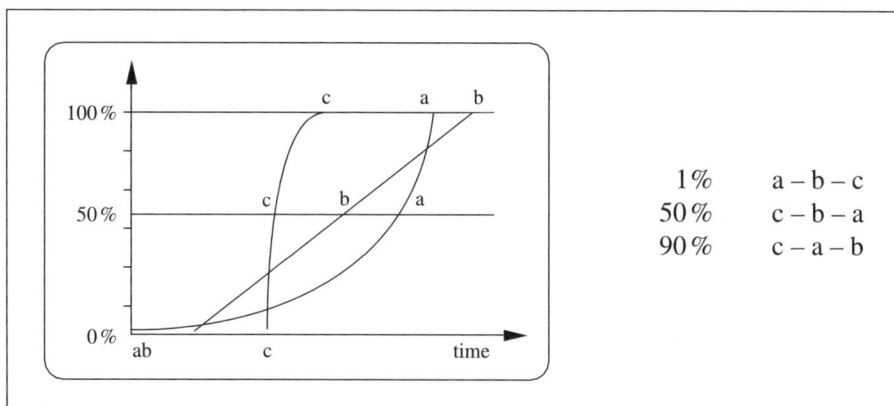

Figure 1. Accuracy and development

The problem is that it is impossible to predict how suppliance in obligatory contexts will develop in any given structure and learner. There are two important things that follow from this: (1) a quantitative acquisition criterion may produce arbitrary orders of accuracy (and acquisition); and (2) chronologies of acquisition cannot be established on the basis of group mean scores. The one cut-off point which remains constant, however, is *the point of emergence,* which is also relevant for other reasons. From a speech processing point of view, emergence can be understood as the point in time at which certain skills have, in principle, been attained or at which certain operations can, in principle, be carried out. From a descriptive viewpoint one can say that this is the beginning of an acquisition process, and focusing on the start of this process will allow the researcher to reveal more about the rest of the process.

Table 2. Adult learners of ESL

Stage Structure	van	IS	my	ks	tam	long	vinh	jr	sang	bb	ka	es	ij	ja	dung	phuc
6 Cancel Inversion	–	–	–	–	–	–	–	–	–	–	–	–	–	–	–	–
5 Aux2nd/Do2nd	–	–	–	–	–	–	–	–	–	–	–	–	–	–	+	+
3sg-s	–	–	–	–	–	–	–	–	–	–	–	–	+	+	+	+
4 Y/N Inversion	–	–	–	–	–	–	–	–	+	+	+	+	/	/	+	+
Copula Inversion	–	–	–	–	+	+	+	+	/	+	+	+	+	+	/	/
3 Neg+V	–	–	–	+	+	+	+	+	+	+	+	+	+	+	+	+
Do Front.	–	–	+	+	+	/	+	+	+	+	+	+	+	+	+	+
Topi	–	–	+	+	+	+	+	+	+	+	+	+	+	+	+	+
ADV	–	–	+	+	+	+	+	+	+	+	+	+	+	+	+	+
2 SVO	–	+	+	+	+	+	+	+	+	+	+	+	+	+	+	+
Plural	–	+	+	+	+	+	+	+	+	+	+	+	+	+	+	+
1 Single words	+	/	/	/	/	/	/	/	/	/	/	/	/	/	/	/

Legend: + acquired   – not acquired   / no context   van, IS, my etc. = names of informants

Table 2 shows an example of an implicational analysis of a cross-sectional second language corpus collected from 16 learners of English as a second language and for 12 grammatical structures (cf. Johnston 1997). The implicational relationship between the 12 grammatical structures constitutes empirical evidence supporting the following developmental trajectory:

Level	Structure	Example
6	Cancel Inversion	I wonder where he is
5	Aux2nd/ Do2nd	When did they get home?
	3 sg-s	She eats
4	Y/N Inversion	Is this ok?
	Particle verbs	I cut it off
	Copula Inversion	Where is it?
3	Neg+V	*She no go home
	Do Front.	*Do she go home?
	Topi	Computers I hate
	ADV	Then he came
2	SVO	The eat at home
	Plural	Two cats
	possessive pronoun	My cat
1	single words	Home

In fact, this developmental trajectory is supported by empirical evidence from a number of further cross-sectional and longitudinal studies of the acquisition of English as a second language (Pienemann 1998b) and it forms a standard point of reference for normal ESL development and can therefore be used as norm for the measurement of second language development.

3.4.   Psychology/ Psycholinguistics

The main thrust of psycholinguistic studies of bilingualism is concerned with how two languages are processed in one mind. One of the old issues that follows from this interest is that of linguistic *dominance* in bilinguals, i.e. which of the two linguistic systems is dominant in the one mind? Generally, psycholinguistic studies of bilingualism focus on issues relating to bilingual language processing.

The notion of 'dominance' is discussed extensively in many introductory texts (e.g. Baetens Beardsmore 1982; Romaine 1989; Hamers and Blanc 2000). The following are only some of the measures of dominance that have been used in the past:

– word naming (for a critical review cf. Cooper and Greenfield 1969)
– self-rating (for a critical review cf. Romaine 1989),
– synonym tests (Lambert, Havelka and Gardner 1959)[3],
– fluency in picture naming (Lambert 1955).

While factors such as fluency in picture naming are readily measurable, they are not connected to the notion dominance in a systematic way. Hence they lack construct validity. Obviously, such a connection could be made only if there was an explicit theory of bilingual representation or of bilingual processing that includes the notion dominance. In the absence of such a theory the above measures remain arbitrary.

Arias, Kintana, Rakow and Rieckborn (2005) point out that dominance has been used with reference to two different concepts, (a) the preferred use of one language by a bilingual individual and (b) the dominance of one grammatical system over the other in the bilingual individual. They review an extensive list of formal measures of dominance and advocate a set of grammatical criteria that can be used in the context of linguistic profiling.

There is a wealth of research on bilingual language processing. Extensive overviews are available in the *Handbook of Bilingualism* (Kroll and de Groot 2005), in the 2005 special issue of *Second Language Research* on "Experimental Psycholinguistic Approaches to Second Language Acquisition" edited by Felser (2005) and in the volume *One Mind, Two Languages* edited by Nicol (2001). Most approaches to bilingual language processing are not directed at developing an overall measure of bilingualism. Instead, their main objective is to gain an understanding of specific aspects of bilingual language processing.

Therefore, the measurement instruments developed in these lines of research serve very specific purposes that are determined by the theoretical framework in which they are used.

Psycholinguistic studies of bilingual or L2 processing can be based on off-line or on-line studies. For instance, Vigliocco, Butterworth and Semenza (1995) use an off-line *sentence completion task* to examine the interplay between conceptual-semantic structure and constituent structure in different languages. In this task informants are to complete sentences referring to multiple tokens (conceptual plural) and to single tokens (conceptual singular), and response differences are measured. The input material is structured as follows:

1 Multiple tokens (conceptual plural):
   The label on the bottles ... → is/are

2 One token (conceptual singular):
   The journey to the islands ... → is/are

The analysis of the responses to this task revealed that the relationship between conceptual-semantic structure and constituent structure is not the same in different languages.

Many psycholinguistic studies of bilingual or L2 processing have in common the assumption that to fully understand L2 processing it has to be measured in real time. Studies based on this assumption therefore utilise on-line techniques in which responses to linguistic stimulus material is measured in terms of response times. One example is the lexical decision experiment (cf. Felser 2005; Marinis 2003) in which the informant is shown a sequence of letters on a computer screen and has to decide if the letters constitute a word in a given language.

Marinis (2003) describes a range of on-line techniques that are used in L2 research and makes recommendations for setting up a psycholinguistics laboratory. The basic setup includes a personal computer, specialised software and some special hardware. One major category of on-line measures is based on the *self-paced reading/listening technique* which requires the informant to trigger the next bit of the stimulus material as quickly as they can process it in the ongoing reading or listening process. The time needed between the last bit of input and the next bit is used as a measure of aspects of the underlying comprehension processes. This technique has been used extensively in studies of L2 grammatical processing (cf. Felser 2005; Juffs 2005).

A number of L2 processing studies (cf. Masterson 1993; Eubank 1993; Clahsen and Hong 1995; Pienemann 1998) were based on *matching tasks*. The design of matching tasks is based on the effect of information encoding on processing speed. For instance, it was found that informants can decide more quickly whether pairs of stimuli are identical if the stimuli are words (e.g. HOUSE/HOUSE) than if the stimuli are non-words (e.g. HSEUO/HSEUO) even though the words and the non-words consist of the same number of characters (e.g. Chambers and Forster 1975).

The general set-up used in *sentence matching experiments* is basically the same: two sentences appear on a computer screen separated by a very short interval; the informant has to decide as quickly as possible if the sentences are identical or not. The test sentences may be grammatical or ungrammatical. In studies with native speakers (Freedman and Forster 1985) it was found that the identity of the sentences can be determined faster with grammatical test sentences. This 'grammaticality effect' is utilised in L2 processing studies (cf. Masterson 1993; Eubank 1993; Clahsen and Hong 1995; Pienemann 1998a).

A further technique used for the measurement of L2 processing is *eye-move-ment recording* (cf. Frenck-Mestre 2005a, b) which requires a more complex technical set-up than that required for reaction-time experiments (as described, for instance by Marinis 2003). The advantage of eye-movement recordings is the increased level of resolution of the timed events. For instance, self-paced reading studies need to rely on single response time measures, whereas eye-movement recordings contain a multitude of measures for each reading. Frenck-Mestre's (2005a, b) papers provide an overview of studies of L2 processing that utilize this technique.

As mentioned at the beginning of this section, all of the above measurement techniques serve very specific purposes in the empirical testing of aspects of theories of L2 processing. Currently they are not designed as overall measures of bilingual performance. It would nevertheless be feasible to develop general measures of bilingual language processing using a combination of these techniques if they were based on explicit and thus operationalisable approaches to L2 processing.

3.5.   Cognitive neuroscience

In recent years research on the cognitive neuroscience of bilingualism has expanded rapidly. This is, in part, due to the development of neuroimaging techniques. Initially, evidence was based on case studies of bilingual aphasia and patterns of recovery from bilingual aphasia (cf. Albert and Obler 1978; Paradis 2001; Hull and Vaid 2005). Hull and Vaid (2005) review the clinical evidence on bilingualism and conclude that, considered on its own, it remains inconclusive about the biological correlates of bilingualism.

Hull and Vaid (2005) also review the entire literature on bilingual laterality. This research is based on a number of measures derived from dichotic listening studies, visual half-field studies and dual task studies. All of these experiments are designed to measure the differential involvement of the two hemispheres of the brain of bilinguals. In earlier reviews results from this line of research were found to be inconclusive (Romaine 1989; Paradis 1990). Hull and Vaid (2005) subject 150 studies of bilingual laterality to a meta-analysis and identify a number of general findings, such as "early bilinguals showed bilateral activation and late fluent bilinguals showed LH (left hemisphere) dominance and did not differ from monolinguals" (p. 486).

A further line of research is designed to identify *electrophysiological correlates* of bilingual language processing (cf. Mueller 2005; Hull and Vaid 2005; Frenck-Mestre 2005a and b). Electrophysiological techniques are based on the measurement of electrical currents (in terms of polarity, peak onset and amplitude) in specific positions on the scalp and how these currents are related to cognitive events, including specific aspects of language processing. In these studies a number of language-related effects have been identified, including the so-called 'N400 effect' that relates to an unexpected semantic event. Other electrophysiological effects have been related to the dichotomy of automatic versus controlled syntactic processing (cf. Hahne and Frederici 1999). A key advantage of electrophysiological techniques is their high temporal resolution and the direct manner in which measurements can be related to linguistic events.

Over the past decade, *neuroimaging techniques* (cf. Gazzangiga, Ivry and Mangun 2002) have yielded a wealth of findings on the spatial and temporal mechanisms of cognitive and linguistic functioning. These techniques can capture online images of neurophysiological processes related to language processing. For instance, in their review of functional neuroimaging studies of bilingualism, Abutalebi, Cappa and Perani (2005) conclude that second language proficiency determines the cerebral representation of languages in bilinguals. One of the intriguing questions that can be pursued in this line of research is the issue of fundamental differences between L1 and L2 acquisition. The basic line of argument underlying these studies is illustrated in Schachter's reasoning: "It would seem, for example, that if the language processor develops in the same way for both child L1 and adult L2 acquisition, then there should be some spatially located area of the brain that processes the same tasks in the same way" (Schachter 1998: 32). Some evidence for differential cerebral representation of aspects of L1 and L2 has been found by Klein, Milner, Zatorre, Meyer and Evans (1995).

It is obvious from this brief review that the measurement techniques developed in cognitive neuroscience require very elaborate technology and laboratory environments and are used to measure very specific aspects of bilingual processing and cerebral representation. These techniques are therefore, at the present time, not suitable for the purpose of screening bilingual populations as would be required for educational and related purposes.

4.   Controversial issues

As we have shown in section 3 of this chapter, there is no single standard for the measurement of bilingualism. Instead, a number of different disciplines have shown an interest in bilingualism and have developed a whole range of measures that focus on very different aspects of bilingualism. Many of these have never been tested for their compatibility because they are based on rather different concepts. Where the compatibility of different measures has been tested empirically, the results are often difficult to interpret.

For instance, Pienemann and Mackey (1992) tested the correlation of proficiency rating scales and developmental stages. In two separate studies they found a significant positive correlation between the two types of measures for the same groups of informants. This is a remarkable result because, conceptually, the proficiency rating scales used in these studies were designed as global measures of linguistic ability aimed at maximum scope, whereas developmental stages were measured focusing entirely on developmental trajectories in morphosyntax designed for maximum precision. Does this mean that proficiency rating relies mainly on morphosyntax? At present the positive correlation between the two types of measures cannot be accounted for in conceptual terms, because the global communicative definition of descriptors for proficiency rating scales cannot be translated into the discrete morphosyntactic definitions used for developmental trajectories.

As the example of proficiency rating scales and linguistic profiling shows, the basic concepts underlying these different research traditions, levels of proficiency and levels of acquisition cannot, at present, be reconciled conceptually although empirical evidence suggests that a link does exist. Given that one approach is aimed at maximum scope and the other at maximum precision, it is presently unclear how the scope-precision dilemma can be resolved within one unified approach to the measurement of linguistic ability.

As we note above, in a number of research contexts the level of linguistic ability needs to be compared across two or more different languages. We also pointed out that measures such as the type-token ratio are skewed by the typology of the languages involved. Daller et al. (2003) propose a method of analysing words and morphemes that counteracts the effect of the typological distance between the pairs of languages involved. In other words, these authors construct a cross-linguistic scoring method on the basis of the structure of the specific languages involved in the comparison. In contrast, our own approach is based on a universal psycholinguistic matrix, namely the hierarchy of language processability (Pienemann 1998a, b).

5.   Contribution of Applied Linguistics

In this section we will summarise our approach to the cross-linguistic comparative measurement of bilingualism which is based on linguistic profiling which in turn is based on Processability Theory (Pienemann 1998a, b; 2005). The principle behind linguistic profiling is rather straightforward. Because language development (first or second) follows a standard schedule, a speech sample is collected from a learner, and this allows the analyst to locate the patterns found in the sample within the overall regularities of the standard developmental schedule. Profile analysis was originally developed by Crystal, Fletcher and Garman (1976) for the measurement of child language development. It was based on an interview, a full transcription of the interview and a detailed analysis of the transcript.

We developed a shorthand version of the original procedure, called Rapid Profile that is based on on-line observation and tailor-made elicitation tasks (cf. Pienemann, Brindley and Johnston 1988; Pienemann 1992; Pienemann and Keßler in prep.). The picture above shows the data-elicitation and on-line assessment process. Rapid Profile produces reliable learner profiles on the basis of learner corpora of 10 to 15 minutes' length. Pienemann and Keßler (in prep.) and Keßler (in press) demonstrate a high degree of reliability of this procedure on the basis of extensive formal trials.

Universal developmental schedules have been found for a wide array of first and second languages (cf. Slobin 1985; Fletcher and MacWhinney 1995; Doughty and Long 2003; Pienemann 2005) and in bilingual first language development (e.g. Meisel 1990; Meisel 1994). Pienemann (1998a, b; 2005; in press) and his associates developed a theory of language development, Processability Theory, which is based on a universal hierarchy of linguistic processability. Processability Theory has been demonstrated to predict developmental schedules of a range of typologically different languages (cf. Pienemann 2005), including Arabic (Mansouri 2005), Chinese (Zhang 2005), English (Pienemann 1998a), German (Pienemann 1998 a, b), Japanese (Kawaguchi 2005), Italian (Di Biase and Kawaguchi 2002), Swedish (Pienemann and Håkansson 1999) and Turkish (cf. Pienemann 2005; Özdemir 2004).

Because all of these developmental schedules can be related to one universal hierarchy of processability, they can also be related to each other. In other words, on this basis it is possible to compare, for instance, the Swedish developmental schedule with the schedule of Arabic L2 development. In this way, Processability Theory constitutes a universal metric for the comparison of linguistic development in bilinguals.

Håkansson, Salameh and Nettelbladt (2003) used this universal metric in the comparative measurement of Swedish-Arabic bilinguals. They studied Swedish-Arabic bilingual children with and without specific language impairment (cf. ch. 9 of this Handbook). Based on the above PT hierarchy for Swedish and Arabic, they were able to measure the language development of bilingual informants using compatible scales for both languages.

Table 3. Cross-linguistic comparison of language development in trilingual speakers (Özdemir 2004)

PT level	Turkish (L2)	German (L1)	ESL(L3)
Intersentential		▓	
Interphrasal	▓	▓	
Phrasal: VP	▓	▓	
Phrasal	▓	▓	
Lexical	▓	▓	▓
Words	▓	▓	▓

Özdemir (2004) applied the comparative profiling approach to the study of trilingual language development in Turkish-German children learning English. She used the existing PT hierarchies for English (SLA) and German (FLA) and developed a Turkish PT hierarchy. All three languages were profiled on the basis of PT hierarchies. This permits a comparison of their levels of development across all three languages as shown in Table 3. In a similar vein, Itani-Adams

(2003) studied the bilingual first language acquisition of a Japanese-Australian child. Her work uses the developmental trajectory of English as a second language established by Pienemann (1998a) and the developmental trajectory of Japanese as a second language established by Di Biase and Kawaguchi (2002) and Kawaguchi (2005). Itani-Adams found that in her data both languages develop following the hierarchy predicted by PT. Using PT as the metric for a comprison of language development across the two first languages of the informant, she found that the two languages of the child did not develop in synchrony. This finding supports De Houwer's (1990) Separate Development Hypothesis.

6.   Research perspectives

In several sections of this chapter we pointed out that some measures of bilingualism achieve high precision at the expense of scope while others are the opposite in design and achieve wide scope at the expense of precision. To some extent the scope-precision dilemma is reduced by the practicalities of measurement. Obviously, the choice of the measure used in practice depends, in part, on the purpose of the measurement. For instance, census data do not need to include information on lexical richness. Hence the scope-precision dilemma does not materialise every time bilingualism is measured.

However, this practical observation does not resolve the conceptual incompatibility of the basic notions that underlie the different types of measures. Many measures aiming at scope are based on proficiency rating scales, which in turn are based on global notions of proficiency. This set of constructs is fundamentally different from the construct of developing linguistic systems used in language acquisition research (cf. Brindley 1998). Future research on the interface between second language acquisition and language testing research (cf. Bachman and Cohen 1998) needs to address these fundamental differences in the concepts used for the construction of the two different approaches to linguistic measurement.

The cross-linguistic validity of linguistic profiling will benefit from the application of SLA theories to further languages (cf. Pienemann 2005), and the scope of this approach will be broadened by including further structural and functional aspects of language in this approach (such as semantic roles and aspects of discourse). Currently these authors also explore ways of including standard measures of word access times into the profiling approach, thus widening the scope of this approach further and yet maintaining its precision. However, it is unrealistic to expect that, within the next few decades, this process of expansion at the descriptive level will yield the kind of scope rating scales are designed for.

The conceptual gap between the two approaches can be narrowed only if the extended scope of profiling is complemented by the construction of rating scales in line with empirical findings from SLA research (cf. Griffin and McKay 1992 for the validation of a rating scale based on SLA research). One would also need to establish how real the intended scope of rating scales is in the everyday use of these scales. In other words, which aspects of language do proficiency raters operate with in the actual assessment process? How many of the large number of descriptors contained in the procedure can they handle in real assessment situations which operate within strict constraints on time? The scope of rating scales achieved in reality would depend to a large extent on empirical answers to these questions.

Notes:

1. Cf. http://www.coe.int/T/E/Cultural_Co-operation/education/Languages/Language_Policy/Common_Framework_of_Reference/1cadre.asp#TopOfPage (17–09–2005).
2. For instance, the English phrase 'in my house' corresponds to the Finnish phrase 'talossani' (*talo-ssa-ni*: literally 'house-in-my'). In other words, this phrase consists of three words in English and one word in Finnish.
3. These tests are based on ambiguous (French/ English) stimuli such as 'pipe'. If the associations consist mainly of French words, the dominant language is assumed to be French. This assumption is based on the strength of the lexical semantic network of the speaker. Obviously, this test design is relevant only to pairs of L1 and L2 with a certain degree of linguistic proximity.

References

Abutalebi, Jubin, Stefano F. Cappa and Daniela Perani
    2005   What can functional neuroimaging tell us about the bilingual brain? In: Judith F. Kroll and Annette M. de Groot (eds.), *Handbook of Bilingualism. Psycholinguistic Approaches*, 497–515. New York: Oxford University Press.
Albert, Martin L. and Lorraine K. Obler
    1978   *The Bilingual Brain*. New York: Academic Press.
Arias, Javier, Noemi Kintana, Martin Rakow and Susanne Rieckborn
    2005   Sprachdominanz: Konzepte und Kriterien. *Working Papers in Multilingualism* 68, 1–21. University of Hamburg.
Bachman, Lyle. F. and Andrew D. Cohen (eds.)
    1998   *Interfaces Between Second Language Acquisition and Language Testing Research*. Cambridge: Cambridge University Press.
Bachman, Lyle. F.
    1990   *Fundamental Considerations in Language Testing*. Oxford: Oxford University Press.

Baetens Beardsmore, Hugo
  1971   A gender problem in a language contact situation. *Lingua* 27: 141–59.
Baetens Beardsmore, Hugo
  1982   *Bilingualism: Basic Principles*. Clevedon, Avon: Tieto Ltd.
Bickerton, Derek
  1971   Cross-Level Interference: The influence of L1 Syllable Structure on L2
            Morphological Error. In: J. L. M. Trim and G. E. Perren (eds.), *Applications
            of Linguistics*, 133–140. Cambridge: Cambridge University Press.
Bley-Vroman, Robert
  1990   The logical problem of second language learning. *Linguistic Analysis* 20:
            3–49.
Bowerman, Melissa
  1973   *Early Syntactic Development: A Cross-Linguistic Study with Special Refer-
            ence to Finnish*. Cambridge: Cambridge University Press.
Brindley, Geoff
  1998   Describing language development? Rating scales and SLA. In: Lyle F.
            Bachman and Andrew D. Cohen (eds.), 1998, 112–140. Cambridge: Cam-
            bridge University Press.
Brown, Roger
  1973   *A First Language: The Early Stages*. Cambridge, MA: Harvard University
            Press.
Chambers, Susan M. and Kenneth I. Forster
  1975   Evidence for lexical access in a simultaneous matching task. *Memory and
            Cognition* 3: 549–559.
Clahsen, Harald
  1990   The comparative study of first and second language development. *Studies
            in Second Language Acquisition* 12: 135–153.
Clahsen, Harald and U. Hong
  1995   Agreement and null subjects in German L2 development: New evidence
            from reaction-time experiments. *Second Language Research* 11: 57–87.
Clahsen, Harald, Jürgen M. Meisel and Manfred Pienemann
  1983   *Deutsch als Zweitsprache: Der Spracherwerb ausländischer Arbeiter*. Tü-
            bingen: Narr.
Clyne, Michael G.
  1982   *Multilingual Australia*. Melbourne: River Seine Publications.
Cooper, R.L. and Lawrence Greenfield
  1969   Word frequency estimation as a measure of degree of bilingualism. *Modern
            Language Journal* 103: 163–165.
Crystal, David, Paul Fletcher and Michael Garman
  1976   *The Grammatical Analysis of Language Disability*. London: Edward Arnold.
Cummins, Jim
  1976   The influence of bilingualism on cognitive growth. *Working Papers on Bi-
            lingualism* 9: 1–43.
Daller, Helmut, Roeland van Hout and Jeanine Treffers-Daller
  2003   Lexical richness in the spontaneous speech of bilinguals. *Applied Lin-
            guistics* 24,2: 197–222.
Dawes, Robyn M.
  1972   *Fundamentals of Attitude Measurement*. New York: Wiley.

DeCamp, David
  1973   Implicational scales and sociolinguistic linearity. *Linguistics* 73: 30–43.
De Houwer, Annick
  1990   *The Acquisition of Two Languages from Birth: A Case Study.* Cambridge: Cambridge University Press.
Di Biase, Bruno and Satomi Kawaguchi
  2002   Exploring the typological Plausibility of Processability Theory: Language development in Italian second language and Japanese second language. *Second Language Research* 18,3: 274–302.
Diebold, A. Richard
  1964   Incipient bilingualism. In: Dell Hymes (ed.), *Language in Culture and Society*, 495–511. New York: Harper and Row.
Doughty, Catherine and Michael H. Long
  2003   *The Handbook of Second Language Acquisition.* Malden, MA: Blackwell.
Dulay, Heidi and Marina K. M. Burt
  1973   Should we teach children syntax. *Language Learning* 23: 245–258.
Dulay, Heidi and Marina K. M. Burt
  1974   Natural sequences in child second language acquisition. *Language Learning* 24: 37–53.
Dunn, Lloyd M.
  1959   *Peabody Picture Vocabulary Test.* Tennessee: American Guidance Service.
Eubank, Lynn
  1993   On the transfer of parametric values in L2 development. *Studies in Second Language Acquisition* 3: 183–208.
Felser, Claudia (ed.)
  2005   Experimental psycholinguistic approaches to second language acquisition. Special issue of *Second Language Research* 21,2: 95–198
Fishman, Joshua A.
  1965   Who speaks what language to whom and when? *La Linguistique* 2: 67–8.
Fishman, Joshua A.
  1968   Sociolinguistic perspective on the study of bilingualism. *Linguistics* 39: 21–49.
Fishman, Joshua A.
  1971   *Advances in the Sociology of Language.* The Hague: Mouton.
Fletcher, Paul and Brian MacWhinney
  1995   *The Handbook of Child Language.* Oxford: Blackwell
Freedman, Sandra E. and Kenneth Forster
  1985   The psychological status of overgenerated sentences. *Cognition* 19: 101–131.
Frenck-Mestre, Cheryl
  2005a   Ambiguities and anomalies: What can eye movements and event-related potentials reveal about second language processing. In: Judith F. Kroll and Annette M. de Groot (eds.), *Handbook of Bilingualism. Psycholinguistic Approaches*, 268–284. New York: Oxford University Press.
Frenck-Mestre, Cheryl
  2005b   Eye-movement recording and syntactic processing in an L2. *Second Language Research* 21: 175–198.
Gazzangiga, Michael S., Richard B. Ivry and George R. Mangun
  2002   *Cognitive Neuroscience. The Biology of the Mind.* New York/London: W.W. Norton.

Griffin, Patrick and Penny MacKay
    1992   Assessment and reporting in the ESL Language and literacy in schools pro-
            ject. In: Penny McKay (ed.), *ESL development: Language and Literacy in
            Schools Project*. Vol. II. *Documents on Bandscale Development and Lan-
            guage Acquisition*, 9–28. National Languages and Literacy Institute of Aus-
            tralia.
Grosjean, Francois
    1997   Processing mixed languages: issues, findings and models. In: Annette M. de
            Groot and Judith F. Kroll (eds.), *Tutorials in Bilingualism: Psycholinguistic
            Perspectives*, 225–54. Mahwah, NJ: Erlbaum.
Guttman, Louis
    1944   A basis for scaling qualitative data. *American Sociological Review* 9:
            139–150.
Hahne, Anja and Angela D. Frederici
    1999   Electrophysiological evidence for two steps in syntactic analysis: early
            automatic and late controlled processes. *Journal of Cognitive Neuroscience*
            11: 194–205.
Håkansson, Gisela, Eva-K. Salameh and Ulrika Nettelbladt
    2003   Measuring language development in bilingual children: Swedish-Ara-
            bic children with and without language impairment. *Linguistics* 41: 255–
            288.
Hamers, Josiane F. and Michel H.A. Blanc
    2000   *Bilinguality and Bilingualism*. 2nd edition. Cambridge: Cambridge Univer-
            sity Press.
Hatch, Evelyn and Anne Lazaraton
    1991   *The Research Manual: Design and Statistics for Applied Linguistics*. New
            York: Newbury House.
Haugen, Einar
    1953   *The Norwegian Language in America: A Study in Bilingual Behaviour*.
            Philadelphia: University of Pennsylvania Press.
Haugen, Einar
    1956   *Bilingualism in the Americas: A Bibliography and Research Guide*. Pub-
            lication of the American Dialect Society 28. University of Alabama Press.
Hockett, Charles F.
    1958   *A Course in Modern Linguistics*. New York: Macmillan.
Hull, Rachel and Jyotsna Vaid
    2005   Clearing the cobwebs from the study of the bilingual brain: converging evi-
            dence from Laterality and electrophysiological research. In: Judith F. Kroll
            and Annette M. de Groot (eds.), *Handbook of Bilingualism. Psycholin-
            guistic Approaches*, 480–496. New York: Oxford University Press.
Itani-Adams, Yuki
    2003   From word to phrase in Japanese-English language acquisition. Paper pres-
            ented at the MARCS seminar, 15 September 2003. University of Western
            Sydney.
Johnston, Malcolm
    1997   Development and variation in learner language. PhD Dissertation, Austra-
            lian National University.

Kawaguchi, Satomi
  2005   Argument structure and syntactic development in Japanese as a second lan-
          guage. In: Manfred Pienemann (ed.), *Cross-Linguistic Aspects of Process-
          ability Theory,* 253–298. Amsterdam/New York: John Benjamins.
Kelly, Louis G.
  1969   *Description and Measurement of Bilingualism.* Toronto: University of To-
          ronto Press.
Keßler, Jörg-U.
  (in press) Assessing EFL-development online: A feasibility study of Rapid Profile.
          In: Fethi Mansouri (ed.), *Bilingualism and Theory-Driven Second Lan-
          guage Acquisition Research.* Cambridge: Scholars Press.
Klein, D., R. J. Zatorre, B. Milner, E. Meyer and A. C. Evans
  1995   The neural substrate of bilingual language processing: evidence from posi-
          tron emission tomography. In: Michel Paradis (ed.), *Aspects of Bilingual
          Aphasia,* 23–36. Oxford: Pergamon Press.
Kroll, Judith F. and Annette M. de Groot (eds.)
  2005   *Handbook of Bilingualism. Psycholinguistic Approaches.* New York: Ox-
          ford University Press.
Labov, William
  1969   Contraction, deletion and inherent variability of the English copula. *Lan-
          guage* 45: 715–62.
Lambert, Wallace E.
  1955   Measurement of the linguistic dominance of bilinguals. *Journal of Abnor-
          mal and Social Psychology* 50: 197–200.
Lambert, Wallace E., Jelena Havelka and Robert Gardner
  1959   Linguistic Manifestations of bilingualism. *American Journal of Psychology*
          72: 77–82.
Leopold, Werner
  1939   *Speech Development of a Bilingual Child: A Linguist's Record.* Vol. I. *Vo-
          cabulary Growth in the First Two Years.* Evanston, Ill.: Northwestern Uni-
          versity Press.
Li, Wei
  1996   Network analysis. In: H. Goebl, P. H. Nelde, Z. Stary, and W. Wolck (eds.),
          *Contact Languages: An International Handbook of Contemporary Re-
          search,* 806–812. Berlin: de Gruyter.
Li, Wei
  (in press) Social network analysis and language maintenance and language shift. *So-
          ciolinguistica.*
Lo Bianco, Joseph
  1987   *National Policy on Languages.* Canberra: Australian Government Publish-
          ing Service.
Macnamara, John
  1969   Comment mesurer le bilinguisme d'une personne? In: Louis Kelly (ed.),
          Description and Measurement of Bilingualism, 80–97. Toronto: University
          of Toronto Press.
Mansouri, Fethi
  2005   Agreement morphology in Arabic as a second language: typological features
          and their processing implications. In: Manfred Pienemann (ed.), *Cross-Lin-*

guistic Aspects of Processability Theory, 117–153. Amsterdam: John Benjamins.

Mansouri, Fethi (ed.)
(in press)   *Bilingualism and Theory-Driven Second Language Acquisition Research.* Cambridge: Scholars Press.

Marinis, Theodore
2003   Psycholinguistic techniques in second language acquisition research. *Second Language Research* 19,2: 144–161.

Masterson, Deborah
1993   A comparison of grammaticality evaluation measurements: testing native speakers of English and Korean. PhD dissertation, University of Hawaii.

Meisel, Jürgen M.
1990   Grammatical development in the simultaneous acquisition of two first languages. In: Jürgen M. Meisel (ed.), *Two First Languages: Early Grammatical Development in Bilingual Children,* 5–22. Dordrecht: Floris.

Meisel, Jürgen M.
1991   Principles of Universal Grammar and strategies of language use: On some similarities and differences between first and second language acquisition. In: Lynn Eubank (ed.), *Point – Counterpoint. Universal Grammar in the Second Language,* 231–276. Amsterdam and Philadelphia: John Benjamins.

Meisel, Jürgen M. (ed.)
1995   *Bilingual First Language Acquisition. French and German Grammatical Development.* Amsterdam: John Benjamins.

Meisel, Jürgen M., Harald Clahsen and Manfred Pienemann
1981   On determining developmental stages in second language acquisition. *Studies in Second Language Acquisition* 3: 109–113.

Mueller, Jutta L.
2005   Electrophysiological correlates of second language processing. *Second Language Research* 21,2: 152–174.

Nicol, Janet L. (ed.)
2001   *One Mind, Two Languages. Bilingual Language Processing.* Oxford: Blackwell.

Oller, John W.
1979   *Language Tests At School: A Pragmatic Approach.* London: Longman.

Oller, John W.
1991   *Language and Bilingualism. More Tests of Tests.* Lewisburg: Bucknell University Press.

Özdemir, Bengü
2004   Language development in Turkish-German bilingual children and the implications for English as a third language. MA thesis, University of Paderborn, Germany.

Paradis, Michel
1987   *The Assessment of Bilingual Aphasia.* Hillsdale and London: Lawrence Erlbaum Associates.

Paradis, Michel
1990   Language lateralization in bilinguals: enough already! *Brain and Language* 39: 576–86.

Pienemann, Manfred
  1992   Assessing second language acquisition through Rapid Profile. MS. University of Sydney.
Pienemann, Manfred
  1998a   *Language Processing and Second Language Development: Processability Theory.* Amsterdam: John Benjamins.
Pienemann, Manfred
  1998b   Developmental dynamics in L1 and L2 acquisition: Processability Theory and generative entrenchment. *Bilingualism: Language and Cognition* 1,1: 1–20.
Pienemann, Manfred
  1998c   A focus on processing. *Bilingualism: Language and Cognition* 1,1: 36–38.
Pienemann, Manfred (ed.)
  2005   *Cross-Linguistic Aspects of Processability Theory.* Amsterdam: John Benjamins
Pienemann, Manfred and Gisela Håkansson
  1999   A unified approach towards the development of Swedish as L2: a processability account. *Studies in Second Language Acquisition* 21: 383–420.
Pienemann, Manfred, Malcolm Johnston and Geoff Brindley
  1987   Constructing an acquisition-based procedure for second language assessment. *Studies in Second Language Acquisition* 10: 217–243.
Pienemann, Manfred and Jörg-U. Keßler
  (in press) *Profiling Second Language Development: Rapid Profile.*
Pienemann, Manfred and Alison Mackey
  1992   An empirical study of children's ESL development and Rapid Profile. In: Penny McKay (ed.), *ESL Development: Language and Literacy in Schools Project. Vol. II. Documents on Bandscale Development and Language Acquisition*, 115–259. National Languages and Literacy Institute of Australia.
Reynell, J.
  1969   *Developmental Language Scale.* Slough: N.F.E.R. Nelson Publishing Co.
Richards, Brian J.
  1987   Type/token ratios: what do they really tell us? *Journal of Child Language* 14: 201–209.
Rickford, John R.
  2002   Implicational scales. In: J.K. Chambers, P. Trudgill and N. Schilling-Estes (eds.), *The handbook of language variation and change,* 142–167. Oxford: Blackwell.
Rietveld, Toni and Roeland van Hout
  1993   *Statistical Techniques for the Study of Language and Language Behavior.* Berlin/New York: Mouton de Gruyter.
Romaine, Suzanne
  1989   *Bilingualism.* Oxford: Blackwell.
Rosansky, E.J.
  1976   Methods and morphemes in second language acquisition research. *Language Learning* 26: 409–425.
Samarin, William J.
  1967   *Field Linguistics. A Guide to Linguistic Field Work.* New York: Holt, Rinehart and Winston.

Schachter, Jaquelyn
    1998   The need for converging evidence. *Bilingualism: Language and Cognition* 1,1: 32–33.
Slobin, Dan I. (ed.)
    1985   *The Crosslinguistic Study of Language Acquisition.* 3 vols. Hillsdale, NJ: Lawrence Erlbaum Associates.
Swain, Merrill and Sharon Lapkin
    1982   *Evaluating Bilingual Education. A Canadian Case Study.* Clevedon: Multilingual Matters.
Tidball, Francoise and Jeanine Treffers-Daller
    2005   Exploring measures of vocabulary richness in semi-spontaneous speech of native and non-native speakers of French: a quest for the Holy Grail? MS. University of the West of England, Bristol.
Valette, Rebecca M.
    1967   *Modern Language Testing. A Handbook.* New York: Harcourt, Brace and World.
Verhallen, Marianne and Rob Schoonen
    1998   Lexical knowledge in L1 and L2 of third and fifth graders. *Applied Linguistics* 19,4: 452–470.
Vigliocco, Gabriella, Brian Butterworth and Carlo Semenza.
    1995   Constructing subject-verb agreement in speech: the role of semantic and morphological factors. *Journal of Memory and Language* 34: 186–215.
Weinreich, Uriel.
    1953   *Languages in Contact. Findings and Problems.* The Hague: Mouton.
Zhang, Yanyin
    2005   Processing and formal instruction in the L2 acquisition of five Chinese grammatical morphemes. In: Manfred Pienemann (ed.), *Cross-Linguistic Aspects of Processability Theory,* 155–177. Amsterdam: John Benjamins.

Recommended readings

Dawes, Robyn M.
    1972   Fundamentals of Attitude Measurement. Wiley: New York.
Doughty, Catherine and Michael H. Long
    2003   The Handbook of Second Language Acquisition. Malden, MA: Blackwell.
Felser, Claudia (ed.)
    2005   Experimental psycholinguistic approaches to second language acquisition. *Second Language Research* 21,2: 95–198.
Kroll, Judith F. and Annette M. de Groot (eds.)
    2005   *Handbook of Bilingualism. Psycholinguistic Approaches.* New York: Oxford University Press.
Marinis, Theodore
    2003   Psycholinguistic techniques in second language acquisition research. *Second Language Research* 19,2: 144–161.
Oller, John W.
    1991   *Language and Bilingualism. More Tests of Tests.* Lewisburg: Bucknell University Press.

Paradis, Michel
  1987   *The Assessment of Bilingual Aphasia.* Hillsdale and London: Lawrence Erl-
            baum Associates.
Swain, Merrill and Sharon Lapkin
  1982   *Evaluating Bilingual Education. A Canadian Case Study.* Clevedon: Multi-
            lingual Matters.

III. Acting multilingual

11. Code-switching as a conversational strategy

Joseph Gafaranga

1.   Introduction

In 1984, a Rwandan linguist wrote:

> Pour nous le français c'est la langue française véhicule de la culture française et ses corollaires belges, canadiennes et suisses. Le kinyarwanda est la langue bantu véhicule de la culture rwandaise. Le français dilué, qu'il se nomme 'Rwandisme' et autre 'Africanisme' cultive en nous un phénomène de rejet. *Il en est de même du kinyarwanda dilué que certains dénomment déjà 'ikinyafaransa', characterisé par un mélange grossier et par des emprunts inopportuns* (Gasana 1984: 224).

> [For us French is the French language, vehicle for the French culture and its Belgian, Canadian and Swiss corollaries. Kinyarwand is the Bantu language, vehicle for the Rwandan culture. Diluted French, whether it is referred to as 'Rwandisme' or any other 'Africanism' evokes a feeling of repulsion. The same feeling is experienced with diluted Kinyarwanda that some are already referring to 'Ikinyafransa', which consists of a rude mixture and inopportune borrowings]

Diluted Kinyarwanda that Gasana was referring to is also known as *code-switching*[1], the use of two languages within the same conversation. In this case, the two languages involved in language alternation were French and Kinyarwanda. According to Gasana, this impure (diluted) Kinyarwanda or language alternation is to be rejected. Such negative attitudes towards language alternation are very common and can be found wherever in the world bilingual speakers draw on their two or more languages in interaction with other bilingual speakers. These attitudes translate a deeply rooted monolingual linguistic ideology.

These negative attitudes towards language alternation have had a profound impact on the nature of studies which have focused on this interactional phenomenon. So far and on the whole, the general thrust of studies has been to rehabilitate language alternation, to demonstrate that, contrarily to common beliefs, language alternation is not random. This effort to demonstrate the orderliness of language alternation has been undertaken from two perspectives. On one hand, researchers such as Poplack (1980), Sebba (1998) and Myers-Scotton (1993a), Musken (2000) have examined language alternation from a grammatical perspective and demonstrated that, at this level, language alternation is very orderly even though its orderliness may be different from that of the languages involved. On the other hand, researchers such as Gumperz (1982), Auer (1984) and Myers-Scotton (1993b) have investigated language alternation from a socio-functional perspective and argued that, rather than being a random phenomenon, the use of two languages in the same conversation serves specific interactional tasks for participants. That is to say, researchers who adopt this perspective argue that language alternation is a conversational strategy or, to use Gumperz' (1982) own terms, one of the "discourse strategies".

The aim of this chapter is to cast a bird's eye view on the main arguments researchers have used to support the notion that language alternation is a conversational strategy, placing them in relevant theoretical contexts and highlighting connections between/among them. Currently, there are too many studies of the interactional dimension of language alternation to be covered in a book chapter of the length I am allowed. Book-length collections of such studies include Heller (1988) and Auer (1998). Therefore, I will not attempt an exhaustive review of this literature. Rather, I will aim to identify general paradigms of research and discuss the works of researchers most commonly associated with them. In thinking about these paradigms, Sebba and Wootton's (1998) distinction between "identity-related" and "sequential" accounts of language alternation is a useful one as is Wei's (2005) distinction between "common sense explanation" and "rational choice" models of language alternation. But, in the following, I will adopt and expand on the more detailed view as found in Torras and Gafaranga (2002: 530):

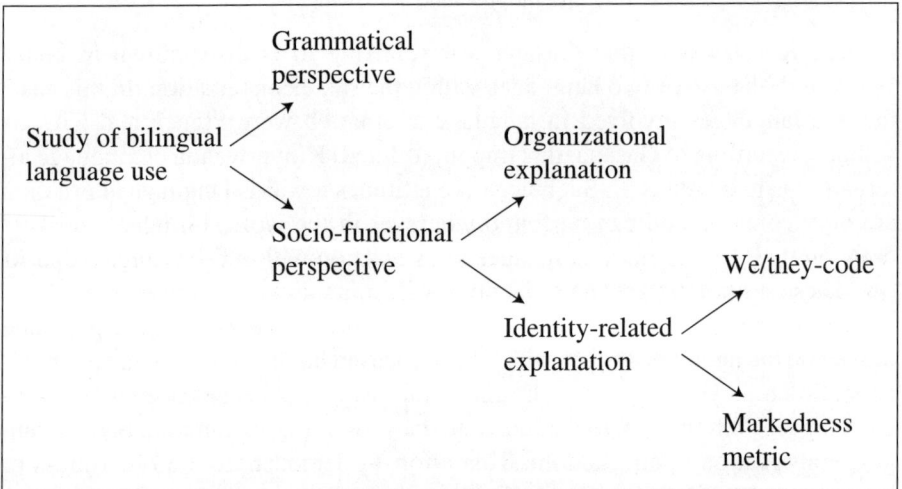

Figure 1. Approaches to language alternation in bilingual conversation

This chapter is structured as follows. In the first section, I will look at the model of diglossia (Ferguson 1959, Fishman 1967) for I think it is a useful theoretical background against which issues in language alternation research can begin to make sense. I will then move on to the identity-related explanation as exemplified by the work of two prominent researchers, namely Gumperz (1982 and Blom and Gumperz, 1972) and Myers-Scotton (1993b). Finally, I will discuss the organisational explanation drawing on Auer's (1984) sequential approach to language alternation and my own take on this approach.

2.   Diglossia: Language alternation in the structuralist/functionalist perspective

By definition (a grossly simplified one), structuralism is a view according to which society consists of different parts. Functionalism, on the other hand is the view that, in a structure (society in this case), parts exist in a state of mutual dependency and complete one another. If one of the parts is removed, either the whole structure crumbles or it is no longer complete. Crucially, the idea of complementarity between parts of the same structure implies that there is very little overlap, if any at all. The model of *diglossia* is a direct application of structuralism / functionalism in thinking about language in society. According to Ferguson, diglossia is

> … a relatively stable language situation in which, in addition to the primary dialects of the language (which may include a standard or regional standards), there is a very highly codified (often grammatically more complex) superposed variety, the vehicle of a large and respected body of written literature, either of an earlier period or in another speech community, which is learned largely by formal education and is used for most written and formal spoken purposes but is not used by any section of the community for ordinary conversation. (1959: 435)

According to Ferguson, in those communities where diglossia obtains, language varieties can be seen as forming a structure. There are two separate varieties (parts) of the language. Furthermore, the varieties stand in a functional relationship vis-à-vis each other. One is used in very specific domains and the other is used in very specific other domains, with little overlap. Depending on the nature of the domains in which each variety is used, one is referred to as the High (H) variety and the other as the Low (L) variety.

Although Ferguson initially intended his model to apply only to communities he considered to be very specific cases of monolingualism, it attracted attention from a variety of researchers, including those with interest in bilingualism. Top among the latter was the sociolinguist Fishman (1967). Fishman's view was that diglossia was a universal phenomenon.

> […] diglossia exists not only in multilingual societies which recognise several languages and not only in societies that utilise vernacular and classical varieties, but also in societies which employ separate dialects, registers, or functionally differentiated language varieties of whatever kind. (Fishman, 1972: 92)

Fishman went even further and worked out the different possibilities in which bilingualism, which he saw as having to do with the individual's linguistic competence, could relate to diglossia, which he considered to be an aspect of society. He came up with four possibilities as shown in figure 2 below.

Diglossia

		+	–
Bilingualism	+	1. Both diglossia and bilingulism	2. Bilingualism without diglossia
	–	3. Diglossia without bilingualism	4. Neither diglossia nor bilingualism

Figure 2. Diglossia and Bilingualism

As far as bilingualism is concerned, according to Fishman, two situations can be observed. Either both bilingualism and diglossia obtain or bilingualism obtains but diglossia does not. Of these two, only the situation of bilingualism with diglossia should be regarded as normal since "[…] bilingualism without diglossia tends to be transitional both in terms of the linguistic repertoire of speech communities as well as in terms of the speech varieties involved per se" (2000: 87). Following Fishman's extension of the model to cover bilingual contexts as well as monolingual ones, other researchers have adopted it and looked at specific contexts, leading to different local variants (Fasold 1984).

The model of diglossia, as briefly sketched above, has important implications in terms of conceptualising language alternation. To understand these implications, we need to operate a short diversion into ethnomethodology and consider briefly the notion of *social norm* (Garfinkel 1967, Heritage 1984). According to ethnomethodology, in the area of social action, a norm must be understood as a 'scheme of interpretation', a grid with respect to which actors make sense of what they are doing, in terms of which social action can be seen to be orderly. In social action, as Garfinkel puts it, "there is no time out" of the norm. Any act is either a direct application of the norm or it is an instance of deviance from it. If an act is deviant with respect to a specific social norm, it is either repairable or it must be seen as functionally motivated.

Keeping this notion of social norm in mind, we can state the first, and probably the most important, implication of diglossia for the concept of language alternation. It is that, under diglossia, language alternation as normative linguistic behaviour is denied. The norm is for the languages to be kept separate in terms of the domains in which they can be used. Language alternation runs precisely counter this norm. The common belief that language alternation is a 'rude mixture', and the resulting negative attitudes (see above), seem to derive from a diglossia view of language in society. The second implication is that, if the norm of *language separateness* (Gafaranga 2000) is deviated from, either of two situations may follow. Language alternation will be seen as repairable deviance or as functional deviance. The first possibility is implied in Fishman's view that bilingualism without diglossia is evidence of a state of transition. Fishman seems also to be aware of the second possibility for he states:

> Once established, […] bilingualism under circumstances of diglossia becomes an ingredient in situational and metaphorical switching patterns available for the purposes of intra-communal communicative appropriateness. (1972: 97–97)

It would seem that it is in this second possibility, where deviance from the norm is functional, that we can correctly speak of *language alternation as a conversational strategy* (see below). It would also seem that one can sensibly speak of a conversational strategy only after the norm has been specified. An act can be seen as strategic only against the background of normative conduct.

2.   Identity-related explanation of language alternation

2.1.   Interactional sociolinguistics: we-/they-codes in language alternation

The perspective of interactional sociolinguistics was pioneered by Gumperz. Gumperz's stated his main concern as in the following:

> There is a need for a social theory which accounts for the communicative functions of linguistic variability and for its relation to speakers' goals without reference to untestable functionalist assumptions about conformity or non-conformance to closed systems of norms. (1982: 93).

In other words, Gumperz was interested, not necessarily in the structure of language in society as was Fishman, but in actual face-to-face communication. According to Gumperz, "communication is a social activity requiring the *coordinated efforts of two or more individuals*. Mere talk to produce sentences, no matter how well formed or elegant the outcome is, does not by itself constitute communication." (1982: 1, my emphasis). Central to this sense of communication as a coordinated activity is obviously the negotiation of meanings between participants. And this is so because actual meaning does not necessarily reside in linguistic forms. The following extract vividly depicts the kind of problems that Interactional Sociolinguistics should help solve. Gumperz wrote this statement referring to a particular study he was conducting:

> (…) individuals who speak English well and have no difficulty in producing grammatical English sentences may nevertheless differ significantly in what they perceive as meaningful discourse cues. Accordingly, their assumption about what information is to be conveyed, how it is to be ordered and put into words and their ability to fill in the unverbalized information they need to make sense of what transpires may also vary. This may lead to misunderstandings (…). (1982: 172)

That is to say, Interactional Sociolinguistics should account for the fact that people may fail to understand each other even when they share a common language, defined as a lexico-grammatical system. Conversely therefore, it should also explicate how participants in interaction manage to communicate successfully. Gumperz answers both questions saying that successful communication, just like the lack of it, is a matter of *contextualization cues*. According to Gumperz, contextualisation cues are "surface features of message form which [...] speakers (use to) signal and listeners (to) interpret what the activity is, how semantic content is to be understood and how each sentence relates to what precedes or follows" (1982: 131). Such cues may be phonetic, syntactic, lexical or stylistic variables. They may consist of formulaic routines, formulaic expressions, discourse routines such as openings and closings, speech delivery features such as prosody (loudness, tempo, stress, intonation, silence, laughter, back channels) and even of language alternation (Gumperz 1982: 129). For Gumperz, contextualisation cues are conventional in the sense that their meanings and their uses can vary from culture to culture. Thus, when these cues are shared by all participants, "interpretive processes are taken for granted and tend to go unnoticed. However, when (they are not shared), interpretation may differ and misunderstanding may occur" (1982: 132).

How does language alternation fit into this analysis of face-to-face communication as developed by Gumperz? In the above, we have seen that Gumperz explicitly states that language alternation itself works as a contextualisation cue.

> Code switching signals contextual information equivalent to what in monolingual settings is conveyed through prosody or other syntactic or lexical processes. It generates the presuppositions in terms of which the content of what is said is decoded. (1982: 98)

Gumperz defines his scheme for interpreting language alternation as follows. In bilingual communities, languages are associated with different values and identities. One is the *we-code*, the other is the *they-code*. He says:

> The tendency is for the ethnically specific, minority language to be regarded as the 'we code' and become associated with in-group and informal activities, and for the majority language to serve as the 'they code' associated with more formal, stiffer and less personal out-group relations. (1982: 66)

Such associations between language varieties and social values come about through frequent language use following patterns of language choice such as those described by models of diglossia (see above). On the other hand, because of this association, language varieties and situations in which they are used, identities they are associated with, social values they communicate, become co-selective. Fishman terms this co-selectivity *congruence* (Fishman, Couper and Ma 1971).

The following example[2] taken from Myers-Scotton (1993b)'s study of language choice in East Africa, can be used by way of exemplifying this. The sociolinguistic context of the example is Kenyan Bilingualism, a situation which, following Mkilifi (1978), can be described as 'double-overlapping diglossia' (Fasold 1984), with English and Swahili as the H's and they-codes and the various local languages as the L languages and we-codes. In the specific examples, the languages involved are Swahili (H) and Lwidhako (L).

Extract 1
At the entrance of the IBM Nairobi office. The visitor (V), from the Luyia area of western Kenya, approaches and addresses the security guard (G). Lwidhako is italicised; otherwise Swahili is used.

1. G: Unataka kumuwona nani?
2. V1:   Ningependa kumwona Solomon I.
3. G: Unamujua kweli? Tunaye Solomon A – Nadhani ndio yule.
4. V1:   Yule anayetoka Tiriki – yaani Luyia.
5. G: *Solomon menyu wakhumanya vulahi?*
6. V1:   *yivi mulole umuvolere ndi Shen L. – venyanga khukhulola.*
7. G: *Yikhala yalia ulindi.*
Another visitor (V2) comes.
8. V2:   Bwana K – yuko hapa?
9. G: Ndio yuko – anafanya kazi saa hii (talk goes on in Swahili).
– – – – – – – – – – – – – – – – – –
translation:
1. G: Whom do you want to see?
2. V1:   I would like to see Solomon I.
3. G: Do you really know him? We have a Solomon A – I think that's the one [you mean].
4. V1:   That one who comes from Tiriki – that is, a Luyia person.
5. G: *Will Solomon know you?*
6. V1:   *You see him and tell him Shem L – wants to see you.*
7. G: *sit here and wait.*
Another visitor (V2) comes.
8. V2:   Is Mr K- here?
9. G: Yes, he's here – he is doing something right now
          (talk goes on in Swahili).[3]

At the beginning of the interaction, participants do not know each other and normatively chose Swahili as the *medium of their interaction* (Gafaranga and Torras 2001). That is, for participants themselves, Swahili is the they-code. In the course of the interaction, they recognise each other as coming from the same region of Kenya where Lwidhako is used. This recognition triggers the shift from speaking Swahili to using Lwidhako, the we-code.

Gumperz' framework as discussed above allows two uses of language alternation as a conversational strategy. First, because of the co-selectivity between language varieties and social contexts, language alternation can be used as a strategy for negotiating a change in the speech situation. He refers to this possibility as *situational code-switching*. Consider extract 1 above again. By switching from Swahili to Lwidhako, the guard is proposing a renegotiation of the speech situation from *doing being* strangers to *doing being* members of the 'local team'. It's important to stress that this is a negotiation process as V1 could have rejected G's identity-switch invitation. Even more subtle cases of language choice such as the following can be seen as instances of situational code switching. The example comes from a study of bilingual service encounters in Barcelona by Torras and Gafaranga (2002). The languages involved are English (Italics) and Castilian (Bold).

Extract 2 (translation in brackets)
At an 'English' pub in Barcelona. Customers (BBB and CCC) and Spanish speakers while the bar attendant (AAA) is taken to be monolingual English.

AAA: *hello*
BBB: *hello* (.) [eh:
CCC: [dues de negra no (addressing BBB) *two of stout right*
BBB: **quires pewueña o grande**
       (would you like it small or large)
CCC: **grande** (large)
BBB: **grande** (large)
AAA: mmm mmm
BBB: *eh: one big (.) one half pint (.) for me (.)*   [*one half pint for me*
AAA: [*one half pint for you*
BBB: *and one pint for him*

As the transcript shows, talk to the bar attendant is conducted in English while customers use Spanish to talk among themselves. Briefly, situational code-switching is a contextualisation cue, and therefore a conversational strategy, because bilingual participants in an interaction may use it to negotiate change in aspects of the context such as participants' identities and topic of interaction.

The second use of language alternation as a discourse strategy that Gumperz' view of face-to-face communication allows is known as *metaphorical code switching*. Just like situational code-switching, metaphorical code-switching draws on the co-selectivity between language varieties and social situations. However, the two are different in the sense that situational code-switching consists of a direct application of co-selectivity while metaphorical code-switching works through "violation of co-occurrence expectations" (1982: 98). That is to say, metaphorical code-switching is an instance of what I have referred to as deviance from the norm. As for the interpretation of this type of code-switching, it is to be understood as consisting of two stages. Initially, deviance from the norm serves as a signal telling the interlocutor that something other than ideational content is being communicated. At the second stage, the shift indicates a candidate interpretation. In this case, as Gumperz says, language alternation is directional, has a semantic value.

> The semantic effect of metaphorical code switching depends on the existence of a regular relationship between variables and social situations [...]. The context in which one of a set of alternates is regularly used becomes part of its meaning so that when this form is then employed in a context where it is not normal, it brings in some of the flavour of this original setting. (Blom and Gumperz 1972: 425)

Extract 3 below illustrates this possibility. The extract was recorded by Gal (1978) during her study of language shift in Oberwaert. The languages involved are Hungarian (plain characters) and German (bold). The general sociolinguistic situation is such that German is H while Hungarian is L. In the extract, a grandfather asks his two grandchildren to stop what they are doing and come to him. Initially, he uses Hungarian. But as the children resist his order, he ups the stakes by switching to German, thus drawing on the force of the language to reinforce his order. In this case, the switch to German is clearly directional.

Extract 3

Grandfather: *Szo! Ide dzsüni! (pause) jeszt jerámunyi*
               (Well, come here! Out all this away)

               mind e kettüötök, no hát akkor! (pause)
               (both of you, well now)

               kum her! *(pause) Nëm koapsz vacsorát*
               (**Come here!**) you don't get supper

However, Gumperz is careful to point out that the directionality of metaphorical code-switching does not always obtain: "In many case [...] it is the choice of code itself in a particular conversational contexts which forces interpretation" (1982: 83). That is to say, in this case, there are no grounds for proceeding to stage two of the interpretation process. The following two extracts from (from Gafaranga 1998) jointly support this. In extract 4, A is saying that he is doing research on French lexical competence among Rwandan secondary school children. He stresses that he has limited himself to the first years, reiterating the French phrase *premières années* in Kinyarwanda as *imyaka ya mbere*.

Extract 4

1. A: hee (.) *donc* nkora muri *lexicologie* (.) *plus précisément muri compe-tence lexicale* muri *école secondaire*
2. B: umh
3. A: (unclear) *je me suis limité aux* **premières années** (.) **imyaka ya mbere**
4. B: umh
5. A: kuko nkeka *hypothèse* yanjye ni uko iyo abana bavuye muri *primaire* nta gifaransa baba bazi

_ _ _ _ _ _ _ _ _ _ _ _ _ _ _ _ _

translation:
1. A: yes (.) so my work is lexicology (.) precisely on lexical competence at secondary school level
2. B: umh
3. A: I have limited myself to the first years (.) first years
4. B: umh
5. A: for my hypothesis is that when children graduate from primary school they do not know French

On the other hand, consider extract 5 below. The topic of the conversation is how difficult it used to be to travel around in Rwanda. To illustrate this, B says that he used to walk for two days and a half to go to the secondary school he attended. By way of stressing the amount of time the walking used to take, he reiterates the Kinyarwanda phrase 'iminsi ibiri n'igice' using the French equivalent 'deux jours et demi'. Clearly, in cases like these, it is doubtful whether one would still be justified to speak of metaphorical code-switching as language alternation does not follow any specific direction.

Extract 5

1. A: mpa dusangire
2. B: kuko twe twakoreshaga iminsi **ibiri hafi n'igice** (.) *deux jours et demi*
3. C: eh nzi nzi abantu bavaga iwacu kakajya wiga (.) iZaza (.) n'amaguru
4. A: umh
5. C: bakoreshagaa icy (.) [icyumweru cyose
6. A: [icyumweru

_ _ _ _ _ _ _ _ _ _ _ _ _ _ _ _ _

translation:
1. A: let's share
2. B: as for us we used to walk for about two days and a half (.) two days and a half
3. C: eh I know people from my village who used to go to school (.) in Zaza (.) on foot
4. A: umh
5. B: they would walk for a whole week
6. A: a week

Briefly, the framework of interactional sociolinguistics as developed by Gumperz allows us to describe two ways in which language alternation can be seen as a conversational strategy. In the first case, referred to as situational code-switching, participants use language alternation as a strategy for negotiating a shift in specific aspects of the speech situation. In the second possibility, known as metaphorical code-switching, language alternation is used to communicate meanings other than ideational by drawing on the symbolic value of the language switched to. Under this second category, Gumperz includes other aspects of strategic language choice which, as the discussion above shows, do not actually fit well in the model. It is such limitations which have motivated later models of language alternation.

2.2.   The markedness model of codeswitching

The markedness model of codeswitching (Scotton 1983, 1988, Myers-Scotton 1993) has its roots in Social Psychology, particularly in the Social Exchange Theory. To put it very briefly, Social Exchange Theory views social action as the result of a balancing act between costs and benefits. These costs and benefits may be material but they may also be symbolic. The influence of the Social Exchange Theory on Myers-Scotton's account of language choice in social interaction is explicitly expressed in the following:

> I argue that a major motivation for using one variety rather than another as a medium of interaction is the extent to which this choice minimises costs and maximises rewards for the speaker. (1993b: 100)

Recently, the markedness model of codeswitching has been 'recast' as the rational choice model (Myers-Scotton and Bolonyai 2001). However, because this new version of the model is not as detailed as the previous one, I will use that previous version.

But Myers-Scotton draws on other theories as well, notably markedness theory. The idea of markedness originated from the Prague School of Linguistics and was initially meant to account for phonological opposites of the sort voiced vs. voiceless. In a pair like this, the element with the feature would be referred to as marked while the one without it would be said to be unmarked. Interestingly, it was also noticed that the unmarked member of the pair was the most natural and commonest. This idea of markedness was then adopted in other areas of linguistic description including morphology, syntax and semantics. Myers-Scotton extends the same idea to language choice among bilingual speakers.

> The markedness model claims that, for any interaction type and the participants involved, and among available linguistic varieties, there is an 'unmarked choice.' [...] Discourses including CS are no different, they also show an 'unmarked choice'. (1997: 231)

Central to Myers-Scotton's argument is the notion of *interaction type* or *conventionalised exchange*.

> A conventionalised exchange is any interaction for which speech community members have a sense of 'script'. They have this sense because such exchanges are frequent in the community to the extent that at least their medium is routinized. That is, the variety used or even specific phonological or syntactic patterns or lexical items employed are predictable. In many speech communities, service exchanges, peer-to-peer informal talk, doctor-patient visits, or job interviews are examples of such conventionalized exchanges. (2000: 138)

In a conventionalised exchange, there normally is a fit between language choice and the rights and obligations set obtaining between participants (also see Fishman's notion of congruence above). When there is congruence between language choice and the rights and obligations set, language choice is said to be unmarked and when there is no congruence between the two, language choice is said to be marked. Consider extract 1 above again. In the extract, two visitors have approached the guard. Each time, the guard has selected to use Swahili when talking to them as if by default. The choice of Swahili is unmarked in this context.

Myers-Scotton also draws on the Ethnography of Communication. A key concept in the Ethnography of Communication is that of *communicative competence* (Hymes 1972; Gumperz 1972). Speaking of this competence and contrasting it with Linguistic Competence as postulated by Chomsky (1967), Gumperz writes:

> Whereas linguistic competence covers the speaker's ability to produce grammatically correct sentences, communicative competence describes his (sic) ability to select, from the totality of grammatically correct expressions available to him, forms which appropriately reflect the social norms governing behaviour in specific encounters. (1972: 205)

Myers-Scotton draws on this notion of communicative competence and formulates what she refers to as the *markedness metric*.

> Speakers have a tacit knowledge of this indexicality (the fact that, in society, language choices index specific rights and obligations sets) as part of their communi-

cative competence. They have a natural theory of markedness. The result is that all speakers will have mental representations of a matching between code choices and rights and obligation sets. That is they know that for a particular conventionalised exchange, a certain choice will be the unmarked realisation of an expected rights and obligation set between participants. (1988: 152)

Finally, Myers-Scotton has been influenced by Gricean pragmatics. In his 'Logic and Conversation', Grice (1975) developed a theory of meaning-making in conversation. According to Grice, conversation, as interaction between participants, is based on a principle he phrased as the *co-operation principle*. The principle is worded as:

> Make your contribution such as is required, at the stage at which it occurs, by the accepted purpose or direction of the talk in which you are engaged.

In turn, this general principle details into four maxims, namely quantity, quality, relevance and manner (see Levinson, 1983 for an extended discussion of this view of communication). According to Grice, in conversation, meanings can be generated either by following the maxims or by flouting, i.e. deviating from, them. In the latter case, he speaks of *conversational implicature*. Two hypothetical examples will help illustrate this.

Extract 6

A: where is Paul?
B: at Sue's house

Extract 7

A: where is Paul
B: there's yellow VW outside Sue's house

The conversation in 6 works by direct application of the maxims. On the other hand, B's response in extract 7 makes sense only by implication because it violates the maxims of quantity.

Myers-Scotton sees the markedness theory of codeswitching as an extension of the co-operation principle. She formulates a *Negotiation Principle*:

> … in addition to relying on a cooperation principle, its associated maxims, and the conversational implicatures which they generate in understanding what is said (Grice, 1975), speakers use a complementary negotiation principle to arrive at the relational import of a conversation. The negotiation principle directs the speakers to 'choose the form for your conversational contribution such that it symbolizes the set of rights and obligations which you wish to be in force between speaker and addressee for the current exchange. (2000: 137)

The example below from Myers-Scotton herself goes along way towards illustrating these claims. The exchange takes place on board a bus in Nairobi (Kenya). The passenger and the bus conductor come from the same region of Kenya (Luyia) where Lwidhako is used. In public places such as the bus, Swahili would normally be the expected choice (see extract 1 above). In the extract, the passenger undertakes to negotiate a favour from the bus conductor. To maximise his chances of success, he claims brotherhood with the conductor and, by implications, the obligations brothers have to help each other. In turn, the claim of brotherhood is reinforced by means of language choice. In other words, the passenger chooses Lwidhako in order to symbolise the set of rights and obligations he wishes to be in force between himself and the bus conductor.

Extract 8 (translation in italics)

L = Lwidhako
S = Swahili
E = English

Passenger: <L> (speaking in a loud voice and addressing the conductor)
                Mwana weru, vugula khasimoni khonyene
                (*Dear brother, take only fifty cents*)

                (laughter from other passengers – no response from conductor)

Passenger: Shuli mwana wera mbaa
                (*aren't you my brother?*)

Conductor: <S> Apana ... mimi si ndugu wako. Kama ungekuwa ndugu
                wangu ninjekujua kwa jina ... lakini sikujui wala sikufahamu
                (*No, I am not your brother. If you were my brother. I would know
                you by name. But I don't know you or understand you*)

Passenger: Nisaidie tu bwana ... Maisha ya Nairobi imeshinda kwa sababu
                bei ya kila kitu imeongezwa ... mimi ninakti Kariobang'i pa-
                hali ninapolipa pesa nying sana kwa nauli ya basi
                (*Just help me mister. The cost of living in Nairobi has defeated
                me – the price of everything has gone up – I live at Kariob-
                ang'i – the fare to get there is very high*)

Conductor: Nimecukua peni nane pekee yake
                (*I have only taken eighty cents*)

Passenger: <E> <u>Thank you very much</u>. <S> Nimeshukuru sana kwa hu-
               ruma ya huyu ndugu wango
               (*I'm very grateful for the pity you showed me, my brother*)

Myers-Scotton's scheme of interpretation as discussed above allows her to address quite a number of strategic uses of language alternation among bilingual speakers. First, Myers-Scotton makes a distinction between marked and unmarked language alternation. Unmarked language alternation can be of two kinds. The first possibility, which she terms *sequential unmarked codeswitching*, is when there is a shift from one unmarked choice to another unmarked choice so as to negotiate a change in the rights and obligation set. Extract 1 is a good example of sequential unmarked codeswitching. As we have seen, the shift from Swahili to Lwidhako corresponds to the shift at the level of participants' relevant identities. A further example is extract 9 below. In the extract, participants are holding a village meeting. The meeting has so far used Lwidhako as the medium in order to reflect the local-ness of the event. However, in turn 1, one member attacks the councillor thus disrupting the so-far-prevalent togetherness. The tone of the meeting shifts from being friendly and becomes confrontational. Reacting to this attack, the councillor distances himself and indexes this by using English, the they-code. In a sense sequential unmarked codeswitching corresponds to what Gumperz was referring to as situational code-switching.

Extract 9

Committee member: (L) Vamemba veru va County Council shikhunyzil vulahi
                      tawe. Inyinga yi tsikura vagadanga vandu vavayinzirira
                      nawutswa numu shivakholanga varia tawe.

                      (*Our councillors don't serve us effectively. During the
                      election campaign, they deceived people, that they will
                      serve them but now they don't*)

Councillor: If there is anyone who wants to take up this post, he
                      should do so now.

Assistant chief: It is not time yet. You know very well it s not yet time for
                      elections. You have just heard we are going to register.
                      Wait and see.

The second possibility, probably Myers-Scotton's most important contribution, is what she refers to as *codeswitching itself as an unmarked choice* or overall codeswitching as the unmarked choice. This pattern is selected when participants

[...] are not satisfied with either the identity associated with speaking (one language) or that associated with speaking (the other) alone when they are conversing with each other. Rather, they see the rewards in indexing both identities for themselves. (...) Thus, codeswitching becomes their unmarked choice for making salient simultaneously two or more positively evaluated identities. (1993b: 122)

Extract 4 above is a good example of codeswitching as an unmarked choice. As we have seen, both participants are Rwandese. Therefore Kinyarwanda (the language of Rwanda) can be seen as indexing this identity. On the other hand, both participants are educated. This identity is particularly relevant here as the very topic of their conversation indicates. They are talking about their research. In Rwanda, French was the medium of secondary and higher education. Therefore, its use in the extract would be explained in terms of it indexing the participants' identity as educated. As both identities are 'relevant' (Schegloff 1991, Gafaranga 2005), Kinyarwanda and French would have been used to index both identities which are simultaneously salient.

It is important to recognise this contribution by Myers-Scotton to the rehabilitation of language alternation among bilingual speakers. Reacting against Gumperz' explanation, a number of researchers including Sankoff (1972) had rejected the idea that each and every instance of language alternation carried a specific meaning. Clearly, the markedness model overcomes such criticisms. However, difficulties still exist. As pointed out in Gafaranga (2001), it is sometimes doubtful whether the identities in terms of which we are asked to interpret the pattern of switching are 'relevant' (Schegloff 1991). Consider extract 10 below. Speakers are talking about the situation of Rwandan refugees in camps across Africa. They agree that refugee camps are breeding grounds for new wars. In talking about this issue, they use both French and Kinyarwanda. As we have said, in the Rwandan context, Kinyarwada is globally held to index the Rwandan identity and French the values of education, power, high social status, etc. None of these values associated with French seems to be relevant in this particular piece of talk where participants are alternating between French and Kinyarwanda.

Extract 10

A: oya (.) bariya bo- bari muri *camp- camp* yo- *quelque soit le camp* iyo ari yo yose (.) yo ni *pepinière* (.) y' intuzaa *du d d'une guerre*
B: *voilà*
A: *camp* iyo ari yo yose (.) *au Rwanda au Burundi et partout ailleurs*
B: umh
A: *camp* ni *pépnière d'une guerre*

_ _ _ _ _ _ _ _ _ _ _ _ _ _ _ _ _ _ _

translation:

A: No those ones – those who are in *camps-* as for a *camp- whatever camp
whatever it is breeding ground* (.) for something *for a war*

B: *That's it*

A: any *camp* (.) *in Rwanda in Burundi and everywhere else*

B: umh

A: a *camp* is *a breeding ground for a war.*

As indicated above, the second category of language alternation is when speakers make marked choices. This is when participants adopt language choices which would not normally index the rights and obligation set currently in force.

> Switching away from the unmarked choice in a conventionalized exchange signals that the speaker is trying to negotiate a different rights and obligations balance as salient in place of the unmarked one, given the situational features. (2000: 150)

An example Myers-Scotton (1988) herself uses to illustrate this possibility is extract 8 above. According to Myers-Scotton, the passenger's choice of Lwidhako is marked because, in this public setting, it is not to be expected (hence other passengers' reaction). Similarly, switching to English in extract 9 would be marked given the fact that the interaction brings together members of the same language community. By the same token, switching to Lwidhako in extract 1 would be marked given the fact that this is a public setting. In other words, this category is seriously problematic for it is not clear how it differs from sequential unmarked codeswitching. As we have seen, most of these examples can also be analysed as instances of sequential unmarked codeswitching. To be sure, Myers-Scotton herself is at pains to distinguish marked switching in this sense and sequential unmarked codeswitching. According to Myers-Scotton, there is sequential unmarked codeswitching if there is "some change in factors external to the ongoing speech event ... the topic changes, new participants are introduced, new information about the identity of participants which is salient in the exchange becomes available, etc." (2000: 156). As Meeuwis and Blommaert (1994) point out, the problem lies in the conventionalisation of speech exchanges. It is as if situations existed before language choices, which are simply mapped onto them. If a more dynamic view of situation is adopted, it becomes clear that language choice is part and parcel of the business of defining the speech situation and that is precisely the reason why Gumperz sees it as a contextualisation cue.

However, some instances of language choice, especially those which are "relatively brief in duration – only a word or two", are clearly marked. Commonest among these, according to Myers-Scotton, is switching for emphasis (2000: 153). In this case, "switching involves repetition (in the marked code) of exactly the same referential meaning conveyed in the unmarked code" (2000:

153). One of the examples Myers-Scotton gives to illustrate this is extract 11 below. Participants are a salaried worker and a farmer and both come from the Luyia region of Kenya. They have met in a bar and the farmer is asking for financial assistance from the salaried worker. Up to this point, talk has been in Lwidhako, the unmarked choice for this type of setting. To express his refusal to help, the salaried worker says 'you have land' thereby meaning that the farmer should earn his own money from the land. In the example, this rejection is expressed in three languages and in this sequence: English, Swahili and Lwidhako. This juxtaposition of three languages is clearly a marked event. However, in this case, as in the cases we have looked at in relation with Gumperz' work, the issue is whether it is the directionality of language choice or whether it is the juxtaposition of language choices itself which is significant. In this example at least, as the direction of switches goes from the most powerful language (English) to the language of intimacy (Lwidhako), the interpretation would be that, through language choice, the rejection is progressively toned down rather than emphasised. The notion of emphasis by means of language alternation is preserved only if directionality is suspended.

Extract 11

Farmer: (finishing an oblique request for money) <Lwidhako> ... inzala ya mapesa, kambuli
         (*Hunger for money. I don't have any*)

Worker: <English> You have got land <Swahili> Una shamba <Lwidhako> Uli mulimi

To summarise, identity-related accounts of language alternation have greatly contributed to the rehabilitation of language alternation. They have demonstrated that language alternation, rather than being random, is a conversational strategy. They have been successful in describing some of the uses to which language alternation, as a conversational strategy, is put and less so in describing some others. For example, both Gumperz and Myers-Scotton have successfully accounted for the possibility of using language alternation in negotiating change in the speech situation (see situational code-switching and sequential unmarked codeswitching). They have also successfully demonstrated metaphorical uses of language alternation. Among the less successful proposals, we can mention the possibility of using two languages as a 'default' choice (Meeuwis and Blommaert 1998) and momentary switches away from the medium which do not communicate metaphorically. As some critics (e.g. Auer 1984, Li Wei 1998) have suggested, the problem might be that these models 'bring along' ideas about macro-societal values of language in the interpretation of specific instances.

I now turn to models of language alternation which claim to 'suspend' those ideas, to be indifferent to them. These are organisational accounts of language alternation.

3.   Organisational explanation of language alternation

Organisational accounts of language alternation divide into two categories: those which focus on the local organisation of bilingual conversation and those which explain language alternation by reference to the overall organisation. Both categories draw on Ethnomethodology and Conversation Analysis (CA). To put it very roughly, Ethnomethodology, a sociological approach associated mostly with Harold Garfinkel (1967), aims to uncover the orderliness of social action by inspecting the methods participants themselves (ethnos) use in accomplishing that very same action. As for CA, associated with sociologists such as Harvey Sacks, Emmanuel Schegloff, Gail Jefferson and others, it aims to account for the orderliness of talk itself as practical social action. Some of the key features of Conversation Analysis are: (i) the view of talk as an activity in its own right, (ii) an emic perspective whereby talk organisation is seen from participants' own perspective, (iii) sequential analysis, etc. (see Psathas 1995, Hutchby and Wooffit 1998 and Ten Have 1999 for some introductory texts).

3.1.   The local order of bilingual conversation: a sequential analysis of language alternation

The sequential analysis of language alternation was pioneered by Peter Auer in a series of publications (1984, 1988, 1995, 1998, 2000, etc.). Auer is explicit about CA influence on his work for he entitles one of his publications 'A conversation analytic approach to code-switching and transfer' (1988). This influence is also explicit in some of his significant statements. For example, he states his view of bilingualism in terms of activities as in the following:

> *I propose then to examine bilingualism primarily as a set of complex linguistic activities* (…). From such a perspective, bilingualism is a predicate ascribed to and by participants on the basis of their visible, inspectable behaviour. [...] We need a model of bilingual conversation which provides a coherent and functionally motivated picture of *bilingualism as a set of linguistic activities*. (1988/2000: 167) (my emphasis)

Announcing his research agenda, he states the following where he commits himself to an emic perspective:

> [...] the procedures we aim to describe are supposed to be those used by participants in actual interaction, i.e. [...] they are supposed to be interactionally relevant and

'real', not just as a scientific construct designed to 'fit the data'. So there is a need for an analytic interest in *members' methods* (or procedures), as opposed to an interest in external procedures derived from a scientific theory. In short, our purpose is to analyze *members' procedures to arrive at local interpretations of language alternation*. (1984: 3) (original emphasis)

Finally, Auer stresses the need for a sequential analysis of language alternation saying:

... any theory of conversational code alternation is bound to fail if it does not take into account that the meaning of code-alternation depends in many ways on its 'sequential environment'. This is given, in the first place by the conversational turn immediately preceding it, to which code-alternation may respond in various ways. (1995: 116)

One of the key concepts in CA is the notion of *preference* (Pomerantz 1984, Bilmes 1988, Schegloff 1988, etc). The easiest way towards understanding the notion of preference is to take a step back and consider the sister notion of *adjacency pair* (Schegloff and Sacks 1973). This is the fact that, in conversation, certain acts tend to condition the relevance of certain other acts. For example, a request makes its granting or denial relevant, an invitation makes an acceptance or rejection relevant, etc. (see Levinson 1983 for a formal description of this organisational pattern). Although, after a particular act, two alternative possibilities are available, they are not equivalent: one is preferred while the other is dispreferred. It is important to note that, in CA, the term 'preference' refers to structural properties of the organisation of talk.

[…] it is a structural notion that corresponds closely to the linguistic concept of markedness. In essence, preferred seconds are unmarked – they occur as structurally simpler turns; in contrast dispreferred seconds are marked by various kinds of structural complexity. Thus dispreferred second are typically delivered: (a) after some significant delay; (b) with some preface marking their dispreferred status; (c) with some account of why the preferred second cannot be performed. (Levinson 1983: 307)

For example, in extract 12 below (from Cameron 2001), two interlocutors (Julia and Anita) have reacted differently to Daphne's suggestion. Observation of the details of talk in the light of Levinson's description of preference makes it clear that Julia's response is preferred while Anita's is dispreferred.

Extract 12

Daphne: I was thinking we could have fish
Julia: Fine
Anita: well actually (.) I've stopped eating fish now because of you know the damage it does to the ocean

Auer extends this notion of preference to language choice among bilingual speakers and speaks of a *preference for same language talk* (1984: 23). That is to say, once a turn or turn constructional unit has occurred in a particular language, participants have to decide either to keep talk going in the same language or in a different language. Of these two options, according to Auer, the preferred choice is to use the same language.

Two implications follow from this extension. First of all, the implication is that language alternation is a dispreferred occurrence. As such, it should be accompanied by dispreference markers. Auer seems to point to this possibility when he says that language alternation, as a contextualisation cue, tends to co-occur with other contextualisation cues (1995: 124). As far as I am aware, there is yet no systematic study of this aspect of bilingual conversation and I will not pursue it any further. The second implication from the view that, in conversation, there is a preference for same language talk is that language alternation is an instance of deviance from this preference. As Auer himself states, "code-switching from this perspective is conceptualised as a divergence from the language of the prior turn or turn constructional unit" (1988/2000: 137). In other words, according to this view, it is against the background of this preference for same language talk that language alternation can be identified and interpreted. The preference for same language talk, "as long as it exists, is an important resource for generating meaning via language use and has to be treated accordingly" (1984: 24). It is because, according to Auer, language choice is to be examined turn by turn and turn constructional unit by turn constructional unit that I refer to his account as based on the local order in bilingual conversation.

Auer's scheme of interpretation allows him to identify two types of language alternation and two dimensions along which each of the two can vary. The four possibilities can be represented in a quadrant as follows:

	Code-switching	Transfer
Discourse-relatedness	X	X
Participant-relatedness	X	X

Figure 3. Code-switching vs transfer in bilingual conversation

As the above representation shows, the first axis of variation is whether language alternation is discourse-related or whether it is participant-related. That is to say, language alternation generates meanings of either of two types: it can generate meanings regarding the organisation of talk (*discourse-related*) and it can generate meanings about participants (*participant-related*). As Auer says, faced with language alternation, participants ask themselves:

Is the language alternation in question providing cues for the organisation of the on-going interaction [...], or about attributes of the participants? (1984: 12)

An example of discourse-related language alternation is extract 13 below (from Torras 1998). The transcript shows the end of a service encounter where a customer (CU) and a shop owner (OWN) engage in some 'small talk' (Coupland 2000) while OWN is working out how much CU will have to pay for the goods she has brought to the check-out. As the transcript shows, small talk is set off from business talk by means of language alternation. The main business is conducted in Catalan while small talk is conducted in Castilian (Spanish) (bold face). Note the relevance of Gumperz' notions of we/they-codes and situational code-switching here.

Extract 13 (translation in italics)

At the butcher's shop
1. Own: què més? (*anything else?*)
2. Cu: re mès (*nothing else*)
3. Own: **anda que sil** (*good*)
4. Own: **se ha quedados en la Gloria** (*you may take a rest*)
5. Own: **qué barbaridad!** (*goodness me!*)
6. Own: **lo que hay que ver lo que hay ver eh!** (*the things you've got to see, the things you've got to see!*)
7. Cu: **esta J** (*this J*)
8. Own: **me ha dejado bueno nueva** (*you've left me well speechless*)
9. Own: dos-centes setanta-dos (*two hundred and seventy two*)
10. Cu: goita què bé (*excellent*)

Other discourse-related functions that language alternation has been observed to serve are preference marking, repair and presequences (Milroy and Wei 1995, Shin and Milroy 2000), but are also included functions such marking quotation, reiteration for emphasis, etc.

As indicated above, the second strategic use of language alternation is participant-related. As I have already indicated, in this case, language alternation leads to inferences about participants. Auer speaks of *language preference* in this case. In turn, language preference may be of two types: linguistic competence or ideological preference.

By preference-related switching, a speaker may simply want to avoid the language in which he or she feels insecure and speak the one in which he or she has greater competence. Yet preference-related switching may also be due to a deliberate decision based on political considerations: (1995: 125)

Consider extract 14 below (from Torras 2002). Talk takes place in an Erasmus office in Barcelona. The participants are a Spanish secretary (SEC) and a German student (STU). STU is complaining about not having an e-mail account yet. The researcher is also present but, practicing participant observation, she has not played any role in the talk so far. In turn 4, SEC experiences difficulties keeping the conversation running in English. She indexes these difficulties in at least two ways, namely the word-search marker (*mmm*), the pause and switching to French (*le droit*). Turning to the researcher, she then switches again to Catalan (*el dret*). In 5, the researcher provides the mot juste and, in 6, SEC ratifies the repair and proceeds on with talk in English. In the example, while the switch to French reveals something about SEC proficiency in the languages involved, is a case of 'competence-related preference', the switch to Catalan is a case of 'ideology-related preference' as both SEC and RES are Catalan.

Extract 14

1. STU: I'm sorry it's not your fault right
2. SEC: no [uh no that's you you you
3. STU: [I'm erm I offended you
4. SEC: mmm (.) **LE LE DROIT LE** (to RES) <u>el dret</u>
   (*the the right the (to RES) the right*)
5. RES: the right.
6. SEC: the right (.) you have the right to protest eh OK
– – – – – – – – – – – – – – – – – –
4. SEC: mmm (.)

This notion of participant-related switching is particularly interesting for it allows to account for language alternation phenomena known as *language negotiation sequences* (Auer 1995, Codó 1998, Torras 1998). In Myers-Scotton (1993b), these phenomena are referred to *codeswitching as an exploratory choice*. Language negotiation sequences are sequences in which speakers use language alternation strategically to negotiate the medium they will be using for the ensuing conversation. A dramatic instance of the sequence is extract 15 below from Heller (1982). In the extract, participants are alternating between French and English by way of testing which of the two languages the interlocutor would like to see adopted as the medium.

Extract 15

At a hospital reception in Montreal, Canada.
1. Clerk: *Central Booking, may I help you?*
2. Patient: Oui, Allo?

3. Clerk: Bureau de rendez-vous, est-ce que je peux vous aider? *May I help you*

4. Patient: [French]
5. Clerk: [French]
6. Patient: [English]
7. Clerk: [English]
8. Patient: [French]
9. Clerk: [French]
10. Patient: Etes-vous française ou anglaise? (are you French or English?)
11. Clerk: n'importe, je ne suis ni l'une ni l'autre ... (it doesn't matter, I'm neither one nor the other ...)
12. Patient: Mais ... (But ...)
13. Clerk: Ça ne fait rien (It doesn't matter)
14. Patient: [French] [Conversation goes on in French]

As we have seen above, according to Auer, when faced with language alternation, bilingual participants ask themselves whether it tells them something about the organisation of the conversation or whether it is a hint to the attributes of the participants. Additionally, Auer says, participants ask themselves the question:

> is language alternation in question tied to a particular conversational structure (for instance a word, a sentence, or a larger unit) or is it tied to a particular point in the conversation? (1984: 12)

If alternation is analysable in terms of a particular point in the conversation, it is said to be *code-switching* and if it is analysable as "tied to a particular conversational structure", it is called *transfer*. In other words, code-switching is a point of departure into another 'language-of-interaction' while transfer is the use of an identifiable stretch of talk (e.g. a specific expression) in another language. An example of transfer can be found in extract 14. In the extract, by using French, SEC is not inviting STU to switch to this language. She is simply indicating that she has a specific problem with a specific linguistic item. In extract 15, on the other hand, by switching from one language to the other, interlocutors are hoping that co-participants will follow them and adopt the switched-to language as the new language-of-interaction. In other words, 15 is a case of code-switching while 14 is a case of transfer although both are participant-related.

To summarise, the sequential explanation of language alternation, as developed by Auer, is an alternative theoretical framework for understanding language alternation as a conversational strategy. In this perspective, language choice can be used strategically because it is a "significant aspect of talk organisation" (Gafaranga 1999). More specifically, language alternation is a conversational strategy for it deviates from the organisational principle of preference for same language talk. Thus, Auer's model can easily account for choices which involve moving from one language-of-interaction to another (see situational CS, sequential unmarked CS) and it adequately handles some momentary departures into another language where language choices are not directional (e.g. reiteration for emphasis). However, the sequential analysis of language alternation also has its own limitations. For example, as Auer himself seems to be aware, the preference for same language talk does not always obtain. He writes:

> ... if more than one participant frequently switches languages within turns (...), it becomes less and less relevant to speak of a language-of-interaction forming the background against which language alternation, must be seen. (1984: 84)

In such cases, it is not clear how speakers' language choices will be accounted for.

3.2.   Overall order in bilingual conversation: preference for same medium talk

As we have noted above, Auer has developed an account of language alternation which is based on the local organisation of talk. At the same time however, Auer works with the notion of 'language-of-interaction' and, as implied in the quotation above, suggests that it is against this language-of-interaction that language alternation becomes meaningful (1984: 84). In other words, Auer seems to hesitate between seeing language alternation as an aspect of the local order and seeing it as an aspect of the overall organisation of bilingual conversation. Recent work by Gafaranga (1998, 1999, 2000, 2005), Gafaranga and Torras (2001, 2002), Torras and Gafaranga (2002) and Torras (2001 and 2005) views language choice, and therefore language alternation, as an aspect of the overall conversational organisation. Evidence of this overall level organisation of bilingual conversation can be found in instances such as extract 16 below.

Extract 16

1. A: noneho rero nka bariya b' impunzi ukuntu bigenda (.) babagira ba (.) a a amashuri hano ni *privé quoi* (.) ni *privé* mbega (.) kuburyo rero kugirango aze muri iyi *université* agomba kwishyura
2. B: umh
3. A: *mais comme* nta mafaranga afite ay yatse *bourse le* (.) babyita **local government**
4. B   umh
5. A: **local authority** *donc* ni nkaaa
6. B: ni nka *municipalité*

7. A: ni nka *municipalité* c'est ça (.) *municipalité* yahano niyo yamuhaye
        bourse
_ _ _ _ _ _ _ _ _ _ _ _ _ _ _ _ _ _

translation:
1. A: refugees like him are (.) schools here are *private* (.) they are *private* so
        that he must pay to study at this *university*
2. B: umh
3. A: *but as* he doesn't have money he has had to apply for a *grant* from the (.)
        they call it <u>local government</u>
4. B: umh
5. A: <u>local authority</u> well it's likeee
6. B: it's like a *municipality*
7. A: that's right it's like a *municipality* (.) he got a *grant* from the local *mu-
        nicipality*

In the extract, three languages are used, French (italics), Kinyarwanda and
English (underlined). However, of the three languages, one seems to have been
treated differently by speakers themselves. Only the choice of English is repaired. If we were to adopt a strictly local view, we would say that the English
element is repaired because it departs from the immediately preceding choice
of Kinyarwanda. However, this would be problematic for we would have to
ask why the Kinyarwanda element itself *babyita*, occurring after the French
item *bourse le*, is not repaired. We then would have to raise the same question
regarding this French element itself as it follows a Kinyarwanda item, and
so on and so forth. In other words, we would have to claim that both French
and Kinyarwanda elements are not repaired because they are functional, and
thus face the criticism raised against Gumperz' account (see section 2). My
claim is that the need for repairing the English element, and not any other,
must be understood with reference to the overall order of the particular conversation.

    One of the big issues in research on language alternation is how to determine
the base language (Auer 2000). In turn, this need arises because, if the base language is not clearly identified, it becomes difficult to tell which elements, in a
bilingual conversation, need interpreting. In other words, the base language is a
scheme of interpretation in the ethnomethodological sense. However, as Auer
(2000) shows, in some cases, it is impossible to tell which of the two or more
languages involved is the base language. In extract 4, for example, there is no
obvious reason why one would want to call either French or Kinyarwanda the
base language of this interaction. Alvarez-Caccamo's (1998) "reconceptualization of communicative codes" is an interesting point of departure for overcoming this difficulty. Alvarez-Caccamo argues that, in looking at language
alternation, the notion of 'language' and that of 'code' must be seen as different.

According to him, the code may or may not consist of one language. In turn, this is in agreement with Auer, who says that, if participants are seen to be alternating frequently between languages, this pattern of alternating, rather one individual language, is the code (1984: 84). To mark the specificity of the linguistic code vis-à-vis other codes that participants draw on while talking, I speak of the *medium of a bilingual conversation* and argue that the medium need not be monolingual, but rather that it can also be bilingual. Note the connection between this and Myers-Scotton's category of code-switching itself as an unmarked choice. In turn, respecifying Auer, I also argue that, in bilingual conversation, there is a *preference*, not for same language talk, but *for same medium talk*. As the medium works as a scheme of interepretation, deviance from it is either functional or repairable. Thus, my analysis of extract 16 above is that participants have adopted a bilingual medium involving French and Kinyarwanda. Given this scheme of interpretation they have repaired the occurrence of English because it deviated from it. In other words, repair and lack of it, of the different elements is understood, not with respect to the immediately preceding element, but with respect to the overall order of the conversation.

This view of language alternation as an aspect of the overall order in bilingual conversation has at least two advantages. First, it accounts for repair mechanisms such as those observed in extract 14 and 16 in a unitary fashion. Both are instances of *medium repair* (Gafaranga 2000); the only difference is that, in 14, the medium is monolingual while, in 16, it is bilingual. Note the parallel between medium repair and Auer's category of participant-related transfer. Secondly, this view allows a functional motivation for language negotiation sequences. A strictly local observation of language alternation can reveal language negotiation sequences, but it does not provide any explanation for them. On the other hand, the view that language alternation is an aspect of the overall organisation of bilingual conversation proposes that participants in a conversation engage in language negotiation sequences so as to determine the medium of the ensuing conversation. And they do this precisely because they need a scheme of interpretation for the language choice acts they might accomplish in the course of the conversation. Thus, in extract 16 for example, if participants had not negotiated to use both French and Kinyarwanda as the medium, they would not know whether to repair the English item 'local government' or not.

The view of language alternation as an aspect of the overall order of bilingual conversation captures various uses of language alternation as in figure 3 below (Gafaranga and Torras 2002: 19). Two of these patterns of language alternation have been discussed above and I will not dwell on them again. These are language alternation itself as the medium or the bilingual medium and medium repair. Examples of the first category are extracts 4, 10, and 16. Examples of medium repair are extracts 14 and 16. As for *medium suspension*, it consists of momentary deviance from current medium which is not oriented to as repairable. Examples of this type are extracts 2 and 11 above as well 17 below. In 17, participants have adopted Kinyarwanda and French as their bilingual medium. In turn 1, A departs from this medium into Swahili to accomplish the specific activity of direct speech reporting in the form of *medium reporting* (Gafaranga 1998). In turn, by medium reporting, A wanted to authenticate the identity of the people reported as Zairians drawing on the association Rwandans (including current participants) make between being Zairian and speaking Swahili. As this deviance from the medium is meant to accomplish a specific interactional task, it is not oriented to as repairable. On the other hand, by using Swahili, A did not mean to invite other participants to adopt Swahili as the new medium. Simply, for the length of the reported element, the medium was temporarily suspended. Note the parallel between medium-suspension and Auer's category of discourse-related transfer.

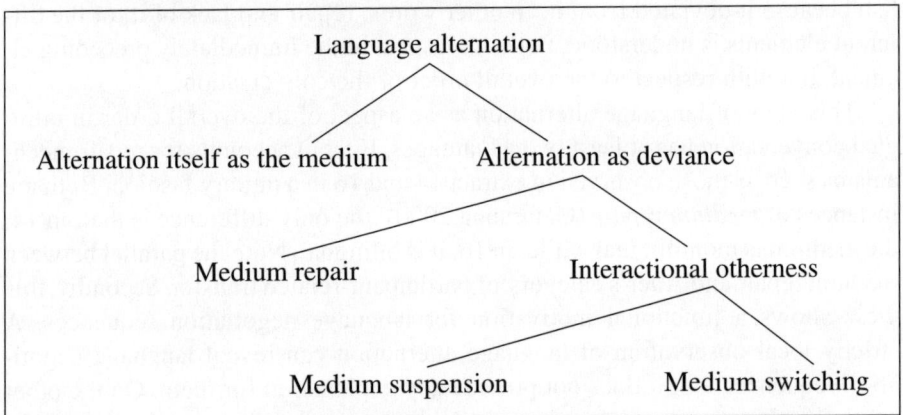

Figure 4. Language alternation as an aspect of the overall order

Extract 17

Civil war has just erupted in Zaire (present day Democratic Republic of Congo) and participants are talking about the consequences this is going to have on Rwandese refugees in that country.

1. A: ubu rero ab (.)[C helping him to wine] buretse (.) abazayuruwa ba-
         giye gutangira ngo (.) **fukuza munyarwanda**
2. B: [*avec raison puisque* turi imbwa
3. A: [xxx (laughter) ariko
4. C: *avec raison* (.) none se none wanzanira ibibazo iwanjye
5. A, B, C: (laughter)

- - - - - - - - - - - - - - - - - - - -

translation:
1. A: now Zairians Zair (.) [C helping him to wine] wait a minute (.) Zai-
          rians are going to start saying **kick out Rwandese**
2. B: [*rightly so as* we do not deserve any respect
3. A: [xxx (laughter) but
4. C: *rightly so* (.) if you brought problems to my door
5. A, B, C: (laughter)

Finally, *medium-switching* occurs when participants stop using one medium and start using another. This corresponds to Auer's category of code-switching, to Myers-Scotton's category of sequential unmarked code-switching and to Gumperz' category of situational code-switching. As I have already amply discussed these categories, I will refrain from recycling the discussion. Extracts 1, 2, 8, 9, 13, etc. are all examples of medium-switching.

4.   Where to from here? In lieu of a conclusion

As indicated in the introduction, my aim in this chapter has been to cast a bird's eye view on the various ways in which researchers have demonstrated that language alternation, rather than being a random phenomenon, is a conversational strategy. Along the survey, we have come across a variety of functions that can be accomplished by means of language alternation. These include: negotiation of aspects of the speech situation such as topics, participants' identities and relationship, negotiation of the medium, use of language alternation itself as the medium, using language alternation to signal repair, to convey metaphorical information, to generate meanings by means of language contrast, etc. As the discussion shows, while some of these uses of language alternation are captured by all the models (e.g. negotiating aspects of the speech situation), others become clear if a specific model is adopted. And this is so because language alternation is a multi-faceted phenomenon. Thus, my conclusion is that the different models of language alternation I have surveyed, rather than being seen as competitive and in terms of one being better than the others, should be seen as complementary. No one approach can claim to be exhaustive.

I also set out to expand on existing maps of the territory of research into the interactional dimension of language alternation. Particularly I have developed the model proposed by Torras and Gafaranga (2002). I can now reveal at a glance the territory of research in language alternation as a discourse strategy by a way of a summary of this discussion.

As I said in the introduction, existing research in language alternation as a discourse strategy can on the whole be described as a rehabilitation effort. This survey shows clearly that language alternation has been rehabilitated. A signifi-

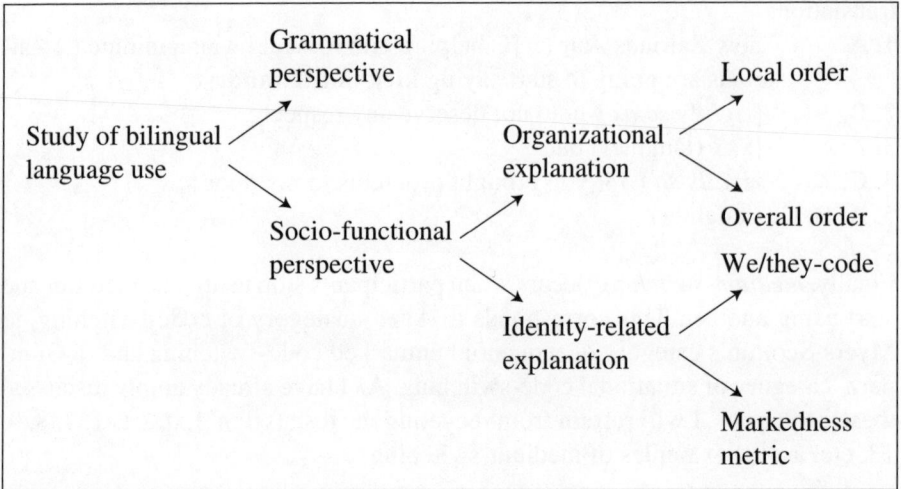

Figure 5. Approaches to language alternation in bilingual conversation

cant amount of evidence, gathered in various sociolinguistic contexts and looked at from powerful theories of social interaction, show that language alternation is a conversational strategy. The question which arises now is: where do we go from here? What prospects for future research into language alternation? It is obviously impossible for me to predict exactly what people with varying backgrounds and different interests will do in the future. Speaking only for those I feel closest to, I can say that those of us who are interested in the organisational dimension of language alternation will continue to inspect talk in detail to see how language choice contributes to the orderliness of bilingual conversation and, by so doing, overcome the so-called dichotomy "using CA" and "doing CA" (Wei 2002). In describing language choice as an aspect of talk organisation, we will not just be using CA, we will be doing CA.

Notes

1. In the literature, the term 'code-switching' is used sometimes with a generic meaning and with a specific meaning some other times. To avoid ambiguity, in this chapter, I will adopt the term 'language alternation' as the generic one and keep 'code-switching' to refer, as appropriate, to specific categories of language alternation.
2. Unless otherwise indicated, original transcription is adopted for all extracts included.
3. Original transcription slightly modified.

References

Alvarez-Caccamo, Celso
  1998   From 'switching code' to 'code-switching': Towards a reconceptualization
          of communicative codes. In: Auer (ed.), 29–48.
Auer, Peter
  1984   *Bilingual Conversation*. Amsterdam: Benjamins Publishing Co.
Auer, Peter
  1988   A conversation analytic approach to code-switching and transfer. In: Heller
          (ed.), 187–214 (reprinted in Li Wei 2000: 166–187).
Auer, Peter
  1995   The pragmatics of code-switching: A sequential approach. In: Lesley Mil-
          roy and Pieter Muysken (eds.), *One Speaker, Two Languages,* 115–135.
          Cambridge: Cambridge University Press,.
Auer, Peter (ed.)
  1998   *Code-switching in Conversation: Language, Interaction and Identity.* Lon-
          don: Routledge.
Auer, Peter
  2000   Why should we and how can we determine the base language of a bilingual
          conversation? *Estudios de Sociolingüística* 1: 129–144.
Blom, Jan-Petter and Gumperz, John. J.
  1972   Social meaning in linguistic structure: Code-switching in Norway. In John J.
          Gumperz and Dell Hymes (eds.), *Directions in Sociolinguistics.* 407–434.
          New York: Holt, Rinehart and Winston (reprinted in Li Wei 2000: 11–136).
Bilmes, Jack
  1988   The concept of 'preference' in conversation analysis. *Language in Society*
          17: 161–181.
Cameron, Deborah
  2001   *Working with Spoken Discourse.* London: Sage Publications
Codó, Ester
  1998   Analysis of language choice in intercultural service encounters. Unpub-
          lished MA dissertation, Lancaster University.
Coulmas, Florian. (ed.)
  1997   *The Handbook of Sociolinguistics.* Oxford: Blackwell Publishers.
Coupland, Justine (ed.)
  2000   *Small Talk.* Essex: Pearson Education.
Fasold, Ralph
  1984   *The Sociolinguistics of Society.* Oxford: Blackwell.
Ferguson, Charles
  1959   Diglossia. *Word* 15: 325–340.
Fishman, Joshua
  1967   Bilingualism with and without diglossia; diglossia with and without bilin-
          gualism. *Journal of Social Issues* 23: 29–38 (reprinted in Li Wei 2000: 81–88)
Fishman, Joshua
  1972   *The Sociology of Language.* Rowley: Newbury House Publishers.
Gafaranga, Joseph
  1998   Elements of order in bilingual talk: Kinyarwanda-French language alter-
          nation. Unpublished PhD thesis, Lancaster University

Gafaranga, Joseph
    2000   Language separateness: A normative framework in studies of language alternation. *Estudios de Sociolingüística* 1: 65–84.
Gafaranga, Joseph.
    2001   Linguistic identities in talk-in-interaction: Order in bilingual conversation. *Journal of Pragmatics* 33: 1901–1925
Gafaranga, Joseph
    2005   Demythologising language alternation studies: Conversational structure versus social structure in bilingual interaction. *Journal of Pragmatics* 37: 281–300.
Gafaranga, Joseph and Torras, Maria-Carme
    2001   Language versus medium in the study of bilingual conversation. *International Journal of Bilingualism* 5: 195–219.
Gafaranga, Joseph and Torras, Maria-Carme
    2002   Interactional otherness: Towards a redefinition of code-switching. *International Journal of Bilingualism* 6: 1–22.
Gal, Susan
    1978   *Language Shift: Social Determinants of Language Change in Bilingual Austria.* New York: Academic Press
Garfinkel, Harold
    1967   *Studies in Ethnomethodology.* Englewood Cliff: Prentice Hall.
Gasana, Anastase
    1984   Bilinguism et traduction: Le cas du Kinyarwanda et du Français. *Mineprisec.*
Grice, Jean Paul
    1975   Logic and conversation. In: P. Cole and J. Morgan (eds.), *Syntax and Semantics 3,* 41–58. London: Academic Press,
Gumperz, John. J.
    1972   Sociolinguistics and communication in small groups. In: J. B. Pride and Janet Holmes (eds), 203–224.
Gumperz, John. J.
    1982   *Discourse Strategies.* Cambridge: Cambridge University Press
Heller, Monica
    1982   Negotiation of language choice in Montreal. In: J. Gumperz (ed.) *Language and Social Identity,* 108–118. Cambridge: Cambridge University Press,.
Heller, Monica (ed.)
    1988   *Codeswitching: Anthropological and Sociolinguistic Perspectives.* Berlin: Mouton Publishers
Heritage, John
    1984   *Garfinkel and Ethnomethodology.* Cambridge: Polity Press.
Hutchby, Ian and Wooffit, Robin
    1998   *Conversation Analysis: Principles, Practices and Application.* Oxford: Polity Press.
Hymes, Dell
    1972   On communicative competence. In: J. B. Pride and Janet Holmes (eds), 269–293.
Levinson, Stephen
    1983   *Pragmatics.* Cambridge: Cambridge University Press.

Meeuwis, Michael and Blommaert, Jan
  1994   The 'Markedness Model' and the absence of society: Remarks on codes-
           witching. *Multilingua* 14: 387–423.
Meeuwis, Michael and Blommaert, Jan
  1998   A monolectal view of code-switching: Layered code-switching among Zai-
           rians in Belgium. In: Auer (ed.), 76–100.
Milroy, Leslie and Li Wei
  1995   A social network approach to code-switching: The example of a bilingual
           community in Britain. In: Lesley Milroy and Pieter. Muysken (eds.) *One
           Speaker, Two Languages,* 136–257. Cambridge: Cambridge University
           Press.
Myers-Scotton, Carol
  1993a   *Duelling Languages: Grammatical Structure in Codeswitching.* Oxford:
           Clarendon Press.
Myers-Scotton Carol
  1993b   *Social Motivation for Codeswiching: Evidence from Africa.* Oxford: Cla-
           rendon Press.
Myers-Scotton, Carol
  1997   Code-switching. In: Florian Coulmas (ed), 1997: 205–217.
Myers-Scotton, Carol. and Bolonyai, Agnes
  2001   Calculating speakers: Codeswitching in a rational choice model. *Language
           in Society* 30: 1–28.
Muysken, Pieter
  2000   *Bilingual Speech: A Typology of Code-Mixing.* Cambridge: Cambridge
           University Press.
Pomerantz, Anita
  1984   Agreeing and disagreeing with assessments: Some features oof preferred/
           dispreferred turn shapes. In: J. Maxwell Atkinson and John Heritage (eds.),
           Structures of Scial Action: Studies in Conversation Analysis, 57–101. Cam-
           bridge: Cambridge University Press.
Poplack, Shana
  1980   Sometimes I'll start a sentence in Spanish *y termino en español*: Towards a
           typology of code-switching. *Linguistics* 18: 581–618.
Pride, J. B. and Holmes, Janet. (eds)
  1972   *Sociolinguistics.* Harmondworth, Midlesex: Penguin Education
Psathas, George
  1995   *Conversation Analysis: The Study of Talk-in-Interaction.* London: Sage
Sankoff, Gillian
  1972   Language use in multilingual societies: Some alternative approaches. In:
           J. B. Pride and Janet Holmes (eds), 33–51.
Schegloff, Emmanuel
  1988   On a virtual servo-mechanism for guessing bad news: A single-case junc-
           ture. *Social Problems* 35: 442–457.
Schegloff, Emmanuel
  1991   Reflections on talk and social structure. In: Deirdre Boden and Don H. Zim-
           merman (eds.) *Talk and Social Structure,* 44–70. Cambridge: Polity Press.
Schegloff, Emmanuel and Sacks, Harvey
  1973   Opening up closings. *Semiotica,* 8: 289–327 (reprinted in R. Turner (ed.)

1974 *Ethnomethodology: Selected Readings,* 233–264. Harmondsworth: Penguin Education).

Scotton, Carol.
1983   Negotiation of identities in conversation: A theory of markedness and codeswitching. *International Journal of the Sociology of Language* 44: 115–136.

Scotton, Carol
1988   Codeswitching as indexical of social negotiation. In: M. Heller (ed.), 151–186 (reprinted in Li Wei 2000: 137–165).

Sebba, Mark
1998   A congruence approach to the syntax code-switching. *International Journal of Bilingualism* 2: 1–20.

Sebba, Mark and Wootton, Tony
1998   We, they and identity: Sequential versus identity-related explanation of code-switching. In: Auer (ed.), 262–289.

Shin, Sarah J. and Milroy, Lesley
2000   Conversational code-switching among Korean-English bilingual children. *International Journal of Bilingualism,* 4: 351–384.

Ten Have, Paul
1999   *Doing Conversation Analysis: A Practical Guide.* London: Sage Publications

Torras, Maria-Carme
1998   Code Negotiation and code alternation in service encounters in Catalunia. Unpublished MA thesis, Lancaster University.

Torras, Maria-Carme
2002   Language choice, social identity and the order of service talk-in-interaction. Unpublished PhD thesis, Lancaster University.

Torras, Maria-Carme
2005   Social identity and language choice in bilingual service talk. In: Keith Richards and Paul. Seedhouse (eds.) *Applying Conversation Analysis,* 107–123. New York: Palgrave Macmillan.

Torras, Maria-Carme and Gafaranga, Joseph (2002) Social identities and language alternation in non-formal institutional bilingual talk: Trilingual service encounters in Barcelona. *Language in Society* 31: 527–549.

Wei L.
1998   The 'why' and 'how' question in the analysis of conversational code-switching. In: Auer (ed.), 156–179.

Wei L.
2002   'What do you want me to say?' On the Conversation Analysis approach to bilingual interaction. *Language in Society* 31: 159–180

Wei L.
2005   'How can I tell?': Towards a commonsense explanation of conversational code-switching. *Journal of Pragmatics* 37: 375–389.

Recommended readings

Auer, Peter
    (1995)   The pragmatics of code-switching: A sequential approach. In L. Milroy and
             P. Muysken (eds.) *One Speaker, Two Languages* 115–135. Cambridge:
             Cambridge University Press.
Fishman, Joshua
    1967   Bilingualism with and without diglossia; diglossia with and without bilin-
             gualism. *Journal of Social Issues* 23, 2: 29–38 (reprint in Li Wei (ed.) *Bi-
             lingualism Reader.* London: Routledge, 81–88)
Gumperz, John
    1982   *Discourse Strategies.* Cambridge: Cambridge University Press, Chapter 4.
Myers-Scotton, Carol
    1988   Codeswitching as indexical of social negotiation. In M. Heller (ed.), *Code-
             switching,* 151–86. Berlin: Mouton de Gruyter (reprint in Li Wei (ed.) *Bi-
             lingualism Reader.* London: Routledge 137–165.
Gafaranga, Joseph and Torras i Calvo, Maria
    2001   Language versus medium in the study of bilingual conversation. *Inter-
             national Journal of Bilingualism* 5, 2, 195–219.
Sebba, M. and Wootton, T.
    (1998)   We, they and identity: Sequential versus identity-related explanation on
             code-switching. In P. Auer (ed.) *Code-switching in conversation* 262–286.
             London: Routledge,.
Wei, L.
    (2005)   'How can you tell?' Towards a common sense explanation of conversa-
             tional code-switching. *Journal of Pragmatics* 37, 3: 375–389.

12. Mixed codes

Pieter Muysken

1. Introduction

This chapter will try to analyze some of the different types of mixed codes that have been discussed in the literature. This literature is growing rapidly and includes the edited collections of Bakker and Mous (1994) and Thomason (1996), as well as analytical studies such as Auer (1999), Bakker and Muysken (1997), Matras (2000), Muysken (2000a), Myers-Scotton (2003), Thomason (1997), and Winford (2003), and special journal issues of the *International Journal of Bilingualism* edited by Poplack and Meechan (1998), Maschler (2000), and Myers-Scotton and Jake (2000). Matras and Bakker (2003a), an important source for the present paper, have collected and contributed a number of comprehensive analytical studies, while Smith (1995) contains a detailed list of a large number of mixed languages. In addition there are a large number of monographs reporting on individual mixed languages and more detailed comparative studies. Indeed, the topic is vast, and I am certain to have neglected some crucial sources. Furthermore, the history of research of the topic remains uncharted, although Peter Bakker has been working on this for some time now.

I will preliminarily define a mixed code as a way of speaking which shows evidence of substantial amounts of morpho-syntactic and/or lexical material from at least two different languages. By itself, this definition excludes the very important domains of semantic, structural, and phonological interference (e.g. the studies in Nichols 2001, such as Dussias 2001). As a consequence, many of the phenomena involved in pidgin and creole genesis (cf. Lefebvre 1998) also fall outside the scope of this paper, since they are primarily semantic, structural, or phonological in nature, and do not necessarily involve lexical elements from different languages. Matras and Bakker (2003b: 1) limit mixed languages to those languages which (a) emerged in the setting of community bilingualism and (b) show a non-marginal etymological split in structures. Criterion (a) is uncontroversial, but criterion (b) is not very clearly formulated. Is the lexicon irrelevant? Do structures have an etymology? Finally, I will not discuss mixed codes that may emerge in bilingual child language development (Meisel 1989; Deuchar and Quay 2000), in second language development, in language attrition and language death, or in the bilingual speech of aphasic or Alzheimer patients. Discussing these would require the consideration of a host of other background assumptions irrelevant to the topic at hand.

The main questions will be treated in four separate sections:

– What are the different types of mixed codes encountered and what are their formal properties (section 2)?
– Under which social conditions did these different mixed codes emerge (section 3)?
– By which psycholinguistic processes did these codes emerge (section 4)?
– Can we account for the properties of these mixed codes and the (a) symmetries in the components of the contributing languages in terms of general models of language processing (section 5)?

It almost goes without saying that I adopt some version of the Uniformitarian hypothesis, holding that given the same circumstances of genesis, the same linguistic results will be produced in different periods of time.

2.   What are the different types of mixed codes encountered and what are their formal properties?

From the perspective of the formal definition of the types of mixing encountered, we can distinguish at least thirteen different patterns:

– heavy borrowing
– slang and jargon-type relexicalization
– insertional code-mixing
– alternational code-mixing
– discourse marker switching
– congruent lexicalization
– Media Lengua-type relexification
– Mbugu-type paralexification
– restructuring and relexification
– Michif-type NP/VP splits
– Australian mixed codes
– Copper Island Aleut-type NP/VP-splits
– Mixed pidgins, trade jargons, and creoles

I will discuss these one by one in the following sections.

2.1.   Heavy borrowing

This type of mixed codes results from heavy borrowing into the non-core vocabulary. This type of borrowing is subject to semantic restrictions: very specific and pragmatically salient terms are borrowed, and to category restrictions: mostly nouns and discourse markers are borrowed, and only later other elements such as verbs and adjectives (cf. e.g. Poplack, Sankoff, and Miller 1988). A typical example from Quechua with heavy Spanish borrowing is the following (cf. also van Hout and Muysken 1994):

(1) Spanish borrowings in Quechua
ñuka *parlu*-wa-da *parla*-gri-ni ñuka Collana-munda *awilu*-guna
I talk-DIM-AC talk-INC-1s I Collana-ABL grandparent-PL
parla-shka-da.
talk-NOM-AC
Chimborazu-mun-shi *primero* shuk *pobre* ri-n k'atu-na-un.
Chimborazo-DAT-REP first one poor go-3s sell-NOM-with
Chi-munda-ga ri-n, ri-n, ri-n, k'atu-na-un.
that-ABL-TO go-3s go-3s go-3s sell-NOM-with
Mana kay-bi k'atu-y *pudi*-sha, chay-mun k'atu-nga-bu ri-n.
not this-LO sell-INF can-SUB that-DAT sell-NOM-BEN go-3s
Chi-munda shuk *amu kaballu monta*-shka *tupa*-sha-ga, ni-shka:
that-ABL one lord horse mount-NOM meet-SUB-TO, say-SD:

'I will tell a story that my grandparents from Collana told. They say that first a poor man goes to Chimborazo with his goods to be sold. Thus he goes, goes, and goes, with his goods. If he cannot sell them here, goes there to sell them. Then upon meeting with a white man mounted on a horse he says: ...'

The beginning of the story contains the following lexical elements from Spanish:

(2) parlu   *parlo   'story'
    parla-   parlar (arch.) 'talk, tell'
    awilu   abuelo   'grandparent'
    primero   'first'
    pobre   pobre   'poor'
    pudi-   poder   'be able'
    amu   amo   'lord, white man'
    kaballu   caballo   'horse'
    monta-   montar   'mount'
    tupa-   topar   'encounter'

In a large corpus of spoken Bolivian Quechua more 'intimate' or 'advanced' borrowing patterns can be observed. Frequent borrowed prepositions include *con* 'with', *como* 'like', and *hasta* 'until'; conjunctions include *cuando* 'when', *porque* 'because', and *si* 'if'; borrowed adverbs include *casi* 'almost'; finally among the frequent borrowed interjections we find *en fin* 'finally', *pues* 'then', and *a ver* 'let's see'. Although the amount and diversity of borrowings is truly remarkable in the corpus, evidence of the historical depth of the borrowing process and the intensity of contact, we should keep in mind that borrowed pronouns of any kind (personal, possessive, demonstrative, relative, interrogative) are very rare, as are borrowed articles, basic prepositions, etc. (Muysken 2000b). Many of these borrowed non-content elements may have entered Quechua as discourse markers (see section 2.5 below).

Poplack and Meechan (1998) have brought together a number of convincing papers showing how productive borrowing can be in bilingual communities. Cases studied are English/Turkish contact in Northern Cyprus, Ukranian/English contact in Lehighton (Pennsylvania), Igbo/English mixed speech in Nigeria, Persian/English mixing among Iranian students in Ottawa, and Acadian French/English contact in Moncton (New Brunswick, Canada). These papers use the same analytical tools as, and confirm the results of, earlier work by the two editors. However, it should be kept in mind that the type of borrowing discussed here has different socio-historical properties from the type of intensive borrowing reported in example (1), which I will take to be characteristic of many such situations. I will also refer to it as 'historical borrowing'.

Time depth. The studies collected in Poplack and Meechan (1998) reflect variable time depth: from longstanding (Acadian French/English in Moncton) to fairly recent contact (Persian/English in Ottawa). In contrast, the Quechua-Spanish contact leading to historical borrowing has lasted now for almost five centuries, and the first Spanish loans entered Quechua in the mid-16th century.

Degree of bilingualism. In the Quechua-Spanish type situation, there need not be community bilingualism (although the percentage of Spanish loan tokens will co-vary with the proportion of bilingual speakers in the community). In contrast, all the settings reported in Poplack and Meechan (1998) involve considerable degrees of bilingualism.

Gradualness. The introduction of Spanish items into Quechua has been a gradual process, while there is no evidence that the emergence of bilingual mixed speech of the type reported in Poplack and Meechan (1998) was a gradual process.

Motivation and variability. Although I am not familiar with explicit studies about this, there is a good chance that the type of bilingual borrowing described by Poplack and Meechan (1998) is variable, subject to level of informality, audience design, etc., in other words, is stylistically motivated. This holds for the type of borrowing in (1), only to a much more limited extent.

These four differences are probably the reason why there has been such resistance in the code-switching research community to accept Poplack and Meechan's conclusions that nonce borrowing is essentially the same thing as other kinds of borrowing. Notice that multi-fragment code-switching patterns with bilingual borrowing on these dimensions, as shown in Table 1:

Table 1.   Historical borrowing, bilingual borrowing, and code-switching compared on four dimensions

	time depth	degree of bilingualism	gradualness	motivation and variability
Historical borrowing	+	−	+	+
Bilingual borrowing	−	+	−	+
code-switching	−	+	−	+

The formal and distributional properties of the two borrowing types are quite similar, but their embedding in the socio-historical context may be quite distinct.

2.2.   Slang and jargon-type relexicalization

Similar to borrowing is what Wälchli (2005) calls relexicalization, the replacement of native vocabulary by words from one or more other languages. This process, like borrowing, is subject to category restrictions: it involves major class items, mostly nouns. However, unlike borrowing, it is not subject to semantic restrictions, and often involves the replacement of core vocabulary. The following example from Stadin Slangi Finnish, a non-standard urban variety of the language, is a typical example. Swedish words are italicized, and the inflection is Finnish.

(3) Swedish words in Stadin Slangi Finnish
   Broid-ien   *mutsi*   ol-I   *nasta*   mimmi.
   Brother-PL.GEN   mother   be-PST.3s   good/nice   woman
   'The brothers' mother was a good woman' (Wälchli 2005).

The process of relexicalization is extremely frequent in a wide variety of urban youth slangs, in jargons, secret and trade languages, etc.

There are several other characteristic features: (a) The process generally involves the replacement of large portions of the native content words, but is not categorical, and there is variation in the content words replaced. (b) Words can come from various languages, particularly in urban youth slangs. In Table 2 a few frequently cited youth slangs are listed:

Table 2. Frequently cited youth slangs

name	matrix or frame	embedded lexicon	location
Sheng	Swahili	English	Kenya
Engsh	English	Swahili	Kenya
Tsotsitaal-Flaaitaal (Makhudu 2002)	Afrikaans	English, Zulu, slang	Johannesburg
Isicamtho (Slabbert and Finlayson 2002)	Zulu/Nguni	English, Afrikaans	Johannesburg
Pachuco/Trilongo/Tirili	Spanish	English, slang	American Southwest
Tex-mex	Spanish	English, slang	Texas

A special type of relexicalization occurs when a special lexicon has been inherited from an older community language. Particularly well-known are the para-Romani languages, in which diverse (mostly European) languages can be combined with a lexicon largely based on Romani. Examples include Anglo-Romani (English grammar, Romani lexicon) and Caló (Spanish grammar, Romani lexicon). Other cases are Lekoudesch, a language of cattle traders in southern Germany with Hebrew words inserted into a German grammatical frame, and Abdal or Äynu, with Persian vocabulary in a Turkish grammatical frame (Matras and Bakker 2003b).

2.3.   Insertional code-switching

Above I used the term code-switching as a generic term. However, a number of authors have argued that there are several kinds of code-switching (Sankoff, Poplack and Vanniarajan 1990). Muysken (2000a), using the cover term code-mixing, has argued that there are three main types, of which insertional code-switching is the first. Here, separate constituents from language B are inserted into a frame constituted by the rules of language A. The main restriction on this process is categorical or semantic congruence or equivalence between the inserted element and the properties of the slot into which it is inserted. A typical example is given in (4), where an (italicized) Dutch adjective + noun combination is inserted into a Turkish clause:

(4) on-dan   sonra lauw   water-nan   yıkayınca ...
    DEM-ABL later lukewarm water-INST wash-GER
    'and then, while you were washing with lukewarm water' (Backus 1996: 103).

Notice that the Turkish postposition or case marker *-nan* is added to the Dutch noun as if it were a Turkish noun.

It is a matter of contention whether insertional code-switching is distinct from the type of bilingual borrowing discussed in section 2.1. The majority of single constituents inserted are either single words or fixed phrases, which could be analyzed under borrowing. However, not all of them are, and in some language pairs multi-word inserted constituents abound.

2.4.   Alternational code-mixing

The second type of code-switching distinguished by Muysken (2000a) is alternation. Here a chunk in language A is combined with a chunk in language B (see e.g. Poplack 1980, 1985, who adopts a slightly different perspective). The principal grammatical mechanism involved is adjunction, since the languages (here, French and Dutch) do not necessarily fit together grammatically.

(5) d'r zit me hier *une femme qui n'est pas drôle*
    there sits me here / a woman who …
    'Here there is a woman who is not funny.' (Treffers-Daller 1994: 224)

Often alternation involves the switching of clause-peripheral elements such as adverbial phrases, dislocated constituents, etc.

2.5.   Discourse marker switching

Possibly a special subtype of switching is discourse marker switching, the topic of a collection of articles edited by Maschler (2000). An example with the discourse marker *donc* (in italic) from a Shaba Swahili/French bilingual conversation (De Rooij 2000: 456) is (6):

(6) Tu-ko   ba-ntu ba-moya b-a   chini. *donc* tu-ko   ba-*faible*. eh?
    we-COP 2-man 2-DET   2-CONN low   so   we-COP 2-weak
    'We're a low kind of people. So we're weak, aren't we?'

There is also a French adjective inserted, *faible* 'weak'.

The use of a discourse marker from a different language often has a highlighting function in structuring the discourse: its very non-nativeness makes it useful to employ a foreign discourse marker. Furthermore, sometimes an element from a different language can help bring the conversation into a more informal domain.

What is important to realize is that the use of discourse markers does not obey the same directionality constraints as e.g. insertion or bilingual borrowing.

While borrowing and insertion generally involve elements from a dominant language put into a community language, this does not hold for discourse marker switching. In some cases, like the Shaba Swahili case mentioned above, indeed the discourse markers are from a dominant language; in other cases, it is the community language that provides the discourse markers, e.g. to make a community variety of the dominant language more ethnic.

Furthermore, it should be kept in mind that discourse marker switching is something very much akin to alternation, in that both involve the periphery of the clause. However, in the case of alternation, there are grammatical structures from the two languages involved, which are oddly combined, while in the case of discourse marker switching, there is the general possibility of clause-peripheral adjunction of separate elements, without internal grammatical structure.

A final point is that the frequency of discourse marker switching probably is the reason for the fact that in so many languages discourse markers have been borrowed from other languages. Frequently switched discourse markers need not become integrated into the native lexicon, but it may happen. An example of a stable non-integrated discourse marker in Dutch is German *überhaupt* 'in any case', used frequently but retaining a distinct, non-native status, which contributes to its pragmatic force.

2.6.   Congruent lexicalization

The final type of code-switching distinguished in Muysken (2000a) is congruent lexicalization, the rapid back and forth switching of loose elements in a structure mostly shared by the two languages. Example (7) is from Sranan Creole / Dutch switching, in this case recorded in the Netherlands:

(7) **soort** *bijdrage*   yu **kan lever**   *op het ogenblik* gi a   *opleving*
     type contribution you can provide at the moment for the revival
     fu a   kulturu
     of the culture?

(Bolle 1994: 78)

The elements in italic are Dutch, those in bold ambiguous between Sranan and Dutch, and the others Sranan. The Sranan word *kulturu* 'culture' is a direct though phonologically adapted borrowing from Dutch. The word *soort* 'type' has a Dutch shape, but is used as a question word the way it would be in Sranan.

Congruent lexicalization is typical of dialect/standard language switching, bilingual settings with considerable convergence, and switching between closely related language varieties.

2.7.   Media Lengua-type relexification

After the phenomena discussed in 2.1–2.6, which are quite common in the languages of the world, and do not necessarily lead to stable varieties, I now turn to a number of mixed codes which are both unique and highly infrequent, and which have a much more stable existence, sometimes as the principal community language. A first such code is Media Lengua, varieties of which are spoken in several communities in Ecuador (Muysken 1981, 1996a). Media Lengua can be characterized in a nutshell as Quechua with Spanish-derived lexical roots.

(8) a. kuyi-buk   yirba nuwabi-shka   (Media Lengua)
        guinea.pig-BEN   grass not.be-SD
    b. kuyi-buk k'iwa illa-shka   (Ecuadorian Quechua)
    c. No ha habido hierba para los cuyes   (Rural Spanish)
        'There turns out to be no grass for the guinea pigs.'

The vast majority of its affixes are Quechua, as is its syntax and most of the phonology. However, over 90 % of the roots are Spanish; the few exceptions can be seen as borrowings from Quechua.

There are people who know Media Lengua but no Quechua, and most Media Lengua speakers at present are also fluent Spanish speakers. Media Lengua is very different, however, from Quechua/Spanish L2 interlanguage, and for a number of speakers it is or was their primary mode of communication.

Matras and Bakker (2003b) cite several languages which have properties similar to those of Media Lengua: Basters Afrikaans (Khoi-khoi structure, Afrikaans root lexicon) and Chindo (Malay/Javanese structure, Peranakan Chinese lexicon). Bakker (2003: 116) suggest that there are about 25 Media Lengua-type mixed codes, which he terms L-G languages (with a Lexicon/Grammar split), and treats as the paradigm case of mixed languages: intertwined languages.

2.8.   Mbugu-type paralexification (co-existence of two lexicons)

Like Media Lengua, Ma'á or Mbugu combines roots, italicized here, from one language (Cushitic in origin) with structures from another language (Bantu), as in example (8).

(9) hé -lo   mw -agirú é -sé -we   kimwéri dilaó w -a
    16 have 1   elder   1 call PS:PF Kimweri king 1 CONN
    'There was an elder called Kimweri, king of ...' (Mous 2003: 9).

Mous (2003) has termed the process involved in the genesis of Ma'á or Mbugu paralexification, because the original lexicon always remains available in another register.

The same holds for Callahuaya (Muysken 1996b), a semi-secret sorcerer ritual language from Bolivia, with a Quechua structure, like Media Lengua, but a lexicon with words from Puquina, in addition to various other Amerindian languages.

2.9.   Restructuring and relexification

Sometimes the process of relexification goes hand in hand with considerable grammatical restructuring. Two cases in point are mixed codes from the island of Java, dating back to the Dutch colonial period, called Petjo (with mostly Malay grammar and mostly Dutch content words) and Javindo (with mostly Javanese grammar and mostly Dutch content words). In the cases of Javindo and Petjo, the 'grammatical' lexicon is split between elements from Dutch and from Malay or Javanese. In addition, there is some variation in this respect. An example is given in (10) from Petjo (van Rheeden 1993: 114, with spelling of the original source maintained):

(10) ja-*itoe*   soesah-*nja*   feel
     yes-DEM   trouble-DET   much
     'Yes that is such a lot of trouble.'

Here the italicized Malay deictic enclitics -*itoe* and -*nja* can be attached to Dutch words. The bold *soesah* is a Malay loan word in Dutch. The overall grammar is Malay, as far as we can see, but the Malay elements in Petjo are simplified with respect to the original Malay system.

2.10.   Michif-type NP/VP split

The next three types of mixed codes all involve a NP/VP split. In Michif, a mixed code currently from the plains of western Canada and the adjacent parts of the US (it originated more to the east), the italicized noun phrases are French, while the verb phrase and the clause are structured with Cree principles and mostly Cree lexicon:

(11) êkwa pâstin -am *sa*   *bouche*   ôhi   *le loup*
     and   open-he.it his.F mouth this-OBV the.M wolf
     ê-wî-otin-ât
     COMP-want-take-he.him
     'and he opened his mouth and the wolf wanted to take him.'

                                                        (Bakker 1997: 6)

2.11.   Australian mixed codes

Another type of mixed code we find in aboriginal communities in northern and central Australia, notably Gurindji Kriol (GK) and Light Warlpiri (LW) (O'Shannessy 2005; Meakins and O'Shannessy, to appear). (12) is a set of examples from Warlpiri, Aboriginal English, and Light Warlpiri, which O'Shannessy (p.c.) would classify as a mixed language. Here roughly the same sentence is presented in three language varieties (data and background information from O'Shanessy, p.c.):

(12) a. Warlpiri:
    Yirra-rni   ka-xafl-xafl   *leda*   watiya-ngka kurdu-pardu-rlu.
    put-NPST   IMPF-3sg-3sg ladder   tree-LO   child-DIM-ERG
    'A child is putting a ladder against the tree.'

   b. Aboriginal English
    Dat   boi   bin   purr-um leda   on   dat   tri.
    DEF   boy   PST   put-TR   ladder PREP   DEF   tree
    'The boy put a ladder against the tree.'

   c. Light Warlpiri
    Kurdu-pawu-ng *i*-m   *purr-um leda*   na   watiya-wana.
    child-DIM-ERG   3sg-NFUT   put-TR   ladder   DIS   tree-PERL
    'The child is putting the ladder against the tree.'

What characterizes Light Warlpiri, among other things, is a more English-type SVO order. Most verbs and verbal morphology derive from Kriol and Aboriginal English (often the difference is hard to see). Nouns can be Warlpiri and English, and nominal morphology is Warlpiri in origin (O'Shannessy 2005). The most striking feature is the innovative auxiliary system, which combines features of Kriol and Warlpiri. Notice the personal reference marker -*i*, derived from 'he', and a non-future marker -*m*, from Warlpiri. The English-etymon verb *purr*- 'put' has a Kriol transitive marker -*um*, ultimately derived from 'him'.

    The NP/VP split in Light Warlpiri, then, is the mirror image of the Michif-type. In Michif, the traditional language Cree provides the verbal system, and in Light Warlpiri the traditional language provides the nominal system. Gerrit Dimmendaal (1998) and Patrick McConvell (1998) have suggested independently from one another that the difference is due to the overall typological difference between head-marking languages like Cree and dependent-marking languages like Warlpiri.

2.12.   Copper Island Aleut-type NP/VP-split

The split in Copper Island (Mednyj) Aleut is again unlike that in Michif: the finite verb morphology is Russian, with Russian pronouns in the Russian past tense (when there is no person marking on the verb):

(13) ya   tibe   cíbu-x   ukagla:ɣa:sa:-l
    1sg.SUBJ   2sg.OBJ   parcel-ABS   bring-PST
    'I brought you a parcel' (Golovko and Vakhtin 1990: 105).

Here the pronouns and the tense marking are Russian; the global structure is Aleut. Only a small minority of the verb roots is Russian, but the number of Russian nouns is much larger. Nominal morphology is Aleut, as well as verbal derivational morphology.

What distinguishes Mednyj Aleut from Light Warlpiri is that the verb roots themselves are largely drawn from the original language, rather than from the new language (Russian), as in the case of Light Warlpiri.

2.13.   Mixed pidgins, trade jargons, and creoles

While many pidgins, jargons, and creoles have lexicons mostly derived from one language source, there is always a fair amount of admixture of foreign vocabulary, and a number of languages actually have quite mixed vocabularies. The process through which this came about has been sketched by Silverstein (1972a, b), among others, in his analysis of the emergence of Chinook Jargon. Speakers of different languages may negotiate a common mixed code when they have roughly equal power and prestige. The example given here is from Russenorsk:

(14) **kak** ju   *wil* skaffom ja   drikke te,   **davaj** på *sjib* **tvoja** ...
    what you want eat   and drink tea, please on ship your
    'If you want to eat and drink tea, then come on board ...'
                                                        (Bakker 1995: 36/7)

Russian is bold, Norwegian italic; the rest is international nautical vocabulary.

Creoles with mixed vocabulary include Berbice Dutch (Dutch, Ijo, Arawak), Saramaccan (English, Portuguese, Fongbe, Kikongo), and Chavacano (Spanish, various Austronesian languages).

3.   Under which social conditions did these different mixed codes emerge?

After enumerating these different mixed codes, the question arises under which social conditions these different mixed codes emerged. Here, Croft (2003) distinguishes five types of mixed languages:

- death by borrowing: as the number of speakers decrease and the contexts of use become more limited, more and more vocabulary and structures from a dominant language enter. The result resembles a mixed language, but not of the type that concerns us here. An example would be Asia Minor Greek, in which Greek grammatical patterns and lexicon were partly replaced by Turkish elements.
- semi-shift: speakers give up a language but relexicalize the new language with the vocabulary of the old one, in order to maintain something resembling their old ethnic identity.
- mixed marriage languages: children born in communities where many fathers speak one language, and many mothers another one, may end up speaking a linguistic variety with a grammar contributed by their mothers' language, and a lexicon derived from their fathers' language.
- new community languages owe their existence to the need to express a new ethnic identity.
- secret languages may be formed by relexicalizing a majority language with lexical elements drawn from an older or a minority language.

We can add several social contexts here:

- urban youth or street languages;
- ritual languages such as Callahuaya;
- trade languages created for inter-ethnic contact, such as the pidgins and jargons mentioned above.

What is striking about many of these cases is that they involve an in-group language. The exception are the trade languages, where we do not find an asymmetric $syntax_a/lexicon_b$ mix, but rather a symmetric $lexicon_a/lexicon_b$ mix.

4.   By which psycholinguistic processes did these codes emerge?

A number of psycholinguistic processes have been suggested in the literature to account for the emergence of mixed codes. Bakker (2003) suggests four fundamental processes, linked to four sociolinguistic scenarios:

Table 3. The four contact processes in the typology of Bakker (2003)

scenario	process	definition
maintenance	lexical mixing or borrowing	add items from one lexicon to another one
shift	interference or transfer	bring structural elements from the old language into the new one
bilingual creation	interwining	matching of the lexicon from one language with the grammar of another one
bilingual resistance	language conversion or metatypy (Ross 2001)	massive grammatical restructuring under the influence of another language

The variety of processes having to do with 'lexical mixing' (relexicalization, borrowing, lexical reorientation, etc.) need not be perceived as problematic in themselves (although the cases where it is semi-categorical are striking, of course). The process of language conversion or metatypy is not at all well understood (cf. e.g. Gumperz and Wilson 1971; Ross 2001), but falls outside the scope of this overview. The same holds for interference in a shift setting: it does not produce a mixed code as defined here. The process of intertwining, which I will take here to include relexification, however, does need a special comment. There are many close links between lexicon and grammar; ideally they go together like hand and glove, even if in a modular view of our language capacities they are seen as essentially distinct cognitive components. So why split them up, and how is this mentally possible?

Two clusters of answers can be found in the literature: conscious creation and transformation of another mixing process. Thomason (2001) suggests that mixed languages must have emerged through a semi-conscious process of creation. The title of Golovko (2003) suggests "'folk' linguistic engineering" in this context. The word 'conscious' should not be taken too literally, since we are dealing with speech communities without a tradition of meta-linguistic reflection. I think it is fair to say that conscious processes of language creation will predominantly involve the lexicon (both borrowing and lexical creation) and

certain aspects of pronunciation of which speakers are sufficiently aware to ma-
nipulate (cf. Labov's 1972 work on variables, markers, and indicators). Thus we
can imagine something like relexicalization and relexification as the result of
conscious creation, but not the adoption of underlying grammatical patterns.

The other suggestion is the transformation of other mixing processes, part of
Saussurean *parole*, into a grammaticalized and stable code, part of *langue*. An
example of this may be what we find in Media Lengua. While Quechua is
spoken in Bolivia, Ecuador, and Peru, completely relexified varieties are found
only in Ecuador. In the other two countries incidental relexification occurs in the
so-called *waynos*, bilingual songs, but as a special register, and not obligatorily.
It may be surmised, but this cannot be proven, that the same psycholinguistic
process responsible for occasional relexification in bilingual songs is used, in
the specific socio-cultural settings of highland Ecuador, to produce various instances of Media Lengua as fixed speech varieties in specific communities.

Likewise, various researchers have suggested that mixed languages such
as Michif, argued to be the result of 'intertwining', may be the result of code-
switching. Auer (1999) develops a complex transitional scenario in which
code-switching leads to 'fused lects' and then on to 'mixed languages'. Indeed, the type of Cree/French code-switching recorded by Drapeau (1995)
in northern Quebec shows the same verb phrase/noun phrase asymmetries as
Michif. McConvell and Meakins (2005) likewise adopt this scenario. Bakker
(2003) disagrees with this general scenario, and presents seven arguments
against it:

(a) The quantity of imported lexical material in code-switching (frequent but
    variable and generally not predominant) is very different from that in inter-
    twining (often categorical). **Comment:** The observation is correct, but
    grammaticalization would lead to the categorical presence of foreign words.

(b) The semantic status of imported lexical material in code-switching (often
    fairly specific content words) is very different from that in intertwining
    (often quite generic). **Comment:** Again, this is generally correct, but fre-
    quent code-switching often involves more generic words.

(c) No documentation has been provided of a transitional stage between code-
    switching and intertwining. **Comment:** Again, this is generally true, but
    the number of documented cases of intertwining is very limited anyhow,
    and the Australian data referred to in section 2.11 may provide just the evi-
    dence for a transitional stages as well (currently, Felicity Meakins and Car-
    mel O'Shannessy are completing their doctoral theses in this area).

(d) When a group speaking a mixed language moves to a new area, the gram-
    mar language is swapped for a new local language; this has not been docu-
    mented for code-switching communities. **Comment:** This may be true, but
    this possibly has to do with the fact that we define code-switching as al-

ways non-permanent. Certain types of bilingual patterns (e.g. bilingual mixed verbs) are carried from area to area (Muysken 2000, forthcoming).

(e) Different typological properties correspond to different types of code-switching: alternation occurs mostly with flexional languages, insertion with agglutinative languages. No such dependence on typology is found in mixed languages; they follow the insertional model independently of the morphological patterns of the component languages. **Comment:** This may be true for the majority of the mixed languages, but the deviant types of Michif, Mednyi Aleut and Light Warlpiri could be analysed as being derived from an alternational pattern since they involve distinct verbal and nominal morphology.

(f) Code-switching as actually documented does not look like intertwining. Peter Bakker illustrates this with data involving Turkish mixed codes. He begins by quoting an example of Turkish/Romani bilingual usage from Istanbul (his own fieldwork data):

(15) Amen   romanes   *konuş-uyor-uz*
     we   Romani-ADV   speak-PRES-1pl
     'We speak Romani.'

This pattern, which Bakker claims to be fairly typical for Turkish/Romani bilingual communities in Turkey and adjacent parts of the Balkan, involves the use of a fully inflected Turkish verb. It contrasts with the pattern encountered in Turkish/German and Turkish/Dutch code-switching (Backus 1996), where alien verbs are introduced by a Turkish 'to do' auxiliary, often *yapmak*. (In addition there is less Turkish in examples such as (15) than in many code-switches reported by Backus (1996).) However, it also contrasts with what we find in 'intertwined' secret languages involving Turkish, where Turkish verbal inflections are added directly to alien verbs. Thus, Bakker concludes, intertwined languages involving Turkish could not have evolved from Turkish/X code-switching patterns. **Comment:** This argument is to some extent circular: the pattern illustrated in (15) and the one involving *yapmak* are also to some extent grammaticalized, in the sense that they reflect an established, non-arbitrary and systematic mixing practice in a particular bilingual community. They are mixed codes in their own right. Arguably, the L-G mixed languages discussed in 2.7 may be more frequent, but this does not make them the only type. Mednyi Aleut and the Australian mixed languages are quite different, and possibly have been overlooked so far in the survey of the mixed codes of the world (cf. also Matras 2003).

(g) Code-switching and intertwining are used in different sociolinguistic circumstances. Code-switching occurs in bilingual communities in which bilinguals have a positive attitude towards both cultures, while intertwining is typical of 'new' ethnic groups. **Comment:** This is only partially correct; both tend to be in-group phenomena. Furthermore, not all code-switching communities have a positive attitude towards both languages; and some of them are in the process of becoming 'new' ethnic groups. It is a more gradual than absolute distinction. Also, we cannot independently reconstruct the attitudes which lead to intertwined languages.

Thus we can conclude that the arguments given by Bakker show that the standard type of intertwined languages cannot be equated with code-switching, but this does not mean that they could not be a grammaticalized and regularized result of code-switching practices. Golovko (2003) suggests that two processes: code-switching and 'lexical reorientation' (termed relexicalization in 2.2 above) independently of each other could lead to two different types of mixed codes: the Media Lengua-type, and the Mednyi Aleut-type. Backus (2003) argues that conventionalization of alternational code-switching (cf. section 2.4) always leads to an output in which full phrases are combined (as e.g. in (15)), never to a grammar/lexicon split. However, this does not mean that insertional code-switching could not lead to this type of 'intertwined' mixed language. This leaves us with two kinds of mixed languages, possibly corresponding to two kinds of code-switching.

5.   Abstract models to account for the asymmetries in mixing patterns

Can we account for the properties of these mixed codes and the (a)symmetries in the components of the contributing languages in terms of general models of language processing? I will start out by summarizing the contribution of the different languages in the mixed codes discussed, in Table 4.

Table 4. Summary of the contributions of the different mixed codes

Asymmetrical patterns	*Components*
heavy borrowing	Grammar and vocabulary from A, many content words and discourse markers from B
slang and jargon-type relexicalization	Grammar and vocabulary from A, possibly a majority of content words and discourse markers from B
insertional code-mixing	Grammar and constituents from A, inserted words, phrases, and small constituents from B
Media Lengua-type relexification	Grammar, including affixes, from A, lexical roots from B
Mbugu-type paralexification	Grammar, including affixes, from A, lexical roots from A and in a different register from B
restructuring and relexification	Grammar mostly from A, with some patterns from neither A nor B, and lexicon from B with some words from A
Michif-type NP/VP splits	Verb phrases from A, noun phrases from B
Australian mixed codes	Noun phrases from A, verbs from B, and a compound auxiliary complex with features of both A and B
Copper Island Aleut-type NP/VP-splits	Noun phrases from A, verbal inflections and related pronouns from B
Symmetrical patterns	
alternational code-mixing	Chunks of A and B in alternation
discourse marker switching	Clauses from A, with discourse markers from B, or the reverse pattern
congruent lexicalization	Mostly shared structures of A and B, with fairly random lexicon from both A and B
mixed pidgins, trade jargons, and creoles	A grammar with elements of A and B, but mostly newly formed, and lexicon from A and B

Leaving aside the trade pidgins and jargons, it is clear that there is an overall asymmetry in the more stable mixed codes. In particular, the distinction functional versus lexical categories and grammatical patterns versus content words play a role here as pointed out by Myers-Scotton (1993) and in a host of other publications.

The way I wish to approach the diversity of the patterns encountered, as well as the frequent occurrence of some patterns, is through a competition model in which a number of independently alternative principles may play a role in creating a mixed code. These principles would include those listed in Table 5.

Table 5. Linguistic processing principles governing the outcome of bilingual strategies

A	N < V Categorial hierarchy	Verbal elements are retained more frequently than nominal elements.
B	lex < func Functional hierarchy	Functional elements are retained more frequently than lexical elements.
C	Core < Non-core Lexical hierarchy	Core vocabulary items are retained more frequently than non-core vocabulary items.
D	func ~ lex	Functional elements are frequently taken from the same language as lexical elements in their immediate environment.
E	Juxtaposition	In language mixing and language creation a frequent strategy is juxtaposing or adjoining chunks from different languages.
F	Discourse	Discourse markers show an entirely separate behaviour, both in terms of their distribution in the clause and the frequency with which they are borrowed, but also in terms of the directionality of borrowing.

Applying these principles to the mixed codes pointed to, however briefly, in this chapter, yields the overview in Table 6. In different bilingual communities, different strategies are adopted, which leads to the different outcomes described here.

Table 6. Examples of mixed codes made possible by the principles A-D in Table 5

Asymmetrical patterns	*Principles operant*
Heavy borrowing	A, B, C
Slang and jargon-type relexicalization	A, B
insertional code-mixing	B, D
Media Lengua-type relexification	B
Mbugu-type paralexification	B
Restructuring and relexification	B
Michif-type NP/VP splits	A, D, E
Australian mixed codes	D, E
Copper Island Aleut-type NP/VP-splits	D, E
Symmetrical patterns	
Alternational code-mixing	D, E
Discourse marker switching	F
Congruent lexicalization	
Mixed pidgins, trade jargons, and creoles	E

6.   Concluding remarks

Quite obviously, the above enumeration of codes, strategies, and principles only does limited justice to the incredibly rich and varied picture of mixed codes that has emerged in the previous sections. The million dollar question that remains to be answered is: can we relate the properties of the different mixed codes to the circumstances of their genesis and use? Various authors have attempted to answer this question (Croft 2003; Matras 2003), but my impression is that the answers are not yet complete. I think it is important to start exploring a richer variation in mixed codes, beyond the grammar/lexicon prototype, before we can answer this question in full.

List of abbreviations used

1s	first, second, etc. person singular
ABL	ablative
ABS	absolutive
AC	accusative
BEN	benefactive/purposive
COMP	complementizer
CONN	connective
COP	copula
DAT	dative
DEF	definite
DEM	demonstrative
DET	determiner
DIM	diminutive
DIS	disjunctive
ERG	ergative
F	feminine
GEN	genitive
GER	gerundial
IMPF	imperfective
INC	inchoative
INF	infinitive
INST	instrumental case
LO	locative
NOM	nominalizer
M	masculine
NFUT	non-future
NPST	non-past
OBJ	object
OBV	obviative
PERL	perlative
PL	plural
PREP	preposition
PS:PF	passive, perfective
PST	past
REP	reportative
SD	sudden discovery evidential tense
SUB	(adverbial) subordinator
SUBJ	subject
TO	topic
TR	transitivizer

References

Arends, Jacques, Pieter Muysken and Norval Smith (eds.)
  1995   *Pidgins and Creoles. An Introduction.* Amsterdam: Benjamins.
Auer, Peter
  1999   From codeswitching via language mixing to fused lects: Toward a dynamic typology of bilingual speech. *International Journal of Bilingualism* 3: 309–332.
Backus, Ad
  1996   *Two in one. Bilingual Speech of Turkish Immigrants in the Netherlands.* Tilburg, Tilburg University Press.
  2003   Can a mixed language be conventionalized alternational switching? In: Matras and Bakker (eds.), 2003a, 237–270.
Bakker, Peter
  1995   Pidgins. In: Arends et al. (eds.), 1995, 25–40.
  1997   *A Language of Our Own. The Genesis of Michif, the Mixed Cree-French Language of the Canadian Métis.* Oxford: University Press.
  2003   Mixed languages as autonomous systems. In: Matras and Bakker (eds.), 2003a, 107–150.
Bakker, Peter and Maarten Mous (eds.)
  1994   *Materials on Mixed Languages.* Amsterdam: IFOTT.
Bakker, Peter and Pieter Muysken
  1995   Mixed Languages and Language intertwining. In: Arends et al. (eds.), 1995, 41–52.
Bolle, Tiba
  1994   *Sranan-Dutch Code-Switching.* Unpublished master's thesis. University of Amsterdam.
Croft, William
  2003   Mixed languages and acts of identity. In: Matras and Bakker (eds.), 2003a, 41–72.
Deuchar, Margaret and Suzanne Quay
  2000   *Bilingual Acquisition. Theoretical Implications of a Case Study.* Oxford: University Press.
Dimmendaal, Gerrit
  1998   Language contraction versus other types of contact-induced change. In: M. Brenzinger (ed.), *Endangered Languages in Africa.* Cologne: Koeppe, 71–117.
Drapeau, L.
  1995   Code-switching in caretaker speech and bilingual competence in a native village of northern Quebec. *International Journal of the Sociology of Language* 113: 157–164.
Dussias, Paola
  2001   Sentence-parsing in fluent Spanish-English bilinguals. In: Janet L. Nicol (ed.), 2001, 159–176.
Golovko, Evgeniy V.
  2003   Language contact and group identity: the role of "folk" linguistic engineering. In: Matras and Bakker (eds.), 2003a, 177–207.

Golovko, Evgeniy V. and Nicolai B. Vakhtin
  1990   Aleut in Contact: the CIA Enigma. *Acta Linguistica Hafniensia*, 22: 97–125.
Gumperz, John and Robert Wilson
  1971   Convergence and creolization: a case from the Indo-Aryan-Dravidian border. In: Dell Hymes (ed.) *The Pidginization and Creolization of Languages*, 151–169. Cambridge University Press.
Hout, Roeland van and Pieter Muysken
  1994   Modelling lexical borrowability. *Language Variation and Change* 6: 39–62.
Labov, William
  1972   *Sociolinguistic Patterns*. Philadephia: University of Pennsylvania Press.
Lefebvre, Claire
  1998   *Creole Genesis and the Acquisition of Grammar*. Cambridge: Cambridge University Press.
McConvell, Patrick
  1988   Mix-im-up: aboriginal code-switching, old and new. In: M. Heller (ed.) *Codeswitching: Anthropological and Sociolinguistic Perspectives*, 97–124. Berlin: Mouton de Gruyter.
McConvell, Patrick and Felicity Meakins
  2005   Gurindji Kriol: A mixed language emerges from code-switching, *Australian Journal of Linguistics*. 25: 9–30.
Makhudu, K.D.P.
  2002   An introduction to Flaaitaal (or Tsotsitaal). In: Mesthrie (ed.), 2002, 398–406.
Maschler, Yael (ed.)
  2000   *Discourse Markers in Bilingual Conversation*. Special Issue of the *International Journal of Bilingualism* 4.4.
Matras, Yaron
  2000   Mixed languages: a functional-communicative approach. *Bilingualism: Language and Cognition* 3: 79–100.
Matras, Yaron
  2003   Re-examining the structural prototype. In: Matras and Bakker (eds.), 2003a, 151–176.
Matras, Yaron and Peter Bakker (eds.)
  2003a   *The Mixed Language Debate. Theoretical and Empirical Advances*. Berlin/ New York: Mouton de Gruyter.
Matras, Yaron and Peter Bakker
  2003b   The study of mixed languages. In: Matras and Bakker (eds.), 2003a, 1–20.
Meakins, F. and C. O'Shannessy
  to appear Possessing variation: age and inalienability related variables in the possessive constructions of two Australian mixed languages. *Monash University Linguistics Papers* Vol. 5, No. 2 (Special issue: Simon Musgrave ed. Language Contact, Hybrids and New Varieties: Emergent Possessive Constructions)
Meisel, Jürgen
  1989   Early differentiation of languages in bilingual children. In: Kenneth Hyltenstam and Loraine Obler (eds.) *Bilingualism Across a Lifespan*, 13–40. Cambridge: University Press.
Mesthrie, Rajend (ed.)
  2002   *Language in South Africa*. Cambridge University Press.

Milroy, Lesley and Pieter Muysken (eds.)
    1995   *One speaker, Two Languages*. Cambridge: University Press.
Mous, Maarten
    2003   *The Making of a Mixed Language: The Case of Ma'a/Mbugu*. Amsterdam:
            Benjamins
Muysken, Pieter
    1981   Half-way between Quechua and Spanish: the case for relexification. In: Ar-
            nold Highfield and Albert Valdman (eds.) *Historicity and Variation in
            Creole Studies*, 52–78. Ann Harbor: Karoma.
    1996   Media Lengua. In: Sarah G. Thomason (ed.), 1996, 365–426.
    2000a   *Bilingual Speech: A Typology of Code-Mixing*. Cambridge: University
            Press.
    2000b   Spanish grammatical elements in Bolivian Quechua: The Transcripciones
            Quechuas Corpus. In: Thomas Stolz and Klaus Zimmermann (eds.), *Lo
            propio y lo ajeno en las lenguas austronésicas y amerindias. Procesos
            interculturales en el contacto de lenguas indígenas con el español en el
            Pacífico e Hispanoamérica*, 59–82. Frankfurt am Main: Vervuert/ Madrid:
            Iberoamericana.
    forthc. *From Colombo to Athens: Linguistic Areas for Bilingual Patterns*.
Myers-Scotton, Carol
    1993   *Duelling Languages. Grammatical Structure in Codeswitching*. Oxford:
            Clarendon Press.
    2003   *Contact linguistics. Bilingual encounters and grammatical outcomes*. Ox-
            ford: Oxford University Press.
Myers-Scotton, Carol and Janice L. Jake (eds.)
    2000   Testing a model of morpheme classification with language contact data.
            Special Issue of the International Journal of Bilingualism. 4 (1): 1–9.
Nicol, Janet L. (ed.)
    2001   *One Mind, Two Languages. Bilingual Language Processing. Explaining
            Linguistics*. Malden, MA: Blackwell Publishers.
O'Shannessy, Carmel
    2005   Light Warlpiri: A new language. *Australian Journal of Linguistics* 25.1:
            31–57.
Poplack, Shana
    1980   Sometimes I'll start a sentence in Spanish Y TERMINO EN ESPAÑOL.
            Linguistics 18: 581–618.
    1985   Contrasting patterns of code-switching in two communities. In: H.J. War-
            kentyne (ed.) *Methods V. Papers From the Fifth International Conference
            on Methods in Dialectology*, 363–386. Victoria, B.C.: University of Vic-
            toria Press.
Poplack, Shana, David Sankoff, and Christopher Miller
    1988   The social correlates and linguistic processes of lexical borrowing and as-
            similation, *Linguistics* 26: 47–104.
Poplack, Shana and Marjory Meechan (eds.)
    1998   Instant loans, easy conditions: the productivity of bilingual borrow-
            ing. Special Issue of the *International Journal of Bilingualism* 2.2:
            127–234.

Rheeden, Hadewych van
 1993   *Het Petjo van Batavia. Ontstaan en structuur van de taal van de Indo's.* Un-
           published MA Thesis, Universiteit van Amsterdam.
Rooij, Vincent de
 2000   French discourse markers in Shaba Swahili conversations. *International
           Journal of Bilingualism* 4: 447–468.
Ross, Malcolm
 2001   Contact-induced change in Oceanic languages in north-west Melanesia. In:
           Alexandra Aikhenvald and R.M.W. Dixon (eds.), *Areal diffusion and Ge-
           netic Inheritance: Problems in Comparative Linguistics,* 134–166. Oxford:
           Oxford University Press.
Sankoff, David, Shana Poplack, and Swathi Vanniarajan
 1990   The case of the nonce loan in Tamil, *Language Variation and Change* 2:
           71–101.
Silverstein, Michael
 1972a, b Multi-level generative systems: the case of Chinook Jargon, I and II. *Lan-
           guage* 48: 137–185, 243–297.
Slabbert, Sarah and Robert Finlayson
 2002   Code-switching in South African townships. In: Mesthrie (ed.), 235–257.
Smith, Norval
 1995   An annotated list of creoles, pidgins, and mixed languages. In: Arends et al.
           (eds.), 1995, 331–374.
Thomason, Sarah G. (ed.)
 1996   *Contact languages. A Wider Perspective.* Amsterdam: Benjamins.
Thomason, Sarah G.
 1997   A typology of contact languages. In: Arthur K. Spears and Donald Winford
           (eds.) *The Structure and Status of Pidgins and Creoles,* 71–88. Amsterdam:
           Benjamins.
Thomason, Sarah G.
 2001   *Language Contact.* Edinburgh University Press.
Treffers-Daller, Jeanine
 1994   *Mixing Two Languages. French-Dutch Contact in a Comparative Perspec-
           tive.* Berlin: Mouton de Gruyter.
Wälchli, Bernhard
 2005   Relexicalization vs. Relexification: The Case of Stadin Slangi Finnish.
           Manuscript. Max Planck Institute for Evolutionary Anthropology, Leipzig.
Winford, Donald
 2003   *An Introduction to Contact Linguistics.* Oxford: Blackwell.

Recommended readings

Matras and Bakker (2003a) contains a number of analytical studies, while Smith (1995)
is a comprehensive list of a large number of mixed languages. Case studies are presented
in Bakker and Mous (1994) and Thomason (1996). Myers-Scotton (2003), Thomason
(1997) and Winford (2003) contain overview chapters on mixed languages (cf. also the
introductory paragraph of the present article).

13.　Multilingual forms of talk and identity work

Benjamin Bailey

1.　Introduction

Language is our primary semiotic tool for representing and negotiating social reality, including social identity categories. Through talk we position ourselves and others relative to co-present interlocutors, the communicative activities in which we are engaged, and various dimensions of the wider world, including social identity categories and their relative value. This positioning of selves is intertwined with the achievement of intersubjective understanding. We speak and interpret language from subject positions (Davies and Harré 1990), i.e., social identities, that are simultaneously a product and contextual frame of our talk.

Some identity negotiations through language are conscious, intentional, and referentially explicit, but most are not, and aspects of social identities are established, reproduced, or contested in even the most fleeting, instrumental, and seemingly trivial social encounters. In the exchange of greetings, for example, we choose the words, timing, and prosody of our utterances – along with facial and corporeal demeanor – to mark our relationship to our interlocutor, thus positioning ourselves and our addressees. This positioning is contingent and interactively negotiated across turns: the people we greet may provide a response to our greeting that positions them as more or less intimate or higher or lower in social hierarchies (Irvine 1974) or they might ignore our greeting entirely. Terms of address in such greetings – *Miss, Ms., Mrs., Dr., Mary*, or none at all – similarly position both speaker and addressee, as do the second-person pronouns, e.g. *tu* versus *vous*, of many European languages (Brown and Gilman 1960) or the multiple status-relationship marking verb endings of such languages as Korean (Lee 1989).

Even the absence of speech positions participants in an encounter. A momentary delay in producing a response to an assessment (Goodwin and Goodwin 1992) can signal disagreement with an interlocutor or something else problematic about the phenomenon or stance invoked by the prior turn. More extended silent co-presence (re)constitutes particular relationships among those who are co-present or displays stances toward widely recognized social categories and who is an authentic member of them (Basso 1972; Wieder and Pratt 1990). To speak – or even not to speak in a social encounter – is always an act of identity (cf. Le Page and Tabouret-Keller 1985).

Turn-by-turn analysis of naturally occurring language and interaction is a means to understanding how individuals, as social actors, socially position themselves and are positioned by others. Interlocutors publicly display and continuously update for each other their on-going understandings of talk – including such positioning. Because they must make these negotiations visible to each other to achieve a degree of intersubjectivity, analysts can 'look over their shoulders' to gain a window onto the understandings that interlocutors, themselves, display of these processes (cf. Heritage and Atkinson 1984: 11).

Compared to monolingual, monocultural individuals, multilingual individuals have an expanded set of linguistic resources for the omnipresent task of positioning self and other, and often a broader range of social categories that can be made relevant through talk. On the linguistic level, bilinguals can draw forms from two languages as well as hybrid forms resulting from language contact. On the social and cultural level, many are familiar with relatively diverse cultural frameworks for interpreting and evaluating the world and positioning themselves and others within it.

Take the following example, in which two Dominican American high school students in a northeastern US city switch languages to negotiate a local meaning of the term *hick*. The use of multiple languages both facilitates coming to a common understanding of the word *hick* and highlights facets of speakers' identities as youthful, relatively acculturated, female Dominican Americans. Their bilingualism is a key to expressing social identity distinctions that are relevant in their multilingual, multicultural immigrant community.

Example 1 [(JS #212:40:58) Janelle (US-born) and Isabella (arrived in US at age 6) are sitting outside of their school and have just referred disparagingly to some male, immigrant students staring in their direction as 'hicks'.][1]

Janelle: What do you call a hick? Cause Jose says a hick is someone ridiculous, somebody stupid. Isn't a hick someone who just came back from the country and they can't really dress, they can't speak English? And they, you know,

Isabella: They be like *loca, loca, //e:::::: pa, epa:::, huepa:* (high pitched and nasal)
            ['honey, honey, he:::::::y, alright!, alri::::ght!, alri:ght!']

Janelle: //Yeah, right?

Janelle offers a candidate understanding of a *hick* in referential terms: as someone who just came from the (Dominican) countryside, is not acculturated to urban American youth clothing fashions, and can't speak English. Isabella confirms Janelle's candidate understanding of 'hicks' not through reference but by giving a representative direct quotation of their speech: *loca, loca, e:::::, epa, epa, huepa.* She squints and scrunches her face, using a nasal, slightly high-pitched register. She introduces this direct quote with the African American English habitual *be* (Rickford 1999), meaning that this category of person *habitually* and *repeatedly* says things of this sort. Janelle displays immediate agreement with this characterization of 'hicks' with an affirmative, overlapping *Yeah, right?,* even before the characterization is completed.

Janelle and Isabella mockingly use these Spanish words and this way of speaking Spanish – associated with a stereotyped island Dominican male style – to position certain recent immigrant male identities and ways of speaking as undesirable in an American urban youth context. *Loca, loca, e:::::, epa, epa, huepa* is associated with the relative directness and intensity of heterosexual Dominican males from the island in approaching females, a style that is being constructed as inappropriate for this US context. 'Hicks' not only know little English and fail to dress according to urban US youth styles, they also fail to adhere to appropriate local cultural frameworks and practices for heterosexual interaction. This code switched characterization of 'hicks' contributes to both a) the achievement of intersubjectivity between Isabella and Janelle, and b) the construction of a desirable category for them to inhabit, even though the category and associated characteristics are not explicitly named.

The relatively indirect linguistic means by which Isabella and Janelle constitute their common, desirable social position is typical of identity work, which is seldom achieved through direct, propositional statements of identity (e.g., 'I am a relatively acculturated Dominican American female teen-ager who would like to distance herself from certain recent immigrant male ways of being'). Much more commonly, speakers exploit non-referential social associations of ways of speaking to position themselves and others. Linguistic forms always include a dimension of social associations or *indexical* meanings (Peirce 1955; cf. "voice" in Bakhtin 1981) in addition to their propositional, or denotive, meanings. Particular ways of speaking, for example, are associated with particular geographic regions, socioeconomic statuses, genders, vocations, etc. These associations, or indexical meanings, vary much more with context than denotive meanings do. In the above example, speaking Spanish is used to disparage a fellow Dominican, but in many other contexts, Janelle and Isabella associate speaking Spanish with a highly valued Dominican identity. Both are bilingual, speak Spanish to monolingual relatives, and regularly code switch in intra-group peer interaction.

The indexical meanings, or active social associations, of linguistic forms are both "brought along" to the interaction as well as "brought about" in the interaction itself (Auer 1992). They are brought along to the interaction in that codes, and specific forms within codes, have social associations that pre-exist particular interactions. They are brought about within interactions in that codes and forms have *multiple* social associations, and interlocutors creatively exploit particular associations in situationally specific ways.

Because they involve both received and negotiated meanings, social identity negotiations provide a means of linking meaning–making processes in interactions at the local level with larger social and historical processes, e.g., racial formation, acculturation, and social stratification, that both inform, and are informed by these social interactions. At a general level, identity work is a perspective from which to examine the encounter of individual social actors with meanings and structures accrued from history. Individuals use language to both resist and reproduce existing meanings and structures, making identity work a lens for viewing the on-going constitution of society in the present (Giddens 1984).

In this chapter, I first define *identity* as I use the term, emphasizing the socially constructed and processual nature of identity negotiations and achievement. I then analyze an example of identity negotiations in monolingual talk. This example illustrates key principles of identity negotiations through language – that they are interactional, indexical, and contingent – that are applicable to both monolingual and multilingual contexts. In the next section, I give four examples of code switching to illustrate the metaphorical implications that some such switches can have for identity, and I situate such metaphorical switches among functional categories of code switching and broader categories of metaphorical language use. In the final section, I argue that what is distinctive about identity negotiations in multilingual contexts is not so much linguistic as social and political, i.e., that the distinctive salience of multilingual talk in Western societies is a function of social and linguistic ideologies rather than the nature of the forms themselves. To analyze identity work in multilingual contexts is thus to analyze the larger social and political systems in which identity options and the value attributed to associated linguistic forms are created, contested, and maintained (Pavlenko and Blackledge 2004).

2.   What is identity?

I use the term *identity* in a specific sense that contrasts with popular psychological and biological uses of the term. In popular psychology terms, identity refers to an individual's subjective sense of self, which is perceived as an enduring quality or essence lodged in that individual. In popular biological terms, identity refers to overlapping essential social, behavioral, and phenotypic qualities that are seen as fixed and heritable, such as ethnicity or race (cf. Carbaugh 1996; Tracy 2002). In both cases, identity is treated as relatively fixed, as located in the individual, and as an analytical prime that affects or explains social behavior and meanings.

This popular notion of identity contrasts sharply with the social constructionist perspective that has been dominant in the humanities and interpretive social sciences since the 1970s. From this social constructionist perspective, social identities are a function not of static attributes of individuals or groups, but rather of on-going processes of social differentiation. The fact that social identity categories have different configurations and meanings across time and space is evidence that they are socially constructed, rather than reflections of essential nature. Even racial categories, which are popularly perceived as biologically-based and thus fixed, can be shown to be a function of time and place rather than attributes of individuals or group members. An individual who counts as White in the Dominican Republic, for example, may count as Black upon immigrating to the United States (cf. Hoetink 1967; Bailey 2002), and the Jewish, Italian, and Slavic immigrants to the United States in the early 1900s who were commonly seen as members of distinct races lost this "racial" distinctiveness over time, becoming White Americans after two to three generations (Waters 1990; Brodkin 1998). From an analytical perspective, social identity is not what one *is*, but what one *counts as* in a particular time and place.

Two subjective processes of ascription serve to constitute social identities: "self-ascription" – how one defines oneself – and "ascription by others" – how others define one (Barth 1969: 13). These two subjective processes, often under other names, are at the core of identity definitions across many academic fields. Discursive psychologists refer to self- and other-ascription as "reflective positioning" and "interactive positioning" respectively (Davies and Harré 1990); in cultural studies, Stuart Hall refers to identity as "the names we give to the different ways we are positioned by, and position ourselves within, the narratives of the past" (1990: 225); and sociocultural linguists Bucholtz and Hall (2005: 586) define identity as "the social positioning of self and other." Individuals typically make reference to empirical attributes of group members in these processes of ascription or positioning, but the membership categories themselves are not based on the sum of objective similarities and differences among individuals or groups. Minor features can be treated as emblems of difference or similarity among groups, for example, and radical differences among group members can be downplayed or denied.

While this conceptualization of identity highlights the subjective, contingent nature of identity constitution and the agency of individuals as social actors, identity construction is fluid only within certain parameters. Our phenomenological understandings develop in an historical world in which history is omnipresent in embodied form, as *habitus* (Bourdieu 1990: 56). Individuals only ascribe identities to themselves, for example, that are imaginable and available in a particular social and historical context, and they are only ratified in identities (through other-ascription) that social history makes available to them. The relative degree of individual agency versus structural constraint experienced by individuals in identity negotiations varies with the specific social histories through which particular categories have been constituted as meaningful. In the US, for example, 3rd or 4th generation Italian or Irish Americans can situationally choose whether to invoke their symbolic ethnicity (Waters 1990;

Gans 1979), while members of non-White racial groups or linguistic minorities have much less control over whether those facets of identity are treated as relevant by others (Mittelberg and Waters 1992). Negotiations of identity thus take place within specific parameters that history has imposed in a particular time and place.

3.   The interactional, indexical, and contingent negotiation of identity

In this section, I present and analyze a segment of monolingual interaction among young Korean Americans in which identity negotiations are salient. This monolingual example illustrates a number of principles, common to both monolingual and multilingual contexts, for relating language use to identities: identities are constituted in talk; identity work is interactional; the indexical dimension of linguistic forms is central to identity constitution; and achieved identities are partial, multiple, contingent, and shifting (cf. Bucholtz and Hall 2005). The continuities between this monolingual example and the multilingual examples in the next section lay a foundation from which to argue, in the final section of this chapter, that the salience of identity negotiations in multilingual contexts is a function of politics and ideology rather than formal linguistic difference.

In this example, adapted from Chun (2001: 60), 1.5[2] and 2nd generation Korean American males in their early 20s negotiate shared and overlapping position for themselves through naming and characterizing the social category 'White people'.

Example 2
1 Jin: I think white people just don't keep it real and that's why
2 Dave: That is- that's true man?
3 Jin: Cause that's why they always back stabbin', like my roommate who
         wasn't gonna pay the last month's rent
5 JH: white
6 Jin: He kicks us out // of
7 Eric: //the prototypical whitey
8 Jin: Ye:::ah ma::n?
9 JH: No social skills.
10 Jin: But that's not true for everyone, I don't think.
11 EC: Uh huh
12 Jin: Cause all those ghetto whiteys in my neighborhood, I think they're
         cool.

In line 1, Jin explicitly names a category *white people* and states a stance toward them, that they *just don't keep it real*, i.e., that they are insincere or dishonest. David, Eric, and JH respond to this initial assessment with various second assessments (Goodwin and Goodwin 1992) of agreement in lines 2, 7, and 9. By displaying this congruent understanding of White people, they position themselves as similar in some respect(s) to Jin and to each other, but different from White Americans.

Jin uses a phrase *keep it real* and a grammatical structure, zero copula *they always back stabbin'*, that are strongly associated with African American identities, in characterizing both White Americans as a group and a particular White individual whose insincerity was characteristic of his social group. While these language forms do not constitute a claim by Jin of being African American, they suggest commonalty of his perspective with African American perspectives on White Americans. This interpretation of these non-referential indexical usages is highly context specific, as the use of forms popularly associated with African American English can have many possible connotations, e.g., such forms can be used by outsiders to mock African Americans.

In line 7, Eric makes the sharing of an African American-like perspective more explicit by referring to Jin's insincere roommate as *the prototypical whitey*. *Whitey* is a disparaging term that African Americans sometimes use to refer to White Americans as well as the privileged, hierarchical social position inhabited by White Americans. In using this term, Eric is positioning himself and, implicitly, his interlocutors, as sharing some dimensions of the experience of African Americans as non-Whites in a racially organized society. This proposed positioning of selves vis-à-vis White and Black Americans is ratified by Jin in line 8, *Yeah man*.

The constitution of identities through talk is always contingent and partial. While these five Korean Americans have initially collaborated in differentiating themselves from a disparaged White identity, the positioning of self and other becomes more complicated in lines 9 and 11 when Jin qualifies the group's criticisms of White Americans *that's not true for everyone* and cites examples of White Americans who do not share the negative attributes that Jin and others have been attributing to them. Jin is thus modifying his subject position as one that can be defined in part through opposition to *certain* White American subject positions, but not all of them. His positive evaluation of *ghetto whiteys* may reflect class solidarity – inhabitants of ghettos being relatively poor and powerless, regardless of color – or an alignment with Whites who live in ghettos and who have adopted hip hop practices and ideologies.

While the identity work in this talk highlights opposition to certain White identities, aspects of gender and age are also being implicitly performed in this segment. The adoption of African American youth, or hip hop, language is much more common among teen-agers and young adults than among older adults, and the adoption of such language by young non-African Americans has been documented primarily among males, for whom it is a resource for enacting masculinity (Bucholtz 1999; Cutler 1999; Kiesling 2001; Zentella 1997). Identities that we claim or enact are always at the intersection of multiple social categories, e.g., race, age, gender, ethnicity, and class, even though only one such dimension may be focal in a given interaction or analysis.

Identities in this short segment of talk are partial, multiple, interactionally negotiated and constituted, and rapidly shifting. The specific social position that is being claimed, 'young Korean American males who see White Americans as disingenuous and inhabiting a position of privilege that excludes non-Whites' does not have a specific category name. This example of social positioning relies almost entirely on indexical meanings. Neither the social positions being enacted – Korean American, male, and young – nor a social identity perspective that informs much of their talk – African American – is explicitly named in this talk.

By their nature, indexical meanings are highly context bound, both in terms of the local interaction and the particular social history that infuses linguistic forms with particular social connotations (Bakhtin 1981). The interpretation of any indexical meaning depends not just on the form and context, but crucially on the interpreter's subject position. While these young Korean American males treat their uses of language and their positioning of themselves as desirable, outsiders might interpret it very differently. Their Korean-raised parents, for example, might find their use of African American English – and their implied solidarity with African American perspectives – undesirable, for example. Many first-generation immigrants to the United States make great sacrifices so that their children can achieve socioeconomic mobility. Aligning oneself with African Americans, who face great obstacles to socioeconomic mobility in the United States, can be directly counter to this desired trajectory (Bailey 2001, 2000; Waters 1994; Chang 1990).

4.   Negotiating identities through metaphorical code switching

Research over the last 35 years has highlighted local meanings and functions of code switches in ways that can be subsumed under three broad headings: situational switching, discourse contextualization switching, and metaphorical switching. Such categories serve as a heuristic for highlighting particular functions of code switching and should not be understood as representing discrete or manifest types. Many switches simultaneously serve more than one of these functions. In this section, I briefly describe these three functional emphases of switches and then give four examples of multilingual talk that highlight identity work through metaphorical switches. While any instance of multilingual speech has implications for identity in Western contexts dominated by monolingual ideologies, I focus here on cases in which speakers exploit local social associations of codes to position themselves vis-à-vis each other and local categories.

In *situational* switching, distinct codes are employed in particular settings and speech activities and with different categories of interlocutors, i.e. there is a direct relationship between code use and observable features of the situation (Blom and Gumperz 1972). Codes are switched as observable changes in the context occur, e.g. to accommodate a monolingual speaker who joins the group or as interlocutors move to a different institutional setting associated with a distinct code. In switching characterized as *discourse contextualization*, individual switches do not necessarily co-occur with external changes in the context or significant shifts in sociocultural framework. Individual switches serve instead as contextualization, or framing, cues to mark off quotations, changes in topic, repair sequences, etc. from surrounding speech (Auer 1984; Auer 1988, 1995; Alfonzetti 1998; Wei 1998; Milroy and Wei 1995; Bailey 2000). These functions in monolingual speech are typically filled through prosody, word choice, and visual cues. In such unmarked discourse contextualization switching, conventionalized associations between particular codes and social worlds are not treated as relevant by participants (although non-member bystanders may see them as relevant), and the act of code switching itself, rather than the particular social associations of given codes, is what helps to organize the interaction.

In the following example, from Bailey (2002: 239), a code switch into Spanish by Dominican American Janelle coincides with a change in footing, a temporary re-framing of talk (Goffman 1979; cf. Zentella 1997: 93):

3) [(JS #210:50:10) Discussing whether she needs new immunizations to do her summer job at a hospital.]

Janelle: I don't know if I- I don't know if I have to go again cause-
dizque no es verdad que ['supposedly isn't it true that'] after a certain time- after a certain time you have to do it again? You gotta get shots again?

Janelle is unsure whether she needs new immunizations before beginning her summer job. She moves from *reporting* this uncertainty in the first part of her turn, to directly *asking* her interlocutor to confirm that one needs to be re-immunized after a certain period of time. This switch from a statement to a question coincides with a cut-off of *cause-* a shift in pitch and tempo, and a change of code, from English to Spanish. Code switching is a linguistic resource – like prosody or body alignment – that can be activated to highlight this shift in footing, or communicative activity, but it is not being treated here by interlocutors as having any greater metaphorical meaning related to identities than the corresponding monolingual change of footing would have.

Neither situational nor discourse contextualizing switching necessarily has *locally* salient implications for identity. Such switching can simply be a means of speaking appropriately to people in ways that they can understand and of managing and organizing conversational sequences.

Metaphorical switches, in contrast to situational switches, partially *violate* conventionalized associations between codes and context, activity, or participants. Elements of setting, participants, activities, or perspectives that are conventionally associated with a code can be invoked by a switch into that code when such elements are not otherwise present or active in the conversation. Changes in language can thus constitute alternative cultural frameworks for interpreting experience and constructing social reality. The switch in Example 1, above, has such a metaphorical import in that Isabella's *loca, loca, epa* brings to life a Dominican male persona and cultural framework for male-female relations that are associated with certain Dominican Spanish ways of speaking but not with American English ways of speaking. This switch simultaneously serves a discourse contextualizing function, i.e. marking off directly quoted speech from the surrounding talk.

Such metaphorically constitutive uses of language can also be monolingual, of course. In Example 2, above, the use of African American English forms by young Korean Americans constitutes them as young non-Whites who see parallels between their racial exclusion and the racial exclusion of African Americans. In both cases, aspects of a sociocultural world that were not demonstrably active in prior talk are invoked and made relevant through use of linguistic forms associated with that particular world.

The following four examples of metaphorical code switches generate meanings about identities, perspectives, and sociocultural frameworks for understanding the world that would not be generated in the same way through continued monolingual speech. In each case, the metaphorical meanings generated depend on specific social and historical associations of language forms and their situated use by speakers.

The first two examples are drawn from Kroskrity's (1993) study of the Arizona Tewa, a small Native American group who are officially members of the Hopi tribe, but who maintain a distinct Tewa language in addition to speaking Hopi. This distinct Tewa language and identity have been maintained despite nearly 300 years of closest proximity to the Hopi.

In Example 4, two middle-aged Tewa men have been discussing, in Hopi, a recent, favorable court ruling on a land dispute between the Hopi and the larger Navajo tribe whose land surrounds Hopi land. The conversation has been proceeding in Hopi, which is common among Arizona Tewa, who live among the numerically dominant Hopi and are always fluent in Hopi. In this particular conversation, their use of Hopi also coincides with their larger tribal interest in confronting the outside Navajos.

Example 4 (Kroskrity 1993: 196–197. In these examples, Hopi language is represented in italics, e.g. *Hopi*, while Arizona Tewa is represented in underlined italics, e.g. *Arizona Tewa*.)

A: *Tenatyava. Tenatyava. Pay-sen 'ita-m nanami pihi:k'yani.*
['It's come true. It's come true. Maybe now we will live peaceably among each other.']
B: *'u̧ to'o wi' he:yu-bí-'í'í-dí han ankhyaw 'u̧-mu:.*
['You are one among the few who think so.']

While *A* expresses optimism about the ruling, *B* suggests that many people are not so optimistic about the eventual outcome. The metaphorical meanings generated by *B*'s switch into Arizona Tewa are a function of the local social connotations of Tewa language, which are directly linked to Arizona Tewa ideologies of identity. Arizona Tewa folk histories position the Tewa as inheritors of a warrior tradition, and the Arizona Tewa view themselves as more pragmatic and realistic regarding issues of conflict than their Hopi brethren, whom they sometimes position as strong in spiritual matters but possibly naïve in more worldly affairs. By switching to Tewa in the above exchange, *B* communicates that he is not just speaking as an individual disagreeing with *A*. He is also positioning himself as representing a more realistic position in such political matters, a position associated with distinctively Tewa perspectives.

The following Arizona Tewa code switch occurs at a *kachina* dance in Tewa village that includes both Hopi and Tewa. The speaker sits among several observers of the dance.

Example 5 (1993: 199–200)
A: *Hi:wo'i díbí-hí-'ó! Loloma, loloma, lomahin-yinʷa.*
[((*in Arizona Tewa*)) 'They are dancing good!'
((*in Hopi*)) 'Beautiful, beautiful, they look good!']

Kroskrity's native consultants found this specific sequence of assessments of the dancing to be highly complimentary. Arizona Tewa see Hopi as highly accomplished in ceremonial, spiritual, and ritual realms. By using Hopi language, the speaker invokes the (implicitly) higher standards of the Hopi for evaluating the dance, and his compliment is thus perceived as communicating relatively greater acclaim than the corresponding Tewa utterances would.

The achievement of intersubjectivity is intertwined with the positioning of selves in these examples. With each of these code switches, there is a shift in sociocultural frameworks for interpreting both the specific words as well as the position from which the words are spoken. In both cases, speakers constitute their identities as both Tewa and Hopi in the process of everyday communicative activities: discussing politics and praising a performance.

Example 6 is one of many instances of Spanish-English code switching in the documentary film *My American Girls* (Matthews 2000), a film about a Dominican immigrant family in New York City. In this segment, Sandra, who immigrated from the Dominican Republic to New York as an adult, confronts her 14-year-old, US-raised daughter Mayra over Mayra's failure to do her homework. Mayra is hanging out in front of her house with a peer, Wendy, when Sandra addresses her.

Example 6

1 Sandra: *Yo te dije que tú fueras arriba para que hacieras algo pero tú dijistes*
2   *que no podías porque tenías muchas tareas. //Métate inmediata-*
           mente.
3   ['Mayra, when I told you to do something upstairs you said you
4   couldn't because you had too much homework. Get in there right
           now.']
5 Mayra: *//Yo lo hice.*
                                                               ['I did it.']
6 Sandra: I don't care. *Vete a estudiar. Tú tienes examenes la semana entera.*
7   ['Go and study. You have tests all week.']
8 Mayra: Wendy *vamo'* ['let's go']
9 Sandra: [   ]
10 Mayra: I'm g̲o̲ing. Wendy *vamo'* ['let's go']
11 Sandra: *Vete*! ['Go']
12 Mayra: I'm g̲o̲ing!
13 Sandra: *Vete*! ['Go']
14 Mayra: Hold on, I'm g̲o̲ing!
15 Sandra: *Mira, yo te quiero abajo ni para un segundo Oístes?*
16   ['Hey, I don't want you down here for even a second. You hear
           me?']
17 Mayra: I'm g̲o̲ing!

Both Mayra's switch into English *I'm going* (line 10) to address her mother, and Mayra's and Sandra's non-reciprocal code use (lines 10 to 17) generate meta-phorical meanings in this exchange. While it is not unusual for bilingual Latino children in the US to respond to their parents' Spanish with English (Zentella 1997: 57), Mayra initially responds to her mother in Spanish and even addresses her peer Wendy in Spanish (while maintaining an English pronunciation of Wendy's name). It is only after her mother reprimands her and uses the impera-tive *Vete* that Mayra responds to her mother in English, a pattern that is repeated across the final four turns.

The non-reciprocal code choice in these six turns reflects negotiations about the sets of rights and obligations between speakers (Myers-Scotton 1993). Dif-fering sets of rights and obligations are implied by Spanish and English in this context. In a Latin American cultural framework, parents have significant au-thority over teen-age children, and parent-child interactions are to be guided by respect for the hierarchical relationship between children and adults. In mainstream US culture, there is much less hierarchy between parents and children, and teen-agers are given considerable individual choice in pursuing friends, interests, and activities. The individualistic nature of US society and the seductive freedoms offered to US youth are a near universal source of tension between first-generation immigrants to the US and their US-raised children.

In this case, the use of Spanish by Sandra represents an effort to constitute a Dominican world, in which parents have authority in the family and children are obedient. It conjures the world of first-generation labor migrants, a world in which children are obligated because their parents work long hours in low-paying, dead-end jobs so that their children, through education, can have a better life. Sandra thus positions herself as a Dominican immigrant mother of a Dominican child.

Mayra's use of English, in contrast, constitutes an assimilated US world in which teen-agers readily talk back to parents and make personalistic choices about activities and work habits, even if such choices undermine opportunities for socioeconomic mobility. She thus positions herself as an American teen-ager.

Competing visions of the world are thus juxtaposed through the juxtaposition of codes across these turns. Neither Sandra nor Mayra accommodates to the other by switching codes because accommodation would be tantamount to acceding to the other's position. It would be difficult for Mayra to talk back to her mother so brazenly in Spanish, because such behavior would constitute a grave offense in Dominican worlds. Sandra does not switch to English, because in the American world thus constituted, children can be relatively disrespectful to parents with impunity.

The final multilingual example in this section is drawn from the same conversation as in Example 1, between Dominican American high school students Janelle and Isabella. In both examples of their talk, code switches into Spanish serve to position them as particular types of Dominican American teen-age females who are different from more recent immigrants. In both examples, Isabella uses direct quotes of a recently immigrated Dominican teen-age male's speech to display negative stances toward the category(ies) of people who talk in such a way. Isabella and Janelle collaborate in coming to a shared perspective on a disparaged category, thus constituting themselves, as interlocutors in the here-and-now, as occupying similar identity positions.

Example 7

[(JS #211:56) Isabella and Janelle are sitting outside of their high school and have been discussing their weekend plans. Isabella has been dating a boy named Sammy for about 10 days, and she is now explaining why she is going to break up with him despite the fact that he is physically attractive. This segment of talk occurs about 40 minutes before the segment in Example 1.]

1   Isabella: He's like- I don't kno:w. He's- he's so jealous.
2   Janelle: Oh
3   Isabella: This kid is sickening! He- he tells me to call him before I go to the
4   club. He- I'm like, I don't have time to call you, pick up the phone,
5   call you while my friends are outside beeping the horn at me so I
6   can jet with them to the club. And he's like- I don't know, he talks-
7   he's like a <u>hick</u>, he talks so <u>much Spanish</u>!
                                                             And he //(   )
8   Janelle: //O::h! ((looks away))
9   Isabella: No, but he speaks Spanish, but- I- the reason- I talk to him- when he
10   talks on the phone he speaks English a lot because I speak English.
11   More. I tell him, speak English, speak English.
12   ((wrinkled face)) *Y que, lo::ca* ['What's up, honey']). He goes,
13   you know, *ni:ña* ['girl'], and you know, and I don't want to hear it.
14   Janelle: You should have found that out before you went out with him.
15   Isabella: I know, he's rushing into it……

Isabella is explaining why she was breaking up with Sammy, a recent immigrant whom she had been briefly dating. She specifies a particular personality deficiency from which Sammy suffers (*he's so jealous*), gives an example of his jealous behavior, and specifies that he's *like a hick* and *talks so much Spanish*.

Janelle responds (lines 2 and 8) to these assessments (Goodwin and Goodwin 1992) of Sammy with *oh*'s and vertical head nods, suggesting a shared understanding of the undesirable nature of a male who is jealous, like a hick, and speaks so much Spanish. Isabella, however, treats some aspect of Janelle's displayed understanding of this as problematic, by initiating a repair *No, but he* ... (line 9). As in Example 1, there are initial, referential descriptions of an undesirable Other, but Janelle and Isabella only treat the characterization as adequate when there is a code switched performance of the speech of this Other. The use of code switching to set off quotations from surrounding talk has often been noted as a function of code switching, and many have noted that the code used for the quotation is not necessarily the same one that the speaker originally used (e.g. Gumperz 1982: 75–76). In this case, the code match between the quoted speech and the antecedent speech is important because the Spanish forms carry social associations for Janelle and Isabella that would not be carried by corresponding English forms. It is only when Isabella enacts Sammy, through a code switched direct quotation of particular Spanish forms – *Y que lo:ca* ('What's up, honey') and *ni:ña* ('girl') – that she treats her characterization of Sammy as complete and definitive, and she and Janelle can proceed to speak about the break up from other perspectives. For Isabella, Sammy's addressing her as *loca* and *niña* may invoke a traditional Dominican social framework for their romantic, male-female relationship, a framework that she wishes to avoid. In establishing the undesirable qualities of Sammy, Janelle and Isabella constitute their own identities – as relatively acculturated, urban, Dominican American teen-age females – as desirable.

While Spanish language can be a unifying emblem of Spanish or Dominican identity in US contexts involving non-Latinos, it can be a key index of difference in local, intra-Latino contexts. The fact that such intra-group boundaries can be situationally highlighted through Spanish use shows that there is not a fixed, one-to-one correspondence between use of a linguistic code and the social affiliation that it expresses. While a notion of 'we-code' versus 'they-code' (Gumperz 1982: 82–95) is appealing from a macrosocial perspective, situated language use reveals no such stable dichotomy, as social meanings and identity associations of particular forms are constituted in specific local contexts.

While language is popularly seen as a referential system for labeling or communicating propositional information, the six examples of talk given in this chapter suggest that direct reference plays only an indirect and often minor role in the enactment of identity. *None* of the social identity positions being claimed by speakers in the six examples in this chapter is referentially named. In three of the examples, a category of Other, who is not present – 'hicks' in Example 1, 'white people' in Example 2, and Sammy (as hick) in Example 3 – is referentially named. The use of explicit category names and a marked style of speaking for constituting an Other against which one defines oneself may be characteristic of relationships between linguistic forms and social identities more generally. One's own identity and ways of speaking are generally treated as normal, natural, and unmarked, so it can be difficult to call attention to them. Identities, like linguistic styles (Irvine 2001) are constituted through meaningful opposition to other identities, so it is through the highlighting of boundaries – through naming and disparaging of an Other or exaggeration of linguistic features seen as emblematic of other identities – that one's own identities and associated ways of speaking are constituted as distinct and discrete (e.g. Basso 1979; Mitchell-Kernan 1972).

5.   Multilingualism as a social and political phenomenon

The examples of metaphorical code switching that I presented in the previous section illustrate the power of multilingual ways of speaking to constitute socio-cultural world and position selves within them. Although I have tried to highlight the partial, contingent, and situated nature of such identity work through talk, the power of language to reflect and (re)constitute identities in these examples can inadvertently reinforce essentialist beliefs about the relationships between language and identity. The assumption of an essential language-identity link is misleadingly reinforced by Western ideologies in which language, race, and nation are seen as forming a natural unity. Westerners tend to see *being* ethnically French, *speaking* French, and inhabiting a French *nation-state* as more or less the same thing, for example, and individuals who fit one or two of these criteria but not all three – e.g. French speaking inhabitants of Paris who are of sub-Saharan African descent – are seen as something other than 'just French'.

This ideology is a function of European nation building projects of the last several centuries, in which links among language, nation, and identity were essentialized and naturalized as parts of political projects. This monolingual ideology informs both popular and academic approaches to multilingualism. The fact that social and cultural linguists have focused so much attention on the meanings and functions of code switching, for example – while paying relatively less attention to corresponding monolingual speech – reflects the monolingual ideology that code switching is not an entirely natural form, but something that is in need of explanation (Woolard 2004).

In the following sections of this chapter, I tease out some of the implications of this ideology for understanding identity work in multilingual contexts. I first show that privileging formal definitions of multilingualism and assuming an essential language-identity link distract attention from a number of multilingual-like forms of talk that have important implications for social identities. I then argue that the distinctiveness of multilingual talk in Western societies has more to do with monolingual ideologies and politics than with the formal distinctiveness of such ways of speaking, and that perceptions of distinctiveness are rooted in particular subject positions and ideologies. At the local, in-group level, for example, most instances of multilingual speech in Western societies do not generate local metaphorical meanings, and for many multilingual speakers, the two (or more languages) they use in some situations do not form a relevant, or meaningful opposition (which undermines the notion of multilingualism as a discrete phenomenon). At the same time, however, such talk is always marked and consequential for identities in the larger context of Western societies. Finally, I argue that the social implications of multilingual ways of speaking are not a function of the formal linguistic distance between forms but of the social histories that have infused forms with particular meanings and varying levels of prestige. The value of analyzing identity negotiations in multilingual contexts is not so much in the details of linguistic forms but in the perspective that such analysis gives on social and political processes and meanings. The notion of 'multilingual' thus becomes a more useful social-analytical construct if it is approached as a socially, rather than formally, based concept.

5.1.   Multilingual-like ways of speaking

Starting from formal definitions of multilingualism or code switching, e.g. the use of two or more grammatical systems in a single speech exchange (Gumperz 1982), distracts attention from the uses to which language is put. From the functional perspective of identity work, multilingual speech is simply one way among many of positioning self and other. A more functional approach to talk can encompass a broader range of multilingual, or multilingual-like phenomena that have implications for social identity but that may or may not meet analysts' more formal criteria for what constitutes multilingualism. If one's starting point is social identity, it may not be central whether a speaker is switching languages, alternating between a dialect and a national standard, register shifting, or speaking monolingually in a variety that highlights language contact. If one starts from a more functional perspective, one is relieved, to a degree, of the questions of what exactly constitutes a language (Alvarez-Caccamo 2001, 1998), and what constitutes the competence level in a second or third language that allows one's speech to count as multilingual (Meeuwis and Blommaert 1998). The focus can thus shift to individuals as social actors using heteroglossic (Bakhtin 1981) sets of linguistic resources to negotiate the social world.

From the perspective of social identity, language alternation may be socially meaningful and worthy of analysis regardless of whether a speaker is a competent speaker of a second language. Rampton (1995), for example, has shown how teen-agers in England use short segments of speech in languages of which they know only a limited number of words or phrases to socially position themselves vis-a-vis their peers and the wider society. Such instances of "crossing" involve the use of language that is strongly associated with an ethnic or racial category to which the speaker does not belong. Thus an Anglo British youth may situationally use words or phrases from Caribbean Creole English or Panjabi to position himself relative both to interlocutors (who may or may not be members of categories popularly associated with those forms), and to the wider, racially organized society (see ch. 14 in this volume).

Similarly, from the perspective of identity work, there is no *a priori* reason why switching among what count as discrete languages should be privileged over switching among what count as dialects. What counts as a language and what counts as a dialect is typically a political question, as captured in the widely-circulated aphorism that a language is a "dialect with a navy." It is not formal or genetic linguistic distance or issues of mutual comprehensibility that differentiates a dialect from a language, but rather the links of a variety to political power, institutions, and states. Varieties, such as Spanish and Portuguese, which are linked to nation states thus count as languages, while varieties that are not at the center of national power typically count, at least popularly, as dialects.

Finally, a more functional perspective can encompass identity work in monolingual speech that has been affected by multilingualism or multilingual situations. Even monolingual speakers may reproduce contact phenomena in their speech from having learned a language in a situation that was formerly multilingual. Thus the English pronunciation of monolingual New York Puerto Ricans, for example, may include a degree of syllable-timing, a feature of Spanish, as opposed to the stress-timing of dominant varieties of Anglo American English (Zentella 1997: 45). Such pronunciation distinguishes the speech of many second- and third-generation US Latinos from more institutionally prestigious varieties and can be used by both in-group and out-group members to constitute a social boundary.

In addition to phonetic effects of language contact, there can also be persistent discourse level patterns inherited from ways of speaking in languages that have been lost through language shift to monolingualism. In such communities, distinctive rhetorical styles can serve as an emblem of social distinction and a locus of both misunderstanding and political struggle in intergroup encounters (Philips 1983; Scollon and Scollon 1981; Tannen 1982).

5.2.   To whom do the languages of multilingual talk represent
         a socially meaningful opposition?

The social meaningfulness of multilingualism is a phenomenological question. While the languages of multilingual contexts are popularly seen as distinct by dominant groups in Western societies, in some contexts multilingual speakers do *not* treat the languages involved in such a way. A growing body of literature since the early 1980s has challenged the assumption that the languages used in code switching are essentially distinct and that code switching necessarily involves social meanings that are different from ones communicated in monolingual talk (Meeuwis and Blommaert 1998; Heller ed. forthc.; Poplack 1980; Woolard 2004). The multilingual practice that most forcefully undermines assumed distinctions among languages is the relatively frequent, intrasentential code switching that has been widely documented in intra-group peer interaction among the children of international labor migrants to Western societies and in many urban, African contexts (e.g. Myers-Scotton 1993; Swigart 1992). When language alternation functions as a discourse mode it its own right (Poplack 1980), it undermines the assumed opposition between languages, and the assumed unity of a single language with identity.

When languages are not compartmentalized and strictly associated with particular social domains (Fishman, Cooper, and Newman 1971), the search for a function of a particular switch may be akin to trying to explain why a monolingual speaker selects one synonym or phrasing over another (Zentella 1997: 101). In a corpus of 1,685 switches among young New York Puerto Rican girls,

Zentella (1997: 101) assigns fewer than half of her switches to specific conversational strategies, or functions, arguing that the motivations and meanings of such switches were no different at the local level than the motivations and meanings of monolingual speakers' choices among synonyms in monolingual speech. Similarly, Meeuwis and Blommaert (1998: 76) argue that the multilingual talk among Zairians in Belgium can represent "one code in its own right," and that the insistence on two distinct languages as the frame of reference for this form of speech is an ideologically-motivated *a priority* that is not useful in terms of interpreting it.

While languages may have lost their distinctiveness to multilingual speakers in particular local contexts, in larger contexts such as Western nation-states where monolingualism is considered normal and natural, multilingual talk is always salient and seen as requiring explanation in ways that monolingual speech is not. The meanings that one finds in such switching vary with one's subject position and analytical perspective. For many adults, including first-generation immigrant parents, code switching is a haphazard jumble of linguistic elements that is emblematic of the inability to speak what those adults see as the correct language, i.e. the ideological standard that is prestigious in institutional contexts (Lippi-Green 1997; Milroy and Milroy 1985; Silverstein 1996). Right-wing nativist groups typically point to immigrant multilingualism as a form of mongrelization and a threat to prosperity and the social fabric (Piatt 1990). Many academics since the 1970s, in contrast, have celebrated the linguistic sophistication displayed in code switching (McClure 1977; Sankoff and Poplack 1981; Lipski 1985) and the social 'strategies' that some forms of it imply (cf. Myers-Scotton 1993: 74; Gumperz 1982; cf. Woolard 2004). For more politically oriented analysts, such code switching can be seen as a form of resistance to dominant discourses of unquestioning assimilation (Gal 1988: 259) and a means to constructing a positive self in a political and economic context that disparages immigrant phenotypes, language, class status, and ethnic origins (Zentella 1997). The meanings and implications of particular forms for identity work are a function of the interpreter's subject position in a larger sociopolitical field.

5.3.   Multilingualism as a dimension of social and political practice

Linguistic approaches to multilingualism can veil the social and political history of which multilingualism is part-and-parcel. The social and political conditions, such as migration and social stratification, that afford the on-going co-existence of multiple languages are the same ones that afford on-going inequality and construction of social difference among groups. In cases of labor migration or refugee streams to Western societies that result in multilingualism, immigrant groups commonly assume lower positions in power hierarchies and their degree of assimilation is a political and contested issue. Often the language, culture, religion, and/or phenotypes of such immigrants are devalued by members of dominant groups, so any expression of identity must engage discourse about the worthiness of those identities. Assimilationist practices are discouraged by group solidarity among oppressed groups, while maintenance of immigrant language and cultural practices are seen by dominant groups as an explanation and justification for on-going inequality. More generally, identity categories and language choice and attitudes are inseparable from power hierarchies and related ideologies about the relative value of identity categories and ways of speaking.

The increased flow of people, goods, and ideas around the world in the last century has made multilingualism and identity negotiations in Western urban centers increasingly visible to Western elites and academics. In relatively stable social and linguistic situations of monolingualism, the social and linguistic categories favored by dominant groups are seen as natural through processes of hegemony or symbolic domination (Bourdieu 1991; Heller 1995). Speakers tend to be relatively unaware of the ways in which their ways of speaking represent performances of identity because speech in stable social situations reproduces what are assumed to be natural, or normal identities. When a member of an ethnic group speaks in a manner popularly associated with that ethnic group, the talk is simply seen as a reflection of a natural, essential, independently pre-existing identity rather than a social negotiation process. The multilingual identity work that is characteristic of more rapidly changing social contexts, in contrast, destabilizes assumptions about an essential unity of language, nation, and identity.

Formal definitions of multilingualism also veil the range of practices and meanings that multilingualism encompasses. The occurrence, form, distribution, and meanings of multilingual talk vary across and within communities, contexts, and interactions. This variation is not random, but rather follows patterns that can be linked to specific questions of power and the construction of social difference. What are relevant social boundaries in a particular context and how did they arise? What are groups' relative and situational interests in boundary-maintenance versus boundary-leveling? How much access to cross-boundary social roles and domains do members of a society have (Heller 1988)?

Patterns and meanings of multilingual talk at the local level can thus be linked to larger sociohistorical questions. Poplack (1988), for example, shows that contrasting patterns of code switching between two communities – a New York Puerto Rican one and a Ottawa-Hull French Canadian one – correlate to contrasting social positions of the two groups. Even though the genetic relationship between French and English is virtually identical to the genetic relationship between Spanish and English, both the form and interpretation of the switching are very different in the two communities. Bilingual New York Puerto Rican switches tend to be smooth and seamless, i.e. unmarked, while French-English switches tend to be highlighted, or marked, through repetition, hesitation, intonational highlighting, and even explicit metalinguistic commentary.

Whereas bilingualism is seen to be emblematic of New York Puerto Rican identity – differentiating members from island Puerto Ricans and non-Puerto Rican Anglophones – Ottawa-Hull French Canadian bilingualism is not associated with a social identity distinct from that of local monolingual French Canadians. For New York Puerto Ricans, use of two languages is both an emblem of a distinctive identity and a practice that draws in immigrant newcomers. In the French Canadian situation, there is no stream of newcomers to incorporate and no distinctive identity bridging disparate communities that needs to be enacted or maintained through language.

Gal (1988: 247) argues that particular code switching ideologies and practices can be linked to even broader political economic and historical contexts. Thus, groups with similar structural positions in the world system – e.g., second-generation labor migrants to Western, industrialized states – will display similarities in code switching meanings and practices. Thus Italian-German switching among the children of Italian labor migrants to German will be similar to that of Spanish-English code switching among second-generation Puerto Ricans in the US, both in terms of patterns and local functions.

Within particular communities, code switching practices and meanings shift over time in conjunction with shifting identity politics. Heller (1992), for example, demonstrates how francophone political mobilization in Quebec destabilized conventional patterns of multilingual speech, resulting in significant negotiations and metacommentary on which language, French or English, to speak and what it means to speak one or the other. In Brussels, where relatively frequent, and intra-sentential code switching was once common, younger generations are switching less than the older generations, in part because of the political polarization between French and Flemish speakers in the country. This polarization makes a joint-French-Flemish Brussels identity – as expressed through frequent French-Flemish switching – less tenable (Treffers-Daller 1992).

The implications of multilingual talk for identity negotiations are thus a function of the history that gives rise to constellations of differently valued identity options and infuses ways of speaking with social meanings and perspectives. If historical social relations among groups are particularly coercive and stratified, ways of speaking associated with those groups will be particularly infused with related social associations, and those ways of speaking will symbolize and reconstitute social difference particularly starkly.

The salience and persistence of distinctions between African American and other varieties of American English illustrate the political and historical bases of social meanings of language. These distinctions have persisted for centuries, despite long-term close contact between speakers of African American and other American varieties of English. It is the distinctively coercive and unjust nature of historical social relations in the US – slavery, systematic Jim Crow laws, segregation, and on-going social and economic inequality – that have both

a) sustained African American and other American English as distinct varieties, and b) made African American English salient as a social marker. In contexts of discrimination and inequality, different ways of speaking will tend to persist as markers of social identity, just as the identities themselves are made to persist. In contexts of relative equality, in contrast, identities and ways of speaking assimilate to each other relatively rapidly, as has occurred among European immigrants to the US across three generations.

5.4.   Multilingualism as social construction

While the notion that identity categories such as race or ethnicity are socially constructed is now an academic commonplace, multilingualism, as both a popular and analytical category, is not generally seen as a social construction. There are fundamental parallels, however, in the social and political processes through which difference is constructed among social identity categories and the linguistic forms that count as separate languages. Both, for example, are popularly seen as having self-evident, empirical bases, and both form parts of the highly naturalized assumption of a language-race-nation unity. In both cases, however, the conceptualizations, salience, and social significance of the categories are a function of social and political processes rather than inherent, or essential characteristics of members of the categories. The fact that multilingual speech draws both popular and academic attention may tell us relatively little about the nature of code switching or linguistic forms, and relatively more about popular and academic language ideologies of Western nation-states.

Conceptualizing bilingual speech as a social construction does not minimize its on-the-ground social implications. An example from social identity categories can help make this clear: the fact that Black-White race in the United States is a social construction, for example, does not make race an illusion or socially insignificant (Omi and Winant 1994). Race has been, and remains, a central organizing principle in the United States and a way of representing, rationalizing, and reproducing tremendous social inequality. Approaching race as a social construction allows one to see, however, that race is not about essential biological difference (which is how race is popularly construed) but about social history. What is socially significant about race is a distinctively violent history of coercion and inequality, not details of hair texture, skin shade, or other morphological features. The social constructionist perspective directs attention to the political and historical processes through which race has been constituted and given such significance in the US.

Similarly, approaching monolingualism and multilingualism as socially constructed does not change their social force at the level of lived experience, but it does show that this social force is not a function of formal, or inherent linguistic differences among what count as languages. If multilingual talk is an especially meaningful mode of speaking, it is not the nature of the forms that make it so but rather particular social and political histories.

Studying identity work in multilingual talk can be a route to understanding society not because of formal linguistic distinctions among languages, but because of the inherent social and political nature of language. In contexts such as Western societies where code switching or multilingual talk has been made to count as particularly socially meaningful, insights into identity negotiations can come from attention to the social and political processes that have made monolingual-versus-multilingual speech a meaningful opposition. The value of analyzing identity negotiations in multilingual contexts is not in the details of linguistic forms but in the perspective that such analysis gives on social and political processes and meanings. Identity work is thus a perspective from which to examine the encounter of individual social actors with history as they resist and reproduce historical meanings and structures in the present.

Notes

1. Transcription conventions are as follows:

Janelle:	The speaker is indicated with a name or abbreviation on the left of the page.
loca	Italics indicate words spoken in languages other than English.
['Jerk.']	Text surrounded by single quotation marks and brackets indicates a translation of the immediately preceding language.
( )	Empty parentheses indicate material that couldn't be heard clearly enough to transcribe.
((smiling))	Double parentheses surround nonverbal, visual, prosodic, or other contextual information.
//I don't- //He said	Text after double slashes that is directly above or below other text after double slashes indicates words spoken in overlap.
(1.5)	Numerals in parentheses indicate periods of time, in seconds, during which there is no speech.
Da::mn	A colon indicates that the preceding sound was elongated in a marked pronunciation.
if I- I	A hyphen indicates that speech was suddenly cut-off during or after the word preceding the hyphen.
stabbin'	A single apostrophe indicates the elision of a single letter.

2. Second-generation Korean Americans are US-born of Korean immigrant parents. The term '1.5 generation' is used to refer to Korean-born individuals who come to the US before adulthood, typically before the end of primary school, thus receiving much of their socialization in the US.

References

Alfonzetti, Giovanna
  1998   The conversational dimension in code-switching between Italian and Dialect in Sicily. In: P. Auer (ed.), *Code-Switching in Conversation: Language, Interaction, and Identity,* 180–211. London/New York: Routledge.

Alvarez-Caccamo, Celso
  1998   From 'switching code' to 'code-switching': Towards a reconceptualisation of communicative codes. In: P. Auer (ed.), *Code-Switching in Conversation: Language, Interaction, and Identity,* 29–48. London/New York: Routledge.

Alvarez-Caccamo, Celso
  2001   Codes. In: A. Duranti (ed.), *Key Terms in Language and Culture,* 23–26. Malden, Massachusetts: Blackwell.

Auer, Peter
  1984   *Bilingual Conversation.* Philadelphia/Amsterdam: John Benjamins.

Auer, Peter
  1988   A conversation analytic approach to codeswitching and transfer. In: M. Heller (ed.), *Codeswitching: Anthropological and Sociolinguistic Perspectives,* 187–213. New York: Mouton de Gruyter.

Auer, Peter
  1992   Introduction: John Gumperz's approach to contextualisation. In: P. Auer and A. Di Luzio (eds.), *The Contextualisation of Language,* 1–38. Amsterdam: Benjamins.

Auer, Peter
  1995   The pragmatics of code-switching: A sequential approach. In: L. Milroy and P. Muysken (eds.): *One Speaker, Two Languages: Cross-disciplinary Perspectives on Code-Switching,* 115–135. Cambridge: Cambridge University Press.

Bailey, Benjamin
  2000   Communicative behavior and conflict between African-American customers and immigrant Korean retailers in Los Angeles. *Discourse and Society* 11 (1): 86–108.

Bailey, Benjamin
  2000   Social/interactional functions of code switching among Dominican Americans. *IPrA Pragmatics* 10 (2): 165–193.

Bailey, Benjamin
  2001   Dominican-American ethnic/racial identities and United States social categories. *International Migration Review* 35 (3): 677–708.

Bailey, Benjamin
  2002   *Language, Race, and Negotiation of Identity: A Study of Dominican Americans.* New York: LFB Scholarly Pub.

Bakhtin, M. M.
  1981   *The Dialogic Imagination:* Four Essays. University of Texas Press Slavic series; no. 1. Austin: University of Texas Press.

Barth, Frederik
  1969   Introduction. In: F. Barth (ed.), *Ethnic Groups and Boundaries: The Social Organization of Culture Difference,* 9–38. Boston: Little Brown and Co.

Basso, Keith H.
  1972   "To give up on words": Silence in western apache culture. In: P. P. Giglioli
          (ed.), *Language and Social Context*, 67–86. Harmondsworth: Penguin
          Books.
Basso, Keith H.
  1979   *Portraits of "the Whiteman": Linguistic Play and Cultural Symbols Among
          the Western Apache*. Cambridge [Eng.]/ New York: Cambridge University
          Press.
Blom, Jan-Peter and J. J. Gumperz
  1972   Code-switching in Norway. In: J. Gumperz and D. Hymes (eds.), *Directions
          in Sociolinguistics*, 407–434. New York: Holt, Rinehart and Winston.
Bourdieu, Pierre
  1990   *The Logic of Practice*. Stanford, Cal.: Stanford University Press.
Bourdieu, Pierre
  1991   *Language and Symbolic Power*. Cambridge, MA: Harvard University
          Press.
Brodkin, Karen
  1998   *How Jews Became White Folks and What that Says About Race in America*.
          New Brunswick N. J.: Rutgers University Press.
Brown, Roger and Albert Gilman
  1960   The pronouns of power and solidarity. In: T. Sebeok (ed.), *Style in Lan-
          guage*, 253–276. Cambridge, MA: MIT Press.
Bucholtz, Mary
  1999   You da man: narrating the racial other in the production of white masculin-
          ity. *Journal of Sociolinguistics* (3-4): 443–460.
Bucholtz, Mary and Kira Hall
  2005   Identity and interaction: A sociocultural linguistic approach. *Discourse
          Studies* 7 (4-5): 585–614.
Carbaugh, Donal A.
  1996   *Situating Selves: The Communication of Social Identities in American
          Scenes*. Albany, NY: State University of New York Press.
Chang, Edward
  1990   *New Urban Crisis: Korean-Black Conflicts in Los Angeles*. Dissertation,
          Ethnic Studies, University of California Berkeley, Berkeley.
Chun, Elaine
  2001   The construction of White, Black, and Korean American identities through
          African American Vernacular English. *Journal of Linguistic Anthropology*
          11 (1): 52–64.
Cutler, Cecilia
  1999   Yorkville crossing: White teens, hip hop and African American English.
          Journal of Sociolinguistics (3-4): 428–442.
Davies, Bronwyn, and Rom Harré
  1990   Positioning: The discursive production of selves. *Journal for the Theory of
          Social Behavior* 20 (1): 43–63.
Fishman, Joshua A., Robert Leon Cooper and Roxana Ma Newman
  1971   *Bilingualism in the barrio, Indiana University publications. Language
          science monographs*, vol. 7. Bloomington: Indiana University.

Gal, Susan
  1988   The political economy of code choice. In: M. Heller (ed.), *Codeswitching: Anthropological and Sociolinguistic Perspectives,* 245–264. Berlin/ New York/ Amsterdam: Mouton de Gruyter.
Gans, Herbert
  1979   Symbolic ethnicity: the future of ethnic groups and cultures in America. *Ethnic and Racial Studies* 2 (1): 1–20.
Giddens, Anthony
  1984   *The Constitution of Society: Outline of the Theory of Structuration.* Berkeley: University of California Press.
Goffman, Erving
  1979   Footing. *Semiotica* 25: 1–29.
Goodwin, Charles and Marjorie Harness Goodwin
  1992   Assessments and the construction of context. In: A. Duranti and C. Goodwin (eds.), *Rethinking Context: Language as an Interactive Phenomenon,* 147–190. Cambridge/ New York: Cambridge University Press.
Gumperz, John Joseph
  1982   *Discourse Strategies.* Cambridge/New York: Cambridge University Press.
Hall, Stuart
  1990   Cultural identity and diaspora. In: J. Rutherford (ed.), *Identity: Culture, Community, Difference,* 222–237. London: Lawrence and Wishart.
Heller, Monica
  1988   Introduction. In: M. Heller (ed.), *Codeswitching: Anthropological and Sociolinguistic Perspectives,* 1–24. New York: Mouton de Gruyter.
Heller, Monica
  1992   The politics of code-switching and language choice. In: C. Eastman (ed.), *Codeswitching,* 123–142. Cleveland/Avon: Multilingual Matters.
Heller, Monica
  1995   Language Choice, Social Institutions, and Symbolic Domination. *Language in Society* 24 (3): 373–406.
Heller, Monica (ed.)
  (forthc.) *Bilingualism: A Social Approach.*
Heritage, John, and J. Maxwell Atkinson
  1984   Introduction. In: J. M. Atkinson and J. Heritage (eds.), *Structures of Social Action: Studies in Conversation Analysis,* 1–15. Cambridge: University of Cambridge Press.
Hoetink, Harry
  1967   *Caribbean Race Relations: A Study of Two Variants.* New York: Oxford University Press.
Irvine, Judith T.
  1974   Strategies of status manipulation in the Wolof Greeting. In: R. Bauman and J. Sherzer (eds.), *Explorations in the Ethnography of Speaking,* 167–191. London: Cambridge University Press.
Irvine, Judith T.
  2001   "Style" as distinctiveness: the culture and ideology of linguistic differentiation. In: P. Eckert and J. R. Rickford (eds.), *Style and Sociolinguistic Variation,* 21–43. Cambridge/New York: Cambridge University Press.

Kiesling, Scott
  2001   Stances of Whiteness and hegemony in fraternity men's discourse. *Journal of Linguistic Anthropology* 11 (1): 101–115.
Kroskrity, Paul V.
  1993   *Language, History, and Identity: Ethnolinguistic Studies of the Arizona Tewa.* Tucson: University of Arizona Press.
Le Page, R. B. and Andrée Tabouret-Keller
  1985   *Acts of Identity: Creole-Based Approaches to Language and Ethnicity.* Cambridge/ New York: Cambridge University Press.
Lee, Hyon-Bok
  1989   *Korean Grammar.* Oxford/ New York: Oxford University Press.
Lippi-Green, Rosina
  1997   *English With an Accent: Language, Ideology, and Discrimination in the United States.* London/ New York: Routledge.
Lipski, John M.
  1985   *Linguistic Aspects of Spanish-English Language Switching.* Tempe, Ariz.: Center for Latin American Studies Arizona State University.
Matthews, Aaron (ed.)
  2000   *My American Girls.* New York: Filmmakers Library.
McClure, Erica
  1977   Aspects of code-switching in the discourse of bilingual Mexican-American children. In: M. Saville-Troike (ed.), *Linguistics and Anthropology,* 93–115. Washington, D.C.: Georgetown University Press.
Meeuwis, Michael and Jan Blommaert
  1998   A monolectal view of code-switching: Layered code-switching among Zairians in Belgium. In: P. Auer (ed.), *Code-Switching in Conversation: Language, Interaction and Identity,* 76–98. London/ New York: Routledge.
Milroy, James, and Lesley Milroy
  1985   *Authority in Language: Investigating Language Prescription and Standardisation.* London/ Boston: Routledge and K. Paul.
Milroy, Lesley and Li Wei.
  1995   A social network approach to code-switching: The example of a bilingual community in Britain. In: L. Milroy and P. Muysken (eds.), *One Speaker, Two Languages: Cross-disciplinary Perspectives on Code-Switching,* 137–157. Cambridge: Cambridge University Press.
Mitchell-Kernan, Claudia
  1972   Signifying and marking: Two Afro-American speech acts. In: J. Gumperz and D. H. Hymes (eds.), *Directions in Sociolinguistics: The Ethnography of Communication,* 161–179. New York: Holt, Rinehart and Winston.
Mittelberg, David, and Mary C. Waters
  1992   The Process of Ethnogenesis among Haitian and Israeli Immigrants in the United-States. *Ethnic and Racial Studies* 15 (3): 412–435.
Myers-Scotton, Carol
  1993   *Social Motivations for Codeswitching: Evidence from Africa.* Oxford: Clarendon Press.
Omi, Michael, and Howard Winant
  1994   *Racial Formation in the United States: From the 1960s to the 1990s.* 2nd ed. New York: Routledge.

Pavlenko, Aneta and Adrian Blackledge
  2004   Introduction: New theoretical approaches to the study of negotiation
            of identities in multilingual contexts. In: A. Pavlenko and A. Blackledge
            (eds.), *Negotiation of Identities in Multilingual Contexts,* 1–33. Clevedon/
            Buffalo/ Toronto: Multilingual Matters LTD.
Peirce, Charles S.
  1955   Logic as semiotic: The theory of signs. In: J. Buchler (ed.), *Philosophical
            Writings of Peirce,* 98–119. New York: Dover Publications.
Philips, Susan Urmston
  1983   *The Invisible Culture: Communication in Classroom and Community on the
            Warm Springs Indian Reservation.* New York: Longman.
Piatt, Bill
  1990   *Only English: Law and Language Policy in the United States.* Albuquerque,
            NM: University of New Mexico Press.
Poplack, Shana
  1980   Sometimes I'll start a sentence in Spanish y termino en espanol – toward a
            typology of code-switching. *Linguistics* 18 (7–8): 581–618.
Poplack, Shana
  1988   Contrasting patterns of codeswitching in two communities. In: M. Heller
            (ed.), *Codeswitching: Anthropological and Sociolinguistic Perspectives,*
            215–244. Berlin/ New York/ Amsterdam: Mouton de Gruyter.
Rampton, Ben
  1995   *Crossing: Language and Ethnicity Among Adolescents.* London/New York:
            Longman.
Rickford, John R.
  1999   *African American Vernacular English: Features, Evolution, Educational
            Implications.* Malden, Mass.: Blackwell Publishers.
Sankoff, David and Shana Poplack
  1981   A formal grammar for code-switching. *Papers in Linguistics* 14: 3–46.
Scollon, Ronald and Suzanne B. K. Scollon
  1981   *Narrative, Literacy, and Face in Interethnic Communication.* Norwood,
            N.J.: Ablex Pub. Corp.
Silverstein, Michael
  1996   Monoglot "Standard" in America. In: D. L. Brenneis and R. K. S. Macaulay
            (eds.), *The Matrix of Language: Contemporary Linguistic Anthropology,*
            284–306. Boulder, Col.: Westview Press.
Swigart, Leigh
  1992   Two codes or one? The insiders's view and the description of codeswitching in
            Dakar. *Journal of Multilingual and Multicultural Development* 13: 83–102.
Tannen, Deborah
  1982   Ethnic style in male-female conversation. In: J. Gumperz (ed.), *Language
            and Social Identity,* 217–231. New York: Cambridge University Press.
Tracy, Karen
  2002   *Everyday Talk: Building and Reflecting Identities.* New York: The Guilford
            Press.
Treffers-Daller, Jeanine
  1992   French-Dutch codeswitching in Brussels: Social factors explaining its dis-
            appearance. *Journal of Multilingual and Multicultural Development* 13
            (1–2): 143–156.

Waters, Mary
  1994   Ethnic and racial identities of second-generation Black immigrants in New
            York City. *International Migration Review* 14 (1): 57–76.
Waters, Mary C.
  1990   *Ethnic Options: Choosing Identities in America.* Berkeley: University of
            California Press.
Wei, Li
  1998   The 'why' and 'how' questions in the analysis of conversational code-
            switching. In: P. Auer (ed.), *Code-Switching in Conversation: Language,
            Interaction, and Identity,* 156–176. London/ New York: Routledge.
Wieder, Larry, and Stephen Pratt
  1990   On being a recognizable Indian among Indians. In: D. Carbaugh (ed.), *Cul-
            tural Communication and Intercultural Contact,* 45–64. London /Hove:
            Lawrence Erlbaum.
Woolard, Kathryn Ann
  2004   Codeswitching. In: A. Duranti (ed.), *A Companion to Linguistic Anthropol-
            ogy,* 73–94. Malden, MA: Blackwell.
Zentella, Ana Celia
  1997   *Growing up Bilingual: Puerto Rican Children in New York.* Malden, MA:
            Blackwell.

14.　Crossing – negotiating social boundaries

Pia Quist and J. Normann Jørgensen

1.　Introduction

Several recent studies have focused on speakers' spontaneous acquisition and fragmentary use of out-group minority and non-standard language varieties. Such linguistic behavior was for a long time unexpected and not given serious attention in linguistic and sociolinguistic studies. However, the spontaneous acquisition and use of languages "that are not generally thought to belong to" (Rampton 1995: 280) a particular person or group seems to be common in local negotiations of ethnic, social and linguistic boundaries. These sociolinguistic processes can be termed 'crossing' (Rampton 1995). Although crossing as a metaphor – that connotes "a step over a heavily fortified and well-guarded linguistic border" (Auer 2003: 74) – is disputable, we will for the sake of convenience use it as a cover-term for the processes we are dealing with in this chapter.

Crossing is related to code-switching, stylization, and double-voicing – terms which we will explain in the following. In the first part of our chapter we approach the phenomenon of crossing in relation to processes of (ethnic) identity and solidarity construction. We refer to studies that examine negotiations of in- and out-group relations and mention a few studies that discuss adolescent use of crossing as a strategy against adults in institutional settings. In the second part we look at studies of crossing as mocking and joking in processes involving stereotyping and stigmatization. In connection to this we discuss the stylization of minority languages and varieties in the media. In the third part we shall look at two examples of crossing in more detail and see how the meanings of crossing, among other things, are related to the local organization of peer network relations. We end our chapter by briefly considering the consequences crossing can have for our understanding of language and speakers in general.

2.　Language crossing and negotiations of (ethnic) categorizations and solidarity

In the 1980s Roger Hewitt conducted ethnographic studies among inter-racial groups of friends in two areas of London (Hewitt 1986, 1992). In his pioneering study of white speakers' use of London Jamaican Creole, Hewitt observed how local cross-linguistic behavior is connected to wider patterns of race and ethnicity in society. He described how the use of Creole by whites in inter-racial

groups sometimes functioned to "neutralize" stigmatized racial differences (Hewitt 1986: 163–164). Whites talking like blacks sometimes achieve "the substitution of a relation to language for the more complex relation to the black community. By temporarily freeing themselves from constraints of their respective
groups, the friends can achieve in language a fictive social relation over and
above their personal relationship of friendship" (Hewitt 1986: 164). Hewitt
distinguished between different strategic modes of outsiders' use of Creole –
modes that, if placed on a continuum, would range from a collaborative inter-
racial friendship mode, over a public cultural mode to a hostile competitive
mode of derision. Such an approach to language use in inter-racial groups was
very different from the ways sociolinguistics had thus far treated white speakers' use of Black English Vernacular. Labov (1980), for instance, studied the
degree to which white speakers were able to acquire more than just a subset of
the vernacular of the black community (see also Le Page 1980 and Sweetland
2002). Hewitt's perspective was also quite different from Gumperz's (1982a
and b) approach to inter-ethnic communication. Gumperz (and his associates)
were mostly concerned with institutionalized interactions, typically between an
applicant and a gate-keeper (interviews with local authorities, job interviews
etc.) – situations with clearly defined roles and power relations. The focus was
on how speakers acted according to their affiliation with predefined social and
ethnic categories, rather than on the (re)construction and (re)negotiation of
these affiliations. Hewitt's interest in the use of a language variety that was not
generally accepted as belonging to the speaker, and resulting in the neutrali-
zation of racial and ethnic hostility, was indeed something new.

Hewitt found that the out-group use of Creole was always somewhat delicate. Blacks were normally sensitive to "the use of creole in derisive ways, and
even just the possibility of its use to serve those ends, [is what] sensitises some
blacks to *any* uses of creole by whites" (Hewitt 1986: 135). The delicacy – or
potential social danger – connected to crossing seemed to be the very basis for
how and why the different modes of conduct resulted in renegotiations of ethnic
and racial positions, i.e. the very transgression sometimes achieved temporary,
new social meanings and positionings. This aspect of crossing was of special interest to Rampton in his study of language crossing in a multiethnic youth club
in London. When defining crossing, he writes:

> Crossing [...] focuses on code alternation by people who are not accepted members
> of the group associated with the second language they employ. It is concerned with
> switching into languages that are not generally thought to belong to you. This kind
> of switching, in which there is a distinct sense of movement across social or ethnic
> boundaries, raises issues of social legitimacy that participants need to negotiate
> (Rampton 1995: 280).

Hewitt's analyses of the political, strategic modes of cross-linguistic practices
were an important source of inspiration for Rampton (1995: 4). Since Rampton

introduced the term 'crossing' scholars have taken it up and analyzed crossing phenomena in different languages and contexts. The term quickly gained popularity, perhaps due to its immediate and intuitive appeal. It seems to provide the analyst with a theoretic and practical tool for dealing with complicated social and linguistic processes in multilingual communities. However, as Rampton's own complex analyses confirm, crossing is a multifaceted phenomenon that takes form and meaning in locally situated interactions and has a different legitimacy and different effects depending on who, where, how, and into which language variety the crossing is done.

2.1.   Ritual and liminality

It is a major point in Rampton's work that *ethnicity* is not a sufficient explanatory category for crossing (1995, 2001). Crossing practices involving the use of Punjabi, Creole, and stylized Indian English by out-group speakers do not correspond with traditional sociolinguistic treatments of ethnicity, since these are profoundly linked to assumptions about 'system', 'coherence' and 'community' (2001: 265) – something which does not make sense when we focus on adolescent language practices in multilingual and multicultural settings. Instead of acting according to the normal expectations of the ethnic group, the adolescents in Rampton's study seemed to be attracted to and aligned with shifting out-group norms and cultural forms. Rather than fitting into or representing one ethnic category, speakers used language to negotiate these affiliations and to challenge them in ways that sometimes made new meanings or "new ethnicities" possible (1995: 297). Instead of approaching the crossing practices with ethnicity as the analytic tool, Rampton found that the sociological and anthropological concepts of ritual and liminality were useful. Ritual is linked to the symbolic conduct in interaction. It "displays an orientation to issues of respect for social order and [...] emerges from some sense of the (actual or potential) problematicity of social relations" (1995: 19). In the case of e.g. stylized Asian English, Rampton found that three different situations or activities involving crossing resulted in different ritual conducts. (1) When adults were the direct or indirect recipients (1995: 141–62), stylized Asian English seemed to serve as an anti-rite – "a small destabilising act counterposed to the categories and conduct that the adult would normally be orienting to" (2001: 281). (2) In more informal interactions among peers, crossing seemed to serve "as a differentiating ritual, focussing on transgression and threatening the recipient with isolation in the marginal zones that AE [Asian English] conjured if the offender did not return to the norms of proper adolescent conduct" (2001: 282–83). Finally, (3) during play or game activities, crossing into stylized Asian English seemed to be a "consensual ritual [...] highlighting the ideals and rules of play rather than their disruption" (2001: 283). Hence, crossing into one language variety, here stylized Asian

English, served quite different ritual functions depending on the status of the interlocutors and the types of activities they engaged in. It is not enough for the analysis of crossing, then, to reveal the attitudes and stereotypes connected to Asian English. It is the concrete, local employment of the variety that tells us how the crossing should be interpreted.

In anthropology the notion of ritual (or rite) is sometimes connected to that of liminality. Rampton borrows the term *liminality* from Victor Turner (1974) and defines it as characterizing a ritual period of transition "*outside* normal social structure", where interlocutors "occupy neither their former nor their future statuses" (Rampton 1995: 19–20). Rampton found that crossing was most likely to occur in such liminal situations when normal routines and structures were temporarily loosened (1995: 192–97). Also, liminality sometimes seemed to be a consequence of language crossing: "Although crossing was often inserted into moments and settings where a breach of the taken-for-granted patterns of ordinary life had arisen independently of ethnic language use, it was also used productively to enhance or create such loosenings" (1995: 196). Hence, crossing was often born out of liminal situations, but it also sometimes led to a liminal situation with temporarily loosened or even reversed social roles and structures. As Auer notes (2003: 75), this is a point where crossing is clearly different from code-switching. Auer and Dirim (2000, 2003) find that Turkish is rarely used by non-Turkish adolescents in liminal situations. Rather, adolescents' shifts between German and Turkish can be described as discourse- and participant-related code-switching (e.g. Auer 1998) which normally do not involve the social risk of transgression which is implied in Rampton's definition of crossing.

2.2.   The spontaneous acquisition of Turkish by non-Turkish adolescents

Auer and Dirim studied the spontaneous acquisition of Turkish by non-Turkish adolescents who grew up in Turkish-dominated neighborhoods in Hamburg. The acquisition of Turkish was "spontaneous" in the sense that the speakers had never taken classes or learned Turkish from their parents or families. Instead, they had picked it up among their Turkish-speaking peers in kindergartens, schools, and during leisure time activities. In order to gain access to the friendship groups in their neighborhood, they used Turkish as an "entry ticket" (Auer and Dirim 2003: 228) – "it seems to be essential to acquire at least a minimum of knowledge of Turkish in order to be accepted in their surroundings" (Auer and Dirim 2000: 160). Although an almost instrumental motivation for acquiring and using Turkish was common, the adolescents diverged substantially with regard to their Turkish cultural orientations and affiliations. Placed in a sociocultural space, the adolescents with non-Turkish backgrounds who used Turkish differed greatly on the dimensions 'mainstream vs. subcultural orientation' and 'youth-cultural vs. anti-youth cultural orientation'. The following finding by

Auer and Dirim is of particular interest: according to the common stereotype, adolescents who grow up in immigrant-dense areas and use ethnically coded language markers (such as Turkish) are identified with marginal (street gang) cultures, face difficulties in school and other state institutions and are involved in criminal acts. This stereotype – as represented in the media (Auer and Dirim 2003: 223) – does not capture the diverse social landscape in which the adolescents who use Turkish position themselves. 13 out of the 25 informants in their study oriented more towards German mainstream culture than towards marginal subculture, i.e. they attended and engaged in school and education and seemed to accept "the rules and regularities of the 'official market'" (2003: 227). Some of the informants oriented themselves towards an adult lifestyle, i.e. they displayed explicit affiliation with their parents' way of living and tried to distance themselves from other adolescents their age. Many of the adolescents had a neutral rather than overtly positive attitude towards what they see as Turkish culture. They did not seem to have acquired Turkish because they valued or praised the Turks and Turkish ways of living. Their motivation seemed more instrumental than symbolic (Auer and Dirim 2003: 227–229). However, other informants explained their motivations with an almost romanticized positive appreciation of Turkish culture. Auer and Dirim conclude that the adolescents' stances and affiliations within socio-cultural space are very diverse. Thus, they argue that the various "ethnic, 'subcultural' and youth cultural affiliations (and, therefore, acts of identity) should be kept analytically distinct" (2003: 223).

Some of the informants with non-Turkish ethnic backgrounds were surprisingly fluent in Turkish (e.g. Hans and Thomas, both of German descent, who even spoke Turkish together without the presence of their Turkish friends), while others seemed to know only a few words and chunks of the language. It is not always clear whether the mixing of German and Turkish should be characterized as code-mixing or code-switching. Auer and Dirim found both in their data. There was evidence that a mixed speaking style involving the alternating use of German and Turkish was common and widespread. Also, partly due to the varying degrees of competence in the involved languages, code-switching was typical. However, Auer and Dirim did not find any qualitative difference between the ethnic groups in their switching behavior – native as well as non-native Turkish speakers code-switched and code-mixed in more or less the same ways (Auer 2003: 84).

2.3.   The spontaneous acquisition of Turkish by non-Turkish adolescents –
        a case of crossing?

Auer (2003) discusses whether or not the use of Turkish by the non-Turks can be characterized as a type of crossing, i.e. as the use of an out-group language. In a broad sense the use of Turkish by adolescents of e.g. Polish, Iranian and German descent is a type of crossing. The speakers employ a language which is associated with an ethnic group that they are normally not considered to belong to. However, the use of Turkish did not have the trespassing character which is implied in Rampton's definition of crossing. The code-mixing was rather part of "an unmarked speaking style" which was "detached from its Turkish roots and [had] instead become part of a general, ethnic, but not Turkish, and sometimes not even ethnic but just fashionable, streetwise youth style" (Auer 2003: 77). Auer's data further includes cases where the alternations could be characterized as code-switching. The switching serves pragmatic and competence-related functions (this resembles the findings in other studies of code-switching, see ch. 11), rather than symbolic, ritual functions in liminal situations. Hence, Auer concludes that crossing in the sense of Rampton is not common among the adolescents in this large immigrant neighborhood of Hamburg. However, Auer claims that crossing occurs among young mainly male speakers with German ethnic backgrounds who usually are not in peer contact with immigrants: "these adolescents do not cross the boundary into Turkish, but rather, they cross into a stereotyped ethnic variety of mock-German (sometimes called *Kanaksprak*) ascribed to Turkish and other migrant speakers" (Auer 2003: 90). We will discuss the mocking use of stereotype varieties in the next section.

Crossing in Auer and Dirim's study seems to be different from that in Rampton's study with regard to its symbolic and transgressing meanings. The reason might be found in the specific type of environment studied in Hamburg. Ethnic hostility and racism do not appear to be at stake to the same extent as in the London immigrant communities. In Hamburg, the adolescents (at least the 25 informants in the study) have positive attitudes towards Turks and Turkish culture (Auer and Dirim 2003: 241). Only one of the informants (Daniel of Capverdian origin) displayed explicitly negative feelings towards Turks. In this generally positive atmosphere where Turkish language and culture seem to be accepted, normal, and unmarked, the use of Turkish by non-Turks is likely to be less problematic. In contrast, in the areas of London where Rampton and Hewitt carried out their studies, racism and ethnic segregation were part of the everyday life of the adolescents (cf. Rampton 1995: 27–30, and Hewitt 1986: ch. 1, especially his "area A" friendship groups were clearly divided between blacks and whites).

2.4.   Crossing and school

It is sometimes argued that the schools' institutional categorizations and reactions to bilingual speakers in multilingual settings neglect speakers' abilities to handle and make creative use of their linguistically and culturally heterogeneous resources (Evaldsson 2002; Hewitt 1989; Rampton 1995: ch 13; Jørgensen 2003; Hinnenkamp 2003). There is a contradiction between the schools' official appraisal of linguistic diversity on the one hand, and their (also often official) monolingual educational policy on the other. The school as an institution often categorizes speakers according to linguistic or ethnic origin, ignoring among other things the fact that many bilinguals in urban, western communities grow up in mixed families with different linguistic and ethnic backgrounds (Evaldsson 2002: 6; Quist 2005).

Evaldsson (2002) describes this categorization of individual speakers as e.g. 'Spanish' or 'Turkish' as a means of controlling and predicting students' behavior and their needs for special teaching. This, she argues, can be described as "ethnic absolutism" (referring to Gilroy 1987). Ethnic categories become exclusive and explanatory at the cost of other possible categories (e.g. gender, age or peer group status). Of course, peer group interaction is not unaffected by these broader institutional framings. In a Swedish school setting investigated by Evaldsson, they make relevant ethnic and linguistic categorization for the activities that take place within the school. This is because (1) they determine which students are grouped together at different times and places (in normal classes as well as classes of special training) and (2) they shape explicit discourses about (what the school thinks to be a lack of) linguistic competence. Evaldsson found that the students challenged and renegotiated the social organization and the monolingual norms of the school. Strategic code-crossing and mixing was one of the ways in which students did so (Evaldsson 2002: 11).

The institutional framing was also decisive for some types of crossing in Hewitt's and Rampton's studies. Hewitt found that the use of Creole by white speakers in London was easier for their black peers to accept when the crossing was used as a sort of anti-language against adults: "A common use of creole by white secondary school children, and one which excites no objections from their black friends, is where it is used deliberately to exclude and mystify teachers and other adults in authority" (Hewitt 1986: 154). Rampton also reports on crossing used strategically in opposition against adult authorities, and he interprets Asian English *I no understand* stylizations within the analytic framework of 'ritual' (Rampton 1995: ch. 3). Especially stylized Asian English was often employed as a ritual contesting the pupil–teacher or youngster–adult power imbalance:

> They switched into an exaggerated Asian English at the threshold of activities like detention or basketball; when they were asking white adults for goods or services; when teachers tried to institute question-answer exchanges; and [...] when interviewers asked for more concentrated attention. These switches seemed to operate as a kind of probe, saying 'if I'm this, then how will you respond?' They conjured awkward knowledge about intergroup relations and in doing so, the purpose seemed to be to disturb transition to the activity being expected (Rampton 2001: 270).

A common feature of these studies (Evaldsson, Hewitt and Rampton) is that crossing does not only challenge (institutionalized) ethnic categorizations, but is also part of the speakers' constructions of youth identities in opposition to adults. This point has been emphasized elsewhere as well (e.g. Auer and Dirim 2003; Cutler 1999; Jørgensen 2003, 2004; Quist 2005). Code-crossing and mixing among adolescents often has to do more with the speakers' constructions of themselves as young people than with displaying specific ethnic identities.

3.   Stylization, mocking and stereotyping

As mentioned above, Auer (2003) found crossing (in the sense of transgressing a social and linguistic boundary) among speakers of German ethnic background. These speakers stylize 'ethnic' German speech, often in ways that are obviously taken from media stereotypes. Some of these instances of crossing can be characterized as mocking, for which there are various examples in the literature. Some studies report on its occurrence in face-to-face interaction (e.g. Hewitt 1986: 170; Hinnenkamp 2003; Quist 2005), others examine mock-type crossing in public media (e.g. Hill 1995; Androutsopoulos 2001; Andersen 2004). Androutsopoulos (2001) demonstrates that these crossing patterns can be followed "from the streets to the screens and back again", i.e. "from their community of origin ('the streets') over mediated discourse ('the screens') to face-to-face-communication of native speakers ('back again')" (Androutsopoulos 2001: 1).

In face-to-face interaction, we can roughly distinguish between out-group mocking, typically performed by members of a majority group who imitate a minority groups' styles of speaking, and in-group mocking, for instance sons and daughters mimicking the non-native accent of their immigrant parents. Hewitt reports the former. When whites use Creole in conversations with other whites, they usually do so with a parodistic and mocking stance (1986: 148), and sometimes for racist purposes (1986: 135). The use of stylized Asian English by speakers of Indian or Pakistani descent is sometimes also used parodistically (Rampton 1995: 142–153). The Bangladeshi adolescents in Rampton's study rank lowest in the peer hierarchy in the youth club. A mocking, stylized use of their language by the others is one way in which the adolescents establish and display this hierarchy.

In-group mocking is mostly based on stylizations of a non-native command of the majority language. Hinnenkamp (2003: 27–33) shows how such stylizations are incorporated by the children of immigrants into their Turkish-German mixed speaking styles (which he calls "code-oscillation"). But the mimicking of "Gastarbeiterdeutsch" is not only used by the second and third generation speakers. Hinnenkamp discusses a conversation between a mother of Turkish descent and her son, who was born and raised in Germany. He shows that the boy *and* the mother stylize the first generation's way of speaking German.

According to Hinnenkamp, "its function is purely phatic: a We that reassures itself of its own identity via an exaggerated and caricatured use of voices that are not their own (anymore) but which become re-appropriated in play [...] stripped of any threatening connotations" (Hinnenkamp 2003: 33). Thus, there is not always a straightforward relationship between the stylized voice and the (ethnic) group which is imitated. Local positions and statuses are also constructed through stylization – something we will find again in the examples in the next section.

Hinnenkamp borrows terminology from Bakhtin for whom language use is always "half someone else's" (Bakhtin 1981: 293): when employing words in interactions, the speaker "appropriates the word, adapting it to his own semantic and expressive intention" (ibid.). However,

> not all words for just anyone submit equally easily to this appropriation, to this sei-zure and transformation to private property: many words stubbornly resist, others remain alien, sound foreign in the mouth of the one who appropriated them and who now speaks them; they cannot be assimilated into his context and fall out of it; it is as if they put themselves in quotation marks against the will of the speaker (Bakhtin 1981: 294).

Crossing might be characterized as a very clear and deliberate case of the re- or ex-appropriation of the words of others. In dealing with crossing, Quist (2005) found it useful to use Bakhtin's distinction between uni- and vari-directional double-voicing (Bakhtin 1984: 193–94). In instances of vari-directional double-voicing, voice and speaker are clearly separated (e.g. irony, parody, joking), whereas in uni-directional double-voicing the voice of the other is integrated into the speaker's own voice (see also Rampton 1995: 221–24).[1]

There are also various examples of stylizations of minority varieties in the media. Androutsopoulos (2001) lists a series of instances of stylized "Türken-deutsch" (Turkish German) from movies, TV and radio. Interviews reveal that these stereotyped stylizations are well known among German adolescents, and that fragments of the stylized voices are often quoted and imitated. In Denmark most adolescents are familiar with *Mujaffa* – a stereotyped young male character with an immigrant background (Turkish or Arabic). Mujaffa was originally a computer game launched by Radio Denmark's youth targeted web-page as *Perkerspillet* (*perker* is the derogatory term for immigrants in Denmark). Due to public complaints and debates about the use of the word *perker,* the name was changed to *Mujaffaspillet* (The Mujaffa Game).[2] The Mujaffa web-page and the Mujaffa game are based on the stereotype of a young male immigrant who is attracted to street gang culture, who wears heavy golden chains and his baseball cap backwards. In the computer game the player takes on the identity of Mujaffa and cruises through the streets of Nørrebro and Vesterbro (the immigrant-dense areas of Copenhagen). The car is a 'top tuned' and heavily decorated BMW (according to a stereotype, the preferred car among young male second generation immigrants). During the cruise, Mujaffa scores points when he collects gold chains, when he crashes into passing police cars and when he succeeds in picking up a blonde girl (a stereotypical 'bimbo'). The Mujaffa game was launched in 2000 and is still a popular site. A quick Google search shows that it has circulated (and is subject to debates) on various Danish web-sites. The attraction seems to be based on the comic representation of 'Mujaffa' alone. Besides serving as an example of the vulgar, stereotyped portrayal of young male immigrants (and young Danish girls), there are two further details which are interesting for our discussion. First, the name Mujaffa has come to serve as a cover-term for this specific stereotype. Andersen (2003) argues that *Mujaffa* is about to assume the state of a noun in Danish, in the same way as *Brian*,[3] and she traces this back to the Mujaffa game web-site. Andersen (2003: 15) reports an example from an interview with a Muslim boy in Denmark who says: "One is forced to pay attention to the effect one has on other people. I try not to look like a Mujaffa" (our translation). In another example taken from Andersen (2003: 15), a reader of the newspaper 'Jyllandsposten' complains in a letter to the editor that the taxis in the town of Århus drive much too fast: "one is not supposed to drive through the Bus Street like Brian or Mujaffa" (our translation).

By coining a noun, *mujaffa*, it becomes possible – with one word – to index 'the whole package', i.e. everything that is associated with and implied in the stereotyped representations of young immigrant males. Part of this 'package' is the speech style of these males (referred to as multiethnolect by Quist 2000). This is the second point of interest in the Mujaffa game: it is a good illustration of the life-circle of crossing which Androutsopoulos (2001) describes. In the first stage, an ethnolectal vernacular is created among speakers of minority backgrounds (Quist 2000; Auer and Dirim 2003; Hinnenkamp 2003). In the second stage, the ethnolect is taken as a source of inspiration for a stereotyped character in the media. In the Mujaffa game the Mujaffa character repeats the same phrase *wolla, min fætter* again and again. It literally means 'vallah, my cousin', with *vallah* derived from Arabic and Turkish and meaning 'by God'. It is a frequent term in immigrant Danish, used as a swearword and intensifier (see examples in the next section). The expression *wolla, min fætter*, however, is not a commonly used phrase among minority youth. *Min fætter* connotes the Danes' stereotype of immigrants' close family relations. In the Mujaffa game 'cousin' is used as a cover-term for all family members (and also evokes the close-knit, family-like organization of gangster and gang culture), and apparently 'Mujaffa' always runs into his 'cousins'. Adolescents who are not familiar with the speech of young second and third generation immigrants in Denmark pick up this phrase (probably assuming that this is what minority youth actually say), and quote and employ it in their conversations. This, then, is the third stage of Androutsopoulos' life-circle. The linguistic source of crossing is not direct communication with the people portrayed, but their stereotyped representation in the media.

The stylized variety 'Mujaffa' speaks can be called mock immigrant Danish. Hill (1995) has investigated Mock Spanish which involves little pieces of Spanish (e.g. *adios, hasta la vista, mañana*) and is used, mostly jokingly, by Anglo-Americans. It can be found in real conversations as well as in movies, on postcards, bumper stickers, mugs, etc. The Spanish-speaking population is – through the use of mock-Spanish – portrayed "with gross sexual appetites, political corruption, laziness, disorders of language and mental incapacity" (Hill 1995: 2). Hill argues that such uses of Spanish in the USA are part of an "elite racist discourse" which is rarely acknowledged as such beause the mocking is only indirect, "in fact [racism] is actively denied as a possible function of their usage, by speakers of Mock Spanish, who often claim that Mock Spanish shows that they appreciate Spanish language and culture" (Hill 1995: 2). Instead, by crossing into Mock Spanish, speakers "signal that they possess desirable qualities: a sense of humour, a playful skill with a foreign language, authentic regional roots, an easy-going attitude toward life" (Hill 1995: 1).

A closer look at the public debate about the Mujaffa web-page (in 2000, when the name was changed from *Perkerspillet* to *Mujaffaspillet*) is likely to reveal a discourse parallel to the one Hill analysizes for Mock Spanish. In fact, the creators of 'Mujaffa' argued that through their 'friendly' comic portrayal, they are promoting the inclusion of young immigrant males in the media representations of society. They saw this as a part of the process of integrating foreigners into Danish society. However, it could be characterized as a racist act as well – Hill's argument being that "the speakers and hearers can only interpret utterances in Mock Spanish insofar that they have access to the negative residue of meaning" (Hill 1995: 2). In other words, crossing into mock immigrant Danish, e.g. in a high school class, would not make sense if it was only connected to knowledge about the classmates with an ethnic minority background. In order to interpret 'Mujaffa's' speech the listener needs to be familiar with (and connect this specific speech style to) the criminal, girl-hunting, etc. stereotype of a young immigrant boy. This is one of the ways in which the stereotype is reproduced and kept alive.

4.   Crossing and peer networks

We shall now look briefly at two examples of crossing. As Rampton points out, organized games involve "an agreed relaxation of the rules and constraints of ordinary behaviour" (1995: 193) – a situation that is likely to trigger language crossing. This was indeed the case in a study of language variation in an ethnically heterogeneous high school in Copenhagen. Quist (2005) analyzes instances of crossing in conversations recorded during a game called *Matador* (a board game, a type of *Monopoly*). In the two examples shown below, 'ritual' and 'liminality' are relevant analytic notions in the description of the situations in which crossing occurs. Furthermore, besides 'ritual' and 'liminality', Quist finds that the roles and positions of the speakers in the local peer network are crucial for (1) who is allowed to do the crossing, and (2) how crossing is interpreted and accepted by the peers.

Extract 1

	Danish		**English**
Amina:	hahaha det er min fød-selsdag jeg skal have to hundrede kroner af jer alle sammen	*Amina:*	hahaha it's my birthday I shall have two hundred kroner from all of you
Phillip:	fuck dig	*Phillip:*	fuck you
Olav:	hold din kæft mand hvad snakker du om	*Olav:*	shut up man what are you talking about
Amina:	to hundrede (.) wallah jeg sværger jeg sværger det er Deres fødselsdag	*Amina:*	two hundred (.) wallah I swear I swear it is your birthday
→ Phillip:	og jeg sagde wallah jeg s:	→ *Phillip:*	and I said wallah I s:
Amina:	modtag af [hver spiller to hundrede] kroner	*Amina:*	receive from [each player two hundred] kroner
→ Phillip:	[wallah jeg sværger]	→ *Phillip:*	[wallah I swear]

Extract 2

	Danish		**English**
Ali:	hvad er nu det for noget?	*Ali:*	now what is this?
Johan:	nej du skal i fængsel mand	*Johan:*	no you are going to prison man
Kristoffer:	næh det er kun hvis han	*Kristoffer:*	no that's only if he
Johan:	du skal være der de næste ti ture uden noget	*Johan:*	you have to stay there for the next ten turns without anything
Kristoffer:	ja og så skal du betale Naweds madpakke	*Kristoffer:*	yeah and then you have to pay for Nawed's lunch box
Johan:	jamen der sker ikke noget du holder der bare	*Johan:*	yes but nothing happens you are just parked there
Ali:	ikke ti ture er du dum eller hvad	*Ali:*	not ten turns are you stupid or what

Johan:	jo ti ture	*Johan:*	yes ten turns
Ali:	det siger den ikke	*Ali:*	it doesn't say that
Johan:	det gør den da	*Johan:*	of course it does
Ali:	you are a liar	*Ali:*	you are a liar
Johan:	skal vi vædde?	*Johan:*	wanna bet?
Ali:	hallo I bliver færdige mand hvad laver du	*Ali:*	hello you are going to finish what are you doing
Kristoffer:	kig i reglerne	*Kristoffer:*	read the rules
→ Johan:	ja jeg siger wallah kig i reglerne	→ *Johan:*	yeah I say wallah read the rules

On the surface, if we look at the linguistic features only, these two examples seem to be similar. The crossings into the multiethnic style (see arrows) are marked by a change of intonation, the use of the intensifier *wallah*, and the phrase *jeg sværger* ('I swear') (cf. Quist 2000: 151–59). From an interactional point of view, however, the two examples are very different. Extract 1 is an instance of mocking, and extract 2 is an example of non-parodistic crossing (i.e. the difference between Bakhtin's notions of uni- and vari-directional double-voicing). These different meanings of crossing relate to the positions of the speakers in the peer-network. Phillip has a Danish ethnic background, and he mostly hangs out with other boys with a similar background. Johan, however, who also has Danish ethnic background, is one of the few who breaks the general pattern and hangs out with boys with ethnic minority background. The different group affiliations are crucial for a proper understanding of the instances of crossing in these examples.

In extract 1 Phillip makes fun of Amina, and he is a bit hostile. Amina has a minority background and is the only girl playing the board game with four boys. Amina tries to hold her own in a discussion during the game. She picks a 'lucky card' which says that 'it is your birthday' (*det er Deres fødselsdag*), and that the other players must pay her 200 kroner. Olav and Phillip protest. Amina insists (reading aloud from the 'lucky card') *wallah I swear I swear it is your birthday*. She says this with an intonation characteristic of immigrant Danish (as e.g. described by Hansen and Pharao 2004) and not unusual for her. Phillip immediately takes up and repeats the phrase *wallah I swear*, in a loud and mocking voice clearly copying Amina. However, his imitation is exaggerated: he says ['swɛwʌ] for Amina's ['svɛwʌ], i.e. instead of a labial dental obstruent he changes [v] to a labial one, which makes it sound exaggerated 'foreign'. This way Phillip manages not only to make fun of Amina and her way of speaking; he also invokes associations of 'foreigners who speak a non-native variety of Danish' – a move which has the effect of positioning Amina as a foreigner, i.e. in a stigmatized position different from Phillip's and Olav's.

Extract 2 is an example of uni-directional double-voiced crossing. Johan uses multiethnic style features to get his way during another disagreement during the game. But Johan does not make fun of the others. On the contrary, although there is a jovial atmosphere, Johan appears rather hostile as he shifts codes. The shift is prosodically signalled by a high rise in intonation, lack of glottal constriction (e.g. omitted 'stød' in the word *reglerne* ['ʁɛ.lʌ.nə] instead of the standard ['ʁɛjʔlnə]), and non-standard stress (cf. Quist 2000: 151–159). Johan does not position himself as Ali's ally (Ali being of a minority background). Rather, he exploits the 'toughness' associated with the minority male youth culture to gain the upper hand in the discussion.

This interpretation is also supported by a look at the sociogram in Figure 1, a graphic representation of the networks of some of the students in the high school. The closer two persons are placed to each other, the more time they spend together in the school during breaks and lessons. The arrows link the students to those of the other students they in the interviews reported to "talk most to", and the gray boxes are the participants of extracts 1 and 2. It is possible for Johan to make use of the style normally associated with Ali as part of his own voice because of his position in the peer network. Johan's friends at school mostly have a minority background. His crossing in this extract, combined with a slightly aggressive tone, seems to borrow from the toughness associated with the group of boys who Johan normally hangs out with, i.e. Mehmet and Ahmet (cf. Quist 2005 for a more detailed analysis of this network). This way Johan also positions Ali as an outsider among the boys who are participating in the game – i.e. as a not-very-tough-guy. Johan is able to do this because of his position in the peer group. In extract 1, however, Phillip would probably not be able to use crossing in this way because of his position in the peer network. Both by themselves and by others, Phillip, Olav, Max, Jakob, and Mads are seen as the 'tough Danish guys', somewhat in opposition to the 'tough foreign guys' ('Danes' and 'foreigners' being the common categorical terms among the students). For instance, Phillip, Olav, Max, Jakob, and Mads drink a lot of alcohol, and they talk a lot about drinking – something Mehmet and Ahmet never do. Phillip never uses double-voicing uni-directionally, but only in a stylized way as in extract 1. Since he does not hang out with boys of a minority background, even a non-stylized crossing would run the risk of being interpreted by his peers as parodistic.

In the case of Johan, one could ask if the multiethnic style is indeed a language "which is not generally thought to belong to Johan". Johan does not use this variety all the time, but often shifts for single utterances, as in extract 2. He does not make fun of his peers, but incorporates their voice into his own. A point we would like to make here is that this practice would not be meaningful if it was *only* connected to ethnicity categories. Arguably, Johan's momentary shifts are a way of performing and presenting himself as a 'Dane-who-is-allowed-to-act-

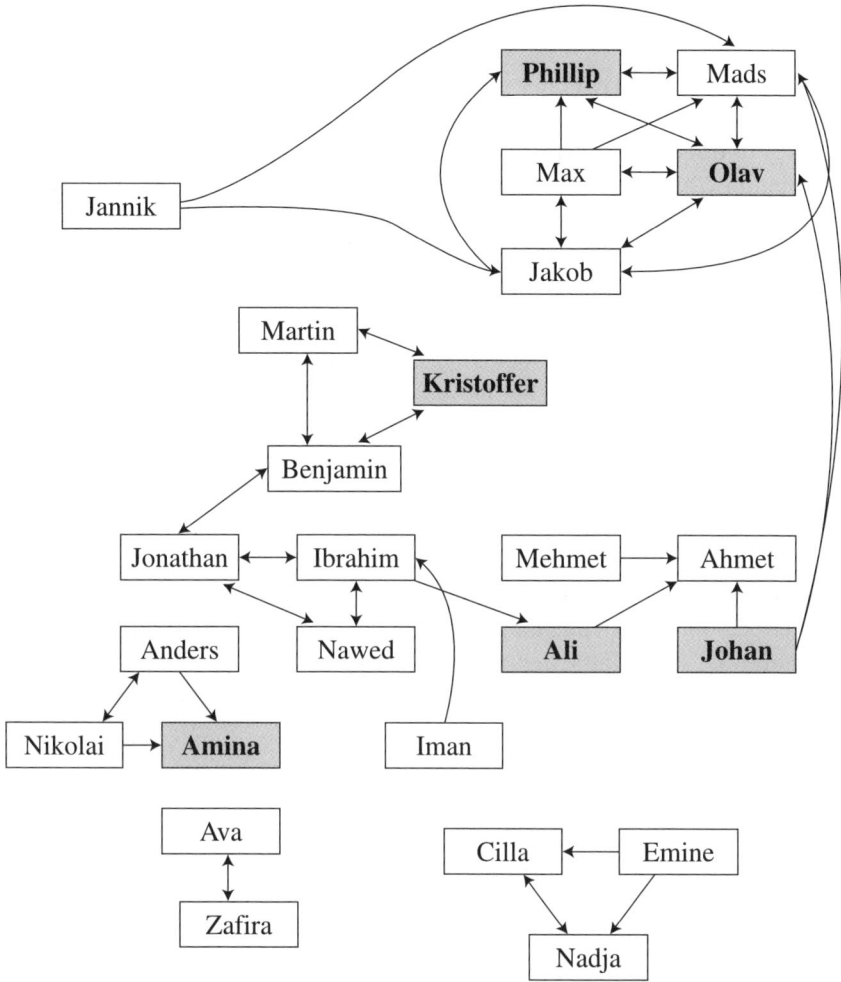

Figure 1. Sociogram of friendship relations. Gray names appear in extracts 1 and 2.

like-an-immigrant-boy' and thereby defining his place in the social peer network. Hence Johan's crossing works in two directions. (1) The incorporation of the minority voice into his own voice is possible (i.e. a legitimate act of identity) because of his position in the peer network. And (2) because of his majority background and his traditional Danish appearance, Johan is not automatically a legitimate or accepted member of his peer group. Hence, crossing may be one means (among many others) available to him to construct a legitimate identity.

5.   Conclusion

In this paper we have used crossing as a cover term for the related but somewhat different processes of crossing, mocking, stylization and double-voicing. These processes of transgression all point to an understanding of language as a human phenomenon which is used by speakers to pursue their goals. Accordingly, we have primarily concentrated on the construction and maintenance of social relations among individual speakers in small groups and networks, but this understanding of language may as well cover any other purpose. The speakers use whatever linguistic means are at their disposal, regardless of the presumed origin of the specific linguistic features. In crossing and mocking, as well as in regular code-switching and code-mixing, speakers use linguistic features which are considered to belong to different sets of linguistic clusters (usually termed *languages* or *varieties*), and the speakers know this. Even to the most 'monolingual' speaker, 'knowing' a word entails not only knowledge of its morphological and syntactic properties, its denotation and connotations. It also involves knowledge of its stylistic value, and its place inside or outside registers and varieties of the 'one' language of the 'monolingual'. The same is true for speakers with access to more than one language. They know where the words belong, and they know the values attached to (the speakers of) each of the involved languages. Furthermore, as we saw in the examples of the last section, speakers in multilingual communities also know about and relate the crossing practices to their local peer group positions and statuses. Transgressing the border between a majority language in a western society and a stigmatized minority language is not in principle different from transgressing the border between a middle class urban standard and a stigmatized rural dialect. Speakers do it all the time, and they do it with a purpose. This is what Jørgensen (2004) terms *languaging*. Crossing and mocking as presented here, i.e. as means to negotiate social relations, are instances of languaging which involve quite separate sets of linguistic features. The transgressions are therefore open and observable *acts* performed with a purpose. This is a fact that makes crossing an ever-interesting source of knowledge about local and global meaning construction and negotiation.

Notes

1. We will refer to the notions of uni- and vari-directional double-voicing in our analyses of the examples of crossing in the next section.
2. http://www.dr.dk/skum/mujaffa/#.
3. In Danish *en brian* ('a brian') is used as a general metaphor for a person with working class background who has little or no education, who is not very smart, and who typically solves his problems through violence instead of talk. To the best of our knowledge this derogatory stereotyping of unskilled working class males has never been an issue in public debate. There are, interestingly enough, more than 19,000 persons in Denmark with the name Brian – who are probably not keen on having their name associated with the stereotype of 'a brian'.

References

Andersen, Margrethe Heidemann
  2003   Om Mujaffaspillet, Mujaffaer og Brianer. In: *Nyt fra Sprognævnet*, 13–15. December. København: Dansk Sprognævn.
Androutsopoulos, Jannis
  2001   From the streets to the screens and back again: On the mediated diffusion of ethnolectal patterns in contemporary Germany. *LAUD Linguistic Agency*, nr. A522. http://www.linse.uni-essen.de/laud/catalogue.htm
  2003   Jetzt speak something about italiano. Sprachliche Kreuzungen im Alltagsleben. In: Erfurt, Juergen (ed.), *'Multisprech': Hybridität, Variation, Identität. OBST Osnabrücker Beiträge zur Sprachtheorie*. 65. 79–109. Duisburg: OBST.
Auer, Peter
  1998   Introduction: 'Bilingual Conversation' revisited. In: Peter Auer (ed.), *Code-switching in Conversation*, 1–24. London: Routledge.
  2003   Crossing the language border into Turkish? Uses of Turkish by non-Turks in Germany. In: Lorenza Mondada and Simona Pekarek Doehler (eds.): *Plurilinguisme – Mehrsprachigkeit – Plurilingualism. Festschrift for Georges Lüdi*, 73–93. Tübingen: Francke.
Auer, Peter and Inci Dirim
  2000   On the use of Turkish Routines by Adolescents of non-Turkish descent in Hamburg. In: Anne Holmen and J. N. Jørgensen (eds.): *Det er Conversation 801 degil mi? Perspectives on the bilingualism of Turkish speaking children and adolescents in North Western Europe*, 159–194. (Copenhagen Studies in Bilingualism. The Køge Series, vol. K7). Copenhagen: The Danish University of Education.
  2003   Socio-cultural orientation, urban youth styles and the spontaneous acquisition of Turkish by non-Turkish adolescents in Germany. In: Jannis K. Androutsopoulos and Alexandra Georgakopoulou (eds.): *Discourse Constructions of Youth Identities*, 223–246. Amsterdam: Benjamins.
Bakhtin, Mikhail
  1981   *The Dialogic Imagination. Four Essays*. Austin: University of Texas Press.

388   Pia Quist and J. Normann Jørgensen

Bakhtin, Mikhail
1984   *Problems of Dostoevsky's Poetics.* Minneapolis: University of Minnesota
         Press.
Cutler, Cecilia A.
1999   Yorkville crossing: White teens, hip hop, and African American English.
         In: Rampton (ed.), 1999, 428–442.
Evaldsson, Ann-Carita
2002   Sociala och språkliga gräsdragningar bland elever i en mångkulturell skola.
         In: *Pædagogisk Forskning i Sverige.* Årg. 7, nr. 1, 1–16. Göteborg: Göte-
         borgs Universitet.
Gilroy, Paul
1987   *'There ain't no black in the Union Jack': The Cultural Politics of 'Race'
         and Nation.* London: Hutchinson Education.
Gumperz, John J. (ed.)
1982a   *Language and Social Identity.* Cambridge: Cambridge University Press.
Gumperz, John J.
1982b   *Discourse Strategies.* Cambridge: Cambridge University Press.
Hansen, Gert and Nicolai Pharao
2004   Prosodic aspects of the Copenhagen Multiethnolect. In: *Proceedings from
         the 9th Nordic Prosody Conference.* August 8–10, 2004, Lund, Sweden.
Hewitt, Roger
1986   *White Talk Black Talk. Inter-Racial Friendship and Communication Amongst
         Adolescents.* Cambridge: Cambridge University Press.
1989   Creole in the classroom: political grammars and educational vocabularies.
         In: Grillo, R. (ed.): *Social Anthropology and the Politics of Language,*
         126–144. London: Routlegde.
1992   Language, youth and the destabilisation of ethnicity. In: Palmgren Cecilia,
         Lövgren Karin and Bolin Göran (eds.), *Ethnicity in Youth Culture,* 27–41.
         Stockholm: Stockholm University.
Hill, Jane
1995   *Mock Spanish: The Indexical Reproduction of Racism in American English.*
         http://www.uta.fi/FAST/US8/SPAN/mockspan.html (Reformatted version of
         original formally at www.language-culture.org/colloquia/symposia/hill-jane)
Hinnenkamp, Volker
2003   Mixed language varieties of migrant adolescents and the discourse of hybridity.
         In: *Journal of Multilingual and Multicultural Development.* 24 (1/2): 12–40.
Jørgensen, J. Normann
2003   Languaging among fifth graders: code-switching in conversation 501 of the
         Køge Project. In: *Journal of Multilingual and Multicultural Development.*
         24 (1/2): 126–148.
2004   Languaging and languagers. In: Christine Dabelsteen and J. Normann Jør-
         gensen (eds.), *Languaging and Language Practices.* (Copenhagen Studies
         in Bilingualism, Vol. 36), 5–22. Faculty of Humanities, University of Co-
         penhagen.
Labov, William
1980   Is there a Creole Speech Community? In: Albert Valdman and Arnold High-
         field (eds.), *Theoretical Orientations in Creole Studies,* 369–388. New
         York: Academic Press, INC.

Le Page, Robert
  1980   Theoretical aspects of sociolinguistic studies in pidgin and creole lan-
          guages. In: Albert Valdman and Arnold Highfield (eds.), *Theoretical Orien-
          tations in Creole Studies*, 331–367. New York: Academic Press, INC.
Quist, Pia
  2000   Ny københavnsk 'multietnolekt'. Om sprogbrug blandt unge i sprogligt og
          kulturelt heterogene miljøer. In: *Danske Talesprog*. Vol.1. Institut for Dansk
          Dialektforskning, 143–212. København: C.A. Reitzels Forlag.
  2005   Stilistiske praksisser i storbyens heterogene skole. Ph.D. dissertation, De-
          partment of Scandinavian Research, Dialectology. University of Copen-
          hagen.
Rampton, Ben
  1995   *Crossing. Language and Ethnicity among Adolescents*. London: Longman.
Rampton, Ben (ed.)
  1999   Theme issue: Styling the Other. *Journal of Sociolinguistics*, 3 (4).
Rampton, Ben
  2001   Language crossing, cross-talk, and cross-disciplinarity in sociolinguistics.
          In: Nikolas Coupland, Srikant Sarangi and Christopher N. Candlin (eds.):
          Sociolinguistics and Social Theory, 261–296. Essex: Pearson Education Li-
          mited.
Sweetland, Julie
  2002   Unexpected but authentic use of an ethnically-marked dialect. *Journal of
          Sociolinguistics*, 6 (4): 514–538.
Turner, Victor
  1974   Liminal to liminoid in play, flow, and ritual: An essay in comparative sym-
          bology. *Rice University Studies* 60 (3): 53–92.

Additional sources

Auer, Peter (ed.)
  1998   *Code-switching in Conversation*. London: Routledge.
Auer, Peter and Aldo di Luzio (eds.)
  1992   *The Contextualization of Language*. Amsterdam: John Benjamin.
Le Page, Robert and Andrée Tabouret-Keller
  1985   *Acts of Identity*. Cambridge: Cambridge University Press.
Jørgensen, J. Normann (ed.)
  2003   *Bilingualism and Social Relations: Turkish Speakers in North Western Eu-
          rope*. Clevedon, England: Multilingual Matters.

Journals

International Journal of Bilingualism. Kingston Press Ltd.
Journal of Sociolinguistics. Blackwell Publishing.
Journal of Pragmatics. Elsevier.

15.   Bilingual professionals

Dennis Day and Johannes Wagner

1.   Introduction

Zinedine Zidane, the aging soccer god in Madrid is one of them, as is his comrade in arms bend-it-like-Beckham. The authors of this paper belong to this group: Dennis Day migrated from Virginia to China and now lives in Gothenburg, Sweden with his family and commutes 500 miles to his workplace in Denmark; Johannes Wagner, who was born and raised in Germany and moved to Denmark 30 years ago, often thinks in German, speaks Danish and writes in English. Suresh Babu Karanam – the friendly Indian software engineer working at the Royal Mail in Copenhagen – is another one of them. They all have specific skills which brought them on the global marketplace. For a while at least they have settled in another country and are confronted with another language. Some of them are constantly moving around as their skills are in high demand – for example software engineers or soccer players – others, like many academics, often settle in their new country.

The movement of highly skilled labor across national boundaries as well as the globalization of modern labor has entailed new empirical circumstances which sociolinguists interested in bi- and multilingualism are just beginning to address.[1] Such circumstances are discussed in studies concerning professional intercultural training, globalization, diversity management, expatriot employment, multinational work teams, and so forth. Linguistic and sociolinguistic issues seldom hold much sway in discussions of these processes, apart from their obvious requirement of communicative efficiency.

The point of departure for this chapter is an interest in the linguistic situation of people – predominately professionals – who, because of their professional skills, are engaged in work with people with different linguistic backgrounds. De Mejía (2002) sorts out the nomenclature concerning the kind of bilingualism we will deal with here. Various terms have been used, such as additive bilingualism, elite bilingualism, voluntary bilingualism, privileged bilingualism, to name a few.[2] All these terms denote the bilingualism of individuals who have the means to voluntarily learn a new language with which they might improve their worklife chances. However, the terms do not refer to the context of use of an individual's bilingual abilities which is also of interest, namely the workplace. Our interests lie in bilinguals who are either dislocated from their country of origin due to their engagement on the labor market, or residents in their home country using a second language in professional environments. For this reason, we will use the term 'bilingual professional' to denote both the above mentioned origins of bilingualism in the individual as well as the particular context of its use. Bilingual professionals use two or more languages in their daily professional lives and are the backbone of the global and virtual economy.

Bilingual professionals have not received much attention in the different research paradigms related to bilingualism. This may be due to the fact that bilingual professionals are transient – that is, they do not always stay long enough to form a minority group ('speech community'), which is a common prerequisite for sociolinguistic research. Furthermore, they are not poor and oppressed, but often well paid and socially secure because of their specific skills. This makes them fall outside studies on intercultural communication at the workplace begun by Gumperz in the 1970s (see Twitchen, Gumperz, Jupp and Roberts 1979; Bremer et al. 1996; Roberts et al. 1992; Roberts, this volume). This group is not of interest for educational research, although their children may go to international schools (de Mejía 2002). Finally, second language acquisition (SLA) research is interested in the linguistic system of the individual, but not in bilingual behavior. A good example is the volume edited by Cook (2002) who refers to a large variety of L2 users: among others, international managers, sports professionals, opera singers, students, street vendors and truck drivers (2002: 1–2). But these professional roles only appear on the first pages of Cook's "portrait of the L2 user". The rest of the book discusses individual competence, individual differences, stages of development, and language attrition. In other words, Cook has edited a book on the L2 user without at any point being specific about the practical issues of bilingual language use.

In sum, the vast majority of sociolinguistic and psycholinguistic work on bilingualism has focused on youth within the context of schooling or on adults in the diaspora, with the latter referring both to 'physical' diaspora, as in the case of immigrants, and to what may be called the 'discursive' diaspora (Belcher and Connor 2001 and Pavlenko and Blackledge 2004). However, we believe there are good reasons to investigate bilingual issues in an increasingly global professional world. As an example of the issues which may arise from such an investigation, we consider the linguistic situation at a workplace under study within a research project led by one of the authors.[3]

'T support' is a unit of 'Build AB' with 80 employees. It is situated in Denmark, as is its corporate headquarters, and provides support globally to the company's computerized administrative systems. Employees are predominately from Denmark with a minority of employees or long-term consultants from, for example, Germany, the United Kingdom, Russia, and India. A survey of communicative routines revealed that communication is overwhelmingly conducted via email, both within the unit itself as well as in its service to other units in Denmark and abroad. Communication is overwhelmingly conducted in English. Language choice can be expressed as a set of general principles and exceptions.

General principles
(i)   If the interlocutor does not speak Danish, use English.
(ii) If the present activity is connected to future activities where a particular language dominates, use that language now.
(iii) If the interlocutor does not speak Danish, but speaks another language you speak, use it, if the activity allows it.
(iv) Switching between English and Danish within an activity is marked and to be accounted for.

Exceptions
(i)   Two categories of people are exempted:
      – people from a particular department and
      – people with a different employment connection to the company.
(ii) If interlocutors in an activity can build groups, 'asides' in the activity may be conducted in a group-specific language.

These principles require a high degree of Danish-English bilingualism, as well as some proficiency in other languages. In other words, given the principles, one is at an advantage as an employee if one has these proficiencies.

Investigating phenomena such as those mentioned above may require some conceptual reorientation within studies of bilingualism. First, the principles of language choice mentioned above seem to be greatly determined by activity type. Language choice is not so much an individual matter as an activity mandate on linguistic resources. Furthermore, two languages, English and Danish, are used as a lingua franca, which again forces a change in perspective from the languages of nation-states to resources for international work-related activities. Finally, especially in connection with new communication technology, linguistic ideology and normativity are in flux, and, again, perhaps best viewed as holding for the domain of a particular institutionalized activity. We believe this perspective is in accordance with Collins and Slembrouck's (2005: 189) questioning of assumptions frequently made in bilingual studies, such as

1. "that language competence is a cognitive property of the individual speaker,
2. that such competence is best and perhaps exclusively assigned at the level of individual languages, and
3. that languages have a clearcut spatial and social provenience" (Collins and Slembrouck 2005: 189).

The spread of language outside 'national areas' is a feature of globalization typically found in bilingual professionals; they are therefore in many respects a new type of category for the social study of language. The category cuts across languages, is activity-based (workplace) and is not bound to a specific geographic area. We will pick up this thread at the end of this article.

2.   Review of the literature

Research on bilingual professionals is distributed across a number of different fields. The bulk of the research, however, comes from studies of organizational communication which have only recently begun to deal with empirical observations of naturally occurring interaction instead of relying on top-down, quantitative studies. The focus has been on questions of language proficiency, and on organizational policy, with communication seen as reflecting organizational structure and function. The following two sections, motivation and training and policy, reflect these concerns. We turn to interaction in the final section, noting a theoretical turn towards language and communication as constitutive of organizational structure and function. While remaining within workplaces, the studies reviewed here are bottom-up discourse analytical attempts to grasp the complexities and subtleties of bilingual professionals' communicative behavior.

2.1.   Motivation and training

In their review of linguistic issues in the literature on management and organization, Barner-Rasmussen and Bor (2005) note that the bulk of research concerns employee acquisition of linguistic skills and, moreover, that even this rather limited view has been superseded and amalgamated into a focus on culture. Culture in turn, we believe it is fair to say, is cast in terms of individual psychology. Language is therefore dealt with in the framework of professional intercultural training. However, the bulk of this work limits its focus to monolingual situations. Issues of language are discussed in terms of competence in a 'host language', and communication seen as one of many behaviors which require 'adaptation'. In spite of what many linguists would view as a rather restricted view of language and communication, Milhouse (1996: 92), in an extensive survey of intercultural training practices, notes that "few training programs deal effectively with the subject of language and culture (only one LC [language and culture] program out of 130 programs dealt with this subject)".

One reason for the paucity of reflection on linguistic and sociolinguistic issues may be its bias towards English and companies based in the United States. The point of reference is the native English-speaking employee dealing with a globalized but English-speaking world.[4] Poncini (2003: 17) notes:

> Despite the range of cultures that may be involved in international business settings, much research into intercultural communication in business has involved two cultures, with one of the cultures often being 'English speaking' (e.g. Halmari, 1993; Murata, 1994; Spencer-Oatey and Xing 1998; Yamada 1990).

It should be noted, however, that such findings stand in stark contrast to a recent survey of executive recruiters where it was found that the ability to speak more than one language is critical to succeed in business in Europe, Asia/Pacific and Latin America. So say 88 percent of executive recruiters from those regions who completed the sixth edition of the quarterly Executive Recruiter Index released by Korn/Ferry International (*Expansion Management*, April 2005).

Turning to a somewhat less anglified Europe, we find that bilingualism is, not surprisingly, the norm rather than the exception. In the *Eurobarometer 54*[5] questionnaire study on foreign languages conducted in 2000, it was found that roughly 15 % of respondents reported active use of a second or third language in their workplace; 74 % of those with children under the age of 20 think it is important that their children learn other European languages to improve their professional perspective. Nonetheless English holds sway as the most frequently learned foreign language, bearing in mind that it is often used as a lingua franca.

Worldwide, recruiters agree that in ten years from now, it will be more important than ever for executives to be at least bilingual. In terms of which foreign languages are in most demand by employers, 88 percent of recruiters in Asia, Europe and Latin America chose English. Recruiters in North America selected Spanish (79 percent), French (43 percent) and Mandarin Chinese (30 percent) (*Financial Executive*, April 2005).

Throughout our investigation, we have found four opposing views: a view of bilingualism where the 'other' speaks English non-natively, a view of bilingialism where everyone speaks English non-natively, i.e. as lingua franca,[6] and a view on bilingualism according to which everybody should speak whatever the dominant language of their 'hosts' is, a 'do as the Romans' approach. And finally, there is the obvious view that one should not be bilingual at all.[7]

These views can also be found in the microcosm of language training in professional football. Kellerman et al. (2005) note that professional sportspeople seem to be very successful language learners. In Dutch football clubs, for example, it was considered important for foreign players to get a command of Dutch since Dutch is used as the language of communication in the clubs. One can assume, however, that English is used as an intermediary lingua franca. Clubs provide language instruction. The players which were approached by the study rated the command of Dutch as important and reported speaking Dutch during training as well as in encounters outside the club. One major argument for learning Dutch was cultural understanding. Resistance to learning Dutch was expressed by players who had set their eyes on clubs outside the Netherlands and intended to leave after a few years in Holland.

A similar survey among English sports clubs faltered due to difficulties in gaining access. Informal observation indicates, however, that English clubs – with Arsenal as a notable exception – seem to leave it up to the players to learn English. Surely, the dominance of English in the world allows English clubs to be less strict in terms of language learning but, as Kellerman et al. (2005: 209) point out, the national agenda may not be relevant in international top clubs, which are 'coincidentally' located in England since "clubs like Chelsea are essentially foreign clubs in a local competition with the players largely closeted away from the directors and administrative staff at their own self-sufficient training centres." In a follow-up study, Wagner et al. (2004) investigated the language policy of different Danish sports clubs. They found that in women's handball, one of the prestigious Danish sports, language skills in Danish are a high priority for foreign players. The clubs have successfully offered language training and social support to newcomers who, as a result, seem to learn Danish fast and effortlessly – apart from players who were just 'passing through'. However, in other sports, most notably men's ice hockey, skills in Danish were neglected and English had become the language of the clubs. This seems to be due to temporary contracts with foreign players who do not stay long enough to learn the host language. But it shows that issues of language choice in the workplace of the professional sportsperson are influenced by pragmatic aspects (effective communication), ideological aspects (team sports, national importance and identification), fluctuation of players, recruitment and money.

2.2.   Policy

Returning to the opposing views concerning the role of dominant languages such as English, we would like to mention two of the relatively numerous Nordic studies in the social sciences on language policy issues within multinational companies. In a series of papers, Marschan et al. (1997, 1999a, 1999b) have presented the case of a Finnish elevator company which encouraged their international affiliates to use their home languages. A contrasting strategy is described in Söderberg and Vaara (2003) concerning a Swedish-Finnish bank merger. Initially, Swedish was chosen as the only language. This was of course advantageous to Swedes, as well as a number of the Finns who were bilingual in Swedish and Finnish.[8] This choice proved to be unsuccessful, however, particularly amongst many Finns who felt they were at a disadvantage with their 'school' Swedish. English was then chosen as the organizational language. These two cases illustrate different language ideologies: the view that bilingualism is unnecessary and the view that English is emancipatory since it is neutral.

The studies reported above are to a great extent based on interviews and questionnaires, and are typical of the view that language and communication somehow reflect organizational reality. In studies of naturally occurring communication, we find not only much greater complexity, but also a fundamental conceptual shift towards the discursive foundations of organizational life and a more holistic, activity-based view of bilingual communication.

2.3.   Interaction in the workplace

Nickerson (1999) shows how email communication within a British subsidary in the Netherlands is written in either English or Dutch depending on organizational needs as well as situational factors. Using audio recordings and observation protocols, Louhiala-Salminen (2002) charts the everyday discursive practices of a bilingual manager in the Finnish branch of a global computer company. It was found that English was used as the lingua franca in the majority of the daily activities, even including writing in a 'Finns only'context.

A closer view of bilingualism in multiparty interactions is provided by Poncini (2003). This study focuses on meetings within an Italian company between company representatives and the company's international distributors. A careful analysis of these meetings reveals the activity-related factors which trigger switches between languages. These triggers are very similar to the principles for language choice presented in section (1) above. Furthermore, the study illustrates a decidedly more European perspective on bilingualism: lingua franca English may be predominately used, but a host of other languages play a subsidiary role (also cf. Lüdi and Heiniger, forthc.; Nussbaum 2003; Unamuno 2005; and Mondada 2004). Mondada, for example, shows how

> linguistic resources are locally selected and used in an accountable way: achieving, sustaining, repairing reflexively the interactional order of international meetings. That order is not dealt with in terms of being difficult/deficient/problematic because of the non-nativeness of its participants, but as an event as it actually emerges and develops (2004: 19).

Mondada's work not only concerns code choice as such; rather it seeks to demonstrate the step by step creation of a bilingual interactional order. We will return to this point below in our discussion of lingua franca studies. Earlier discourse analytical work on communication involving bilingual professionals has mainly sought to investigate interactional challenges due to linguistic and cultural differences.

Linguistic differences are discussed in a volume edited by Ehlich and Wagner (1995). In this volume, Rehbein (1995) describes the institutionalized pattern of buying and selling within French-Dutch business encounters. The study analyzes core activities and ways of handling trouble. Mariott (1995a) takes a similar discourse analytical stance and describes topic development and structure in interactions between an Australian seller and Japanese buyers. Both studies show how linguistic difficulties affect the overall structure of the business interaction. As Rehbein remarks, the success of business interaction can depend on linguistic problems: "My analysis [...] points to the obvious conclusion that the seller should use the buyer's native language if he wishes to influence the latter's decision-making process by verbal means" (1995: 98). The consequence for Rehbein is a plea for multilingual language competence.

Work concerning cultural differences is perhaps best represented in a volume edited by Bargiela-Chiappini and Harris (1997a). Here, in a study of meetings conducted in English within a Hong Kong-based airline, Bilbow (1997) argues that, despite a significant amount of similarity between British and Chinese interactants with regards to the speech acts of directing and requesting, cases of dissimilarity are seen as reflecting the differences between Western and Confucianist value systems. Equivocal findings such as these, especially when juxtaposed with findings from cross-cultural comparisons, such as Bargiela-Chiappini and Harris (1997b), lead the following observation by Bargiela-Chiappini and Harris (1997a: 8): "It would also be fair to assume that native speakers' verbal (and non-verbal) behavior in intralinguistic situations is likely to be different, and possibly very different, from their behavior in interlinguistic ones." It seems that the closer researchers look at interaction in their analysis, the more equivocal their results become. This equivocality is explained in conversation analytical and ethnomethodological work as being due to the fact that cultural difference is a topic of inquiry, rather than a resource for explaining certain phenomena. Another explanation is that interlocutors are 'etically' from different cultures, but 'emically' this difference is apparently not always oriented to by interlocutors. It is this rather fundamental theoretical reorientation which seems to inform a growing body of work within what can be referred to as studies of lingua franca interaction. Much of this work concerns bilingual professionals.

Firth's work (1991, 1995, 1996) has been very influential in this area.[9] Firth (1996) analyzes English as a lingua franca within international commercial workplaces. He maintains that, in spite of the 'non-native', 'marked' or 'abnormal' appearance of work-related talk, interlocutors routinely rely on general, arguably universal, principles of interaction in order to "imbue talk with orderly and 'normal' characteristics", and that interlocutors adapt to each other's language use regardless of its fit with the norms of the relevant cultural groups (i.e. English native speakers). A similar perspective on lingua franca discourse as well as native/non-native interaction is taken, for example, in Meierkord 2000; Gramkow 1993, 2001; Rasmussen and Wagner 2000; Rasmussen 1998, 2000; Wagner 1995a, 1995b. An example is Rasmussen's (1998) study of phone calls in German between a Danish company and a French subsidiary. The thrust of her study is a critique of previous studies of intercultural conflicts which are said to emerge from differences in pragmatic rules between different languages and speech communities. Rasmussen carefully describes how the 'normative' formal address patterns of French and German do not apply, and how interlocutors let "cultural differences pass" (1998: 69). Employees in their talk flout normative principles, as it were. So-called informal address forms are used in the lingua franca German business encounters and do not lead to trouble and conflict, but are contextualized in the intercultural situation.

Similarly, Ramussen and Wagner (2002) show that speakers in the international marketplace have routinized ways of choosing the language of telephone calls. As a default, the language chosen by the answerer in the first turn becomes the language of the call. If a caller wants to change the language which has been offered by the answerer, he may repair the language choice in the first turn. Alternatively, language choice follows person identification – that is, by identifying a known speaker, the language which was used in earlier encounters is chosen again.

3.   Conclusion

Our review reveals that the close analysis of the communicative worklife of bilingual professionals is just beginning. There is much work to be done in exploring the relationships between communicative activity and the interlocutors' use of bilingual resources. Future work in this area should enable us to better understand what bilingual communicative competence entails for professionals, and should provide the basis for more informed decisions concerning company language training and language policy.

As mentioned in the introduction, research on bilingual professionals as summarized in this chapter questions the idea of language as the property of speech communities, of communication outside an activity, and of culture as given: this fits in nicely with current theorizing on language and communication in an increasingly globalized world. Blommaert (2003: 610) sees the challenge of a sociolinguistics of globalization as follows: "We have to deal with niched sociolinguistic phenomena related to the insertion of particular varieties of language in existing repertoires, and also with the language ideological load both guiding the process and being one of its results." The bilingual professional and his or her communicative doings would appear to be a part of just the sort of sociolinguistic phenomena to which Blommaert is referring.

Notes

1. Hereafter we will use the terms 'bilingual' and 'bilingualism' despite the fact that they may refer to individuals and situations involving more than two languages.
2. 'Elite bilingualism', for example, has been used for middle class children who are sent to international schools to acquire high prestige languages (de Mejía 2002: 5, quoting Paulston 1975 and Skutnabb-Kangas 1981). Heller (1994) describes middle class families in Canada who view an education in the other Canadian language as a way of giving their children more symbolic capital – and thus an edge in the pursuit of professional success.

3. The project *Global Communication in Danish Organizations* is led by Dennis Day and is partially funded by a grant from the Danish Humanities Research Council.
4. This is evident in Kubota's (2001) report of attempts to train American managers in 'International' English.
5. Eurobarometer 54 Special: Europeans and Languages is the report of a large-scale questionnaire study produced for the The Education and Culture Directorate-General of the EU by International Research Associates (INRA). It is available at http://europa.eu.int/comm/education/policies/lang/languages/barolang _en.pdf.
6. A challenge to this distinction between non-native and lingua franca use of a language is offered in Day (2003).
7. The first two views are not new to scholars of the sociology of language, since they encapsulate the two opposing views of the role of English as either hegemonic or emancipatory in an increasingly globalized world. The linguistic situation of bilingual professionals should provide an interesting empirical ground for studying these views. For a cogent discussion see Lysandrou and Lysandrou (2003).
8. Finland is officially bilingual (Finnish and Swedish) and Swedish is an obligatory subject in Finnish schools.
9. For a different perspective on lingua franca discourse, see Knapp and Meierkord (2002).

References

Bargiela-Chiappini, Francesca and Sandra Harris (eds.)
  1997a   *The Languages of Business: An international perspective.* Edinburgh: Edinburgh University Press.
Bargiela-Chiappini, Francesca and Sandra Harris
  1997b   *Managing Language: The Discourse of Corporate Meetings.* Philadelphia: John Benjamins.
Bargiela-Chiappini, Francesca and Catherine Nickerson
  2003   Intercultural business communication: a rich field of studies. *Journal of Intercultural Studies*, 24 (1): 3–15.
Barner-Rasmussen, Wilhelm and Sanne Bor
  2005   Language in multilingual organizations – a review of the management and organization literature. Paper presented at *The 18th Scandinavian Academy of Management Meeting* (NFF), Aarhus School of Business, Denmark 18–20 August.
Belcher, Diane and Ulla Connor (eds.)
  2001   *Reflections on Multiliterate Lives.* Clevedon: Multilingual Matters
Bilbow, Grahame T.
  1997   Cross-cultural impression management in the multicultural workplace: the special case of Hong Kong. *Journal of Pragmatics* 28: 461–487.
Blommaert, Jan
  2003   Commentary: A sociolinguistics of globalization. *Journal of Sociolinguistics* 7 (4): 607–623.
Blum Kulka, Shoshana, Juliane Edmondson-House and Gabriele Kasper (eds.)
  1989   *Cross-Cultural Pragmatics: Requests and Apologies.* Norwood, N.J.: Ablex.

Boxer, Diana
  2002   *Applying Sociolinguistics: Domain and Face to Face Interaction.* Amsterdam/Philadelphia: John Benjamins.
Bremer, Katharina, Celia Roberts, Marie-Thérèse Vasseur, Margaret Simonot and Peter Broeder
  1996   *Achieving Understanding: Discourse in Intercultural Encounters.* London: Longmans.
Brouwer, Catherine E., Gitte Rasmussen and Johannes Wagner
  2004   Embedded corrections in second language talk. In: Rod Gardner and Johannes Wagner (eds.), 2004, 75–92.
Collins, James and Stef Slembrouck
  2005   Multilingualism and diasporic populations: Spatializing practices, institutional processes, and social hierarchies. *Language and Communication* 25: 189–195.
Cook, Vivian (ed.)
  2002   *Portraits of the L2 User.* Clevedon: Multilingual Matters.
Davis, K. and R. Henze
  1998   Applying ethnographic perspectives to issues in cross-cultural pragmatics. *Journal of Pragmatics* 30: 399–419.
Day, Dennis
  2003   Owning a language and lingua franca discourse. In: Alan Firth (ed.) *Language Travels: A Festschrift for Torben Vestergaard,* 77–88. Aalborg: Department of languages and intercultural studies, Aalborg University.
de Mejía, Anne-Marie
  2002   *Power, Prestige and Bilingualism.* Clevedon: Multilingual Matters.
Drew, Paul and John Heritage (eds.)
  1992   *Talk at Work. Interaction in Institutional Settings.* Cambridge: Cambridge University Press.
Ehlich, Konrad and Johannes Wagner (eds.)
  1995   *The Discourse of Business Negotiation.* Berlin: Mouton de Gruyter.
Firth, Alan
  1991   *Discourse at Work. Negotiating by Telex, Fax and Phone.* Unpublished Ph.D. dissertation, Aalborg University, Denmark.
Firth, Alan (ed.)
  1995a   *The Discourse of Negotiation.* Oxford: Pergamon.
Firth, Alan
  1995b   Talking for a change: commodity negotiating by telephone. In: Alan Firth (ed.), 1995a, 183–222.
Firth, Alan
  1995c   Telenegotiation and sense-making in the 'virtual markedplace'. In: Konrad Ehlich and Johannes Wagner (eds.), 1995, 127–149.
Firth, Alan
  1996   The discursive accomplishment of normality: On "lingua franca" English and conversation analysis. In: Johannes Wagner (ed.) Special issue *of Pragmatics* Volume 26: 237–258.
Gardner, Rod and Johannes Wagner (eds.)
  2004   *Second Language Conversations.* London: Continuum.

Global companies look for more bilingual executives
   April 2005   *Expansion Management.* p. 2.
Gramkow Andersen, Karsten
   1993   *Lingua Franca Discourse: An Investigation of the Use of English in an International Business Context.* Aalborg: Aalborg Universitet.
Gramkow Andersen, Karsten
   2001   *The Joint Production of Conversation: Turn-Sharing and Collaborative Overlap in Encounters Between Non-Native Speakers of English.* Aalborg: Centre for Languages and Intercultural Studies, Aalborg University.
Gumperz, John J.
   1982   *Discourse Strategies.* Cambridge: University Press.
Halmari, Helena
   1993   Intercultural business telephone conversations: a case of Finns vs. Anglo-Americans. *Applied Linguistics* 44(4): 408–430.
Harzing, Anne-Wil
   2001   Of bears, bumble-bees, and spiders: the role of expatriates in controlling foreign subsidiaries. *Journal of World Business* 36/4: 366–379.
Heller, Monica
   1994   *Crosswords. Language, Education and Ethnicity in French Ontario.* Berlin: Mouton de Gruyter.
Kasper, Gabriele and Merete Dahl
   1991   Research methods in interlanguage pragmatics. *Studies in Second Language Acquisition* 13(2): 215–247.
Kellerman, Eric, Monique van der Haagen and Hella Koonen
   2005   'Feet speak louder than the tongue'; A preliminary analysis of language provisions for foreign footballers in the Netherlands. In: M. Long (ed.) *Second Language Needs Analysis*, 200–224. Cambridge: University Press.
Knapp, Konrad and Christiane Meierkord (eds.)
   2002   *Lingua Franca Communication.* New York: Peter Lang.
Kubota, Ryuko
   2001   Teaching world Englishes to native speakers of English in the USA. *World Englishes* Volume 20:1: 47–64.
Lakha, Salim and Michael Stevenson
   2001   Indian identity in multicultural Melbourne. Some preliminary observations. *Journal of Intercultural Studies* 22, 3.
Louhiala-Salminen, Leena
   2002   The fly's perspective: discourse in the daily routine of a bisness manager. *English for Specific Purposes* 21: 211–231.
Lüdi, Georges and Monika S. Heiniger
   (forthc.)   L'organisation de la communication au sein d'une banque régionale bilingue. *Sociolinguistica* 19.
Lysandrou, Photis and Yvonne Lysandrou
   2003   Global English and proregression: understanding English language spread in the contemporary era. *Economy and Society* 32, 2: 207–233.
Mariott, Helen
   1995a   The management of discourse in international seller-buyer negotiations. In: Konrad Ehlich and Johannes Wagner (eds.), 1995, 103–126.

Mariott, Helen
  1995b   'Deviations' in an intercultural business negotiation. In: Alan Firth (ed.), 1995a, 247–270.
Marschan-Piekkari, Rebecca, D. Welch and L. Welch
  1999a   In the shadow: the impact of language on structure, power and communication in the multinational. *International Business Review* 8: 421–440.
Marschan-Piekkari, Rebecca, D. Welch and L. Welch
  1999b   Adopting a common corporate language: IHRM implications. *The International Journal of Human Resource Management* 10/3: 377–390.
Marschan, Rebecca, D. Welch and L. Welch
  1997   Language: the forgotten factor in multinational management. *European Management Journal* 15, 5: 591–598.
Meierkord, Christiane
  2000   Interpreting successful lingua franca interaction. An analysis of non-native-/non-native small talk conversations in English. *Linguistik online* 5, 1/00. http://www.linguistik-online.de/1_00/MEIERKOR.HTM
Milhouse, Virginia H.
  1996   Intercultural Communication education and training goals, content, and methods. *International Journal of Intercultural Relations* 20, 1: 169–95.
Mondada, Lorenza
  2004   Ways of 'doing being plurilingual' in international work meetings, In: Rod Gardner and Johannes Wagner (eds.), *Second Language Conversations*, 27–60. London: Continuum.
Murata, K.
  1994   Intrusive or co-operative? A cross-cultural study of interruption. *Journal of Pragmatics* 21: 385–400.
Nickerson, Catherine
  1998   Corporate culture and the use of written English within British subsidiaries in the Netherlands. *English for Specific Purposes* 17, 3: 281–294.
Nickerson, Catherine
  1999   The use of English in electronic mail in a multinational corporation, In: Francesca Bargiela-Chiappini and Catherine Nickerson (eds.), *Writing Business: Genre, Media and Discourses,* 35–56. Harlow, Essex: Longman.
Nussbaum, L.
  2003   Immigration et dynamiques polyglossiques en Catalogne. In: L. Mondada and S. Pekarek-Doehler (eds.), *Plurilinguisme – Mehrsprachigkeit – Plurilingualism. Enjeux identitaires, socio-culturels et éducatifs. Festschrift pour Georges Lüdi*, 15–28. Francke. Tübingen.
Pavlenko, Aneta and Adrian Blackledge (eds.)
  2004   *Negotiation of Identities in Multilingual Contexts*. Clevedon: Multilingual Matters.
Poncini, Gina
  2003   Multicultural business meetings and the role of languages other than English. *Journal of Intercultural Studies* 24, 1: 17–32.
Rasmussen, Gitte
  1998   The use of address forms in intercultural business conversation. *Revue de Semantique et Pragmatique* 3: 57–72.

Rasmussen, Gitte
  2000   *Zur Bedeutung kultureller Unterschiede in interlingualen und interkulturellen Gesprächen.* München: Iudicium.
Rasmussen, Gitte and Johannes Wagner
  2002   Language choice in international telephone conversations. In: K. K. Luke and Th. Pavlidou (eds.), *Telephone Calls. Unity and Diversity in Conversational Structure Across Languages and Cultures,* 111–131. Amsterdam: John Benjamins.
Rehbein, Jochen
  1995   International sales talk. In: Konrad Ehlich and Johannes Wagner (eds.), 1995, 67–102.
Roberts, Celia, Evelyn Davies and Tom Jupp
  1992   *Language and Discrimination. A Study of Communication in Multi-ethnic Workplaces.* London: Longman.
Söderberg, A.-M. and E. Vaara (eds.)
  2003   *Merging Across Borders: People, Cultures and Politics.* Copenhagen: Copenhagen Business School Press.
Spencer-Oatey, Helen and Jianyu Xing
  1998   Relational management in Chinese–British business meetings, In: Susan Hunston (ed.), *Language at Work: Selected Papers from the Annual Meeting of the British Association for Applied Linguistics Held at the University of Birmingham,* September 1997, 31–55. Clevedon: Multilingual Matters.
Twitchen, J., J. Gumperz, T.C. Jupp and Celia Roberts
  1979   *Cross Talk.* BBC.
Unamuno, Virginia
  2005   L'entorn sociolingüístic i la construcció dels repertoris lingüístics de l'alumnat immigrat a Catalunyas. *Noves SL. Revista de Sociolingüística,* http://www.gencat.net/presidencia/llengcat/novese, Primavera-estiu 2005e.
Wagner, Johannes
  1995a   What makes a discourse a negotiation? In: Konrad Ehlich and Johannes Wagner (eds.), 1995, 9–36.
Wagner, Johannes
  1995b   Negotiating activity in technical problem solving. In: Alan Firth (ed.), 1995a, 223–246.
Wagner, Johannes et al.
  (2004)   Sportsmigrants and their clubs. Paper given at the 12th Sociolinguistic Symposium, Newcastle.
Yamada, H.
  1990   Topic management and turn distribution in business meetings: American versus Japanese strategies. *Text* 10(3): 271–295.

16. Multilingualism in the workplace

Celia Roberts

1. Introduction

The multilingual workplace has been a site for educational intervention rather than for research. Indeed much of the research has arisen out of practical issues that relate to language training for workers. So, this chapter will look both at research projects and at the larger and often more informal literature from project evaluations and descriptions of educational programmes. Since much of the research is dependent on opportunities for workplace education, the studies of workplace multilingualism depend upon the vicissitudes of government policy initiatives on adult basic skills training. So, for example, in the English speaking world, during the 1980s and 1990s, Australia took the lead in developing second language programmes in the workplace and consequently there is a richer research literature from that area. The more critical accounts of language use and training in these settings also connect to the literature on linguistic ideologies as it relates to 'linguicism' (Skutnabb-Kangas and Phillipson 1995) and the dominant language requirements of the workplace. Applied linguistics in these contexts is not just about using linguistics to analyse real world contexts but about the practical relevance of applied linguistic studies in bringing about change.

This chapter will focus on shopfloor and service industry settings, including the health service, where, traditionally, migrant workers have found jobs and where status and work identity has been constructed not by their educational and background qualifications but by gaps in the labour market: a teacher may be a postal worker, a farmer may be a factory worker, a doctor may be a care assistant. These are also contexts where the factory line or the supermarket may be truly multilingual or where 'ethnic work units' mean that only one minority language is spoken. The research on intercultural communication in international settings will not be included as this is the subject of chapter 15 of this handbook.

The following brief case study illustrates some of the research and practical issues raised in the chapter. A large engineering company in the UK was investigated because a group of mainly Gujarati speakers had accused it of discriminating against them in promotion interviews. The shopfloor workers were predominately Gujarati speakers with some local English speakers but the company required those seeking promotion to foremen to go through a formal interview in English. Ethnographic observations and recordings of shopfloor communication and promotion interviews were collected to establish whether the latter required greater skills than the former. The research showed that the interview, characterised by indirectness and stylised truthfulness, in which issues of face were paramount, was discriminatory. The South Asian applicants, who could communicate clearly on the shopfloor, both in English and Gujarati, were disadvantaged by the linguistic demands and implicit conventions of the interview. This case illustrated the legal and wider political dimensions of the multilingual workplace – there is a linguistic dimension to discrimination and exclusion – and used interactional sociolinguistic theory and method to illuminate this process (Brierley et al. 1992).

2.   Overview of the field

The workplace has been transformed over the last fifty years, particularly but by no means exclusively in the western world, from a monolingual to a multilingual setting. The response to this has been a largely functional one: how can organisations run effectively and safely unless workers can communicate in the dominant language of the workplace (Alcorso 2002)? Most activity has centred on language training or, more widely, on attempting to change the communicative environment. However, employers have also adapted to the multilingual workforce in other ways: translating notices and manuals, using both professional and informal interpreters and using bilingual supervisors (Dicker 1998; Collins and Slembrouck in press; Mawer 1999). As well as descriptions of educational interventions, there has also been a critical strand which has raised questions about who benefits, and which critiques the hegemony of 'English/ Danish/German etc. only' policies in the workplace.

As the makeup of the workforce has changed, so has the whole work context. Increased use of technologies, more multi-tasking, more flexible work practices, flattened structures and a more textualised workplace have created new language and literacy demands which affect even the manual worker. The 'new work order' (Gee, Hull and Lankshear 1996) has created a 'new word order' (Farrell 2001) which often takes little account of the multilingual workplace. Similarly, as part of the development of new work genres, there is an increase in the oral and literacy demands of the selection, promotion and appraisal of basic manual and service jobs. These 'gatekeeping' functions (Erickson and Shultz 1982) have also been a focus for research both at manual and professional levels where linguistic minorities are required to perform in the majority language, often in discourses not required in the job itself, as the brief example above shows.

Since the 1980s there has been a burgeoning literature of discourse-based sociolinguistic studies of workplace interaction in healthcare, business and law (Coleman 1989; Fisher and Todd 1983). This literature has been dominated by Conversational Analysis (CA) and has particularly focused on professional communication in healthcare and medicine and decision making (Drew and Heritage 1992). Virtually none of these studies are based in the multilingual workplace and there have been virtually no variationist sociolinguistic studies of workplace multilingual language use. More recently, studies of language/interaction in the workplace, for example the New Zealand Language in the Work-Place Project, have studied the wider issues where multilingualism is the norm and so is a factor in examining the communicative environment.

The studies of the multilingual workplace have drawn on three main theoretical/methodological approaches: pragmatics, interactional sociolinguistics and linguistic ethnography. Many of the studies blend aspects of all three and are broadly informed by a critical perspective and how workers "engage critically with the conditions of their working lives" (Cope and Kalantzis 1995: 26). A critical discourse analysis examines the new work order and how it is constructing new work roles and identities (Fairclough 1989; Sarangi and Slembrouck 1996). The colonisation of workplace practices by competing discourses may have a particular impact on the culturally and linguistically diverse workplace where, for example, gatekeeping interviews are turned into 'little chats' (Fairclough 1992; Wodak 1996).

The Pragmatics literature on speech acts has been used in contrastive analyses of lingua franca settings where workers from both European and Asian backgrounds have to manage shopfloor interaction and meetings (Clyne 1994; Day 1992; Willing 1992). Levinson (1983) argues that there are systematic pragmatic constraints which largely determine how speakers make inferences from each others' contributions. These are partly determined by Gricean assumptions of rational efficiency and 'face' wants and needs (Brown and Levinson 1987). The New Zealand project has made a particular study of facework in multilingual workplaces (Newton, Daley, Holmes and Stubbs 2004). Some of the pragmatics studies (for example Clyne 1994, see below) identify patterns of difference between different cultural groups whereas others, for example Day 1992, argue that orientation to the workgroup and the specific demands of workplace meetings often override cultural factors.

Drawing on pragmatics and the ethnography of communication, interactional sociolinguistics (IS) links macro issues of inequality and sociological notions of ethnicity and social identity with micro issues of the 'interaction order' and CA ideas of sequential organisation (Gumperz 1982a and b, 1997). Small interactional moments can have large social consequences when inferential processes and conditions for negotiating are not shared, as is often the case when the majority language is the required means of communication in the linguistically diverse workplace (Roberts et al. 1992; Holmes 2000). Misunderstandings and negative social evaluations arise when the 'contextualisation cues' (Gumperz 1992a and b) that channel the inferential process are not agreed on. These cues signal what is to be expected in an exchange, what meanings can be implicitly conveyed and how interpersonal relations and social identities are to be managed (Gumperz 1996: 396). The most important, and paradoxically most hidden, are prosodic cues and for this reason intercultural awareness programmes for multilingual workplaces (see below) include quite technical matters. Whereas the methods for pragmatically informed studies focus on audio taped recordings and speech act analysis, interactional sociolinguistic methodology includes a period of ethnographic observation to establish the 'communicative ecology' of the workplace (Gumperz 1999). Decisions on what recorded material to focus on and feedback accounts of interaction are also ethnographically informed.

IS methodology links to the last of the three approaches: linguistic ethnography. Studies of workplace multilingualism have drawn on traditional anthropological ethnography (Wallman 1979; Westwood and Bhachu 1988) but use ethnographic tools (Green and Bloome 1997) rather than full blown ethnographic studies, and micro-ethnography (Erickson and Shultz 1982). Practitioners engaged in language audits of an organisation (Mawer 1999) have also used ethnographic methods to establish the range of languages spoken/used in organisations. Two of the studies described in more detail below, Goldstein's and Hull's, have used linguistically informed ethnography (see Goldstein 1997; Hull 1996).

3.   Controversial issues

The focus here is on three areas of debate: the relative paucity of research on multilingual workplaces, the controversies around the relationship between language and cultural practices and the tensions around the scope and stance of the practitioner in these workplaces. Firstly, why are workplaces so little used as research sites compared with educational, community and family settings? There are both ideological and practical reasons which interconnect. Many organisations will not allow access unless they can see the benefits and researchers may be ill-equipped or uncomfortable as business consultants. Practically, these are difficult sites to research in because of noise, work routines and issues of confidentiality. And yet these are some of the most exciting research sites where language practices and struggles over social, political and legal language rights are constantly evolving.

Secondly, there are the perennial debates around language/cultural practices which are of course by no means confined to multilingualism at work. Both practically and theoretically, there has been a tension between separating language and culture, on the one hand, and, on the other, seeing them as "wired in together" (Agar 1994). Constructivist theories, critical cultural studies and talk in interaction studies both critique homogenising notions of 'culture' and treat language and cultural practices as interconnected through discourse. Urban argues for "a discourse-centred approach to culture" (Urban 1991: 1) in which "culture is localised in concrete, publicly accessible signs, the most important of which are actually occurring instances of discourse" and this is similar to Gumperz's notion of "discourse-centred cultural knowledge" (Gumperz 1996: 402). Essentialist notions of culture, many of which stem from stereotypes of different language groups, have to be engaged with and "recognised for what they are: ideological formations" (Gumperz 1996: 401).

A common sense view of 'culture' widely held on the shopfloor assumes that everyone belongs to one culture which explains differences and problems. Language and cultural differences are seen as brought into interactions from the outside rather than "talked into being" (Auer and Kern 2000). The explanatory power of language and culture as opposed to other factors such as workplace identities, the functional demands of the job and the team and so on remains open to debate.

Addressing the commonplace ethnicised discourses of the workplace raises the third area of controversy: the scope and stance of the workplace-based practitioner. One position is that of the second language trainer who, relatively unproblematically, uses the workplace as a context for improving the second language skills of workers. Another position is one that more closely aligns to the concerns of the organisation and which holds that any educational intervention must be linked to wider initiatives which benefit both the employer and the workforce (Mawer 1999). A third position takes a more critical stance, challenging the hegemony of the dominant language and questioning who really benefits from language courses and language audits (Goldstein 1997; Harper, Pierce and Burnaby 1996; Tollefson 1991). All three positions are illustrated in current practice but the second and third are more frequently found since the 1990s.

4.   Applied research perspectives

This section will look at three sets of studies which exemplify some of the issues raised above: pragmatics studies based in Australian workplaces, ethnographic studies in North America and gatekeeping studies set in the UK.

4.1.   Pragmatics

The first of these is Clyne's study of English as lingua franca in multilingual workplaces in Australia (Clyne 1994). The analysis concentrates on speech acts of complaints, commissives, directives and apologies. The systematic ways in which speech acts are realised cross-culturally are related to turn-taking and negotiating. Three different communicative styles are identified: style A represented by European speakers and Spanish speaking Latin Americans, style B represented by speakers from South Asia and style C from South-East Asia. The latter group is claimed to be at a particular disadvantage since they are less likely to assert themselves, and directives and complaints addressed to them tend to be longer and more explicit than those directed to other groups (Clyne 1994: 153).

The different discourse patterns across the groups can be attributed to "sociocultural international parameters" such as harmony and uncertainly avoidance and to "discourse cultural parameters" such as explicit orientation to topic and degree of linearity (203). These patterns vary as much across different ethnic groups as they do between these groups and the majority Anglo-Australian group. As a result, Clyne argues that educational interventions should include dealing with different communicative styles and dealing with pragmatic breakdowns (see also Duff, Wong and Early 2000; Roberts et al. 1992; and Li 2002).

A second study is Willing's research on professional problem solving in Australia (Willing 1992, 1997). Here English is the dominant language and Willing is contrasting linguistic problem solving strategies between the white majority and linguistic minority staff. In white-collar problem solving there are a range of subtle linguistic skills which make the speaker relatively persuasive or not. For example, the degree of cognitive commitment to suggestions depends crucially on modality. He argues that it is difficult to distinguish clearly between epistemic and politeness modality and recommends that there should be more concentration on modality in language courses.

4.2.   Ethnographic studies in North America

The first of these is a study of Portuguese factory workers and their relationship with supervision and quality assurance staff (Goldstein 1997). This study challenges the assumption that English competence is necessary to communicate in the workplace or indeed for promotion. Drawing on the notion of the political economy of language choice from a feminist perspective, Goldstein argues that language choice is not a purely practical one. The choice between Portuguese or English depends upon the symbolic value of each language and the structural positions of the workers. Within the factory, there is a "Portuguese manufacturing family" and Portuguese serves as a means of maintaining ethnic identity and solidarity. Language choice helps to maintain boundaries, with code-switching used strategically to cross boundaries. However, since most workers choose to remain on the line, Portuguese is endowed with authority as the language of friendship and survival on the shopfloor.

English classes improve language ability but are unlikely to lead to promotion since a high level of education is required. Goldstein concludes that if English language training is only part of the hegemonic process that gives English even more power and marginalizes limited speakers of English then it needs to be challenged. A somewhat similar conclusion from Harper et al.'s study in a Canadian garment factory (1996) suggests that the newly acquired English language skills reinforced traditional relationships between workers and management and men and women. A more critical pedagogy is required (Belfiore and Burnaby 1984; Bell 1995) which does not undercut the values of the minority language.

The second study is of literacy practices within the "new work order" (Hull 1997) in a computer components company in Silicon Valley (Hull 1996). The restructuring of the workplaces with new forms of organisation and new technologies requires new literacy skills and finely-tuned oral language abilities both for the production line and in training. The new focus on literacy often entails literacy assessment which can label workers as less competent than they are in doing the job and can block promotion (Hull 1996, 1997; Katz 2000). Hull's study of the language and literacy requirements of training for teamwork and of the team meetings themselves showed that no account had been taken of the linguistically diverse workforce, many of whom had no voice in the proceedings.

4.3.   Gatekeeping studies in the UK

The multilingual workplace is also a site where indirect discrimination can take place as formal means of assessment and selection become increasingly common. The job interview is a high-stake encounter in which different communicative styles (Gumperz et al 1979) and different discourses (Birkner 2004) can lead to negative evaluation and failure. The search for a coherent version of the candidate which is bureaucratically processible disadvantages the linguistic minority candidate since both their communicative style and previous experience are read as inconsistent and/or incoherent (Roberts and Campbell 2006).

There are many other oral assessment sites particularly in the health service. The preparation, training and assessment of minority ethnic healthcare professionals, particularly those educated overseas, raises questions about the adequacy and fairness of these high-stake intercultural encounters. Routinely, the linguistic and socio-cultural demands of these encounters are played down and the potential for indirect discrimination overlooked (Duff et al. 2000). The discursive resistances that linguistic minority nurses and doctors face include language testing (McNamara 1997), interviews for supervised practice and for additional training.

An example of this in the UK is the oral examination for membership of the Royal College of General Practitioners (Roberts and Sarangi 1999). Video recordings of the examinations were analysed using interactional sociolinguistic methods. The study concluded that the "hybrid discourses" of the exam were particularly problematic for non-traditional candidates, especially those trained overseas. The exam consisted of three different modes of question: institutional, professional and personal. However, the exam criteria were institutionally driven. For those candidates not used to the institutional discourses of gatekeeping oral assessments, however proficient they were as doctors, the examination remained an unfair hurdle.

5.   The contribution of applied linguistics

Most of the workplace studies already referred to have practical relevance in terms of educational and training programmes. In this section, we will look at second language teaching and learning and at awareness training for gatekeepers and management. We will also look at the contribution applied linguistics has made to the legal issue of majority-language-only requirements in the workplace.

Where language courses have been run using the multilingual workplace as a convenient setting, there has been little opportunity to analyse the communicative environment and there is often little impact on either individuals or the environment as a whole. However, where "the workplace is the curriculum" (Mawer 1999), there has been much greater involvement in researching the workplace and consequently more influence from applied and sociolinguistic theory and methodology. One example of this broader approach is illustrated in the Odysseus project which describes second language projects in Finland, Germany, Latvia, Poland, Spain, Sweden and Switzerland. However, the project report concludes that "the participating countries are relatively weak on (...) research into workplace language in our own countries" compared with the developments in the English speaking countries (Grünhage-Monetti et al. 2003: 66).

Another significant source of insights into multilingualism in the workplace comes from evaluation reports of second language training. For example, some studies suggest that language courses provide a level of economic protection and improve chances of new employment (Belfiore 1993; Goldstein 1993) and that they can reduce reliance on language brokers and give workers more of a voice when dealing with conflicts over production (Pierce, Harper and Burnaby 1993). Other studies have concentrated on workers' perceived benefits for themselves and their families (Benseman 1998). Some evaluations have been more critical of the status quo – aligning with the studies mentioned above. The more limited language courses are criticised for too narrow a focus (Bell 1995; Katz 2000). Some authors report a gap between workers' perceptions and government policy on the one hand and employers' demands for high levels of the second language on the other (Hawthorne 1997).

A common recommendation from these evaluations is for some intervention which will have an impact on those with relatively more communicative power, more linguistic capital, in the workplace: managers, supervision, trade unions and the gatekeepers who control access to jobs and promotion. Since interactions are jointly accomplished, it is argued that speakers of the majority language need to change as well. However, the capacity to reflect consciously on language and to develop a metapragmatic awareness is not a regular part of people's analytic repertoire. Pauwels (1994), for example, found that Australian health workers on awareness courses could identify broad differences in beliefs and values and could talk about different 'accents', but were much more challenged by the analysis of discourse and pragmatic features and prosody.

There have been resistances to workplace language/cultural awareness courses over the last twenty years. Nevertheless, there have been persistent attempts to use awareness raising to challenge linguistically based negative ethnic stereotyping (Belfiore and Heller 1992; Byrne and Fitzgerald 1996; Cope et al. 1993; Gumperz and Roberts 1980; McGregor and Williams 1984; Pauwels 1994; Roberts, Davies and Jupp 1992). The contribution to these courses from interactional sociolinguistics led to a series of BBC films between 1979 and 1992 which used naturally occurring and reconstructed interactions to show the interconnection of cultural assumptions, discourse level processing and features, particularly prosodic features, of the linguistic code.

6.   Linguistic rights in the workplace

The right to use minority languages in the workplace is a matter both of tolerance and rights and organisational efficiency. Many organisations make local decisions but the issue of linguistic human rights (Skutnaab-Kangas and Phillipson 1995; Phillipson, Rannut and Skutnaab-Kangas 1995) in some countries, most notably the USA, has been widely debated (Dicker 1998). The extent to which organisations adapt to or suppress multilingualism (Thomas and Gregory 1993) reflects their more general attitude to minority ethnic workers. For example, Burger King is praised for allowing interpreters into the job selection process but there is doubt over whether the company as a whole has adapted to being a multilingual, multicultural organisation at all levels (Dicker 1998).

By contrast with companies that adapt, there are those that have adopted 'English only' practices. Although employees have sued their companies for this and have been supported by the Equal Employment Opportunity Commission, the courts have by no means always supported these claims: "English-only work rules have received favourable review by the courts; they represent a viable, although perhaps not widely popular solution to workplace multilingualism" (Dicker 1998: 296). Arguments used to bolster English-only and Official-English legislation and use – that the status of English is being eroded, that immigrants are not making efforts to fit in – are not supported by the literature (Dicker 1998: 297). Similar arguments and counter arguments are currently played out in other English speaking countries such as the UK and Australia. And, as in the USA, the changes in attitude and policy and economic demands over successive periods have an impact on how multilingualism is viewed in the workplace and therefore also on the opportunities (or not) for greater tolerance, or even encouragement of linguistic diversity, and for second language learning and wider changes in the communicative environment.

7.   Conclusion

The multilingual workplace is an important and underresearched strategic site. Most applied linguistic research in this area has been practitioner-led, and this has been both a strength and a weakness. It has encouraged practical relevance in a discipline area where, despite the name 'applied', contribution to change has often been more honoured in the breech than in the observance. However, it has also limited the scope and stance of research, and because provision is so vulnerable to the vicissitudes of political and economic trends, it is hard to sustain and grow a body of literature.

Multilingual institutions, such as workplaces, are prime sites for exploring multilingual language use and for examining the processes of second language socialisation (Clyne and Ball 1990; Duff et al. 2000). In the case of the latter, they provide opportunities for researching lingua franca use as well as the more traditional models of language socialisation. However, second language socialisation with its apprenticeship model is increasingly problematised in workplaces where the dominant language of the country or region is not heard in its 'native speaker' variety on the shopfloor. So newcomers are not socialised into the standard or local variety of the dominant language but hear many languages and much 'crossing' between languages. More research is clearly needed here.

This raises questions of methodology. The interactive patterns of workplace language are audio and occasionally video recorded, as these recordings are necessary to undertake any detailed discourse analytic work and are increasingly used in interlanguage pragmatics studies. However, as Cicourel (1992) and Hak (1999) have argued, such recordings limit what is to be counted as relevant data; the recorded data becomes the object of scrutiny and everything else is backgrounded. Rather, as Hak argues, we should think about how the particular environment we are studying looks from the perspectives of those who work in it. Ethnography and specifically linguistic ethnography allies the focus on recorded and analysed discourse with a study of the communicative ecology of the workplace and the subjectivities that sustain it.

Access to the shopfloor, the meeting place or the job interview room continues to be difficult and the price of entry is often to produce findings that may benefit the employer as well as improving the life chances of minority workers. However, there is also a critical dimension, which consists both in helping to develop a critical understanding of participants' own working lives and a critical stance on the hidden effects on relations of power (Kalantzis and Brosnan 1993; Goldstein 1993; Pierce 1989, Pierce et al. 1993). Awareness training, particularly in gatekeeping settings, is one area where the adaptive employer can meet the more critical stance of the applied socio-linguist. However, intercultural communication itself can feed into essentialising notions of language/culture unless the notion of interculturality is itself critiqued. Cultural or ethnic background is not a given in intercultural/interlingual encounters, it is only significant if made relevant in the interaction. For example, Day's analysis shows that identities that relate to a particular work group override cultural or national identities. What mattered in the workplace meetings was how to construct the event as a meeting rather than any particular cultural take on the interaction (Day 1992).

The multilingual workplace is increasingly the norm in our evermore globalised economy. However, access to it as a research site may remain difficult, and it is likely that the imperatives of organisational efficiency, particularly in the form of second language training, will continue to be the main pathway in. It will remain a site of struggle with the relationship between dominant and minority language use played out across issues of identity, rights and opportunities. Practical and ideological positions continue to be in tension both for workers, organisations and applied linguists in an area of multilingualism where we still know relatively little.

References

Agar, Michael
    1994   *Language Shock.* New York: William Morrow.
Alcorso, Caroline
    2002   Improving occupational health and safety information to immigrant workers in New South Wales. *Working Paper 78.* ACIRRT. University of Sydney.
Auer, Peter
    1998   Learning how to play the game: An investigation of role-played job interviews in East Germany. *Text* 18 (1): 7–38.
Auer, Peter and Aldo di Luzio (eds.)
    1992   *The Contextualization of Language.* Amsterdam: Benjamins.

416   Celia Roberts

Auer, Peter and Frederike Kern
    2000   Three ways of analysing communication between East and West Germans
            as intercultural communication. In: Aldo di Luzio and Susanne Günthner
            (eds.), *Culture in Communication: Analysis of Intercultural Situations,*
            89–116. Amsterdam: John Benjamins.
Belfiore, Mary
    1992   *The Changing World of Work Research Project.* Toronto: Ontario Ministry
            of Citizenship.
    1993   The changing world of work research project. *TESL Talk* 21: 2–20.
Belfiore, Mary and Barbara Burnaby
    1984   *Teaching English in the Workplace.* Toronto: OISE Press/Hodder and
            Stoughton.
Belfiore, Mary and Monica Heller
    1992   Cross-cultural interviews: Participation and decision making. In: Barbara
            Burnaby and Alisdair Cumming (eds.), *Socio-political Aspects of ESL,*
            233–240. Toronto: OISE Press/Hodder and Stoughton.
Bell, Judith
    1995   Canadian experiences of training linguistically diverse populations for the
            workplace. *Australian Review of Applied Linguistics* 18 (1): 35–51.
Benseman, John
    1998   *Voices for the Workplace.* Aukland: Workbase: The National Centre for
            Workplace Literacy and Language.
Birkner, Karin
    2004   Hegemonic struggles or transfer of knowledge? East and West Germans in
            job interviews *Journal of Language and Politics* 3 (2): 293–322.
Brierley, Clarice, Sardul Dhesi and Valarie Yates
    1992   Ethnographic and linguistic analysis applied: a case study. In: Celia Ro-
            berts, Evelyn Davies and Tom Jupp, 224–245.
Brown, Penelope and Stephen Levinson
    1987   *Politeness: Some Universals in Language Usage.* Cambridge: Cambridge
            University Press.
Byrne, Margaret and Helen Fitzgerald
    1996   *What Makes You Say That?* Canberra: Special Broadcasting Services.
Cicourel, Aaron
    1992   The interpenetration of communicative contexts: examples from medical
            encounters. In: Alessandro Duranti and Charles Goodwin (eds.), *Rethinking
            Context: Language as an Interactive Phenomenon,* 291–310. Cambridge:
            Cambridge University Press.
Clyne, Michael
    1994   *Inter-cultural Communication at Work: Cultural Values in Discourse.* Cam-
            bridge: Cambridge University Press.
Clyne, Michael and Martin Ball
    1990   English as a lingua franca in Australia, especially in industry. *ARAL* 7: 1–15.
Collins, James and Slembrouck, Stef
    (in press) 'You don't know what they translate': Language, contact, institutional pro-
            cedure, and literacy practice in neighbourhood health clinics in urban
            Flanders. *Journal of Linguistic Anthropology* 16/2.

Coleman, Hywel (ed.)
   1989   *Working with Language: A multi-Disciplinary Consideration of Language
             Use in Work Contexts*. Berlin: Mouton de Gruyter.
Cook-Gumperz, Jennifer and John Gumperz
   1976   Context in children's speech. *Papers on Language and Context*. Working
             Paper *46*. Berkeley: Language Behaviour Research Laboratory.
Cope, Bill and Mary Kalantzis
   1995   A pedagogy of multiliteracies: Designing social futures. Paper presented
             at the Twenty-first Australian Reading Association National Conference,
             Sydney, July 1995.
Cope, Bill, Anne Pauwels, Diana Slade, Daphne Brosnan and Deborah Neil
   1993   *Local Diversity, Global Connections: Six Approaches to Cross-Cultural
             Training*. Canberra: Office of Multi-cultural Affairs.
Daley, Nicola, Janet Holmes, Jonathan Newton and Maria Stubbs
   2004   Expletives as solidarity signals in FTAs on the factory floor. *Journal of
             Pragmatics* 36: 945–964.
Day, Dennis
   1992   Communication in a multicultural workplace: Procedural matters. In:
             H. Crischel (ed.), *Intercultural Communication: Proceedings of the 17th In-
             ternational L.A.U.D. Symposium*, Duisburg, Germany.
Dicker, Susan
   1998   Adaption and assimilation: US business responses to linguistic diversity in
             the workplace. *Journal of Multilingual and Multicultural Development,* 19
             (4): 281–302.
Drew, Paul and John Heritage (eds.)
   1992   *Talk at Work: Interaction in Institutional Settings*. Cambridge: Cambridge
             University Press.
Duff, Patricia, Paul Wong, and Margaret Early
   2000   Learning language for work and life: The linguistic socialization of immi-
             grant Canadians seeking careers in health care. *Canadian Modern Lan-
             guage Review* 57 (1): 9–57.
Erickson, Frederick and Jeffrey Schultz
   1982   *The Counselor as Gatekeeper*. New York: Academic Press.
Fairclough, Norman
   1989   *Language and Power*. London: Longman.
Fairclough, Norman (ed.)
   1992   *Critical Language Awareness*. London: Longman.
Farrell, Lesley.
   2000   Ways of doing, ways of being: Language, education and 'working' iden-
             tities. *Language and Education* 14 (1): 18–36.
   2001   'The new word order': workplace education and the textual practice of glo-
             balisation. *Pedagogy, Culture and Society* 9 (1): 57–74.
Firth, Alan
   1994   Talking for a change: Commodity negotiating by telephone. In: Alan Firth
             (ed.), *The Discourse of Negotiation: Studies of Language in the Workplace,*
             183–222. Oxford: Pergamon.
Fisher, Susan and Alexandra Todd
   1983   *The Social Organisation of Doctor-Patient Communication*. Washington,
             DC: Centre for Applied Linguistics.

1986   *Discourse and Institutional Authority: Medicine, Education and Law.* Norwood, NJ.: Ablex.

Gee, James, Glenda Hull and Colin Lankshear
1996   *The New Work Order: Behind the Language of the New Capitalism.* Sydney: Allen and Unwin.

Goldstein, Tara
1993   The ESL community and the changing world of work. *TESL Talk* 21: 56–64.
1997   *Two Languages at Work: Bilingual Life on the Production Floor.* Berlin: Mouton de Gruyter.

Green, Judith and David Bloome
1997   Ethnography and ethnographers of and in education: a situated perspective. In: James Flood, Shirley Brice Heath and Diana Lapp (eds.), *Handbook of Research on Teaching Literacy Through the Communicative Visual Arts,* 181–202. New York: IRA Simon Schuster Macmillan.

Grünhage-Monetti Matilde, Elwine Halewijn and Chris Holland
2003   *Odysseus: Second Language in the Workplace.* European Centre for Modern Languages, Strasbourg: Council of Europe Publishing.

Gumperz, John
1982a   *Discourse Strategies.* Cambridge: Cambridge University Press.
1992a   Contextualisation and understanding. In: Alessandro Duranti and Charles Goodwin (eds.), *Rethinking Context: Language as an Interactive Phenomenon,* 229–252. Cambridge: Cambridge University Press.
1992b   Contextualisation revisited. In: Peter Auer and Aldo di Luzio (eds.), 39–54.
1996   The linguistic and cultural relativity of conversational inference. In: John Gumperz and Stephen Levinson (eds.), *Rethinking Linguistic Relativity,* 374–406. Cambridge: Cambridge University Press.
1997   A discussion with John J. Gumperz. In: Susan Eerdmans, C. Previgagno and Paul Thibault (eds.), *Discussing Communication Analysis 1: John Gumperz,* 6–23. Lausanne: Beta Press.
1999   On interactional sociolinguistic method. In: Srikant Sarangi and Celia Roberts (eds.), *Talk. Work and Institutional Order,* 453–472. Berlin: Mouton de Gruyter.

Gumperz John (ed.)
1982b   *Language and Social Identity.* Cambridge: Cambridge University Press.

Gumperz, John, Tom Jupp and Celia Roberts
1979   *Crosstalk.* London: National Centre for Industrial Language Training.

Gumperz, John amd Celia Roberts
1980   *Awareness training in intercultural communication.* SEAMO, Regional English Language Centre, Singapore.

Hak, Tony
1999   'Text' and 'con-text': Talk bias in studies of health care work. In: Srikant Sarangi and Celia Roberts (eds.), 389–400.

Harper, Helen, Bonny Pierce and Barbara Burnaby
1996   English in the workplace for garment workers: a feminist project. *Gender and Education* 8 (1): 5–20.

Hawthorne, Lesleyanne
1997   Defining the target domain: What language skills are required for engineers and nurses? *Melbourne Papers in Language Testing* 6 (1): 5–20.

Holland, Chris, Fiona Frank and Tony Cooke
  1998   *Literacy and the New Work Order.* Leicester: National Institute of Adult and
          Continuing Education.
Holmes, Janet
  2000   Talking English 9 to 5: challenges for ESOL learners at work. *International
          Journal of Applied Linguistics* 10 (1): 125–140.
Hull, Glenda
  1996   *Changing work, changing literacy. A study of skills requirements and devel-
          opment in a traditional and a restructured workplace.* Final Report. Berke-
          ley, California: National Centre for the Study of Writing and Literacy, Pitts-
          burgh.
Hull, Glenda (ed.)
  1997   *Changing Work, Changing Workers: Critical Perspectives on Language,
          Literacy and Skills.* Albany: SUNY Press.
Kalantzis, Mary and Daphne Brosnan
  1993   *Managing Cultural Diversity.* Sydney: Centre for Workplace Communi-
          cation and Culture, University of Technology.
Katz, M.
  2000   Workplace language teaching and the intercultural construction of ideo-
          logies of competence. *Canadian Modern Language Review* 57 (1):
          144–172.
Levinson, Stephen
  1983   *Pragmatics.* Cambridge: Cambridge University Press.
Li, D.
  2002   The pragmatics of making requests in the L2 workplace. *Canadian Modern
          Language Review* 57 (1): 58–87.
Mawer, Giselle
  1999   *Language and Literacy in Workplace Education: Learning at Work.* Lon-
          don: Longman.
McGregor, Graham and Mark Williams
  1984   Cross-cultural communication in the employment interview. *Australian Re-
          view of Applied Linguistics* 7 (1): 203–219.
McNamara, Tim
  1997   Problematizing content validity: the occupational English test (OET) as a
          measure of medical communication. *Melbourne Papers in Language Test-
          ing* 6 (1): 19–43.
Newton, Jonathan, Nicola Daley, Janet Holmes and Maria Stubbs
  2004   Face threatening talk on the factory floor: implications for intercultural
          communication *Journal of Pragmatics* 36: 945–964.
Pauwels, Anne
  1994   Applying linguistic insights in intercultural communication to professional
          training programmes: An Australian case study. In: Anne Pauwels (ed.),
          Cross-Cultural Communication in the Professions. Special issue of *Multi-
          lingua* 13 (1/2): 195–212.
Pierce, Bonny
  1989   Toward a pedagogy of possibility in the teaching of English internationally:
          People's English in South Africa. *TESOL Quarterly* 23 (3): 401–420.

Pierce, Bonny, Helen Harper and Barbara Burnaby
  1993   Workplace ESL at Levi Strauss: Dropouts speak out. *TESL Canada Journal*
            19 (2): 9–32.
Phillipson, Robert, Mart Rannut and Tove Skutnabb-Kangas
  1995   Introduction. In: T. Skutnabb-Kangas and Robert Phillipson (eds.) 2005,
            133–139.
  1993   ESL in the changing world of work. *TESL Talk* 21.
Roberts, Celia, Evelyn Davies and Tom Jupp
  1992   *Language and Discrimination: A Study of Communication in Multi-Ethnic
            Workplaces.* London: Longman.
Roberts, Celia and Sarah Campbell
  2006   Fitting stories into boxes: Rhetorical and Textual constraints on candidates'
            performances in Job interviews. To appear in *Journal of Applied Lingustics.*
Sarangi, Srikant
  1994   Intercultural or not? Beyond celebration of cultural differences in miscom-
            munication analysis. *Pragmatics* 4: 409–427.
Sarangi, Srikant and Stef Slembrouck
  1996   *Language, Bureaucracy and Social Control.* London: Longman.
Sarangi, Srikant and Celia Roberts (eds.)
  1999   *Talk, Work and Institutional Order: Discourse in Medical, Management
            and Mediation Settings.* Berlin: Mouton de Gruyter.
Skutnabb-Kanagas, Tove and Robert Phillipson
  1995   *Linguistic Human Rights: Overcoming Linguistic Discrimination.* Berlin:
            Mouton de Gruyter.
Thomas, R. and T. Gregory
  1993   A diversity perspective on the language challenge. *Employment Relations
            Today* 20 (4): 363–376.
Tollefson, James
  1991   *Planning Language, Planning Inequality: Language Policy in the Commu-
            nity.* London: Longman.
Urban, Greg
  1991   *A Discourse-Centred Approach to Culture.* Austin, TX: University of Texas
            Press.
Wagner, Johannes
  1994   'Negotiating activity' in technical problem solving. In: Alan Firth (ed.),
            1994, 223–246.
Wallman, Sandra
  1979   *Ethnicity at Work.* London: Macmillan.
Westwood, Sallie and Parminder Bachu (eds.)
  1988   *Enterprising Women.* London: Routledge.
Willing, Kenneth
  1992   *Talking it Through: Clarification and Problem-Solving in professional work.*
            Sydney: National Centre for English Language Teaching and Research.
Willing, Kenneth
  1997   Modality in task-orientated discourses: The role of subjectivity in 'getting
            the job done'. *Prospect* 12 (12): 33–42.
Wodak, Ruth
  1996   *Disorders of Discourse.* London: Longman.

Additional Sources

The following recommended reading highlights some texts referred to in the chapter and adds some others.

Books

Clyne, Michael
   2003   *Dynamics of Language Contact.* Cambridge: Cambridge University Press.
Firth, Alan (ed.)
   1995   *The Discourse of Negotiation: Studies of Language in the Workplace.* Oxford: Pergamon.
Gee, James, Glenda Hull and Colin Lankshear
   1996   *The New Work Order: Behind the Language of the New Capitalism.* Sydney: Allen and Unwin.
Goldstein, Tara
   1997   *Two Languages at Work: Bilingual Life on the Production Floor* Berlin: Mouton de Gruyter.
Holmes, Janet and Maria Stubbs
   2003   *Power and Politeness in the Workplace: A Sociolinguistic Analysis of Talk at Work.* London: Pearson.
Mawer, Giselle
   1999   *Language and Literacy in Workplace Education: Learning at Work.* London: Longman.
Roberts, Celia, Evelyn Davies and Tom Jupp
   1992   *Language and Discrimination: A Study of Communication in Multi-Ethnic Workplaces.* London: Longman.

Special issues and articles from journals

Belfiore, Mary
   1993   The changing world of work research project. *TESL Talk* 21: 2–20.
Bell, Judith
   1995   Canadian experiences of training linguistically diverse populations for the workplace. *Australian Review of Applied Linguistics* 18 (1): 35–51.
Coleman, Hywel (ed.)
   1984   *Language and Work 1: Law, Industry and Education.* (Special Issue of the *International Journal of the Sociology of Language*, 49). Berlin: Mouton de Gruyter.
   1985   *Language and Work 2: The Health Professions.* (Special Issues of the *International Journal of the Sociology of Language*, 51). Berlin: Mouton de Gruyter.
Farrell, Lesley
   2000   Ways of doing, ways of being: Language, education and 'working' identities. *Language and Education* 14 (1): 18–36.
Pauwels, Anne (ed.)
   1994   Cross-cultural communication in the professions. Special issue of *Multilingua* 13 (1/2).

Reports

Benseman, John
    1998   *Voices for the Workplace.* Aukland: Workbase: The National Centre for
            Workplace Literacy and Language
Kalantzis, Mary and Daphne Brosnan
    1993   *Managing Cultural Diversity.* Sydney: Centre for Workplace Communi-
            cation and Culture, University of Technology.

17.   Multilingualism and commerce

David C.S. Li

1.   Language and the multilingual business environment in a globalized economy

In a broad sense, the word 'commerce' refers to activities that involve an exchange of goods or services for a profit. As such, it is indistinguishable from a closely related term, 'business'. From barter to e-commerce, humans have come a long way in terms of the mode of exchange of consumables (in the modern sense) and artistic objects of appreciation, be it driven by a need for subsistence or a desire to accumulate wealth. Capitalism evolved when the latter became the sole objective of economic activities, bringing with it social problems such as conflicts over the ownership of precious resources. The benefits and value of trade across national and ethnic boundaries have long been recognized since Adam Smith, while Karl Marx made us aware that a great deal of human misery in nineteenth-century Europe could be traced to immoral capitalists' greed and the ensuing unequal and unethical distribution of wealth, at the expense of the working class who had neither control over the means of production nor any say about the abuse and exploitation of their physical labour. Since the end of the Second World War, the volume of international trade has increased by leaps and bounds. Free trade, or freedom from cross-border restraints in the flow of capital, merchandise, services and labour, is looked upon by many nations in the west, notably the USA, as the most profitable and productive way of doing business. It is the cause of many an international dispute over preferred trading terms. Today, such disputes are arbitrated by the World Trade Organization (WTO), whose raison d'être is to promote and facilitate free trade around the world. Unlike its predecessor GATT,

> WTO serves as a global commerce agency. The stated objective of the WTO is to ultimately create a fully integrated global economic system in which not only goods, services, and capital flow without any interference or control of local national governments, but the property rights of corporations, both physical and intellectual, are fully protected. (Peoples and Bailey 2003: 328)

What is the relationship between commerce, conducted increasingly on a global scale, and language choice and language use patterns worldwide? Three recent examples collected from the press in different parts of the world may help illustrate how commerce, invariably driven by a profit motive, has the potential to influence language use patterns at the institutional and individual levels in multilingual business environments. The first example shows how a high level of English proficiency in English-L2 societies enables its speakers to take jobs away from their English-L1 counterparts. In a special Indian Republic Day sponsored feature in *South China Morning Post* in Hong Kong (26 January 2005, C11), it is reported that

> the world's second most populous nation [India] is picking up the phone for British and US companies seeking cost savings [...]. India has emerged as the leading location for western firms to outsource their call centres [...] claiming 150,000 of the 350,000 offshore call centre jobs [...]. Britain's Communication Workers Union fears that 200,000 British jobs may be lost by 2008. The trend is becoming an issue in the United States too, where about 400,000 jobs have already shifted abroad and studies suggest 3 million may disappear by 2015.

The feature attributes this glaring business success to the availability of some 50 million skilled English speakers in India, most of whom being university graduates. This is an instructive example showing how a high level of English proficiency in non-native settings is a valuable 'linguistic capital' (Bourdieu 1991) that gives its L2 speakers an edge in an increasingly globalized and competitive labour market – an edge that also helps account for India's tremendous success in a growing software industry.

The second example comes from a news report on the main reason why hundreds of shopkeepers and restaurant owners in Trier, a 'sleepy' town in Germany, were eager to study a Chinese language course organized by 170 business-minded shop owners. For several years, Trier has reportedly become a hot tourist destination for visitors from mainland China. According to the news story, the single attraction to these visitors is Marx House where Karl Marx was born. This attraction lures thousands of Chinese tourists to visit Trier, whose spending has almost quadrupled since 1999. This is the background against which many restaurant owners, waiters, opticians and jewellers signed up for Chinese language lessons (10 two-hour sessions), because they want "to welcome the Chinese tourists and tell them how much things cost" (*South China Morning Post*, 29 May 2005, A1).

The third example is also concerned with tourism, which is the second-largest sector in Malaysia in terms of foreign-currency income. In early June, 2005, it was reported that a new 'Arab Square' would be inaugurated in the shopping district of Kuala Lumpur. The purpose is to make high-spending, Arabic-speaking holiday-makers from the Middle East – notably Saudi Arabia, the United Arab Emirates, Kuwait, Lebanon, Turkey, Syria, Oman and Jordan – feel completely at ease during their stay in Malaysia. The report also indicates that an increasing number of Muslim holiday-makers choose to visit Malaysia, which to them is a more friendly and modern Islamic state compared with Western countries, many of which are considered anti-Arab. According to one Malaysian official interviewed, special measures would be introduced to attract

Muslim tourists, including a red-carpet welcome at the Kuala Lumpur International Airport, special fast-track immigration lanes for Middle Eastern families, and welcome signs and announcements in Arabic. In addition, "more than 500 Arabic-speaking university students will work in Kuala Lumpur's five-star hotels and tour agencies to help make travellers comfortable". The 'Arab Square', which was inaugurated by the Prime Minister in summer 2005, is to be "a permanent landmark showcasing Middle Eastern food and culture amid the city's backdrop of mosques and Islamic museums blended with cosmopolitan facilities" (*Bangkok Post*, 4 June 2005, B2). Examples such as these are good illustrations of how language use patterns may change in response to changing needs in the business environment.

Globalization encompasses multiple dimensions, for example, economic, political, cultural, environmental, and security (national as well as in cyber space), but it is perhaps the most visible in the realm of business and commerce. Today's commercial activities and business transactions increasingly take place within the framework of a global economy or market. Language and geographical boundaries are no longer insurmountable barriers to consumption, including products for entertainment. For instance, deep in the jungle of Central Africa the US movie *Basic Instinct* could be watched from a video before it was shown in the cinema in London (Giddens 2000: 24). In a fast food shop in Hong Kong, a buzzling Chinese city, Bollywood movies dubbed in Thai are routinely the favourite pastime of the Thai speakers working there. While the root of globalization as a worldwide phenomenon may be traced back to the days of Columbus's 'discovery' of North America, there is general consensus that the global economy as we know it today gradually took shape after the Second World War (Kottak 2004, Peoples and Bailey 2003). Several factors contributed to this development: the collapse of the British Empire; technological innovations that significantly lower production costs and allow for speedier delivery of consumables and transportation of people in greater volumes and numbers; and above all, the unrestrained circulation of electronic money and capital in international finance, making it possible to transfer billions of dollars at the click of a mouse (Peoples and Bailey 2003, chapter 16; Giddens 2000: 27). As Peoples and Bailey (2003: 160) point out: "In essence, market globalization means that the entire world is increasingly integrated into a single economic system based around market exchange: labor, capital, technology, consumer products, and services move with fewer and fewer restraints across national boundaries". In some real sense, globalization has rendered the world smaller and geography irrelevant, as evidenced in the development of telecommunications using video conferencing, international phone calls using 3G technology and the Internet. Like 'global village', the idea of the entire human species living in one world is fast becoming a cliché, as shown in the slogan 'One World, One Dream' adopted for the 2008 Olympic Games in Beijing.

Whether one is critical or sympathetic, issues pertaining to globalization are a matter of concern for political leaders, NGOs and the powerless alike. As Giddens (2000: 25) puts it, "I haven't been to a single country recently where globalization isn't being intensively discussed. In France, the word is *mondialisation*, in Spain and Latin America, it is *globalización*. The Germans say *Globalisierung*. The global spread of the term is evidence of the very developments to which it refers". When it comes to the organization of global events, however, English tends to be chosen as the working language, at least for writing banners and slogans for international media consumption. One recent example is the international campaign 'Make Poverty History' targeting leaders of the G-8 summit in Scotland in July, 2005, which is a sober reminder of the state and magnitude of a central concern for many, namely global socioeconomic inequality.

Many critics believe that globalization is westernization (often equated with Americanization) in disguise, imposing Western (notably US) values and practices onto economically less developed countries and cultures. This impression, which is encapsulated in the catchphrase 'the West and the rest', is partly supported by trade statistics. According to Bailey and Peoples (2002: 238), in addition to the global presence of American cultural products such as Coca-Cola and McDonald's, the entertainment industry – comprising movies, television programs, and music – constitutes the largest export industry of USA in dollar terms, which is one good reason why the US government is so concerned about the infringement of intellectual property rights (IPR). As is well-known, the item 'IPR crimes' is high on the agenda of ongoing Sino-US trade negotiations. The global spread of infotainment products from the USA has attracted criticisms of cultural and linguistic imperialism (e.g. Phillipson 1992). Critics argue that globalization has brought about many evils, from an ever-deepening and -widening wealth gap to the dominance of English, the latter being a pervasive threat against the ethnolinguistic well-being and sociocultural heritage of minority groups. Such beliefs are periodically translated into protests punctuated by G7 (now G8) summits, often resulting in violence, the latest being occasioned by the G8 summit in Scotland in July, 2005. In the age of telecommunications, images of large-scale civil disobedience and violent street protests transmitted via satellites and the Internet reach millions of households instantaneously around the world, prompting other sympathizers to take to the streets. Televised images of angry protesters and 'people's power' have been shown to have considerable potential to bring down governments, witness the first 'television revolutions' in Eastern Europe in 1989 (Giddens 2000: 32–33). More recently, the series of anti-Japanese protests in several cities of mainland China in April, 2005 were similarly sparked by electronic messages from cell phones and mass email shots sent via MSN. Advances in communications technology thus constitute another important dimension of globalization.

The purpose of this chapter is to examine the role of language in a multilingual business environment. It aims to show how people from different language backgrounds with varying levels of multilingual proficiencies cope with language-related problems when engaged in commercial activities. In particular, the following themes will be covered: language and economy, the cost of translation in multilingual business transactions, language communication in the multilingual workplace, multilingualism as a key to business success, the emergence of English as a 'world lingua franca' and symbol of modernity, problems involving a brand name in the global market, and cross-border advertising for multilingual audiences. Our discussion will naturally draw on the relevant literature to date. Given the space limitation, I regret that some of the references that are found useful could not be included. The relevant literature accessible to me will be supplemented by clippings from the international press and footages of Cantonese news broadcast in Hong Kong, which were consciously collected during the first half of 2005 as they came to my attention.

2.   Language and economy

Several scholars have pointed out the intimate relationship between the vitality of a nation's economy and the vitality of its national language(s) (see, e.g. Coulmas 1991, 1992, 1993; Edwards 2004). The motivation to learn a non-native language is largely determined by its perceived *Kurswert*, or 'market value'. In this regard, Coulmas (1992, 1993) speaks of *Sprache als Ware* – 'language as commodity'. As is well-known, the emergence of English as a 'world lingua franca' is due historically to the economic strengths of countries where English is spoken as a native language, notably the USA and the UK (Brutt-Griffler 2002). The demand for Japanese as a foreign language may be similarly explained by Japan's economic success in the post-war era (Coulmas 1992). This is confirmed by a recent news story in *Hong Kong Economic Times* (15 June 2005, A11), which indicates that Japanese continues to be among the most popular foreign languages among local students. The vitality of German as a second language is also very much in evidence in Eastern Europe with the creation of undergraduate degree programmes in the German language and the expanding operations of Goethe Institut in the former satellite countries of the now defunct Soviet Union (Coulmas 1992, 1993). A more recent example is Mandarin Chinese which, following China's robust economic growth since the early 1980s, is learned by as many as 30 million people around the world, and the number is expected to reach 100 million within four years (*China Daily*, overseas edition, 26 April 2005, p.10).

Many other instructive examples of the intimate relationship between language and economy may be found in Viv Edwards's (2004) monograph *Multi-*

lingualism in the English-speaking world. The linguistic independence and political power of French speakers in Quebec, Canada, is another case in point. Despite their numerical strength, French-speaking Québecois had until recently little political influence and were thus subordinated to Anglophone elites in the province. This was largely due to the fact that, being mostly Catholics, they were discouraged by the church to engage in commercial activities beyond agriculture. For a long time, therefore, a lack of economic strength prevented Québecois to play an active role in national decisions pertaining to the maintenance of the French language and culture in a sea of English. The situation was gradually reversed after the 'Quiet Revolution' in the 1960s, whereby more and more Francophone Quebeckers owned businesses and occupied high-level positions (Edwards 2004: 151). Enhanced economic strength gives them a stronger voice in their assertion of language rights, including those in the workplace (2004: 161). The way such rights are enforced is generally resented by the minority English-speaking population in Quebec. Members of the English-rights Equality Party, for example, put up a fight in the media against the attempt by the 'language police' to dub *Kentucky Fried Chicken* as *Poulet frit Kentucky* allegedly for the convenience of French sign language users (Edwards 2004: 73). The struggle over symbolic domination (Bourdieu 1991) aside, it is interesting to note that the scholarly inquiry of bilingual education owes much to the economic success of Francophone Québecois. As Edwards (2004: 149) points out, "[t]he greater economic power of Quebec has given birth to French-immersion education in English-speaking Canada". For various minority groups in English-dominant societies, economic success is also an important factor contributing to the maintenance of their ethnolinguistic and cultural heritage. This, for example, is clearly the case of 'Indigenous economies' in some Canadian and Australian Aboriginal communities (see Edwards 2004: 150–151).

3.   Commerce in a multilingual business environment: Translation costs

Translation, especially from or into English, is an expenditure item that has to be factored into the costing of multilingual business operations, making translation per se an increasingly attractive business (Coulmas 1992, Sprung 2000). For example, Sprung (2000: ix) observes that "[i]n fiscal 1998, over 60 percent of Microsoft's revenues came from markets outside the United States. In that same period, revenue from translated products exceeded US$5 billion. Microsoft executes over 1,000 localization projects a year". One recent Microsoft initiative is the launching of a low-cost, starter version of Windows XP operating system in Hindi targeting non-English users in India. The expected sales volume is around 200,000 copies in the first year, and support for nine other languages in India will be added later (*Bangkok Post*, 4 June 2005, B2). Similarly, the translations of media products originated in English represent a sizeable market in its own right: "*Newsweek, Glamour, Discover, People*, and *Rolling Stone* magazines are now available in Spanish or Portuguese. *Reader's Digest* reached 600,000 Brazilian readers in 1998, with 1.7 million reading the publication in Spanish and Portuguese; *Glamour en español* now sells 500,000 copies" (Sprung 2000: ix; cf. Rodriguez 1999). Sprung further adds that "[b]illions of dollars are spent each year on translation and related services – tiny fraction of the value of the actual products being sold" (Sprung 2000: xii).

In terms of language choice in the multilingual workplace, there is also evidence that English is increasingly being used in some European companies as a working language for internal communication purposes, in part to avoid translation costs. This for example is the case of some Swiss companies which opt to use English "not only for their international business relations but also for communications within the company, on the grounds that this is cheaper than paying for the translations that would otherwise be necessary" (Chesire and Moser 1994: 453–454).

4.   Language communication in the multilingual workplace

In an increasingly globalized business environment, a high level of proficiency in the world's major languages of wider communication is one of the most frequently cited requirements for the multilingual workplace. For example, one feature in the business pages of *Bangkok Post* (31 May 2005, B4) headlined "Chinese look for partner to penetrate market in Thailand" cites a Chinese executive director of a Bangkok-based international architectural design group as saying "We need a lot of Thai designers as they are skilful in interior and landscape design. They're also talented, artistic, polite and congenial. But they should improve their English and learn Chinese in order to add [sic] their competence". At the same time, knowledge of foreign languages in addition to one's mother tongue often means job opportunities and prospects not available to monolingual competitors. For instance, in two small Chinese Muslim communities Tong Hai and Nagu in Yunnan province, China, students of a community college reportedly learn the Qu'ran, Arabic and the history of Islam in addition to computer science and other academic subjects. Knowledge of Arabic is an advantage in China as there is an increasing demand for Arabic interpreters for private companies and as tourist guides, both being well-paid jobs by mainland standards. For graduates conversant in Arabic, therefore, unemployment appears to be a non-issue (*Bangkok Post*, 26 May 2006, pp. 1,6). Likewise, recruitment adverts of the recently opened Disney Hong Kong specify fluent English and Putonghua (Mandarin) in addition to Cantonese, obviously in anticipation of international visitors and holiday-makers in Greater China. Applicants who are tri- or bi-lingual in these languages will therefore have an edge over their monolingual counterparts. Conversely, a lack of language skills tends to make one less competitive in the job market. However, a lack of language skills is sometimes no more than a smoke screen to hide the boss's dislike of the applicant's ethnicity. This for example is sometimes true of minority groups of South Asian descent in Hong Kong, who are often denied jobs, including menial labour, on the grounds that they don't speak Cantonese (cf. Tinker-Sachs and Li, in press).

For language planners working in communities where the minority language is under threat of extinction, the promotion and use of the endangered language in the work domain is absolutely crucial for reversing the trend of language loss or even language death. One exemplary case is the successful maintenance of Welsh in Wales, an "established minority language" (Edwards 2004) in the UK. Thanks to the initiatives of concerned sociolinguists and concerted efforts of its speakers, Welsh has regained considerable vitality in the last decade. The Welsh Language Board plays an instrumental role in implementing "grounded language action planning", publicizing tangible incentives for speaking Welsh and educating the public about the cognitive, linguistic and cultural benefits of bilingualism (Baker 2003). The Board also actively promotes Welsh in such domains as law and business. Ingenious grounded actions include identifying Welsh-speakers using *Iaith gwaith/Working Welsh* badges, signs and stickers (e.g. in a bank); using Welsh in marketing activities such as adverts, brochures and leaflets; and bilingual packaging and labelling of goods made in Wales (Edwards 2004: 162). All these efforts appear to have paid off; recent census figures show that the number of Welsh-speakers is steadily on the rise, which in turn attracts more people to learn it after discovering that English-Welsh bilingualism gives them additional employment opportunities in such fields as education, the media, government, and of course business and commerce. There is some indication that many Welsh-speaking parents and English-speaking parents "believe their children will have better employment prospects in a country where increasing numbers of jobs in both the public and private sectors require bilingual and bilterate skills" (Edwards 2004: 109–110). A similar development involving Māori-English bilingualism is taking place in New Zealand (2004: 149).

At the institutional level, where the workforce is made up of staff coming from multilingual and multicultural backgrounds, communication – both linguistic and intercultural – problems are to be expected. Problems of this kind are especially acute when business conglomerates originated from very different "languacultures" (Agar 1994: 58) merge into still bigger transnational enterprises. One recent example may be found in the comments of Liu Chuanzhi (柳傳志), the CEO of Lenovo, at a press conference on the main problems confronted by the company after merging with IBM. One of the three problems mentioned concerns 語言衝突 (*yuyán chōngtū*, 'language conflict') and communication problems between the management of both sides. To resolve that problem, he appeals to Lenovo (Chinese) personnel to brush up their English, which he considers to be the key to reducing communication problems with (American) IBM staff (*Hong Kong Economic Times*, 15 June 2005, A9).

5.   Multilingualism: Key to success in a multilingual business environment

From the point of view of a business enterprise, knowledge of the client's preferred language is a lubricant in the process of negotiating for a deal. Thus, for example, the new Commerce Bank branch in Chinatown in Lower Manhattan, New York, reportedly prides itself on trilingual automatic teller machines (Chinese, English and Spanish) as well as trilingual employees (Cantonese, Mandarin and English) (*Taipei Times*, 10 July 2005, 12). In a hospitality industry such as airliners, the employees' multilingual communication skills is seen as a selling point. One good illustration is a quarter-page Cathay Pacific advert that appeared in *Hong Kong Economic Times* (6 April 2005, A8), where the headline reads 微笑 無須翻譯 (mei[21] siu[33] mou[21] seoi[55] faan[55] jik[22], 'smile, no translation needed'). The illustration in the middle of the advert shows a charming, smiling flight attendant, surrounded in the background by the word *Welcome* and its translation equivalent in six other languages: (clockwise) Japanese, German, Chinese, Dutch, French and Korean. The body copy (in Chinese) stresses that the Cathay Pacific crew are all polyglots, and that their smile is the best signal of their readiness to serve – a non-verbal cue that naturally transcends their multilingual communication skills.

In imports and exports, success in global business depends largely on making the product information available in the language(s) of the community of target consumers. Thus to enter a lucrative market such as mainland China, knowledge of Chinese languages is seen as crucial. For example, an executive director of a vermicelli factory in Thailand points out that an ability to speak Mandarin "makes it easier for you to do business there and understand the spending habits of Chinese consumers if you speak Chinese languages". He further reminds other Thai exporters to label their products clearly using simplified Chinese characters because failure to do so may result in problems at the Chinese customs (*Bangkok Post*, 30 May 2005, B3).

For the key players of the extremely competitive cell phone market, there is evidence that a user-friendly multilingual interface gives a cell phone manufacturer an edge to outperform competitors. This is arguably the case of the market success of Nokia 6108, a cell phone model recently launched in China. Its outstanding market performance is attributed largely to its localized product design, which is characterized above all by a range of multilingual facilities: in addition to a built-in Chinese-English dictionary, it also recognizes the handwriting of both Chinese and Latin characters for message sending and note-taking. Such language facilities add value to the product and are seen as the key to the success of Nokia 6108. The monetary returns are tremendous given the huge number of cell phone users in China, which is currently estimated at 350 million, or some 27 per cent of the total population of about 1.3 billion (*China Daily*, overseas edition, 20 June 2005, p. 7).

One relatively recent technological development is the growing significance and popularity of e-commerce. The last two decades witnessed a rapid expansion of the Internet as a platform for information dissemination and exchange, offering thereby exciting business opportunities. When the Internet was first introduced, English was the only language through which one could gain access to cyber space, putting English in a privileged position vis-à-vis other languages. This however is changing. Websites now appear in many other languages, with Arabic being a relatively recent addition. According to a feature article in *South China Morning Post* (14 May 2005, A14) headlined "Netting the Middle East", most speakers of Arabic used to have no access to the Internet because they have little knowledge of English: "People either don't speak English or simply would like to use their native language". This sociolinguistic barrier was recently overcome with the launching of Maktoob (literally 'message') in 1998, the first Arabic-language website similar in status to Yahoo in the Chinese-speaking world. To be sure, there were technical and language-related hurdles to overcome in the outset. For example, since Arabic-language keyboards were rare, Arabic stickers had to be sent out for clients to fasten onto English-language keyboards. But soon a solution was found as the number of subscribers quickly multiplied, and the Arabic language played a crucial role in this process. One instructive example is Maktoob's campaign to attract subscribers using the slogan *Sajel Ana Arabi* ('Proud to be an Arab'), which resulted in "a roaring commercial success" and "led to an emotional outpouring from delighted users across the Middle East". The founder of Maktoob, a Jordanian from Anman called Samih Toukan, was quoted as saying that "even today subscribers send e-mails saying how proud they are that we've been able to compete with international websites". The sheer number of Arabic subscribers made it possible for Toukan to gradually introduce a range of other commercial services, such as the world's first Arabic online auction site, a prepaid shopping card for online purchases, and an online match-making service. The market success of Maktoob is thus a good illustration of how an accurate understanding of the ethnolinguistic identity of target language groups may be turned into a lucrative business opportunity.

6.   English: The 'world lingua franca' and symbol of modernity

English has emerged as the 'world lingua franca' after the Second World War. In international events where people from different language backgrounds get together, English is often assumed to be *the* working language by default. The same is true of international travel, notably in Asia. This helps explain why, in preparation for the 2008 Beijing Olympic Games, taxi drivers in the Chinese capital are required to take an English test to ensure that they can understand and respond to simple questions raised by English-speaking visitors, and that they should be familiar with the English terms for the new Olympic facilities (e.g. Olympic Stadium or Bird's Nest; TVB Jade morning news, 15 June 2005, Hong Kong).

The role of English as a world language, notably in the multilingual workplace, fuels a global demand for it, making English language teaching (ELT) a multi-billion enterprise for ELT course providers in countries where English is spoken as a native language (for a critical discussion of the ethical problems arising from the spread of English in language education worldwide, see, e.g. Phillipson 1992, 2003, Pennycook 1994, 1998, Skutnabb-Kangas 2000, Li 2003). The global spread of English is also evident in multilingual adverts. For example, commenting on the increasingly pervasive role of English in German-English TV commercials and print adverts in Germany, Piller (2001: 181) describes English as "the lingua franca of the marketplace". To norm providers such as the UK, such a "language advantage" is generally believed to be one important factor sustaining the position of international business and financial centres such as Hong Kong and London. This point is made unabashedly in a rhetorical question by the author of a feature article (*South China Morning Post*, 23 June 2005, A17):

> No one should be in any doubt as to the importance of English in the context of Hong Kong's role as a centre for business and finance. Would London have held on so well to its pre-eminent financial position in Europe after Britain opted not to join the euro, were it not for the language advantage? Almost certainly not.

In non-English-L1 settings, it has been shown that the use of English is often associated with prestige and power, symbolizing progress, modernity and technological advancement. There are plenty of examples in the literature. Thus in Hogan's study of the social significance of English usage in Japan, he observes that Mr. Kanno, one of his informants who was a home electronics salesman in a rural community in Hokkaido, "preferred to use English-derived terms because they are conveniently short and sound more interesting than the equivalent Japanese terms" (Hogan 2003: 50). When talking to prospective clients, Mr. Kanno found it useful to allude to English-derived terminology "to give the impression of professional expertise, to make the products themselves seem trendy and attractive, and to coax non-specialists into asking for more information about his products" (Hogan 2003: 50).

One correlate of the emergence of English as a global language is that it is often the preferred (additional) language in international protests. In mid-June, 2005, for example, representatives of European shoemakers were seen protesting outside the EU headquarters in Brussels against the alleged dumping of cheap Chinese shoes below the production price. Those marching in front were seen hoisting a big banner carrying a slogan in English: "Stop the Chinese footwear invasion" (TVB Jade morning news, 16 June 2005, Hong Kong). The presence of the international media ensured that the images would be broadcast worldwide, which is probably the main reason behind the protesters' language choice when wording the banner, in this case against what many European shoemakers perceive to be unfair trading practice. Examples such as these suggest that English is generally looked upon as a language which has the potential to carry one's message far and wide through the international media.

7.   Positioning a product/service in the global market: What is in a brand name?

The brand name is one of the most valuable assets of a product or service, as shown in the estimated value of some of the most prestigious brand names in global commerce such as Coca-Cola (US$69 billion) and Microsoft (US$65 billion) (Interbrand 2001, cited in Usunier and Shaner 2002: 212). A good brand name "can save millions of dollars over the product's life because it carries its own meaning, describes the product's advantages, is instantly recognized and serves to differentiate the product significantly from competition" (Stern 1983, cited in Chan 1990: 81). There is a sizable body of literature, notably in the field of advertising, focusing on how to localize the brand name of a global product or service with a view to ensuring market success. There is no shortage of examples of poorly selected brand names in the localization process, largely as a result of a lack of sensitivity to the linguistic contexts and sociocultural values of target consumers. Several such examples are reported by Usunier and Shaner (2002: 219). Thus the German hair spray product Caby-Net did not sell well in the French market probably because, pronounced in French, it is reminiscent of *cabinet*, meaning 'toilet'. Similarly, one of the main reasons why the car model Nova launched by Chevrolet was poorly received by Spanish-speaking consumers in Latin America had to do with Nova being homophonous with *no va* (literally 'does not run') in Spanish. The stakes involved in cross-border branding are therefore very high, which is why transnational corporations all consider it a top priority to create a nice-sounding, easy-to-remember brand name with positive associations in the process of localizing their products or services, and to manage it with care in their day-to-day business operations.

Usunier and Shaner (2002) propose a theoretical framework to assess the linguistic values of a given brand name with regard to phonetics and phonology, etymology and rhetoric, and explore the conditions under which these values may be transferred to other languages. It is not the only study focusing on linguistic problems involved in the localization of a brand name (see, e.g. Chan 1990, Huang and Chan 1997). In general, all studies agree that to ensure easy recognition and retention by target consumers, as a rule of thumb a good brand name should be easy to spell and pronounce, preferably with positive connotations and free from unwanted associations. Yet easy pronunciation, good denotations and positive connotations are linguistic traits that tend to be lost when transferred to another language, particularly when the target consumers have little knowledge of the denotative meaning of the source language. For instance, part of the market success of the French orange juice Fédor is attributed to the play on words – the brand puns on *fait d'or*, meaning 'made of gold' – a connotation that is generally obscure to non-French speakers (Usunier and Shaner 2002: 220). Thus there is sometimes a need to devise a brand name that evokes a rather different set of attributes and perceived benefits in the target language brand name compared with those in the source language counterpart. This is arguably the case of the following western products marketed in mainland China:

Product name	Chinese brand name		Literal translation of Chinese brand name
Coca-Cola:	可口可樂	kěkǒu kelè	'tasty and enjoyable/happy'
Pepsi-Cola:	百事可樂	báishì kělè	'hundred happy things'
Mercedes-Benz:	奔馳	bēnchí	'striving forward fast'

In examples such as these, there is one additional language-related problem, namely the use of a different writing system (script) in Chinese. Unlike in Europe, marketers of these products have to cope with the problem that the Roman alphabet on which the western brand name is based is generally less familiar to target consumers in mainland China. A similar literacy problem is also found in other parts of Asia such as India, where local people accustomed to the Devanagari script of Hindi may or may not be able to read English words written in the Roman alphabet (Bhatia 2000: 32).

Another related strategy to localize a brand name is linguistic reduction or simplification. Three examples may be cited: to global consumers worldwide, products or services from Proctor & Gamble, Louis Vuitton, and The Hongkong and Shanghai Banking Corporation are no doubt better known to them as P&G,

LV and HSBC, respectively. In the adverts, the acronym or abbreviation of these brands appears like a logo, with or without the brand name spelled out in full. Not only are these shorter forms easier to spell and pronounce regardless of the target consumer's language background, but they are also more economical to write and thus easier to remember, which is crucial in the business world where time is money.

To forestall the problem of branding in the global market, some transnational corporations deliberately choose a name that has a high degree of transferability across language and national boundaries. One such example mentioned in many studies is Sony. It fits in very well with the general linguistic criteria of a good brand name: bisyllabic with a simple structure (CV), semantically neutral and with no known negative associations in any language (Usunier and Shaner 2002: 221, cf. Huang and Chan 1997: 323). Another example is Kinder (literal meaning: 'children'), a German brand name for milk- and chocolate-based products targeting young consumers. Although the brand name is a German word, it is really part of a global lexicon by virtue of the popularity of the word *kindergarten* in many languages (Usunier and Shaner 2002: 225).

There is general agreement that relatively easy spelling and pronunciation facilitate quick recognition and retention of a brand name. But there are exceptions. Sometimes 'difficult' names may derive their appeal exactly from their 'foreignness', which is arguably the case of the ice-cream brand Haågen-Dazs. The letter with Umlaut (*å*) and letter combination *d-a-z-s* look exotic to consumers outside of Scandinavia. Thus sometimes a difficult brand name "may paradoxically be favourable (…) because of positive associations of foreignness" (Usunier and Shaner 2002: 219, 224). Few consumers realize, however, that Haågen-Dazs is a nonsense word contrived by a US firm deliberately to invite associations with some Nordic language and culture (e.g. Danish). Thus in addition to foreignness, the market success of Haågen-Dazs worldwide is also attributable to "product ethnicity" (Lock 2003). Similarly, foreignness and product ethnicity are probably the main motivations behind such brand names in garment as Baleno, Bossini and Giordano, which are all Hong Kong brands despite their unmistakable Italian-sounding pronunciation (Lock 2003: 199).

Finally, some brand names are designed to invite association with positive attributes through word play or punning (e.g. the French orange juice *Fédor* puns on 'fait d'or', meaning 'made of gold'). To my knowledge, there has been no mention in the literature of how the effect of some amusing association, produced by the typical pronunciation of a source language brand name by consumers of a target language, enhances the visibility and popularity of the brand and its products. One such example is Salvatore Ferragamo, a prestigious Italian brand name for deluxe fashion and leather products, notably shoes. This brand name is generally known to Hong Kong Chinese consumers by the second polysyllabic word: Ferragamo. Because this four-syllable word sounds very much like a meaningful Cantonese phrase fei^{55} lat^{55} gai^{55} mou^{21} (飛甩雞毛, literally 'fly-fall off-chicken-feather'), it is a favourite target of word play among Cantonese-speaking Hongkongers – probably after being popularized in some TV soap opera or movie. In effect, it is as if the brand name Salvatore Ferragamo gets free publicity every time it is invoked in Cantonese word play. It would be interesting to find out whether, and if so to what extent such free publicity in language play influences product sales and marketability.

8.   Cross-border advertising for multilingual audiences

Without a doubt, the ideological root of globalization is capitalism, or profit-making in naked terms. Mass production fuels "a global, transnational culture of consumption" (Kottak 2004: 473). Since the pace of consumption generally falls short of that of production, manufacturers would resort to all kinds of strategies within limits of their resources to advertise and promote their product or service. Increasingly products and services are advertised on the web and transactions made directly through email. One consequence of globalization is that "advertising has infiltrated even remote places such as the interior mountains of New Guinea" (Peoples and Bailey 2003: 191).

Like in many other domains, English is spreading far and wide in global advertising. In India, for example, "the use of English as a marker of global and marketing discourse is growing rapidly" (Bhatia 2000: 59). Bhatia (2000: 10) laments an imbalance between research on Indian as opposed to English adverts, and that the latter are clearly prospering at the expense of the former. He also deplores the "slavish" mentality of Indian advertisers which consists in the widely shared belief that "[t]he advertisement is written in the English language", and that such an obsession about advertising in English "has turned some Indian newscasters into the worst offenders in the pronunciation of Indian names (personal and place names), unmatched even by foreign newscasters" (2000: 11). In addition, the use of English in adverts in rural India breeds deception. Since most villagers in India have little or no literacy skills in English, and the Roman alphabet in general, they are often easy prey of deception when counterfeit products are sold using names that are spelled slightly differently than leading brand names such as Lifebuoy [Lifeboy] and Boroline [Boriline] (p. 125). Deception, however, is not limited to the medium of English; the same is true of Hindi in the tobacco industry (Bhatia 2000: chapter 7).

Successful marketing depends on effectively designed adverts, and language choice plays a key role in the market effectiveness of an advert, or a lack of it. There is a sizeable body of literature on the language of advertising in multilingual settings, where it has been shown that English, among other languages of wider communication, is often assigned symbolic meanings, while referential meanings may or may not be intended. For instance, Harald Haarmann observes that a foreign language may be used in Japanese television commercials mainly for its symbolic meanings in association with the wider community's perception of ethnocultural stereotypes (Haarmann 1984, 1986, 1989). He shows that English and French expressions are often displayed in the middle of a commercial, with no expectation of such expressions being understood by Japanese viewers. One instructive example involves cosmetics products of a French brand, Cacharel de Paris. Except for the setting featuring a beautiful and fashionably dressed Japanese woman smiling to the camera, everything else is in French, including background music. On the right side of the screen is a running text that says:

> Je suis une femme indépendante ['I am an independent woman']
> Je suis une femme qui aime la vie ['I am a woman who loves life']
> Je suis une femme qui sait ce qu'elle veut ['I am a woman who knows what she likes']
> Je suis Japonaise ['I am a Japanese woman'] (Haarmann 1984: 107–108)

The commercial culminates in the only speech act: the naming of the product Cacharel de Paris by a female voice with native French accent. Given the fact that Japan is largely a monolingual society, Haarmann characterizes this type of multilingualism in Japanese TV commercials as "impersonal", in the sense that it has little reality beyond the mass media. In addition, "[i]t is not intended by the [advertiser] management that the text should be understood. All items only serve as requisites for stimulating the illusion of 'Frenchness'" (1984: 108). In other words, the commercial appeared to have been designed deliberately to match the ethnocultural stereotype, or ethnosymbolism, of French charm, chic, elegance, refined taste, and the like – all being attributes which are widely shared among Japanese viewers. French also figures commonly in Japanese fashion magazines, with *élégance* being a high-frequency word (Haarmann 1986: 112). More recently, the symbolic function of English and other 'chic' western languages, as manifested in brand names and mixed code, has also been attested in fashion magazines in Hong Kong (Lee 2000).

In a similar vein, in their study of 1,242 adverts from two weekly magazines *L'Hebdo* (targeting an educated readership) and *L'Illustré* (a popular magazine targeting general readers) in French-speaking Suisse Romande, Chesire and Moser (1994) found that English is sometimes used in print adverts ostensibly for a symbolic or display function. This is without exception the case of credit cards, but it is also largely true of adverts for Swiss watches: 46.7% of them use English to different extents. Horlogerie being a national heritage that the Swiss are proud of, this finding struck the authors as somewhat unexpected. In the analysis, however, Chesire and Moser (1994: 465) believe it makes very good sense not only because English symbolizes modernity and technological sophistication, but also because English indexes the implied reader's identity as a multilingual whose repertoire includes English. At the same time, since a majority of the Swiss population has at least some knowledge of English, and that the English in their sample adverts tends to be worded in simple language, clearly English also serves a referential function – in addition to its symbolic function. Chesire and Moser (1994: 458) further suspect that readers who have no problem understanding the English message may feel flattered by the relative simplicity of syntax and vocabulary in the advert. Only some 15 per cent of the 390 adverts that contain English are believed to be elusive to French-speaking Swiss readers. One such example involves punning, as shown in the slogan of Pierrot ice-cream, which is spelled as *Paradice*. It takes both knowledge of the English word *paradise* and the recognition that the slogan contains the shorter word *ice* to appreciate the pun (Chesire and Moser 1994: 458). Finally, Chesire and Moser (1994: 466) analyze the "problematic identity" of the Swiss and conclude that English – the language of international tourism – serves as "a mirror for Switzerland", in that it allows the Swiss, in Suisse Romande at least, "to construct a self-image that is consistent with the favourable image that they present to tourists" (p. 467).

An appeal to ethnocultural stereotypes through manipulating the voices and identities of the narrator and narratee (implied reader) is also attested in Piller's (2000, 2001) studies of TV commercials and print adverts in Germany. Based on an analysis of over 600 commercials and 400 print adverts collected in February, 1999, Piller found that multilingualism is very common in German advertising, but unlike previous studies, her focus is not limited to lexical borrowing; rather, she presents strong evidence of multilingual commercials being a discourse phenomenon when other dimensions such as brand names, setting, background songs, the written mode and spoken mode – in any combination – are taken into account (Piller 2000: 264, 2001: 158; cf. Cook 1992). German-English bilingualism, by far the most common, is set up "as the strongest linguistic currency for the German business elite" (Piller 2001: 153), as shown by a number of indicators. One such indicator consists in the common "intertextual allusion" to the phrase 'Made in Germany', as in the signature line of 'GOLD⁄PFEIL GERMANY 1856', a brand name for deluxe leather goods and sophisticated craft products such as briefcases (Piller 2001: 154). Another indicator is the use of English in the headline and slogan positions (of print adverts) and the voice of a narrator (in TV commercials). In both cases English is vested with "the meaning of authority, authenticity, and truth" (Piller 2001: 160), deliberately intended to conjure up a number of attributes of the bilingual narratee, in any combination: internationalism, future orientation, success and elitism, fun, youth, and maleness (Piller 2001: 173). Piller (2000, 2001) further notes that the English variety alluded to and the accompanying paralinguistic cues are rarely uniquely American or British, but international, thereby further confirming that English appearing in German adverts is associated with transnational consumerism rather than national elitism. As for bilingualism involving other languages, Piller (2001: 169) found that two Romance languages are also represented: in print adverts, French is still occasionally used to connote *joie de vivre* but this function is increasingly taken over by English; in TV commercials, whereas French continues to carry aphrodisiac or erotic connotations (e.g. chocolate snacks), Italian remains a symbol of the good life (e.g. pasta; see also Piller 2000: 277).

9.   Coda

One recurrent theme that pervades the intimate link between multilingualism and commerce is the dominance of English in multilingual societies, plus the ethical problems thus arising, especially in former British and American colonies. Such problems have been deliberated under different theoretical frameworks depending on the scholar, for example, linguistic imperialism (Phillipson 1992, 2003), cultural politics and the discourse of colonialism (Pennycook 1994, 1998), and linguistic genocide (Skutnabb-Kangas 2000). The focus may vary, but the issues all revolve around the notion of English as a 'killer language', past as present: the polarization of 'English-speaking haves' versus 'non-English-speaking have-nots'; the presumed universality of native-speaker norms of usage for ESL/EFL learners, from pronunciation to sociopragmatic rules of speaking; and the gradual disappearance of minority languages following the death of the last speakers – along with the world-views and cultural heritage encoded in the dying languages. To arrest the world's dependence on English in its ever-expanding role as a world lingua franca, it has been suggested that Esperanto be promoted as a universal second language (see e.g. Phillipson 2003, Skutnabb-Kangas 2000), starting from international institutions such as the General Assembly of UN and UNESCO. There are however practical difficulties with this scenario, notably the limited number of communicative functions that Esperanto has been put to use, and the relatively small community of Esperanto users, hence a vicious circle (Li 2003). In the foreseeable future, it is estimated that English will continue to prevail in inter-ethnic encounters and cross-border communications.

Toward the end of her book *Multilingualism in the English-speaking World*, Viv Edwards (1994: 222) echoes the intriguing question attributed to the British Classicist Richard Porson in the eighteenth-century: "Is life too short to learn German?" With that question, Edwards wants to dispel two popular and deep-seated misperceptions whereby (a) languages are looked upon as "pedigrees of nations", and (b) acquiring a language in addition to one's mother tongue up to native-like proficiency is impossible. Of these two myths, the former is debunked by the bulk of her book, which provides strong evidence showing how, "[t]hanks to the efforts of minority communities to keep their languages alive, the inner-circle countries [where English is the first language of the majority] have a competitive edge in international trade". As for the latter, Edwards underscores empirical evidence from research on bilingual education, which suggests that with careful planning and implementation, an additional language may be acquired by being used for teaching content subjects to young learners at no expense of their first language. In an increasingly globalized world where multilingualism is the norm, therefore, there is no question about the benefits – cognitive, linguacultural as much as economic – that multilingualism will bring to the individual as well as to the organization that he or she works for.

References

Agar, Michael
  1994   *Language shock / Understanding the Culture of Conversation.* New York: William Morrow and Co.
Bailey, Garrick and Peoples, James
  2002   *Essentials of Cultural Anthropology.* Belmont, CA: Wadsworth.
Baker, Colin
  2003   Language planning: a grounded approach. In: Jean-Marcus Dewaele, Alex Housen and Li Wei (eds.), 88–111. *Bilingualism: Beyond Basic Principles.* Clevedon: Multilingual Matters.
Bhatia, Tej K.
  2000   *Advertising in rural India. Language, Marketing Communication, and Consumerism.* Tokyo: Tokyo University of Foreign Studies.
Bourdieu, Pierre
  1991   *Language and Symbolic Power.* Cambridge: Polity Press.
Brutt-Griffler, J.
  2002   *World English. A Study of its Development.* Clevedon, UK: Multilingual Matters.
Chan, Allan K.K.
  1990   Localization in international branding. A preliminary investigation on Chinese names of foreign brands in Hong Kong. *International Journal of Advertising* 9: 81–91.
Chesire, J. and Moser, L.
  1994   English as a cultural symbol: the case of advertisements in French-speaking Switzerland. *Journal of Multilingual and Multicultural Development* 15, 451–469.
Cook, Guy
  1992   *The Discourse of Advertising.* London and New York: Routledge.
Coulmas, Florian (ed.)
  1991   The economics of language in the Asian Pacific. *Journal of Asian Pacific Communication* 2(1).
Coulmas, Florian
  1992   *Language and Economy.* Oxford: Blackwell.

Coulmas, Florian
 1993   Was ist die deutsche Sprache wert? In: J. Born, G. Stickel (eds.), *Deutsch als Verkehrssprache in Europa*. 9–25. Berlin: De Gruyter.
Edwards, Viv
 2004   *Multilingualism in the English-speaking World*. Malden, MA and Oxford, UK: Blackwell.
Giddens, Anthony
 2000   *Runaway World. How Globalization is Reshaping our Lives*. New York: Routledge.
Haarmann, Harald
 1984   The role of ethnocultural stereotypes and foreign languages in Japanese commercials. *International Journal of the Sociology of Language* 50: 101–121.
Haarmann, Harald
 1986   Verbal strategies in Japanese fashion magazines – a study in impersonal bilingualism and ethnosymbolism. *International Journal of the Sociology of Language* 58: 107–121.
Haarmann, Harald
 1989   *Symbolic Values of Foreign Language Use. From the Japanese Case to a General Sociolinguistic Perspective*. Berlin: Mouton de Gruyter.
Hogan, Jackie
 2003   The Social Significance of English Usage in Japan. *Japanese Studies* 23: 43–58.
Huang, Yue Yuan and Chan, Allan K. K.
 1997   Chinese branding name: from general principles to specific rules. *International Journal of Advertising* 16: 320–35.
Kottak, Conrad Phillip
 2004   *Cultural Anthropology*. 10th ed. Boston: MaGraw Hill.
Lee, Micky
 2000   Code-switching in media texts: its implications on society and culture in postcolonial Hong Kong. In: David C.S. Li, Angel Lin and Wai King Tsang (eds.), *Language and Education in Postcolonial Hong Kong*. 95–129. Hong Kong: Linguistic Society of Hong Kong.
Li, David C.S.
 2003   Between English and Esperanto: What does it take to be a world language? *International Journal of the Sociology of Language* 164: 33–63.
Lock, Graham
 2003   Being international, local and Chinese: advertisements on the Hong Kong Mass Transit Railway. *Visual Communication* 2: 195–214.
Pennycook, Alastair
 1994   *The Cultural Politics of English as an International Language*. London: Longman.
Pennycook, Alastair
 1998   *English and the Discourses of Colonialism*. London: Routledge.
Peoples, James and Bailey, Garrick
 2003   *Humanity. An Introduction to Cultural Anthropology*. 6th edn. Melbourne: Thomson.
Phillipson, Robert
 1992   *Linguistic Imperialism*. Oxford: Oxford University Press.

Phillipson, Robert
2003   *English-Only Europe? Challenging Language Policy.* London and New York: Routledge.
Piller, Ingrid
2000   Multilingualism and the modes of TV advertising. In: Friedrich Ungerer (ed.), *English Media Texts Past and Present. Language and Text Structure.* 263–279. Amsterdam/Philadelphia: John Benjamins.
Piller, Ingrid
2001   Identity construction in multilingual advertising. *Language in Society* 30: 153–186.
Rodriguez, América
1999   *Making Latino News. Race, Language, Class.* Thousand Oaks, CA: Sage Publications.
Skutnabb-Kangas, Tove
2000   *Linguistic Genocide in Education – or Worldwide Diversity and Human Rights.* Mahwah, NJ. and London: Lawrence Erlbaum Associates, Publishers.
Sprung, Robert C. (ed.)
2000   *Translating into Success. Cutting-edge Strategies for Going Multilingual in a Global Age.* Amsterdam / Philadelphia: John Benjamins.
Tinker-Sachs, Gertrude and Li, David C.S.
in press   Cantonese as an additional language: problems and prospects. *Multilingua.*
Usunier, Jean-Claude and Shaner, Janet
2002   Using linguistics for creating better international brand names. *Journal of Marketing Communications* 8: 211–228.

Recommended readings

Coulmas (1991, 1992) offers a comprehensive overview of the 'economics of language', showing how the vitality of a language (e.g. German and Japanese) is closely related to the economic well-being of the speech community in question. For an insightful theoretical analysis of language as a form of capital ('linguistic capital' and 'symbolic capital'), see Bourdieu (1991). Sprung (2000) is a highly readable collection of case studies exemplifying the role – in particular the cost – of translation in transnational business enterprises such as Microsoft, Eastman Kodak, and Ericsson. Usunier and Shaner (2002) is an updated and informative account of various aspects of brand name research in cross-border multilingual advertising practices. On the use of language in increasingly multilingual adverts in Japan, Germany and Hong Kong, see Haarmann (1984, 1986, 1989), Piller (2000, 2001), and Lock (2003), respectively. Viv Edwards' (2004) monograph is an interesting and accessible account of the historical circumstances leading to the state of multilingualism in the English-speaking world today. It also offers, among other things, an insightful analysis of the critical factors behind the survival and demise of various minority languages, including those in the UK, North America and Australia. Brutt-Griffler (2002) is an insightful historical study of the global spread of English. Finally, for a general introduction to globalization and how it impacts on transnational business practices, see Kottak (2004) and Peoples and Bailey (2003).

IV. Living in a multilingual society

18.   Societal multilingualism:
reality, recognition and response[1]

John Edwards

1.   Introduction

The maternal tongue of a Bombay spice merchant is a Kathiawari dialect of Gujerati; he usually speaks Kacchi at work, however. In the market place he speaks Marathi and, at the railway station, Hindustani. English is the medium when he flies with Air India to New Delhi, and he sometimes watches English-language films at the cinema. He reads a Gujerati newspaper written in a dialect more standard than his own. He sometimes has dealings with a Bengali colleague who routinely speaks both "high" and "low" Bengali – a man whose "primary" wife speaks a dialect strongly marked as a female variant, and whose "secondary" wife normally speaks Urdu. His office manager speaks Dhaki and his servants variously use Bhojpuri, Awadhi, Maithili, Ahiri and Chatgaya. This Bengali businessman has a cousin in Orissa, an Oriya speaker married to a Tamil: they use English at home, but their children are more likely to speak Bengali; they employ a Hindustani nurse and a Nepali watchman.[2]

I possess a general acquaintance with the languages and literature of the Aryan and Syro-Arabic classes […] with several [languages] I have a more intimate acquaintance as with the Romance tongues, Italian, French, Catalan, Spanish, Latin and in a less degree Portuguese, Vaudois, Provençal and various dialects. In the Teutonic branch I am tolerably familiar with Dutch […] Flemish, German, Danish. In Anglo-Saxon and Moeso-Gothic my studies have been much closer […] I know a little of the Celtic, and am at present engaged with the Sclavonic [sic], having obtained a useful knowledge of Russian. In the Persian, Achaemenian Cuneiform and Sanscrit [sic] branches, I know for the purposes of Comparative Philology. I have sufficient knowledge of Hebrew and Syriac to read at sight the O.T. […] to a less degree I know Aramaic Arabic, Coptic and Phenician [sic].[3]

Each of the two little vignettes presented above demonstrates something of the multilingual reality. In the first, we have a glimpse of contexts that elicit the multiple language skills of many 'ordinary' people; in the second, we read of the abilities of the young James Murray – in 1866, before becoming the editor of the *Oxford English Dictionary* – abilities that, in *his* context, were not ordinary at all. Each description reveals a spectrum of competence, either a normal and unremarked-upon one, or a more formal and unusual acquisition – and, whether the multilingual repertoire is a product of the street or the study, each vignette also reveals the broad potentials that are within the grasp of all people of average intelligence.

Multilingualism is a powerful fact of life around the world, a circumstance arising, at the simplest level, from the need to communicate across speech communities. Important *lingua francas* have always acted as aids to cross-group understanding; these typically represent the language of some potent and pres-tigious society – Greek, Latin, French, Arabic, English, and so on. As well, pidgins, creoles and 'artificial' or constructed languages (like Esperanto) have served in more restricted contexts. But the strong and obvious attractions of such trans-group varieties have generally coexisted with, rather than eliminated, more local forms, and they have not spelled the death of multilingualism so much as they have been a product of it and, indeed, a contributor to it.

To be multilingual is not the aberration supposed by some of those who speak a 'big' language – indeed, in global statistical terms at least, monolingual-ism is much less common than the sorts of expanded repertoires illustrated in the opening vignettes. The linguistic myopia that is so often a feature of mono-lingual perspectives is sometimes accompanied by a narrow cultural awareness and – if we move from the personal to the social level – can be seen to be rein-forced by state policies which typically elevate only one language to official status. Thus, while there exist something like five thousand languages in about two hundred countries, only a quarter of all states recognise more than one lan-guage. As well, even in those countries in which two or more varieties have legal status, one language is usually predominant, or has regional limitations, or carries with it disproportionate amounts of social, economic and political power. Switzerland, for example, with its recognition of German, French, Ita-lian and Romansch, shows clear linguistic dominance for one variety at the can-ton level and the four languages are not anything like equal in cross-community utility. Singapore also has four official languages – English, Mandarin, Tamil and Malay – but the latter two are much less important than the former pair (see ch. IV.4 of this handbook). Ireland constitutionally recognises both Irish and English but the first has, increasingly, only symbolic significance in the general life of the country.

In countries where more than one language has legal status, it would still be unwise to assume that multilingual encounters are common. One might live in India, where eighteen varieties are now constitutionally recognised as 'sched-uled' languages (and where one of these – Hindi – shares federally official status with English), and experience the daily multilingualism shown in the first vi-gnette – but one might also have a full life completely within a monolingual en-clave. On the other hand, such encounters may not be at all uncommon in states officially recognising only one or two varieties. Many African countries, for example, are so linguistically complex that multilingual interaction is a mun-dane occurrence – this is certainly in so Nigeria, where eighty million people speak four hundred languages, but where only English has the official imprima-tur. Even in America, where no variety is official at the federal level, but where English has all the *de facto* clout a language could wish for, you might work in a linguistically heterogeneous city like New York and spend a great deal of your time code-switching between English and Spanish.

2.   The development of multilingualism

Multilingual realities 'on the ground' arise in a number of ways. With simple population movement, for instance, immigrants bring their languages into contact with each other, and with those of existing populations (cf. ch. IV.3 of this handbook); territorial expansion is another type of migration, with similar results (cf. ch. IV.2 of this handbook). Sometimes, as with imperialist and colonial expansion, it is unnecessary for large numbers of people to physically move; they may 'move' their language into contact with others through military and economic pressures which require only a handful of soldiers, merchants and bureaucrats – thus, a few thousand people controlling the Indian sub-continent brought about a massively expanded base for English among a (current) population of more than a billion: some forty million use English on a regular basis, and many more have some ability in the language. Language spread and contact, and the resultant multilingualism, have always been closely allied to trade, to imperialist military ventures and to hopes for religious conversion and proselytism. Some cultures have had more explicit policies here than have others – compare, for instance, the *mission civilisatrice* of the French with the more pragmatic attitude of the English – but all imperial powers have, directly or indirectly, made their languages attractive and sometimes necessary to conquered or colonised groups. The languages of expansionist regimes often become intertwined with pragmatic advantage and cultural prestige, factors which coexist with the simpler and more brutal trappings of dominance – and which often long outlive the initial colonial influence. The continued adherence to European varieties which exists in former colonial areas is an example here (cf. ch. IV.4 of this handbook). English in India is, again, another instance – although we should note that the continued global power of English has been immeasurably heightened by the rise of the United States; it is quite atypical for former 'world' languages to gain a renewed lease on life in this way.

Multilingualism can also arise as a result of political union among different linguistic groups: Switzerland (as noted above) incorporates German, Italian, Romansch and French populations; Belgium unites (sometimes precariously) French and Flemish speakers; Canada has English and French 'charter' groups. In addition to this sort of political association, there are also multilingual federations based upon more arbitrary arrangements, often the result of colonial boundary-marking and country-creation; modern examples are found in Africa and Asia. Multilingualism is also commonly observed in border areas: two North American examples can be found along the Mexican-American border in the south, and on that between New England and Quebec in the north.

These are the primary circumstances underpinning the development of multilingual competences but they are not, of course, the only ones. As the James Murray vignette illustrates, cultural and educational motivations can also expand linguistic repertoires – not only on an individual basis, but in more widespread fashion as well, as historical examples of so-called élite bilingualism make clear (cf. ch. III.5 of this handbook). Also relevant here is the degree to which a language community is open to the use of 'its' variety by others: consider the differences between the English and the French in this regard. The latter have traditionally been much more possessive of their language and, while working hard to bring it to those unfortunate enough not to already speak it (the *mission civilisatrice*, again), have also been zealous in protecting its 'purity', both at home and abroad. English, on the other hand, has not been treated in the same guarded way; while there are books and journals devoted to the 'new' Englishes and to 'world' English, there are no such treatments for French. English is thus becoming 'internationalised' in a way that French is not, and an important consequence is that a language once tainted by imperialism is rapidly becoming 'ours' in many parts of the world; India (again) provides perhaps the best example of a broadly accepted indigenised variety of English.

English and French also illustrate another point in the linguistic expansion of competing varieties: the position taken by 'third parties'. While the expansion of English became marked in the twentieth century, French initially retained some diplomatic privileges, endorsed as the language of record at important conferences, negotiations and treaties. After the second world war, however, the shifting sands of global policies and alliances favoured English, with the result that, today, it is the dominant diplomatic vehicle, in addition to being globally central in science and technology, finance and popular culture. This is an appropriate juncture at which to point out that the spread of one language is typically at the expense of another (bilingual accommodations notwithstanding). Since all languages are potentially capable of filling all roles, it is easy to see that those whose varieties are threatened by others may quite understandably feel aggrieved. Their language, after all, has not been edged aside because of any inherent defects; there is no fatal linguistic here that has to be grudgingly acknowledged. Rather, the power of a competing variety derives from the strength of its community and it is this which is most difficult to accept, particularly to those who were once dominant themselves. The lack of any inherent linguistic hindrance, and the changeability of global power structures, might be thought to provide a glimmer of hope: few people, after all, would have predicted the present scope of English in 1500, when it had only four or five million speakers (well behind German, Spanish, French and Italian). It has to be said, however, that so far we have not seen the re-emergence of a 'world' language after its eclipse.

3.   The recognition of multilingualism

The Hungarian prime minister, Pál Teleki (1879–1941), who committed suicide when he realised that his signature on the 1940 Berlin Pact (an extension of the Italo-German axis of 1936) committed his country to invade Yugoslavia, related an interesting anecdote about a disputed border district: Cieszyn (Polish) / Těšín (Czech) – formerly under Habsburg rule (as Teschen). Asking how many Poles lived in the area, Teleki was told that the number varied between 40,000 and 100,000. His informant explained that many villagers changed their stated nationality, almost on a weekly basis, according to individual and community interests.[4]

3.1.   Censuses

Whether or not a language is an 'official', 'national' or 'scheduled' variety, many societies make regular attempts to assess the type and extent of multilingualism within their borders: this is most obviously done by census. Unfortunately, census information is often limited in important ways, and an initial difficulty arises in the phrasing of questions. If we ask respondents, "What is your mother tongue?", how do we know that they will all understand 'mother tongue' in the same way? What of those who feel they have more than one mother tongue, or of those who have forgotten the language first learned in childhood? Questions are sometimes even murkier: in the 1986 Canadian census, respondents were asked "Can you speak English or French well enough to conduct a conversation?", a statement open to a huge degree of interpretation. To further complicate matters, census questions often change over time, making comparability problematic. In Canada, for example, censuses up to 1941 defined mother tongue as "the language first learned and still spoken"; from 1941 to 1976, it was "the language first spoken and still understood"; in 1981, informants were asked about "the language first learned and still understood". In other national censuses, mother tongue has been defined as the language spoken in the informant's home when he or she was a child; in this case, a 'mother tongue' might never have been actually learned by the informant.

Perhaps it would be better to ask the central question in simpler form: something like, "What is the first language you spoke?" – but this may not provide us with the current information required. A question like "What language do you most often speak now?", however, rather alters the thrust of the enquiry and, besides, this sort of probe gives rise to other difficulties; how, for example, should or would it be answered by those who speak two or more varieties more or less equally? Problems are compounded by census practice which, for ease of data coding, often permits one response only, without any room for elaboration or explanation, and which may offer options that are inadequate to cover all important circumstances; such problems are of course inherent in tightly structured or closed-format questionnaires. (It will also be noted here that, even in situations in which informants can discuss possible answering options with census officials, the end result is often the same, since responses must still be recorded in essentially very simple ways.) And we have not even touched upon inaccurate self-reporting, whether innocent or not. See de Vries (1985, 1990) for further information on censuses and census difficulties.

Censuses may also be influenced by official policy, and this is particularly so in linguistically heterogeneous states. All Singaporeans are placed in one of the four linguistic groupings noted earlier – which can result in 'mother tongues' being assigned. Even though Indians in Singapore may speak Malayalam or Gujerati (for example), the policy selects Tamil as 'their' language; similarly, although relatively few Chinese are Mandarin mother tongue speakers (Hokkien, Teochew and Cantonese are the major variants), that variety is 'assigned' to them. In 1980, a case was reported of a civil servant who was ethnically Chinese but who had Malay as a mother tongue and English as a second language. Permission was refused for him to sit an examination in Malay because it was deemed 'only natural' that one should be competent in one's mother tongue – designated here, on Singaporean principles, as Mandarin (see Edwards 1995). Of course, official language policies may sometimes interfere with recording in much blunter ways: some groups of speakers may be ignored altogether, or their linguistic data may be manipulated for political ends. And in certain instances, language data (and sometimes other sensitive information, too) are simply not collected: all language-related questions were eliminated from post-1947 Belgian censuses, as the gathering, reporting and interpretation of such data were seen to be too politically hot.

One obvious implication of all these actual and potential confusions is that, when accurate language data are needed, specialised tabulations are required. These may build upon census information and, in some countries (like Canada), it is possible to have custom-made tables prepared by central statistical authorities; but some specific field-work is often called for. Serious students of multilingualism may begin by looking at census information, but they must inevitably go well beyond it.

3.2.   Language legislation and language rights

The numerous ecological organisations formed expressly for the protection of endangered languages typically have a charter or a statement of intent stressing language rights: Terralingua, for instance, observes that "deciding which language to use, and for what purposes, is a basic human right" (1999). As well, existing language associations have argued for rights, the most recent example being that of Teachers of English to Speakers of Other Languages (TESOL) which, in November 2000, passed a resolution advocating that "all groups of peoples have the right to maintain their native language ... a right to retain and use [it]". The other side of the coin, they argue, is that "the governments and the people of all countries have a special obligation to affirm, to respect and support the retention, enhancement and use of indigenous and immigrant heritage languages [...]". Such specialised manifestos are typically inspired by the conventions and charters endorsed by the United Nations, the European Union and other international bodies; a good recent example is the *Oegstgeest Declaration* on immigrant, regional and minority languages, the first article of which explicitly acknowledges the *Universal Declaration of Human Rights*, as well as the more specifically focussed European *Charter for Regional or Minority Languages* and the *Framework Convention for the Protection of National Minorities* (see Extra and Gorter 2001).

Within an ever-growing literature on rights in general there now also exist several useful overviews of language-rights claims and legislation, the most exhaustive being de Varennes (1996; see also the collection edited by Kontra *et al.* 1999, as well as the rather more pointed contributions by Phillipson 1992, 2000). The brief historical overview by Ruiz Vieytez (2001) focuses upon the concerns of language minorities, noting in particular the Council of Europe's convention and charter. These and other legislative provisions are more fully discussed by de Varennes (2001), and several generalities can be extracted.

First, virtually all the frameworks, conventions and charters having to do with language minorities that are underwritten by the European Union or the United Nations see minority rights as particularised applications of what de Varennes calls "basic human rights" (freedom of expression and non-discrimination being the most immediately relevant here) – hence he argues that language rights are not collective rights. Second, the documentation is generally not of a legally binding nature, reflecting rather the "political and moral obligations" that signatory states have acknowledged. There are no judicial remedies for sins of omission here. Third, the various charters typically distinguish between rights to the private use of languages by individuals and the public use of such varieties in official or authoritative contexts (as de Varennes [1999] points out elsewhere, there currently exist no unqualified rights to use a minority language). Most modern societies accept private usage and, indeed, public usage where no official ramifications exist. (Of course, those who are most concerned with rights for the speakers of 'small' varieties are typically interested in much more than private, within-group discourse.) Fourth, language rights are typically restricted to 'national minorities'. Quite apart from difficulties in defining this term, the deeper issue here has to do with de Varennes's first point: if rights for speakers of 'small' languages are, in fact, logical extensions of basic human rights, then on what grounds can they restricted in this way? Why shouldn't immigrant minority groups, for instance, benefit from legislation?

Government resolutions and charters dealing with language rights are often outlined ways so general as to be virtually useless. There are reasons for cynicism, too, for believing that the commitment they represent is essentially lipservice only. As well, many modern governments, while possibly more tolerant of diversity than before, still consider that toleration need not imply positive action, and arguments linking linguistic uniformity with efficiency, documenting a need for one language to bind disparate groups within state borders, and so on, are frequently encountered. Consequently, supporters of language rights typically find existing legislation to be frail. Phillipson (1992: 95) notes, for example, that "existing [...] declarations are in no way adequate to provide support for dominated languages" (see also de Varennes 1999). Simpson (2001: 29) says that not only are "arrangements for the domestic protection of human rights" weak and inadequate, but "at an international level the situation is much worse: for most ill-treated people, most of the time, human-rights instruments are not worth the paper they are written on." This is not to say, of course, that language conventions and the like are always weak. Where they appear effective, however, they are inevitably a reflection of larger social trends and pressures, tending to add a particular linguistic endorsement to some broader *projet de société*; thus, language legislation in Québec has had a clear effect – on non-francophone immigrants to the province, for example. But these are not the sorts of settings of greatest interest to supporters of 'small' languages – their concerns are with more or less immediately threatened varieties and their aspirations, therefore, are for legislation that is more 'pro-active'. It is in *these* circumstances that legislation typically proves lacking in their eyes.

Beyond official cynicism, or a reluctance to act based upon immediate and mercenary assessments, there are deeper issues. Linguistic rights are usually meant to have an effect at the group level – indeed, their existence is generally motivated by the plight of small groups whose languages and cultures are considered to at risk – and this may sit uneasily with traditional liberal-democratic principles that enshrine rights in individuals, not collectivities. For some, of course, the liberal essence *can* be reconciled with differential group treatments; indeed, for those who argue that language rights are in essence individual rights, the need for such a reconciliation never arises (see again de Varennes 1999, 2001). But it is surely the case that language rights, in any but the most rarefied of contexts, involve more than the individual; language itself generally presupposes a social context. All internationally underwritten rights may be individual ones, as de Varennes suggests, but "their manifestation may involve more than one individual" (1999: 118). And this *does* create difficulties, since it raises the individual-collectivist matter once again, and in a pointed way: while it may be possible to legislate freedom of individual language choice, it is rather more difficult to guarantee its utility. This is perhaps the nub of the difficulty suggested by statements like those of the TESOL organisation (noted above): can a right to be *understood* be reasonably expected (see Coulombe, 1993; Wright, 2001)? This returns us to a collective context – and, indeed, one without which more purely individual rights would be rather vitiated. A more nuanced position accepts that language rights necessarily comprise a sort of 'hybrid' category. On the one hand, language may be considered an individual characteristic, arguably of some importance to personal identity; on the other, it is group membership that leads to demands for language rights, and language is seen as a pivotal marker of group identity (see Coulombe 1993; MacMillan 1982, 1983).

With reference to what has already been mentioned – particularly the important matter of the nature of rights – we can perhaps understand why some (Kukathas 1992, for instance) have said that 'rights' (some? all?) would be better understood as cultural 'claims'. A recent overview by Brumfit (2001) brings the matter squarely to linguistic rights. These, he points out, are typically *assertions* of things that ought to be, rather than statements which, through general or longstanding agreement, have become objectified (in legal terms). Rights to language, then, are not of the same order as, say, those which proclaim freedom from slavery. While legal rights imply moral ones, the reverse does not necessarily hold – although, of course, what is merely desirable today may become lawfully codified tomorrow.

4.   Dealing with multilingualism

Although the exigencies of language contact give rise to multilingual abilities, there are obviously many occasions when limitations in such abilities necessitate some means of bridging a language gap. There are two main methods here. The first, the use of lingua francas, is either part of the existing multilingual picture, or necessitates an extension of it. These 'link languages' fall into three categories: so-called 'languages of wider communication', varieties that have achieved regional or global power; restricted or limited linguistic forms whose diminished scope is at once easy to master and sufficient for communicative purposes which are, themselves, quite circumscribed; and constructed or 'artificial' languages.

There are many historical examples of existing languages becoming important lingua francas – not, of course, because of any intrinsic qualities setting them above other varieties, but because of the power and prestige of their speakers. Greek and Latin are the 'classical' link languages, but French, Italian, Arabic and – today – English have all played bridging roles. Pidgins and creole varieties comprise the second category here. The limited vocabularies and grammars of pidgins are sufficient for basic communication – and they are, then, a rather good example of a much more general tendency, the development of multiple fluencies up to, but not beyond, the requirements of use. If the social contacts that give rise to pidgins remain, themselves, of a rudimentary nature, then those pidgins may have considerable longevity; if contact situations persist, however, and become more complicated, pidgins may evolve into *creoles*. The developments here stem from the need for richer and more expressive forms, and these, in turn, often arise because nobody's mother tongue (a pidgin) is in the process of becoming somebody's mother tongue (a creole). Constructed languages are a third potential bridge across linguistic divides: although there have been a great many schemes over the centuries, the best known and the most successful constructed variety is Esperanto (initiated by Ludwig Zamenhof in 1887). In most cases, the initial desire has been to produce a 'neutral' auxiliary – easy to learn because of structural simplicity and regularity – a role that powerful 'natural' languages are seen to be unable to play. But Zamenhof and others like him have also believed that constructed link languages, untainted by imperialist pasts, might contribute to some 'trans-national' identity, and thus to global harmony. Although there are several important reasons for the lack of acceptance of constructed languages, a basic problem is this: Esperanto (for example) might be more appealing if there were a community of speakers one could join. Without such a community, however, motivating potential learners to take the plunge is of course difficult – yet how else will a speech community come into being?

The other great bridging method is translation. While it is clear that the services of translators and interpreters are of practical benefit, it is perhaps less obvious that psychosocial tensions may arise. As George Steiner put it (1975: 202), "there is in every act of translation – and specially where it succeeds – a touch of treason. Hoarded dreams, patents of life are being taken across the frontier". The old Italian proverb was blunter: *traduttori, traditori*. This suggests that concealment is as much a feature of language as is communication and this, too, has been expressed in many ways and for a long time (Talleyrand, for instance, once observed that "la parole a été donnée à l'homme pour déguiser sa pensée": cited by Steiner 1975: 225). Privacy, the construction of fictionalised myths, legends and stories, and outright dissimulation are at once important and threatened by translation and translators; one modern theme is the 'appropriation' of native stories by outsiders, for in many cultures – particularly ones with powerful and rich oral traditions – stories belong to the group or, indeed, to some designated story-teller.

Apart from an almost useless word-for-word exercise, every act of translation involves interpretation and judgement. For this reason, it has sometimes been supposed that 'true' translation is impossible; however, although a perfect version which captures *every* nuance and allusion is rather unlikely – and becomes more so as the material to be translated becomes less prosaic – we have nonetheless translated, for practical purposes, throughout history. (Seeing translation as interpretation also links, incidentally, cross-language exercises with communications within the same language. That is, even the simplest of conversations between two speakers of the same language involves interpretation, and is analogous to 'reading between the lines' in written language.) If, as is generally the case, the aim is to adhere to what the well-known classical translator, Émile Rieu, once called the "law of equivalent effect" (see Tancock 1954: 16), then the greatest threats to accurate translation appear at opposite ends of the literary continuum. At the 'lower' end, the nonstandard language of the streets, heavy with ever-changing slang and obscenity, poses real problems; at the 'higher', poetic or philosophical productions lay traps in their use of metaphor, allusion or dense, abstract reasoning.

Beyond the bridging that multilingualism necessitates, languages in contact can also generate moat-building. The most interesting form of this defensive strategy is linguistic prescriptivism or purism, which, given free rein, would often lead to proscription. Concern about the 'contamination' of one language by another, about infiltration and borrowing and about the bullying of small languages by larger ones is an historically longstanding worry; the desire to keep one's language 'pure' has always been strong. Linguists note, quite correctly, that the prescriptive urge is generally both unrealistic and undesirable – languages have always borrowed from one another – but it is the powerful link between language and identity that is crucial here; that is, prescriptivism is a psychological matter, one in which the linguistic specifics are often just badges or team jerseys.

The classic instruments of linguistic prescriptivism, the drive to maintain 'standards', are academies and dictionaries. The first institution devoted specifically to language was the *Accademia della crusca* of Florence, founded (or, at least, given royal blessing) in 1572: *crusca* means 'bran', so the name implies a desire to separate linguistic grain from chaff. The *Académie française* was established in 1634. The *Real Academia Española* followed in 1713 – its royal motto, *limpia, fija y da esplendor*, emphasises the desire to clarify, purify and glorify a language. And after these came many more – in fact, language academies (or similar bodies) are very much the rule. Conspicuous by its absence is any English-language academy. There was certainly interest in one: as early as 1605, for example, Richard Verstegan was emphasising, in *A Restitution of Decayed Intelligence*, a renewed and nationalistic pride in the language; later on, the Royal Society took an interest, as did important individuals like Dryden, Evelyn, Defoe and Swift (see Ayto 1983). If an English academy was not to be, however, there remained the perceived need for standards – and the solution involved Samuel Johnson and his famous dictionary of 1755 (in England) and, a little later, Noah Webster and *his* dictionary of 1827 (in America). In each case, an English-speaking population had rejected standardisation by committee, and endorsed a one-man academy.

5.   Bilingualism and diglossia

Bilingual or multilingual competence has traditionally reflected and supported upper-class boundaries. In earlier times, not to have known Latin or Greek or French in addition to one's mother tongue would have been unthinkable for educated people. This so-called élite bilingualism, however, is far removed from the mundane necessities fuelling the more common 'folk' variety: humbler citizens have also been bilingual from earliest times. We know it was necessary under the Ptolemies to acquire Greek, even for quite minor posts, and Athenian slaves – representatives of the lowest class of all – were often bilingual as they were pressed into domestic service and teaching (Lewis 1976).

There are important differences between individual bilingualism and collective or social bilingualism, regardless of whether the latter is officially endorsed (as in Canada) or simply a fact of ordinary life (as in Taiwan, where Mandarin is official but where most speak Fukienese as a mother tongue). Collective bilingualism can be an enduring quantity, or it can be impermanent. In many immigrant contexts – in the United States, for example – bilingualism has been a generational way-station on the road between two monolingualisms. A less ephemeral collective bilingualism implies a continuing necessity, one that usually rests upon different social functions and different domains of use for each language. This situation is now commonly referred to as *diglossia*. This word is simply the Greek version of 'bilingualism' and, on the face of it, would not seem to be a useful innovation; it does not logically encompass the social, collective aspect that, in practice, it refers to. Near the end of the nineteenth century, hellenists wishing to describe the roles of dialects in Greek society introduced the idea of *diglossie*; thus, *demotic* Greek (the ordinary spoken variety) and *katharévusa* (the 'purer', more classic form) exist in a diglossic relationship. It soon became apparent that modern Greece was not the only setting where a functional differentiation existed between 'higher' and 'lower' varieties of the same language. Later, the scope of diglossia was extended, from two dialects of the same language to separate languages altogether (or, indeeed, to styles and registers). The important matter remains functional differentiation among co-existing varieties. Thus, one can now find examples of *triglossia* – in North Africa, for instance, where classical and vernacular Arabic co-exist with French – or *tetraglossia*: in Morocco – to stay in North Africa – one finds the three varieties just mentioned augmented by Berber. In fact, a 'polyglossic spectrum' is the norm in many parts of the world. While diglossia, as collective bilingualism, is seen to be a stable condition, it should be remembered that even stability is relative: the French-English diglossia that prevailed in England after the Norman conquest eventually broke down, with the 'lower' variety (English) achieving dominance (see Ferguson 1959; Mackey 1986, 1989).

6.   Classifying multilingualism

Examination of various language-contact settings reveals that the uniqueness of every context arises because of the differential weightings and combinations of elements that are, themselves, recurrent across settings. This suggests the possibility of frameworks within which settings might be assessed and compared. A classification of language situations is at once an attempt to impose theoretical order, and a means of codifying and facilitating cross-community comparison; indeed the comparison of cases can often indicate what more we need to know about individual cases themselves. Some have criticised typological exercises, on the grounds that they embody prevailing assumptions, have limited analytical utility and imply permanence or stasis. These are certainly appropriate cautions, but my view is simply that – since people will obviously continue to be interested in describing and accounting for language situations, since it makes no sense to assume that different contexts are unique in every element, and since scholars are properly drawn to the task of theory construction or generalisation – a comprehensive and well-specified typology could be a useful guide. Cross-context comparisons might well be facilitated, for example, if attention was given to the same variables in all settings; any student in the area will have experienced frustration in attempting comparisons and contrasts where this sort of attention has not been paid. Prominent figures in linguistics have made similar points:

> It is frustrating to read a stimulating case study and find that it lacks information on what the reader regards as some crucial points [...] what I have in mind is not so much a well developed theoretical frame of reference as something as simple as a checklist of points to be covered. (Ferguson 1991: 230)

> most language descriptions are prefaced by a brief and perfunctory statement concerning the number and location of its speakers and something of their history. Rarely does such a description really tell the reader what he ought to know about the social status and function of the language in question. Linguists have generally been too eager to get on with the phonology, grammar, and lexicon to pay more than superficial attention to what I would like to call the "ecology of language". (Haugen 1972: 325)

Indeed, Haugen and Ferguson (and others: see below) have paid some attention to typological work themselves.

Building upon the work of these and other researchers, I have constructed a typological framework of minority-language situations. The model clearly does not cover all important instances of multilingual contact; however, because contact often involves stronger and weaker varieties, it is descriptive of many settings. In its geographical underpinning, the framework represents an adaptation of a scheme first proposed by Paul White in 1987 (see White 1991). It makes three basic distinctions. The first is among minority languages which are unique to one state, those which are non-unique but which are still minorities in all contexts in which they occur, and those which are minorities in one setting but majority varieties elsewhere; thus, we have *unique*, *non-unique* and *local-only* minorities. The second distinction deals with the type of connection among speakers of the same minority language in different states; are they *adjoining* or *non-adjoining*? Thirdly, what degree of spatial cohesion exists among speakers within a given state? Here, the terms *cohesive* and *non-cohesive* can be used. Given that the adjoining/non-adjoining distinction does not apply to unique minorities, it follows that a ten-cell model emerges. Table 1 provides some examples, of both indigenous and immigrant minority-language settings.

Table 1. Examples of minority-language situations

	TYPE	INDIGENOUS MINORITIES	IMMIGRANT MINORITIES
1.	Unique Cohesive	Sardinian (Sardinia); Welsh (Wales); Friulian (Friuli-Venezia-Giulia)	Dialect communities (often religiously organised) in which the variety is now divergent from that in the region of origin (e.g., Pennsylvania 'Dutch')
2.	Unique Non-cohesive	Cornish (Cornwall)	As above, but where speakers are scattered
3.	Non-unique Adjoining Cohesive	Occitan (Piedmont and Liguria, and in France); Basque (France, and in Spain); Catalan (Spain, and in Andorra)	Enclaves of immigrants found in neighbouring states
4.	Non-unique Adjoining Non-cohesive	Saami (Finland, Norway, Sweden and Russia)	Scattered immigrants in neighbouring states
5.	Non-unique Non-adjoining Cohesive	Catalan (Spain, and in Sardinia)	Welsh (Patagonia); Gaelic (Nova Scotia)
6.	Non-unique Non-adjoining Non-cohesive	Romany (throughout Europe)	Scattered immigrants of European origin in 'new-world' receiving countries
7.	Local-only Adjoining Cohesive	French (Valle d'Aosta, and in France)	French (in New England town enclaves); Spanish (southwest USA); Italian gastarbeiter (in Switzerland)
8.	Local-only Adjoining Non-cohesive	German (Piedmont, and in Switzerland)	French (scattered throughout New England)
9.	Local-only Non-adjoining Cohesive	French (Apulia, and in France)	Immigrant enclaves in 'new world' countries
10.	Local-only Non-adjoining Non-cohesive	Albanian (throughout the Mezzogiorno, and in Albania)	As above, but where speakers are scattered

The model is, of course, far from perfect. Consider, for example, the immigrant-indigenous dimension. In one sense, only Amerindian languages are indigenous to Canada yet, in another sense, French (along with English) has a four-hundred-year claim on Canadian territory. There are also problems with the cohesiveness dimension: if a minority language is spoken sparsely over a wide area, but also possesses a concentrated centre, then it could be seen as either cohesive or non-cohesive. Yet another difficulty arises when considering a minority which is found in adjoining states; while each group can be classified as cohesive or non-cohesive, the degree of cohesion of its neighbour may also be important. Issues also arise concerning the adjoining/non-adjoining dichotomy itself. For Basques in France and Spain, the adjoining label seems appropriate, but what of minority groups found in neighbouring states but not in their common border areas? More generally, while a geographical framework might be quite useful, it is clear that information of other types is required to more fully understand the complexities of minority languages and their speakers.

The functions and status of competing language varieties are clearly central here, and have engaged the attention of Ferguson (1962, 1966), Stewart (1962, 1968), Haugen (1972), Haarmann (1986), Giles (see, e.g., Giles and Coupland 1991) and others; many of the specifics discussed in their models fall under the general rubric of the 'ecology of language', an area devoted to the interactions between a language and its environment. I have closely examined all these existing efforts as part of my own attempt to construct a comprehensive scaffolding of ecolinguistic factors. It builds upon three basic categories of variables: *speaker, language* and *setting*. These are not, of course, watertight and mutually exclusive dimensions, but they may serve as benchmarks. A second categorisation takes into account different substantive and disciplinary perspectives (history, demography, education, and so on). Combining these two classifications produces the framework shown here as Table 2.

For each of the 33 cells in Table 2, questions of interest can be formulated. As examples here, I have drawn attention to five cells. Cell A would alert us to consider urban-rural distinctions of importance for language maintenance or decline, for instance; cell B, the matter of within-group or without-group marriage; cell C, the nature and degree of dialectal variation or fragmentation; cells D and E, the matter of language attitudes and beliefs; and so on. It is obvious that these questions are not nearly specific enough to comprise a completed and applicable typology; they are merely suggestions of the sort of items which could be grouped together by cell (some questions could fit reasonably well in more than one cell). Much more work remains to be done in the production of a comprehensive typology useful for description and comparison, leading to a more complete conceptualisation of language-contact situations, perhaps even contributing to predictions of shift/maintenance outcomes. Given that many individual case-studies, however rich and many-layered, are essentially one-off

Table 2. A Framework for Language-contact Situations

	SPEAKER	LANGUAGE	SETTING
Demography			A
Sociology	B		
Linguistics		C	
Psychology	D	E	
History			
Politics/Law/Government			
Geography			
Education			
Religion			
Economics			
The Media			

exercises, it is clear that typological exercises can be useful, even if they do no more than rationalise data gathering.[5]

7.   Conclusion

Multilingualism is an aspect of what might be called the 'social life of language' and, as such, it has both a *de facto* existence and an important place in the psychological, political and social debates that define nations and states. The 'reality' of multilingualism is that it is a widespread phenomenon that arises for a number of well-understood reasons. It is also, in the main, an unremarkable phenomenon, fuelled by necessity up to, but rarely beyond, appropriately useful levels of competence. It implies both heightened and lessened opportunities for exchange: multilingual capacities at a personal level obviously increase the range here, but it is also clear that a world of many languages is a world in which communicative problems exist. In such a world, various sorts of *lingua francas* and for translation are required.

The recognition of multilingualism at a group level involves, first, some informed idea about its scope and prevalence and, second, some legislative reaction (or, of course, none at all). If the modern census is prone both to practical difficulties and to political interference, more basic problems can affect less 'developed' states. For instance, a language can have different names: Ubykh – an extinct Caucasian language of Turkey – is Oubykh to francophone writers, and it has also been styled Ubyx and Pekhi. Multiple names are particularly likely to occur for remote, 'small' varieties, but even better-known languages may have several, and it is not at all the case that the various names are similar (as with Oubykh-Ubykh-Ubyx): consider examples like Kituba/Fiote (from the Congo), or Ambonese/Haruku (Indonesia), or Desano/Kusibi (Colombia), or Gwichin/Loucheux (Canada) – see Grimes (2000) and Heine (1970). Multiple names arise for a number of reasons, but one of the most common is confusion between language and dialect. Accurate assessments of varieties spoken can by no means be taken for granted.

Legislation about languages and their speakers may rest, then, upon shaky pillars. In addition, questions of language 'rights' are of course subject to the same political winds that affect the very acceptance or assessment of speech communities. Much of contemporary interest revolves around questions of how language rights, and linguistic legislation generally, might best be allocated. It is a commonplace, for example, to read that 'indigenous' groups have stronger claims than do 'immigrant' population but – as I have pointed out in the previous section, matters of 'indigenousness' are hardly clearcut; besides, the moral-legal grounds on which allocations could be made to indigenous people but denied to immigrants – who are in many cases (in urban Canada, for example) now numerous and legal state citizens – are questionable.

Those concerned with multilingual practices and multilingual rights should bear in mind Kedourie's dictum about language and power:

> It is absurd to think that professors of linguistics [...] can do the work of statesmen and soldiers [...] academic enquiries are used by conflicting interests to bolster up their claims, and their results prevail only to the extent that somebody has the power to make them prevail [...] academic research does not add a jot or a tittle to the capacity for ruling. (Kedourie, 1960: 125)

This does not vitiate, of course, the usefulness for accurate data – and it is the desire to provide useful and, above all, comparative, information that has led several researchers to look for cross-contextual generalities. But it is useful to remember that – when dealing with official responses to multilingual realities – much of what appears in the literature under the heading of 'language planning' will never leave the academic cloisters.

Notes

1. For fuller details on the topic, see Edwards (1985, 1995).
2. For this Indian vignette, I have adapted information found in Pandit (1979) and Pattanayak (1986).
3. This self-description of James Murray is found in his grand-daughter's delightful biography (1977, p. 70).
4. The story related by Count Pál Teleki is found in Kedourie (1960: 124); I have supplemented it with some geographical and political information.
5. For some examples of work involving the typology outlined here, see Grenoble and Whaley (1998), King (2001) and Yağmur and Kroon (2003).

References

Ayto, John
    1983   English: Failures of language reforms. In: Istvan Fodor and Claude Hagège
               (eds.), *Language Reform: History and Future* (Volume 1), 48–67. Ham-
               burg: Helmut Buske.
Brumfit, Christopher
    2001   *Individual Freedom in Language Teaching.* Oxford: Oxford University Press.
Coulombe, Pierre
    1993   Language rights, individual and communal. *Language Problems and Lan-
               guage Planning* 17: 140–152.
Edwards, John
    1985   *Language, Society and Identity.* Oxford: Blackwell.
Edwards, John
    1995   *Multilingualism.* London: Penguin.
Extra, Guus and Durk Gorter
    2001   *The Other Languages of Europe.* Clevedon: Multilingual Matters.
Ferguson, Charles
    1959   Diglossia. *Word* 15: 325–340. [reprinted in: Pier-Paolo Giglioli (ed.), 1972,
               Language and Social Context. Harmondsworth, Middlesex: Penguin].
Ferguson, Charles
    1962   The language factor in national development. In: Frank Rice (ed.), *Study
               of the Role of Second Languages in Asia, Africa and Latin America,* 8–14.
               Washington: Center for Applied Linguistics.
Ferguson, Charles
    1966   National sociolinguistic profile formulas. In: William Bright (ed.), *Socio-
               linguistics,* 309–315. The Hague: Mouton.
Ferguson, Charles
    1991   Diglossia revisited. *Southwest Journal of Linguistics* 10: 214–234.
Giles, Howard and Nikolas Coupland
    1991   *Language: Contexts and Consequences.* Milton Keynes: Open University
               Press.
Grenoble, Lenore and Lindsey Whaley
    1998   Toward a typology of language endangerment. In: Lenore Grenoble and
               Lindsey Whaley (eds.), *Endangered Languages,* 22–54. Cambridge: Cam-
               bridge University Press.
Grimes, Barbara (ed.)
    2000   *Ethnologue: Languages of the World* (14th edition). Dallas, Texas: Summer
               Institute of Linguistics.
Haarmann, Harald
    1986   *Language in Ethnicity.* Berlin: de Gruyter.
Haugen, Einar
    1972   *The Ecology of Language.* Stanford: Stanford University Press
Heine, Bernd
    1970   *Status and Use of African Lingua Francas.* Munich: Weltforum.
Kedourie, Elie
    1960   *Nationalism.* London: Hutchinson.

King, Kendall
    2001   *Language Revitalization: Processes and Products*. Clevedon, Avon: Multi-
            lingual Matters.
Kontra, Miklós, Robert Phillipson, Tove Skutnabb-Kangas and Tibor Várady
    1999   *Language: A Right and a Resource*. Budapest: Central European University
            Press.
Kukathas, Chandra
    1992   Are there any cultural rights? *Political Theory* 20: 105–139.
Lewis, E. Glyn
    1976   Bilingualism and bilingual education: The ancient world to the Renais-
            sance. In: Joshua Fishman, *Bilingual Education*, 210–223. Rowley, Mas-
            sachusetts: Newbury House.
Mackey, William F.
    1986   The polyglossic spectrum. In: Joshua Fishman, Andrée Tabouret-Keller,
            Michael Clyne, Bh. Krishnamurti and A. Abdulaziz (eds.), *The Ferguso-
            nian Impact*, 77–89. Berlin: de Gruyter.
    1989   La genèse d'une typologie de la diglossie. *Revue québécoise de linguistique
            théorique et appliquée* 8: 11–28.
Macmillan, Michael
    1982   Henri Bourassa on the defence of language rights. *Dalhousie Review* 62:
            413–430.
    1983   Language rights, human rights and Bill 101. *Queen's Quarterly* 90: 343–
            361.
Murray, Katherine
    1977   *Caught in the Web of Words*. New Haven: Yale University Press.
Pandit, P.
    1979   Perspectives on sociolinguistics in India. In: William McCormack and
            Stephen Wurm (eds.), *Language and Society,* 55–71. The Hague: Mouton.
Pattanayak, Debi
    1986   On being and becoming bilingual in India. In: Joshua Fishman, Andrée Ta-
            bouret-Keller, Michael Clyne, Bh. Krishnamurti and A. Abdulaziz (eds.),
            The Fergusonian Impact, 119–136. Berlin: de Gruyter.
Phillipson, Robert
    1992   *Linguistic Imperialism*. Oxford: Oxford University Press.
Phillipson, Robert (ed.)
    2000   *Rights to Language*. Mahwah, New Jersey: Erlbaum.
Ruiz Vieytez, E.
    2001   The protection of linguistic minorities: A historical approach. *MOST* [Man-
            agement of Social Transformations Programme] *Journal on Multicultural
            Societies* 3(1) [see at www.unesco.org/most].
Simpson, A.
    2001   In rights we trust. *Times Literary Supplement* 8 June, 17.
Steiner, George
    1975   *After Babel*. London: Oxford University Press.
Stewart, William
    1962   An outline of linguistic typology for describing multilingualism. In: Frank
            Rice (ed.), *Study of the Role of Second Languages in Asia, Africa and Latin
            America,* 15–25. Washington: Center for Applied Linguistics.

1968   A sociolinguistic typology for describing national multilingualism. In: Joshua Fishman (ed.), *Readings in the Sociology of Language*, 531–545. The Hague: Mouton.

Tancock, Leonard
1954   Introductory notes to *Germinal* (Émile Zola). Harmondsworth, Middlesex: Penguin.

Terralingua
1999   *Statement of Purpose* (a single-page declaration). Hancock, Michigan: Terralingua.

TESOL
2000   *TESOL Board of Directors Reaffirms Position on Language Rights* (a single-page declaration). Alexandria, Virginia: TESOL.

de Varennes, Fernand
1996   *Language, Minorities and Human Rights*. The Hague: Nijhoff.
1999   The existing rights of minorities in international law. In: Miklós Kontra, Robert Phillipson, Tove Skutnabb-Kangas and Tibor Várady (eds.), *Language: A Right and a Resource*, 117–146. Budapest: Central European University Press.
2001   Language rights as an integral part of human rights. *MOST* [Management of Social Transformations Programme] *Journal on Multicultural Societies* 3(1) [see at www.unesco.org/most].

de Vries, John
1985   Some methodological aspects of self-report questions on language and ethnicity. *Journal of Multilingual and Multicultural Development* 6: 347–368.
1990   On coming to our census. *Journal of Multilingual and Multicultural Development* 11: 57–76.

Verstegan, Richard
1605   *A Restitution of Decayed Intelligence, in Antiquities*. London: Norton & Bill.

Yağmur, Kutlay and Kroon, Sjaak
2003   Ethnolinguistic vitality perceptions and language revitalisation in Bashkortostan. *Journal of Multilingual and Multicultural Development* 24: 319–336.

White, Paul
1991   Geographical aspects of minority language situations in Italy. In: Colin Williams (ed.), *Linguistic Minorities, Society and Territory*, 15–39. Clevedon, Avon: Multilingual Matters.

Wright, Sue
2001   Language and power: Background to the debate on linguistic rights. *MOST* [Management of Social Transformations Programme] *Journal on Multicultural Societies* 3(1) [see at www.unesco.org/most].

Recommended readings

Blommaert, Jan (ed.)
   1999   *Language Ideological Debates*. New York: Mouton de Gruyter.
Fishman, Joshua A.
   1989   *Language and Ethnicity in Minority Sociolinguistic Perspective*. Clevedon:
            Multilingual Matters
   1991   *Reversing Language Shift*. Clevedon: Multilingual Matters
Nettle, Daniel and Romaine, Suzanne
   2000   Vanishing Voices: The Extinction of the World's Languages. Oxford: OUP
Spolsky, Bernard
   2004   *Language Policy*. Cambridge: CUP

19. Multilingualism of autochthonous minorities

Penelope Gardner-Chloros

1. Introduction

What distinguishes the multilingualism of autochthonous minorities from that of other comparable ones, in particular from minority language groups of immigrant origin? One answer is that the multilingualism of such groups is, almost by definition, superfluous to practical requirements – the country's majority language is almost guaranteed to be more widely spoken, more useful in the job market, more prestigious, and more acceptable for communication with the outside world. Immigrant languages, by contrast, provide an essential link with the country of origin and confer the advantage of bilinguality in a language related to the wider world. But the multilingualism of autochthonous groups should, paradoxically, be of particular interest to linguists, because it is for its own sake – its *raison d'être* is to be an act of identity.

Let us first consider what is meant by the title 'autochthonous minorities'. How long must an ethnically/linguistically distinct group live in an area to qualify for the title 'autochthonous'? As May (2003) points out, both national and minority languages were created out of the politics of European state-building, and not vice-versa. For example, Norwegian was regarded as a dialect of Danish until the end of Danish rule in 1814, and only became a fully independent language after independence from Sweden in 1905 (2003: 212).

By the 3rd/4th generation, immigrant minorities face many of the same issues – and should probably be accorded many of the same rights – as those who have been implanted for longer. Historically, both English and French could be considered non-autochthonous since they both arose as a result of invasions and, following decades of language contact, displaced Celtic languages, which were themselves the product of earlier invasions. It has also often been pointed out by linguists that the concept of 'minorities' has little to do with actual numbers. The French-speaking populations of Switzerland and Belgium are rarely referred to as minorities because their populations are a) at least partially territorially distinct from other groups, and b) more significantly, traditionally powerful and influential.

In a chapter on 'Language Minorities', Edwards (2004) refers to claims that indigenous groups have a greater right to special attention for the continuation of their culture than immigrant ones (e.g. Kymlicka 1995). As Edwards points out, in fact, the basic issue of identity maintenance is the same for both types of minority – and indeed for majorities also. In the 21st Century, pretty much all ethnic groups face difficulties in preserving valued traditions in the face of pressures for assimilation and homogenization. The additional difficulty faced by minority groups, as Edwards states, is that of a split between the communicative and symbolic functions of their language.

While the over-arching problem of identity maintenance is shared with other types of languages, the specific problems faced by autochthonous languages are extremely varied, and tied to their individual historical, geographical, economic, demographic and ideological circumstances. This of course makes it harder to formulate appropriate policies for them. Autochthonous groups may speak varieties closely related to the national or majority language of the country where they are spoken (e.g. Frisian in the Netherlands) or to that of a neighbouring state (French in Belgium) or totally dissimilar to either of these (Basque in Spain). They may straddle national frontiers (e.g. Saami in Finland, Norway, Sweden and Russia) – and the relevant circumstances in the different countries might differ – or be contained within them. Edwards' (1995: 140) table (again on p. 460 of this handbook) subsumes both indigenous and immigrant minorities,[1] and ranks minority language situations according to a) whether they are 'unique/non-unique/local only' (i.e. whether they are spoken in one country only, in another country as well, and whether they are minorities in all the countries where they are spoken or not); b) their cohesiveness, i.e. whether speakers are concentrated or scattered; c) whether they are adjoining or non-adjoining to groups across the border where the same language is spoken. As soon as one takes an individual case and looks at it in greater detail, it becomes clear that many varied and complex factors affect the vitality and maintenance of any individual autochthonous language. This illustrates the difficulty of making generalizations – such as those schematized in the table above – which are sufficiently informative to predict the fate of any individual language and to allow for effective language planning – particularly at the supra-national level.

In the next section the case of Alsatian will be described, in order to illustrate the complexity of relevant factors affecting autochthonous languages in a concrete manner.

2.   A case-study: Alsatian

2.1.   Background

France's autochthonous regional languages were, notoriously, repressed for decades by successive French governments (Judge 2000). One of these, Alsatian, is the traditional language of the region on France's Eastern border, which changed hands between France and Germany five times between 1648 and

1945. Since Alsace became French again after the Liberation, any suggestion of allegiance to Germany has been generally shunned. French is the language of the State, of education and the media and increasingly the mother-tongue of the younger generation.

However Alsatian, a form of Alemannic, is still widely spoken (Office pour la langue et la culture d'Alsace (OLCALSACE) 2005; Gardner-Chloros, 1991; Tabouret-Keller 1988). Recent figures indicate that 61% of the population (which is approximately 1.7 million) claim to be dialect-speaking – admittedly a big drop from 95% in 1900 and 90.8% in 1946 (OLCALSACE 2005). Alsatian has always been an important element of the area's identity, distinguishing it from both its French and German-speaking neighbours. Like other regional varieties, it is used in the country rather than in town, and most of all by *NORMS*.[2] In Strasbourg it functions as an in-group marker of Alsatian identity, as opposed to the French from other parts of France and also to the sizeable foreign population associated with European institutions and other employers. Alsatian has recently enjoyed a revival among younger generations, including young parents when speaking to their offspring. It is used in adolescent groups as well as by local comedians, playwrights and poets – and has been for centuries – for humorous, emotional and vernacular purposes of all kinds.

In spite of this, surveys document a slow but inexorable falling off in its use among younger age groups. Whereas 86% of those over 60 claim to speak the dialect, this falls to 38% among 18–29 year-olds (OLCALSACE 2005; Bister-Broosen 2002).[3] In Strasbourg, the dialect is more often than not mixed with French, i.e. it is heard more in the context of code-switching than in its unmixed form. It should be noted that this in itself is not a sign of language shift to French; on the contrary, it may show that the dialect continues to be used in a relevant and socially up-to-date manner (Gardner-Chloros 2001). In the educational sphere, gradual progress has been made in introducing some German teaching at primary/nursery school level. A proportion of pupils now receives three hours of German classes per week; and a smaller number (13,000) are in 'bilingual' schools where half the curriculum is delivered in German. The aim is to gradually extend this teaching through the system.

2.2.   The maintenance of Alsatian as an autochthonous language

Alsatian is an archetypal autochthonous language, i.e. traditional, territorially linked, and long-standing. It is also – if the above figures are even approximately correct – too widely spoken to be overlooked. Disingenuous centralists have at times argued that it is not a language, but 'merely' a dialect of German. Linguists appear to have had some influence here, at least at the international level, in rectifying such misinformed views. This is evidenced – admittedly somewhat negatively – by the fact that the European Charter on Regional or Minority Languages (see below) sees the need to wash its hands of this problem: "The charter does not concern local variants or different dialects of one and the same language. However, it does not pronounce on the often disputed question of the point at which different forms of expression constitute separate languages. This question depends not only on strictly linguistic considerations, but also on psycho-sociological and political phenomena which may produce a different answer in each case" (*European Charter*, 1992, Article 1 para.32). The solution adopted by the Charter is to allow each signatory country to define for itself which languages to include. Measures taken in France to protect regional languages, such as the *loi Deixonne* in 1951, excluded Alsatian, along with Flemish and Corsican, on the basis that these were not regional languages of France but national languages of neighbouring states. The *loi Toubon* (1994) reasserted the primacy of French and its fundamental place in the character and heritage of France.

Whatever the part played by the French state in sabotaging the health of Alsatian, historical and attitudinal factors have probably played as great a part in its decline – to a point which, in spite of its healthy demographics, seems likely to be terminal within a few generations. The psychological turning point was probably the end of World War II, when, sick of the Occupation and sick of being assimilated – by both sides – to the Germans, transmission of the dialect to children tailed off. This was heavily encouraged by the French state, which waged a campaign to encourage people to speak French (the slogan was "*C'est chic de parler français*"). The teaching of German at school was also prohibited. Those who are in their fifties/sixties at the time of writing still learned the dialect, since it was almost universally spoken by their parents' generation, but they also increasingly learned French. Their own children, born roughly in the seventies, heard more and more French around them. They also lived in an ever more urban and cosmopolitan world, went to schools where many pupils were bilingual in other languages such as French and Arabic, worked increasingly in offices and less and less on the land, watched television (almost entirely in French), and were influenced, like young people all over Europe, by British and American pop culture. Not surprisingly, the majority chose English and not German as a second language at school. Not many young people would make a deliberate choice to speak like their grandparents, and young Alsatians were no exception.

A final relevant factor is the relationship between Alsatian and German. Alsatians were in several ways 'cut off' from a Standard language in the period since the War. Naturally, Germany geographically adjoins Alsace, and German tourists pour into Strasbourg – but this does not mean that dialect-speakers are anxious to look to German as a model. Many have cultivated a state of denial, claiming for example that Alsatian bears no relationship to German. Even now, it is not clear what effect the growing teaching of German in schools will have on dialect use. Although dialects should in principle be reinforced by the presence of the relevant standard language in the educational system, which gives them prestige and legitimacy, in this case the link between the two has been so eroded both by historical events and by speakers' attitudes that no easy conclusions can be drawn.

This brief overview of the complexities attendant on multilingualism in this setting shows some of the difficulties of maintaining an ancestral language. These are well illustrated by the Alsatian case, even though the particular relevant factors are idiosyncratic. Those familiar with other cases, that of Welsh, for example, or Catalan, will recognize the relevance of internal divisions and psychological associations which can undermine the battle to maintain autochthonous languages from within.

3.   Central concepts

3.1.   Nationalism and territoriality

As mentioned above, it was the creation of nation-states which brought about a category of 'minority languages'. The relationship between the concepts of nation, nation-state and language is explored in Barbour and Carmichael (2000). Whereas the nation-state is a legal entity, a nation is generally identified with a population. This coincides more or less with an ethnic group, the difference being that the latter may not occupy a specific territory – it may, for example, include immigrant groups in the diaspora. The particular relevance of Europe in this debate is emphasized. It is in Europe that the underlying philosophy of 'one nation, one language' developed, and it is also in Europe that a high proportion of ethnic groups and nations have names virtually identical to the names of their languages (though the same applies, say, in Japan). As Barbour (2000) points out, this situation is misleadingly simple, as it fails to recognize the tensions between 'languages' and 'dialects', with the former being sometimes on a linguistic continuum and mutually comprehensible (e.g. the Scandinavian languages), whereas some 'dialects' of the same language may be mutually incomprehensible (e.g. in Germany). It also fails to recognize the differences in status within dialects, some having a high profile and being used increasingly in the domains formerly reserved for national languages (e.g. Swiss German). Nation states, which Anderson (1991) referred to as 'Imagined Communities', still arouse loyalty – and affect the linguistic situation in many ways since their shared sense of identity necessitates a minimum level of communication. Indeed the impulse for new state formation in recent times has come chiefly from autochthonous groups, such as the Albanians in former Yugoslavia and the Basques in Spain. This leads Barbour to conclude, perhaps with a degree of optimism, that "autochthonous cultures are simply not on the wane any more" (2000: 287).

From a linguistic point of view, it is clear that there is no intrinsic difference between what are referred to as 'autochthonous languages' and majority, or national languages. The languages of majorities and states are also autochthonous – though they may, in some cases, be historically more recent than minority languages which have been eroded by them (e.g. English is more recent than Welsh in Great Britain). The reasons why a particular variety is selected and codified for use in educational and official spheres are political and geographic – usually it is the variety spoken in the capital or by the elite which is elevated in this way. In France for example, it was, somewhat ironically, the variety spoken by the aristocracy which was imposed on the masses, of whom only about half were French-speakers at the time of the Revolution in 1789 (Judge 2000). In other cases, political events result in decisions having to be taken to *select* particular forms to constitute a national language, leaving a parallel, popular form of speech which coexists in a *diglossic* relationship with that variety (Ferguson 1959). This was the case for example in Greece after its Independence from the Ottomans, and in colonial states where the colonial power imposed its variety on the population, as in Papua New Guinea (Romaine 1989). After the demise of colonialism, even in a highly multilingual situation like that of Papua, a more 'autochthonous' variety, in this case Tok Pisin, the pidginised language which had developed and started to fulfil the role of lingua franca, gained ground and took over some of those functions.

In recent times, autochthonous groups have become less willing to leave the status of their language to the vagaries of history and a power struggle has sometimes developed, with people fighting for their 'linguistic rights' (see below). In order to achieve their ends, various groups have focussed on their traditional implantation in an area and staked claims based on their ancestral presence (e.g. Maoris in New Zealand, Skutnabb-Kangas and Phillipson 1995a; Canadian Aboriginal groups, Sachdev 1995; Saamis (Lapps) in Scandinavia, Décsy 2000).

Grin (1995) discusses what he refers to as the 'territorial principle' at length, and suggests that, with some adjustments, it can provide a solution for protecting all minority languages, autochthonous and immigrant. The territorial principle is the basis for countries like Switzerland or Belgium allocating language rights to different languages in different parts of the country. Grin claims that some principle of territoriality underlies all language policies to some extent, but that the principle needs to be adjusted in order to protect the rights of immigrant minorities as well as autochthonous ones – in effect a proposal for positive discrimination. His proposal is based on the idea that minority languages are bound to be minorised still further if a simple territorial principle is applied, since within any given territory, the majority language is bound to be more powerful/useful overall. He suggests that language rights be considered within a devolved framework where several layers of decision-making and government are relevant. In this way a scattered minority, which is nevertheless reasonably numerous overall, will receive some proportional representation at relevant levels. Skutnabb-Kangas and Phillipson (1995b) point out the huge discrepancies which currently exist in national provisions: in Finland, for example, there only have to be thirteen children from the Swedish-speaking minority within a local authority for them to be able to claim education through the medium of their mother-tongue for the first nine years of compulsory schooling. At the other extreme there are still many groups in the world which are punished, physically or in other ways, for using their mother-tongue – the Kurds in Turkey being an extreme example of such human rights abuse (Skutnabb-Kangas and Bucak 1995). This, along with the attitudinal aspect of language maintenance, forms the subject of the next section.

3.2.   Language rights

Skutnabb-Kangas and Phillipson (1995b) define the primary Linguistic Human Right as the right to identify with your mother-tongue(-s) and to education and public services through the medium of it/them. They suggest that the right to learn a second language – including the national language of one's country of residence – is a secondary Linguistic Human Right. The importance of stating and upholding these rights is that, they claim, "most minority language speakers are discriminated against on grounds of language", contrasting well-established national or regional minorities which enjoy extensive rights in education and public life, for example in Belgium, Canada and India, with other substantial minorities worldwide such as the Saamis or the Kurds who have had to fight for generations for the most basic concessions for their language.

Sometimes, within the same country, one vocal minority has achieved advanced legal protection for its language whereas others are still struggling for recognition. This is the case, for example, of the aboriginal speakers in Canada, consisting of over a million people or 3.8 % of population, who can be broken down into over 50 language groups, only three of which have more than 5,000 speakers. (Edwards 2004). By contrast, the French-speaking minority has achieved a stable and well-protected status. Similarly, in Spain, Catalan, though heavily repressed under Franco, now has an established status and has even sought representation at the EU level. On the other hand the protection of Bable, the traditional language of the Asturias region, is far less developed and the language is in a state of decline.

Skutnabb-Kangas and Phillipson (1995b) review the various historical stages of recognition of Linguistic Rights, starting in the 19th Century with the Congress of Vienna, which was the first international instrument to recognize the rights of national (and not merely religious) minorities, and progressing up to the present day with the signature and ratification by a number of European states of the Council of Europe's Charter for Regional or Minority Languages (1992), and the creation of various official and semi-official bodies in Europe and elsewhere for the promotion of particular (groups of) languages, such as the Welsh Language Board, the Gaeltacht Authority in Ireland, the European Bureau of Lesser Used Languages, the Fryske (Frisian) Akademy, etc. Their book includes a lengthy Appendix including a number of relevant legal or quasi-legal documents on the protection of language rights, but from a legal point of view they fail to make a sufficiently clear distinction between enforceable and unenforceable rights. For example they dismiss the Belgian Linguistic Case brought before the Court of Human Rights in 1968 as being of limited signifi-cance, and fail to point out that, because the relevant right was enshrined in the European Convention on Human Rights, a legally binding document, the plain-tiffs had an enforceable right – to education without discrimination on grounds of language – to redress, which was bound to affect the Belgian Government's future policies. By contrast the European Charter, though specifically designed to cover linguistic matters only, allows ratifying states – ratification itself being voluntary – to choose which clauses to apply (though there is a minimum). Fur-thermore, there is no mechanism of external control after ratification.

Grin (2003) and Craith (2003) devote chapters to the workings of the Euro-pean Charter. Grin (2003) provides a table of 'Policy Indicators' as a guide to deciding how effective the protection of regional and minority languages (RMLs) is in a variety of official spheres, including the cultural sphere, the media, the judicial system etc. This provides a useful contribution to the grow-ing number of initiatives for cataloguing and assessing threatened languages, and an extract is reproduced below (cf. Tab. 1). The Appendix also provides a list of selected internet resources, some of which are listed in the titles for further consultation below.

3.3.   Language planning and ethnolinguistic democracy

Attitudes and policies towards the languages of autochthonous as opposed to im-migrant minorities are determined by different types of historical circumstances. As we have seen, many autochthonous groups have suffered centuries of oppres-sion (e.g. Aborigines, Arvanites). Whereas apathy/prejudice might characterize governmental attitudes to the maintenance of immigrant minority languages, targeted repression has often characterized the treatment of autochthonous ones. This repression has often been tied up with fears about separatism, or, in the case of adjoining minorities, about annexation by the neighbouring state.

Immigrant groups, on the other hand, are largely a 20th Century phenom-enon, and while they have certainly not always been well-treated in their host-

Table 1. Policy Indicators for the protection of regional and minority languages (RML) (from Grin 2003)

Art.	Area	Main condition targeted	Indicators
8	Education	Capacity	81 – Number and percentage of RML users at different levels of competence, in different age groups
			82 – Competence levels of RML learners at different stages in the education system
9	Judicial system	Opportunity	91 – Number and percentage of court cases proceedings requested and supplied
10	Administration and public services	Opportunity	101 – Number and percentage of RML oral (face-to-face and telephone) interactions
			102 – Number and percentage of RML written (mail, e-mail, etc.) interactions
			103 – Percentage of official forms available in RMLs.
			104 – Time spent by RML-users interacting with officials in the RML
			105 – Percentage of civil servants fluent in RML
			106 – Average competence level of civil servants in RML
			107 – Percentage of RML signs and information displays in public administration premises
11	Media (audiovisual)	Opportunity	111 – Total number of RML radio and TV programming, differentiated by genre as well as between new programmes and replays
			112 – In case of bilingual stations: relative share of RML programming in prime time
			113 – Audiences of RML, radio and TV programmes, differentiated by genre of programmes and by viewer profile (age, sex, etc.)
12	Culture	Opportunity	121 – Total number of RML books published per year
			122 – Sales figures of RML books © Number of RML periodicals dailies, weeklies, monthlies, etc.)
			123 – Circulation figures of RML periodicals
			124 – Reader profile of RML materials
			125 – Amount and distribution of state subsidies to RML publishing and distribution
			126 – Total number of RML live arts productions per year
			127 – Number of RML films showed (usually majority language works with dubbed in RML or with RML subtitles)

Art.	Area	Main condition targeted	Indicators
			128 – Attendance figures for RML live arts and cinema shows, with audience profile
			129 – Amount and distribution of state subsidies to RML arts, film production, dubbing or subtitling
13	Economic and social life	Opportunity (Desire)	131 – Percentage of RML and/or bilingual commercial signs visible from the street
			132 – Percentage of RML and/or bilingual signs visible inside shops and other commercial establishments (restaurants, etc.)
			133 – Percentage of consumer goods with RML or bilingual packaging and labelling
			134 – Percentage of consumer goods with RML safety instructions (e.g. electrical appliances and drugs)
			135 – Share of RML or bilingual advertisements in written and audiovisual media
			136 – Type of goods and services advertised in RML or bilingually
			137 – Frequency of RML use on the workplace, by economic sector, position held and language of owners or managers
			138 – Ownership of firms by language group
			139 – Usefulness of RML skills for access to employment
			140 – Amount of wage premia for bilingual workers

countries, they have arisen in the context of a world where governments pay lip-service, at the very least, to the notion of human rights and where differences between people have, at least in some contexts, been welcomed – a superficial example is the popularity of ethnic cuisine, dress, etc. Immigrant groups have a 'homeland', however unhelpful this may sometimes have been to them, to look towards and sometimes to long for (viz. 'the myth of return'). On the other hand, autochthonous minorities have sometimes the double grievance of being marginalized by a richer/more powerful majority in economic, educational etc. terms, and at the same time of having their longer-standing historical status in their country of origin disregarded. The claims which they make are also of a different nature to those made by immigrant groups. While the latter may request some educational support for language teaching – and there is plenty of evidence that it is in everyone's interest to provide this (Sneddon 2000) – much of this is organised on a community basis, and claims for political rights, other than the right to vote in the case of long-term residents, are unlikely.

Autochthonous groups, on the other hand, may make a variety of claims for the representation of their language in public life as well as in the educational sphere – or not, as we saw in the case of Alsace described above where speakers' own reticence to make claims for their language, and to pass it on to their children, has been their own worst enemy. Where there are claims, on the other hand, these are decided, clearly, partly on matters of principle and partly on matters of practicality. In a paper entitled 'On the limits of ethnolinguistic democracy', Fishman (1995), one of the most significant champions of ethnolinguistic rights, details the problems in representing what he terms the 'smallest mother tongues' – those which are non-governmental everywhere that they are spoken – at the level of international organizations. Turi (1995) describes the different types of language legislation which can be found and discusses their comparative effectiveness. As suggested above in relation to the European Declaration of Human Rights, from a legal point of view – though this may be hard for linguists to accept – it may be best for language rights to be enshrined along with a variety of other rights (freedom of religion, etc.) in legal instruments which are directly geared in with a system of enforcement. Declarations such as that of the Linguistic Society of America or the TESOL teachers' Resolution on Language Rights (in Skutnabb-Kangas and Phillipson 1995) are, unfortunately, unlikely to be translated into effective action by governments.

3.4.   Language attitudes and language maintenance

There is important work going back to the 1960s at least on the psychological/ attitudinal, as well as the political preconditions for language maintenance. As we have seen, Fishman has been the most significant figure defending threatened languages against shift and suggesting both diagnostic criteria and revitalization measures (1990, 1991, 1997, 2001, 2004). Others, however, have contributed substantially to this effort: see for example Dorian (1988, 2004), Nettle & Romaine (2002), Grenoble and Whaley (1998), Crystal (2000), and Projects such as the Endangered Languages Project based at the School of Oriental and African Studies in London (for other similar projects, see the websites listed in the Appendix of Grin 2003). The other important contribution to our understanding of these issues has been made by linguists describing specific threatened language situations from an ethnolinguistic perspective, such as Gal (1979) on Hungarian in Austria, Dorian (1981) on Scottish Gaelic, or Aikhenvald (2002) on the languages of the Amazonian Basin.

The other side of language maintenance is the attitudinal aspect. Social psychologists of language have shown with reference to many different contexts that language is one of the most significant aspects of group identity (Giles,

Bourhis and Taylor 1977; Sachdev and Bourhis 1990; Fishman 1989). Traditional languages have such an important identity function that they may be valued in that capacity even by groups where the majority do not actually speak the language. The case of Irish Gaelic, promoted by the Government and taught in Irish schools, is an example of this. Where feeling is sufficiently strong, a dead language may even be revived and re-disseminated, as was the case of Hebrew in Israel. Spolsky (1989) cites a recent notable example of such revival – the increase in knowledge of Maori among children of Maori heritage in New Zealand. Giles et al. (1977) introduced the notion of Ethnolinguistic Vitality to cover the significant factors at play in such cases. The three most significant aspects of this were held to be Demography (both absolute numbers and the concentration of speakers), Status (including prestige in the community and outside it, sense of historicity, the presence of a respected literature/culture in the language, etc.), and Institutional Support (the presence of the language in public life, its use in education and the media etc.). These concepts have proved robust in relation to findings in many different parts of the world and continue to form the basis of Ethnolinguistic Vitality questionnaires and surveys (e.g. Sachdev 1995).

The issue of bilingual education is related to these factors and is highly significant in its own right. Where effective bilingual education programmes have been introduced (e.g. the French Immersion schools in Canada; Ikastolas in the Basque country) and have progressed beyond the experimental stage to be considered relatively mainstream, this has of itself created a positive snowball effect for the relevant languages (Hamers and Blanc 2000).

4.   Problems and solutions

4.1.   Standardization

One of the principal problems faced by autochthonous languages in their maintenance efforts is that of standardization, since many autochthonous languages comprise several dialects. A recent article in the *Times* about Cornish, which is undergoing something of a revival in Britain (the last monolingual speaker of Cornish having died in the late 18th Century), stressed that progress towards the teaching of Cornish and its recognition in public places (road signs etc.) was being seriously hampered by the revivalists' inability to agree among themselves the most appropriate spelling system. Many autochthonous languages have never had a written form, yet the creation of one is essential to their survival in the modern age. The problem with respect to teaching extends to the variations in the spoken form, each speaker assuming their own dialect to be more correct or preferable to the others. National languages have all faced the same difficulty at some stage, and languages such as English seem if anything strengthened by the continuing variety which they encompass. But for a small language struggling to survive, the issue of internal diversity can seem like a major mountain to climb.

4.2.   Normativeness and code-switching

Another major problem, not unconnected with the first, is the issue of the normative attitudes of the older generation towards younger people with incomplete levels of competence in the traditional language. It is reported for example that young Greek-Cypriots in London arc sometimes driven to avoid speaking the Cypriot Dialect altogether, or to exaggerate their incompetence, by the ridiculing attitude of the older generation (Gardner-Chloros, McEntee-Atalianis and Finnis 2005). In Community schools for 2nd/3rd generation children from this community, teachers from mainland Greece struggle to teach Standard Modern Greek, a variety which the majority of these children have scarcely been exposed to. The children's work is marked down for 'Cypriotisms' which are perfectly correct within the Dialect which they hear at home.

Code-switching, itself often a subject of disapproval or amusement in such communities, often characterizes the younger generation. There is little doubt that a liberalization of attitudes in this respect, and encouragement to speak the language however imperfectly, would encourage the survival of many such languages. Interestingly, Aikhenvald (2002) reports in her study of languages in the Amazon that whereas code-switching was scrupulously avoided between the traditional local languages, even by multilingual individuals, code-switching to English is not so uncommon now that this language is beginning to intrude on the linguistic scene.

4.3.   The political pecking order

The final problem which needs to be mentioned in this brief survey is of course that of the priorities and attitudes of those in power at the national level. As we have seen through the extreme example of the Kurds and the much milder one of the French, if a governmental regime is sufficiently determined to stamp out a language, it can go a long way towards doing so. This is partly a matter of specific political measures – for example both the Turks and the French have traditionally only permitted citizens to be given traditional Turkish or French first names – and partly a matter of spreading an ideology, through propaganda and in particular through the school system. A pupil who is consistently punished for speaking their home language (e.g. Bretons, Welsh, etc.) will eventually give up the unequal struggle and adopt the majority language, despite the cultural and identity loss which that may entail. This leads us on to the final section where we consider, rather than political measures as such, the question of the 'market value' of different languages and the role which this plays in the maintenance of autochthonous languages.

5.   Applied research perspectives: Cypriot Greek in two contexts

At various points in this chapter, comparisons have been drawn between autochthonous and immigrant minorities. This is because many of the problems which the two kinds of groups face in maintaining their language(s) are the same, although, as has been pointed out, there are also some crucial socio-political differences. The points of similarity are obvious: both are in a weak position compared with a state-promoted, standard language. Either can be linguistically related to the majority language, and either can be internally divided between different dialects or sub-groups. Both are likely to suffer from a lack of self-confidence faced with the economic power and advantages associated with the majority culture.

Thanks to a recent research project aimed at comparing the fate of the Greek Cypriot Dialect (GCD) in its home context (Cyprus) and in the large immigrant community in London (some 200,000 people), we have an opportunity to directly compare the position of an autochthonous language in its 'home' setting and as an immigrant language, and consequently to compare the effect of the differing socio-economic pressures which it faces in each (Gardner-Chloros, McEntee-Atalianis and Finnis 2005).

It may seem surprising to refer to the Greek Cypriot Dialect as an autochthonous language in the Cypriot context, since, while clearly autochthonous as such, it is the traditional language of the *majority* of the population, and most autochthonous languages considered so far have been minorities, operating within the sphere of more prestigious, majority, state-sanctioned languages. However, as the Alsatian case-study showed, each case is *sui generis* to some extent. Alsatian is unusual in being spoken by such a high proportion of the population and yet being of somewhat dubious ethnolinguistic vitality owing to its particular historical circumstances. In the case of GCD, in spite of the fact that Cyprus has been an independent state since it ceased to be a British colony in the 1960s, it nevertheless continues to operate within the ambit of the Greek-speaking world and to look to mainland Greece for cultural and linguistic models. Schoolchildren are taught Standard Modern Greek (SMG), not GCD – as we saw above, this is extended to the transplanted setting, with Cypriot community schools importing teachers from Greece to teach a variety which continues to have a direct relevance in Cyprus, but has little or no relevance for children born in England, who hear only GCD at home.

Papapavlou and Pavlou (1998) describe the Greek Cypriot community of Cyprus as di- or tri-glossic in the Greek Cypriot Dialect (GCD), Standard Modern Greek (SMG) as spoken in mainland Greece, and Katharevousa/Puristic Greek. English also continues to enjoy a prestigious presence, more so than in Greece itself where its importance is merely due to the forces of modernity, as everywhere in Europe. In Cyprus, English retains some importance as the ex-colonial language and is widely present. To this we should add the presence of Turkish, a language which co-existed peacefully with Cypriot Greek until the Turkish invasion of 1974, which led to the partitioning of the island; of Russian, due to the presence of numerous Russian second-home owners – many road-signs are trilingual in Greek, English and Russian – and of English, again, along with numerous other languages, owing to the heavy reliance of the island on tourism.

The first Greek Cypriot immigrants to arrive in London were of low socio-economic status; they spoke GCD, but due to limited education, were not competent in SMG. They never needed to acquire ENG in Cyprus or London as all aspects of their lives revolved around the Greek Cypriot community. Recently, as in reports of the Greek Cypriot community in Cyprus, concern has been expressed regarding the future of SMG/GCD in the London community. Most of the younger Greek Cypriots, particularly those born in the UK, consider ENG as their mother tongue, whilst GCD is used for interaction mainly with grand-parents, whose knowledge of ENG is limited. However families still have access to, and communicate via GCD in other domains, e.g. satellite television, radio and in local institutions such as banks, travel agencies, community centres, and restaurants.

Analysis of language attitudes and use within the Greek-Cypriot population of London, and comparisons with findings in Nicosia, reflect the symbolic forces operating in two distinct settings. In Britain, young people especially use their mastery of the national language in a much larger market enabling them to participate in more varied and lucrative transactions than those within the smaller Greek Cypriot community. By contrast, in Nicosia, the national codes (GCD/SMG) "afford speakers the benefits of group solidarity, in addition to cul-tural, economic and symbolic capital in all domains of use" (McEntee-Atalianis and Pouloukas 2001: 33). Different market forces are therefore operating in the Greek-Cypriot communities of Cyprus and Nicosia. The results of this study suggested that these capital forces may lead eventually to language shift in the Greek-Cypriot community of London: the youth report comparatively little use of the community codes. Whilst acknowledging the benefits of the more classi-cal ethnographic approaches (e.g. Milroy 1987 and Li Wei 1994), this study drew on a different paradigm – attitude studies, this technique being used to examine the relationship between ethnic/social identity and language use by in-dividuals in varied linguistic markets. Our research design and interpretation of the data was informed by 'the theory of practice' (Bourdieu 1997). In very dif-ferent ways, the language shift taking place both in this community and in Alsace show how the concept of what is autochthonous is by no means absolute, but instead contingent on a variety of contextual factors.

6.   Conclusion

The multilingualism of autochthonous minorities is enormously varied in its manifestations, just like that of indigenous groups and of immigrant communities. Our two case-studies, of Alsace on the one hand, and the comparative case-study relating to Greek Cypriot on the other hand, show the complexity of historical and economic forces which bring their weight to bear on the maintenance of these languages today. Their future will depend not only on the sentimental attachment of their speakers to these idioms, nor even on their legitimate cultural aspirations being recognised. It will depend on their own ability to overcome internal divisions – for example regarding orthography – and to push for legally binding forms of protection as opposed to more linguistically complete, but ultimately ineffectual, expressions of political will.

Notes

1. 'Autochthonous' and 'indigenous' are used here as synonymous terms. Stephens (1976) made a distinction, suggesting that 'indigenous' meant 'native to a particular place' and 'autochthonous' meant 'aboriginal, from the soil', but the usefulness of such a distinction is not apparent. The Council of Europe Charter, which sets out targets for the protection of these languages, refers to them as 'historical regional or minority languages of Europe'. It distinguishes them from the languages of immigration – in this volume *new minorities* – even when the speakers of such languages have acquired the nationality of the European country where they live. On the other hand, it does claim that some parts of the Charter can be applied to traditionally spoken languages which lack a specific territorial base, such as Yiddish and Romany (Council of Europe, 2002).
2. Non-mobile Older Rural Males – a Labovian term.
3. These figures are derived from various surveys which have been summarised on the OLCA website. Most were not designed by linguists. Apart from questions of statistical validity, they are contingent on the exact way in which the question was asked, and how it was interpreted. For example, does: "Do you speak the dialect?" mean: "Are you able to?" *or* "Do you ever?" *or* "Do you regularly?" For a discussion of the problems of carrying out reliable linguistic surveys, see Milroy (1987).

References

Aikhenvald, Alexandra Y.
  2002   *Language Contact in Amazonia.* Oxford: Oxford University Press.
Barbour, Stephen
  2000   Nationalism, language, Europe. In: Stephen Barbour and Cathie Carmi-
          chael (eds.), 2000, 1–18.
Barbour, Stephen and Carmichael, Cathie (eds.)
  2000   *Language and Nationalism in Europe.* Oxford: Oxford University Press.
Bister-Broosen, H.
  2002   Alsace. In: J. Treffers-Daller and R. Willemyns (eds.) *Language Contact a
          the Romance – Germanic Language Border.* 98–111. Clevedon: Multilin-
          gual Matters, 98–111.
Bourdieu, Pierre
  1991   *Language and Symbolic Power.* Cambridge, England/ Malden, MA: Polity
          Press.
Council of Europe
  1968   Case relating to certain aspects of the laws on the use of languages in edu-
          cation in Belgium (Merits), Judgment of 23 July 1968, Registry of the Court.
          Publications of the European Court of Human Rights, Volume 6, Strasbourg.
Council of Europe
  1992   *Charter on Regional and Minority Languages.* Council of Europe, Stras-
          bourg.
Craith, M. Nic
  2003   Facilitating or Generating Linguistic Diversity: the European Charter for
          Regional or Minority Languages. In: Gabrielle Hogan-Brun and Stefan
          Wolff (eds.), *Minority Languages in Europe*, 56–73. Basingstoke/New-
          York: Palgrave.
Crystal, David
  2000   *Language Death.* Cambridge: Cambridge University Press.
Décsy, Gyula
  2000   *The Linguistic Identity of Europe.* Bloomington, Indiana: Eorolingua.
Dorian, Nancy C.
  1981   *The Life Cycle of a Scottish Gaelic Dialect.* Philadelphia: University of
          Pennsylvania Press.
  1988   *Investigating Obsolescence.* Cambridge: Cambridge University Press.
  2004   Minority and endangered languages. In: Tey K. Bhatia and William C. Rit-
          chie (eds.), *The Handbook of Bilingualism*, 437–460. Oxford: Blackwell.
Edwards, John
  1995   Multilingualism. Harmondsworth: Penguin.
  2004   Language Minorities In: Alan Davies and Catherine Elder (eds.), *Handbook
          of Applied Linguistics*, 451–476. Oxford: Blackwell.
Ferguson, Charles A.
  1959   Diglossia. *Word*, 15: 325–40. Reprinted in Pier Paolo Giglioli (ed.), 1972,
          Language and Social Context, 232–252. Harmondsworth: Penguin.
Fishman, Joshua A.
  1989   *Language and Ethnicity in Minority Sociolinguistic Perspective.* Clevedon:
          Multilingual Matters.

1990   What is reversing language shift and how can it succeed? *Journal of Multi-lingual and Multicultural Development* 11: 5–36.

1991   *Reversing Language Shift: Theoretical and Empirical Foundations of Assistance to Threatened Languages.* Clevedon: Multilingual Matters.

1995   On the limits of ethnolinguistic democracy. In: Tove Skutnabb-Kangas and Robert Phillipson (eds.), *Linguistic Human Rights*, 49–63. Berlin/New York: Mouton de Gruyter.

1997   *In Praise of the Beloved Language: A Comparative View of Positive Ethnolinguistic Consciousness.* Berlin/New York: Mouton de Gruyter.

2004   Language maintenance, language shift, and reversing language Shift. In: Tey K. Bhatia and William C. Ritchie (eds.), *The Handbook of Bilingualism*, 406–437. Oxford: Blackwell.

Fishman, Joshua A. (ed.)

2001   *Can Threatened Languages be Saved? Reversing Language Shift Revisited, a 21st Century Perspective.* Clevedon: Multilingual Matters.

Gal, Susan

1979   *Language Shift: Social Determinants of Linguistic Change in Bilingual Austria.* New York: Academic Press.

Gardner-Chloros, Penelope

1991   *Language Selection and Switching in Strasbourg.* Oxford: Oxford University Press.

2001   Code-switching and language shift. In: Tom Ammerlaan, Madeleine Hulsen, Heleen Strating and Kutlay Yagmur (eds.), *Sociolinguistic and Psycholinguistic Perspectives on Maintenance, Shift and Loss of Minority Languages*, 127–139. New York/Munich/Berlin: Waxmann.

Gardner-Chloros, Penelope, Lisa McEntee-Atalianis and Katerina Finnis

2005   Language attitudes and use in a transplanted setting: Greek Cypriots in London. *Journal of Multilingualism* 2 (1): 52–80.

Giles, Howard, Richard Y. Bourhis and Donald M. Taylor

1977   Towards a theory of language in ethnic group relations. In: Howard Giles (ed.), *Language, Ethnicity and Intergroup Relations*, 307–348. London: Academic Press.

Grenoble, Leonore A. and Lindsay J. Whaley

1998   *Endangered Languages: Current Issues and Future Prospects.* Cambridge: Cambridge University Press.

Grin, François

1995   Combining immigrant and autochthonous language rights: a territorial approach to multilingualism. In: Tove Skutnabb-Kangas and Robert Phillipson (eds.), *Linguistic Human Rights*, 31–49. Berlin/New York: Mouton de Gruyter.

2003   *Language Policy Evaluation and the European Charter for Regional or Minority Languages.* Basingstoke/New York: Palgrave.

Hamers, Josiane and Michel Blanc

2000   *Bilinguality and Bilingualism.* Cambridge: Cambridge University Press.

Judge, Anne

2000   France: 'One State, one nation, one language?' In: Stephen Barbour and Cathie Carmichael (eds.), *Language and Nationalism in Europe*, 44–83. Oxford: Oxford University Press.

Kymlicka, Will
1995   *Multicultural Citizenship.* Oxford: Oxford University Press.
Li Wei
1994   *Three Generations, Two Languages, One Family: Language Choice and Language Shift in a Chinese Community in Britain.* Clevedon, Avon: Multilingual Matters.
McEntee-Atalianis, Lisa and Stavros Pouloukas
2001   Issues of Identity and Power in a Greek-Cypriot Community. *Journal of Multilingual and Multicultural Development,* 22 (1): 19–38.
May, Stephen
2003   Language, nationalism and democracy in Europe. In: Gabrielle Hogan-Brun and Stefan Wolff (eds.), *Minority Languages in Europe: Frameworks, Status, Prospects,* 211–232. Basingstoke/New York: Palgrave.
Milroy, Ann Lesley
1987   *Observing and Analysing Natural Language.* Oxford: Blackwell.
Office pour la Langue et la Culture d'Alsace (OLCALSACE)
2005   http://www.olcalsace.org
Nettle, Daniel and Suzanne Romaine
2002   *Vanishing Voices: The Extinction of the World's Languages.* Oxford: Oxford University Press.
Papapavlou, Andreas and Pavlou, Pavlos
1998   A review of the sociolinguistic aspects of the Greek cypriot dialect. *Journal of Multilingual and Multicultural Development* 19 (3): 212–220.
Pauwels, Anne
2004   Language maintenance. In: Alan Davies and Catherine Elder (eds.), *The Handbook of Applied Linguistics,* 719–737. Oxford: Blackwell.
Romaine, Suzanne
1989 (^{2}1994)   *Bilingualism.* Oxford: Blackwell.
Sachdev, Itesh
1995   Language and identity: ethnolinguistic vitality of aboriginal peoples in Canada. *The London Journal of Canadian Studies,* 11: 41–54.
Sachdev, Itesh and Richard Y. Bourhis
1990   Language and social identification. In: Dominic Abrams and Michael Hogg (eds.), *Social Identity Theory: Constructive and Critical Advances,* 101–124. Hemel Hempstead: Harvester-Wheatsheaf.
Skutnabb-Kangas, Tove and Sertac Bucak
1995   Killing a mother tongue – how the Kurds are deprived of Linguistic Human Rights. In: Tove Skutnabb-Kangas and Robert Phillipson (eds.), 1995b, 347–370.
Skutnabb-Kangas, Tove and Robert Phillipson
1995a   Linguistic human rights, past and present. In: Tove Skutnabb-Kangas and Robert Philipson (eds.), 1995b, 71–110.
1995b   *Linguistic Human Rights: Overcoming Linguistic Discrimination.* Berlin/New York: Mouton.
Sneddon, Raymonde
2000   Language and literacy: children's experiences in multilingual environments. *International Journal of Bilingual Education and Bilingualism* 3 (4): 265–282.

Spolsky, Bernard
    1989   Maori bilingual education and language revitalization. *Journal of Multilingual and Multicultural Development* 10: 89–104.
Stephens, Meic
    1976   *Linguistic Minorities in Western Europe.* Wales: J. D. Lewis.
Tabouret-Keller, Andrée
    1988   La situation linguistique en Alsace: les principaux traits de son évolution à la fin du XXe siècle. In: *L'Allemand en Alsace/ Die deutsche Sprache im Elsass.* Presses universitaires de Strasbourg, 77–109.

Additional sources

Selected Internet Resources (from Grin 2003)

Aménagement linguistique dans le monde
    http://www.tlfq.ufaval.ca/ax/
Centre for Multilingual Multicultural Research (CMMR)
    http://www.use.edu/dept/education/CMMR
COMIR
    http://lig.osi.hu/comir/
eLandnet: Europe
    http://www.elandnet.org./
Endangered Languages Fund
    http://www.sapir.ling.yale.edu/~elf
Ethnologue
    http://www.sil.org./ethnologue.introduction.html
Eurolang
    http://www.eurolang.net
Euromosaic
    http://campus.uoc.es/euromosaic/
European Centre for Minority Issues (Flensburg, Germany)
    http://www.ecmi.de/
European Language Council/Conseil Européen pour les Langues
    http://www.solki.jyu.fi/elc/ekm.htm
European Languages Resources Association (ELRA)
    http://www.icp.inpg.fr/ELRA/home.html
European Minority Languages
    http://www.smo.uhi.ac.uk/saoghal/mion-chanain/en/
European Research Centre on Migration an Ethnic Relations (ERCOMER)
    http://www.ercomer.org/
Foundation for Endangered Languages
    http://www.ogmios.org/
GeoNative
    http://www.geocities.com/Athens/9479/tables.html
Gesellschaft für bedrohte Sprachen
    http://www.uni-koeln.de/gbs/index.html

I love languages
   http://www.ilovelanguages.com/
INCORE: Initiative on Conflict Resolution and Ethnicity
   http://www.incore.ulst.ac.uk/
Language futures Europe
   http://web.inter.nl.net/users/Paul.Treanor/eulang.html
Linguasphere
   http://www.linguasphere.org/
Mercator-Education
   http://www.mercator-education.org/
Mercator-Legislation
   http://www.troc.es/ciemen/mercator/index-gb.htm
Mercator-Media
   http://www.aber.ac.uk/-merwww/
MINELRES – Minority Electronic Resources
   http://www.rigal.lv/minelres/
Minorities at Risk Project
   http://www.geocities.com/~patrin/marp.htm
Minority Languages Links
   http://biblioteca.udg.es/fl/aucoc/min_link.htm
Minority languages of Russia on the Net
   http://wwwl.poeples.org.ru/eng_index.html
MOST Clearing House
   http://www.unesco.org/most/
Red Book of the Peoples of the Russian Empire
   http://www.eki.ee/books/redbook
Terralingua: Language Diversity and Biological Diversity
   http://www.terralingua.org/
UCLA Languages Materials Project
   http://www.lmp.ucla.edu/default.htm
UC Linguistic Minority Research Institute
   http://lmri.ucsb.edu/abtlmri/tocabout.htm
UNESCO Red Book on Endangered Languages: Europe
   http://www.helsinki.fi/~tasalmin/eur_indes.html
Yamada Language Centre
   http://babel.uoregon.edu/yamada/guides.html

Selected internet journals on language and/or education

Annual Review of Applied Linguistics
   (Editor: Mary McGroarty)
   http://uk.cambridge.org/journals/apl/
Bilingual Family Newsletter
   (Editor: Marjukka Grover)
   http://www.multilingualmatters.com/
Current Issues in Language Planning
   (Editors: Robert B. Kaplan & Richard B. Baldauf Jr.)
   http://cilp.arts.usyd.edu.au/

Current Issues in Language & Society
    (Editor: Sue Wright)
    http://www.multilingualmatters.com
DiversCité Language – Revue et forums interdisciplinaires sur la dynamique des languages
    http://www.teltq.uquebec.ca/diverscite/entree.htm
    (Editor: Angéline Martel)
Estudios de Sociolingüística
    (Editors: Xoan Paolo Rodrigues-Yanez, Anox M. Lorenzo Suarez, Fernando Ramallo)
    http://www.linguistlist.org/issues/11/11–2619.html
Evaluation & Research in Education
    (Editor: Steve Higgins)
    http://www.multlingualmatters.com/
Internationsl Journal of Bilingual Education and Bilingualism
    (Editor: Colin Baker)
    http://www.multlingualmatters.com/multi/
International Journal of the Sociology of Language
    (General editor: Joshua A. Fishman)
    http://www.degruyter.de/journals/ijsl/
Journal of Multilingual & Multicultural Development
    (Editor: John Edwards)
    http://www.multlingualmatters.com/
Journal of Sociolinguistics
    (Editor: Allan Beli and Nikolas Coupland)
    http://www.blackwellpublishers.co.uk/journals/JOSL/descript.htm
Language Awareness
    (Editor: Peter Garrett)
    http://www.multilingualmatters.com/
Language, Culture and Curriculum
    (Editor: Eoghan Mac Agáin)
    http://www.multilingualmatters.com/
Language and Eduction
    (Editor: Viv Edwards)
    http://www.multilingualmatters.com
Language and Intercultural Communication
    (Editors: Michael Kelly and Alice Tomic)
    http://www.multilingualmatters.com/
Language Policy
    (Editors: Bernhard Spolsky and Elana Shohamy)
    http://www.kluweronline.com/issn/1568-4555/current
Language Problems and Language Planning
    (Editors: Probal Dasgupta and Humphrey Tonkin)
    http://www.benjamins.com/jbp/jornals/Lplp_info.html
Language, Society and Culture
    (Editors: Thao Le and Quynh Le)
    http://www.educ.utas.edu.au/users/tle/JOURNAL/JournalF.html
Llangua I Ùs
    http://cultura.gencal.es/Llengcat/publications/liu.htm

Mercator Media Forum
  (Editor: George Jones)
  http://www.aber.ac.uk/~merwww/engintro.htm
MOST Journal on Multicultural Societies
  (Editor: Matthias Koenig)
  http://www.unesco.org/most/jmshome.htm
Multilingua
  (Editor: Richard Watts)
  http://www.degruyter.de/journals/multilin/
The Linguist List – Journals
  http://www.linguistlist.org/journal.html

Selected international organisations dealing with regional or minority language issues

Council of Europe
  http://www.coe.int/
European Bureau for Lesser-Used Languages
  http://www.eblul.org.
European Union
  http://europa.eu.int/comm/education/langmtn.html
Organisation for Security and Cooperation in Europa
  http://www.osce.org/
United Nations
  http://www.un.org/

Selected official or semi-official language policy bodies in Europe

Bwrdd yr Ilaith Gymraeg/Welsh Language Board/(Wales, UK)
  http://www.bwrdd-yr-iaith.org.uk
Comunn na Gáidhlig (Scotland, UK)
  http://www.cnag.org.uk/
Délégation générale à la langue francais et aux langues de France/Gerneral Delegation to
  the French Language and languages of France (France)
  http://www.dglf.culture.gouv.fr/
Direcció General de Política Lingüistica / Directorate Genreal of Language Policy (Catalonia)
  http://www.cultura.gencat.net/Llengcat.
Hizkuntza Politikarako Saiburuordetza/Viceconsejería de pliítica lingüística/Deputy
  Minisory for Language policy (Basque Contry)
  http://www.euskadi.net/euskara_hps/indice_c.htm
Ùdarás na Gaeltachta /Gaeltacht Authority
  http://www.udaras.je/

20. Multilingualism of new minorities (in migratory contexts)

Peter Martin

1. Introduction

John Edwards (1995: 1) reminds us that multilingualism is "a normal and unremarkable necessity for the majority in the world today". The aim of this contribution to the Handbook is to focus on this "unremarkable necessity" within the context of new immigrant communities, often referred to as 'new minorities', and to show how these new minorities manage their multilingualism. The particular focus will be on new minorities in countries where English is the 'native' language or, to use the term introduced by Kachru (1985), in 'inner-circle' countries, with emphasis on the UK context. The contribution reviews several emerging themes from recent and current research on 'new minorities' and their sociolinguistic patterns. It explores initiatives taken by the communities themselves to maintain their languages against the backdrop of the policies (and ideologies) of the state. Of central importance here is the management of multilingualism in the face of the "monolingualising" (Heller 1995: 374) or 'homogenising' tendencies which exist in several inner-circle countries where new minorities have settled. The conclusion outlines several possible directions for future research in the intersection between applied linguistics and the multilingualisms of the new minorities.

In the context of this chapter, 'new minorities' refer to those peoples who, in the period following World War II, moved to 'inner-circle' countries such as Australia, Canada, the UK and the USA. In the immediate aftermath of the war, displaced refugees entered the UK and the USA from Europe. However, the major sources of immigration into these countries were from the Indian subcontinent, from East Africa and the Caribbean. In the final three decades of the twentieth century, other groups moved from their home countries to escape from political upheavals, war or famine. A general picture of the "roots of diversity" in the inner-circle countries is provided by Edwards (2005). Others have provided more detailed accounts of particular communities. For example, Ghuman (2003), in a chapter evocatively sub-titled "From the Ganges to the Thames and the Hudson", reviews the history of the migration of South Asians to the US, Canada, the UK and Australia. Clyne and Kipp (2002) provide a brief account of Australia's changing language demography with particular reference to the new minorities in the country.

The actual numbers of languages spoken by new minorities in inner-circle countries is considerable. In the capital city of the UK, for example, Baker and

Eversley (2000) have noted that more than 300 languages are spoken by children in the city's schools. They go on to add that for more than one-third of London's 850,000 schoolchildren, English is not a language they speak or hear spoken at home. This is a very significant fact and one which has important implications for the way multilingualism is managed. There has been an increase in multilingualism in other cities in Europe, too. Extra and Yağmur (2004) have investigated the increase of urban multilingualism in six cities in Europe. They not only consider the distribution of "immigrant minority languages" spoken at home, but also on their vitality, and on the status of the languages in the school systems.

Away from Europe, Edwards (2005: 9) notes that one in five of the population in the USA speaks a language other than English. Clyne and Kipp (2002) provide details of the multilingual situation in Australia. They examine the 1996 census data on home language use and relate that 14.6% of the population use a language other than English in the home, with the two traditionally multicultural cities of Melbourne and Sydney (25.4% and 26.4% respectively) having the highest proportion. The statistical data provided by Clyne and Kipp demonstrate a considerable increase in Australia's diversity, with several new ethnolinguistic minorities appearing for the first time, such as Tagalog, Indonesian, Malay, Hindi, Urdu, Korean and Japanese.

What is clear, then, is that, just as internationalisation and globalisation have increased the position of English around the world, the processes of migration have led to a greater diversity of languages in Europe, Australia and North America, and the emergence of new minorities and new multilingualisms in these contexts.

2.   Migration histories

The movement of peoples over the last 60 years, a process which is on-going with the issue of refugees and asylum seekers hardly out of the news in recent years, has resulted in large groups of new minorities in the inner-circle countries. Following World War II, Britain encouraged immigration, in part to help in the massive reconstruction process that was required. In the last 50 years political upheaval, persecution and war, famine and other ecological catastrophes have led to a widespread movement of peoples from different geographical and political contexts. Immigration policies in the inner-circle countries have also changed, not only due to the need for labour for economic growth, but also due to a softening of the racist tendencies inherent in many of the earlier policies. Edwards (2005: 34), for example, makes reference to the "greater concern for human rights" following the civil rights movement in the USA, as well as the Racial Discrimination Act of 1975 in Australia.

The presence of new minority groups in their new environments has significantly changed the language ecologies in the receiving countries. Several interlinking factors contribute to the changing language ecologies including, of course, the pre-migration experiences of groups and individuals (Kipp, forthcoming), such as the linguistic background of individuals (their languages and literacies), but also, importantly, the migration histories of the groups and their associated linguistic and sociolinguistic experiences. A general account of the linguistic and migration histories of the new minorities in one context is provided in a volume entitled *The Other Languages of England* (Linguistic Minorities Project 1985). This volume categorises the new "linguistic minorities" according to, on the one hand, the main reasons for their migration and settlement, and on the other hand, their place of origin. Included in the discussion is information on language and literacy background, and educational provision for the languages of the new minorities.

Migration histories sometimes involve more than a country of origin and a country of settlement in that some groups pass through an intermediary country either in the short term or for a longer period of time. For example, a large number of Somalis have to come to Britain from the Netherlands over the last decade. A more well-documented case is that of the "East African Asians" who were expelled from Kenya and Uganda between 1968 and 1973 (Linguistic Minorities Project 1985). These groups can be considered "twice migrants" (Singh 2003: 45) in that after settling in East Africa for a considerable amount of time, they were again uprooted due to the policies of Africanisation. As noted in Linguistic Minorities Project (1985: 48) though, these migrants came to Britain from a totally different sociolinguistic ecology than those who came directly from the sub-continent. For example, in East Africa many of them became fluent in Swahili while others did not become literate in their own languages due to lack of educational provision at the time of their initial or subsequent migration.

There appears to be little published material on the migration histories of the new minorities and, specifically, how these histories have influenced the linguistic habits of the new minorities. In addition, there is a dearth of information on the sociolinguistic status of the languages and varieties of languages that the new minorities brought with them to the country of settlement and what influence, if any, the new linguistic environment has on people's attitudes to their languages or varieties. For example, with regard to the Chinese communities, little is known about what might be called 'minorities within minorities', such as speakers of Hakka and Hokkien, their sociolinguistic relationship with speakers of Cantonese and Mandarin, and how this might be affected by the new linguistic ecology in which they find themselves. A further, major topic which needs exploration is how the migration trajectories have affected literacy practices of the new minorities. Attitudes to literacy may vary between different communities, but the new linguistic ecologies in which they settle may also influence their attitudes to literacy and whether they will continue to take the steps to maintain and pass on literacy skills to the next generations.

3.   Government policies towards the languages of new minorities

There is no standard terminology for the languages of the new minorities in inner-circle countries. In Britain, the term 'community language' is often used whereas the term 'heritage language' is favoured in the USA. In Australia the term LOTE (Languages other than English) has gained acceptance, although 'community language' is also used (Clyne et al. 2004). Recently, Hornberger (2005) has suggested that the composite term 'heritage/community language' (HCL) provides some common ground but, at the same time notes that there are shortcomings and ambiguities in both terms.

Within inner-circle countries there is similarly a plethora of terms used to describe the position of English in the linguistic repertoires of speakers of HCLs. In Britain, at least, the terms English as a second language (ESL) and English as a foreign language (EFL) have been superseded by the term English as an additional language (EAL).

In the inner-circle countries, although there is some official recognition of the languages of the new minorities, their status is uncertain, and they have largely been left to fend for themselves without any government support. Edwards (2005: 39) notes how Australia "has showed the most radical and progressive approach to multilingualism" through its policy of "unity within diversity" and official language maintenance efforts. In Britain, however, government discourse which highlights the importance of multilingualism does not appear to be backed up by concrete action. For example, the rhetoric in the Bullock Report (Department of Education and Science 1975: 293–294), although positive in its affirmation of bilingualism, did not lead to any real change in the status of the languages of new minorities. The Report states that the bilingualism of inner city students:

> is of great importance to the children and their families, and also to society as a whole. In a linguistically conscious nation in the modern world we should see mother tongue as an asset, as something to be nurtured, and one of the agencies which should nurture it is the school. Certainly, the school should adopt a positive attitude to its pupils' bilingualism and whenever possible should help to maintain and deepen their knowledge of their mother tongue.

Ten years later, however, a new report (The Swann Report) notes that linguistic and cultural maintenance was seen as beyond the remit of mainstream education and, instead, as "best achieved within the ethnic minority communities themselves" (Department of Education an Science 1985: 406). Discussion of how the new minorities have managed the issue of language and cultural maintenance is provided later in this chapter.

The discourse of 'assimilation' rather than integration can be found in many of the government documents which make reference to the languages of the new minorities in Britain and, indeed, in other contexts. For example, the Swann Report (Department of Education and Science 1985) would appear to be supporting a transitional model of bilingualism within an overall assimilationist framework, that is, the 'other' language is used as a resource until full proficiency in English has been achieved. This is perhaps linked to what Baetens Beardsmore (2003: 10) has referred to as the "deep-seated and widespread fear of bilingualism" and the "all-pervading tendency to couple the notion of 'problems' to that of bilingualism". It is also linked to what Rassool has referred to as "the notion of a monolingual, English-speaking people" which, he states, has "remained a potent variable in shaping common understandings of British nationhood". This, despite the fact that "bilingualism has been a reality for different social groups ... throughout the centuries" (Rassool 1997: 114). The important point here is that although official documentation would appear to endorse and even celebrate bilingualism, multiculturalism and linguistic diversity, they do so "without recourse to the social experiences of the speakers of these languages" (Rassool 1995: 288, cf. Hall et al. 2002). A similar point is made by Leung et al. (1997) with reference to official government discourses which construct language diversity in ways that do not necessarily reflect many people's daily experiences. To put this into perspective and take it one step further, such multilingual interactional experiences have even been categorised as "schizophrenic" by one former senior member of the British government:

> Speaking English enables parents to converse with their children in English as well as in their historic mother tongue, at home and to participate in wider modern culture. It helps to overcome the schizophrenia which bedevils generational relationships. (Blunkett 2002: 76)

What Blunkett is referring to here with his association between mental sickness and the non-compartmentalisation or mixing of languages neatly encapsulates the official discourses and what Bourne (1997: 56) has referred to as the "ideology of homogeneity that is so powerfully being constructed" in the UK. A similar point is made by Heller (1995: 374) in her reference to the "monolingualising tendencies" in the Canadian linguistic environment.

Despite the sentiments expressed above, there clearly has been a shift in the inner-circle countries from viewing the languages of the new minorities as a "problem" to viewing them as a "resource", although not always as a "right". These terms are taken from the influential article by Ruiz (1994) on the various orientations in language planning. Certainly the discourses in countries where there are large numbers of new minorities have moved away from problematising the languages of new minorities, and they are now recognised as an important resource (or 'asset') and, in some contexts, as a right. As early as 1981, for example, a British government document noted that the languages of new minorities were not just a valuable resource for the child/learner, but also as a valuable "national resource" (Department of Education and Science 1981), although what this actually means is not clear. In a recent article, Ricento (2005: 357) has been critical of the "language-as-resource" discourse in the promotion of heritage languages in the USA, particularly what he refers to as the "discourses of the heritage language movement". For example, he notes how such discourses have a tendency to "perpetuate a view of language as instrument" (rather than as an identity marker), which leads to a view of language being promoted as a "commodity displaced from its historical situatedness, a tool to be developed for particular national interests". He suggests that there has been a downplaying of the human side of things such as how the languages are used and issues to do with maintenance and loss of these languages. Ricento (2005: 349) argues that for a resources-oriented approach to succeed, "hegemonic ideologies associated with the roles of non-English languages in national life would need to be unpacked and alternative interpretations of American identity would need to be legitimised".

4.   Community initiatives in language and cultural maintenance

Given the lack of status accorded to the languages of new minorities in inner-circle countries generally, and the fact that mainstream education in many contexts neglects the real-life social experiences of cultural and linguistic diversity, it is not surprising that the communities themselves became involved in the setting up of schools in order to promote their cultures and languages. Indeed, in the UK context, as noted above, the government has put the issue of language and cultural maintenance in the hands of the new minorities themselves, and such educational provision has been set up in addition to the education provided by the state.

Different terms are in use to refer to this form of education. In Britain alone there are several terms, such as community language education, supplementary schools, complementary schools, and out of hours learning. Hornberger (2005), based on discussions with educators in the USA and Australia, has adopted the term 'heritage/community language education' (HCLE).

This form of community language education has, for well over a century, provided a 'safe' but largely 'hidden' space in which specific communities can learn about their own cultures and languages. Although the history of such education is relatively long in Britain (cf. McLean 1985), little was known about this form of education outside the communities themselves (Rampton et al 1997) until recently. According to Verma et al (1994: 12), the initial aim of community language education is to strengthen "cultural and religious identity in the face of the threat of cultural assimilation". Hall et al (2002: 415) take this further by making reference to the roles that such schools play in "correcting" the rather "subtractive" approach to learning language in the mainstream sector. In addition, certain communities have set up community schools in order to counteract the perceived deficiencies in state education for particular communities. For example, Mirza and Reay (2000) and Reay and Mirza (1997, 2001) make reference to the "spaces and places of back education desire" in "black supplementary schools".

Although there has been a large amount of work in Britain, North America and Australia which points to crucial connections between minority communities and their languages, cultures, religions, literacy practices and identities, as noted above, there is a dearth of studies which focus specifically on community language education initiatives. Much of the work which is available demonstrates how ethnic minority children benefit from their multilingualism and the bilingual opportunities which the schools provide. For example, Hall et al. (2002: 409) note how attendance at supplementary schools provides "a way of reclaiming the specificity of cultural and social identity ... missing from mainstream schooling". In their comparative study of provision, purposes and pedagogy of supplementary schooling in Leeds (UK) and Oslo (Norway), they found that supplementary education "imbues its participants with a sense of belonging to a community that supports them practically, culturally, socially, emotionally and spiritually" (Hall et al. 2002: 410). These are important issues and they can be linked back to the discussion above about the social experiences of using languages, rather than simply the celebration of linguistic diversity. Such educational opportunities provide a safe haven for young people from the new minorities to use their bilingualism in creative and flexible ways (cf. Martin et al. 2006). Critically, little is still known about the educational pedagogies of such schooling as well as the relationship between mainstream and supplementary education.

It appears that, in Britain at least, the government is beginning to notice the potentiality of supplementary education for new minorities. A recent report entitled *Aiming High* (Department for Education and Science 2003) highlights the potential benefits of supplementary schooling. With reference to mainstream schools, the document states:

> Successful schools reach out to their communities. They often make premises available for community use, which can build bridges and develop dialogue. *Many pupils have also benefited greatly from out-of-school-hours learning in community-run initiatives such as supplementary schools.* Some supplementary schools focus on the curriculum, others on cultural, mother tongue or religious faith instruction. Attendance can enhance pupils' respect, promote self-discipline and inspire pupils to have high aspirations to succeed.
> (Department for Education and Science 2003: 26, emphasis added)

The particular initiative of the new minorities, that is, the provision of supplementary education is, then, beginning to receive some official recognition in the UK. This type of education, set up in response to a historically monolingual ideology which ignores the complexities of the modern multilingual state (cf. Creese and Martin 2006), is still under-researched and under-theorised, although some literature is available.

The important work on black supplementary schools by Mirza and Reay (2000) and Reay and Mirza (1997, 2001) has already been referred to, as has the comparative study of supplementary schooling in Leeds (UK) and Oslo (Norway) by Hall et al (2002). Other literature includes Li Wei's (1993) study of the role of Chinese supplementary schools in the northern British city of Newcastle in the maintenance of Chinese, and Arthur's (2003) study of Somali literacy teaching in Liverpool. Recent work in the British midlands city of Leicester has been reported in Creese et al (2006) and Martin et al (2006). The former focuses on three identity positions which emerge from the work in Gujarati supplementary schools in the city: these are "multicultural", "heritage", and "learner" identities. The study explores the importance of ethnicity as a social category for students in supplementary schools, but also the important role of the schools in promoting successful learner identity. The importance of community schools, particularly in their "identity-forming" and "identity-providing" purpose has been noted by Fishman (1989). The other study demonstrates how the participants in the school manage bilingualism and bilingual learning in the school context. The bilingual Gujarati-English interaction found in these schools, particularly the way that the participants spontaneously and purposely juxtapose Gujarati and English in order to create learning/teaching opportunities plays an important part in the negotiation and management of the linguistic, social and learning identities of the classroom participants. The Leicester study (Martin et al. 2004) shows that these schools are important sites for the acquisition of linguistic and literacy knowledge; add value and enhance learning across other educational settings; play an important role in community cohesion; and provide a positive and uncontested model for bi- or multilingualism.

5.   New multilingualisms

In the final section of this chapter a brief overview of some of the new multilingualisms that are emerging in the language ecologies of inner-circle countries are reviewed. Despite the rather monolingual official discourses found in these contexts, multilingualism is alive and well. As Sneddon (2000a: 103) notes, "[c]hildren all over Britain live their daily lives in two, three or more languages". This contemporary multilingualism comes through in a plethora of studies in different contexts, for example, in studies such as Hansen et al. (2003)

titled "Sometimes Dutch and sometimes Somali", and that of Hall (1995) titled "A time to act English and a time to act Indian". However, although multilingualism certainly is a reality in contemporary Britain, and in other contexts where new minorities have settled, there is surprisingly little literature which demonstrates the nature of this multilingualism. This, surely, is an area where further work is required. Despite the paucity of information on the ways new minorities actually use their languages and the new multilingualisms which are evolving, there are several strands of research reported in the literature which are of interest.

The contact between the speakers of the new minority languages and the speakers of the existing language(s) in the receiving countries has influenced the linguistic ecologies in these countries in several ways, and code-switching and 'crossing' between languages, hybrid forms of languages, and new creative forms of English are common phenomena found in such countries.

Although there is a plethora of work on code-switching and code-mixing in many different linguistic contexts (cf. Auer 1998, Myers-Scotton 1993), there is a dearth of studies which focus on switching or mixing of languages among new minorities and, in particular, how new minorities use their languages in their daily interaction. Critically, this does not simply refer to how they use their languages as a resource, as something to be brought out for show, so to speak, but rather as an identity marker and how this allows speakers to promote different identities at different times and in different contexts (cf. Ricento 2005, Hall 1995).

Rampton (1998) has added a new slant to research into code-switching, following fieldwork on young people of Indian, Pakistani, African Caribbean and Anglo descent. He introduces the notion of "language crossing", that is, the use of a language that is not usually thought to "belong" to the speaker. According to Rampton (1998: 291, 299), language crossing is "poised at the juncture of two competing notions of group belonging" and "involves a sense of movement across quite sharply felt social or ethnic boundaries". Rampton (1998: 300) therefore argues that language crossing opens up the possibility of "exploring other people's ethnicities, embracing them and/or creating new ones". This, then, is clearly an area that deserves further exploration.

Pennycook (2003) has extended Rampton's work on crossing, by focusing on rap music. Although specifically focusing on Japan, the study is relevant to the discussion of new multilingualisms in the linguistic ecologies of contexts in which new minorities exist. He notes how recent sociolinguistic work has helped to replace the "fixed and static categories of class, gender and identity membership" with "more fluid ways of thinking about language, identity and belonging" (Pennycook 2003: 514–515).

As well as the work referred to above, there has been a whole range of work carried out on the literacies of the new minorities, for example, Gregory and

Williams' (2000) study on "unofficial" literacies in the lives of East London communities, and Sneddon's (2000a, b) work on language and literacy practices in multilingual environments. Studies from North America (such as Zentella 1997), Australia and elsewhere (Durgunoglu and Verhoeven, 1998) have demonstrated crucial connections between new minorities and their language, cultures, religions, literacy practices and identities. More recent work, by Kenner (2000, 2004), has focused on how children from new minorities "experience their worlds not as separate linguistic and cultural entities but as 'simultaneous' [and how they] consequently tend to integrate and synthesise their linguistic resources" (Kenner 2004: 44). As noted in the discussion above, and also by Kenner, the monolingualising society in which we live tends to try and keep children's worlds separate, with different, compartmentalised codes for each separate context.

There are, then, interesting strands of research into the ways members of new minority communities manage their multilingualism and on the new forms of multilingualism that are evolving. There is a need, though, for more detailed analyses of these multilingual practices.

6.   Conclusions and directions for future research

This chapter has provided a brief discussion of the multilingualism of the new minorities, with particular reference to new minorities in inner-circle countries. Emphasis has been given to official government policies towards the languages of the new minorities and the steps the new minorities themselves have had to take in order to maintain their own languages in contexts which are ideologically monolingual, despite government rhetoric which celebrates multilingualism and diversity.

Within the field of multilingualism of the new minorities, there are several areas which would surely repay further study, and these have been referred to in the discussion above. Although demographic information about numbers of speakers of different languages is important, we need to move beyond quantitative data and provide micro-ethnographic analyses to explore the interaction of new minorities. This is important on several levels, not least of which is to begin to move away from the ideologically positioned viewpoint that mixing of languages is inherently problematic. We need to explore how languages are brought together to communicate and to express identities. We need to consider the issues of spontaneity and simultaneity in language choice and move away from the ideology of putting discrete languages into separate compartments. As noted above, it is also essential to examine the linguistic and sociolinguistic contexts during the migration trajectories of the new minorities, and the statuses and histories of the languages and varieties of languages in the linguistic ecologies of these contexts. A further area of research is the whole question of literacies and, as pointed out above, there is already some major work in this area. Finally, there is a need to look at how language choice is changing inter-generationally, and the issue of language maintenance and shift.

References

Arthur, Jo
    2003   'Baro Afkaaga Hooyo!' A case study of Somali literacy teaching in Liverpool. *International Journal of Bilingual Education and Bilingualism* 6, 3 and 4: 253–266.
Auer, Peter (ed)
    1998   *Code-Switching in Conversation. Language, Interaction and Identity.* London: Routledge.
Baetens Beardsmore, Hugo
    2003   Who's afraid of bilingualism. In: Jean-Marc Dewaele, Alex Housen and Li Wei (eds) *Bilingualism: Beyond Basic Principles*, 10–27. Clevedon: Multilingual Matters.
Baker, Philip and Eversley, John
    2000   *Multilingual Capital, the Languages of London School Children and their Relevance to Economic, Social and Educational Policies.* London: Battlebridge Publications.
Blunkett, David
    2002   Integration with diversity: globalisation and the renewal of democracy and civil society. In: P. Griffith and M. Leonard (eds) *Reclaiming Britishness*, 65–77. London: The Foreign Policy Centre.
Bourne, Jill
    1997   "The grown-ups know best": language policy making in Britain in the 1990s. In: William Eggington and Helen Wren (eds) *Language Policy: Dominant English Pluralist Challenges*, 49–65. Amsterdam: John Benjamins.
Clyne, Michael, Hunt, Claudia R. and Isaakidis, Tina
    2004   Learning a community language as a third language. *International Journal of Multilingualism* 1, 1: 33–52.
Clyne, Michael and Kipp, Sandra
    2002   Australia's changing language demography. *People and Place* 10, 3: 29–35.
Creese, Angela and Peter Martin
    2006   Interaction in complementary school contexts- developing identities of choice: An introduction. *Language and Education* 20, 1: 23–43.
Creese, Angela, Arvind Bhatt, Nirmala Bhojani and Peter Martin
    2006   Multicultural, heritage and learner identities in Complementary schools. *Language and Education* 20, 1:
Department of Education and Science (DES)
    1975   *A Language for Life.* [The Bullock Report]. London: HMSO.
    1981   *The School Curriculum.* London: HMSO.

1985   *Education for All.* Report of the Committee of Inquiry into the Education of Ethnic Minority Groups, Chairman, Lord Swann [The Swann Report]. London: HMSO.

2003   *Aiming High. Raising Attainment for Minority Ethnic Pupils.* London: DfES.

Durgunoglu, Aydin Y. and Verhoeven, Ludo (eds.)

1998   *Literacy Development in a Multilingual Context. Cross-Cultural Perspectives,* Mahwah, NJ: Lawrence Erlbaum Associates.

Edwards, John

1995   *Multilingualism.* Harmondswoth: Penguin

Edwards, Viv

2005   *Multilingualism in the English-Speaking World.* Oxford: Blackwell.

Extra, Gus and Kutlay Yağmur (eds)

2004   *Urban Multilingualism in Europe. Immigrant Minority Languages at Home and School.* Clevedon: Multilingual Matters.

Fishman, Joshua

1989   *Language and Ethnicity in Minority Sociolinguistic Perspective.* Clevedon: Multilingual Matters.

Ghuman, Paul A. Singh

2003   *Double Loyalties. South Asian Adolescents in the West.* Cardiff: University of Wales Press.

Gregory, Eve and Ann Williams

2000   Work or play? 'Unofficial' literacies in the lives of two East London communities. In: Marilyn Martin-Jones and Kathryn. Jones (eds) *Multilingual Literacies. Reading and Writing Different Worlds*, 37–54 Amsterdam/Philadelphia: John Benjamins.

Hall, Kathy

1995   "There's a time to act English and a time to act Indian": the policy of identity among British Sikh teenagers. In: Sharon Stephens (ed.) *Children and the Politics of Culture*, 243–264. Princeton, NJ: Princeton University Press.

Hall, Kathy, Kamil Özerk, Mohsin Zulfiqar and Jon Tan

2002   "This is our school": provision, purpose and pedagogy of supplementary schooling Leeds and Oslo. *British Educational Research Journal* 28 (2), 399–418.

Hansen, Mylène, Boogaard, Marianne and Herrlitz, Wolfgang

2003   "Sometimes Dutch and sometimes Somali". Children's participation in multicultural interactions in Dutch primary schools. *Linguistics and Education* 14, 1: 27–50.

Heller, Monica

1995   Language choice, social institutions, and symbolic domination. *Language in Society* 24: 373–405.

Hornberger, Nancy

2005   Heritage/Community language education: US and Australian Perspectives. *International Journal of Bilingual Education and Bilingualism* 8 (2 and 3): 101–108.

Kachru, Braj

1985   Standards, codification and sociolinguistic realism: the English language in the outer circle. In: R. Quirk and H. Widdowson (eds) *English in the World.* Cambridge: Cambridge University Press.

Kenner, Charmian
  2000   Biliteracy in a monolingual school system? English and Gujarati in South
          London. *Language, Culture and Curriculum* 13 (1): 13–30.
  2004   Living in simultaneous worlds: difference and integration in bilingual script
          learning. *International Journal of Bilingual Education and Bilingualism* 7,
          1: 43–61.
Kipp, Sandra
  (forthcoming) Australia's community languages. In *Encyclopedia of Language and
          Education*. Volume 9. *Ecology of Language*. Angela Creese, Peter Martin,
          Nancy Hornberger (eds). Springer.
Leung, Constant, Roxy Harris and Ben Rampton
  1997   The idealised native speaker, reified ethnicities and classroom realities.
          TESOL Quarterly 31, 3: 543–560.
Li Wei
  1993   Mother tongue maintenance in a Chinese community school in Newcastle
          upon Tyne: Developing a social network perspective. *Language and Edu-
          cation* 7 (3): 199–215.
Linguistic Minorities Project
  1985   *The Other Languages of England*. London: Routledge and Kegan Paul.
McLean, Martin
  1985   Private supplementary schools and the ethnic challenge of state education
          in Britain. In: C. Brock and W. Tulasiewicz (eds) *Cultural Identity and Edu-
          cational Policy*, 326–345. London: Croom Helm.
Martin, Peter, Angela Creese, Arvind Bhatt and Nirmala Bhojani
  2004   Final Report on Complementary Schools and their Communities in
          Leicester. University of Leicester/University of Birmingham. Unpublished
          Document. (ESRC R000223949). Also available at: http://www.le.ac.uk/
          education/research/complementary_schools/index.html
Martin, Peter, Arvind Bhatt, Nirmala Bhojani and Angela Creese
  2006   Managing bilingual interaction in a Gujarati complementary school in
          Leicester. *Language and Education* 20, 1: 5–22.
Mirza, Heidi Diane Reay
  2000   Spaces and places of black education desire: rethinking black supplemen-
          tary schools as a New Social Movement. *Sociology* 34, 3: 521–544.
Myers-Scotton, Carol
  1993   *Social Motivations of Code-Switching*. Oxford: Clarendon Press.
Pennycook, Alastair
  2003   Global Englishes, Rip Slyme, and performativity. *Journal of Sociolinguis-
          tics* 7 (4): 513–533.
Rampton, Ben
  1998   Language crossing and the redefinition of reality. In: Peter Auer (ed.) 290–317.
Rampton, Ben, Roxy Harris and Constant Leung
  1997   Multilingualism in England. *Annual Review of Applied Linguistics* 17,
          224–241. (Also published as Occasional Paper, CALR, Thames Valley Uni-
          versity.)
Rassool, Naz
  1995   Language, cultural pluralism and the silencing of minority discourses in
          England and Wales. *Journal of Education Policy* 10 (3): 287–302.

1997   Language policies for a multicultural Britain. In: Ruth Wodak and David Corson (eds.) *Encyclopedia of Language and Education. Volume 1: Language Policy and Political Issues in Education*, 113–126. Kluwer Academic Publishers.

Reay, Diane and Heidi Mirza
1997   Uncovering genealogies of the margins: black supplementary schooling. *British Journal of Sociology of Education* 18, 4: 477–499.

Reay, Diane and Heidi Mirza
2001   Black supplementary schools: spaces of radical blackness. In: R. Majors (ed.) *Education our Black Children: New Directions and Radical Approaches*. London: RoutledgeFalmer

Ricento, Thomas
2005   Problems with the 'language-as resource' discourse in the promotion of heritage languages in the U.S.A. *Journal of Sociolinguistics* 9 (3): 348–368.

Ruiz, Richard
1984   Orientations in language planning. *National Association for Bilingual Education (NABE) Journal* 8 (2): 15–34.

Singh, Gurharpal
2003   Multiculturalism in contemporary Britain: reflections on the 'Leicester model'. *International Journal on Multicultural Societies* 5, 1: 40–54.

Sneddon, Raymonde
2000a   Language and Literacy Practices in Gujarati Muslim Families. In: Marilyn Martin-Jones and Kathryn Jones (eds.) *Multilingual Literacies. Reading and Writing in Different Worlds*, 103–126. Amsterdam: John Benjamins.
2000b   Language and Literacy: Children's experiences in multilingual environments. *International Journal of Bilingual Education and Bilingualism* 4, 3: 265–282.

Verma, Gajendra, Zec, Paul, and Skinner, George
1994   *The Ethnic Crucible. Harmony and Hostility in Multi-Ethnic Schools*. London: Falmer Press.

Zentella, Ana C.
1997   *Growing Up Bilingual*. Oxford: Blackwell.

Additional readings

Baumann, Gerd
1996   *Contesting Culture, Discourses of Identity in Multi-ethnic London*. Cambridge: Cambridge University Press.

Bhatt, Arvind, David Barton and Marilyn Martin-Jones
(1994) Gujarati literacies in East Africa and Leicester: changes in social identities and multilingual practices. *Working Paper Series* No 56. Centre for Language in Social Life. University of Lancaster, UK.

Creese, Angela and Peter Martin (eds)
2006   Interaction in complementary school contexts: developing identities of choice. Special Issue of *Language and Education* 20, 1: 1–4.

Heller, Monica
   1999   *Linguistic Minorities and Modernity. A Sociolinguistic Ethnography.* Harlow: Addison-Wesley Longman.
Martin-Jones, Marilyn and Kathryn Jones
   2000   *Multilingual Literacies. Reading and Writing Different Worlds.* Amsterdam/Philadelphia: John Benjamins.
May, Stephen
   1999   *Indigenous Community-based Education.* Clevedon: Multilingual Matters.
   2001   *Language and Minority Rights. Ethnicity, Nationalism and the Politics of Language.* Harlow, UK: Pearson Education.
Norton, Bonny
   2000   *Identity and Language Learning; Gender, Ethnicity and Educational Change.* London: Longman.
Rampton, Ben
   1995   *Crossing: Language and Ethnicity among Adolescents.* London: Longman.

21.   Multilingualism in ex-colonial countries

Christopher Stroud

1.   Introduction

Multilingualism in ex-colonial countries is constituted as an object of reflection and study in many different, partially overlapping, discourses that vary considerably over time and across geographical and semiotic space. One salient discourse is that of linguistics, which constructs multilingualism as particular relationships of inclusion and exclusion of linguistic systems, or in terms of overlapping and distinct networks of communication. Historically, colonial linguistics was a prominent tool in the colonial project of governmentality, where a politics of 'divide and rule' encouraged the multiplication of languages and the creation of unbridled linguistic diversity – an African 'Tower of Bable' – that was seen to rationalize strict colonial regulation of linguistic realities (Errington 2001; Makoni 1998; Mazrui and Mazrui 1998). This particular discourse has undergone considerable change with the transformation of colonial states into independent nations, and has ceded to a dominant strand of contemporary linguistics that is actively seeking to 'disinvent' (Makoni and Pennycook in press), or at the very least reduce, colonial linguistic diversity. So, for example, Prah (1998: 7) remarks that many of the 1250–2100 languages claimed to be spoken in Africa are "in reality dialects that can be put into wider clusters enjoying significant degrees of mutual intelligibility" (cf. also Mühlhäusler 1996 for Papua New Guinea).

Framing linguistic discourses of multilingualism are political and economic discourses, with their associated ideological conceptions of language. Political stances on multilingualism in colonial contexts varied with the philosophy of colonialism entertained by the state in question; in French and Portuguese Africa, a principle of assimilation allowed 'natives' a controlled access to French and Portuguese respectively in order that they may become bona fide, assimilated, citizens rather than mere subjects. British Africa, on the other hand, was run according to principles of linguistic colonial management developed in India. Here, only a handful of intermediaries (in the contact zone) were deemed to need a proficiency in English, while the colonized population in general managed its day-to-day affairs through local languages. In India, the politics of colonialism shifted between Orientalism and Anglicism with clear ramifications for the status accorded to local languages (Pennycook 1998). A similar controversy spiraled in Portuguese Mozambique, where Catholics and Protestants held widely divergent views on the use and development of African languages for educational, administrative and religious purposes (Helgesson 1991); Catholics, in alliance with the Portuguese state, stood firmly behind the sole use of (civilized) Portuguese for all formal functions, whereas Protestants conducted their missions in local languages. These different colonial policies reverberate today in the status of local languages (developed orthographies and grammars) in British Africa as opposed to French and Portuguese Africa. In these latter contexts, however, indigenous varieties of French (and to some extent Portuguese) have evolved as a historical consequence of earlier contact through popular access to these languages – something that is true although to a lesser extent also for English.

In each of these colonial countries, we find competing educational discourses on multilingualism (cf. Junod 1905, 1946; Loh Fook Seng 1970). In many colonial contexts, religious insistence that 'natives' be taught morality and manners through the word of God in the metropolitan language provided the ideological glue that linked the hierarchization of languages (Portuguese, French, English) to an ethics of the colonial project (cf. Fabian 1986). At times, official stance was characterized by an alignment and 'ideological fit' across educational, political and religious discourses that created a more or less hegemonic understanding of multilingualism.

On independence, many countries chose to deal with their colonial legacies in one of two main ways, either keeping a metropolitan language as official language, or opting for one or more indigenous languages in this role. In the majority of cases, however, linguistic discourses were taken over wholesale from the colonial project. Issues of linguistic hierarchy, adequacy and level of technical development of local languages for formal functions, and political considerations, such as the extent of the links that should be retained to old colonial metropoles, or type of citizenship sought, were core concerns of post-independent language planning. In more recent times, the legacies of traditional political (and economic) constructions of discourses on multilingualism have met with new political discourses informed by Western liberal understandings of citizenship and rights. The politization of multilingualism in terms of "linguistic human rights" (Skutnabb-Kangas and Phillipson 1997) lends itself to metaphorization in terms of contemporary discourses of ecology, framing problems of language maintenance, survival shift and death in terms of the value of natural human diversity (cf. Romaine and Nettle 2001). Contemporary educational perspectives on multilingualism highlight the importance of mother tongue education to the survival of minority languages, which in turn is viewed as a prerequisite for the audibility of minority voice and a broad popular participation in governance.

Susan Gal has suggested that historical and contemporary variation in the organization of multilingualism may at root be accounted for in terms of a political economy of language, noting how "political economic systems of dependency and inequality" such as "colonization, state and class formation, the expansion of capitalism, and transnational labor migration" (Gal 1989: 356) underlie forms of linguistic change. From the standpoint of a political economy of language, multilingualism in ex-colonial societies can be viewed as a set of practices and perceptions about languages and their interrelationships (political, educational, cultural, etc), that serve as one means whereby contact and competition over scarce symbolic and material resources is managed, regulated and organized.

In today's world, ex-colonial nations remain embroiled in structures of (hegemonic) dependency or reciprocity with other nations in a world system network of exchange and appropriation, and much of the current dynamics in ex-colonial multilingual situations is entwined with global, transnational processes (cf. also Heller 1999a; Journal of Sociolinguistics, 7 (4), 2003 for papers on the sociolinguistics of globalization). Importantly, the effect of global processes on multilingual dynamics varies from context to context or nation-state to nation-state, suggesting that the lived linguistic and cultural realities of speakers are mediated by a significant interaction between global macrostructural political and economic institutions, on the one hand, and the local structures of state and civil society, and their ideologies and practices, on the other. The specific location of an ex-colonial context in the global political economy generates the structural and ideological conditions for the formation, transformation, and reproduction of different types of citizenship, that is, alternative or vernacular modernities. Multilingualism, therefore, can be framed politically in terms of citizenship, voice and agency, on the understanding that the nature of the relationship between state and citizen depends on the types of markets and institutions hosted in a particular community (cf. e.g. Haeri 1997; Stroud 2002 for accounts that explore issues of multilingualism against a Bourdieuian conception of market/field).

Different types of linguistic markets have different outcomes in terms of local linguistic forms of multilingualism. In some cases, speakers' attempts to access the resources of more powerful segments of society result in contact languages such as pidgins and creoles (Fabian 1986), and in other cases, second language acquisition may result in a near-native competence of a target language. Whereas some contexts may encourage retention of original mother tongues – in cases where these languages are given value on the linguistic market – other situations serve as a catalyst for language shift and create subtractive conditions for first language acquisition. Competition between different groups in society may also result in the formation of distinct, class-based varieties of a dominant language, and in specific cases, local and less prestigious languages may become the object of purist activity for political purposes. In all cases, multilingualism involves some form of functional ideological division of labor between languages, captured in notions such as diglossia or domain.

This chapter attempts a detailed account of multilingualism in ex-colonial countries in terms of the local politics and economics of globalization, on the one hand, and their mediation in linguistic structures and sociosymbolic uses of language on the other. In keeping with this, sections 2 to 5 discuss the organization of multilingual practices and perceptions in terms of three framing factors: first of all, how the local political institutions and ideologies that mediate global economic processes at the national level organize multilingualism differently as a political resource, as well as how the state employs discourses on multilingualism to (re)configure the (imagined) place of a nation in globalization; secondly, how real economic and material developments in the global system order languages, varieties and multilingual practices directly into (competing) structures of linguistic value; and thirdly, the ideologization of languages that puts multilingual practices and perceptions to sociosymbolic use in creative (and occasionally subversive) stylization and identity work on local symbolic markets.

The chapter concludes in section 6 with some remarks on the implications of this approach for a practical politics of multilingualism.

2.   Two ex-colonial multilingual nations[1]

Globalization is far from a uniform process throughout the world, and multilingual practices are inseparable from the local interplay between state, market and forms of life. In order to illustrate this "internal diversity of globalization" (Hannerz 1996: 9), I have chosen to review multilingualism in two nations at diametrically opposite ends of the economic continuum, Mozambique and Singapore.

2.1.   Ex-colonial Mozambique

In Mozambique, a population of 14 million people speak an estimated 20 Bantu languages (NELIMO 1989),[2] and a handful of Indian languages with Portuguese as the official language (Lopes 1999). In recent years, the status of local languages has changed from 'patrimonial' acknowledgement to their more substantial recognition and use in official contexts such as political debates and education. The number of speakers who claim Portuguese as a mother tongue is over 3%, and as a second language more than 40%. According to the latest census conducted in 1997, Portuguese continues to remain principally a language of the towns, with over 90% of speakers found in urban areas, although it is gaining a small foothold in rural areas as well. Portuguese is a young language, spoken predominantly in the age bracket 15–39. It exists in a variety of (second language) forms that vary according to parameters such as age, education, occupation and gender (Firmino 1995, 2000, 2002; Gonçalves 1996; Stroud and Gonçalves 1997). There are no syncretic varieties comparable to what is found in Nairobi and DRC, and no attested pidgins or creoles.

The largest Bantu language, Emakua, is spoken by approximately 25% of the population in the north of the country on the border to Tanzania. Many Mozambican languages share with Emakua the status of cross-border languages, for example, CiChewa (also spoken in Malawi), XiShona and Ndebele (Zimbabwe) and Tsonga (South Africa). Speakers of Xironga, the original language of the capital Maputo, have undergone considerable language shift to XiChangana/ Tsonga – a language virtually identical to Xironga. A variety of Indian and Chinese languages are spoken in small numbers principally among trades-people throughout the country, although with a concentration in urban areas.[3]

In a world systems perspective, Mozambique is on the periphery of global development and is one of the world's poorest (although fast expanding) economies. It is modernizing via an informalization of its economy and a retraditionalization of politics (Chabal and Daloz 1999), two processes behind an extensive reorganization of the relationship between state and civil society. The history of multilingualism in Mozambique since independence has produced a non-unified market in Bourdieu's terms, where competing norms and conceptions of linguistic legitimacy characterize a highly polycentric and linguistically heterogeneous community.

2.2.   Singapore

The population of Singapore (3.2 million) comprises the ethnic Chinese, making up 76.8% of the population, Malays at 13.9%, 7.9% Indians, and 1.4% Others, that is, mainly Eurasians and Europeans. Four official languages are spoken (English, Mandarin, Tamil and Malay), with Malay as the national language serving primarily ceremonial functions, chosen in recognition that Malay fisher-folk comprised the original population of the island, and to honor the fact that Singapore was once part of the Federation of Malaysia. An original contact language, Bazaar Malay, is spoken by a few semi-speakers only (Daw Khin Khin 2005). Mother tongues are assigned on the basis of the father's ethnicity and are not necessarily the actual languages used in the family. Up until the mideighties, the Chinese community spoke an estimated 25 mutually unintelligible dialects. During the course of Singapore's independence, most Chinese speakers have shifted to Mandarin and, today, only the largest dialect groups (e.g. Hokkien, Cantonese, and Teochew) retain speakers who admit any degree of fluency at all in their ancestral languages. Among the ethnic Indians, likewise only a small number actually master their officially designated language, Tamil, acknowledging proficiencies in Bengali, Punjabi, and Gujarati, among others, especially English. Local, basilectal varieties of English, so-called Singlish or Colloquial Singaporean English (Bao 2003, 2005; Lim 2004) are spoken widely across the ethnic groupings, organized into diglossic (Gupta 1998a, b) or lectal continua (Ho and Platt 1993) with Standard Singaporean English.

Singapore is very much at the opposite end of the global systems continuum to Mozambique. The history of contemporary multilingualism in Singapore has roots in the nation's economic ambitions as a global player and its communitarian political ideology. In Singapore, developments since independence have catapulted the country into a late modern condition with a strong state built on the foundations of economic pragmatism. This has resulted in a situation of ordered multilingualism and the commodification of language, and to a marked emphasis on an exo-normative and tightly managed standard of English.

3.   The politics of multilingualism in globalization

The spread of languages and language contact is a salient aspect of the global economy. As political processes and relations also govern the workings of economic markets (Irvine 1986), the exact way in which globalization is manifest in linguistic diversity and multilingualism is determined by available political institutions, type of modernity, local ideologies and perceptions of language – current and historical – as well as statal and institutional narratives (Wee and Bokhurst-Heng 2005). However, multilingualism is not only manifested and refigured in political framings of citizenship, but is also the very materials out of which states envisage and rhetorically constitute themselves in the global economy. Arnaut (2005) has employed the notion of discourses of scale to capture how talk about events (and language) across global space serves to position these spaces in a world system matrix.

3.1.   Mozambique

3.1.1.   Multilingualism in the development of the nation-state

Many formative and conspiring factors contributed to the multilingual dynamics of Mozambique at independence. Foremost among these was a colonial legacy in the form of a bifurcation between citizens and subjects. Citizens had access to strict forms of Portuguese, were considered civilized, and lived in the urban sprawl of Maputo, whereas subjects were ruled in 'native' (rural) lands by traditional chiefs (regulos) according to customary law through the medium of local African languages. The newly independent government of President Samora Machel immediately set about constructing a homen novo – a new man – who, while cognizant of tradition and custom, would nevertheless be foremost a citizen of the modern, nation-state of Mozambique, and celebrate tradition through the medium of Portuguese (Stroud 1999).

In the first years of independence, language figured as an integral part of the cultural nation-building project. Language ideological debates constructed Portuguese as a language of consensus, and, not surprisingly, it was declared the sole official language of the country immediately upon independence. Discourses on multilingualism, specifically with respect to ascription of competence and linguistic proficiency, were powerful tools in the cultural project of nation-building. For example, early on the government sought ways to positively reevaluate forms of 'broken' Portuguese spoken by the largely Bantu language speaking population as a way to represent the genuine language of revolutionary spirit, a political position that later gave way to a concern that speakers emulate the norms of standard European Portuguese. In this latter context, hybridity in language and use of local languages in formal, public arenas was frowned upon, and rhetorically constituted, as evidence of the inimigo interno (the internal enemy). This was tantamount to morally managing the relationship between citizen and state by indexically configuring a relationship between linguistic contact phenomena and type of citizenship.

Debates continue on the 'authenticity' of Portuguese in Mozambique, and on the role of metropolitan languages vis-à-vis African languages (Firmino 2002; Lopes 1999). This is an issue that is pervasive on the African continent generally (cf., e.g., Ngugi wa Thiong'o 1986; Tengan 1994), and is very much an instance of competing elite discourses around the linguistic imaginary of the new nation.

There was initially no substantial political or economic role reserved for African languages at independence, although they were treated as objects of patrimonial interest and cultural value. This was most certainly a consequence of a colonial legacy that saw African languages as divisive to the state imaginary, and as 'lesser', incomplete and less functional systems (but cf. references in Lopes 1999).

3.1.2. Multilingualism in the post-independent weak state

The hierarchical relationship between Portuguese and African languages has gradually shifted over time, due to a confluence of factors. First of all, the marginal position in the world economy that Mozambique today shares with many African countries has had felt ramifications for the functioning and legitimacy of its state apparatus. These developments have fanned an inefficient administration that is no longer able to provide the populace with economic benefits – not even able to pay the salaries of its functionaries, resulting in a situation where people have had to seek recourse to alternative structures and institutions for their livelihood, and generating competing foci of power and legitimacy in the process.[4] Local social aggregates such as kinship networks, churches, and practices such as sorcery not only alleviate material necessity, but also provide alternative routes to social mobility, and serve as channels for popular forms of dissatisfaction (Alfredsson and Linha 1999). A diminished role for the state as an economic actor, as employer and as provider of goods and services has been followed by a mushrooming of foreign-funded NGOs, many of which are addressing reform in public sector services such as transport, health and education (cf. Nugent 2005: 366).

This transformation of the Mozambican state has been reinforced by its ongoing retraditionalization, embodying a revamped role for traditional practices of government (Chabal and Daloz 1999) based on an understanding of political power in terms of particular notions of legitimacy and accountability. The legitimacy of African elites is a patrimonial legitimacy (Chabal and Daloz 1999: 15), which derives from the ability of the elites to nourish clients on which their power rests. The transactional nature of the patron-client links make politicians' obligations to their kin, clients, community, region and religion foremost, and so power brokers strive to be perceived as "a worthy embodiment of the community" (Chabal and Daloz 1999: 55). In this type of African modernization, the boundaries of the political have been extended, with citizens balancing traditional and 'modern' worlds and beliefs in their everyday existence (West and Kloeck-Jenson 1999; Buur and Kyed 2003).[5] The advent of multiparty politics in the early nineties and the vernacularization of Mozambican politics, evident in a concern on behalf of politicians to couch national issues as locally relevant, is a further factor reinforcing a weakening of central state power.

The fragmentation and deconstruction of the Mozambican state is mirrored in the fragmentation of the linguistic hegemony of Portuguese, and a reinforced role for African languages. The re-traditionalization and recent vernacularization of African politics has brought about their (re)framing as local languages of politics, and local voices are now heard in local languages voicing local political concerns (Liphola 1996). One of the most important and productive aspects of local language cultivated is the link nurtured between African languages and sorcery, which comprises an extensive political discourse of responsibility and accountability, offering alternative interpretations and solutions to practical and ethical problems of everyday politics (West 2005). The extended civil society role taken up by religious institutions also carries implications for language. Churches are historically important institutions in the development of prestigious forms of African languages, and as the various denominations employ distinct languages (Cruz E. Silva 1996), including in some cases Portuguese, they have come to play an important part in disseminating alternative, civil society discourses on language, sometimes in conflict with official state perceptions of local languages. Radio Mozambique is another important institution for the development and dissemination of Bantu languages, currently transmitting in 12 Bantu languages, with the further development of community radios in the pipeline (Lopes 1999). Finally, NGO activity is also ushering in more frequent use of African languages, in attempts to engage the community in processes of development (cf., e.g., Robinson 1996). NGO influence has been most significant in the education sector, where one of the predominant activities has been the promotion, evaluation and design of mother tongue programs in African languages for elementary level schooling and adult literacy. Such activities not only create literacies in African languages in a range of areas, but also increase the reach of relevant technical and educational registers in Portuguese. For African languages, the range of different markets and stakeholders generates a situation of polycentricity and competition, where political stances on African languages may conflict with religious interests, and where uses of language in sorcery discourses may stand in opposition to political discourses of linguistic human rights (cf. West 1997, 2003, 2005).

3.2.   Singapore

3.2.1.   Multilingualism in the development of the nation-state

In 1965, a tearful prime minister Lee Kuan Yew announced that Singapore was leaving the Federation of Malaysia with which it had had a stormy co-existence since the withdrawal of the British in 1959. At the time, Singapore, like the region in general, grappled with a colonial legacy of a highly multiracial and linguistically complex society, and the constraints and possibilities of its geographical and politico-economic position. Up until its de facto separation from Malaysia, few seemed to have seriously entertained the idea of Singapore as an independent nation, judging this to be an unfeasible proposition considering the small size of the island (600sq km) and its lack of natural resources.

With Singapore cast adrift from its Malaysian hinterland 'with no other resources than its people', the government set about discursively conceptualizing Singapore as a nation in crisis fighting for its survival in a rallying trope of government that is productive to this day. In this highly fragmented society – politically, religiously, ethnically and, not least, linguistically – a major task for the new government was thus to "develop a sense of the 'nation' and 'national interests' and to enable the multiethnic population to 'imagine' a common faith and destiny" (Beng-Huat 1995: 5). An important part of this task was the development of a principle of multiracialism that accorded equal recognition to the different ethnic groups officially constituted by the state as representative of Singapore's population, namely the Chinese, Malays, Indians and Others (Benjamin 1976). At the same time, policy makers initiated a cultural transformation that aimed to instill in the population the "cultural requirements of capitalist industrialization" (Beng-Huat 1995: 1); this was buttressed by an "ideology of pragmatism couched in a carefully crafted rhetoric of crisis and survival" (Beng-Huat 1995: 5).

Language came to play an important role in a postcolonial political search for racial and religious harmony, ethnic consensus, tolerance, and national development (PuruShotam 1998; Tan 1998). Government emphasis on economic development went hand in hand with the promotion of English as a so-called 'neutral language', a tool essential for broader participation in the global market that was rhetorically construed as accessible to all Singaporeans through education. On the other hand, the state imperative to provide due acknowledgement to Singapore's principle of multiracialism dictated the simultaneous official recognition of three other languages, Mandarin (designated as the ethnic language of the Chinese group), Malay, and Tamil (for the Indian group). The choice of Mandarin as the official language of Chinese ethnicity meant that the many various 'dialects' (an estimated 25 more or less mutually unintelligible varieties) spoken by this group as bona fide mother tongues at independence were subject to official erasure.[6] Likewise, the Indian group was uniformly assigned Tamil as its ethnic language, despite the fact that many ethnic Indians speak other Indian languages (Punjabi, Banglasdeshi, Hindu etc), and even claim English as their 'native language'.

3.2.2.   Multilingualism in the postindependent strong state

The development of Singapore in the 40 years following independence has seen the continued expansion of a strong, interventionist state in pursuit of accelerated economic development; the growth of an individualized middle-class, or meritocracy, and the consolidation of forms of modernity based on a communitarian notion of citizenship.

A consistent policy on multilingualism has been one of the major tools with which the Singapore government has sought to transpose issues of economic management into structures of communitarian democracy. The tension between modern individualism and Western values on the one hand, and a reinvented tradition of Confucianism emphasizing family values, respect for authority and communitarian ideals on the other, has been rhetorically managed by ideologically constructing English as the language of modernization, and South East Asian languages as essential carriers of traditional values. In other words, the fabrication of (linguistic) authenticity for local languages and an ideology of non-ownership of English is very much attuned to economic imperatives that demanded inter- and intra-ethnic cohesion.[7] Language ideological debates and state campaigns, such as the 'Speak Mandarin Campaign' (SMC) (Bokhurst-Heng 1999) – ongoing since the eighties – or the 'Speak Good English Movement' (Rubdy 2001) comprise the powerful and all-encroaching instruments for normalization and implementation of the policy.

3.2.3.   Multilingualism in discourses of scale

In Singapore, the nature and status of English has comprised an on-going subtext to the discourse of globalization and the position of Singapore in the global scenario. An important aspect of this discourse has been the thrashing out of positions on the local variety of Colloquial Singapore English, or Singlish, which, according to the previous PM, Goh Tok Chong, "reflects badly on us and makes us seem less intelligent or competent" (Time, July 29, 2003). The political desire to avoid acknowledging the legitimacy or viability of Singlish has been reinforced by the government's unwillingness to concede that English may be the mother tongue of any Singaporeans or that norms of English may be intrinsic to the Singaporean community (cf. Rappa and Wee 2006).

As noted above, Singaporean language policies were expressly formulated to position the nation in the ideological crossroads of tradition and modernity. In recent years, with the influx of 'foreign talent', and the growth in number of resident foreigners, the 'global' has encroached increasingly upon the traditional. This impacts upon the current Asian languages versus English dichotomy, as the majority of this workforce cannot be assigned a traditional Singaporean ethnic mother tongue (with many claiming English as their home language). In time, this development could involve a shift towards a more "'open' bilingual policy", where, in addition to English, all students will learn another language, the choice of which would be optional as opposed to prescribed (Wee and Bokhurst-Heng 2005: 170).

4.   The economics of multilingualism

The material foundation for types of modernity laid down in state structures, specific institutions and forms of citizenship and representation are to be found in processes that order the world economy. As language provides access to scarce resources, it itself becomes a resource to be acquired and coveted (cf. Gal 1989).

4.1.   Mozambique

4.1.1.   Trade networks

Ten years into independence, the Mozambican economy underwent the beginnings of a formidable transformation (Fauvet 2000). The rapid disintegration of the socialist Eastern bloc countries that had provided the prime economic (and ideological) support to Mozambique had deleterious implications for the country – as it did for many African nations – by opening a space for the gradual disengagement of Western support for an Africa that had lost its strategic importance. The economy was further undermined by the civil war driven by RENAMO (The National Resistance Movement) with wanton destruction of infrastructure, hospitals and schools, the pillaging and burning of rural areas, and general disruption to industrial production. Most importantly, there was a significant and growing division between formal economies and informal, as material necessities obliged individuals to form extensive networks based on local kinship and neighborhood networks outside of formal institutions in order to satisfy basic needs and aspirations.

With respect to multilingualism, one of the main implications of the informal economy has been a newfound utility and market value for local African languages, especially larger cross-border languages linked to networks of trade. The reevaluation and increase in multilingualism has been a gendered affair; labor migration into cities reinforced pre-colonial trends privileging male above female employment, where jobs usually reserved for women, such as street vendor, were co-opted to the new subsistence needs of men. Informalization of the economy led to a 'grassroots globalization' in the formation of associative networks and trade across regions. This involved a significant investment in local languages, especially larger regional and cross-border languages, such as Tsonga and Zulu in South Africa. Continued patterns of migrant labor to South Africa (a development actually unintentionally reinforced by Mozambican politics of land collectivization) also contributed to the more comprehensive functions of African vernaculars as languages of economic contact, and stimulated the incorporation of a range of new languages into local repertoires.

The main impact on Portuguese has come from economic developments in the formal economy. The establishment of Portuguese-speaking television stations, the growth of the hotel and tourist industries, and increased trade with Lusophone organizations has ushered into Mozambique a range of non-Mozambican varieties of Portuguese. Although Brazilian soaps are highly popular, their influence on viewers' language is predominantly confined to the incorporation of lexical items. The biggest impact of external norms of Portuguese can be found among members of the Brazilian *Igreja national/* national church who are moved to speak by the Holy Spirit in fluent sounding Brazilian Portuguese.[8]

4.1.2.   Demographics of multilingualism: urbanity as a sociolinguistic dynamic

According to the latest census in 1997, distribution and use of languages have changed little since the first mapping in 1980. Bantu languages, spoken predominantly in the rural regions of Mozambique, are still the mother tongues of the majority of the population, while Portuguese remains a predominantly urban language and the mother tongue of a small percentage of people. More men than women overall claim knowledge of Portuguese, and it remains a language of youth. In urban areas, a wide variety of Bantu languages are spoken, whereas in the rural parts of the country, the number of languages represented is greatly diminished (Firmino 2000).

The informalization of the economy and the concomitant displacement of populations to urban areas have resulted in the growth of the informal city. One aspect of the expansion of the urban environment has been a distinct pattern of multilingualism in cities when compared to outlaying rural areas.[9] Preliminary studies suggest that this urban-rural split in multilingualism figures differently depending upon region, and interacts with social variables such as gender and age, as well as function/register and context of language use (Stroud ms). For example, in the northern province of Cabo Delgado where the city of Nampula is situated, speakers of every age claim to use Portuguese in formal meetings, where local political, administrative and related issues are discussed. In other contexts and for other functions, such as sports, intimate friends, and colleagues, there is an age distribution from the use of local Makua among the older population, to more frequent use of Portuguese among the younger generation. In Vilanculos, a much smaller metropole, Portuguese is likewise used mainly in formal meetings. However, in contradistinction to Nampula, the local language XiCitswa is used across all age groups for all other functions.

Urban-suburban differences in language use interact with age and gender differently for different languages. In both Nampula and Vilanculos, Portuguese is more often a second language for women than for men. The number of languages mastered by speakers in urban areas is greater than in rural areas; men in all age groups report knowing more African languages than women, and younger speakers know more languages than older. In other words, urbanity and mobility translate into a gendered and age differentiated access to linguistic resources, introducing social stratifications around multilingualism that we do not find in the rural areas.

4.1.3. *Portuguese*

The importance of urbanity is also apparent in frequency of use and knowledge of Portuguese, as well as in the ideologies attached to different types of Portuguese. The capital Maputo falls into at least three types of space from a linguistic perspective. First of all, the bairro of Xipaminine where the older, pre-independence residents of the city live; these residents were functionaries in the lower administration, such as teacher, clerk, etc., and were often assimilados in colonial times; secondly, the bairro of Polana Cimento where the new nomenclature and noveau riche occupy the parts of the cement city that were abandoned by the whites at independence; and thirdly, areas such as Maxaquene where newly arrived migrants have moved in since independence, either as displaced refugees or labor migrants, settling into neighborhoods where other members of their various ethnic groupings live (cf. Firmino 2002).

Of particular interest to the urban framing of Portuguese is the interaction of age, education, and employment in the formal economy for level of Portuguese proficiency attained. Studies suggest that whether or not a speaker has employment is an important factor in the extent to which s/he uses European Portuguese (EP) normed speech – this is especially the case for those who are less educated (Stroud 1996: 201). In fact, among speakers with the same level of education (year 5), those who were in gainful employment were generally considered to be more proficient speakers of EP on an attitude test.[10] This suggests that the Portuguese linguistic market is non-unified (Bourdieu 1991) and that the school is not producing a Portuguese proficiency that tallies with the requirements of the formal labor market.

In general, the ideological conception of Portuguese vis-à-vis African languages is one where Portuguese voices are judged as formal, urban, cultivated and modern. Local discourses on African languages, on the other hand, are associated with the informal, and the local/traditional/rural. Interestingly, this division of ideological labor is remarkably similar to how these languages were perceived (and organized in relation to each other) during colonial times. Furthermore, whereas there is a recognition among large segments of the population of Maputo that there is a 'correct', standard way of speaking Portuguese, African languages are clearly represented as polycentric, where speakers concede that one and the same language may be spoken in different ways depending on the locale of the speaker. This symbolic significance of Portuguese and local African languages is available for use in performances of identity and to signal aspirations such as gender and urbanity.[11]

4.1.3.1. Proficiency and its ideologization

The different residential groupings show clearly different patterns of acquisition and use of Portuguese with varying degrees of Bantu substrate influence (cf. Stroud 1996; Firmino, 2002). So, for example, the more established pre-independence residents in Maputo tend invariably to show less Bantu substrate influence and speak a more EP-normed Portuguese than the migrant groups or the residents of Polana Cimento. Many of the older population would have acquired Portuguese in colonial times as a prerequisite to becoming *assimilados* – a resource that they would have passed on to their children. The in-migrated residents in the neighborhood of Maxaquene, on the other hand, exhibit typical across-the-board Bantu uptake in their varieties of Portuguese and span a wide range of proficiencies. What is of interest here is how the Bantu substrate in this case, comprising fairly low level morphological 'errors', is stigmatized and perceived to be indicative of bad education and an uncultivated manner. This contrasts with the Bantu substrate in the speech of Polana Cimento residents that is not only free from stigma, but widely believed to comprise core features of Portuguese.[12] In this case, the Bantu substrate is part of a refiguring of linguistic repertoires that came about through social exchanges in the contact zone between the formal and informal economy, as PC speakers are reliant on the informal market for vital economic supplements in the form of material goods and non-material benefits, such as contracts and land tenure deeds. The fact that different indexical meanings are attributed to different types of substrate suggests that proficiency is a situated notion that is ideologized differently in ways that may function to provide a linguistic rationale for the organization of social inequality.

4.1.4.   African languages

The end of colonialism saw rapid language shifts within a newly mobile population. Anecdotal evidence has it that families might shift linguistic allegiances between different African languages depending on the linguistic nature of the social networks they were part of. The churches and their social organizations played a particularly prominent role here in determining what languages were used both within the congregation and without. In modern Mozambique, soap operas and sitcoms in local XiChangana have gained in popularity, and there is also limited media coverage in other African languages at specific time-slots. Mobility is encouraging the development of contact varieties of African languages (such as Tsonga influenced Ronga).[13]

Little is presently known about how these languages are being acquired among the younger generation in both urban and rural contexts. Commonly, African languages are learnt in the extended family network from grandparents or older caretakers, whereas younger caretakers use Portuguese.

4.2.   Singapore

4.2.1.   Commodification

Singapore's central position in global networks of trade has clear implications for its politics and practices of multilingualism. The long-term emphasis on English is one such obvious implication, and the fact that English is spoken extensively (and fluently) in Singapore has also become one of the country's more important immaterial assets. As Singapore offers education at all levels in English, it is fast becoming an educational hub for the rest of the region, especially mainland China, Thailand and Vietnam. Its affluence has also created a popular middle-class demand for English-speaking maids. English as a capital resource is currently generating a domestic, extracurricular market with a rapidly growing infrastructure of private schools and tutors for the middle class family. It is one of the mainstays of the recent consumerist trend of 'self-improvement'; Singapore youth across all classes cite the activity of 'self improvement' as their main reason for reading books, magazines, and newspapers in English.

Heller (1999b: 5) has noted how globalization has created a situation with respect to language where "the old politics of identity" is increasingly being abandoned "in favor of a new pragmatic position" where language and culture become refigured as a commodifiable resource (cf. Wee 2003: 211). This is increasingly evident in Singapore, where the official mother tongues (especially Mandarin) are slowly being re-entextualized into narratives of the economic value of languages in the world economy, with a shift of emphasis away from their value as icons of culture and heritage (cf. Wee 2003). The Chinese group in particular has long made the claim that a pragmatic (economic) motivation for learning Mandarin is necessary for the continual survival of the language, and other ethnic groups in Singapore have been voicing demands since 1994 that they be given access to Mandarin in order that they may become more economically competitive. The government, caught between its multiracial ideology and the need not to be seen as economically discriminating against non-Mandarin speaking groups, has subsequently tried to play up the instrumental value of Tamil and Malay, a strategy that may not be successful, as these languages lack the global market that mainland China can boast (Wee 2003). Wee, following Heller, notes that an emphasis on instrumental value promotes an exonormative stance towards these languages, raising the question of how tensions between local and more dispersed, non-local varieties will be resolved, and what variety to teach in schools. In general, an exonormative norm may lead in time to a rift between those speakers of Malay/Tamil with local features and those who master the economically viable, exonormatively approved variety.

4.2.2.   Demographics of multilingualism

Not surprisingly, the government's energetic and encompassing language policy has been credited with promoting massive language shift over a period of 30 years. Li Wei et al. say:

> Large scale complex changes in sociolinguistic patterns in Singapore can be largely attributed to the deliberate and often forcefully-implemented government policies towards language and language varieties (1997: 368).

English, on the other hand, is consolidating its foothold in the linguistic terrain and growing as a home language, especially in its more vernacular forms of Colloquial Singaporean English, despite the government's explicit multiracial and multilingual policy (Pakir 2000: 262; Li Wei et al. 1997; Saravanan 1994; Kwan-Terry 2000). The rise of English is most pronounced in Chinese and Indian homes, with an increase in Chinese homes citing English as the home language from 10.2% in 1980 to 23.9% in 2000. For Indian homes, the corresponding figures are 24.3% and 35.6% respectively. Although Malay homes also show a discernible shift towards English, it is much less pronounced than the other groups, possibly due to the close affiliation between the Malay language and Islam (Rappa and Wee 2006).

The shift of speakers away from Chinese dialects or ancestral, ethnic languages implies massive capital transference away from the resources of the socially most dispossessed and elderly, as their languages are no longer viable means of exchange on the linguistic market.[14] Furthermore, those groups that can be seen to be shifting to English with advantage are those who are upwardly mobile and who bring a range of resources (social, cultural, economic) to the linguistic market. In other words, shifting languages gives these groups access to valued resources, and those who shift successfully are those who have the capital to access the requisite linguistic resources, and make good of them.

4.2.3.   English

Despite the 'wide availability' of English in society at large, its acquisition and use is largely socially determined. Statistics show that its status as a class language – a language associated with higher income and more qualified education – has been an unchanging feature of the language for many years (Leow 2001).

English furthermore is the site of highly competitive strategies of acquisition. Singaporean middle class children are subject to increasing pressure "to begin formal schooling [in English] outside the family at an increasingly early age; certainly younger than in many other urban societies" (Thompson 2003: 302). Many children will have already completed 4 years of pre-school prior to enrolment in the primary school. On top of this, many children throughout their lives will be taught through private tutors, and will engage in a range of social and educational activities, such as piano-lessons or tennis tutoring, that come packaged with English.

4.2.3.1. Proficiency and its ideologization

Discourses around English play a specific role in how Singapore imagines itself as a community and in how the state reproduces itself as a consensual meritocracy. Young secondary school students recognize the power and importance of English, in terms that simultaneously naturalize their own linguistic inabilities in the language.[15] The many direct and indirect ways in which the importance of English is promoted contributes to the de facto dominance of a monolingual ideology in the face of a multilingual Singaporean reality.[16] As success on the English language market is recognized as conferring privilege, the 'consensual' reproduction of the legitimate English language market is at the same time a legitimation of social class differences in terms of (linguistic) ability.

4.2.3.2. Reflexivity and performance in language acquisition

Late modern societies such as Singapore are characterized by reflexivity (Giddens 1991: 1), where actors are "highly deliberate and self-aware" (Bucholtz and Hall 2004: 380). In line with this, we find a construction of multilingualism in Singapore through strategies of acquisition that emphasize 'artful performance'. Artful performance as an acquisition mode, attends to detail and pronunciation, imaginative use of linguistic items in novel contexts, improvisation and (monitored) rehearsal in the service of reflexive identity construction.

4.3.   Other languages

Little is known about actual patterns of acquisition and levels of proficiency in the different languages (cf. Mani and Gopinathan 1983). In a survey of 1407 Singapore youth, Chew et al. (1998: 5) found that most of their respondents considered themselves either bilingual (86.8%) or trilingual (5.3%), in the case of reading and writing. Only about 7.9% claimed to read and write exclusively in English. Despite this multilingualism, Chew et al. (1998: 146) report that while Chinese youth enjoy both English and Chinese television programs, Malay and Indian youth prefer to watch mainly English programs. Thus, among young Singaporeans, at least where information and entertainment are concerned, the Malay and Tamil languages are clearly losing out significantly to English.

Gupta and Yeok (1995) and Thompson (2003) show how a potentially great degree of multilingualism in Singaporean families may come about through incidental socialization. Children grow up learning English, the official ethnic language(s) of the parent, Mandarin, Tamil or Malay (with either an active or a receptive competence in these languages) and also perhaps the ancestral languages of the grandparents, should this differ from the official ethnic language (e.g. Teochew, Hainanese, Hokkien for the Chinese groups). Besides this, the chances are that the child will have access to other varieties of English (e.g. Philippino English), as many middle class families employ foreign maids as household help. The family will also allow for many patterns of communication and associated language choice between siblings and across and within generations. Besides this, many children will also be attending day-care centers and kindergartens where English (and possibly another language) will comprise their first order network contacts from the age of 30 months onwards.

Notwithstanding official government functional compartmentalization of languages, Chinese dialects continue to play an important role in many speakers' everyday, modern orientation to life as part of living and working in modern Singapore society (Hing 2004). A cursory glance at the small ads section in the national daily *The Straits Times* reveals many an employer (ranging from supermarket chains to individual entrepreneurial plumbers) seeking employees with knowledge of Chinese dialects. These languages also have value in the face of all odds in that they provide the means for speakers to step outside a strict and formalized interaction order, thereby allowing participants in potentially face-threatening encounters to defuse tension that would have been underscored through use of English (Chuah 2003). In other words, the continued vitality of Chinese 'dialects' has to do with their functional allocation to the private and non-official arenas of social life (e.g. language of local commerce and bonding), rather than any role they may be assigned on formal arenas.

A new development on the local language scene with interesting potential implications for multilingual dynamics is the use of different languages (Tamil, Malay, Punjabi) in internet media such as blogs, on-line journals and customized web-sites. Virtual arenas for many languages are fast becoming trend-setting with respect to linguistic norms, moving processes of linguistic innovation and standardization away from governments and official bodies and increasingly into the private sphere.

5.   Multilingualism in local construction of identities

The representations, ideologies and discourses associated with specific languages in a multilingual matrix may be exploited for the (re)construction of social identities through stylization (e.g. Pennycook 2003; Hill 2001), reproducing, and sometimes also subverting and transforming indexical values of languages in the process.

5.1.   Mozambique

5.1.1.   *The politics of ascription of competence and ownership*

In the Mozambican context, multilingualism figures prominently in the telling of life histories that frame the way in which speakers position themselves in terms of time and space. Speakers may, for example, represent themselves as XiRonga-speaking, with a Chope linguistic ancestry on the father's side, whose grandparents worked in the South African gold mines and mastered the mine-pidgin Fanagalo. Here, languages may stand proxy for a range of other issues, such as tradition (local language) – modernity (Portuguese), labor history (Fanagalo), colonial migration, etc. Family history is thus traced through the listing of languages and varieties contextualized in narratives on multilingualism.

5.2.   Singapore

5.2.1.   Language and identity

Not surprisingly, the media is a powerful force in the regulation of linguistic identities. In Singapore, Chinese dialects are not permitted in the media, and all imported programs that may use other varieties of Chinese are dubbed into Mandarin. In a recent Singaporean sitcom production, Heartlanders, characters that should be represented as speaking a multilingual mix of languages are instead portrayed as speakers of (cosmopolitan) standard English, and the work of signifying transgressive identities such as youth gangsters is linguistically accomplished through the use of Americanisms and British slang. In contradistinction to Mozambique, 'heritage' languages (such as Hokkien, Teochew) are not generally considered to be 'necessary for cultural identity', this role being reserved for Mandarin (Hing 2004). On the informal market, the construction of youth lects in the stylization of identities is a prominent feature of young Singaporeans such as Malay hiphoppers and skateboarders who incorporate salient markers of Black English vernacular into their speech.

5.2.2.   Detraditionalization: Cross-ethnic language acquisition

In late modernity, the meaning of sociostructurally determined forms of identity, such as class, gender, and sexuality, are increasing becoming matters for individual decisions (e.g. Giddens 1991). In Singapore, individuals can be seen to fashion and reinvent identities that cross-cut structural categories such as ethnicity by positioning themselves in a multilingual and multivariate space, and using language choice in stylization of identity. This means that speakers are acquiring languages to which they have no direct 'officially' designated right – according to the language policy. Nevertheless, anecdotal data suggest countless examples of young Malay Singaporeans who are proficient speakers of Hokkien, of Indian speakers who have acquired Malay, and, of course, speakers in the Chinese group who learn each others' languages and dialects (cf. Stroud and Wee forthc.). Such unofficial multilingualism is quite likely pervasive, as government funded housing policies and school policies provide structural and institutional encouragement for spontaneous language acquisition across ethnic groups.

6.   Conclusion

Global economic development – the (trans)national flow of people, products and services – is culturally mediated through institutions and representations. These are ultimately determined by the position of a nation in the fundamentally uneven and fragmentary reach of the world system, on the one hand, and the cultural and historical specifics of the polity, on the other. In this nexus, different types of modernity come to host different ideas of the relationship of the individual to the state that mediate the local multilingual practices of individuals and groups. Particular patterns of mother tongue and second language acquisition, the development of new varieties of indigenous and metropolitan languages, the ideological values associated with each language in a multilingual matrix, and the sociosymbolic use of multilingual practices structured along local parameters of social class, gender and ethnicity, can be understood in terms of a political economy of language.

The broad approach to the political economy of language illustrated here potentially carries a number of both theoretical and practical implications for our understanding of multilingualism. From a theoretical perspective, this approach reiterates an informative critique of overly simplistic models of transnational language contact, such as early work that takes as its point of departure the notion of linguistic imperialism (e.g. Phillipson 1992). In seeking to explain the sociolinguistics of multilingualism in ex-colonial contexts, this notion implies a specific focus on the politico-economic macrostructures and institutions that undergird the role of English. Multilingual ecologies are conceptualized fundamentally in terms of language maintenance and language loss, and the exercise of hegemonic power through English and its global institutions is seen as silencing and marginalizing alternative languages and discourses, thereby emasculating local voice and agency. By way of criticism, other work (e.g. Pennycook 1994) has underscored the creative appropriation of metropolitan languages and the stylized refiguration of local languages and linguistic ecologies in situations of contact. This perspective highlights the important role of local agency in the formation of contact situations and emphasizes how resulting multilingualism may enhance linguistic voice in ways that defy a simple analysis in purely structural and economic terms. From the account offered in this chapter, it appears that the limitations of the one approach – that is, a failure to take into account cultural factors in the organization of multilingualism – is compounded by the myopia of the other – that is, a blindness to how cultural and identity factors (voice) are tightly integrated with the historical and material conditions of the specific ex-colonial context in the global economy.

From a practical perspective, an awareness of alternative, vernacular modernities also encourages a critical stance on some popular language political discourses. Currently, the paradigm in vogue is built on the edifice of linguistic human rights. However, the LHR paradigm requires a specific type of relationship between a state and its citizens, such that the state distributes resources on formal markets on the basis of citizen recognition. States that for whatever reason – either lacking resources and/or structures of distribution (as in many African states) or with different conceptions of citizenship (e.g. communitarian, as in Singapore) – cannot be easily accommodated in a LHR program.

The multilayered and centrifugal nature of multilingualism revealed in this chapter also raises some issues for conventional practices of language planning and intervention. With respect to retraditionalized communities, an imperative question is what role the state can ever play in the regulation and distribution of languages. A case in point is the inadequacy of traditional diffusionist models of language in education to solve the problem of access to valued language resources. For example, why is the uptake of government sanctioned Portuguese or mother tongue so poor in Mozambique? Is the cause to be found in a mere lack of opportunity, or in technical reasons such as lack of trained teachers or dearth of teaching materials? Or are there more fundamental issues of politics and participation at play? In general, providing official recognition to a previously ignored language will mean little to its speakers unless the move is part of a more extensive and in-depth transformation of these speakers' relationship to structures of state power and resource distribution (cf. Stroud and Heugh 2004). Similar issues of lack of fit between political tools and multilingual realities can be seen in late modern societies, such as Singapore, where popular or commercial agents and institutions may dictate language norms in cooperation with users on virtual arenas – a distributed type of linguistic authority far removed from traditional planning bodies and the reach of nation-states.

Notes

1. A caveat: it is difficult to get comparable language data on multilingualism from different contexts. This is not surprising, given the very political and ideological nature of census studies and the questions asked of them (cf. Gal 1995). Also, just as some contexts allow certain types of research to be carried out, other contexts refuse access to researchers.
2. Etnologue, SIL, suggest there may be as many as 48 different languages spoken. Cf. Lopes (1999) for a number of references to alternative enumerations.
3. Lopes (1999) notes how Mozambique is among the 15 most linguistically diverse countries in the world, where 'linguistic diversity' is defined as "a situation where no more than 50 % of the population speak the same language" (Robinson 1993: 52).
4. See Pitcher for an account of the Mozambique state since the 1980s.
5. A recent USAID project supported an African American Institutes Project called 'Democratic Development in Mozambique' built on traditional authority (cf. Fry 1997).
6. A shift to Mandarin was also motivated by an educational discourse that highlighted the relative difficulties children would encounter in schooling switching from 'dialect' to Mandarin at the same time that they would be expected to learn English.
7. As a large part of the population is ethnically Chinese and historically was seen as potentially susceptible to communist infiltration, it was seen as important to secure their loyalty during nation-building. Part of the problem was the historical divisions between the so-called English-educated and Chinese-educated ethnic Chinese. The Chinese-educated held a deep-seated resentment against what they considered the

privilege and prestige given to the English-educated Chinese; it was feared that this dissatisfaction would kindle further revolt in this very important group (cf. Kwan-Terry 2000). Incidentally, this was also a rationale for the multiracial policy – comprising a signal to the world that Singapore would not be a Chinese puppet state.

8. Recent increased trade regionally and globally has highlighted the role of English which introduces many new aspects to the multilingual scene in Mozambique (Matusse 1997).

9. What follows is based on preliminary analysis of a multilingual questionnaire study conducted on studies of a small (2,500) but sampled population in different parts of the country. There is currently no information from the National Census on multilingualism in the population according to age, gender, or urbanity. The census did contain one question of interest in this respect, namely P17B asking what other languages than the most frequently used that informants employed, but the information remains to be analyzed.

10. The instrument was administered to 250 informants selected from different social backgrounds and bairros of Maputo as part of a larger study on developing varieties of Portuguese.

11. Stroud (2004) explores how code-switched juxtaposition of utterances in Portuguese and Ronga by Mozambican tradeswomen play on the contrasting values associated with each of these languages for subtle politically transgressive purposes.

12. In this latter case, many of the Bantu inspired variants found in Portuguese are in some sense expanding the expressive repertoire of the EP lexicon, e.g. re-subcategorization of certain verbs to allow passive forms.

13. I am grateful to Feliciano Chimbutane for sharing this information with me.

14. This was especially evident during the recent SARS crisis when the government found itself forced to use local languages/Chinese dialects with the elderly population to get information across.

15. The reasons students give for not being proficient English speakers are often in the form of factors outside their control, such as family background, innate talent or lack of opportunities for travel (cf. Stroud and Wee forthc.).

16. These comprise methods of teaching that (un)intentionally highlights the importance of English vis-à-vis other languages, government campaigns such as the Speak Good English Movement, and advertising and marketing slogans etc.

References

Alfredsson, Ulla and Carlisto Linha
  1999   Onde dues vive. Introduçao um estudo en Igrecia Independente em Maputo [Where God lives. Introduction to a study of the Independent Church in Maputo]. Maputo: INDE.
Arnaut, Karel
  2005   'Our Baka brothers obviously do not speak French': Siting and scaling physical/discursive 'movements' in post-colonial Belgium. *Language and Communication* 25: 217–235.
Bao, Zhiming
  2003   Social Stigma and grammatical autonomy in nonnative varieties of English. *Language in Society* 32: 23–46.

2005   The aspectual system of Singapore English and the systemic substratist explanation. *Journal of Linguistics* 41: 237–267.

Beng-Huat, Chua
1995   *Communitarian Ideology and Democracy in Singapore*. London/New York: Routledge.

Benjamin, Geoffrey
1976   The cultural logic of Singapore's multiracialism. In: Riaz Hassan (ed.), Singapore: *Society in Transition*, 115–133. Kuala Lumpur: Oxford University Press.

Blommaert, Jan, James Collins and Stef Slembrouck
2004   *Spaces of multilingualism. Working Papers on Language, Power and Identity No. 18*. Gent University, Brussels.

Bokhorst-Heng, Wendy
1999   Singapore's Speak Mandarin Campaign: Language ideological debates and the imagining of the nation. In: Jan Blommaert (ed.), *Language Ideological Debates*, 235–266. Berlin/New York: Mouton de Gruyter.

Bourdieu, Pierre
1991   *Language and Symbolic Power*. Cambridge, MA: Harvard University Press.

Bucholtz, Mary and Kira Hall
2004   Language and identity. In: Alessandro Duranti (ed.), *The Blackwell Companion to Linguistic Anthropology*, 369–394. Oxford: Blackwell.

Buur, Lars and Helene Kyed
2003   *Implementation of Decree 15/2000 in Mozambique: The consequences of state recognition of traditional authority in Sussundenga*. Copenhagen: Centre for Development Research.

Chabal, Patrick and Jean-Pascal Daloz
1999   *Africa Works: Disorder as Political Instrument*. Oxford: James Curry Press.

Chuah, Charlene
2003   An ethnographic study of the role of dialect in a Singaporean Teochew family. MA thesis, Department of English Language and Literature, National University of Singapore.

Chew, Soon Beng, Mike Leu, Guo-Jiun and Kin Heng Teng
1998   *Values and life-styles of young Singaporeans*. Singapore: Prentice Hall.

Cruz E. Silva, Teresa
1996   Protestant Churches and the formation of political consciousness in Southern Mozambique (1930–1974). Ph.D. Thesis, Department of Social and Economics Studies, University of Bradford.

Daw Khin Khin, Aye
2005   Bazaar Malay: History, grammar and contact. Ph.D. dissertation, Department of English Language and Literature, National University of Singapore.

Errington, J. Joseph
2001   Colonial Linguistics. *Annual Review of Anthropology* 30: 19–39.

Fabian, Johannes
1986   *Language and Colonial Power. The Appropriation of Swahili in the Farmer Belgian Congo 1880–1938*. Cambridge: CUP.

Fauvet, Paul
  2000   Mozambique: Growth with poverty. A difficult transition from prolonged war to peace and development. *Africa Recovery* 14 (3): 12–19.
Firmino, Gregorio
  1995   O caso do Português e das Linguas Indigenas de Moçambique. [The case of Portuguese and the indigenous languages of Mozambique]. *Revista International de Lingua Portuguesa* 13: 33–43.
  2000   *Situação Linguística de Moçambique* [The Linguistic Situation in Mozambique]. Maputo: Instituto National de Estatística.
  2002   *A Questão Linguística na Africa Pós-colonial: O Caso do Português e das Linguas Autoctones em Moçambique* [The Language Question in Postcolonial Africa: The Case of Portuguese and the Indigenous Languages of Mozambique]. Maputo: Promedia
Fry, Peter
  1997   Final Evaluation of the Decentralization/Traditional Authority Component of the African American Institute Project "Democratic Development in Mozambique" (Cooperative Agreement #656-A-00-4029-00). Maputo: USAID.
Gal, Susan
  1989   Language and political economy. *Annual Review of Anthropology* 18: 345–367.
  1995   Linguistic theories and national images in 19th Century Hungary. *International Journal of the Sociology of Language* 111: 93–102.
Giddens, Anthony
  1991   *Modernity and Self-identity.* London: Polity.
Gonçalves, Perpetua
  1996   *Português em Moçambique: Uma Variedade em Formação.* [Portuguese in Mozambique: A Variety in Formation]. Maputo: Livraria Universitária & Faculdade de Letras da UEM.
Gupta, Anthea Fraser
  1998a   The situation of English in Singapore. In: Joseph Foley, Thiru Kandiah, Bao Zhiming, Anthea F. Gupta, Lubna Alsagoff, Ho Chee Lick, Lionel Wee, Ismail Talib and Wendy Bokhorst-Heng (eds.), *English in New Cultural Contexts: Reflections from Singapore*, 106–126. Singapore: Oxford University Press.
  1998b   A framework for the analysis of Singapore English. In: S. Gopinathan, Anne Pakir, Wah Kam Ho and Vanithamani Saravanan (eds.), *Language, Society and Education in Singapore: Issues and Trends*, 119–132. Singapore: Times Academic Press.
  2001   English in the linguistic ecology of Singapore. Paper presented at The Cultural Politics of English as a World Language, Freiburg, Germany 6–9 June 2001.
Gupta, Anthea Fraser and Siew Pui Yeok
  1995   Language shift in Singapore society. *Journal of Multilingual and Multicultural Development* 143: 301–14.
Hannerz, Ulf
  1996   *Transnational Connections.* London: Routledge.
Haeri, Niloofar
  1997   The reproduction of symbolic capital: language, state and class in Egypt. *Current Anthropology* 38 (5): 795–816.

Helgesson, Alf
  1991   Catholics and Protestants in a clash of interests in Southern Mozambique.
          In: Carl F. Hallencreutz and Mai Palmberg (eds.), *Religion and Politics
          in Southern Africa*, 194–206. Scandinavian Institute of African Studies,
          Uppsala.
Heller, Monica
  1999a   *Linguistic Minorities and Modernity: A Sociolinguistic Ethnography.* Lon-
          don: Longman.
  1999b   Alternative ideologies of la francophonie. *Journal of Sociolinguistics* 3 (3):
          336–359.
Hing, Kevin
  2004   Chinese dialects in Singapore: Reversing language shift. Honors thesis, De-
          partment of English Language and Literature, National University of Sin-
          gapore.
Hill, Jane
  1999   Styling locally, styling globally. What does it mean? *Journal of Socioling-
          uistics* 3 (4): 542–556.
Ho, Mian-Lian and John T. Platt
  1993   *Dynamics of a Contact Continuum. Singaporean English.* Oxford: Oxford
          University Press.
Irvine, Jane
  1986   When talk isn't cheap: Language and political economy. *American Ethnol-
          ogist.* 16 (2): 248–267.
Junod, Henri
  1905   *What should be the place of the native language in native education.*
          Morija: Sesuto Book Depot.
  1946   *Usos e costumes dos Bantos. A vida duma tribo Sul-Africana.* Tomos 1 e 2.
          [Habits and Traditions of the Bantus. Life in a South African Tribe. Vol-
          ume 1 & 2]. Imprensa Nacional de Moçambique, Lourenço Marques.
Koh, Fook Seng
  1970   The nineteenth century British approach to Malya education. *Jurnal Pen-
          didekan* 1 (1): 105–115.
Kwan-Terry, Anne
  2000   Language shift, mother tongue and identity in Singapore. *International
          Journal of the Sociology of Language* 143: 85–106.
Leow, Bee Geok
  2001   Census Population 2000 Statistical Release 2: Education, Language and
          Religion. Singapore: Department of Statistics, Ministry of Trade and In-
          dustry.
Liphola, Marcelino M.
  1996   The use of Mozambican languages in the elections. In: Brazao Mazula
          (ed.), *Mozambique: Elections, Democracy and Development.* Maputo:
          Inter-Africa Group.
Li Wei, Vanithamani Saravanan and Julia Ng Lee Hoon
  1997   Language shift in the Teochew community in Singapore: A family domain
          analysis. *Journal of Multilingual and Multicultural Development* 18 (5):
          364–384.

Lim, Lisa (ed.)
2004   *Singapore English. A Grammatical Description*. Amsterdam/Philadelphia: John Benjamins.
Lopes, Armando J.
1999   The language situation in Mozambique. In: Robert B. Kaplan and Richard Baldauf Jr. (eds.), *Language Planning in Malawi, Mozambique and the Philippines*, 86–132. Clevedon: Multilingual Matters.
Makoni, Sinfree
1998   In the beginning was the missionaries' word: The European invention of an African language. The case of Shona in Zimbabwe. In: Kwesi Prah (ed.), *Between Distinction and Extinction: The Harmonization and Standardization of Languages*, 157–164. Johannesburg: University of Witwaterstrand Press.
Makoni, Sinfree and Alistair Pennycook (eds.)
(in press) *Disinventing and Reconstituting Language*. Clevedon: Multilingual Matters.
Mani, A. and S. Gopinathan
1983   Changes in Tamil language acquisition and usage in Singapore: A case study of subtractive bilingualism. *Southeast Asian Journal of Social Science* 11 (1): 104–117.
Matusse, Renalto
1997   The future of Portuguese in Mozambique. In: Robert K. Herbert (ed.), *African Linguistics at the Crossroads*, 541–554. Cologne: Rudiger Koppe Verlag.
Mazrui, Ali and Alamin Mazrui
1998   *The Power of Babel: Language and Governance in the African Experience*. Chicago: University of Chicago Press.
Mühlhäusler, Peter
1996   *Linguistic Ecology: Language Change and Linguistic Imperialism in the Pacific Region*. London: Routledge.
NELIMO
1989   1 Seminario sobre a Padronizão da Ortografia de Linguas Moçambicanas. Universidade Eduardo Mondlane: Faculdade de Letras.
Ngugi wa Thiong'o
1986   *Decolonizing the Mind: The Politics of Language in African Literature*. London: James Curry.
Nugent, Paul
2004   *Africa Since Independence*. London: Palgrave Macmillan.
Pakir, Anne
2000   Singapore. In: Wah Kam Ho and Ruth Y. L. Wong (eds.), *Language Policies and Language Education: The Impact in East Asian Countries in the Next Decade*, 259–84. Singapore: Times Academic Press.
Pennycook, Alistair
1994   *The Cultural Politics of English as an International Language*. London: Longman.
1998   *English and the Discourses of Colonialism*. London: Routledge.
2003   Global Englishes, Rip Slyme and performativity. *Journal of Sociolinguistics* 7 (4): 513–533.
Phillipson, Robert
1992   *Linguistic Imperialism*. Oxford: Oxford University Press.

Pitcher, M. Anne
  2002   *Transforming Mozambique: The Politics of Privatization, 1975–2000.*
          Cambridge: Cambridge University Press.
PuruShotam, Nirmala S.
  1998   *Negotiating Language, Constructing Race: Disciplining Difference in Sin-*
          gapore. Berlin: Mouton de Gruyter.
Rappa, Tony and Lionel Wee
  2006   *Language Policy and Modernity in Southeast Asia, Malaysia, the Philip-*
          pines, Singapore, and Thailand. New York: Springer.
Robinson, Clinton R. W.
  1996   *Language Use in Rural Development: An African Perspective.* Berlin and
          New York: Mouton de Gruyter.
Romaine, Susan and Daniel Nettle
  2000   *Vanishing Voices: The Extinction of the World's Languages.* New York: Ox-
          ford University Press.
Rubdy, Rani
  2001   Creative destruction: Singapore's Speak Good English Movement. *World*
          Englishes 20: 341–355.
Saravanan, Vanithamani
  1994   Language and social identity amongst Tamil-English bilinguals in Singa-
          pore. In: Rosemary Khoo, Ursula Kreher and Ruth Wong (eds.), *Towards*
          Global Multilingualism. European Models and Asian Realities, 79–93.
          Clevedon: Multilingual Matters.
Skutnabb-Kangas and Robert Phillipson
  1997   Linguistic human rights and development. In: Cees J. Hamelink (ed.),
          Ethics and Development. On Making Moral Choices in Development Co-
          Operation, 55–69. Amsterdam: kok Kampen.
Stroud, Christopher
  1996   The development of metropolitan languages in postcolonial contexts: Lan-
          guage contact and language change and the case of Portuguese in Maputo.
          In: *Nordic Journal of Linguistics* 19 (2): 183–213.
  1999   Portuguese as ideology and politics in Mozambique: Semiotic (re)construc-
          tions of a postcolony. In: Jan Blommaert (ed.), *Language Ideological De-*
          bates, 343–380. Berlin/New York: Mouton de Gruyter.
  2002   Framing Bourdieu socioculturally: Alternative forms of linguistic legit-
          imacy in postcolonial Mozambique. Multilingua 21: 247–272.
  2004   The performativity of codeswitching. *International Journal of Bilingualism*
          8 (2): 145–166.
Stroud, Christopher and Kathleen Heugh
  2004   Language rights and linguistic citizenship. In: Jane Freeland and Donna
          Patrick (eds.), *Language Rights and Language Survival. Sociolinguistic*
          and Sociocultural Perspectives, 191–218. Manchester, UK: St Jerome Pub-
          lishing.
Stroud, Christopher and Perpetua Gonçalves (eds.)
  1997   *Panorama do Português Oral de Maputo. Volume 1: Objectivos e Métodos*
          [Panorama of Oral Portuguese in Maputo. Volume 1: Objectives and
          Methods]. Maputo: INDE.

Stroud, Christopher and Lionel Wee
(forth-   Identity, English language literacy and remedial double-crossing: Explor-
coming)   ing liminalities in social positioning. *TESOL Quarterly.*
Tan, Su Hwi
1998   Theoretical ideals and ideologized reality in language planning. In: S. Gopinathan, Anne Pakir, Wah Kam Ho, and Vanithamani Saravanan (eds.),
Language, Society and Education in Singapore; Issues and Trends, 45–64.
Singapore: Times Academic Press.
Tengan, A. B.
1994   European languages in African society and culture: A view on cultural
authenticity. In: Manfred Pütz (ed.), *Language Contact and Language Conflict*, 125–137. Amsterdam: John Benjamins.
Thompson, Linda
2003   Becoming bilingual in Singapore: A sociolinguistic study of family environments. In: Kenneth Hyltenstam and Kari Fraurud (eds.), *Multilingualism in
Global and Local Perspectives. Papers from the 8th Nordic Conference on
Bilingualism*, November 1–2, 2001, Stockholm-Rinkeby, 281–305. Stockholm: Rinkeby Institute of Multilingual Research and Centre for Research
on Biingualism, Stockholm University.
Wee, Lionel
2003   Linguistic instrumentalism in Singapore. *Journal of Multilingual and
Multicultural Development* 24 (3): 211–224.
Wee, Lionel and Wendy Bokhorst-Heng
2005   Language policy and nationalist ideology: Statal narratives in Singapore.
Multilingua 24: 159–183.
West, Harry G.
1997   Creative destruction and sorcery of construction: Power, hope and suspicion in Post-war Mozambique. *Cahiers d'Etudes Africaines* XXXVII(3)
(147): 675–698.
2003   'Who rules us now?' Identity tokens, sorcery and other metaphors in the
1994 Mozambican elections. In: Harry G. West and Todd Sanders (eds.),
*Transparency and Conspiracy: Ethnographies of Suspicion in the New
World Order*, 92–124. Durham: Duke University Press.
2005   'Govern yourselves!'. Democracy and carnage in Northern Mozambique.
Ms.
West, Harry G. and Scott Kloeck-Jenson
1999   Betwixt and between: "Traditional authority" and the democratic decentra-
lization in post-war Mozambique. *African Affairs* 98 (393): 445–484.

Recommended readings

For more information of the Mozambican linguistic situation, one of the few comprehensive overviews is Armando Lopes (1998) *The language situation in Mozambique in Language Panning in Malawi, Mozambique and the Philippines*, edited by Robert Kaplan
and Richard Baldauf (Clevedon: Multilingual Matters). Among the many overviews of
the Singaporean situation, the most recent is Rappa and Wee's forthcoming *Language*

Policy and Modernity in South East Asia, Malaysia, the Philippines, Singapore, and Thailand. Good studies of the concept of high and late modernity is provided in Anthony Gidden's (1991) *Modernity and Self-identity* (London: Polity Press) and for explorations of language in late modernity, albeit with a particular regional bias, Monica Heller's (1999) *Linguistic Minorities and Modernity: A Sociolinguistic Ethnography* (London: Longman). For recent studies on the sociolinguistics of globalization, good sources are *Journal of Sociolinguistics* 3 (4), 1999, *Journal of Sociolinguistics* 7, 2003, and a recent edition of *Language and Communication* 25, 2005.

22. Multilingualism and transnationalism

Monica Heller

1. Are we living multilingualism in new ways?

Much has been made in recent years of opposing linguistic tensions held to be produced by globalization: on the one hand, we are supposedly at risk of being drowned by English (cf. Maurais and Morris 2003; Phillipson 2003), and on the other, globalization is held to represent new conditions for the maintenance and development of various kinds of multilingualism (cf. Cronin 2003; Dor 2004; Swaan 2001; Wright 2003). While there are many senses in which such tensions are not new (after all, language is one of the ways in which groups seek to dominate and resist, and the hallmarks of globalization – the planet-wide circulation of goods, ideas and people – are not in and of themselves new either), there are ways in which the current conditions of life for many people involve multilingualism in somewhat different ways.

It can be argued that what is really new is not the globalization of language practices per se, but rather the centrality of language in the new economy (Gee et al. 1996; Cameron 2001; Castells 2000; Heller 2003), which happens also to be globalized. Thus Boutet (2001: 56) argues that the new economy (one based on services, symbolic goods and information, not on industrialized manufacturing or the exploitation of primary resources) places a premium on communication, in contrast to the old economy which controlled, and indeed often suppressed, it:

> Dans le taylorisme, parler et travailler sont considérés comme des activités antagonistes. Parler fait perdre du temps, distrait, empêche de se concentrer sur les gestes à accomplir. (…) La mise en place de nouveaux modes de production et en particulier l'automation, la robotisation et l'informatisation des activités, comme la mise en place de nouveaux modes de gestion des salariés (management participatif, responsabilisation, équipes semi-autonomes, auto-contrôle …) auront deux conséquences majeures en ce qui concerne le statut du langage au travail. L'une c'est la généralisation du recours à l'écrit (lecture et écriture) dans tous les métiers et activités y compris déqualifiées (…). L'autre c'est l'émergence d'une compétence de communication.
>
> (In taylorism, talking and working are considered antagonistic. Talking makes you lose time, distracts you, prevents you from concentrating on the (physical) action you need to perform. (…) The introduction of new modes of production, and in particular of automation, robotization and computerization of activities, along with the introduction of the management of workers (participative management, responsibilization, semi-autonomous teams, self-direction …) end up having two major conse-

quences for the place of language at work. The first is the general spread of engagement with the written word (reading, writing) in all activities and trades, including
unskilled ones (…). The second is the emergence of a work-related communicative
competence.)
(Translation M.H.)

So, language itself is now at the centre of economic activity, both as a process
and as a product. The workplace produces and disseminates information, provides services, and markets authentic cultural artefacts whose authenticity is
frequently guaranteed by linguistic forms. Language is increasingly central to
lived experience if only because of shifts in economic processes.

However, this is not the whole story. The new economy is also globalized,
such that not only is communication important, it also entails dealing with linguistic variety in all its many manifestations; here we will focus on multilingualism as one of the more salient ones. Certainly globalization, in the form of
circulation of people, goods and ideas, has been around for a long time; but it
seems clear that the speed of such processes has accelerated: workers of various
kinds circulate rapidly around the world, whether as élites in first class airplane
cabins or as the poorest of displaced people stowing away in airplane wheel
wells or navigating the Straits of Gibraltar at night; information circulates instantaneously; goods are produced in one corner of the world and sold the next
day in another. It seems likely that fewer people are protected from these processes; more and more, we all have to deal with the multiplicity of material and
symbolic resources, language(s) among them, as part of our daily lives.

Finally, these processes have no linear, clear-cut direction. Rather, they contain tensions. In the realm of language, there are tensions between uniformization
and standardization, in the service of control of resources, and the importance of
reaching diverse markets. Every push towards monolingualism is countered by a
pull towards multilingualism; every push towards standardization is countered
by a pull towards diversity. These tensions have both local and transnational dimensions, of course, as people draw on linguistic resources from a wide variety
of sources to address both local and translocal issues under specific, and variable,
conditions. Thus overall we have new economic conditions which: 1) place communication at the heart of economic activities; 2) entail confronting multilingualism; but 3) contain tensions between trying to find strategies which fully embrace
linguistic and cultural diversity and strategies which suppress or erase it – tensions which may be resolved quite differently in different spaces.

Ethnographic descriptions of these emerging processes are only beginning
to be undertaken, and so it is difficult to say exactly what shape these processes
are taking, and what kind of impact they are likely to have, whether on specific
fields (such as translation, interpreting, language policy or language teaching)
or on sociolinguistic theory. Most work is coming out of studies of immigration
(a sampling of relevant studies might include Birken-Silverman 2004; Gold-

stein 2003; Auer 2003; van den Avenne 2004; Martin-Jones and Jones 2000; Meng 2001; Woods 2004), which is not surprising given that research funding is driven by State interests, and that immigration is tied to economic and political shifts central to State concerns while challenging the State's ability to control its borders and its relations with other States. It is also perhaps the most public face of the processes in question, given the multiple ways it intersects with the lives of so many people. Some of these focus on the trajectories of immigrants themselves, some on language use in public places (whether face-to-face or virtual) or popular culture, some on key sites such as education, the workplace or forms of regulation of movement such as asylum hearings (see several of the contributions to this volume). Fewer focus on ways in which transnational multilingualism has seeped into the very process of work (but cf. Cronin 2003 on translation; cf. Boudreau 2003; Roy 2003 on bilingual call centres; cf. Wagner 2004; Phillips 2000; Roy and Gélinas 2004 or Moïse 2003 on tourism; or Heller 2005 for a more general discussion). Fewer still have examined what this might mean for the expertise connected to knowledge about languages, notably as concerns language learning, although it is clear that the role of the "language worker" (translator, interpreter, language teacher, developer of translation software or technologies of voice recognition) is not only rapidly evolving but also becoming more and more important (but see Yarymowich 2003, Yarymowich 2005 on language 'edutourism'). In what follows I will discuss the kinds of findings that are nonetheless beginning to emerge, and the kinds of paradoxes they seem to point to.

2.   The varied faces of transnationalism

First, it is abundantly clear that the experience of language in the globalized new economy varies widely depending on how people are positioned both with respect to their place in it and to the related issue of their access to unequally distributed linguistic resources. At the very least, we see very different profiles emerging between those who are directly involved in that economy and those whose experience of multilingualism is still informed by the old one (as in labour migration in agriculture or mining, for example). Among those involved in the new economy we see differences between the élite managers of the global economy and the actual providers of service at the chalk face; cross-cutting this distinction we have one which divides those who have access to linguistic resources of global currency, such as English, French or Spanish, from those who do not, with further distinctions to be made regarding the value of the specific varieties people master or can learn.

For those involved in labour migration, the question of transnational multilingualism has everything to do with survival strategies. Economic integration is in fact precarious in host countries, and labour migration is often in any case intended to support people in the places of origin. Multilingualism is a matter, on the one hand, of gaining or maintaining access to new spaces and new resources, especially when it is regulated by the monolingualism of the gate-keepers as part of long-established mechanisms of State-building and the construction of citizenship; and on the other, it is a matter of maintaining access to the networks of solidarity to which one is obliged, and on which one counts in case of failure. This is not a very new phenomenon, but it is certainly accentuated now by the increasing possibilities for the circulation of people (it is simply easier to get around than it used to be) and of communication (whether by telephone, which can cost significantly less than in the past, and for which it is increasingly easy in countries of origin to provide the basic infrastructure; or by internet, which is increasingly publicly available, although it does require literacy skills).

For those more directly involved in the new economy, much depends on the ideology of language as it connects to the ideology of the activity involved, and on the position of individuals with respect to that activity. Both monolingualism and multilingualism can work as means of regulating resources and positioning oneself advantageously with respect to them, but both also entail some risks. In most of what follows, we will see this ambivalence playing out again and again.

There are a number of angles one can, indeed should, take to understand transnational multilingualism. One can, for example, look at it from the perspective of the mobile speaker-subject, whether in élite or marginalized spaces. Hannerz (1996), for example, followed journalists around; van den Avenne (2004) has followed migrant workers.[1] One can look at specific transnational communication practices, such as the use of the internet (Androutsopoulos in press). One can look at institutionalized spaces which exist largely for the management of transnational encounters, notably through immigration, such as the various settings for the provision of services to immigrants, including education (cf. Pujolar, forthc.; Rojo et al. 2004). Language learning itself as a (frequently institutionalized) social practice is an obvious site (cf. Yarymowich 2005; Pavlenko and Blackledge 2003). Tourism (cf. Baider et al. 2005; Macdonald 1997; Jaworski and Pritchard 2005; Moïse 2003; Phillips 2000; Roy and Gélinas 2004) has also become an increasingly popular space for understanding the role of language in managing new experiences of transnationalism, in part because it allows for connecting the trajectories of mobile speaker-subjects (tourists) to those of the producers of the tourism product, to the management of their encounter, and to the circulation of tourism-related discourses through a wide variety of mediated means (postcards, television shows, in-flight magazines, travel supplements in newspapers, and so on; Jaworski and Pritchard 2005). While (The Pet Shop Boys notwithstanding) the private sector is clearly an important site as well, most work here has focussed on call centres (Boudreau 2003; Budach et al. 2003; Roy 2003); my own research team however has recently collected data on multilingualism in a multimedia company and a fair-trade/ecology NGO doing business across North America, and a biotech company with links across Canada and Europe (Heller and Boutet, in prep., 2007). The relative paucity of research in this key area is likely due to reasons that have held for decades; the private sector is simply not as open to sociolinguistic research as the public sector, given the principles of transparency that legitimate the public sector and the principles of competition that constrain the private sector.

What we see emerging, I think, is a necessarily multiple approach which attempts to connect language practices to the spaces of their performance and to the trajectories of speakers, with a variety of research questions at the fore: questions about how language is involved in the social construction of settings, spaces and relations; how transnational multilingualism is involved in the construction of relations of difference and inequality; or how it connects to new and usually multiple and complex forms of social organization, calling into question old categories and old boundaries. In what follows, however, I will focus mainly on the tensions and paradoxes that traverse transnational multilingualism. I will places an emphasis on the globalized new economy workplace, largely because it is a characteristic of our times that economic activities drive political and social ones. The discourse and logic of capitalism permeate political and public discourse and social organization, and are hence important to understand. The paradoxes experienced in the workplace are then, I believe, not only characteristic of the social changes we are currently living through, they can also tell us a great deal about what is at stake, and for whom, in a wide variety of sites.

3.   Language, commodification and authenticity

The globalized new economy values language(s) (indeed language varieties of all kinds) in two major, but radically different, ways. It values language as a technical skill which facilitates the management of workforces, contacts with clients and suppliers, and the provision of services worldwide. It is also valued as a mark of authenticity, whether in the marketing of cultural goods and services (notably, but not exclusively, in tourism), or in the construction of the legitimacy of authority of one particular group versus others in specific domains (for example, in the appeal to the specific importance and value of indigenous ethnobotanical knowledge which is generally argued, admittedly in a rather Whorfian manner, to be inscribed in the lexicon of indigenous languages); in some ways these are merely two sides of the same coin, two ways of constructing who gets to define what counts as authentic and of putting into play the value of authenticity as commodity in a globalized market (Heller 2003).

This contrast is traversed by another one, which flows directly from the dominant ideology of the new economy, namely that the value of a product is derived from a notion of quality of service. The problem with that driving notion is that there are two contradictory ways of injecting service with quality. One derives from (still active) Fordist ideas about standardization: producers should assure that all clients get the same quality of service (and product) by making sure that all products (and services) are the same (Cameron 2001). As a consumer, I should know what to expect. The other derives from post-Fordist ideas about flexibility and variability (cf. Gee et al. 1996), which foreground the importance of meeting the consumer on his or her own ground and of adapting quickly to conditions as they change. Hence McDonald's sells poutine in Quebec and lobster rolls in Maine, while endeavouring all the while to remain recognizably McDonald's. Similarly, call centres waver between trying to teach their staff in India how to sound like New Yorkers or Londoners, or focussing on the standardized script and leaving the accent out of it.

These two contradictory ideologies of economic production necessarily have an impact on the management of multilingualism. One way of ensuring standardized quality is by making sure that everything is done in the same language; but if you do that, then you fail to provide consumers with products or services they can identify as being appropriately, and authentically, aimed at them. While the 19th and 20th century nation-State tried valiantly to produce the homogeneous citizen (and movements like the one that led to the development of Esperanto wanted to produce universal ones), the 21st century is coming face-to-face (or screen-to-screen) with the difficulty of that enterprise, and alternately trying to save it or trying to turn impossibility to advantage. On the one hand, we see major investments in English as a world language, and on the other we see major gestures in the direction of multilingualism (language learning, the language of supranational organizations like the European Union, and advertising are probably the most evident examples of both, but they also turn up in interesting ways in other kinds of markets; Kelly-Holmes 2000; Phillipson 2003; Piller and Takahashi in press).

The conditions of the globalized new economy thus place an emphasis on the commodification of language one way or another, with constant tensions between standardization (and monolingualism) and flexibility and diversity (and multilingualism[2]). These can be managed in a variety of ways, notably by treating language either as a skill, or as a talent.

If you treat language like a skill, you can manage it by measuring, evaluating, and, eventually, remunerating it. You can also remove it, separate it out from, the rest of the activities you are involved in. Or, alternatively, you can market it as a commodity in and of itself. We see this manifested concretely in a number of ways. One is the use of translators and interpreters in the management of multilingual communication. Producers themselves therefore need not be multilingual; they can produce in their own language, and rely on others (whether humans or machines) to transform the communicative wrapping of their product or service. The activity of translation or interpretation (which in this scenario obviously relies on an ideology of language as either neutral and transparent, or, in a Chomsky-inspired mode, as derived from universal sets of principles) can thus be made, more or less literally, accountable; they become technical professions, requiring specialized training, and the attribution of monetary value to their products. The professionalization of translation and interpretation of course is a way of guaranteeing legitimacy, authority and therefore quality. Another is the development of standardized tests for use in recruitment for multilingual jobs, or in performance evaluation in these same sectors. Finally, we see linguistic knowledge treated in the workplace in the same way as any other form of technical knowledge, with similar forms of remuneration (in Canadian call centres, when there are specific amounts attached to knowledge of both French and English, they tend to vary between 25 cents and one dollar an hour, which gives an idea of the market value of bilingualism).

If language is treated as a talent, there are some distinct advantages, the first of course being that there is no need to pay for it. Indeed, within Canada's so-called bilingual belt, Quebec seems to be competing with New Brunswick and Ontario for the call centre industry precisely along the lines of whether or not to treat labour force bilingualism as a remunerable skill or as just one of the many talents local workers bring to the job: in 2004, on a Government of Quebec website, companies were urged to establish themselves in Montreal because: "Québec's bilingual labour pool, the biggest in Canada, is a key advantage for businesses that wish to gain access to 7 million French-speaking Canadians without paying bilingualism bonuses".[3]

The downside of this strategy is that it is impossible to control the nature of the linguistic product, and indeed, in accounts we have heard in our fieldwork, this is a source of problems for bilingual workers and their managers.[4] In some cases, workers do not know in advance what language(s) their interlocutor speaks or prefers, and often need to navigate pragmatic minefields when multilingualism is a fraught terrain. For example, receptionists in an insurance office in a small town in Ontario described how some callers dislike being greeted in English (the company owner is francophone, and some clients think of the office as a francophone space where francophone rights can and must be asserted), some dislike being greeted in French (because English is the dominant language and French can feel threatening), and some dislike being greeted bilingually (because one or the other dispreferred language is still present, and no strong stance one way or the other is taken). Call centre representatives in a variety of sites in Ontario and New Brunswick described how even within French (although notably not within English), there were tensions over the legitimacy of the varieties they speak, as opposed to those of their callers; one representative went so far as to invent an English persona for herself so that francophone callers would not hold her responsible for mastering whatever variety of French they happened to think ought to be the norm, and would congratulate her instead on her excellent second-language skills.

In tourism, the issue is also one of credibility for different audiences. For example, in northeastern New Brunswick, there is a village museum containing buildings from different moments of Acadian history, from the 18ᵗʰ and 19ᵗʰ centuries. In each, employees dress in period costume, and indeed live in the houses on site during the season: they are meant to enact former occupants. We find them moving back and forth through different voices. Sometimes they speak as the person they are meant to be (say a 19ᵗʰ century general store manager), and sometimes as the local person whose job is it to enact that character (hence stories about having themselves grown up in the village when their parents used to work there, for example). They also cannot predict what languages will be spoken by the tourists who enter the building; on the days we visited the majority were Canadian francophones, but many were English-speaking North Americans or Europeans, some of whom had English and some French as an additional language. Some English-speakers want to practice their French and some do not, or have no French to practice; some visitors, whether English- or French-speakers, care about language as a mark of authenticity and some do not.

In a language-as-skill approach, these tensions are lessened. There are no claims to personal responsibility for cultural knowledge and social loyalties linked to language choices; one can be angry at a technician for not being able to fix the computer, but one can't accuse him or her of betrayal. At most, one can accuse the employer of inadequate training.

The reality of multilingualism is that it is about not only diversity, but also about inequality and struggle, and the ideal clientèle and the ideal workforce behind most management strategies simply do not exist. Faced with dilemmas such as those I have just described, most workers we have met say that they are left on their own to figure out how to respond; such issues are beyond what management can address.

Whether language is treated as a talent or as a skill, we can see that dealing with multilingualism in the new economy is full of unforeseen contradictions. Largely this is because the ideologies and practices we have inherited assume homogeneity: at best, multilingualism is understood as multiple monolingualism, as a string of distinct systems to be mastered and used separately. The private sector strategies we have seen show how difficult it is to use that frame for coping with messy reality; and indeed, the private sector is not the only place where the dominant ideologies of multilingualism are only now being challenged. State practices, including in such key State agencies as education, also are sites where such confrontations occur. For example, in Switzerland, debates currently rage over whether to add English to the elementary school curriculum, replacing a second national language for some years or in addition to it; in Quebec, francophone parents fight over whether to permit intensive English instruction in elementary school; in Alberta, there are debates over whether to abandon French in favour of Mandarin or Spanish. Transnational multilingualism is thus a challenge for the forms of social organization that currently dominant ideologies underlie and help reproduce. What remains to be seen is whether the strategies we have discovered serve to neutralize these tensions, or whether they will force a reexamination of what we understand by multilingualism, and of what forms of social organization we seek to build through (or around or despite) it.

In the last section, I will explore what this might mean for our own disciplines, since academic understandings of multilingualism are part and parcel of the construction of ideologies and practices. I alluded above to different ways in which it might be possible to explore how transational multilingualism works these days; in what follows, I will focus more generally on what a sociolinguistics of transnational multilingualism might need to look like.

4.   A multisited sociolinguistics of transnational multilingualism

What we have seen of transnational multilingualism raises several issues. First, it asks us to address the question of how multiple kinds of linguistic resources circulate across time and space, not as the possessions of speakers, but as resources circulating in spaces to which some people have access and some do not, and which some make use of and some do not. That is, do we think about speakers as having languages in their heads, or as having access (or not) to spaces where linguistic resources may be available? Second, it forces us to recognize that the idea of multilingualism is in the eye of the beholder; it is in speakers' confrontation with dominant ideologies of language, in which linguistic resources are understood to belong to distinct systems and sets of speakers, that we see how those ideologies constrain what is imaginable and concretely possible in the navigation of speakers across social spaces. Finally, we get a sense of the stakes of the game: how linguistic resources are deployed does make a difference, but how they are judged also depends on the connection between ideologies of language, nation, State and more local legitimating ideologies in specific settings, such as those of service and production discussed above. (Clearly, ideologies of gender, race, sexuality and class matter greatly here too, as do those informing many other kinds of institutions, like religion, or the family.)

This leads us perhaps to thinking of how to approach the question empirically through the kinds of multi-sited ethnographies increasingly emerging in anthropology (cf. Burawoy et al. 2000; Marcus 1995; Hannerz 2003). Transnational multilingualism is indeed, as I argued above, partly a matter of trajectories (of speakers, of institutions, of resources) and partly a matter of discursive spaces; it is also a matter of legitimating ideologies and forms of social organization. The question is how to put them together.

Some versions of multi-sited ethnographies argue for a kind of comparative study that tries to understand globalized processes as they manifest themselves simultaneously in a number of sites. I want to argue here for a more contingent and dynamic understanding that sees social processes as linked in complicated ways across time and space, not simply as simultaneous manifestations of the same thing in different places. The tools of sociolinguistics can help us make the connections we need to make in order to understand processes which link people and resources across time and space. Communicative processes are central to transnational movements, and looking at how people draw on their communicative resources, in conjunction with other symbolic and material ones, allows us a glimpse into how those resources are distributed and into what happens when they are deployed.

Tracing trajectories and focussing on spaces they traverse is one way to grasp what is at stake, and for whom. It is one way to identify key producers of discourses of language and identity, and to discover how value gets attributed to linguistic practices and their practitioners. It can help analysts decide what position to take about states of affairs, notably about the regulation of access to linguistic resources, and about how those resources are understood.

This is a historical moment of discursive shift, one in which the political economic conditions of the globalized new economy are intimately tied to new ways of using language, and new ways of understanding what language is, and how it is connected to social identity and social relations. Transnational multilingualism is a first sign, and a key site for discovering what those changes are all about.

Notes

1. The British rock group The Pet Shop Boys captured something of the thrill of the new multilingual élite in their 1996 song "Bilingual" (Cage Music Ltd., 1996):
   They call this a community
   I like to think of it as home
   Arriving at the airport I am going it alone
   Ordering a boarding pass
   Travelling in business class
   This is the name of the game
   I'm single bilingual
   Single bilingual
   I come to the community from U.K. p.l.c.
   Arriving at my hotel there are faxes greeting me
   Staying in a junior suite so there's room to meet and greet and after work explain how I feel
   "Perdoneme me llamo Neil" (sic)
   I'm single bilingual

Single bilingual
In Brussels Bonn or Barcelona I'm in demand and quite at home there
"Adelante!" Through the door
"Un momento por favor"
This is what I get paid for
"Muchas gracias senor"
I'm a player in the continental game with unlimited expenses to reclaim
Information's easy
Tapping at my PC
That is the frame of the game
I'm single bilingual
Single bilingual
I'm single bilingual
Single bilingual
"Hay una discoteca por acqui?" (sic)

2. Of course, even that distinction is too simple, since in either case one is still faced with the problem of varieties within what are conventionally accepted as different languages; cf. Boudreau 2003.

3. This is from www.invest-quebec.com/en/int/secteur; thanks to Joan Pujolar for drawing my attention to it.

4. I draw here on two projects funded by the Social Sciences and Humanities Research Council of Canada, *Prise de parole II: La francité canadienne et la nouvelle économie mondialisée*, (2000–2004) and *La francité transnationale: pour une sociolinguistique de la mouvance* (2004–2008). My collaborators and assistants include: Annette Boudreau, Lise Dubois, Normand Labrie, Patricia Lamarre, Mathieu Leblanc, Deirdre Meintel; Claudine Moïse, Peter Auer, Werner Kallmeyer; Emanuel da Silva, Mélanie Le Blanc, Darryl Leroux, Sonya Malaborza, Mireille McLaughlin, Mary Richards, Chantal White, Natalie Zur Nedden.

References

Androutsopoulos, Jannis
    in press   Language choice and code-switching in German-based diasporic web forums. In: B. Danet and S. Herring (eds.), *The Multilingual Internet*. Oxford: Oxford University Press.

Auer, Peter
    2003   "Crossing" the language border into Turkish? Uses of Turkish by non-Turks in Germany. In: L. Mondada and S.P. Doehler (eds.), *Plurilinguism/Mehrsprachigkeit/Plurilingualism*, 73–94. Tübingen: A. Francke.

Baider, Fabienne, Marcel Burger and Dionysios Goutsos (eds.)
    2005   *La communication touristique. Approches discursives de l'identité et de l'alterité*. Paris: L'Harmattan.

Birken-Silverman, Gabriele
    2004   Language crossing among adolescents in a multiethnic city area in Germany. In: C. Hoffman and J. Ytsma (eds.), *Trilingualism in Family, School and Community*, 75–101. Clevedon UK: Multilingual Matters.

550   Monica Heller

Boudreau, Annette
    2003   *Le vernaculaire comme phénomène de résistance. L'exemple d'un centre d'appel.* Contacts de langue et minorisation. Systèmes, pratiques et représentations. Sion (Suisse).
Boutet, Josiane
    2001   Le travail devient-il intellectuel? *Travailler. Revue internationale de psychopathologie et de psychodynamique du travail* 6: 55–70.
Budach, Gabriele, Sylvie Roy and Monica Heller
    2003   Community and commodity in French Ontario. *Language in Society* 32 (5).
Burawoy, Michael, et al.
    2000   *Global Ethnography: Forces, Connections and Imaginations in a Postmodern World.* Berkeley, LA: University of California Press.
Cameron, Deborah
    2001   *Good to Talk?* London: Sage.
Castells, Manuel
    2000   *The Information Age: Economy, Society and Culture* (3 volumes). Oxford: Blackwell.
Cronin, M.
    2003   *Translation and Globalization.* London: Routledge.
Dor, D.
    2004   From Englishization to imposed multilingualism: globalization, the internet, and the political economy of the linguistic code. *Public Culture* 16 (1): 97–118.
Gee, James, Glynda Hull and Colin Lankshear
    1996   *The New Work Order: Behind the Language of the New Capitalism.* Boulder, CO: Westview Press.
Goldstein, Tara
    2003   Contemporary bilingual life in a Canadian high school: choices, risks, tensions and dilemmas. *Sociology of Education* 76: 247–264.
Hannerz, Ulf
    1996   *Transnational Connections: Culture, People, Places.* London: Routledge.
    – 2003   On being there ... and there ... and there! Reflections on multi-site ethnography. *Ethnography* 4 (2): 201–216.
Heller, Monica
    2003   Globalization, the new economy and the commodification of language and identity. *Journal of Sociolinguistics* 7 (4): 473–492.
    – 2005   Language, skill and authenticity in the globalized new economy. NOVES–SL Winter: (online).
Heller, Monica, and Josiane Boutet
    in prep   Vers de nouvelles formes de pouvoir langagier? *Langage et société* 118.
Jaworski, Adam, and Annette Pritchard (eds.)
    2005   *Discourse, Communication and Tourism.* Clevedon/Buffalo/Toronto: Channel View Publications.
Kelly-Holmes, Helen
    2000   Bier, parfum, kaas: Language fetish in European advertising. *Cultural Studies* 3 (1): 67–82.
Macdonald, Sharon
    1997   A people's story: heritage, identity and authenticity. In: C. Rojek and J. Urry

(eds.), *Touring Cultures: Transformations of Travel and Theory,* 155–175. Oxford: Routledge.

Marcus, George
    1995   Ethnography in/of the world system: the emergence of multi-sited ethnography. *Annual Review of Anthropology* 24: 95–117.

Martin-Jones, Marilyn and Kathryn Jones (eds.)
    2000   *Multilingual Literacies.* Amsterdam: John Benjamins.

Maurais, Jacques and Michael Morris (eds.)
    2003   *Languages in a Globalising World.* Cambridge: Cambridge University Press.

Meng, Katharina
    2001   *Russlanddeutsche Sprachbiographien. Untersuchungen zur sprachlichen Integration von Aussiedlerfamilien.* Tübingen: Narr.

Moïse, Claudine
    2003   *Le rôle du tourisme en Ontario dans la redéfinition de la minorité franco-ontarienne.* Contacts des langues et minorisation, Sion (Suisse).

Pavlenko, Aneta and Adrian Blackledge (eds.)
    2003   *Negotiation of Identities in Multilingual Contexts.* Clevedon, U.K.: Multilingual Matters.

Phillips, Dylan
    2000   We'll keep a welcome? The effects of tourism on the Welsh language. In: G.H. Jenkins and M.A. Williams (eds.), *"Let's do our best for the ancient tongue": The Welsh language in the 20th century,* 527–550. Cardiff: University of Wales Press.

Phillipson, Robert
    2003   *English-Only Europe? Challenging Language Policy.* London/ New York: Routledge.

Piller, Ingrid and K. Takahashi
    in press   A passion for English: desire and the language market. In: A. Pavlenko (ed.), *Bilingual Minds: Emotional Experience, Expression and Representation.* Clevedon, UK: Multilingual Matters.

Pujolar, Joan
    forthcoming   African women in Catalan language courses: struggles over class, gender and ethnicity in advanced liberalism. In: B. McElhinny (ed.), *Words, Worlds and Material Girls: Language, Gender and Global Economies.* Berlin/ New York: Mouton de Gruyter.

Rojo, Luisa Martin, Luci Nussbaum, and Virginia Unamuno
    2004   Special issue: Escuela e immigracion/School and immigration. *Estudios de Sociolinguistica* 5 (2).

Roy, Sylvie
    2003   Bilingualism and standardization in a Canadian call center: challenges for a linguistic minority community. In: R. Bayley and S. Schecter (eds.), *Language Socialization in Multilingual Societies,* 269–287. Clevedon, UK: Multilingual Matters.

Roy, Sylvie, and Chantal Gélinas
    2004   Le tourisme pour les Franco-Albertains: Une porte d'entrée au monde. *Francophonies d'Amérique* 17: 131–140.

Swaan, Abram de
    2001   *Words of the World: The Global Language System.* Cambridge: Polity.

552 Monica Heller

Van den Avenne, Cécile
2004   *Changer de vie, changer de langues. Paroles de migrants entre le Mali et Marseille.* Paris: L'Harmattan.
Wagner, Lauren
2004   *Tourism and Representations of Morocco: The Mediation of Authenticity Through Language, Interaction and Video.* Ph.D., University of Texas at Austin.
Woods, Anya
2004   *Medium or Message? Language and Faith in Ethnic Churches.* Clevedon, U.K.: Multilingual Matters.
Wright, Sue
2003   *Language Policy and Language Planning: From Nationalism to Globalisation.* New York: Palgrave Macmillan.
Yarymowich, Maia
2003   *Language Tourism in Canada: Theorizing Language Education as a Global Commodity,* Unpublished Ph.D. Thesis University of Toronto.
Yarymowich, Maia
2005   Language tourism in Canada: a mixed discourse. In: F. Baider, M. Burger, and D. Goutsos (eds.), 257–273.

Recommended readings

Appadurai, Arjun
1991   Global ethnoscapes: Notes on queries for a transnational anthropology. In: R.G. Fox (ed.), *Recapturing Anthropology,* 191–210. Santa Fe, N.M.: School of American Research.
Appadurai, Arjun
1996   *Modernity at Large: Cultural Dimensions of Globalization.* Minneapolis: University of Minnesota Press.
Bauman, Zygmunt
1998   *Globalization: The Human Consequences.* Cambridge: Polity Press.
Bayley, Robert and Sandra Schecter (eds.)
2003   *Language Socialization in Bilingual and Multilingual Societies.* Clevedon, UK: Multilingual Matters.
Block, David and Deborah Cameron (eds.)
2002   *Globalization and Language Teaching,* London: Routledge.
Coupland, Nik
2003   Sociolinguistic authenticities. *Journal of Sociolinguistics* 7 (3): 417–431.
Coupland, Nik (ed.)
2003   Sociolinguistics and globalization. Special issue of the *Journal of Sociolinguistics* 7 (4): 465–623.
Coupland, Nik, Peter Garrett and Hywel Bishop
2005   Wales underground: discursive frames and authenticities in Welsh mining heritage tourism events. In: A. Jaworski and A. Pritchard (eds.), *Discourse, Communication and Tourism,* 199–222, Clevedon, UK: Channel View Publications.

Craik, Jennifer
   1997   The culture of tourism. In: C. Rojek and J. Urry (eds.), *Touring Cultures: Transformations of Travel and Theory*, 113–136. London: Routledge.
del Valle, Jose
   In press   U.S. Latinos, la hispanofonia, and the language ideologies of high modernity. In: Clare Mar-Molinero and Miranda Stewart (eds.), *Globalization and the Spanish-Speaking World*. London: Palgrave.
Macdonald, Sharon
   1997   A people's story: heritage, identity and authenticity. In: C. Rojek and J. Urry (eds.), *Touring Cultures: Transformation of Travel and Theory*, 155–175, Oxford: Routledge.
Pries, Ludger
   2001   The approach of transnational social spaces. In: L. Pries, ed., *New Transnatioinal Social Spaces: International Migration and International Companies in the Early Twenty-First Century*, 3–33. New York: Routledge.
Pujolar, Joan
   In press   Bilingualism and the nation-State in the post-national era. In: M. Heller (ed.), *Bilingualism: A Social Approach*. London: Palgrave.
Vertovec, Steven
   2001   Transnationalism and identity. *Journal of Ethnic and Migration Studies* 27 (4): 573–582.

Biographical notes

Peter Auer
received his academic training at the universities of Cologne, Manchester and Constance, where he also worked as an assistant professor of General Linguistics. From 1992 to 1998, he was professor of German linguistics at the university of Hamburg. Since 1998, he has held a chair of German linguistics at the University of Freiburg (Germany). He has done extensive research on bilingualism, phonology and dialectology, prosody, interaction and spoken language from a syntactic point of view. He is the author of *Bilingual Conversation* (1984), *Phonologie der Alltagssprache* (1990), *Language in Time* (1999, with Elizabeth Couper-Kuhlen and Frank Müller), *Sprachliche Interaktion* (1999) and *Türkisch sprechen nicht nur die Türken: über die Unschärfebeziehung zwischen Sprache und Ethnie in Deutschland* (with inci Dirim, 2004). He has (co-)edited eight academic books (among them, *Code-Switching in Conversation,* 1999) and written about 100 articles in linguistic journals and edited volumes.

Benjamin Bailey
received his PhD in Linguistic Anthropology from the University of California Los Angeles. His research focuses on negotiations of ethnic and racial identity in face-to-face interaction, particularly in urban US contexts. His publications include *Language, Race, and Negotiation of Identity: A Study of Dominican Americans* (2002, NY: LFB Scholarly) and various articles and chapters on race, code switching, bilingualism, immigration, and intercultural communication.

Colin Baker
is Professor of Education at the University of Wales, Bangor. He is the author of 14 books and over 60 articles on bilingualism and bilingual education. This includes the 'Foundations of Bilingual Education and Bilingualism' (2006, 4th edition) which has been translated into Japanese, Spanish, Latvian, Greek and Mandarin, and the Encyclopedia of Bilingualism and Bilingual Education (Multilingual Matters, with S.P. Jones, 1998). He edits two Multilingual Matters Book Series and is Editor of the International Journal of Bilingualism and Bilingual Education.

Patricia Baquedano-López
is Assistant Professor in Language and Literacy, Society and Culture at the Graduate School of Education, University of California, Berkeley. Her research investigates the literacy and language socialization practices of culturally diverse children in and out of school. Her work has been published in the Anthro-

pology and Education Quarterly, Annual Review of Anthropology, Journal of Linguistic Anthropology, and Narrative Inquiry among others.

Dennis Day
is Associate Professor at the Institute for Language and Communication, University of Southern Denmark, Odense. He is currently leading a research project entitled 'Global Communication in Danish Organizations' with funding from The Danish Research Council for the Humanities.

Jean-Marc Dewaele
is Reader in French and Applied Linguistics at Birkbeck, University of London. He has published on psycholinguistic, sociolinguistic, pragmatic and psychological aspects of SLA. He is also interested in the complex interplay between multilingualism and emotions in a variety of contexts. He is member of the Executive Committees of EUROSLA, the IAM and AILA, where he is Research Network Coordinator.

John Edwards
was born in England, educated there and in Canada, and received a PhD (in psychology) from McGill University in 1974. After working as a Research Fellow at the Educational Research Centre, St Patrick's College, Dublin, he moved to Nova Scotia, where he is now Professor of Psychology at St Francis Xavier University. His research interests are in language, identity and the many ramifications of their relationship. He has lectured and presented papers on this topic in some thirty countries. Professor Edwards is on the editorial boards of a dozen language journals, and is the editor of the Journal of Multilingual and Multicultural Development; he also edits a companion series of books. Professor Edwards's own books include Language in Canada (Cambridge, 1998), Multilingualism (Penguin, 1995), Language, Society and Identity (Blackwell, 1985) and The Irish Language (Garland, 1983). He is also the author of about 200 articles, chapters and reviews. Professor Edwards is a member of several psychological and linguistic societies, as well as scholarly organisations for the study of ethnicity and nationalism. He is a fellow of the British Psychological Society, the Canadian Psychological Association, and the Royal Society of Canada.

Guus Extra
studied Linguistics at the University of Nijmegen in the Netherlands. From 1970 to 1981 he was senior lecturer at the same university. After defending his dissertation on second language acquisition at Nijmegen University (1978), he was a postdoctoral fellow at Stanford University (Department of Linguistics) and UC Berkeley (School of Education) in 1978/1979. Since 1981 he has held the Chair of Language and Minorities in the Faculty of Arts at Tilburg University. In

2002 he was appointed Director of Babylon, Centre for Studies of the Multicultural Society, at the same university. In Babylon, the Faculty of Arts, the Faculty of Social and Behavioural Sciences, and the Faculty of Theology cooperate in the domains of linguistic, cultural and religious diversity (guus.extra@uvt.nl / www.tilburguniversity.nl/babylon).

Joseph Gafaranga
is Lecturer in Linguistics in the Department of Linguistics and English Language at the University of Edinburgh. His main interests are in the area of language and interaction, with focus on bilingual conversation and on doctor-patient interaction.

Ofelia García, Lesley Bartlett and JoAnne Kleifgen
are faculty members at Columbia University's Teachers College in the Department of International and Transcultural Studies. García and Kleifgen co-direct the Center for Multiple Languages and Literacies. García is professor and coordinator of the program in Bilingual-Bicultural Education. Her research and publications are in the area of sociology of language, especially language education policy and bilingual education. Bartlett is assistant professor of international and comparative education. She focuses on social studies of literacy and critical literacy. Kleifgen is associate professor of linguistics and education. Her research interests are in the area of multimodal discourses and literacies in schools and the workplace.

Penelope Gardner-Chloros
started her career as a conference interpreter, working for the EU and the Council of Europe. Since 1991, she has been Lecturer in the School of Languages, Linguistics and Culture, Birkbeck, University of London. She is the author of 'Language Selection and Switching in Strasbourg' (OUP 1991) and co-editor of 'Vernacular Literacy: A Re-Evaluation' (OUP 1997). Her latest book, 'Code-switching', is forthcoming in 2007 with CUP. Her main interests are in the fields of Sociolinguistics, Bilingualism and Code-switching.

Monica Heller
is Professor in the Department of Sociology and Equity Studies in Education and the Centre de recherches en éducation franco-ontarienne at the Ontario Institute for Studies in Education of the University of Toronto (Canada). Her research interests focus on the role of language ideologies and practices in the construction of social difference and social inequality, with a focus on francophone Canada. Her most recent publications include *Linguistic Minorities and Modernity: A Sociolinguistic Ethnography* (London, Longman; 1999),*Voices of Authority: Education and Linguistic Difference* (co-edited with Marilyn Martin-

Jones; Westport, CT, Ablex; 2001), *Éléments d'une sociolinguistique critique* (Paris, Didier, 2002), and *Discours et identités. La francité canadienne entre modernité et mondialisation* (co-edited with Normand Labrie, Cortil-Wodon, Belgium, Éditions EME, 2003). She is currently preparing two edited volumes: M. Heller (ed.), *Bilingualism: A Social Approach* (London, Palgrave Macmillan), and M. Heller and A. Duchêne (eds.), *Discourses of Endangerment: Ideology and Interest in the Defense of Languages* (London, Continuum).

J. Normann Jørgensen
1978–79 University of Texas. 1980–1995 Danish University of Education. Since 1995 Department of Scandinavian Studies and Linguistics, University of Copenhagen. Currently professor of Danish as a second language. Studies in sociolinguistics, including language variation in Danish, multilingualism and youth language. Former Danish and Scandinavian champion in saber fencing.

Shlomy Kattan
is a Doctoral student at the Graduate School of Education at the University of California, Berkeley. His research examines language socialization practices and ideologies of language among Israeli emissaries on two-year assignments in the United States, focusing on their binational transitions and the ways these transitions are negotiated by family members in everyday practices.

Jörg-U. Keßler
worked as a secondary school teacher and is currently seconded to the University Paderborn. He worked on the evaluation and calibration of Rapid Profile for his PhD and is a member of the State Committee for the evaluation of English in Primary Schools in the State of North-Rhine Westfalia.

Elizabeth Lanza
is Professor of Applied Linguistics at the University of Oslo, Norway. She has a Ph.D. from Georgetown University, USA. Her main research interests and publications are in bilingualism especially from sociolinguistic and interactional perspectives. She is currently involved in a collaborative research project on multilingual education in elementary schools in Ethiopia.

David C.S. Li
is an associate professor at the Department of English and Communication, City University of Hong Kong. He obtained his BA in Hong Kong, MA in France, and PhD in Germany. He has published in three main areas: Hong Kong English, English as a global language, Cantonese-English code-switching, and Hong Kong Chinese EFL learners' learning difficulties and correction strategies.

Li Wei, PhD
is Professor of Applied Linguistics at Birkbeck, University of London. He is author of *Three Generations Two Languages One Family,* and editor of *The Bilingualism Reader, Opportunities and Challenges of Bilingualism* (with Jean-Marc Dewaele and Alex Housen,) *Bilingualism: Beyond Basic Principles* (with Jean-Marc Dewaele and Alex House) and *The Blackwell Guide to Research Methods in Bilingualism and Multilingualism* (with Melissa Moyer). He is the Editor-in-Chief of the *International Journal of Bilingualism.*

Peter Martin
is Professor of Education and Linguistics at the University of East London. He previously worked at the University of Leicester and Universiti Brunei Darussalam. His major research interests are language shift and minority and endangered languages, bilingual interaction, multiliteracy, new varieties of English, classroom discourse, complementary schooling, bilingual education and language planning.

Pieter Muysken
is professor of linguistics and director of the Centre for Language Studies at Radboud University Nijmegen, after having previously taught at the Universities of Amsterdam and Leyden, all in the Netherlands. He has published in the field of Quechua, Andean linguistics, creole studies, morpho-syntax, and language contact and bilingualism.

Johanne Paradis
is an associate professor in the Department of Linguistics at the University of Alberta, Canada. Her research interests include bilingual first language acquisition, childhood second language acquisition and child language disorders. She is currently conducting comparative research on the morphosyntactic acquisition in bilingual and monolingual children, with and without language impairment.

Manfred Pienemann
is Professor of Applied Linguistics at the University of Paderborn and the University of Newcastle-upon-Tyne. Previously he worked at the University of Sydney and the Australian National University. He is the author of many books and papers and the designer of Processability Theory and Rapid Profile.

Pia Quist
2000–2002 Osaka University of Foreign Studies. Since 2002 at the Department of Scandinavian Research, University of Copenhagen. MA in Danish and Political Science, PhD in Sociolinguistics. Quist has studied language variation in

multilingual settings with particular focus the emergence of new multiethnic speech varieties. In her PhD-study she explores how social, ethnic, and linguistic heterogeneity is handled and negotiated by multilingual speakers in interaction.

Celia Roberts

is a Senior Research Fellow in the Department of Education and Professional Studies at King's College London. Her publications in the fields of urban discourse, including medical discourse, second language socialisation and intercultural communication include: *Language and Discrimination* (Longman 1992 with Davies and Jupp), *Achieving Understanding* (Longman 1996 with Bremer et al.), *Talk, Work and Institutional Order* (Mouton 1999 with Sarangi) and *Language Learners as Ethnographers* (Multilingual Matters 2000 with Byram et al).

Monika Rothweiler

studied Germanic Philology and Biology at the University of Cologne. She did her PhD on the acquisition of subordinate clauses in German, and her habilitation on lexical acquisition in normal develoment and in SLI children. The primary focus of her research is that of language acquisition (grammar) in various contexts. Since 1999, she has been professor of Applied Linguistics in the Department of Special Needs Education at the University of Hamburg, and since 2006 director of the Collaborative Research Center on Multilingualism in Hamburg where she is conducting a project on "Specific Language Impairment and Early Successive Language Acquisition" supported by the DFG.

Christopher Stroud

is professor of linguistics at University of Western Cape, South Africa and professor of bilingualism at Stockholm University, Sweden. His research interests are language and education in transnational development, the historiography and politics of multilingualism, issues of identity and social transformation in language contact, specifically codeswitching, and sociolinguistic ethnographies of literacies. He has worked with these issues in Sweden, Papua New Guinea, Mozambique, and more recently, South Africa.

Johannes Wagner

is Professor of Language and Communication at the University of Southern Denmark. He has studied at the Universities in Tübingen and Uppsala and received his doctorate in 1982 from Odense University, Denmark. Since 1997 he has been the director of the International Graduate School in Language and Communication. He has recently (2004) edited Second Language Conversations (London: Continuum, with Rod Gardner).

Name index

Subject index